PEREGRINE BOOKS

Y 54

ROMAN VERGIL

W. F. JACKSON KNIGHT

W. F. Jackson Knight

ROMAN VERGIL

PENGUIN BOOKS

Penguin Books Ltd, Harmondsworth, Middlesex, England
Penguin Books Pty Ltd, Ringwood, Victoria, Australia

—

First published by Faber and Faber 1944
This revised edition published in Peregrine Books 1966

—

—

Made and Printed in Great Britain
by Hazell Watson & Viney Ltd
Aylesbury, Bucks
Set in Monotype Garamond

DISCIPVLIS
DISCIPVLVS

CONTENTS

PREFACE 9

1 THE WORLD BEFORE VERGIL,
AND VERGIL'S WORLD 13

2 VERGIL'S LIFE AND WORK 52

3 TRADITION AND POETRY 99

4 FORM, AND REALITY 143

5 LANGUAGE, VERSE, AND STYLE 225

6 POETRY AND MANUSCRIPTS 342

7 VERGIL AND AFTER 362

APPENDIX 1: VERGIL'S LATIN 399

APPENDIX 2: VERGIL'S SECRET ART 419

INDEXES 441–63

PREFACE

THIS book was partly written under some pressure during a few weeks in the summer of 1939, when I was expecting soon to be posted to a military appointment in Greece, and completed during another short period in the ensuing winter. However, though there were signs of haste and other deficiencies, Mr T. S. Eliot and Messrs Faber and Faber Ltd approved the work for publication; and sales, which were and continued to be good, endorsed their trust. I thank them, a number of generous reviewers and critics, and the public, too, for their kind support: I recall now particularly Professors Luigi Alfonsi, R. G. Austin, Ettore Bignone, Sir Maurice Bowra, Mr B. Goulding Brown, Professors Karl Büchner and Quintino Cataudella, Mr Cyril Connolly, Mr J. J. Dwyer, Professor Francisco Rebelo Gonçalves and the late Professor P. J. Enk, Professor T. J. Haarhoff, Mrs E. M. Hatt, Professor Lewis Horrox, Mr H. F. Hose, the Rev. Bruno Scott James, Mr L. G. James, Professor Felisberto Martins, the late R. W. Moore, Professor Ettore Paratore, Mr J. R. Thornhill Pollard, Professors Emanuele Rapisarda and L. J. D. Richardson, the late Professor H. J. Rose, Mr H. W. Stubbs, Mrs G. Swannick, and Dr Piero Treves.

Several debts were individually acknowledged in the first and second editions. I have now to express thanks to all who have helped me to prepare the present Peregrine edition, especially to Mr John D. Christie of Glasgow University, who has once again given me his indispensable aid, unsparingly drawing on his time, his energies, and his rigorous scholarship to assist in the revisions and in the organization of the indexes; to Dr Ernst Badian of Durham University who has read the proofs and given me the advantage of his immense and precise learning in furnishing me with many necessary corrections and improvements; to Miss J. E. Southan, Mr Brian Shefton of Newcastle University, and Mr

John Glucker of Exeter University for some highly skilled library research; and to Mr Terence J. Hunt of Exeter University, who has also read the proofs, sharpsightedly checking references, effecting many necessary alterations, and compiling indexes; and to Mr Keith Prowse.

There remains a special obligation, to Professor George E. Duckworth and to Professor E. A. Robinson, the Editor of *The Classical World*, for sending me in good time proofs of the current *Vergil Survey*, by Professor Duckworth, which appears first in *The Classical World* and is obtainable separately. This *Survey* is very complete and accurate. I like to hope that it may save some readers from the ill effects of my own too scanty documentation; the plan of my book made it necessary to dispense, or nearly to dispense, with citations of modern authorities in notes. They can, of course, easily be traced, with or without the help of the few works which I have cited. In the notes I refer to the *Eclogues*, or *Bucolics*, of Vergil by *E*, to the *Georgics* by *G*, and to the *Aeneid* by *A*, with numerals indicating poems or books, and lines. The name of an ancient commentator prefixed indicates that commentator's note on the specified passage. Except when warning is given, the last numerals in references represent the pages of modern works in prose, or the chapters or sections of ancient works in prose, or the lines of works in verse. Very short texts, such as the ancient *Lives* of Vergil, are cited without numerical references. I have used for Vergil and the *Appendix Vergiliana* volumes in the series of Oxford Classical Texts, *Publi Vergili Maronis opera*, recognovit . . . Fredericus Arturus Hirtzel, Oxford, 1900, and *Appendix Vergiliana* . . . recognovit . . . R. Ellis, and the ancient *Lives* of Vergil . . . recognovit . . . C. G. Hardie (issued together in one volume), Oxford, 1954; for Ennius, *Ennianae poesis reliquiae*, recensuit Iohannes Vahlen, Leipzig, 3rd ed., 1928; and for Naevius, E. H. Warmington, *Remains of Old Latin*, Loeb Series, London and Cambridge, Massachusetts, II, 1936. I have sometimes diverged slightly from the Oxford Text of Vergil, but except very rarely only in punctuation; I suggest comparison with the latest critical edition, *P. Vergili Maronis opera*, R. Sabbadini recensuit, Rome, 1930, and the revision of this work by L. Castiglioni and R. Sabbadini, Turin and else-where, 1945.

To the present edition I have added two Appendices containing material which seemed to be required but could not be inserted among the chapters within the time available. They are therefore in the form in which I had them. I gratefully thank the Editors of *Acta Classica*, Proceedings of the Classical Association of South Africa, Vol. I, 1958, an issue dedicated to Professor T. J. Haarhoff, for permission to reprint Appendix 1, and to the Editors of the *Proceedings of the Virgil Society* and *Rivista di Cultura classica e medioevale* for permission to reprint Appendix 2.

My brother G. Wilson Knight, that genius who has never done harm to any one but only good, has never wasted a minute, has always been there, helping; he has helped the present book from years before it was written, until now.

Exeter   W.F.J.K.
October 1964

It has been found necessary to smoothe out certain inconsistencies in my brother's proofs with regard to the dating of Etruscan migrations, the relevant adjustments occurring on pages 53 and 198–201.

Consequent perhaps on the anxiety shown in his preface on page 10, his last proof-revisions (which included the comment on myself, of which I knew nothing) involved many new references to various 'modern authorities'. These had been done under pressure while his strength was failing. Numerals and even titles were often erratic, and much more checking was found to be necessary. Had it not been for the penetration, expertise and devotion of Mr John D. Christie, for so many years my brother's chief adviser and support, who has laboured strenuously in the detection and removal of inaccuracies, undertaken the amplification and finalizing of our indexes, and given weeks of research to the identification and perfecting of references to books and articles, many of them foreign and hard of access, this edition might have been indefinitely delayed.

Exeter   G.W.K.
July 1965

CHAPTER I

THE WORLD BEFORE VERGIL, AND VERGIL'S WORLD

SEVEN centuries of extraordinary deeds by ordinary men had made a city a world. Nothing else in history has been like that. Plenty of human groups, tribes and nations, have imposed their power on neighbours over great areas. Sometimes they have acted through dynasties powerful in a chief city. Sometimes, too, city states have dominated other city states, or even considerable tracts of country along and behind sea shores. There is the experience of the riverine cultures of Egypt and Asia; and the experience of Athens, Phoenician cities, and cities of Italy, especially Venice and Genoa, in the Middle Ages. But nothing has been like Rome – the village that became a city and a great city, and a great power; and then became much more; something hard to describe, as there has been nothing else like it, a kind of unity, a focus, a belt round the lands round the Roman sea.

They say that Rome is not a name for a place or for a people, no local or national name, but a name for a government. That is true, if by a government is meant much more than the mechanics of rule. The government that was Rome was instinct with the emotions and habits and willing sacrifice on which order depends in societies. The Roman idea has never been quite explained. Cicero goes farthest when he says that the Romans and Italians, not excelling other races in courage, brains, or genius, yet prevailed over all by their deep emotional attachment to their homes.

The Romans revered their homes. Their gods were there, and the relation was perhaps at first cold and contractual – Livy and Horace knew what bad luck would follow if the site of Rome were changed – but their fathers, and, still more, their mothers, too, were in those homes revered, and also loved, in the reticent Roman way; and it is as true to say that these emotions of the home gave the Romans their strength as it is to agree with Horace that they held their sovereignty from their humility under heaven. But the Romans had to wait long for a poet who could tell the full truth about them, although, and because, he could keep the Roman reticence too.

And yet the dreadful times of most Roman history shew another side. The Romans themselves in some moods believed the greatness and loveliness of their destiny. But they had to tell themselves, or be told. In the middle of things it is hard to see the broad lines which point to the future, and to the permanent, perhaps even the eternal. Strangely, what we see happening flatly contradicts the truth. It is a familiar paradox. There never were any good old days. The spacious times of Queen Elizabeth I were times of corruption and moral decay, almost bestiality, of every kind; it was obviously not God but luck that fought and won against Spain; yet nevertheless it was God, after all. It can be persuasively argued that the record of the march of Rome by heroic virtues to greatness needs no other explanation than the emotional mind of Livy, with which he uniformly sentimentalized the past, anachronistically deducing its nature from Stoic creeds. The Romans were hard, cynical materialists. Bloodshed was what you saw and the news that you heard. Shameless exploitation was accepted as normal. We could say the same of our times. But just occasionally, even to contemporaries, a window is opened on to the soul of an age. There are hard things, and there are soft things, which last and in the future have their command. These are the things which it takes a poet to see and say.

Between about the twentieth and the eighth centuries before Christ the Greek nation was made in Aegean lands from old cultures of the south blent with new from the north. Then, within a few more centuries, the Greek nation made the wider Greek world, by settlements from Syria and Egypt to Spain; and when Alexander had marched to India and the Western Desert, the Greek world was spread for thousands of miles, and a Greek empire was created. But Alexander was not quite a Greek. If he had been, his empire would never have started. Perhaps great empires are not really meant for Greeks; but rather for others, who learn from Greeks, but whose own experience is in a strange sense deeper, and less articulate; pent in reticence, and not too soon discharged in brilliant light. The real Greek empire came when the Greek essence worked through kindred but different material, slowly and for centuries; till the flash of Greece was disciplined to burn in the steadier Italian flame. The process was long. It is hard to find a time in Roman history when there were no Greeks yet in Rome; Aristotle called Rome a Greek city. The Greeks themselves were a blend; and the Romans who were first Italians, but soon themselves a blend of a blend, gave the future what Greeks and Italians, each alone, could not have given. And indeed during her early period as a city Rome was part of the Etruscan world, subject to the Greek influence with which Etruria was permeated.[1]

About five hundred years before Christ, in 508 B.C., Rome became a republic, with a strange 'mixed' constitution, destined to allow, as Chesterton saw, a kind of permanent revolution, going on for centuries without ever quite stopping. Round Rome were the lands and cities of Latium, to the south, and Etruria, to the north; they were hers in the fourth century B.C.; and meanwhile the mountaineers of the farther south, especially the Samnites, and also other peoples, not least the Campanians, of whom many were more than half Greek, were coming first under Roman influence and then under Roman rule. When, as if by destiny, the preparations had been made, Rome met a foreign enemy on her own soil, Pyrrhus, own relative of Alexander, claiming descent from Achilles himself; and he, when he met Romans, saw that these barbarians were 'no barbarians in battle'; and in fact, though he won victories, he lost the war (275 B.C.). Next, still with the mark of destiny on events, there was a foreign foe to meet, on foreign soil and seas; but finally, after two generations of antagonism, Carthage too fell (202 B.C.). Rome had Sicily, African lands, and Spain. The east came next; Rome conquered Macedon and Greece, and in the same year as Carthage, in arms again for the last time, Corinth was destroyed (146 B.C.). There was too much success; and the resistance of foreign foes no longer held together in harmony the forces at work in Rome. The constitution, based on the

1. Arnaldo Momigliano, 'An Interim Report on the Origins of Rome', *The Journal of Roman Studies*, LIII, 1963, Parts i and ii, 95–121, with references, especially to the important views of Professor E. Gjerstad.

family and the home, took the easy way; authority, sorely needed, was given to single men, and passed beyond control and recall; great men met their match; and there were six civil wars in the years which ended with the principate of Augustus, the first Roman Emperor; and with the *Aeneid* of Vergil.

Sir S. Radhakrishnan writes[1] of the present century: 'Modern civilization with its scientific temper, humanistic spirit, and secular view of life is uprooting the world over the customs of long centuries and creating a ferment of restlessness. The new world cannot remain a confused mass of needs and impulses, ambitions and activities, without any control or guidance of the spirit. The void created by abandoned superstitions and uprooted beliefs calls for a spiritual filling.'

It was not unlike that when Vergil was born seventy years before Christ. The horrors of life had come to be not only actual but real. In most 'good old days', for all the horrors, something good was going on, towards a brighter future, and a poet can see it, as Shakespeare did, and said so in *Macbeth*, at the vision of kings to come, and in *Henry the Eighth*, in Cranmer's prophecy. We think we are wronged, and that all is wickedness, but the poets can tell us to stand, and look to the end.

Vergil took up the strands of all the past that preceded his time. Immediately after him, Christianity started weaving new strands. Vergil so nearly fastened the skeins that he has been thought a prophet of Christ. World history had indeed brought man to the point where Christianity, after Vergil, need not be a surprise.

The background of Vergil can be divided roughly into the topics of philosophy, politics, religion, and poetry. These can be made to include all experience, as the mind registers and uses it.

For us it is Socrates who first saw the truth of the moral soul; first described and defined, perhaps, what we should mean by the spiritual life and the spirit. For thousands of years, partly from experience, partly from superstition, partly from imagination, and partly from mechanical excogitation, thoughts that the individual soul might be immortal had been developing in the world. There

1. S. Radhakrishnan, *Eastern Religions and Western Thought*, Oxford, 1939, Preface, vii.

were myths of its experience after death, devised from ritual meant to assure survival. But the true, permanent conception of the soul as a life principle deriving strength and reality from a certain moral health is due to Socrates – in so far as Dr O. G. S. Crawford's epigram, 'No one was ever the first to say anything', can be evaded.

The epigram is worth bringing into a book about Vergil, since it is important for understanding the nature of things; and to the nature of things, Vergil, through his power of continuity, is very near. And, to bridge the eras, and guard the gate to Christian times, Vergil had to know the soul.

Greek philosophy always sought monism or something near it. The Ionian originators reduced the world to four elements, or to strife and love, all things attracting or repelling each other, or to a perpetual flow. The first and sharpest unity was Plato's; he, developing the presuppositions of Socrates – here, perhaps, though there is always uncertainty, not adding so very much of his own – held the moral soul to be the great reality; but it was a soul instinct with rationality in intellectual contact with the real. 'Virtue is knowledge'; and the real is real in proportion as it is intelligible to the pure intellect; moral evil belongs to the false and to the unreal or partly real; moral good belongs to truth and first reality. There was no sufficient distinction between the moral will and the intellectual apprehension of truth; but Plato, actually influenced to this by the necessity to shew how the soul could acquire knowledge, which seemed impossible on his presuppositions, firmly adopted a theory of reincarnation, which helped to disguise the need for a distinction between the intellectual and the moral, and for a conception, not yet reached, of a moral will.

Reincarnation has been called a theory universal to humanity over all the world, except for a small part of it in Western Europe; and even here many or even most of the great poets are said to have been inclined to it. Plato, when he passes beyond the reach of constructive reasoning, habitually presents his beliefs in the form of myths, and among them his belief in reincarnation. But he reaches this belief by reasoning also, and it is a real belief, farther from emotively expressed and suggestive fancy than much that Plato's myths contain. Vergil made of reincarnation an explicit, not merely an implicit, answer.

Plato's philosophy is hard to understand but in outline easy to remember; Aristotle, or the 'two Aristotles, the follower and the critic of Plato', treating Plato with 'massive common sense', produced a philosophy hard to remember, but, in some sense, easier than Plato's to understand. Perhaps it is intelligible that Vergil did not accept very much from 'the master of those who know'. Vergil, indeed, would not have claimed to be one of them; but he desired to be, and planned to devote his life to philosophy after the *Aeneid* was done.

One way of denying the infra-rational world of experience was asceticism. Plato's moral theory included a self-denial that was subject to reason, but not asceticism at all times for its own sake, though he firmly held that the 'aristocratic man', in distinction from the 'tyrannical' and 'democratic' men, was necessarily beyond risk of enslavement to one, or to many, of the passions of sense. But soon afterwards the Cynical school, founded by Diogenes, and owing something to the earlier Eleatics, exalted asceticism into a rule. In that tradition after four or five centuries came Epictetus; it is not always remembered that Cynic experience and experiment matched Christianity in the intensity of its abnegations, and sometimes produced an almost Christian sweetness of temper and charity The Cynics helped to make Vergil.

But the great successors to Plato were Epicureans and Stoics; Stoics by direct affiliation, but Epicureans, perhaps, rather by descent from the whole tradition of Ionian physics. Socrates started from the world within, but the Ionians from the outer world of nature, persistent in their faith that observation would disclose principles; though some, especially Heraclitus, if he can be counted among them, had much to say about the dark places of the mind. The exaltation of matter into a monistic principle, however, was left to Democritus, an earlier contemporary of Plato; and Epicurus, who lived just after Plato, fitted a moral system to the new explicit materialism.

Epicurus was a saint, and he started a kind of religious community, intensely bound together by friendship. Ostensibly the one moral principle was pleasure, but the theory was several stages away from crude hedonism, which had already been tried. To the early Epicureans pleasure was most itself when it was shared in society by people of sensibility and unselfishness. Such was originally the herd of which Horace claimed to be a pig. The Epicureans gave something to Vergil.

Vergil owed a debt to the Stoics also, a debt variously estimated. The Stoics were influenced by eastern thought, perhaps ultimately Zoroastrian, which had somehow even affected Socrates himself. Zoroastrianism was notable among ancient religions as a highly moralized monotheism; it was in harmony with the Jewish religion, and partly parental to it. The Stoics continued Platonism, and especially its moral absolutism and intellectualism. But they went farther, partly by accepting other influences, especially from the physicists, and partly by deducing what followed from Platonism; they thought for themselves, but without brilliance, and their systems are not sufficiently coherent to have 'high technical merit as philosophy'.

The main Stoic emphasis was, of course, on morals; and the main contribution was the deduction of a detailed, practical system of moral maxims from the principle that the world is ruled according to a rational law. The Logos of St John is usually said with some truth to have been derived from the Stoics, through Philo of Alexandria.

It is an old story, how Stoicism was adopted at Rome because the practical Roman world view was best fitted to assimilate and use a practical philosophy. Romans were attracted to Greek thought; and quite early, as early as the third century, to judge from Ennius, and his taste for Euripides, Euhemerism, scepticism, and for other very un-Roman things, they were ready to listen to daring and experimental ideas. But either because of the 'conservative reaction' which happened in the second century B.C., or because a deeper inclination prevailed, Stoicism became the characteristic form in which Romans assimilated Greek thought.

The famous Scipionic Circle, the set of aristocratic Romans, led by Publius Cornelius Scipio Aemilianus, the younger Africanus, the destroyer of Carthage (146 B.C.), and the first Roman to shave, and have a bath as often as once a week, adopted and spread Greek culture with energy and effect. They were Stoics, but not extremists in Stoicism; extreme Stoicism came to be more characteristic of the later party of reaction in the first century B.C., which found Stoicism an ally against the more dangerous tendencies in Greek thought. This party, especially Marcus Porcius Cato the younger, believed in the old Roman rule of duty, simplicity, conservatism, and habit. In these republican centuries the Roman legend or rather myth was developing. The story that the Romans had come originally from Troy was growing; and the Romans were becoming self-conscious about their own achievements. In this they were helped by Polybius, the exiled Greek historian who lived in Rome for many years till his death about 120 B.C., and, conceiving a great admiration for the Roman way, and a great curiosity about it, wrote forty books of history in which he included reflections on Roman greatness and Roman methods. Polybius and other Greeks helped the Romans to discover more about their own merits. But they had been to some extent aware of them before. The speech of Appius Claudius Caecus, extant in Cicero's time, in which he formulated a principle of Roman policy, 'No peace with an enemy on Italian soil', was delivered early in the preceding century (280 B.C.). Plautus in his plays, some presented during the Second Punic War (218–202 B.C.), apostrophizes the audience, and praises their courage in war and justice in peace. The Roman myth, mainly true in outline and value, was fairly spontaneous and indigenous. The Romans had a sense of time and history unique in antiquity. More than others, they relied on precedent, and kept records. They felt responsible to the past for the future, and lived their lives under a sense of destiny; not every individual, all the time, but many of those who counted most, in the main. It was a new and extraordinary political continuity, partly aware of itself, but only partly, till writers of great penetration could be created by it, and interpret it.

From the second century Stoicism helped. Stoicism gave a code for the behaviour of the sage, or the saint, or however we translate *sapiens*, 'wise man'. The Romans found that this matched their own ideals of dignity, loyalty, steadiness of will, and moral leadership – *gravitas*, *pietas*, *constantia*, and *auctoritas*. They rationalized their own social habits, and when Livy, Vergil's later contemporary, wrote his prose-epic of the history of Rome he wrote it half as a tale of Stoics, guided by destiny. Stoicism gave the Romans reasons for what they did instinctively, and coloured their story of themselves.

The Stoic rule appears almost comical, as satirized not inaccurately by Cicero. The sage is never angry, never pities, never grieves, and thinks all sins equal. This is all because he follows reason. From here the step is soon taken towards determinism. Some Stoics were inclined to believe in a fixed fate, with possibilities of accurate prophetic prediction. This fitted the Romans, in whose politics official prophecy exerted a powerful control. Other Stoics, however, avoided such strict consequences, and preferred a system more loosely reasoned. Another Stoic doctrine of which not so much is heard under the Republic is the doctrine of the brotherhood of man. Here the Stoics and Epicureans converged, and Vergil, according to a particular tendency that he had, could follow both at once.

Under the Roman emperors, Stoicism became a republican orthodoxy of aristocrats discontented with the Empire. It was an unpractical and annoying orthodoxy then, not always as sincere as it was ostentatious; though Roman Stoics with political interests such as Seneca, Lucan, and Thrasea Paetus, met death bravely enough, if sometimes rather theatrically, for their beliefs. Stoicism has always been found unsatisfactory for the whole of life; but it is a powerful reserve for arduous times.

Meanwhile Epicureanism was having a strange history. Epicureans were discouraged as atheists, and on the whole rather disingenuously. Cicero says that Epicurus was an atheist really, but, in order to escape religious persecution, pretended to believe that the gods existed, but had no care for men. It is beginning to appear, partly from a newly discovered letter of Epicurus himself, that the true Epicurean view was that the gods existed, and cared, not for all men, but for good men. At Rome, Epicureanism was revolutionary under the Republic, more really and more sincerely than Stoicism under the Empire. It was considered anti-social because for obvious reasons it discouraged, or might be said to discourage, obedience to authority.[1] One sign of this is a certain neglect of the great philosophical poem of Titus Lucretius Carus, the *De*

1. B. Farrington, *Science and Politics in the Ancient World*, London, 1939, *passim*.

Rerum Natura, 'The Nature of the Universe', in which he argued for Epicureanism. Lucretius was hotly debated in the fourth century A.D., but sometimes before that seems to have been ignored. Indeed, a conspiracy of silence has been suspected.[1] Cicero, who was said to have edited Lucretius' poem, mentions it only once, in a letter to his brother Quintus, in which, if the text is right, he praises it for its inspiration but adds that it also shewed technical competence. That, surprisingly enough, is the only reference to it in Cicero's extant works, though many of them deal freely with philosophy and mention very many other philosophers.

Stoicism and Epicureanism both started from the impulse towards a rational personal religion. This impulse became powerful when the Greek city state, with its religiously fierce and satisfying social allegiances, died away. The city state was weakened by the Peloponnesian War (431–404 B.C.); and after the rise of Macedon and especially the battle of Chaeronea, at which Athens was defeated (338 B.C.), it lost its vitality for ever in Greece. Culture was advanced, and individuals of keen self-consciousness had to depend on themselves, and find an individual's world view, in order to face the world alone. In both the new systems there was some sort of individual salvation to be found.

Stoicism was normal among Roman society, but Epicureanism was in fashion for a short period more or less corresponding to Vergil's life-time. And that, too, was when the Roman myth was being perfected. This meant that one task of thinkers and poets was to fit one or both of the two Greek philosophies, designed to satisfy the consciousness of individuals who had lost the sustaining faith in the old Greek city state, to another society, the society of Rome, past and present, real and ideal. The Stoic sage could stand alone; now he stood in order that Rome might stand; not for selfish domination as Alexander designed but in a carefully delimited system. Still, the Stoic sage might be too absolute, an obstruction, not a support; there were ironic situations in politics, in which the Stoic morality, that is, the ideal morality of old

1. See the volume of selections from Lucretius by Paratore and Pizzani, *Lucreti de rerum natura locos praecipue nobiles collegit et illustravit* Hector Paratore *commentariolo instruxit*, Hucbaldus Pizzani, Rome, 1960, 8–44.

Rome, seemed to be doing more harm than good. The sovereignty really resided with powerful individuals who controlled or obeyed social or financial groups or families; government depended on complicated negotiation to achieve sufficient balance and stability, if only for a moment, to get work done. The rapid increases in the scale and complexity of the Roman system had really removed it beyond control, like a chariot stampeding, as Vergil thought. Every one was 'doing evil that good might come'; and the more evil they did the more they had to do. The younger Cato was obstructive when (60 B.C.) he refused to connive at the scandalous revision of a bargain with the tax-farming 'equestrians'. Led by Crassus, they were willing to support Julius Caesar and Pompeius, if they were excused the full price which they had agreed to pay for collecting the taxes of Asia, when the yield was less than expected. The arrangement was made, and Cato's policy failed through its consistency. Even the mild and humane Cicero had to pretend to support Brutus, who, to recover interest owed to him at a terribly high rate, positively starved out respected gentlemen of an eastern province, Cyprus, who took refuge in a temple. And Cicero, though he gently mocked Stoicism in Cato, was, if not Stoic, at least Platonic in his general, declared outlook. Clearly, Stoicism raised more problems than it settled. You had to be un-Stoic and un-Roman, up to a point, to take part in affairs. It was, in fact, a well-known problem in Stoic theory, in fact a kind of regular essay question, whether the Sage could take part in politics at all. Cicero, together with most people, thought that the Sage could, but the task of making the answer logical was beyond them all; until Vergil poetically stated the problem, and by stating it solved it.

Epicurean theory did not obviously help. It was not very applicable to traditional Rome. It openly recommended a peaceful, retired life, of refined pleasure or at least of untroubled calm. It has often been misunderstood; but there is not much doubt that, as normally stated, it was not an impulse towards success in empire building.[1] Yet the empire builders came to look more and

1. Cf. F. W. Clayton, 'Some Aspects of Later Stoicism', Exeter, 1948, a very amusing Inaugural Lecture.

more Epicurean. Sulla, the libertine, was morally the opposite to a Stoic; Julius Caesar could be unscrupulous and lax whenever it suited him; Antonius pretended to be a Greek god, Dionysus Omestes, 'Eater of Raw Flesh', and appeared to devote himself to a life of Greek and eastern pleasure; all were much more addicted to personal satisfactions than to anything that might be supposed the Reason that is behind the world; and if Epicureanism meant to many materialism and the life of pleasure, and it probably did, Rome was in its power. But in the life-time of Julius Caesar, Epicureanism had a more authentic claim. Five teachers of it came to settle in Italy, and won the active assent of many powerful Romans. It became less narrow and more human, and developed as one side of Roman life was developing, in the direction of kindliness and sensitivity. It offered an escape from excessive consciousness of responsibility, and a unifying commentary with which the inherited intellectual world could be explored again, without the need to take any of it too seriously. Art, daily life, and nature could be a decoration and an entertainment, after Epicureanism had dispelled the threat in them. The moment could be enjoyed, without too much thought of the next. It was on the whole a healthy and civilizing influence, and a mitigation of the intensity of living. It admitted soldiers and statesmen to cultural activities and interests, and gave them a humanity to which they could react from civil war. Perhaps it made possible the Augustan peace. But it did not settle everything. The riddle of the universe was not answered. Death and God were sure to be questioned again.

Ancient societies were intensely self-conscious; and religions, superstitions, and tabus, that usually hold simple and early societies together, were so recurrently questioned, and the need and legitimacy of political inquiry so frequently extended, that, especially in the eventful history of classical antiquity, theories of the relation of man to men were easily formulated and tested.

On the whole, though it is scarcely a subject to dismiss in a few words, the riverine cultures of nearer Asia and Egypt and the partly derivative Minoan culture of Crete, during their long if intermittent prosperity between outer dates of 4000 and 1000 B.C., were helped in civil coherence by theocracy. The divine king, or human medicine man, or rain-maker, in some sense representing, or coming to represent, the magic power of the sky, which eventually became a personified supreme god, who was supposed at home in the sky or on the mountain tops, is in simple tribal societies sufficiently general; and the scheme of this religion remained in the riverine cultures.

General, also, was the religion of a great Earth Mother, but it was varyingly emphatic in dependence on, or competition with, the religion of the Sky Father. Not everything is known; in many places the two powers may have begun as a pair of human officiants, mating together in sacred union, in order, by sympathetic magic, to compel the sky to fertilize the earth. When culture settled in a river basin, so that crops depended on the rivers, not on the rain, the Sky Father tended to lose allegiance. This happened in Egypt; and there were revivals of the Old Religion, enforced by powerful priests, who drove kings to the old sacrificial death.[1] The worship of the sun is uncertain in origin, and was afterwards introduced as a royal religion, useful to the kings, because it excused them death by sacrifice. In the city states, first of Sumeria and soon after of Egypt, where in spite of organization by districts city states were usually important units, elaborate polytheisms were developed mainly from the primary personalities of sky and earth and later the sun, and in Egypt also of Osiris, who is the Egyptian river.

Simple tribal societies were normally held together by the Custom that is King, and the ready obedience of all to the inherited and sanctified wisdom which reposed in the elders of the tribe. Later, in the first civic societies, the divinity of an individual king, of violently effective sanctity, and the prestige and power of an increasingly numerous priesthood, regularly contributed that 'majesty' to law and order which the Romans were the first to understand. Ovid, expressing more explicitly if less profoundly what Vergil declares less in allegory than in symbol, lightly tells us that there was chaos and uproar among the Olympic gods, each trying to gain the highest place, till suddenly 'Majesty' entered, and took her seat; then all deferred to higher dignity, and there

1. G. A. Wainwright, *The Sky-Religion in Egypt*, London, 1938, *passim*.

was order, and calm. Political order and harmony cannot always or even often depend on right reason and clear thought alone; it needs, as Rousseau not less than Plato saw, an ancient awe and a divinity to hedge the civil rule.

The difficulty is that divine sanctions come to be questioned, and with good reason. Those who once accepted, fairly enough, the idea of a divine king and a priestly caste, might find that the idea did not work for ever. The king did not ensure good harvests always. He might 'devour the people', in Homer's expression. So might the priests, who devoured people, land, and king under the nineteenth Egyptian dynasty. Further, cities mean organized war, and the Sumerians invented armed, disciplined soldiers soon after civilization began (*c.* 3000 B.C.). It is said that before then humanity was peaceful, and even that the cities of the very ancient Mohenjo-Daro culture of the Ganges valley are proved to have had no defences. In this there is exaggeration, if some truth; in Sumeria, at least, cities soon had to face the need for defence against the pressure of desert dwellers upon the rich river basins.

Consequently, a class of fighting men developed, and was sometimes important, though in Egypt, where according to Herodotus there were well defined castes, it was always kept in subjection. So, in China, soldiers have usually been despised, and it used to be proverbially a folly to make a good man a soldier. But everywhere civilization has had to fight and to be armed; and a different kind of monarchy and caste-prestige, military not religious, arose at an early stage. The two sorts, then, had to be combined somehow.

An opportunity already existed.[1] Temples and cities were divine in the east, and sometimes in Egypt. The eastern temple-tower, the ziggurat, 'bound earth and heaven and hell together'. Round it the city was built; it was the centre of all things, to the inhabitants. Divinity defended the city, aided by strange human methods of magic and ritual. The magic circle about the city must not be pierced, nor the divine protection, in the person of an inviolate

1. For this subject see W. F. J. Knight, *Cumaean Gates*, Oxford, 1936; idem, 'The Holy City of the East in Vergil', *Vergilius* II, Jan. 1939, 6–16; Joseph Rykwert, *The Idea of a Town*, St George's Gallery, London, w1, 1964.

maiden goddess, lured away. Such in short were the ideas of ancient Babylonia; and they remain strong in the Greek tale of the siege of the eastern city, Troy. They were lost in historic Greece; but somehow they came to Italy, before Italian history begins, and survived in magic circles round Italian towns, and in Vesta who is both the central hearth, and the city's protecting goddess too; and they survived in the mind of Vergil, always in close touch with most ancient things.

Economic necessity prevented the conditions of the old divine monarchies from lasting. In the beginning it seemed simple and satisfactory to kill and replace the medicine man or divine king if the food supply failed. But before four thousand years ago the literature of complaint at oppression had begun. In Sumeria economic need produced an appeal from a poor peasant that is still extant; and the writings of Imhotep in Egypt contain bitter regret for contemporary demoralization, and impoverishment, and the collapse of civilization. It is like the poetry of the Greek poets Hesiod and Theognis, lamenting the effects of economic pressure which they could not understand; like the literature of Gaul, when in the fifth century A.D. law and loyalty and morals had gone, with economic and political disorganization, and under barbarian pressure, too; and like the literature of our own epoch, in the last few years before hope and energy and positive interest revived – for a time – in 1938 and 1939, and there was something for which to fight, and sing, and smile again.

In Mesopotamia, the legal Code of Hammurabi (?c. 2100 B.C.) set a standard for the rationalization of civil intercourse. There are prayers at the beginning and end; but it is a secular document, ordaining for practical utility a justice of requital, stern, but for the time fair, and an immense advance. The Hittites who not long after began a long rule in Cappadocia (c. 1800–c. 1250 B.C.) apparently achieved civil harmony, and a peace lasting even longer than the Roman peace, with some system of justice that was milder and not less successful than Hammurabi's. There was thus much experience for the Greeks to inherit; they were nearer to contact with the ancient experience of mankind than has been thought, and it has even been said that they owed more to it than we in modern Europe owe to theirs. But the contribution of their unique analysing thought remained to be made; even the Egyptians, for all their gifts and right-mindedness, their good manners and fairly good morals, and their religious sense, were comically at a loss to find reasons why we should be good and obedient, and behave well, when tempted otherwise. Not that the question is easy.

From the fourteenth century B.C. or earlier the Greeks began with something like a feudal monarchy supported and controlled by a council of elders, and a popular assembly. This may be called usual to speakers of Indo-European dialects. In the Dark Age after the Dorians came at about 1100 B.C., monarchy gradually broke down, in most of the cities, and aristocracies governed. The aristocracies were often selfish and unimaginative. Economic revolutions, partly due to the invention of coinage in Lydia (c. 700 B.C.), produced unemployment and destitution. Some Greeks were sharp enough to see the obvious, but dangerous, way to relief; and tyranny, unconstitutional autocracy, unchecked sometimes by custom, religion, or even common morality, arose. This autocracy, like the party strife, almost the class war, which occasioned it, might be called something new in the world; and both, like warfare, have been part of the price paid for progress. New problems are always raised by progress which only new progress can solve. These anxieties were very much alive in Vergil's reflection.

Greek thinkers worked hard to rationalize the relation of the individual to society, and to justify, from the point of view of the individual, that limited deference to the group which is sometimes more clearly desirable for the group than for the individual. To Plato, the health of the individual soul depended on a balance of qualities and impulses, which constituted justice; and justice, of the same kind, appeared also in the balance of parties and interests in the community. The best thing for a human being was to be just and wise and brave and good; and, if he thus achieved his own highest aim, and therefore happiness, he must inevitably act justly towards others. To be loyal and disciplined, and so serve the community, was therefore in the interest of the individual, both in this life, and after death. It was Plato's tragedy, or part of it, as Solovyef shewed, to find what steady faith such a theory needs, even if – the rare chance that came to both Plato and Aristotle – the philosophers have an opportunity to make philosophers of kings. In brutal, unjust societies it was hard to believe what could be believed very easily, at certain moments, amid the grace and affection of aristocratic friends in 'violet-crowned' Athens, in her brightest days. But it is something like Plato's old faith that we are still trying to recapture.

Aristotle and his assistants wrote monographs on the constitutions of a hundred and fifty Greek cities. They therefore had facts, and faced them. To Aristotle, the facts might be hard to explain, or even deplorable; but the main task was to find and define the facts, without either forcing them, or indulging in myth and fancy and abstraction. Virtue alone was not enough for happiness, the aim of all; but some virtue, as well as some material prosperity, and above all good activity in good conditions, were necessary ingredients. This is admirable, and might be called incontestable; but fortunately for humanity some spirits could never be content with such a view alone. And even then, it has been said, Aristotle is sometimes, in spite of himself, more abstract and even more mystical than Plato.

But it was well to insist on the many accidents which condition that human life, for which 'the city comes into existence', and that 'good life' also, 'for which the city continues in existence'. Aristotle, brilliantly seeing these 'final causes', yet did not know, what his pupil Alexander proved, that the city state was not enough. It depended on too many fortunate accidents. Its harmony and efficiency and intensity of living must be kept, but in a wider harmony, so that the mere accidents of a neighbour's powers and propensities need not distort policy at home from its best way. We must be ready to fight to make a world in which our pacifism can live, as Vergil, seeing more still, was compelled to see.

Plato and Aristotle left certain things clear. Society is not a fortuitous, contractual organization; it is rather organic than merely organized; it is natural. It is right, if it is just to all; and all – that is, all who have the right to do so, which is a difficulty – must help to decide, and to control. The highest good of the individual is in some relation to his relation to society; 'only a

beast or a god can live alone'. Something had been done to replace unthought religious sanctions with an intelligible principle
of cooperation, recommended by reason. But Aristotle was in
some danger of leaving his favourite type of society 'watery', and
lacking in the spontaneous impulse to cohere; the very criticism
which he made against Plato's communism. Something must be
done to channel our spontaneous energies, so that their flow increases the good of all.

The great Greek thinkers left it clear that societies tend to
change according to a kind of law. Monarchy naturally devolves
into aristocracy, aristocracy into democracy, and democracy into
monarchy; probably 'tyranny'. The cycle often starts again. The
rule of the one, of the few, or of the many may be good, or bad.
There are good constitutions of each sort, and bad ones, that
are distortions of the good kinds; tyranny is a distortion of monarchy; rule of a clique or 'oligarchy' of aristocracy; and mob-
rule of democracy.

Italian and Roman political experience may have owed much to
Greek suggestion at the start. Possibly the Twelve Tables really
were compiled (451–450 B.C.) with help from the Laws of Solon of
Athens (594 B.C.); possibly individual Greeks advised early Italian
statesmen. Certainly, Greek influence flowed plentifully from
Etruria when Rome was an Etruscan city. But Italian politics were
peculiarly Italian. There was an instinct for cooperation between
cities or tribes, and therefore leagues were natural, and there was
an instinct for cooperation within cities and tribes, and therefore
party strife was less intense and constitutions more permanent. It
is a long story; but Rome behaved in the Italian way, making sure
and going slowly; maintaining religious sanctions in reverence,
until – and this is important – political development had gone far;
avoiding tyranny with suspicious caution, dependent undoubtedly
on Greek experience; and tempering avarice and sometimes
cynical self-interest with a god-fearing regard for the feelings of
others, and a responsible sense of personal honour.

The Greeks of Homer had a word for the strange impulse of
self-respect combined with respect for the opinions of others,
αἰδώς, 'shame', though the word means more than that; and a
word meaning the righteous indignation which must be expected

from others if this impulse fails, νέμεσις, 'vengeance', 'vengefulness', or 'retribution'. But here as often the public politics of Greece do not display the Greek inspiration as well as the public politics of Rome. There is an important extension of this. Thucydides says that in the beginning there was no distinction between Greeks and foreigners, 'barbarians' as they called them. Herodotus explains that there came a time when the Greeks emerged from 'barbarian' simplicity and foolishness, and became themselves, distinct from others. During their most creative centuries the Greeks were almost too confident in their superiority to others, and were narrow in their national self-consciousness. Alexander, not quite a Greek, was exceptional in his broad-minded admission of all races to respect and consideration. In Roman politics he would have been less an exception than the rule. Romans long used to bargaining with foreigners, independent or not fully subdued, came to respect other races by habit. The story has been worked out by Professor T. J. Haarhoff – how Rome at last achieved harmonization of different races and cultures,[1] and got from each a free contribution of something like the best that was there to give; and, herself a blend, blended creatively the diversities of many lands.

Religion inevitably has points of contact with these political subjects. Religion, of course, is everywhere; but it is more obviously present in early than in later philosophy and politics. 'The two sources of morality and religion', as M. Bergson[2] traces them, the static, conventional 'myth', or religious and moral system, enshrined in each society, and the new, combatant discoveries of individual initiative, constitute, like many other polarized pairs of ideas, a useful help towards the comprehension of ancient thinking. The Greeks loved and trusted the old, and never ceased to explore and exploit the new. There has therefore been an argument, whether they were, or were not, conservative. They both were and were not; for ages and peoples are characterized by

1. T. J. Haarhoff, *The Stranger at the Gate*, London, 1938, 2nd ed. Oxford, 1948, *passim*.
2. Henri Bergson, *The Two Sources of Morality and Religion*, English translation, London, 1935, *passim*.

their typical contrasts and oppositions, not by single qualities alone.

The individual Greeks, under stress of need, rapidly outgrew restraint. The poets and thinkers added to inherited mythology new turns. The poets led. But the Greeks themselves thought that their first poets, long before Homer, were religious teachers; especially the mythical Orpheus. They composed 'oracles'; Orpheus, according to Aristophanes, invented 'initiations', or 'religious services', and taught them. Early poets were to some extent leaders of the religious dances, and composers and singers of the hymns, with which Olympian gods, especially Apollo, were worshipped. These worships must have been peculiarly satisfying, with the brightness everywhere, rhythm, colour, sound, nothing to frighten or to bore; activities in which all joined, sinking personality into united joy, sealed by a faith, a distraction from care, yet with little selfishness, little thought of personal salvation, but rather a rest from both hope and fear at once. And there was real feasting; Olympian gods, like their part-ancestors, pre-Homeric heroes, enjoyed roast beef, which was an unusual luxury to their worshippers who shared it with them, and might prove even intoxicating to people who are not used to it. And with the festivals sometimes went athletic sports, races and other competitions, joyful to watch and to win and to celebrate in song. The perfection of the golden, momentary present belongs in its fullest pride to Olympia in Elis and the Olympian Games, as Pindar, its highest poet, who helped to create it, knew.

There were festivals not quite so Olympian, which seem to have descended from very ancient cults, half-magical, spontaneous, meant to keep active the fertile processes of earth and sky. Hence drama grew; and hence also 'the mysteries', at Eleusis in Attica, and elsewhere. 'The mysteries' were not for the pride of the golden moment; they spoke to Greeks who knew and remembered that the golden moment is not all. They were, in fact, whatever the uncertainties about them may be, a religion, or several religions, which tried to guard and save individuals, and give them a hope for themselves. He who died returned to the Earth Mother; and, if the rites were true, and if he himself were true, he could live again; for the Mother would remember, if the Father God forgot.

She would remember to send the fruits and flowers, and remember her human children also. Women, besides men, could be initiated into the Mysteries. There were two places on earth, said Pausanias, more blessed by Heaven than any others: Olympia and Eleusis. Pindar was the poet of Olympia; and the poet of Eleusis was Aeschylus, the poet not of the proud moment, but of suffering time and triumphant eternity. Perhaps even Vergil could hardly be the poet of both – at least, hardly of both at once.

Greece had its great Olympian cults and their festivals, and their permanent faith and joy, and the quickly progressive art, in marble and in sound. Greece too had the mysteries. And there were thinking and talking, speculation and philosophy. The Olympians maintained the myth, the sanctification by custom and belief of the fabric of common life. The mysteries, reaching back perhaps to an older past, also pushed on, and held open a way of hope, if any could take it. But hard thinking was wanted; and the poets, principally, reached from their own experience new conclusions with which religious systems might have to make terms. There was one very obvious issue between established religion and independent thinking. It concerned Fate. In Homer Zeus is supreme, but in some degree Fate is also supreme. On the whole, the two powers agree, but Zeus is limited by Fate; as he is, too, by the temporary oppositions of other divinities. Scientists, philosophers, and poets, especially Aeschylus, were inclined to make Fate supreme, even over Zeus. Later, Chance in various forms almost took the place of Fate. God, said Pindar and Aristotle, could not do everything; he could not make what had happened not to have happened. Plato's myths recognize Fate, and Stoicism was inclined to exalt it. But Fate, if really supreme, needed a purpose and a content, which might be shewn incarnate in human lives, and that meant that this Fate, which was also the supreme, divine will of the universe, the Stoic Reason, must be revealed in active reconciliation, and some myth, some picture, some parable found. The Stoic philosophers went far. But they left a task for a Roman poet to do.[1]

1. For the difficult question of these philosophers and Vergil's relation to them and to others, cf. Ettore Paratore, *Virgilio*, Rome, 1945, second edition Florence, 1954, *passim*, and Luigi Alfonsi, 'L'Approdo di Vergilio alla Filosofia', *Rivista di filosofia neo-scolastica*, LVI, 1964, 197–201.

Then there is the inescapable riddle of the universe, the problem of the divine justice. In Homer there is plenty of criticism of Zeus, some serious, some flippant, and some just dramatically required. But a deeper feeling, an advance on the existing myth, lies behind; Zeus protects strangers, and the helpless; prayers are the daughters of Zeus, lame and slow, but in the end they prevail; Zeus assents to a mother's prayer for her son; he approves and gives decision, when a righteous man is to be saved; and when someone has gone too far in transgression, he accepts the plea of other divinities that a high power must interpose, and chooses the milder way. Odysseus comes to his home, and prevails; Thetis, sure of the help of Zeus, saves her son Achilles in her own fashion. Homer has a real faith which speaks in his poetry quite distinctly from the fashionable flippancy about things divine, which is more a satire on the talk of men than on the existence of God; and distinctly, too, from the archaic beliefs and established cults which were to be real to many for centuries yet, but could not yield to Homer the God of his heart and his mind.

This, however, concerns poetry as much as religion; though it may be absurd to separate the two even in discussion.

The Homeric faith is explicitly pessimistic, like the faith of other heroic ages, at least in the beliefs represented as held by characters. There was no hope after death, and in life endless hardship of fighting and travelling, with only the pride of it all for consolation, a consolation which Odysseus and Sarpedon perfectly express. But others, lesser men perhaps, were less content. Hesiod, who is usually still more pessimistic than Homer, made Justice a daughter of Zeus. Some earlier elegiac poets, Mimnermus and after him Xenophanes and Theognis, are sad at the doom of mankind, and the shortness of youth, the only lovely thing; Zeus is challenged for his injustice, and the gods are doubted, or allegorized. The Sophists, rationalistic professional teachers, continued the doubts and increased them; but old faiths went on all the time, and are clear again, for example, in Xenophon. An attempt to spread beliefs that were intellectualized beyond the possibility of instinctive adherence was the cause of the death of Socrates. As the late J. B. Bury saw, 'There have been no better men than Socrates;

and yet his accusers were perfectly right'.[1] It is not safe to disturb too quickly the 'myth' on which the coherence of society depends. This is a dilemma; and it is surprising that a solution was ever found, and that a poet came who had the instinctive depth and the advancing vision and the sheer brilliance and subtlety of intellect to find it.

There is another dilemma, concerned with the emotions. Keats said that the heart should be the 'horn-book' of the mind, but the Stoics did not think so. There are still the two views, and still people who will never agree about the question; and so it was in antiquity. On the other hand, the question did not look quite the same then. The effect of the ancient symbolic polytheism was subtle. The divinities were known from cult, cult-myth – stories told at temples – and poetic myth, especially in Homer and Hesiod. Those two poets, according to Herodotus, fixed the names, prerogatives, and relationships of the gods. Without the poets there would certainly have been no very clear conception of what the gods meant. Several would mean more or less the same thing, and without contrasts it would never be very certain what each did mean, especially as many were developed from similar spirits or still less personified sanctities, or were tended in different places. Greek worships eventually had the effect of removing repressions. Specially good behaviour was required at some festivals, as the festivals at Olympia and Delphi. But there were cults which involved the withdrawal of tabus. Attic comedy sprang from some fertility cult in which remarks which seem improper to us had to be made in order to help forward magically the productivity of the world. Religious worship of gods whose myths told of their passionate acts confirmed the morality of similar acts among worshippers. But orthodoxy is conservative, and sure to seem old-fashioned sometimes. The gods behaved as men once thought it right to behave. Naturally this was noticed by Heraclitus, who had a rare sense of time in history. 'Man lives because the Gods die.' But even Heraclitus had an imperfect historical sense, and like many thinkers with similar antecedents he allegorized Homer, calling Athena the air, and so on. This saved the credit of the gods at the cost of their reality, and their religious existence.

1. J. B. Bury, *History of Greece*, London, 1958, 581.

The alternative was to decide that 'the gods have their own laws'. It was not, however, unusual to realize that the available departments of religion were not a perfect moral guide. Conscience was alive, and had to depend largely on itself. But it found an ally in tabu. Ritual purity, a practical affair of magic, not particularly moral, was enlisted, and transformed, especially by Orphism at its best, into a moral purity required for salvation in the after life. But there was still plenty of opportunity to obey the instincts and believe that this obedience was sanctioned by Apollo, or Artemis, or Aphrodite, or even that indulgence was an act of worship.

There was plenty of moral restriction, especially at special times and special places. Murder in a temple was sacrilege, but murder outside might be natural and justifiable revenge, especially if there was a political excuse. The mind and observation of the great historian and sociologist Thucydides were needed to disclose the terrible risk of this dependence on narrow codification, with no conviction that any law held good 'for all rational beings', and at all times. The disclosure is in his account of the demoralization at Corcyra resulting from party strife, and the ruin of the religion of the city state. Then as now, inflamed sectional loyalties, and forces released by false rationalization shielding selfishness and impatience, could quickly devastate a human society where Custom was no longer King.

The moral efficacy of Greek religion looks, in fact, accidental. Religion could be used by men of conscience for high moral and social ends. Good advice, the wisdom of experience, was given under divine sanction, such as the Delphic maxims of moderation, and the doctrine of inevitable vengeance for sin, especially the sin which is typical in Attic tragedy, *hybris*, ὕβρις, an un-Christian lack of consideration for others. Attic tragedy worshipped Dionysus, a god of unrestraint. But the tragedy which was part of his cult was restrained. Then, too, city cults, meant to protect the city, had the effect of moralizing intercourse within it. There had to be some union in the worship. So, also, family cults, starting with tabus, developed a morality that could work in a wider field. Kindred bloodshed was perilous, and the ghosts and furies would avenge it. But the religion of the family might confront a higher law, and sometimes it must be suspended. Or it might widen its maxim, and help the world to know that all murder is wrong, within the city, or within the Greek nation, even, in some cities, the murder of a slave; but scarcely, for this was beyond the reach of imagination, among all mankind, including barbarians, at all times. City and family cults might conflict; and the conflict was serious indeed, if it should be between minor sanctities and Zeus who was the god of fidelity, and already beginning to be high god of all the world.

It was easy, then, for Greeks to obey their emotions, but also easy, for many of them, at many times, to need and seek and perhaps apply some systematic rational law of behaviour, which went far beyond custom, and far beyond the old, simple Egyptian precept 'Do rightly in order to get a good reputation'. With brilliant insight and economy, Greeks kept more or less present to themselves the maxim of moderation in all things, with a special fear of *hybris*. But they were fatally able to discard the maxim under stress, partly perhaps because of their sad fear of the jealousy of the divine, supposed to persecute the fortunate no less than the sinful. The Greeks never came near enough to understanding how much the heart should, or should not, direct the mind; they came nearest to it in simple cultivated households, where custom, old faith, rule of moderation, and natural affection made life smooth for a time. The household of Cephalus, the dramatic scene of Plato's *Republic*, was like that; but it was devastated after the dialogue is supposed to have occurred, in the revolution of the Thirty (403 B.C.). It must have seemed hard to make and keep a world in which the heart could rule. It generally is hard.

In Italy experience was in a way quite different. It looks as if an early stage of religion became petrified, and stopped from further development. There were high gods, some of them Greek originally, such as Artemis-Diana, Bacchus-Liber, and also the three gods, Jupiter, Juno, and Minerva, worshipped together at Rome; they were really 'the Etruscan triad', Tinia, Uni, and Menwra, though Jupiter and Juno, with their Indo-European names, were more than half northern, and Menwra may have been an Etruscanized Minerva, whose name is Latin, and whose content owes something to Athena.

But the characteristic Latin deities are functional, like Levicula, goddess of taking up a newly born baby and so recognizing its membership of the family, or Adolenda, Commolenda, and Deferunda, three goddesses for burning, breaking down, and carrying away a tree that has to be removed from the roof of a temple. Such deities are known elsewhere, especially in Rumania. They matter, and therefore exist, only at occasional moments. They are actions which have taken a short step only on the way to personification. One result was that the Romans and others were used to tending, or regarding, powers with few if any human qualities. They were not models for action, for they never did anything; they were mechanical in so far as they were effective, and, not having capricious human wills, they had to be set in automatic action rather than persuaded. For these and for other reasons early Roman religion was hard, formal, and contractual, with no claim on emotion or use for beauty, and only an insistence on the strict discharge of obligations, however unintelligible. This provided a framework of reliability within which loyalty could grow out of natural affection within a wide sphere untouched by technical obligations, but regularly in harmony with them. But rational religion with a place within it for the emotions, such as the later regard for Jupiter, 'most good and most great', *optimus maximus*, and in general for the 'immortal gods', *di immortales*, needed that fusion of Greek thinking and Roman doing which Vergil was concerned to perfect; helped here by something else, hard to fix, which may even have been the Hebrew experience of a single God, and the Hebrew vision that God and goodness go together, and can go together in this world.

Poetry, and also other arts, but especially poetry, are concerned with the subjects of politics, morals, philosophy, and religion, each of which is, however, in its own particular way concerned with all the others. Each in fact must obviously subordinate the rest under its own treatment. But poetry is, among other things, the way to deal with all the others simultaneously, for in it the experience of the past and the wider world can hasten and check and guide the moment's individual thought.

The history of poetry before Vergil is nearly, but not quite, impossible to review in outline.

There were songs to help work, and to express sorrow and joy, when work could not, or need not, help. Song is almost as physically spontaneous as dancing and language itself; they all may well begin as reflex actions, almost short-circuiting the thinking mind. The natural, everyday quality of song can be guessed from considerable evidence collected among simple tribes, especially in North America. Such may be the start of lyric. It becomes religious when words are set to the rhythm of a magical dance, which has come to be thought a dance in honour of a divinity; the divinity is probably the supposed power behind the leader of the dance, or a projection from the mental state of the dancers. That is on the way to choral poetry, drama, and church services.

There is also story-telling, itself an emotional, almost sacramental performance, reacting between the teller and the hearers. It has been observed illuminatingly among simple tribes, for example in East Africa. In such emotional conditions rhythm and metre may be generated spontaneously, as when two men in America, condemned to death, unintentionally spoke their last words in blank verse. So much is enough to start poetic story-telling; but it is possible that verse has sometimes been purposely employed because it is easy to remember, and especially for genealogies, orally transmitted, which, as for centuries in Iceland and New Zealand, have sometimes been the only legal title to land and rank.

Story-telling may deal in fairy tales, some going back even to a time early in the Stone Age, having started as tales about people and things in a primitive hut told by a mother to keep the children quiet. Objects are personified, and the stories seem to be about giants and wonders in the wide world. There are also tales of adventure, starting as accounts of what really happened to energetic people encountering things that they did not understand. Eventually this kind of narrative may become the epic saga of a chief's exploits in battle, perhaps recited by minstrels, more or less extempore, on the very evening of the fight, to the chief himself; as to Attila according to Saxo, and to earlier German chiefs according to Tacitus.

With increasing culture ritual is elaborated. Ritual must be right. To get it right it needs a libretto to remind officiants what to do. Oral, remembered versions are some use, but written versions are better. These versions are found to take the form of narrative, not instructions. A good example is from Ras Shamra, in North Syria, and dated to the thirteenth or fourteenth century B.C. – the libretto of a kind of miracle play, a ritual against drought. Dr Theodor Gaster[1] has published and explained it. In it directions for officiants to pour water as a rain charm are expressed. 'Then the goddesses came . . .', and so on, in narrative form, and with the transition from human performer to divine, mythical being complete. Such an expression of stage directions occurs also in old English texts.

This is one kind of literary original which operated on Greek poets from the east; it is at least hard to believe that this kind of play, very old in the east, is in no sense ancestral to Greek drama. There was much more.[2] The Sumerians had other literature which, by whatever way, affected Greek poetry, especially the *Epic of Gilgamish* and *The Descent of Ishtar*. Saga, which consists of stories of fact, and true myth, developed normally from cult, and plain fairy tales also, all affect each other; and certain favourite forms are found which attract into themselves new material. The *Iliad* of Homer, perhaps finished in the eighth century B.C., reflects the siege of Babylon that occurred before 2000 B.C.; and the *Odyssey* of Homer the stories, earlier still, about journeys of both Gilgamish and Ishtar to the world of the dead, stories that were originally cult-myths, designed to secure happiness after death.

From a time soon after the first Greeks arrived in Greece (? *c.* 2000 B.C.), for a thousand years, the preparation for the work of Homer went on, and Greek poetry, containing saga, myth, and fairy tales, developed, till the metre of the long hexameter verse, a special poetic language and style, and the art of choosing and combining material were all, in Homer, perfected. What went before Homer can only be guessed; but Homer, the first known

1. Theodor Gaster, *Thespis*, New York, 1950, 3–72 and elsewhere; Dr Gaster discusses a great number of such texts.
2. W. F. J. Knight, *Vergil and Homer*, Presidential Address to The Virgil Society, 1950; Oxford, 1950; idem, 'The Holy City of the East in Vergil', *Vergilius* II, Jan. 1939, 6–16; T. B. L. Webster, *From Mycenae to Homer*, London, 1958, 64–158, with references, especially in 64 note 2.

European poet, has already achieved perfect epics – that is, long poems of adventure expressing the relation of man to other men, to God, and to nature, in narrative which is partly dramatic. The style and method were clearly developed, as many analogies shew, especially the South Slavonic epic of the last six hundred years, from centuries of oral recitation. This recitation left many fixed formulae of words, and also fixed formulae of thought and incident, to be altered gradually and slightly, or retained as the alphabet of poetic mood. Here began the characteristic practice of European poetry, the release of poetic force in a poet's mind by the action of former poetry. Words and rhythms suggest, and seem to create, ideas and visions quite different from any in the poetry from which they came, even if sometimes the recollection of the original or originals helps the effect or contributes something new and different to it. This poetic creation out of earlier poetry is very important in Vergil. It arose mainly from two things, the conditions of early Greek oral recitation, and the origin of true Latin literature in translations from Greek.

Epic belongs to a feudal and aristocratic and adventurous time – a 'Heroic Age' is the name given to the kind of age in which it arises. Epic is strongly individualistic. Heroes forcibly have their way. Interests are few, fighting, robbery, farming, and simple but often exquisite handicraft; and minstrelsy. The thrill of epic is in the music of the verse, in the release of strong emotions, as in imagined fear and rescue, revenge, or victory, in the interest of strange or familiar tales of strange or familiar people and lands, and in the wonder at miraculous adventures. There is the thrill and pride of courage against odds, courage that must fail in the end before death, with honour the only prize. But in Homer there is already much more, the exquisite moral truth of human personalities, facing sin and pain, and somehow winning; with manifold varieties of character, and with all the appropriate ways in which evil is faced or fled, and some good won. As after a tragedy, you feel in Homer that somehow it is well with Achilles after all the sin and disgrace, and well with Odysseus, after the agonies of disappointment and fear. Homer has contrived for ever the two sorts of great book, conflict-tragedy and the journey to a destination, perhaps a Quest or a Pilgrim's Progress; the ending that seems sad, and the ending that is shiningly happy; which are both, somehow, equally happy endings, by the artist's power. And on the way, as poets must, but reticently, Homer tells what it is like to be man, revealing secrets of the heart and mind that only a great poet knows well enough to reveal.

Homer sets forth a pattern of loyalty, and order, and courage in battle, and harmony and happiness in the home, and kindly rule by wise kings. He makes it clear how thus life can work well and be worth while.

That is not merely flat and obvious. There is a real secret here, which Homer partly discloses, at least confirming the facts so that they become credible; the secret that in some conditions those who deserve luck have luck, and God helps those who help themselves. There are guardian angels, or something very much like them. Homer found them for his age. But when culture grows more complex they have to be sought anew. So the city state demanded answers other than Homer's.

Aristocracies succeeding monarchies, and more settled life in cities succeeding perpetual adventure, meant, for obvious reasons, a different kind of individualism, introverted and repressed, perhaps, rather than extraverted, enjoying the epic freedom of action. Such individualism led naturally to lyric. Perhaps it was really a return to poetic impulses which had preceded the epic period; but the new lyricism of Sappho, Alcaeus, and Anacreon in the seventh and sixth centuries B.C. was of course more subtle and complex.

This direct, personal poetry, the statement without dramatization of the feelings of the poet, common in European and other literature, for example and especially the Chinese, is exceptional in Greek. Far more often there was dramatization of some kind. The reason is given by Father Aurelio Espinosa Pólit, s.J. [1] The Greeks had a way of making the subjective and the objective, the ideal and the real, fit and coincide to perfection. The outlines of the thought and the thing were somehow precise and identical without that penumbra of uncertainty and suggestion, on which the poetry of other societies has greatly relied.

1. Aurelio Espinosa Pólit, s.J., *Virgilio, el poeta y su misión providencial*, Quito, 1932, 134–68, especially 150–9.

There are in this sense two kinds of poetry.[1] The intellectual kind, Greek, and French also, with some exceptions, especially the poetry of Villon and Ronsard and, long after, of the Romantics, depends on meanings internal to words and phrases; the suggestive kind, Latin poetry, with exceptions, especially in the poetry of Ovid, German poetry, and English poetry too, with exceptions among some, but some only, of the 'classical' poets, depends on meanings external to the words, which the words themselves, especially in their unexpected combinations, and their sound and rhythm, induce, evoke, create, or otherwise make apparent. The distinction is like, but not identical with, the distinction between Classical and Romantic poetry. Aeschylus, more than other Greeks, used a penumbral language, with recessions of meaning beyond the words. But Sophocles himself was not purely precise. He may even have helped Vergil to use words with attention to their ambiguities, and their etymological meanings, and make them mean more than words are ordinarily intended, especially by Greeks, to mean. Interest in words has, in fact, already begun. The Sophists encouraged it; and presently Plato in the *Cratylus* shewed how far in this direction Greeks could go. 'Analogy', the normal ancient view, that a word belonged like a shadow to a thing, and by a law of nature corresponded to it, was already threatened by something like 'anomaly', the theory which was to replace it, that words are more conventionally than naturally attached to the things that they mean. Sophocles and Vergil imply the ideal existence of both analogy and anomaly. There is a reality about a word, but it is more than a reality which exactly and permanently fits at a single moment a single thing. Meanwhile the almost religious puns, characteristic of early culture and most obvious of all in the Bible, were having a history. The comedian Aristophanes could have taught Vergil the art of getting simultaneous and contrasting meanings from words, and sentences too.

On the whole intellectual poetry works more through the conscious mind and reason than does the suggestive, penumbral kind,

1. The following generalization may perhaps need some defence, which might, in fact, be available: for example Racine may seem to write suggestive poetry, but it is in fact known that he intentionally avoided penumbral meanings often, if not always.

which is inclined to have its way by awaking the quicker, more discursive, reasoning below the threshold of consciousness. Further, the intellectual kind is often, perhaps most often, inclined to give very direct accounts of things experienced, and the thoughts suggested by them, especially thoughts which are themselves dramatic, unexpected, epigrammatic even, satisfying to the reason, because discovering for it a new activity. The suggestive kind is naturally more associative, and is therefore inclined to associate not only thoughts but moods, sounds, rhythms, and images. The apparent source of this poetry is often in former poetry, verbal reminiscences giving the impression that the later poet is simply copying a predecessor. The truth is that poetry is normally generated from the storage, in William James's 'deep well of unconscious cerebration', of impressions, which, like 'hooked atoms', according to M. Poincaré, combine of themselves, and find new meanings which ultimately are expressed in a new poem. This process, which I call 'integration' in distinction from conscious 'composition', is the method of all genius, and specially belongs to the suggestive kind of poetry. It was first scientifically described by Professor John Livingston Lowes from an examination of the poetry and sources of Coleridge; and first applied by the late E. K. Rand to Vergil. I write more fully of all this later. Vergil owes his greatness and inclusive power and range to countless things, but not least to the poetic process of integration.

Now Greek lyric poetry tends to integrate; as when Sappho rehandles similar thoughts and words in two poems, one of which is specially praised by Dionysius of Halicarnassus for its smooth harmony of expression. The process is not materially different if a poet is sustaining this influence from the words and thoughts of others or of himself or herself. In this, lyric is unlike much later Greek poetry, but like Greek epic; it was the perpetual reproduction and readaptation by old oral recitation which developed for us the integrating process, and it was on this process that for all its long life of perhaps two thousand years Greek epic creation relied. It was, however, characteristically Greek, in the precision with which it fitted ideal to real; there was not normally the dark depth of suggestion, beyond the outline of the thing seen, which lyrical integration, by its own nature, will find. Using Nietzsche's terms, we could say that much of Greek poetry is more Apolline than Dionysiac.

Greek epic habitually enjoyed a healthy spontaneity and freedom and it worked on a wide canvas. The poets, it is clear, kept themselves healthy by the actual exercise of recitation, as Cicero by making speeches, according to his own confession. Originally the minstrels may have become minstrels because through physical defects they were denied the usual direct satisfactions of fighting and other activities; and so sought them in saying, or singing about, what they could not do. There was then some psychological pressure pent by this abnegation, which they released by minstrelsy, in themselves and in their hearers. But the inhibitions of the lyric poets were stronger; they had found the hard frustrations and bitterness of party politics, economic restraint, and love; and their poetry was deeply pent – it was only for a short time, however, and mainly on the fringe of the Greek world.

This deeply pent and held poetry, therefore, with its tendency to long gestation and resulting intensity, and its tendency, too, to integration, has a cognate tendency to self-repetition. Self-repetition is rhythm in a wide sense; and emotion creates rhythm and rhythm emotion. There are plenty of kinds; repeated sounds, in rhyme or assonance, repeated metrical feet, and repeated words or even thoughts can all constitute rhythm. The thought-parallelism of the Hebrew psalms is one extreme instance; another is the verbal repetition of Catullus, when he builds a verse of words used in a former verse, or in two former verses, so creating his best and intensest poetry, as Dr Jan van Gelder[1] has acutely shewn. Self-repetition *is*, he says, lyric style; it is part, or perhaps all, of the rhythm which intensity gives. As the delicacy and force of feeling grow with human culture and experience, the kinds of rhythm gather and combine; and in Vergil they come to their filigree miracle, and their surge of all time's ocean in the world. But that was after the Roman way had made its own a poetry of pent force, which was never fully Greek, the poetry of waiting under con-

1. J. van Gelder, *De Woordherhaling bij Catullus*, The Hague, 1933, *passim;* cf. Thomas Halter, *Form und Gehalt in Vergils Aeneis*, Munich, 1963, who actually reveals a similar schematism in Vergil.

straint, the poetry of men who know themselves, and face steadily their end.[1]

Then there is translation. What is usually meant by Roman literature started about 240 B.C. when Livius Andronicus translated the *Odyssey* into Saturnians, so that, as a schoolmaster, he might have something more interesting than the Twelve Tables of Roman law to teach to the children of the Roman nobility. For a century, in fact for centuries, this translation went on, varying between translation and adaptation, with an important step when Naevius, Plautus, or Terence, whoever it may have been – Terence is quarrelsome about the question, in self-defence – started combining plots to make a single play. One objection to this, as the late W. Beare[2] shewed, was that the plots of Greek plays would give out sooner, if they were thus unfairly and wastefully used. So they might, but such combination, *contaminatio* as it was called, was important to Homer, and still more important to the very life of Roman poetry; it became a kind of integration on a great scale, broad characters and incidents and whole plots being integrated with increasing spontaneity, till Vergil, and the poets in the general European tradition of literature, were reached.

The poetry of the ancient world, therefore, developed in significant relation to the integrating dependence on poetic originals. That was natural and inevitable in oral recitation, and had its share in the lyric movement. Choral lyric, more intellectual and dramatized and less spontaneous, integrated less, though Pindar has notable instances of the verbal integration of the lost Cyclic Epic. He in particular, however, appealed for evocation to the habitual

1. Cf. Brooks Otis, *Virgil, A Study in Civilized Poetry*, Oxford, 1964, Chapter III 'The Subjective Style', 41–96, who cites Richard Heinze, *Vergils Epische Technik*, Leipzig (1928, 145–70) and shews how all is seen through the mind of Vergil himself, or the mind of a character, or both; and how this 'psycho-dramatic approach governs the smallest detail of the language', 43–4; cf. 385; he observes, 43–9, 98–100, how the nature of the Latin Language, and Latin thought, in contrast to Greek, helped Vergil; cf. here also D. J. G. Leech, 'In Praise of Vergil as a Friend', *The Classical Journal*, Malta, IV, 1950, 36–44, who indicates that more than most poets Vergil has the ability to become the intimate friend of his readers; he cites especially C. A. Sainte-Beuve and F. W. H. Myers, two basic authorities for all true appreciation of Vergil.

2. W. Beare, *The Roman Stage*, London, 1955, 2nd ed., Chapter II.

mental tendencies and general mental currency of social groups, the coherent aristocracies of the earlier fifth century, whose members were susceptible of an appeal to rational and emotional assumptions, including myths which all shared.

Comedy assumed this kind of social uniformity also; but it also included verbal allusions to earlier writing by way of parody, a kind of integration not without prospects of enriching future poetry. Much can be done by subtle contrasts of old words with new, and not quite direct, meanings, as Vergil was to shew. Tragedy was different. Tragedy certainly adopted with slight change verbal inspiration from the past, especially the recent past. But its appeal to tradition and to emotive awareness in the audience was not mainly through familiarity, conscious or unconscious, with forms of words, or even common social assumptions. Perhaps it was addressed to something as universal as the larger interest of Homer, to the interest of the great simplicities of life and death, but now in the more complicated conditions of city life requiring more elaborate analysis. A hope in religious faith, older, newer, perhaps deeper than Homer's, had returned, and there was less chance of satisfaction by pride of battle, or rescue for a short moment. Minds had learnt subtlety, and yearning; and contemplation had brought hope rather than despair. The religion of drama is a quest for optimism, and Aeschylus found it.

Aeschylus, with the high hope of an initiate, the delicacy of an Attic aristocrat, and the strength of a victor of Marathon, in his plays set forces in progressive conflict, and proved, by the issue, that sanctities of family, city, and individuals, in their pride, or their hope in their gods, must all give way before a supreme high power, a power that is truly itself only in the process by which time goes to meet eternity, and at no single moment of time is complete. The answer comes by the activity of a good life. Athena – in Jane Harrison's translation – is 'all for the Father', the Father of all the world; and she is a symbol of active living in the restraint and the light of bright Attic days. The white fire of Apollo, clear lines to the eye and clear thought in the brain, is no more sufficient than the dark reluctance of the Furies, who drink blood in vengeance, challenged now to resign the dark horrors of a blind, habitual past to advancing day. It is to Athena that Apollo and the

Furies defer. In Aeschylus, each problem is solved not algebraically but by living. It turns, as you watch, into a new problem. This vitality, restraint, and energy, not timeless, but in time, as time passes on, redeem both Prometheus, who is advancing civilization itself with its sin and danger, and also Zeus; both are saved generations after by Heracles, human good sprung of the divine evil, which was the rape of Io.[1]

It is not certain that any other ancient poet went quite so far; but the truth of Aeschylus, almost too profound to see, must not be forgotten when the poets that were to come are read. Perhaps even Aeschylus left something out. He went too far towards Stoicism; and did not say where loyalty and affection, spontaneous good in a kind of action that is both natural and more than moral, belong.

Sophocles found the answer in the peace after pain, felt as in Homer, not proved as in Aeschylus. He pursued suffering and decay, and so far followed the true tragic experimental method. The loveliness in tiny moments of verse, the music, the pattern in a rhythm of sound, with the sympathy and the gentleness there, even if they were bound to fall, must for Sophocles bear all the weight of the world. So they are made ready for that, and the plays of Sophocles are, I suppose, the most Greek books in existence. Aristotle might well say that Sophocles told of grave actions in language carefully made to be attractive – a strange way of saying it, but true. Vergil learnt from Sophocles how lovely a sound could be. But he gained more from him than that – pictures of stories which carried force and range in their very structural lines, and especially the one answer which we know that Sophocles directly gave in the last of his plays to all the questions of all his plays; and more still, the tragic irony of Sophocles, and his vision of moral law, awaiting its temple on earth.

In Sophocles it is not always possible to see the trees for the wood, and sometimes this makes him seem almost too universal; but there was his younger contemporary Euripides, to reveal places in the human mind still dark, and shew how far, for good and evil, tiny things can go; for evil, little irritations and frustra-

1. W. F. J. Knight, 'The Tragic Vision of Aeschylus', *Greece and Rome*, v, 1935, 29–40.

tions, little unkindnesses and stupidities, inclinations to go too far even in apparent goodness, and the folly of trusting too much the terrible powers of nature in man, and the mercy of gods, man-made; and for good, simplicities of homes, the rightness, conscience, and beauty of ideal Athens, and the relief, in times of pain, of the woods, and the mountains, and streams.

The Alexandrians went on with this work in their own way. Apollonius put the subtlety of feeling, which in Euripides belongs to failure, into the thrill of a happy emotion of love, which Euripides had not yet elaborated. Callimachus told in poetry of myths and ancient cult and mystery. Euripides had also liked the past for its interest. And Theocritus brought the country itself out from the mere relief of the choric ode, and normal, active love out from the background of a story, on to the central stage, where highly complex urban communities needed it most. The *Idylls* that he and others wrote were something new, several of them something Sicilian, and on the way from Greece to Italy.[1]

The poets of Rome, therefore, had much to translate, but they soon gave special attention to the almost contemporary New Comedy of Athens, plays by Menander, Diphilus, and others, which, in the surprises of plot, frivolity, and irresponsibility, gave serious Romans, who were attractively shocked by what they were now finding out about Greek life on Italian and Sicilian soil, an undoubtedly pleasant release, and indeed the lowest comedies were the greatest success. This release may well have helped, after generations passed, to liberate the Roman mind for satire and lyric. Latin comedy helped to generate tensions which could well be needed for work of grander scale.

On a different side, Rome in the third and second centuries had begun to talk about herself. The *Odyssey* and the Twelve Tables were marrying each other. Naevius made a poetic chronicle of the First Punic War, which included some of the Roman foundation legends in some form, and Ennius adapted the hexameter to a similar purpose in his long poem of Annals. This use of epic ex-

1. For the literature available to Roman poets, and the literary situation, Greek and Roman, which they inherited, see Kenneth Quinn, *The Catullan Revolution*, Melbourne, 1959, and Brooks Otis, *Virgil, A Study in Civilized Poetry*, Oxford, 1964, Chapter II.

ample is the more extraordinary the more it is contemplated. Perhaps the most remarkable thing is the adaptation of epic for an intensely national and moral purpose in a poem which is in a special way the production and possession of a whole people – almost as it would have been if Homer had positively planned his poems to be the Bible of the Greeks. That, however, would have been a calamity. Poets, it is now almost too well known, must not preach; by some obscure law, preaching spoils their poetry and their purpose. It was a remarkably difficult problem how to make national, moralizing, and eventually propagandist poems succeed in being poetry at all. The earlier Latin poets had plenty of success, partly because, so far as we can see, the national and the moral tendencies had not gone very far, and propaganda was absent. The answer to the question proved to lie in myth, and myth of a subtle and elaborate kind.

The first century before Christ was a solemn time, when the work for the world of the Greek city state and the Republic of Rome was finishing. And it was a time of terror and despair, wickedness and decay of order and faith, retrogression, and violent development forward in directions of dread. It was a time of the failure of advanced ideas, such as the Gracchan conception of democracy, rationalized according to Greek systems of thought, which had held out hope before.

In reaction, there was a return to personal loyalties and what seemed to humanists and rationalists old-fashioned insufficiencies. The partly Stoic conception, and partly very un-Stoic concession, of the law of reason as a personal law, the will of a leader, was something like a resurgence of divine kingship or blind theocracy, passed to Rome from the remains of Alexander's East. It filled a lack in democracy and aristocracy, Greek and Italian. But it was dangerous. As Dr John Murray has said, 'There is no democracy without aristocracy.' Cicero was much exercised by the problem of finding leaders, perhaps just a few leaders, of high enough quality to stave off the domination of single men.

The movement towards personal rule, superstitiously exaggerated, practically useful, or richly and progressively religious, should be connected with the special Roman expansion of self-consciousness, and the enhancement of the value of personality.

It all goes back to the beginnings of Rome, and much of it beyond or aside from them; and results are seen in the Roman sensitivity to friendship in the first century, and also in the poetry then. The wild pathos and depth of Lucretius, the grace and appealing strangeness and intimacy of Tibullus, the expressive, active vitality and self-awareness of Propertius, and the passion of Catullus, quick-minded, humorous, fanciful, for all his hot blood and hot, hopeless tears, shew that man had become something new. Even Euripides looks in a way impersonal beside them. Yet perhaps Euripides, and many Greeks, got much farther than they. It was another dilemma, with a solution to come.

The young poets among whom Vergil grew up were noted for their devotion to Alexandrian precedent. They followed Callimachus, Euphorion, and perhaps Theocritus[1] and other pastoral poets, attending particularly to poetry in elegiacs, hexameters and pentameters alternately, a metre which had been useful already for the premature reflective pessimism of Callinus and Mimnermus in the seventh century B.C., and became no less useful for the Roman poets, men of a personality more complex and more aware. Theirs was a poetry of mood, rather assuming, than seeking, by great structures of patterned design, answers to the great questions. This Roman genius went deeply down, but did not spread wide, or soar upwards, yet.[2]

1. J. S. Phillimore, *Pastoral and Allegory* ... , Oxford, 1925, 10–13, argues that it was a very important move on the part of Vergil when he deliberately abandoned Euphorion and the rest for Theocritus – there being little from any other Hellenistic poet in the *Eclogues* at all; cf. now Viktor Poschl, *Die Hirtendichtung Virgils*, Heidelberg, 1964. For a recent, sharp-sighted, treatment of the literary situations and movements half-concealed in the *Eclogues*, see Otto Skutsch, 'Zu Vergils Eklogen', *Rheinisches Museum* . . . . , LXXXXIX, 1956, 193–201.

2. Propertius, perhaps a greater poet than these, was perhaps on the brink of the Vergilian vision; there is no room here for any fair treatment: see Luigi Alfonsi, *L'Elegia di Properzio*, Milan, 1945.

CHAPTER 2

VERGIL'S LIFE AND WORK

VERGIL'S life is much better known than Shakespeare's, but not nearly so well known as Milton's. The contemporary information is very slight. It includes internal evidence, and whatever of contemporary evidence is transmitted in later documents. The internal evidence in Vergil's poetry is direct and indirect. The poetry is full of indirect references to events and conditions, but they need other evidence to be interpreted. The direct internal evidence consists in mentions of important people by name, such as Octavianus (Augustus), Maecenas, Pollio, and Gallus, and allusions to events, such as the confiscation of Vergil's farm and the expedition of Octavianus to the East. The internal evidence alone could furnish about one page of statements. The external evidence is much fuller but of uncertain value.[1] It consists firstly of several *Lives of Vergil*, mainly transmitted with manuscripts of Vergil himself or his commentators, especially the *Life* attributed to Aelius Donatus the famous Grammarian of the fourth century, probably in part derived from a *Life of Vergil* written by Suetonius in the early second century. Secondly there is the information contained in commentaries, especially the commentary of Servius, mainly of the fourth century A.D., but expanded, the most important additions being known by the name Daniel and so cited, though some or all may have been written by Aelius Donatus. Thirdly, there are mentions in later writers, especially Macrobius, who wrote in the fifth century A.D. his *Saturnalia*, the only extant ancient work, apart from commentaries, principally devoted to Vergil. Vergil

---

1. For powerful treatments of this very intricate question, and other associated questions, see especially Ettore Paratore, *Una nuova ricostruzione del 'De poetis' di Suetonio*, Rome, 1946, and Karl Büchner, *P. Vergilius Maro, Der Dichter der Römer*, Stuttgart, 1955 (a monumental article reprinted from Pauly-Wissowa, and a constant resource, especially on the most intricate Vergilian problems), 1–41.

became famous in his life-time, and his poetry a school book. Much information about him was preserved. Even the commentary of Servius may go back often to contemporaries; and Macrobius verbally quotes from correspondence between Vergil and Augustus. The information from all these sources is often contradictory or otherwise suspicious. Some, however, is reasonably trustworthy; especially as it is used by the late Professor Tenney Frank in his life of Vergil,[1] a work of which I have availed myself here with great freedom, and most often with assent to its conclusions.

Late in Italian prehistory, and probably not long before the foundation of Rome (? 753 B.C.), Celts from beyond the Alps had settled in what is now north Italy, the valley of the river Po and the Plains of Lombardy. They expanded farther, and pressed the Etruscans, who had probably come from Asia Minor in two main waves in the late thirteenth and the eighth to seventh centuries;[2] and, having thus helped the Romans, still farther to the south, but almost surrounded at that time by Etruscans, to break the Etruscan domination, continued on their way till they captured Rome itself (? 390 B.C.). Whether the raiding bands of Celts hoped to retain the site of Rome or not, they did not do so. Rome revived, and during the fourth and third centuries B.C. steadily forced her way into Celtic territory. Just before the Second Punic War (218–202 B.C.), she established colonies in the Celtic country not far south of the Alps; Placentia, Cremona, and Mutina. At first these and other outpost cities were hard to maintain, and some had to be partly resettled in the second century. But they survived and prospered, and in the first century B.C. there existed in Cisalpine Gaul an advanced and vital culture, sustained economically by the energetic cultivation of rich soil, and based on the old Latin tradition of home life and service. After the Marsic War 'Gaul' between the Po and the Alps received 'Latin rights' (89 B.C.); and it received full Roman citizenship forty years later (49 B.C.), by one of Julius Caesar's very first acts, when he became master of Rome.

1. Tenney Frank, *Vergil, A Biography*, Oxford, 1922; H. J. Rose, *The Eclogues of Vergil*, Berkeley, California, 1942.

2. G. A. Wainwright, 'The Teresh, the Etruscans and Asia Minor', *Anatolian Studies*, IX, 1959, 197–213.

The 'waveless plains of Lombardy', as Shelley called them, have always been a good place for a productive mixture of races. The upper-class society there in the first century B.C. was Latin, like society at Rome, and probably more Latin still, and at any rate healthier, for in the capital the pace was quicker and there were more influences working for decadence. But there were other racial traditions in the north which necessarily affected the Latin families there. The population was mainly Celtic. To the west near the sea was a pre-Celtic population, the Ligurians, who gave their name to Livorno, Leghorn. To the east, destined also to leave their name behind them, were Veneti, who in very early times, perhaps not many generations after Rome was founded, came from an uncertain place, possibly Paphlagonia in Asia Minor, to settle the site where Venice still stands. And, though Etruscan power had fallen and Etruscan culture was being absorbed by the Latin and Greek culture of Rome, Etruscans still lived in the north, and Etruscan greatness was remembered there. Greek influence was less forceful in Cisalpine Gaul than in South Italy; but Marseilles had been founded as the Greek city Massilia about 600 B.C., nearly a hundred years before Rome expelled her kings.

The city of Mantua, on the Po, near its mouth, was according to Vergil[1] a city of mixed culture; and it was at Andes, a village near Mantua, that in 70 (or possibly 71) B.C., he was born. Vergil says that at Mantua there were three racial elements, each constituted by four different communities, but that it was from the Etruscan blood that she drew her strength. Whatever the precise meaning may be, and it can scarcely be fully ascertained, it is clear that Vergil attributed a mixture of races to his own city.

Vergil himself has been supposed an Etruscan, a Venetian, a Celt, and a Jew; and he has been thought to have had some Greek blood in him. The reasons for these views are not equally conclusive. Vergil's praise of the Etruscan strain at Mantua need not of course mean that he himself had, or thought that he had, Etruscan connexions. Nor need the 'romantic' quality which is sometimes attributed to his poetry suggest that he was a Celt. Renan and others have rightly estimated the Celtic love of what is strange, remote, and mysterious; and it may even be legitimate to

1. *A.* x, 198–203.

call this tendency or preference romantic. But the word 'romantic' is not sufficiently precise to be safely used in classifying writers, still less races; and again, if Vergil has some of the qualities which are sometimes included under that word, there are plenty of other poets, ancient and modern, who also have qualities that may be called romantic, but who were certainly not Celts. On the whole, both Vergil's father and his mother may well have been Italians, though it is not improbable, from what is known of the family names,[1] that both had some Etruscan blood.

From the evidence that exists it is safe to regard Vergil as a Latin, with probable Etruscan connexion, belonging to a Latin family settled, perhaps already for generations, in Cisalpine Gaul. His name, Vergilius, is common among Latins, in the north and elsewhere. The spelling with an *e* is certainly right, but the wrong spelling with an *i* occurs already at about Vergil's own time.

There is an interesting hint that Vergil's own name was sometimes spelt and pronounced as 'Virgilius'. When he lived at Naples, he was nicknamed Parthenias, a name which in Greek means 'maidenly'. Perhaps the nickname was partly due to Vergil's known nature and partly to a similarity between his name spelt with an *i* and the Latin word *virgo*, 'virgin', 'maiden'. There may have been other influences too, such as the name, Parthenope, of a village near his house in Campania; and perhaps also, though we cannot now see just how such a suggestion worked, the name of one of his teachers, Parthenius.

Much more obvious is the later history of the name. 'Virgilius' suggested not only *virgo* but also *virga*, 'rod', or 'magic wand'. That made it easier for Vergil, regarded as 'man of the magic wand', to gain a reputation as a magician. His mother's name may have helped also. By a strange coincidence she was Magia Polla; and 'Magia' contained the element *mag-*, which in ancient Persian, Greek and Latin, as in modern languages, could mean or connote 'magical'.

Vergil's praenomen Publius is of course one of the most common. His cognomen, or family name, Maro, is more interesting. It occurs in the *Odyssey* as the name of a priest of Apollo. So far as we know, that is a pure coincidence, and however attractive the

1. Mary L. Gordon, *The Journal of Roman Studies*, XXIV, 1934, 1–12.

coincidence may be it is not legitimate to argue from it, as has been urged, that Vergil had Greek or Balkan connexions. The name has a meaning in Etruscan and Umbrian speech also; it was originally a word denoting Etruscan magistrates, sometimes translated by the Latin term aedile. Possibly some ancestor of Vergil held such an appointment.

Vergil's father was said to have been a yeoman farmer, originally a servant, who, like the father of Keats, married his employer's daughter. He certainly worked a farm, with bees and cattle. He is also said to have manufactured pottery – a pottery-factory was part of the farm, and thus an honourable source of livelihood – or managed a local postal and delivery service, or to have been a bailiff for a landowner. Clearly, he was, or at least became, a prosperous owner of land. That was likely to involve also the ownership of a pottery works, for then, though not under the later empire, pottery-making was often a home industry. Cicero owned a pottery-factory. Vergil's father must have been a man of some standing, and not altogether poor, for he planned for Vergil an upper-class career, and could afford to educate him for it.

What is known of Vergil's physical and other characteristics allows the suggestion that he was partly Etruscan, but does not contradict the probability that he was of Latin stock. He is described in the *Life* by Donatus as tall and dark, countrified in appearance, unready in speech, untidy in dress, and of weak health; it is suggested that he suffered from tuberculosis, and eventually died of it. With this general description two portraits that exist agree.[1] One is very remarkable, and early. It is a mosaic of the second century A.D., found in north Africa. Vergil is seen seated, reading a copy of his *Aeneid* open near the beginning at *musa mihi causas memora*, 'Muse, tell for me this tale, how all began . . .'[2] Behind him, one on each side, are the muse of epic, here and here only Euterpe, and the muse of tragedy, Melpomene. Vergil is shewn with close-cropped black hair receding from a low, sloping forehead, a rounded chin, full lips, and hollow, ill, visionary eyes. It may well be an authentic portrait of Vergil at the age of about forty-five.

1. J. F. Crome, *Das Bildnis Vergils*, Mantua, 1935; Tenney Frank, *Vergil, A Biography*. Oxford, 1922, Chapter 1, with references.

2. *A.* 1, 8.

The other portrait, which is possibly but not certainly a portrait of Vergil, shews Vergil, if it is Vergil, as he was when he was much younger. The portrait is a bust which exists in several copies; it is hard to say who can be represented if it is not Vergil, but the identification is not certain.

Vergil is known besides from scattered notices. Horace mentions him more than once, calling him *anima candida*, perhaps 'a nature pure and bright, through and through',[1] and attributing to him what is *molle atque facetum*, 'a wit that is sensitive, tender, and expressive'.[2] It is sad that here, even more than usually, our knowledge of the Latin language fails us. These two expressions are a severe test of scholarship. No one can be sure of translating them exactly, and thus we cannot know as precisely as we should wish how Vergil appeared to one of his closest friends. There is even a view resting on the authority of Quintilian,[3] that *facetum* does not here imply humour or a sense of the comic, but something like 'eloquent', or 'expressive', an older meaning. But the other meaning is common,[4] and remains possible. The adjective *mollis* in a context of Augustan poetry is inclined to mean tender, sensitive, sentimental, or even immorally passionate and sensual. Here there is no need to press it. 'Sympathetic' may be a large part of its meaning.[5] The two adjectives stand alone, with no noun. It is not legitimate to supply *ingenium*, a word which tends in classical Latin to have an intellectual rather than a moral meaning, 'brains' rather than 'character'. Even if it were legitimate to supply it, it would not add much, since Horace is indicating the styles of several poets, and means his adjectives to describe Vergil's. The phrase is certainly inadequate to the Vergil of the *Aeneid*; which is not surprising, since when Horace used it the *Aeneid* was not

1. Horace, *Satires*, I, 5, 41–2.   2. ibid., I, 10, 44.
3. Quintilian, VI, 3, 20.
4. Cicero, *De Officiis*, I, 29, 104; I, 30, 108; etc.
5. J. S. Phillimore, *Some Remarks on Translation and Translators*, English Association Pamphlet No. 42, London, January 1919, 12–13, thinks Vergil is being called 'the sentimental humorist' with implication of humour and irony, and he quotes Servius, *Introduction to A.* IV, *paene comicus est stilus*, 'almost in the manner of comedy'. Cf. also id. *Ille ego: Virgil and Professor Richmond*, London, 1920, and *Pastoral and Allegory, a re-reading of the Bucolics of Virgil*, Oxford, 1925.

written, and Horace only knew the early poems, the *Eclogues*, and perhaps the *Georgics* also.

Vergil is recorded to have been born at Andes, now Pietole, in the first consulship of Pompeius and Crassus (70 B.C.), and lived there, uneventfully so far as is known, with his father, mother and one brother, till he went to school. There is no doubt that he regarded his family, his home, and the farm with intense interest and devotion.

When he was about ten to twelve years old, he started going to school at Cremona (? 60–58 B.C.). That was the time when Julius Caesar was beginning his ten-year conquest of Gaul beyond the Alps. Caesar was recruiting his army at Cremona and elsewhere in Cisalpine Gaul, always a good recruiting ground. Soon his famous *Commentaries* on the Gallic War began to appear; it has been attractively suggested that Vergil read them 'in serial form', with an interest increased by the occasional sight of Julius himself.

The education at Cremona was from the Roman point of view primary education, that is, grammatical and literary. Probably the education in Cisalpine Gaul reached a high standard, with a catholicity of literary taste not permissible at Rome; for there, as now sometimes at our own older universities, fashion rigidly and exclusively prescribed what must be admired and what neglected.

In the year (55 B.C.) when Lucretius his great predecessor is sometimes said to have died, the year when Pompeius and Crassus were consuls together for the second time, Vergil is supposed, but doubtfully, to have assumed the *toga virilis*, the dress of manhood; and apparently in the same year he left the school at Cremona for a school of the same kind at Milan. There it is safe to think that he continued his grammatical and literary education at a higher standard. Milan, Mediolanum, was a big centre, then as afterwards, and before: it had been the chief city, in a sense the capital, of Cisalpine Gaul before any Romans were there. The opportunity at Milan for wide culture and wide reading must have been excellent.

In the next year (54 B.C.), Catullus died, and then or not long after Vergil went to Rome for the second stage of his education. He was to learn rhetoric, to fit himself to practise at the bar, and perhaps qualify for the political career to which the bar was an admission. Like Ovid, for whom such a career was also planned, Vergil could not face so uncongenial a prospect for long. He spoke in the courts once only, and his performance was bad. The rhetorical education was very narrow, specialized and technical. Examples of sixty figures of speech had to be learnt by heart. Everything was planned for efficiency, and for the successful achievement of the main purpose in the face of fierce competition. It was not even certain that efforts so spent would not be wasted. At about the time when Vergil first went to Rome, the capital was in a ferment of lawless rioting; Pompeius, most unconstitutionally sole consul, without a colleague, was attempting to maintain order by force (52 B.C.). And when in that year Cicero tried to defend Milo, the leader of one riotous gang, against the charge of murdering Clodius, the leader of another, freedom of speech, and the practical use of rhetoric, were already becoming farcical. This Vergil may have had the perspicacity to see; but his distaste for rhetoric was sufficient without any such reflections. Apparently, his father afforded Vergil the best facilities to be had, if there is truth in the record[1] that he attended the classes of Epidius, the teacher of Antonius and Octavianus himself,[2] and there met Octavianus. This is not impossible. Octavianus was about seven years younger, but he was advanced for his age, since when he was twelve years old he prepared to deliver a funeral speech for his grandmother.

Events now moved fast in the Roman world, but, so far as we know for certain, Vergil's life remained surprisingly unaffected by them. Julius crossed the Rubicon, swept down Italy, and occupied Rome (49 B.C.); the government, led by Pompeius, escaped across the Adriatic just in time. Perhaps Vergil remained in the capital throughout the first year of the civil war. Or perhaps he was conscripted by Julius. The evidence for such a supposition is a poem[3] just possibly by Vergil about the hardships of war, supported by suggestions in Vergil's undoubted work – a knowledge of the Adriatic, and a clear picture of the battlefield of Pharsalus where Julius defeated Pompeius (48 B.C.). It is possible that Vergil served for a year, and was discharged as medically unfit after the

1. The *Life of Vergil* heading the Berne MS.
2. Suetonius, *De rhetoribus*, IV.   3. *Catalepton*, XIII.

hard winter of the first year of the war; but it is just as likely, or perhaps more likely, that his health prevented him from serving at all.

Soon his movements are clear again. Immediately after the battle of Pharsalus, or even before, he left Rome and settled in Campania, where he lived for most of the rest of his life. He went there to join a philosophical school or circle, called 'the Garden', where he meant to enjoy what seemed then the satisfying reality of Epicurean philosophy, a pleasant change from the unrealities of rhetoric.

The school was founded by Phaedrus, and continued by Philodemus and Siro. Some years before Vergil went there Cicero expressed a high opinion of its learning. Philodemus was a very cultured man, an Epicurean who let himself go beyond the orthodoxy of Epicurus himself, and also a writer of Greek verse, especially epigrams in the Alexandrian tradition; the Syrian Epicureans, from whom 'the Garden' originated, were less rigid than others. Books of Philodemus' library, including partly burnt rolls containing works written by himself, have been found at Herculaneum. In Vergil's time 'the Garden' was directed by Siro, who must have been a good and inspiring teacher; it is only fair to concede him some influence in forming Vergil's mind. Vergil was with Siro for about six years, till his death (42 B.C.); and even then he seems to have remained at his villa, which he perhaps inherited.

So Vergil stayed quietly in Campania while the great events of the civil war were passing. After Caesar's victory at Pharsalus in Greece (48 B.C.) came his further victories at Thapsus in Africa (46 B.C.) and Munda in Spain (45 B.C.); next the assassination of Caesar (44 B.C.), the usurpation of Antonius, and simultaneously the emergence of Caesar's great-nephew Octavianus, who accepted the inheritance of Caesar and took command of his army.

Then (43 B.C.) came the momentary revival of the Senate's power, led by Cicero with his bitter attacks on Antonius; the complicated war centred in north Italy, where Octavianus, in association with the Republican consuls, besieged Antonius at Mutina and later (41–40 B.C.) the brother of Antonius, Lucius, at Perusia; the agreement of Marcus Antonius, Octavianus, and Lepidus to form a 'triumvirate', and their 'proscriptions', in which among many others Cicero lost his life (43 B.C.); the mobilization of armies in the east by the 'liberators', Brutus and Cassius; and the Battle of Philippi in Macedonia (42 B.C.), where they lost all, and Octavianus and Antonius prevailed.

After Philippi, an event occurred which seriously concerned Vergil. Octavianus wanted to settle some 100,000 demobilized troops on the land, and ruthlessly confiscated farms in Italy, among other places in Campania where Vergil lived, and also near Cremona and Mantua, including probably enough his own old home. In his first certainly authentic poetry, the *Eclogues*, Vergil introduces the emotions which the evictions stirred, sadness at loss, and joy at unexpected restoration. Once he appeals to a friend, Alfenus Varus, a member of the commission for the redistribution of land, to save Mantua. It is possible that Varus, or some other powerful friend, saved Vergil's home from confiscation, but little can be asserted; Servius and other ancient commentators, too boldly interpreting the *Eclogues*, and reflecting back into history the conditions of patronage and flattery existing in their own days, give an account of what happened that is altogether fanciful and misleading.

There was now little resistance to the conquerors except from Sextus Pompeius, who dominated the Sicilian Seas and threatened the food supply of Rome until his defeat seven years later (35 B.C.). But there was danger to each of the two victors from the ambition and jealousy of the other. Soon after Philippi the antagonism was marked by an attempt to end it, the Treaty of Brundisium (40 B.C.), sealed by the marriage of Antonius to Octavia, sister of Octavianus. Octavianus was to govern Italy and Antonius the East.

These were the years when Vergil began his poetic career. He is not known to have written any poetry before the death of Cicero; but soon after the Treaty of Brundisium he was already famous. These were the three years, within which, according to Donatus, he wrote the ten *Eclogues*. Their publication established Vergil's reputation immediately.

The *Eclogues*, the *Georgics*, and the *Aeneid* are the only extant poems certainly known to have been written by Vergil. But there exist others, collected under the name of the *Appendix Vergiliana*, which are attributed to him with varying probability. Many of these poems were written during Vergil's early years, whoever actually wrote them. If they were known to be authentic, they could throw much light on the story of his early life, and on his mental and artistic development. But not one is certainly by Vergil.

The ten *Eclogues*, 'Selections', otherwise *Bucolics*, 'Poetry of cowherding', are short pastoral pieces in hexameters, the metre of all Vergil's certain work. They can be to some extent dated from internal evidence in relation to the history of the time. First in or before 42 B.C. came *Eclogues* II, III, VII, and VI, probably in that order; then, in 41 B.C., X, V, VIII, IX, and I, again probably in that order; and lastly, in 40 B.C., IV. The order depends on arguments of varying strength. *Eclogue* V refers to *Eclogues* II and III, quoting their opening words. *Eclogue* IV belongs to 40 B.C. because it refers to Pollio as consul for the year, and a baby to be born of a marriage then taking place, possibly the dynastic marriage between Antonius and Octavia arranged at or about the time of the Treaty of Brundisium. These indications may be called certain. The other *Eclogues* fall into place with some probability. *Eclogues* I and IX mention the evictions after Philippi (42 B.C.). The supposed history of Vergil's friends, Messalla and Gallus, helps to date *Eclogues* II and X respectively, where they are mentioned. *Eclogues* II, III, and VI seem to be all in a similar early style, with strongly dramatic dialogue. *Eclogue* X has an introduction, designating it as the last of the *Eclogues*, and also a conclusion, quoting the first line of the first *Eclogue* as the start of the series. These passages are not organic, and were added when the poems were arranged for publication in their present order.

After the *Eclogues* were published, Vergil is not known to have written poetry for a few years. He read and perhaps travelled with Maecenas; he may have travelled with him again later, on a mission of appeasement to Antonius (37 B.C.), and it may have been then that he gained much of his geographical knowledge. Maecenas, the statesman and patron of letters, whom he had met when he was in Rome, admired him greatly, and after the *Eclogues* were published gave him a house there, in his own gardens on the Esquiline Hill. Vergil always however preferred to live near Naples and came to Rome very rarely. But it was in some sense at the suggestion of Maecenas that he planned his next great work, the *Georgics*, four books ostensibly for the instruction of farmers. It was, he says, the command of Maecenas.[1] The *Georgics* were written in seven years (37–30 B.C.), at an average rate of less than one line a day.

These were years of dawning hope but unsolved problems. Octavianus, helped especially by Maecenas in home affairs and by Agrippa in war, was trying to secure order and prosperity in Italy. He had bad times. There were food riots, and his authority was sometimes openly defied. There was at first the pressure of Sextus Pompeius and his fleet on the communications of Italy; and in a campaign against him Octavianus himself had a narrow escape and suffered some loss of personal dignity. It is hard to recognize in the Octavianus of these early years the benign and majestic sovereign whom the world remembered. But before the *Georgics* were finished he had already changed, and was no longer the engaging but disreputable and coldly ferocious young creature[2] who at Perusia had brutally 'sacrificed' three hundred of the city's nobility (40 B.C.).

The complicated history of these years involved other tensions. The Peace of Brundisium could not last. The east of the Roman world was in sharp cultural and political competition with the west; and old and new aspirations were strengthened and focalized by the combined leadership of Antonius of Rome and Cleopatra of Egypt, heiress to the Pharaohs and the Macedonian kings. At the Battle of Actium (31 B.C.) two Roman forces met; the fighting itself, such as it was, before propaganda overlaid it, is not altogether easy to understand; but Octavianus and Agrippa quickly won.

After Actium, the *Georgics* were soon finished, and the *Aeneid* begun, with a confidence in its message which Actium had helped to impart. The *Aeneid* was written in eleven years (30–19 B.C.), and destined to undergo revision for another three. The twelve books were all but finished but not revised when Vergil planned a voyage to Greece, to see the places there which came into his

1. *G.* I, 2; III, 41; IV, 2.
2. Sir Ronald Syme, *The Roman Revolution*, Oxford, 1939, *passim*; W. F. J. Knight, *The Classical Review*, XLVI, 1932, 55–7; XLVII, 1933, 169–71.

story. He travelled as far as Megara and there met Octavianus, now Augustus. At Megara he suddenly suffered an attack of illness, perhaps connected with the habitual cause of his weak health, whatever that may have been. He returned to Italy and died at Brundisium. Before he died he anxiously wished the *Aeneid* to be burnt, for reasons that cannot be recovered now. Augustus either overruled the desire or more probably persuaded Vergil to consent to the publication of the *Aeneid* by his old friends Varius and Tucca, who were to edit the work, adding nothing not already in the text, and excising passages which were in the text but which in their judgement Vergil would have removed. Within a year or a little longer the work was done and the *Aeneid* published. Vergil was laid to rest near his home, in a tomb by the sea and now under deep bright water, on the now submerged coast road from Naples to the north. His epitaph, written by some friend, and quoted by Donatus, his biographer, had his own reticence: '*Mantua me genuit*; *Calabri rapuere*; *tenet nunc Parthenope*; *cecini pascua, rura, duces*' – 'Mantua gave me life, and from life Calabria stole me; but to Parthenope I now belong; my singing was of pastures and farms, and chieftains at their wars.'

Little is known of the details of Vergil's ordinary life beyond this outline. But information is available about the mental experiences which helped to make his poetry, and the intellectual and artistic influences which he underwent can be detected. The names and characteristics of some of his friends are known. To a few of them he refers in his poems, and many have a place in the history of the time. There were others who may or may not have known Vergil or who certainly did not know him, personally, but who must have contributed to the quality of the mental world in which he lived.

From Vergil's country in the north came many poets at about his time. There was Valerius Cato, who exercised a strong influence towards Alexandrian style on his younger contemporaries; Gaius Valerius Catullus himself, from Verona; Varius Rufus, Quintilius Varus, Alfenus Varus, and Furius Bibaculus, all from Cremona, where Vergil first went to school; there was Caecilius of Novum Comum; and Helvius Cinna, probably from Brixia.

Vergil spent his life among poets and thinkers, many of whom were men of action also. It was a fascinating and brilliant society, vital with energy and devotion to objects of great endeavour. There was real enthusiasm for reading and writing prose and verse.

The first few years of Vergil's life were the years when Lucretius and Catullus were founding classical Latin poetry. Catullus was neglected afterwards, and Lucretius too, in some periods at least. Lucretius (99 [? 95]–59 [? 52–51] B.C.) was unique. His poem, in six books of hexameter verse, *De rerum natura*, 'The Nature of the World', was a philosophical poem. There were many philosophical poems in Greek and some in Latin (mainly translations), as there are in other languages. Robert Bridges' *The Testament of Beauty* shews that they are still wanted, and can still be written. Among ancient philosophical poems was a work of Manilius, a contemporary of Vergil, who wrote with dexterity and sometimes humour on astrology and astronomy. Lucretius was unique for two reasons which go together, his real scientific ardour for close reasoning and for truth, and the deep poetic emotion which impelled him to seek in science that union between the mind and the outer world for which all poetry contends.

Lucretius, for his philosophical poem, adopted the form of the Greek poem on nature by Empedocles (who lived in the fifth century B.C.); his subject was the physical and still more the moral philosophy of Epicurus (who was active from about 300 B.C.), based on the physical and metaphysical theory of Democritus (of the fifth century), atomistic materialism. There had been no Epicurean poem; the literature of the school was in prose, usually very plain in style. However, a certain Sallust, perhaps the historian and the later contemporary of Lucretius, wrote a Latin poem, now lost, on the philosophy of Empedocles; one poem may have helped to provoke the other. (This Sallust may be, if not the historian, the Gnaeus Sallustius of Cicero's letters.)[1] The poem of Lucretius, unlike other ancient philosophical poems, except perhaps the poem of Empedocles himself, is intensely poetic, with the pressure of violent emotion. Lucretius longed to make humanity at home in the universe, and conquer sadness, and

1. Sir Ronald Syme, *Sallust*, Berkeley, California, 1964, 10–12.

the fear of death and of gods. He hoped to explain all terrors away by his science, and to give calm to the world. But, like Epicurus himself, he had for his motive pity and love. Both cared most for human happiness, and only afterwards for knowledge. Epicurus was a saint and a prophet, and could be a poet too. 'All the world is dancing with friendship' is his most famous saying. But Lucretius, in an Italian way, saw with passion the majesty of nature and her changeful power no less than the pathetic loveliness of human things. He was too honest to see a human heart in nature; unless, perhaps, he was not quite sufficient in prophetic greatness.

Lucretius stands alone, strongly individual, because he had assimilated and blended many different things, especially the science of Greeks, the old Latin language and verse of Ennius, the spoken Latin of his time, which he used with a true poet's violence, the depth of reflective Italian passion, and a sympathy that was partly Greek and partly of his own civilized and sensitive world.

The more general and characteristic tradition of Latin poetry was different. It was detached from old Latin and from the early Greek language and thought, and it blended current Italian impulses with current and recent Greek literary achievement. The Alexandrian, Hellenistic poetry of the last three centuries B.C. could certainly pretend to satisfy, by its interest, facility, and complexity, and by the sensitivity of its literary forms, the strong mental needs of Italians. For all that, there was a certain simplicity too, a regularity of mood and resource. The same kind of complexity, mainly complexity of feeling and balanced structure, recurred. But for Italians, the satisfaction that came from the style was not wholly real.

At the very beginning of the century Lutatius Catulus was writing short love poems, like Alexandrian epigrams, and Laevius was also writing love poetry under the same influence. The work of Laevius may have been more considerable in range and in influence on future poetry, especially the poetry of Gaius Valerius Catullus (87 [? 84]–54 B.C.), next to Lucretius the greatest poet of the century before Vergil.

Catullus, unlike Lucretius, worked not alone but as one of several poets all developing the same Alexandrian method in Latin poetry, and called the *'neoterici'*, 'the moderns', or 'the innovators'.

He was not the most influential; that was Publius Valerius Cato, who is called in an anonymous fragment 'the Latin Siren, the only reader and maker of poets'. The writer of the fragment may be Marcus Furius Bibaculus, another of the 'neoterics'.[1] Two others, friends of Catullus, were Gaius Helvius Cinna and Gaius Licinius Calvus. 'Cinna was perhaps the most "Alexandrian" member of the school, if we may judge by the references to his celebrated poem, *Zmyrna*. We are told that he spent nine years on polishing this piece of erudite affectation, which gave material for commentators as soon as it was published.'[2] Calvus was probably a better poet; Ovid classes him with Catullus himself.

Calvus was not less successful as an orator. The orators of the time were normally poets also. Even Cicero's contribution to the development and refinement of Latin verse was considerable. He was derided as a poet more than he deserved; some of his fragments have real merit, especially a passage from his translation of the lost *Prometheus Unbound* of Aeschylus and another from his translation of the *Odyssey*. His other main poetical works were a poem called *My Consulship*, and translations of the *Phaenomena* and *Prognostica* of Aratus. But though Cicero translated these Alexandrian poems into refined Latin verse, he was unsympathetic to the 'neoterics', whom he calls 'poets who write out Euphorion'. Euphorion was perhaps a more than usually erudite and sentimental, and also influential, Alexandrian poet of love and the country, and of elaborate mythology. Cicero himself firmly believed in the older Latin poets, Ennius, Accius, Pacuvius, Plautus, and Terence.

The 'neoterics' or 'moderns' took the methods and preferences of Alexandrian poetry and based their Latin poetry on them. Accordingly, they wrote short narrative poems with an elaborate structure, and a strong emotional interest. Emotion was elaborated and developed at length, and sometimes without much organic relationship to the whole. There was interest in the feminine mind, and in the sort of masculine mind which has feminine qualities. The characters tend to form picturesque tableaux; in general Alexandrian poetry is decorative and pictorial.

1. E. E. Sikes, *The Cambridge Ancient History*, ix, Cambridge, 1935, 745.
2. ibid., ix, 751.

The neoterics were comparatively numerous.[1] They were under the influence both of Greek books and of Greek teachers, who were the living exponents of the same tradition. The romantic and introspective habit of thought which resulted from it helped to modify Roman society. The Alexandrian world, through books and living contact, helped to make part of the Roman world romantic, introspective, sympathetic, and affectionate. A further result of this and other causes was a rapid development of tastefulness in everyday affairs. Quick wit, sensitivity, sympathy, good manners, and humour were valued highly.[2] Romantic love became an occupation. Roman society lived a poetic life. Their daily intercourse readily turned into poetry in the minds of people highly educated in Alexandrian habits of thought. There next resulted a partly new, colloquial poetry, which made little use of a traditional framework.[3] Catullus wrote this kind of poetry too, and it was his best. He and others sometimes followed and sometimes violently renounced the Alexandrian discipline. The restraint brought its reaction, and they expressed some of their feelings on their own behalf, not only on behalf of inherited mythical characters, in remotely decorative tableaux, helped by foreign names from far lands.

This alternative manner gave Catullus his place as one of the world's greatest lyric poets.[4] He made personal poetry direct and simple and powerful by the compression of emotion in his unconscious mind. For this direct poetry he often used, not the hexameters and elegiacs which Alexandrian poetry mainly preferred, because they were simple, but old Greek lyric metres which had become difficult for Greek poets because the pronunciation of the Greek language had changed. Catullus, reacting

1. See the account by Luigi Alfonsi, *Poetae Novi*, Como, 1945.

2. This was in fact the beginning of Roman 'Humanism'; on this see for example Karl Büchner in Karl Büchner and J. B. Hofmann, *Lateinische Literatur und Sprache in der Forschung seit* 1937, Berne, 1951, 185–98 and see Index 289.

3. For a fuller treatment, with an application of modern methods of literary criticism, see Kenneth Quinn, *The Catullan Revolution*, Melbourne, 1959; cf. idem, *Latin Explorations*, London, 1963.

4. J. Granarolo, 'Catulle, ce vivant', *Annales de l' Académie du Var* (Toulon), CXXV, 1957.

from Alexandrianism, not only went forward to his own time and place for the content of his new lyric, but back, also, to early Greek poetry for its force and freedom, and to some degree for its form.

Competition between the two styles or methods within the work of Catullus himself was a manifestation of a wider general tendency. There is always convention and revolt in poetry, though sometimes the revolt is a return to an old convention, or the rapid creation of a new. Another manifestation was the contemporary competition between the two styles of oratory, the florid Asianic and the purer Attic. In Vergil's early years Attic was beginning to win.

The Greeks distinguished two styles of oratory, the austere and simple, and the ornate, with an intermediate style halfway between. The Romans adopted these classifications, using the words *tenuis* or *exilis*, *grandis* or *ornatus*, and *medius*.[1] At the beginning of the first century B.C. the ornate style had been developed further in Asia Minor and was called Asianic. The plain style was associated with the earlier, Athenian orators, especially Lysias, and was called Attic. The plain direct oratory of Gaius Gracchus, discussed by Cicero, was being replaced in Cicero's early years by the Asianic. His great elder contemporary Quintus Hortensius always used an Asianic style, even when the reaction was already making it obsolete. Cicero himself, though he did not go to extremes, was an Asianist; and so were Marcus Antonius and also Marcus Varro, the great scholar; and so probably, since he taught Antonius, was Epidius, who is supposed to have taught Vergil. The Asianic style had elaborate antitheses, and exploited the internal meanings and similarities of words; it was a free flow of exalted language, with a strong rhythm, declaimed in a formal manner with musical intonation.

The reversion to a plainer, more direct style had begun before Vergil was old enough to be interested. Calvus was an Atticist, and so was Calidius. Julius Caesar was, too; he could not fail to

---

1. E. E. Sikes, *The Cambridge Ancient History*, IX, 757. My treatment of this question here is much abbreviated and perhaps over-simplified: see further U. von Wilamowitz-Möllendorff, 'Asianismus und Atticismus' in *Hermes* XXXV, Berlin, 1900, 1–52.

prefer a style which allowed language to be practical, direct, and in touch with the world of daily and violent activity. Julius was counted second only to Cicero as a speaker, and he must have exerted a strong influence; but he himself contributed most of all by his destruction of the Republic to the quick recession of public speaking from its place of high importance.

The classification of styles applied to oratory was also applied to poetry. It had been elaborated in text books by Greeks and Romans. Horace classes Latin writers, old and new, in four categories,[1] which were also used by others. The first style, 'grand and ornate', was represented by Hortensius and Pacuvius, the second, 'grand but austere', by Cornificius in prose and Varius and Pollio in verse, the third, 'plain and austere', by Calvus in speeches and Catullus (to us, very oddly) in lyrics, and the fourth, 'plain but graceful', by the speeches of Calidius, and by Catullus in Alexandrian poems such as *Peleus and Thetis*; by the writer of the *Ciris*, of which more will be said; and by Vergil in the *Eclogues*. The first two styles were for important speeches at law or in politics, and for epic and tragedy; the second two were for less formal prose, and for comedy, or 'little epics', of the sort now called 'epyllia',[2] and other minor poems.

'In choosing between these two, Horace, of course, sympathizes with the ideals of the severe and chaste style, which he finds in the comedies of Fundanius. Vergil's early work, unambitious and "plain" though it is, falls, of course, into the last group; and though Horace recognizes his type with a friendly remark, one feels that he recognizes it for reasons of friendship, rather than because of any native sympathy for it.'[3] Horace likes the classical second and third styles best, and dislikes extreme sensitivity or sentiment, *mollitudo*. On this principle, Horace regards Vergil as more or less outside classification; he might almost have ignored him, as he ignores Gallus and Tibullus, or disparaged him, as he

1. Tenney Frank, *Vergil, A Biography*, Oxford, 1922, 145–6; Horace, *Satires*, I, 10, 40–91; cf. *Epistles*, II, I, 247.

2. The word *epyllion*, plural *epyllia*, is first found in Aristophanes who used it three times to mean 'a scrap of poetry'; the meaning 'little epic' was first given to it by Haupt while lecturing on Catullus in 1855: see C. J. Fordyce, *Catullus*, Oxford, 1961, 272.

3. Tenney Frank, *Vergil, A Biography*, Oxford, 1922, 147–8 with references.

disparaged Catullus, for Alexandrianism. The other Augustans were more strictly classical than Vergil; but Vergil retained their reverence and the reverence of Propertius too; and he never renounced Gallus and Catullus.

'The strict classicists are Horace the satirist, Varius a writer of epics, Pollio of tragedy; while Varus, Valgius, Plotius, and Fundanius, though less productive, employ their influence in the support of this tendency as does Tibullus somewhat later.'[1]

The influences on Horace were the Greeks whom he met during his stay at Athens (45–43 B.C.), especially Stoics, and Apollodorus, the teacher of Octavianus. Horace vigorously returned to classical Greek poetry, though the Alexandrians influenced even him. Perhaps the attacks of Catullus and Calvus on Julius helped to make the Augustan poets react from them with dislike, but that is doubtful. The Augustans knew that there were two sides to the political question.

Prose was now fully 'classical'. Pollio and Messalla were the leading orators; Pollio was influenced by Calvus and Caesar, and Messalla by Brutus. Augustus himself agreed. Only Maecenas retained, and indeed developed to extravagance, the style of fancy and elaboration.

Vergil must have spared much attention, in his early years and after, for the controversy of style. His solution was characteristically universal and catholic. He followed every model, and by combining the different methods made each singly, and all together, reach greater success than ever before.

The Latin conception of poetry did not fully fit the facts of Latin poetry. This is a universal occurrence; neither poets nor readers ever quite understand what is going on. Posterity may see more clearly; but Latin poetry is little more understood even now than the poetry of our own time. The process of poetic communication is mainly a mystery.

To us the Roman view seems peculiarly inadequate, perhaps more inadequate than it really was. Romans exalted form over matter and style over poetic reality. It was a question how to say

1. ibid. 148: Valgius, ibid. 145, counts as a 'classicist' because he translated the 'classical' Apollodorus, and Plotius apparently because he was with Vergil at Naples and a close friend.

things rather than what to say. Incidentally, much that was new was, of course, said; but rather as if that was incidental. Concentrating on one thing, the poets did another. Poets perhaps always do.

That is how the controversies about Alexandrianism and the Asianic style came to seem as important as they certainly did. Perhaps it was only when systems of external ornamentation were consciously abandoned that their true poetic value could emerge; and perhaps it was only when the alternative of direct statement was tried that a high, intense personal reality could be found, to make tradition the true vehicle of the unique and the new that it ought to be.

Vergil was brought up in a poetic society, and he was in a poetic society when he came to Rome. And the poets were active men, many with a place in history. Poetry was less detached from active life than it had been. It went with it, as in the Elizabethan age. Even though the current and favoured Epicurean philosophy was inclined to discourage active political life, most of the greater poets except Lucretius are known to have fulfilled some of the functions, in government and war, of the ruling class.

The poets whom Vergil knew at home, at Rome, or later, were not all on the same side in the civil wars. Quintus Cornificius, a great friend of Catullus,[1] first joined Caesar, but was then persuaded by Cicero to join Brutus instead. After Philippi he continued to fight in Africa, but he was defeated and executed. It has been thought that the Seventh *Eclogue* alludes to him, since Valgius, another friend of Vergil, is said to have written elegies to 'Codrus', a name which, in the *Eclogue*, was believed to represent Cornificius[2]; and that he is represented by the Daphnis of the Fifth *Eclogue*. Cornificius was treated with respect by Cicero as an Atticist[3] and his poetry is supposed to have influenced Vergil's. He wrote lyrics and at least one epyllion in the manner of Catullus.

Vergil met Cornelius Gallus at Naples. He may or may not have been a Celt. He was certainly brilliant and reckless. He was about

1. Catullus, xxxviii.
2. Tenney Frank, *Vergil, A Biography*, Oxford, 1922, 116; The Verona Scholiast, *E.* vii, 22.
3. Cicero, *Ad Familiares*, xii, 17, 2.

Vergil's own age; and he began his career, as Vergil his, by leaving rhetoric for philosophy and philosophy for poetry. He followed Catullus, and Euphorion, and wrote amatory elegies, and perhaps epyllia, one closely dependent on Euphorion and possibly a translation from him. Octavianus appointed him to organize Egypt, but his head was turned, and he forgot duty in personal satisfactions and self-assertions. He was removed from his appointment, and committed suicide. In the Tenth *Eclogue* Vergil makes poetry of Gallus himself, then possibly on service somewhere in Greece, and of his poetry, and his love. The later elegists attributed the invention of lyrical elegies about personal love not to Catullus but to Gallus.

Little is known, but much has been invented, about the activities of Vergil's friends in Vergil's home country. Gallus certainly made a speech, which is quoted in part by Servius,[1] against Alfenus Varus, accusing him as follows: 'When ordered to leave unoccupied an area of three miles outside the city, you included in the area an expanse of water round the city walls eight hundred paces in extent.' Gallus and Varus, therefore, were concerned in the confiscations.[2] Alfenus, as Servius says, was a commissioner on the colonial board; but Servius was wrong to say that he was Pollio's successor as Governor of Cisalpine Gaul after it became autonomous, or that he had been generous to Vergil in some way; it was rather the opposite. Vergil in the Ninth *Eclogue*[3] promises him glory if he shews mercy to Mantua. Whether he did is not known; Vergil never mentions him again. The Sixth *Eclogue* is not addressed to him, as Servius thought, but to Quintilius Varus.

Gallus had to exact money from cities that escaped confiscation.[4] Alfenus may thus have invaded his sphere. He anyhow wanted to save Mantua, and so may have appealed to Octavianus on behalf of Vergil. Vergil's property may even have lain, as Probus says, if the reading 'thirty' is really a mistake for 'three', within the three mile limit.[5] Some words of a character, Menalcas, in the Ninth *Eclogue*[6] who might possibly represent Vergil himself, started a story, later

1. Servius-Daniel, *E.* IX, 10.
2. Tenney Frank, *Vergil, A Biography*, Oxford, 1922, 124–5.
3. *E.* IX, 26–9.   4. Servius-Daniel, *E.* VI, 64.
5. Probus, *Life of Vergil*.   6. *E.* IX, 11–16.

current, that Vergil quarrelled with a soldier sent to dispossess him; but in three out of the five *Eclogues* in which the name is met there is little or no reason for any but a tenuous identification. The low hills and beeches mentioned in the Ninth *Eclogue*[1] up to which the property was saved were the boundaries of Mantua, not Vergil's estates on the low river plains. So, too, in the First *Eclogue* a character, Tityrus, has been wrongly thought to represent Vergil himself, grateful to Octavianus for the restoration of his farm. That *Eclogue* might, however, even have displeased Octavianus; still, he is called a god in it, and the idea is central to the structure.[2] There may be truth in the traditional view that it was written out of special courtesy to him.

Vergil addresses Gaius Asinius Pollio in two *Eclogues*, the Eighth[3] and the Fourth.[4] In some sense he dedicated the *Eclogues* to him.[5] They were written at his command, Vergil says, and he must accept them, for he is their end and their beginning. In the Fourth *Eclogue*[6] Vergil asserts that Pollio's consulship will mark the beginning of the Golden Age to be. Vergil addresses others, too, very cordially, and there may be some exaggeration. But Pollio may well have encouraged Vergil most of all, when he began the *Eclogues*, and while he was writing them. He was a man already distinguished in literature and war. He was only six years older than Vergil, but he had already served on Caesar's staff. He was a writer of tragedies, and Vergil compared him to Sophocles.[7] Catullus and Cinna both refer to him in poems. There is a letter from Pollio in Spain to Cicero (43 B.C.) mentioning literary conversations between Pollio and Gallus.[8] Perhaps it was Gallus who first introduced Vergil to Pollio.

After Caesar's assassination Pollio fought in Spain. When the 'triumvirate' was formed (43 B.C.), he was made Antonius' *legatus* in Cisalpine Gaul, and promised the consulship for the year after the appointment ended. After Philippi Cisalpine Gaul was declared

---

1. *E.* IX, 7–9.
2. Franz Altheim, *A History of Roman Religion*, translated by Harold Mattingly, London, 1938, 327–49.
3. *E.* VIII, 6–13.   4. *E.* IV, 11–14.   5. *E.* VIII, 11–12.
6. *E.* IV, 11–14.   7. *E.* VIII, 9–10.
8. Cicero, *Ad Familiares*, X, 32, 5.

a part of Italy, and so was no longer under Pollio's control. However, he waited, encamped near the mouth of the Timavus, and even prepared to take some obscure part in the Perusine war. At this time Octavianus was besieging Lucius Antonius in Perusia (41–40 B.C.). Pollio was *legatus* of Marcus Antonius. After the Perusine War he joined Marcus Antonius at Brundisium and spoke for him at the conference (40 B.C.).

Servius has a tradition that Vergil wrote in Pollio's honour through gratitude to him for pleading with Octavianus against the confiscation of Vergil's first home. At this time, however, Pollio was no longer governor of Cisalpine Gaul. Nor was he likely to be on good enough terms with Octavianus. He was closely associated with Antonius, whose brother Octavianus was besieging about this very time. Vergil's friendship with him was rather literary than practical. He addressed him in the Fourth *Eclogue* because he was consul that year, and all the more freely since Octavianus and Antonius were to be reconciled. However, it is quite probable that Pollio introduced Vergil first to Maecenas, who then, unless Vergil met the future emperor independently, introduced him to Octavianus.

Marcus Valerius Messalla was for some time (45–44 B.C.) at Athens, finishing his education. There he wrote 'eclogues', pastoral poems in Greek. It is almost certain that Vergil knew him well and accepted influence from him in *Eclogues* II, III, and VII. The very first line of the First *Eclogue* is probably derived from Messalla, to whom Vergil may well have owed the very idea of writing the *Eclogues*.

Messalla joined Brutus and Cassius the year after Caesar's assassination, much to Cicero's approval. He was a good barrister, even opposing the great Servius Sulpicius in one case. At Athens he wrote Greek verse and listened to the philosophers. He helped Cassius to gain support in Asia, and at the first of the two battles of Philippi he led a cavalry charge, which captured Octavianus' camp. Three weeks later the second battle was a decisive victory for the other side. Messalla, now in command of the defeated, surrendered. He remained with Antonius in the East.

Plotius Tucca is said to have been a poet; he and Varius were Vergil's literary executors.

Vergil's friends in 'the Garden' and for life were, according to Probus, Quintilius Varus, the critic, Varius Rufus the writer of epics and tragedies, and Plotius Tucca. Horace mentions them together.[1] It is also possible to identify the four names together on the rolls of Philodemus.

Quintilius Varus was mainly a critic. He helped to form Augustan taste. He was older than Vergil, a friend of Catullus and Calvus, and he too, like Varius, came from Cremona and Vergil's country beyond the Po. He took some part in the civil wars. Horace's poem[2] to Vergil on Quintilius' death shews that he was, as Servius says, one of Vergil's most devoted friends.

Horace, Quintus Horatius Flaccus, who was born five years after Vergil (65 B.C.) and died eleven years after his death (8 B.C.), was the son of a freedman who however gave him a very good education. He lived at his home in Venusia till he was nineteen. He was taught by the best masters at Rome, and then went to Athens to learn philosophy. There he joined Brutus, but at Philippi he cast his shield away and fled. He returned to Rome, accepted the rule of the victors, obtained employment as a clerk in the treasury, and wrote poetry. By his early work he contrived to attract the interest of Vergil and Varius, who introduced him to Maecenas and Octavianus. They gave him a life of comfort and leisure. He lived for poetry and good pleasures, especially friendship. He even refused a position as secretary to Augustus, who was not offended at the refusal.

Horace was a member of the party of literary men on a famous journey to Brundisium (? 37 B.C.) which he himself described.[3] The other members were Maecenas, Vergil, Varius, and Plotius Tucca. Presently it seems that Vergil was accepting in the *Georgics*[4] suggestions from the Sixteenth *Epode*, a poem which Horace wrote partly under inspiration from the Fourth *Eclogue*, and to solicit Vergil's interest. Though it is hardly ever certain which of the two poets has influenced which, this time it is at least clear that there is an exchange of thoughts on the Golden Age; indeed, it is now considered that Professor Bruno Snell has proved that it was

1. Horace, *Satires*, 1, 5, 40; 1, 10, 43–5 and 81; *Odes*, 1, 24.
2. Horace, *Odes*, 1, 24.   3. Horace, *Satires*. 1 5.
4. *G.* 11, 109–76. Also cf. *G.* 11, 82 with *Epode* XVI, 46.

Horace who wrote in answer to Vergil, Vergil's poem being written before Horace's.[1] Horace puts it far away, but Vergil, more optimistic than the rest, puts it in Italy. Vergil never mentions Horace by name; but Horace refers to Vergil more than once. They seem to have been friends of unbroken loyalty; but their meetings must have been occasional since Horace lived nearly always at or near Rome, and Vergil liked to keep away from the capital as much as he could.

Horace became known first for *Satires*, but he soon began composing his *Odes*, beautifully finished short pieces in old Greek lyric metres. The first volume of *Satires* appeared in 35 B.C., when the *Georgics* were being written; the second, and the *Epodes*, five years later (30 B.C.); but the first three volumes of *Odes* years afterwards (23 B.C.), not long before Vergil's death. The first volume of *Epistles* followed (20 B.C.); then, probably, the fourth book of *Odes* (17–13 B.C.), and the *Carmen Saeculare*, the 'Song for the Century' written for the great 'Games for the Century' of Augustus (17 B.C.); and the *Ars poetica*, 'The Poet's Art', at an uncertain date (perhaps about 20 B.C. or about 13 B.C.).

Sextus Propertius (*c*. 50–? 15 B.C.) was born in Umbria, the son of a Roman equestrian who supported Antonius and whose land was confiscated by Octavianus. The son soon won his favour for his poetry, and the friendship of Maecenas, Vergil, and Gallus. Maecenas wanted him to write an epic on Augustus. Propertius wrote love poetry in elegiacs; unlike Tibullus, he retained strongly the influence of the Alexandrians, and he wrote with less neatness and finish but with far more passion, as he gives us the *journal intime* of his unhappy love for Cynthia – whoever she may have been. Unlike Vergil but like Catullus he at first lacked a profound moral interest in the wider world. But he had the force of a poetic tradition which has not forgotten its youth. When his love betrayed him, he transferred his ardour to myth and the truth in myth, to a pride in Roman glory, and to the life beyond the

1. Eduard Fraenkel, *Horace*, Oxford, 1957, 50–3, citing, 51 note 2, Bruno Snell, *Hermes* LXXIII, 1938, 237–42. Professor Fraenkel's major work should always be indispensable on any question concerning Horace.

grave[1] – Vergilian themes indeed. Propertius mentions Vergil, especially in a poem written about 26 B.C.[2] There he heralds the *Aeneid*, of which all knew though few if any had seen any of it, as something greater than the *Iliad*. The praise cannot be taken quite literally since he writes in similar terms of the forgotten *Thebaid* of Ponticus.[3] Next, in the former poem, he deftly describes Vergil and his work, some written, as he implies, near Tarentum.[4]

Albius Tibullus (*c*. 60–*c*. 19 B.C.) was a younger contemporary of Vergil, and an Augustan. He was a Roman of rank, an equestrian. After some short service in the Civil Wars, he settled at Rome and wrote of love and the country in elegiac verse. He is said to have lost his estates in the confiscations, and to have been too unwilling to ingratiate himself with the court to recover them. He never mentions Augustus or Maecenas, but he knew the literary men, including Vergil, Horace, and Ovid, well. His poetry is charming enough, and of special interest as a strong reaction from Alexandrianism to a natural, neat, and pure style, free from recondite imagery and learning. He followed in his different way the lyrical, direct Catullus, without, like Vergil, retaining the influence of the Catullus of Alexandrian inspiration. But his love of home life in Italy and his sympathy are, within his narrower span, in touch with the Vergilian spirit.

After these poets, a literary revolution has occurred. The poet Ovid already belongs to the succeeding age; but the great prose poet Livy might be called a true Vergilian. Of these writers there will be more to say.

How much the poets owed to the court, and above all Maecenas, who has become the permanent type of literary patron, it is hard nowadays to comprehend. Gaius Maecenas was an Etruscan descended from the Etruscan prince Elbius Volterrenus, who was killed at the battle of Lake Vadimo (309 B.C.). Other ancestors had been Roman equestrians, who held high commands in the Roman army. Proud of this rank, Maecenas refused to become a

1. See the profound statement in Luigi Alfonsi, *L'Elegia di Properzio*, Milan, 1954.

2. Propertius II, 34, 61–80, especially 65–6.

3. ibid., I, 7, 1–3.   4. ibid., II, 34, 67–8.

senator. His early years are obscure. Perhaps he was educated at Apollonia across the Adriatic and there met Octavianus and Agrippa. He is first mentioned as coming to Rome with Octavianus after the Battle of Mutina (43 B.C.), and as present with him at the Battle of Philippi (42 B.C.). He helped in the campaign against Sextus Pompeius (38–36 B.C.) and perhaps at Actium (31 B.C.), and sometimes in these years quelled disturbances at Rome. His tact, united with great political wisdom and ingenuity, and a firm belief in mild government, was of still greater value in the years of reconstruction; the Roman world may have owed him as much as it owed Augustus, whom he guided. He himself was perhaps partly guided by Vergil, who directly or indirectly without doubt influenced Augustus. Maecenas is very important in the context of Vergil's life and work. He is an example of the mild humanity to which the world was growing, for all the brutality of the times. A single spirit touched him and Vergil. There was another side to Maecenas. He was luxurious, both by taste and policy, to excess, and a sensualist. His own style in writing was offensively florid, though other writers were purifying the language. Augustus parodied his style in a letter partly preserved by Macrobius. He wrote occasional poems. He was unhappily married to a beautiful but capricious wife, to whom he was devoted, and illness afflicted his later years. Vergil, Horace, and other poets were very sincerely devoted to him, and in 8 B.C. he died in touching circumstances, commending Horace, who died a few months later, to the emperor.

But not all the great men of the time shewed favour to the poets. Marcus Vipsanius Agrippa (62–12 B.C.) was very different from Maecenas. He was one of the ablest military and naval commanders in Roman history, and Augustus mainly owed his victories to him. Augustus designated him as his successor. Agrippa seems to have been a strong and grave man, with an able but limited mind. He was out of sympathy with the poets, and Donatus says that he criticized Vergil for a fault hard to interpret from the Latin, *nova cacozelia*, 'an original kind of affectation'; the statement goes on to suggest that he blamed Vergil for seeking to create a false impression by a method of his own invention, concealed by its use of clichés, and emphasized by neither richness nor poverty of style.[1] Like many since, Agrippa saw to some extent the nature of Vergil's poetic process, but was prevented by presuppositions from realizing its authentic greatness and submitting to Vergil's power. Of this there will be more to say.

Of Augustus himself (63 B.C.–A.D. 14), a few words are needed here, and a few must be enough. He was great somehow by virtue of his whole self, not individual good qualities. He had prudence, energy, insight, cunning perhaps; a certain not quite reliable generosity and unselfishness; a sense of humour; but perhaps most of all a power of inspiring loyalty in others and a mysterious capacity for moral development in himself. He had most of the faults. He was wantonly and vindictively cruel time after time in his early years, and never quite lost his cruelty; he could be treacherous; in purity of life he did not always practise what he preached; he even lacked power of command and courage. Perhaps in later life, though scarcely in old age, he was a better man. We shall never know quite how much he and Rome owed to Vergil, Horace, and Maecenas, who could feel some mysterious force in their leader, and whatever he did refused to despair of him, so that they made his virtues grow and overcome his faults.

A strong influence on Vergil was exerted by 'the Garden', the academy founded by Phaedrus near Naples, where he was taught by Philodemus and Siro, Epicureans of the less rigid Syrian school. Philodemus wrote ornate Alexandrian poetry, especially epigrams, and elegies paraphrased by Catullus, Horace, and Ovid. Cicero is thought to have criticized him anonymously in the *In Pisonem*,[2] but he probably used his essays and his work on theology for his *De finibus*. 'The Garden' gave Vergil, besides much else, his Epicurean and Oriental sympathies and knowledge, and an astonishing, sensitive system of human relationships, which we should be proud to call modern.

1. J. W. H. Atkins, *Literary Criticism in Antiquity*, Cambridge, 1934, Vol. II, 171: 'Thus Vergil was in general accused of affectation and bad taste, his metaphors, his coinages, and his uncommon grammatical usages being all alike condemned.' Cf. an original elucidation by J. J. H. Savage, Jr, *Translations and Proceedings of the American Philological Association*, XCI, 1960, 371ff.

2. R. G. M. Nisbet, *Cicero, In Pisonem*, Oxford, 1961, 186: 'The pomposity of the rebukes need not be taken too seriously: Cicero is amusing himself at the cost of his Epicurean friends.'

'The Garden' had a great influence on many Romans, including Julius Caesar, Piso his father-in-law and the patron of Philodemus, Manlius Torquatus, Hirtius, Pansa, Dolabella, Cassius, Trebatius, Atticus, Paetus, and Gallus. They all belonged to it. Living near were many important Greeks, Andronicus, Archias, Parthenius who taught Vergil and influenced Octavianus Augustus, and probably Alexander and Timagenes.

The years that Vergil spent among these thinkers and poets, amateurs and professionals, acquainted him with the sympathetic friendliness of Epicureanism, with its conception of the unity of man and nature, and its vision of the beauty of both, however its scientific background might seem to conflict with its real poetic resource. These years, too, opened to Vergil much learning of the east. This influence, apparent in the Fourth *Eclogue*, even led to a view that he had read Isaiah, a view not in itself impossible, though it is not proved. It further gave him a certain sympathy with the oriental principle of deifying rulers, which was one day to dominate the theory of the Roman principate. Vergil could see the strange truth in it, and he soon began to admit this deification into his earlier poetry. Yet, surprisingly, it never appears in the *Aeneid*. Perhaps he had seen the immense dangers of the doctrine, and had gone beyond it now.

It is possible to give a very full and fascinating account of Vergil's life by accepting as his the poems of the Vergilian *Appendix*. But there is a serious risk; not one of these poems is certainly genuine, and most of them are certainly not.

The *Appendix* includes twenty-seven poems, some very short, and some as long as a book of the *Georgics*. Of these poems two[1] are sometimes counted as one, perhaps rightly; two others[2] are also sometimes counted as one, but wrongly. Another poem[3] is sometimes without sufficient reason included. Of the twenty-six, there are some[4] which scarcely anyone believes Vergilian. Many of the remainder are the subject of hot controversy. Several[5] are thought by many to be genuinely Vergil's work, but for none is the evidence conclusive.

---

1. *Catalepton*, XIV, XIVa.   2. *Lydia, Dirae*.   3. *Rosetum* or *Rosae*.
4. *Est et non, Vir bonus, Maecenas*.
5. *Ciris, Culex, Aetna, Copa, Catalepton*, III, V, IX, XIV.

The poems can be classified in various ways. They are mentioned in two different early lists. One is given by Servius in his
general introduction to the *Aeneid*.[1] He quotes an early epigram,
on a robber called Ballista, and adds that Vergil also wrote poems
called *Ciris, Aetna, Culex, Priapea, Catalepton, Epigrammata, Copa,*
and *Dirae.* The other is given by Donatus in his *Life of Vergil.* He
too starts with the epigram on Ballista, and then says that Vergil
wrote also the *Catalepton, Priapea, Epigrammata, Dirae, Ciris,* and
Culex; here Donatus, after saying that Vergil wrote the *Culex* at
the age of sixteen, gives a short précis of the poem, and then he
adds that Vergil also wrote a poem *Aetna,* but that his authorship
of it was doubted. Donatus omits the *Copa;* and both he and
Servius omit the *Moretum.* These and a few more poems, *Est et
non, Maecenas,* and *Rosetum* or *Rosae,* are attributed to Vergil in their
headings in the manuscripts. The remaining poem, *Lydia,* is
counted in the lists, and written in manuscripts, as a part of *Dirae.*

Fourteeen, or, if the last two should each be divided into two,
sixteen of the smaller poems are classed together as *Catalepton,* or
possibly, if '*Catalepton*' is a Greek genitive plural, *Catalepta,* which
means something like 'morsels' or 'shreds' of poetry. The name is
taken directly from the Greek poems, called *Catalepta,* of Aratus.
Some of them are sometimes called *Priapea,* poems to the god
Priapus, and some *Epigrams.* The *Catalepton* includes the poems
which are most likely to be by Vergil, and which would tell us
most about Vergil, if we were sure that he wrote them.

One, the Fifth *Catalepton,* in 'limping' iambic Alexandrines,
fourteen lines long, says good-bye to the rhetoricians, and continues: 'I am setting sail for that happy haven, to hear Siro's learned
talk, and rescue my life from every anxiety. And, Muses, you go
away from me too, go away, but good luck to you, dear Muses – I
shall admit the truth, you were once dear to me – yes, and in
spite of all come back sometimes to my pages, but modestly, and
seldom.' That is altogether like Vergil, and exactly fits his feelings,
as they almost must have been, when he left Rome for Naples
(? 48 B.C.).

Another, the Third *Catalepton,* in elegiacs, laments the fall of

1. Servius, *Prologue to the Aeneid;* cf. Servius, *A.* 111, 571; Servius-Daniel,
E. vi, 3.

some great man who might have enslaved Rome. It is a poem that Vergil might have written on Pompeius after Pharsalus (48 B.C.).

Not all these poems are free, like Vergil's certain work, from unpleasant and even disgusting language; such language is possibly necessary in some poems, and there is no need either to assert or deny that; the point is that Vergil's authentic poems are in this respect different. One of these, the Thirteenth *Catalepton*, in a lyric iambic metre, describes the horrors of active service in the army. If it is by Vergil, it implies that he served in Caesar's army at the beginning of the Civil War (49 B.C.). But there is no proof whatever, and no particular probability.

Another interesting poem, in elegiacs, the ninth, is addressed to Valerius Messalla, foretelling a triumph for him, and further success afterwards in Africa; and, still more interestingly, referring to his poetry. The writer says that some of Messalla's poems, Greek in language and wit, have found their way on to his own pages. Then, most dramatically, he writes a couplet[1] of which the first line contains three, out of seven, words in common with the first line of Vergil's First *Eclogue*; and the second line contains the names *Moeris* and *Meliboeus*, characters who occur in the *Eclogues* of Vergil. And the reference is to Greek poems of Messalla. It is very tempting to think that the writer of the little poem is Vergil himself, acknowledging the most important inspiration which his *Eclogues* owed to Messalla. The poem must have been written when Vergil was beginning the *Eclogues*, and just before the second battle at Philippi; afterwards, there was no talk of a triumph or African successes for Messalla; he went to serve with Antonius, whom Vergil never liked, in the east. There is one thing more to say about this little piece. In it shepherds of Messalla's *Eclogues* lie under an oak; the description is in Vergilian words, which recur in the first line of Vergil's First *Eclogue*. But there the tree is a beech, *fagus*. There are reasons. The Greek for an oak tree is the same word as the Latin for a beech tree. And there were beeches near Mantua. Vergil, by reversing one of his own changes, commits an apparent mistranslation and thereby gets something exactly right. That is precisely Vergil's way, as will appear.

1. *Catalepton*, IX, 17–18.

In the fourteenth poem, also in elegiacs and perhaps more interesting still, Venus and her Cyprian home are addressed; she is to come to Surrentum, across the bay from Naples, where Caesar was inviting her to his new temple. This new foundation is well known. In September 46 B.C., Julius Caesar was asserting his descent from Venus Genetrix and acknowledging her protection, after his fourfold triumph had celebrated his victories in Gaul, Egypt, Pontus, and Africa. The poem must have been written soon after. In it the writer talks of his plan to make Trojan Aeneas travel in poetry through Italian towns.[1] Again, it is tempting to think Vergil the author. Here might be the first known words in which Vergil wrote of Aeneas, and of what he should become. Again characteristic of Vergil is his further use of words and thoughts which he had already used in this poem, if it is his. Trojan Aeneas is to 'pass through Roman towns in poetry fit for him', *Romana per oppida digno . . . carmine . . . eat*. In the Second *Georgics*, perhaps ten years later, Vergil wrote, *Ascraeumque cano Romana per oppida carmen*, 'I sing poetry of Ascra', that is, Hesiodic poetry, 'through Roman towns'.[2] By a characteristic change, not the *Aeneid*, but the *Georgics* are described; not the Homeric Trojan hero, but Hesiodic verse is to come to Italy. But the similarity of words cannot be missed.

The poems of the *Appendix* outside the *Catalepton* are better known, but they are very hard to prove Vergilian.

The *Culex* or 'Gnat' is said by Donatus to have been written when Vergil was sixteen, which would date it to 54 B.C., the year after Vergil is said to have assumed the dress of manhood. The figures XVI are sometimes emended to XXI, which would date the poem to a time when he was about to leave Rome for Naples (49 B.C.).

The poem is an Alexandrian 'epyllion' in Latin hexameters. The story is this: A shepherd went to sleep. A snake came up to bite him. He was saved by a gnat, which stung him and woke him up. He hastily killed it, and it travelled to the land of the dead, seeing in some detail the sights of the other world. In remorse, the shepherd composed an epitaph for it. The *Culex* is not much admired. It makes much of little, in the Alexandrian way, and

1. ibid., XIV, 3–4.   2. *G*. II, 176.

has little or no strong poetry. It contains many Ovidian phrases, and has been thought to have been written by Ovid or a poet later than Ovid. On the other hand, the incidence of stress-accent in the fourth feet of the verses is exceedingly Vergilian. Latin writers of the Empire thought that the *Culex* was by Vergil, and sometimes compared it with their own early work, arguing in self-defence that, as Vergil began with the *Culex*, they need not be ashamed of the insufficiencies of their own youth. The poem which we have may be an altered and expanded version of a poem by Vergil. It is not by Vergil in its present form.

The *Ciris* is another epyllion, perhaps modelled on Callimachus, and perhaps a positive translation of an Alexandrian poem. It is more lively than the *Culex*, and more like the poetry of Catullus. It describes how Scylla, daughter of Nisus, king of Megara, fell in love with Minos, who was besieging the city. The safety of the city magically depended on a talisman, a bright lock of hair on the head of Nisus. She cut it off; and the city fell. But divine retribution came. In the end, she was turned into a bird, a 'Ciris', and Nisus into a bird too, but keeping his name; and he perpetually pursues her still.

The *Ciris*, whether it is by Vergil or not, may well be taken to indicate the poetic atmosphere in which he began to develop his own style. Servius and Donatus accepted it as Vergil's work but they can hardly be right. The mind behind the *Ciris* is just not like Vergil's.[1] It is frequently supposed that, since the *Ciris* contains so many words and phrases which occur in Vergil's certainly authentic work, it is by a later poet who copied Vergil. If so this poet need not be much later. The *Ciris* seems to have been composed about the time when Vergil was beginning to write. There is also an elaborate and skilful theory[2] that Cornelius Gallus wrote the *Ciris*, and that Vergil adopted expressions from it out of

1. Karl Büchner, *P. Vergilius Maro, Der Dichter der Römer*, Stuttgart, 1955, 89–109, especially 105–7; cf. also for a different theory Auguste Haury, *La Ciris, poème attribué à Virgile*, Bordeaux, 1957 and C. G. Hardie, 'The Pseudo-Virgilian *Ciris*', *Virgil Society Lecture Summaries*, No. 34, 1954, a powerful and interesting statement of arguments for dating the *Ciris* considerably after Vergil.

2. F. Skutsch, *Aus Vergils Frühzeit*, Leipzig, 1901, *passim*, especially volume II.

compliment to him. But the reasons for denying it to Gallus, and indeed to Vergil, are sufficiently strong – however neatly it would fit into Vergil's biography if it could be accepted as his work.

According to Tenney Frank's account[1] Vergil wrote the *Ciris* just before he went to Naples (48 B.C.). When he went, it was not finished. He left it aside, and returned to it some years after. Then he wrote the introductory lines, explicitly saying that he wrote them in Siro's 'garden'. Then he laid it aside again, and it was only published, like most of the *Appendix*, after his death. The preface, like the Ninth *Catalepton* written about the same time, is addressed to Messalla, who was either at Athens (45–44 B.C.) or serving with Brutus and Cassius (43–42 B.C.). The author apologizes for such a trivial, romantic poem, written when he ought to be describing Epicurean philosophy. The introduction was written not long before Philippi. After the battle, we might imagine that Vergil lost interest in Messalla, now with Antonius; and again set the poem aside, but used many lines from it for his own later work. But Vergil can hardly be the author.

Alexandrian poetry was the primary influence for Vergil, and the *Ciris* has the typical Alexandrian qualities. It is built on a principle of digressions and hints, half replacing and half concealing the main line of the story. It analyses mental processes for their own sake, especially processes in the feminine mind. It is pictorial and decorative. The verse is slightly monotonous, with few elisions and with too regular divisions within it. But it has music and rhythm, quite startling sometimes; and a weird strange beauty all its own. But the mind behind it is not Vergil's. We could almost say that the *Ciris* is the kind of poem Vergil might have written, but not the kind of poetry. He retained the Alexandrian interest in moods of the mind; but in his certain work the significance of mental states is immensely more. Characters have a universal, commanding appeal before all humanity. The mind and its moods are not isolated playthings any more. The Alexandrian detail is used, subordinated to the grand, dramatic moral structures planned out of the great classics of Greek and Roman poetry. So too Alexandrian organization grew in Vergil's

1. Tenney Frank, *Vergil, A Biography*, Oxford, 1922, 35–46.

art into an organization far more full of meaning, not merely entertaining by an intricacy little more than decorative.

The *Aetna*, a scientific account of the volcano Etna, is also attributed to Vergil by Servius and Donatus, but in some manuscripts of Donatus the words, *de qua ambigitur*, 'about which there is a controversy,' are added. Seneca[1] refers to a complete treatment of Mount Etna by Vergil. It is certain that part at least of the existing poem must have been written while Vergil was young. The Lucretian language proves it later than the publication of the poem of Lucretius (? 54 B.C.). Further, it mentions a statue of Medea by Timomachus as being abroad; and the statue was brought to Rome (46–44 B.C.) while Vergil was under Siro's instruction. The *Aetna* is therefore strongly held by some critics to be Vergil's work. Grave doubts, however, remain. Phrases in the *Aetna* that are like phrases in Vergil's authentic work are regularly found at a later stage of development in the *Aetna*, and seem derived from Vergil in the same degree as other phrases clearly derived from other poets, such as Manilius. The *Aetna* is intensely Lucretian, but there is little of Vergil's quality to be seen in it. However, Vergil could be most unlike himself when he was not writing very spontaneously. Perhaps a view sometimes held of the *Culex* is probable for the *Aetna*; the *Aetna* which now survives may contain Vergil's *Aetna* in a much changed and simplified form, by no means identical with the poem which Vergil wrote and to which he may conceivably refer in the *Georgics*,[2] and possibly elsewhere also.

Of the other poems in the *Appendix*, the most interesting are the *Moretum* or '*Salad*', a detailed and amusing description of a countryman preparing a meal, the *Copa*, a delightfully realistic and well observed short poem about a Syrian woman who kept an Italian inn, and how she invited travellers to stop, the *Dirae*, a poem of 'curses' against those who evicted Italian farmers to make room for demobilized soldiers – a theme of the *Eclogues*, here less tactfully treated – and the *Lydia*, a charming but rather too romantic poem of love and the country. Of these the *Copa* is most probably Vergilian, and the *Dirae* least probably. In all it is possible to

1. Seneca, *Ad Lucilium*, 79, 5.　　2. *G.* I, 471–3.

fancy the presence of Vergilian qualities or signs of Vergil's future development.

The formative period for Vergil might be said to end well before the Peace of Brundisium, and before he wrote the earlier *Eclogues*. He was then already a very finished artist, and the true Vergilian quality had come into the world. He continued, of course, to develop and expand his powers, continuously, and perhaps quickly. But the style which is the man was made. The depth of tone belonging to Vergilian epic can be heard already in the *Eclogues*, in which epic lines and movements can be detected.

A characteristic of great poets, strongly exemplified by Vergil, is the continuity of their mental process. This characteristic is equally clear in Shakespeare, who in the early play *Richard II* forecasts with astonishing precision the course which his work would take during the many remaining years of his life.[1]

Even if the *Ciris* is not Vergil's, it appears to contain the beginning of much that he did afterwards. The four consecutive lines that end it[2] occur again in the First *Georgics*,[3] and many single lines are used in various places in Vergil's work. Vergil used the *Ciris*, especially in the third book of the *Aeneid*, just as he used earlier poems known to be his. The mood and method are exactly the mood and method likely to have preceded the *Eclogues*, and started the whole development of Vergil's style. In music, and knowing how to make it, the *Ciris* is just one stage back. And some of the qualities there are the same that are developed for mighty use after.

Not much, therefore, is certain concerning Vergil's earlier years; and still less is known of his later life. He wrote the *Georgics* at Naples (37–30 B.C.), and soon afterwards read them to Augustus on his return from the East, at Atella in Campania (? 29 B.C.).[4] The *Georgics* are unlike the *Eclogues* in the greater self-sufficiency of their creation. They are not so much the result of personal contacts and the sudden impressions made by events and by reading. Vergil put into them his life-long interest in farming, and perhaps too the technical knowledge of science, which according to Don-

---

1. G. Wilson Knight, *The Imperial Theme*, London, 1931, 355–67.
2. *Ciris*, 538–41.   3. *G.* I, 406–9.   4. Donatus, *Life of Vergil*.

atus he learnt with great success in his early education. The *Georgics* are the result of long, quiet reading, reflection, and hard work. There are in them a few mentions of contemporary people and events. There is at the start an address to Maecenas, and a suggestion that Octavianus will be a god;[1] later, in the third book, the poem is called an arduous task, which Maecenas commanded.[2] At the end of the first book, a splendid passage[3] recalls the prodigies at the death of Julius, and Vergil mentions an eruption of Etna as if he or his contemporaries had seen it; there is a reference to Philippi, and an appeal for, and to, Octavianus, joined to a lament for the civil wars. In the second book, a gorgeous passage[4] in praise of Italy mentions the new 'Julian Harbour', by the Lucrine lake, a great feat of engineering, by means of which Agrippa meant to train a fleet in safety to defeat Sextus Pompeius. Mantua, and the land which she had lost, have a passing reference.[5] In the third book, Vergil very interestingly says[6] that he will bring home to Mantua the prize of his poetry, and will build by the river Mincius a temple, and Caesar shall be in the middle of it – clearly a prophecy of the *Aeneid*, conceived as a poem on Augustus, a poem being represented under the Pindaric symbol of a building. In the following lines,[7] Vergil in luxuriant imagery pictures the lands reached by Caesar's fame and the long descent of his line from Troy and the gods of Troy, and here it is that he calls his work the arduous command of Maecenas. There is later[8] a hint of the hard resistance which the Spaniards opposed to Rome; and at the end[9] a terrible description of a plague among farm animals in Vergil's home country, near the river Timavus. The fourth book begins with an address to Maecenas,[10] like the first. Soon Vergil charmingly writes[11] of a garden near Tarentum, kept by an old man once a Cilician pirate. He says that he remembers it; he must have seen it when he stayed in the neighbourhood, as apparently he did, for a short time, while he was writing the *Eclogues*.[12]

There is one very interesting suggestion about a connexion between the *Georgics* and external events. Servius says that the

1. *G.* I, 24–42. 2. *G.* III, 41. 3. *G.* I, 466–514.
4. *G.* II, 136–76. 5. *G.* II, 198. 6. *G.* III, 12–16.
7. *G.* III, 17–48. 8. *G.* III, 408. 9. *G.* III, 471–503.
10. *G.* IV, 1–7. 11. *G.* IV, 125–48. 12. Propertius, II, 34, 67–8.

fourth book originally ended with a passage in praise of Cornelius Gallus, but that after his disgrace and death Vergil replaced the passage with another. In one place[1] Servius says that the passage later inserted was a shorter passage,[2] about Orpheus and Eurydice, and in another[3] that it was the whole present ending of the book,[4] from the start of the story how Aristaeus lost his bees and repaired the loss; he adds that Vergil made the change at the command of Augustus. The date (26 B.C.) of the fall of Gallus is known; it was three or four years after the *Georgics* were finished. The style of the present ending is very grand and finished, like, perhaps, the later parts of the *Aeneid*, but that is a precarious question. If Vergil removed the passage in praise of Gallus, his motive is debatable. Perhaps he was angry with Gallus; perhaps he was angry with Augustus, who, however unwillingly, was the cause of his death; or perhaps he acted in some more general sadness and disillusionment. Servius is, however, almost certainly wrong in his story.[5]

The *Georgics*, therefore, refer to a few events affecting Rome and Octavianus, and also to Vergil's memory of his first home, and his visits to south-east Italy, and to Sicily, where Donatus says that some of his poetry was written. Thus there is not much internal evidence for Vergil's life in the *Georgics*.

Nor is there in the *Aeneid*. Vergil seems to have stayed in Campania, occasionally coming to Rome. Events in the world moved fast.

In the next year after the Peace of Brundisium, there was a conference at Misenum (39 B.C.) and a treaty with Sextus Pompeius. War began again the year after, and the fleet of Octavianus met disaster at Cumae and Scyllaeum. Ventidius defeated the Parthians, and Herod was made king of Judaea. The next year (37 B.C.), Octavia barely allayed a new quarrel between Octavianus and

1. Servius, *G.* IV, 1.   2. *G.* IV, 453–566.   3. Servius, *E.* X,1.
4. *G.* IV, 315–566.
5. W. B. Anderson, *The Classical Quarterly*, XXVII, 1933, 36–45; but cf. now clever articles by T. J. Haarhoff, 'The Bees of Vergil', *Greece and Rome*, VII, 1960, 155–70, and Robert Coleman, 'Gallus, the *Bucolics*, and the ending of the Fourth *Georgic*', *The American Journal of Philology*, LXXXIII, 1962, 55–71, where by recognizing Vergil's symbolic method, an interesting compromise-solution is reached.

Antonius; and Agrippa was meanwhile practising his fleet in the new Julian Harbour. In another campaign against Pompeius, another fleet was lost (36 B.C.), but Agrippa then won a decisive victory at Naulochus (36 B.C.). Octavianus was given the authority of a tribune for life. There were more threats. Veterans mutinied; Antonius prepared for war and divorced Octavia (33 B.C.). War was declared, but against Cleopatra (32 B.C.); and next year she and Antonius were defeated by Agrippa at Actium. Immediately there followed more revolts in Italy itself (30 B.C.). But soon, for the third time in Roman history, the Temple of Janus was shut, to symbolize peace (29 B.C.); and not long after (27 B.C.) regular government returned at last, the Roman world was reorganized, and Augustus, for so he was now to be called, restored, as he said, the republic. He did not rest, however, but visited Gaul (27 B.C.), and Spain (26 B.C.), where he fought a war, indecisively, for trouble there continued after he returned to Rome. He there further defined his constitutional position (23 B.C.), and in the same year had to endure the death of the young Marcus Marcellus, who already for two or three years had been recognized as his heir. Soon after (22 B.C.), he went with Agrippa to Sicily and Greece; but there were more disturbances in Italy and Agrippa had to return to quell them (21 B.C.). Augustus now went to Asia, and Agrippa to Gaul (20 B.C.). In Asia, the Parthians surrendered to Augustus the standards which they had captured years before (53 B.C.) when they annihilated the army of Crassus. Augustus returned to Greece (19 B.C.), happy at his success, and at the prospect of meeting Vergil there; but Vergil's last illness had come, and soon after they reached Brundisium together he died (21 September 19 B.C.). Before he died, Vergil anxiously wished to burn the *Aeneid*, for reasons which cannot now be recovered. Augustus either overruled this desire or persuaded Vergil to consent to the publication of the Aeneid by his old friends Varius and Tucca. They were in fact entrusted with the task of editing and publishing it on the understanding that they were to add nothing, and to remove whatever Vergil would have removed from the text. They seem to have done the work quickly and loyally, and published the *Aeneid* within two years or less. Before, Vergil's friends at court and elsewhere had heard or seen some passages, including whole books, and the progress of the work was widely known and followed. But no other arrangements for publication are recorded.

Of Vergil's life in these later years little can be said; at most a mainly conjectural account can be given of the progress of his great work, the *Aeneid*. It was fully begun after Actium and after the publication of the *Georgics*; after ten or eleven years, three more years, for the revision of the poem, were still needed when Vergil died.

The history of the *Aeneid* from its first conception to its publication is so obscure that sharply contradictory views are held. The same book, the fifth, is sometimes supposed the first to be written and sometimes the last, and differing opinions are possible about the changes which Vergil made in the plan of the poem. There is, however, some precise evidence, both external, in the ancient tradition, and internal, within the poems of Vergil.

Before Vergil had finished the *Eclogues*, he had planned an epic. He says himself, in one of them, *cum canerem reges et proelia, Cynthius aurem vellit* . . . 'when I tried to make a poem of warring kings, Apollo twitched my ear (and told me to write with the humility that befits a shepherd)'.[1] This is explained credibly by Donatus, who says that Vergil designed an epic on Roman history, but gave it up and started the *Eclogues* instead, *offensus materia ad Bucolica transiit*, perhaps 'conceiving a dislike for the subject', but possibly 'bored with such a voluminous topic' – as usual the mere translation of the notice is tantalizingly uncertain; Servius says that Vergil dropped the subject, *nominum asperitate deterritus*, 'frightened off it by the unmusical sound of the characters' names'. According to him this epic was to be either about Aeneas, or about the early kings of Alba Longa.[2]

That, then, is the first stage, and the information can be trusted. Before he was thirty, Vergil began a historical or prehistorical epic poem, but abandoned it in dislike. The information can be amplified, but only by uncertainties.

If Vergil wrote the *Culex*, he was already, at a much earlier age, interested in some of the epic material which he treated years after; and made poetry of it, mock heroic poetry. And it was largely

1. *E.* VI, 3–5.   2. Servius, *E.* VI, 3.

material about the other world, important in one of the most finished books, the sixth, of the final *Aeneid*, which is apparently unconnected with any intermediate plan. But, once again, the extant *Culex* is almost certainly not by Vergil.

Nor is *Catalepton* XIV certainly his, although it may well be. Here there is a clear conception of emotional values which determined the main lines of the final *Aeneid*. Apparently under the strong impression made by Julius Caesar's fourfold triumph, and the new temple of Venus Genetrix which he founded at Surrentum (45 B.C.), the writer of the poem formed a poetical conception of the Julian line and its destiny, originating with Venus and with Troy, and symbolized by Aeneas and his journey to Italy. It would be most characteristic of Vergil if he formed this conception and planned an *Aeneid*, abandoned it in favour of a different poem to which the Sixth *Eclogue* refers, and then returned to it years later.

All this is quite uncertain, and it remains uncertain in spite of some apparent confirmation in the existing *Aeneid*. For in its first book there is a fine passage[1] in which Jupiter prophesies the greatness of the Julian line. Servius commenting on it says that Vergil is thinking of Julius Caesar, not Augustus, and the language of the passage confirms him. If Servius is right, the lines were probably begun and partly finished while Julius was alive, about the time when the new temple of Venus was dedicated. There are other parts of the *Aeneid* also, which may well be early, in the fifth book.[2] There certain references to republican families are appropriate to an early time, and so is the description of the Trojan Game, a kind of old musical ride which had been revived by Julius for performance after his triumph (46 B.C.).

The next stage of the plan is also known from Vergil's own words. In the *Georgics*[3] he says that he will build a temple with Caesar in the middle, and then[4] more clearly, and after further imagery, that he will describe Caesar's battles and give him long renown. Caesar is of course Octavianus Augustus. Apparently this plan still stood when Vergil read the *Georgics* to Augustus (? 29 B.C.), about the time when he actually began the extant *Aeneid*.

1. *A*. I, 254–96.   2. *A*. v, 116–23.   3. *G*. III, 12–16.
4. *G*. III, 46–8.

The poem was to be contemporary history. Servius[1] says that Augustus set Vergil the task of writing an *Aeneid*. He probably means by the name '*Aeneid*' this proposed poem on contemporary history, 'The Deeds of Romans', *Gesta populi Romani* as Servius[2] says the name was, or, perhaps, 'The Deeds of Octavianus', *Gesta Octaviani*. It might have started with Aeneas and continued through the intermediate history before the real subject began.

It is possible that Vergil started such an *Aeneid*, but fortunately his poetic imagination refused to work on a purely historical subject. He may even have tried for a long time. Three years after he started the *Aeneid*, Propertius[3] in 26 B.C. wrote of it as if Augustus and the Battle of Actium were still the main subjects, and the arrival of Aeneas secondary. There is a still more fascinating piece of contemporary evidence in a letter to Augustus by Vergil himself. Macrobius[4] relates that Augustus, while in Spain (26–25 B.C.), wrote to Vergil asking him to send some of the *Aeneid*, and he quotes part of Vergil's reply – 'About my Aeneas-poem, if I had had any to send, I should gladly have been sending it. but it is such an immense task that I think I must have been out of my senses to start any such thing.' Perhaps it is worth recalling that Milton planned and started a historical epic on King Arthur, before he decided on the more mythical *Paradise Lost* instead.

However, soon afterwards, Vergil's great poem must have caught fire. At some time he saw that he must make it mythical through and through. Progress must have been quick, for he soon (? 24 B.C.) read to Augustus the third and fourth books, or possibly the second and fourth books, if the numbers, as Servius thinks,[5] were changed; and, soon after that, the sixth also (23 B.C.). When he read the Sixth *Aeneid*, Octavia, sister of Augustus, and mother of Marcellus, heir to the principate and lately dead (23 B.C.), fainted, at the passage where Vergil mentions him. That helps to date this part of the poem.

Naevius and Ennius had combined myth and history. But the change which Vergil made, in confining his poem's whole structure to myth, followed, or started, a lively traditional principle. It

1. Servius, *Prologue to A.* 1.   2. Servius, *A.* VI, 752.
3. Propertius, II, 34, 61–4.   4. Macrobius, *Saturnalia*, I, 24, 11.
5. Servius, *Life of Vergil*.

interested Servius greatly, and he often refers to it. He explains[1] that Vergil summarizes all Roman history to his day, partly in the visions of the Sixth *Aeneid*, and partly in the pictures on the shield of Aeneas at the end of the Eighth. Of course there are historical references throughout the poem. In a passage in the first book, where Aeneas shortly says that his divine mother guided him from Troy, Servius says[2] that Vergil here lightly hints at a story, *historia*, perhaps 'history' or 'true legendary tradition', which by an artistic law of poetry he cannot openly state; and adds that the later poet, Lucan, who disobeyed that law, composed a history, not a poem at all.

Servius had an exacting taste in these matters. He thought[3] that a poet who wrote anything completely untrue is to blame. Elsewhere[4] he praises Vergil for not openly using 'poetic licence', but pretending, by the use of the word for 'tradition says', *fertur*, that he is strictly following an accepted version. Servius had, however, noticed[5] the main principle of Vergil's story-making, how he regularly transfers attributes and actions from one character to another. It all looks like a game; but really the ancient critics were trying hard and creditably to analyse the psychological process of poetry, never so fully achieved, perhaps, by any ancient artist as by Vergil. Of this there will be more to say.

The *Aeneid* then, after many adventures in Vergil's mind, came alive at last. But even as the story of Aeneas it had adventures.

There are many opinions about the order in which the books were composed.[6] Donatus credibly says that Vergil wrote out a prose draft, divided already into twelve books, and then worked at different parts of the story as he pleased, not keeping to any order. A prose draft of a poem is not altogether unusual. The old Indian epic the *Mahabharata* was first constructed in prose; so was some poetry of Goethe. But it is not known whether Vergil's prose draft was long, or a mere outline.

Not much is certain about the order in which the books of the *Aeneid* were composed. It is to some extent an unreal question. Part of a book may be very early and part very late. Vergil worked

1. Servius, *A.* VI, 752.   2. idem, *A.* I, 382.   3. idem, *A.* III, 46.
4. idem, *A.* I, 15.   5. Servius-Daniel, *A.* III, 10.
6. A. Gercke, *Die Entstehung der Aeneis*, Berlin, 1913.

over much of the poem again and again, and almost infinite adjustments were possible, as the poem evolved and grew. But he had found the right form for his story, and that may have been more important than all the rest.

On the stages by which the poem in its existing form was evolved only a few things can be said with confidence. Some passages seem to be later than others, because the style is more mature and the finish and unity are more perfect. The second, sixth, and twelfth books are admitted, on the whole, to be late, at least in their present condition.

Most of the opinions are more precarious. The fourth book is sometimes supposed early because of its small discrepancies and incongruities, and so, too, is the first, on the very questionable ground that it is weak. The fifth book has been thought on the whole the earliest and on the whole the latest. Similar opinions have been held of the eighth. All the first six books have been supposed earlier than all the others; and they have also been supposed later.

The most certain theory is that there is something strange about the Third *Aeneid*, in which Aeneas tells Dido the story of his travels from Troy to Carthage; it is at present a narrative told by Aeneas in the first person, like the second book on the fall of Troy, but originally it was in the third person, told, like all the other books, by Vergil. There are sufficient signs that the book has been altered, and was once part of a different plan for the whole *Aeneid*. I hope a short account of this will not be confusing here.

The poem now begins where Aeneas is sailing from Sicily to Carthage, and continues with two books of the narrative of Aeneas before it returns to direct narrative by Vergil in the fourth book. The second and third books, therefore, go back in time to events before the first book opens. There is little doubt that the third book was written early, and meant to form part of a narrative in unbroken sequence. And it seems to assume a different course of events.[1] In the other books the Trojans know from the start

1. M. M. Crump, *The Growth of the Aeneid*, Oxford, 1920, 16–40, especially 27–8, with references, especially to Remigio Sabbadini *Il primitivo disegno dell' Eneide e la composizione dei libri I, II, III*, Turin, 1900. Cf. idem, *Studi critici sulla Eneide*, Lonigo, 1889, 70 ff. I have failed to find copies of either book in Britain.

that they are going to Italy and Latium, but the geography is vague; a prophecy, that they will have to eat their tables, is given by Anchises, and is a sign that their destination is reached; the Trojans are to see a white sow with thirty young as an omen for the later foundation of Alba Longa, thirty years after the death of Aeneas; Anchises prophesies war in Italy; the anger of Juno is the cause of the afflictions of the Trojans; Venus is their guide; Acestes, a Trojan who has settled in Sicily, entertains the Trojans of Aeneas on their first landing there; and the journey takes seven years.

The third book contradicts each of these suppositions. Latium is not mentioned, and the name of Italy is not known at first but only gradually revealed; however, the geography is clear, and the position of Italy is known; Celaeno, a harpy or evil spirit in the form of a human-headed bird, prophesies that the Trojans must eat their tables, and it is a bad omen; the white sow is a sign for the foundation by Aeneas of Lavinium, if that is the name of his city; the Sibyl at Cumae is to prophesy the wars in Italy; Juno's anger is not mentioned; Apollo is the guide; Acestes does not appear at the first landing in Sicily; and the journey takes two years only.

These and other reasons are enough to shew that Vergil wrote the Third *Aeneid* early, perhaps while he still designed a more historical poem than he eventually wrote; and that he did not fully adjust the book, either by revising it, or by rewriting it, to the scheme which he finally chose.

Among the supporting arguments for this theory are some which are of great interest. Vergil treated the third book as he treated earlier poems of his own, possibly including the *Ciris*, and took from it many lines to use elsewhere in the *Aeneid*. It was believed in antiquity that the order of the books in the *Aeneid* had once been different. Donatus records a tradition that Varius changed the order of two books, and made the original second book the third in the new order. Servius, in his *Life of Vergil*, cites, without assenting to it, an opinion that the second book is really the first, the third the second, and the first the third. Donatus says that Vergil read to Augustus the second, fourth, and sixth books, but Servius that the books read were the third, fourth and sixth.

Perhaps it is not possible to make sure what, exactly, the original order was. But there is here at any rate traditional support for the theory that the present third book was designed to fit an early plan, which was afterwards altered.

Of Vergil's life as a sequence of events in history there is not much to say; and all the time his work for which he lived forces itself into the sequence of the few external facts. His real history is mental, a sequence and a spatial pattern in the imagination. Far more engaging is the direct approach to his poetry; but for that some attention must be given to the manner in which it was made.

CHAPTER 3

TRADITION AND POETRY

ALL who think much about Vergil are nearly certain to become involved in the question of his derivations from earlier poets. The attractive force which this question exerts is surprising, until we recognize that it is a necessary result of Vergil's greatness. In the discussions of this subject, one side usually argues that Vergil copies other writers, and is therefore a plagiarist, and a bad poet, while the other side contends either that Vergil does not precisely depend on derivations from other writers, or that if he does he is yet so great that he can do so without spoiling his poetry. In the present state of knowledge, it is possible to see that the question is more important even than has been supposed, but that the discussions of it have usually taken wrong directions and have often been conducted with wrong motives. It should soon become hard to believe that there could ever have been surprise at Vergil's method, or any talk about plagiarism in connexion with him.

There seems to have been current for generations the false assumption that a poet can either write down his own sentiments in his own words, which is praiseworthy, or he can derive his words, and therefore his thoughts, from other writers, which is certainly suspicious, and probably quite enough to condemn him. The facts which contradict this assumption are obvious enough, and there would be no need to revive the controversy, if it were not that the present position of it is enlightening, and that there is further progress to be made.

The most obvious fact is the excellence of the poetry written by the derivative poets. Even Voltaire said that if Homer made Vergil, Vergil was the best thing that ever he did make. Father Aurelio Espinosa[1] has well explained that if it is clear, as indeed it is, that Vergil depends verbally on an immense number of

1. Aurelio Espinosa Pólit, s.j., *Virgilio, el poeta y su misión providencial*, Quito, 1932, 36–113, especially 40.

literary reminiscences, that does not prove that his poetry is dead, since it is just as clear that his poetry is very much alive. Domenico Comparetti[1] is among those who have used a similar argument. Father Espinosa firmly asserts that imitation, as he calls it, is the universal law of poetry; and that is the right place to start. He explains that even the supposedly original Homer was just as dependent on his sources as Vergil himself. Yet not many generations ago Dr Johnson held that all the stories in the world were derived from the uniquely original Homer; and still more recently Mr Gladstone believed that when Homer's descriptions of works of art correspond with objects that have been actually found, that is because Homer first imagined them and described what his imagination saw, and the Greek artists simply copied the Homeric descriptions.

Father Espinosa's warning was greatly needed, since respected scholars regularly express surprise that Vergil should have been able to improve what he borrowed, and even copy several originals at once. He 'copied' Lucretius, on two different computations, once in every four to five, or twelve, lines;[2] but he 'improved on' Lucretius regularly. He depended still more on Homer; he 'copied' both the beginning of the *Iliad* and the beginning of the *Odyssey* for the beginning of the *Aeneid*; and to the surprise of many made the result great.

There is, meanwhile, a frequent assertion, not from scholars but from poets, of the importance of tradition, whatever that may mean. Goethe is particularly insistent; and Shelley, followed by Mr T. S. Eliot, went some of the way towards explaining it. Artists, to be artists, says Mr Eliot,[3] must explicitly place themselves in their true relation to the dead artists; they must feel and shew their presence within the whole coherent sequence of world art, which is altered for ever by the new work of each new artist. That does not explain everything. But it reveals that derivation is rather essential to the arts than accidental and unfortunate.

1. D. Comparetti, *Vergil in the Middle Ages*, translated by E. F. M. Benecke, London, 1908, 13–14.

2. W. F. J. Knight, *Vergil's Troy*, Oxford, 1932, 24, with references 142, note 23.

3. T. S. Eliot, *Selected Essays*, 1917–32, London, 1932, 13–22.

Mr E. E. Kellett[1] has observed that the best poets are also the best borrowers. Chaucer, Shakespeare, Milton, Gray, Coleridge, Tennyson, and Eliot are among English poets most distinguished for borrowing. But why poets should want to borrow is still left obscure. However, there is also an instructive theory of Mlle A.-M. Guillemin[2] for the 'borrowing' of Latin poets. She regards them as following a convention which would not nowadays be understood, and pitting their brains against each other, to say the same thing more and more exactly and beautifully. The poets, according to Professor R. B. Steele,[3] were in search of the matchless word or phrase, and trying to improve on the work of their predecessors. They were not trying to say anything that had never been said before.

There is much truth in this. Still, it is not always easy to distinguish the saying of the same thing in a new way and the saying of something different. Nor is it always a question of what the poet intends. Landor,[4] in so many words, and other poets regularly in their different ways, have recorded that this is the question least worth considering about poetry. But Mlle Guillemin is right to say, as she does, that the Latin poets were in 'competition', ἀγών, to reach perfection, by a rehandling, *retractatio*, of the same idea with slight changes of words again and again. She cites Horace, Seneca, and Pliny as explicitly saying that this happened; Seneca explaining that Vergil's 'thefts' were of a special kind, since he wanted them to be recognized. Perhaps it was a new and wrong kind of just this emulation that Agrippa blamed Vergil for inventing.

Common sense, however, with help from detailed examination of poetry, shews that all derivations are not due to conscious competition. Possibly poets trained themselves that way; Horace implies it. But they hardly stopped there; though much of their conscious thought may have been directed to the ambition to excel each other with similar words, and that was anyhow a healthy discipline, if not carried too far. And there is meanwhile

1. E. E. Kellett, *Literary Quotation and Allusion*, Cambridge, 1933, 31–43.
2. A.-M. Guillemin, *L'originalité de Virgile*, Paris, 1931, 5–9, 125–54.
3. R. B. Steele, *Classical Philology*, xxv, 1930, 328–42.
4. W. S. Landor, *Imaginary Conversations*, London, 1846, 82.

the probability that Latin poets quoted each other, without change of words, as a compliment; not to excel, but to shew admiration.

Besides these views, there are also 'allusive' theories, perhaps going back to Aristotle's observation that recognition gives pleasure.[1] According to the 'allusive' theories poets refer openly to earlier poetry, because the recognition of the allusion gives pleasure. Familiarity and recognition may be effective either for their own sake, or because the context gives added point to familiar words or thoughts. Allusive theories are certainly true sometimes, but they are not, except in a much elaborated form, applicable always, since in the great poets by far the greater number of the allusions are unlikely to be noticed. Donatus reports that Quintus Octavius Avitus compiled eight volumes of Vergilian parallels, and Perellius Faustus an anthology of his 'thefts'.

All the theories work towards the recognition that, somehow, available earlier poetry helps the poets, and should help them to create new poetry. The derivations clearly help the poet to write quite as much as they help the reader to enjoy, or more; and they help the poet not to evade but to discharge his responsibilities. The ordinary theories are, however, insufficient. Still, each of them is true of some poetic passages. Much poetry is conscious retractation, much is allusion meant to be recognized, and some even unsuccessful, deplorable copying, for there is such a thing, even if it is rare. But these conceptions are only approaches to the real problem, which is not so simple as any one of them implies.

The real question has been opened and partly solved by Professor E. K. Rand, who has applied to Vergil the results of Professor John Livingston Lowes' work on Coleridge.[2] Vergil's method is seen to be characteristic of many of the greatest poets; he could not help remembering words, sounds, and rhythms from earlier poetry, and letting them start new poetic complexes in his own mind, subtly different from the poetry which he remembered. That is how Coleridge worked also.

1. E. E. Kellett, *Literary Quotation and Allusion*, Cambridge, 1933, 17–30; W. A. Edwards, *Plagiarism*, Cambridge, 1933, 45–61.

2. E. K. Rand, *The Magical Art of Virgil*, Cambridge, Massachusetts, 1931, 10–15, 269–70, etc.; John Livingston Lowes, *The Road to Xanadu*, New York and London, 2nd ed., 1933, *passim*.

Professor Lowes proved from Coleridge's notebooks that countless ideas and words derived from his reading, mainly in poetry and in the literature of travel, were accepted by Coleridge, and retained by him in the part of the mind called by William James 'the deep well of unconscious cerebration'. They were like 'hooked atoms', as M. Henri Poincaré, the French mathematician, described such fragments of reminiscence; and they gradually coalesced in the unconscious mind into new expressive wholes, till one day, quite suddenly, they emerged into consciousness as poetry. The process does not apply to poetry only, but to all discoveries. M. Poincaré described his own mathematical discoveries as made in this way. It is the same in classical scholarship; problems are consciously stated, and stored, apparently forgotten, in the unconscious; and it may be twenty years after that the answer, having pieced itself together unseen, appears in the conscious mind.

Professor Lowes considers that the acceptance of 'hooked atoms' of experience, from life or from books, and their self-combination into new wholes, are in varying degrees normal to everyone. For Lowes, the peculiarities of the poet are his shaping will and intelligence, by which he organizes into a larger scheme the units delivered to his conscious mind. Coleridge in *Dejection* wrote of the 'shaping spirit of imagination', and in *Biographia Literaria*, XIII, of the 'esemplastic power', power 'which shapes into one'. It seems that Coleridge himself supposed that a larger part of the process is unconscious than Professor Lowes assumes it to be.

This leaves something to be said. There is a theory of Dr I. A. Richards[1] that the poet is distinguished by his greater psychological vigilance, that is, readiness to accept impressions, a readiness which he has the power to communicate. Further, *Kubla Khan* was delivered to Coleridge's consciousness ready made; it is well known that he composed it in his sleep, and, when he woke up again, wrote down as much as he could, before he was interrupted. Conscious organization had nothing to do with it whatever. And, as Professor G. Wilson Knight[2] has shewn, the poem is a perfect

1. I. A. Richards, *The Principles of Literary Criticism*, London, 1934, 183–5, 204, 248.
2. G. Wilson Knight, *The Starlit Dome*, London, 1941, 90–8.

whole, fully organized, and intensely and profoundly significant; it is not in the least the meaningless fragment which it was once supposed to be. Further, discoveries in other branches than poetry, such as mathematics or botany, are also given in this way, ready made; though of course much conscious thought is used to express them, afterwards. It is to be noticed, too, that ordinary people do not make great discoveries. The hooked atoms in their minds combine to form a dream world, which they may certainly know in sleep; but normally the dream world does not produce material of importance to waking life, such as great poetry, or scientific discoveries.

I suggest, therefore, that the shaping will and intelligence that are characteristic of genius, poetic or other, may operate consciously or unconsciously. There may or may not be much left for the conscious mind to do; sometimes the units delivered by the unconscious are already comprehensive and fully organized. The large structural lines of an epic may conceivably be unconsciously invented, no less than small phrases may be, through the combination of remembered elements; though there is sure to be at least some conscious work in the organization of long poems.

The poets who mainly 'integrate' – a word is needed for the process and this one will do – from literary originals appear to be awakened to the productive poetic mood by the effect of earlier poetry on them. In that mood they create their own poetry, and it is likely to contain words and thoughts from earlier work, which reappear more or less altered. Coleridge might fuse and blend a dozen memories of various books in one stanza of *The Ancient Mariner*, scarcely a phrase being quite new, but scarcely a phrase being exactly what he had read.

Not all poets depend preponderantly on literary derivation. Some take inspiration from the common ideas and talk of a group, as Pindar, Catullus in most of his colloquial lyrics, Donne, Auden, and Day Lewis. Among the poets who depend on literary derivation are Homer, perhaps Sappho, Vergil, more than any, most of the great English poets, and now Ezra Pound and Eliot, who are unusually conscious in their derivations. The method of the ancient poets was developed naturally from the endless repetitions, with gradual slight changes. through centuries of Greek epic poetry; with a new start in the loose kind of translation which began literary work in Latin. After the great periods of Latin poetry, the later Latin poets depended too literally on former work, saying too nearly the same thing in only slightly different ways. An extreme was reached in the *centones*, poems entirely made by the redistribution of old lines. This may have helped to set the fashion for the Middle Ages, which in ballad, epic, and court poetry were inclined to go on doing the same thing with increasing elaboration. Medieval epic, at first fresh with a new inspiration, declined into repetitions and expansions. Then, out of the Middle Ages, grew the more constructive integration, comparable to Vergil's, of Dante and Chaucer. The other tradition, of statement according to words and thoughts current not in literature but in the talk of a social group, might be said to emerge most noticeably in the informal work of Skelton,[1] which is in contrast to his more traditional poems, and to appear again, after a gap, in Elizabethan lyrics and sonnets. The tradition might be said to pass through Donne, Wordsworth, and Browning to several of the moderns.

Vergil's integration could be called inspiration from former poetry, which might equally be the poetry of others, or poetry of his own. He probably tried direct colloquial lyric, following Catullus, but poems of that kind in the *Appendix* are not certainly his. Of course, Vergil and the 'new poets' or 'moderns' made close contact with the Alexandrians, in particular Apollonius Rhodius; and the true derivative method, then as at other historical moments, grew out of attempts at reproduction, and translation. It became a habit to try to say what had been already said, but if possible with improvements; and eventually, almost by mistake, to create poetry of the best and most original kind. in which numerous reminiscences are fused and blended.

The exact truth about this process is elusive; but it is now quite clear that in integrative method Vergil was like, but not exactly like, Coleridge. Vergil used all methods, but the integrative tendency nearly always conditioned the others. The process worked apparently as follows.

1. L. J. Lloyd, *John Skelton* ...., Oxford, 1938, *passim*.

Vergil read something. The emotional charge, in the sound, the rhythm, the words, the ideas, the sequence of events, the grand structure – anything, in fact, on whatever scale – communicated itself to him, never to be dispelled altogether from his conscious or at least his unconscious memory. The impulse was to say the verse or tell the story over and over again, partly because there was a mysterious, self-sufficient delight in the poetry, and partly because it fitted Vergil's own feelings, expressed them, clarified them, and made them acceptable and friendly to himself. These feelings were strong, and ever developing. They exerted force on what had at first seemed the perfect expression of similar feelings, in the poetry of Theocritus, or Euphorion, or Hesiod, or any of the others. The scheme and structure might remain; or the sounds and rhythms; but everything could not remain; and in general, as with Coleridge, nothing at all was ever reproduced entirely without alteration. Everything went into the dream world, into the 'deep well'; the 'hooked atoms' parted and recombined. Vergil's supposed mistranslations of Greek are characteristic. Superficially, the process of getting poetry right is almost indistinguishable from the process of getting anything else wrong; but, though the poetic process may resemble hallucination,[1] really it is a discovery of truth, like other sorts of discovery.

The process declares itself with unusual clarity in Mr Ezra Pound's poem, *Homage to Sextus Propertius*. Pound lets Propertius suggest ideas. But, as Mr Martin Gilkes has shewn in detail,[2] there is nothing in the poem obviously like Propertius. The mistakes in Latin, if they are mistakes, are perhaps the most glaring on record anywhere. *Canere*, 'sing', will reappear as if it were *canis*, 'dog'; and so on, in countless instances. The spirit, also, is quite different, and so is everything else. The truth is that the poem is a poem and not a translation. It has travelled perhaps a little further than Vergil's *Eclogues* along the way that started with the loose, active renderings of Greek works by Livius, Plautus, Ennius, and the rest.

The natural human tendency towards forgetfulness and con-

1. Charles Baudouin, *Suggestion and Autosuggestion*, translated by Eden and Cedar Paul, London, 2nd ed., 1921, 48–55.
2. Martin Gilkes, *English*, 11, 1938, 74–83.

fusion normally produces error, but in poets it may produce poetic truth. Their unconscious mind is full, not only of imaginative impressions, but also of a latent reason. The 'hooked atoms' combine according to it. The reason in it all is missed, because it is too quick, and too compressed and elliptic. Poets seem to talk nonsense because they talk so much truth all at the same time.

The poetry of ancient Italy, and Europe since, was fortunate in that Naevius, Plautus, and Terence combined, or 'contaminated', plots of different Greek works. It was fortunate, too, that Vergil combined different *Idylls* of Theocritus into one *Eclogue*. Vergil remembered everything but the organization of details; and his personal feelings provided a new organization, which was, however, not too new to allow their expression to be generalized, in touch with tradition, and so artistic.

Donatus in his *Life of Vergil*, most of which is by Suetonius, explained how Vergil worked, and Professor Rand has shewn how Donatus is to be understood.

Vergil wrote each morning a large number of lines. He spent the day, as he himself is recorded by Donatus to have said, licking them into shape, as a she-bear is supposed to lick her cubs. In the evening he had just a few perfect lines – perhaps an average, for his writing life, of well under twenty a day; less than one finished line a day was the pace of the *Georgics*.

Possibly following Vergil himself, Donatus used the word *retractatio* to mean the process of polishing and improving verses already roughly made. The other sense, which was emphasized by Mlle Guillemin, is also legitimate; the word can mean the act of rehandling, and either improving, or merely changing for use in a different context, verses or parts of verses used already either by the same poet or by one or more other poets.

Vergil's practice as Donatus describes it looks at first sight like very conscious work. So does the further fact recorded by Donatus that Vergil wrote the *Aeneid* in a prose draft, with the sequence of events divided into twelve books. But he adds that Vergil created the poetry as the fancy took him, any passage at any time; and that when the right line did not come readily, he invented any kind of line, however bad, temporarily, 'so that nothing might stop the flow of creation'. Vergil called such a line a *tibicen* or 'prop', something to hold up the edifice for a time. Sometimes, too, he might leave a line uncompleted, where the inspiration stopped, intending to fill in the rest of it later.

How he filled the gaps is one of the most significant facts about his method. Donatus also records that Vergil had left uncompleted a line in the Sixth *Aeneid:* . . . *ut venere, vident indigna morte peremptum Misenum Aeoliden* . . ., 'they saw, when they came, lifeless, of a death unfair, Misenus, of Aeolid line . . .'.[1] Eros, Vergil's secretary, was reading the passage to him one day. Suddenly the answer came, and Vergil told Eros to write down . . . *quo non praestantior alter aere ciere viros* . . ., 'than whom no second had been more supreme, to wake the heart of fighting men with notes of bronze . . .'.[2] Apparently, though here the interpretation is uncertain, the inspiration stopped again, and was renewed later in exactly the same way; as Eros was reading, the final completion suddenly occurred to Vergil, and he told him to write down, *Martemque accendere cantu,* 'and light the fire of battle with his music'.[3] There is no need to doubt that the story contains the truth about the completion of at least one of the two lines.

As Vergil read, and thought, and watched, and felt, impressions from life and letters sank into his memory and combined, unseen. Meanwhile he worked and planned, and decided at least what he thought that he wanted to do, however much the wayward poetic drive might distort his human planning. But the planning itself was contributing to the unconscious integration. 'Take care of the conscious' is a psychologist's advice, 'and the unconscious will look after itself.' It is not all mad, mysterious, automatic, or fortuitous. Hard thinking, facing facts, planning, and reasoning were just as important in the unconscious centre of Vergil's creation as old heard melodies, not understood, but caught and held; lovely, but with little meaning that we, or Vergil either, could have defined.

The unconscious process, therefore, was not independent of the conscious processes of thinking and planning and choosing – even down to the mere choice of what to read; and it was also followed by a conscious process, of judging, criticizing, and correcting what the unconscious mind had delivered. There is something uncon-

1. *A.* vi, 163–4.   2. *A.* vi, 164–5.   3. *A.* vi, 165.

scious still in such criticism and correction. Taste is involved. Sometimes, it is a matter of consciously applying truth, which has been acquired from the unconscious in another mood. There is little doubt, either, that Vergil, like living poets whom I have known, consciously planned to make, or to let, the unconscious mind work for him; though he would not have described it like that.

There are, of course, difficulties. It is hard to say, sometimes – Plato thought, always – what is inspiration, and what is just madness. W. B. Yeats was careful to leave his early poems unaltered in his 1912 collected volume, 'fearing', he said, 'some stupidity in my middle years'. Coleridge, in a footnote to a passage of splendid poetry which was never understood till a few years ago,[1] wrote, with apology, that he printed it because it was clearly good, though he himself could see no meaning in it.

Vergil also misunderstood himself sometimes. For example, according to Servius in his *Life*, the famous passage in the Second *Aeneid*,[2] where Aeneas sees Helen in burning Troy and wants to kill her, was rejected by Vergil's editors, clearly according to his known wishes, but not less clearly to the disadvantage of the poem. There is scarcely anything finer than the passage, or more necessary to the *Aeneid*. Poets, at dull moments, make mistakes. Coleridge refused to publish *Kubla Khan* for years till Byron made him, and he persuaded Wordsworth to remove very necessary lines from the ode *Intimations of Immortality*.

According to Shelley, the greatest poet cannot create poetry just when he wishes. The poetry comes 'from whence 'tis nourished', in the words of Shakespeare, like 'a gum which oozes,' not like 'the fire i' the flint' which 'shews not till it be struck'.[3] So Noel Essex,[4] a contemporary writer of unusual power, says that much of her best poetry comes 'without going through my head at all'; and that its meaning sometimes only becomes clear, for the first time, weeks afterwards. Of the same writer it can be observed

1. G. Wilson Knight, *The Starlit Dome*, London, 1941, 139, 143.

2. *A.* ii, 567–88.

3. *Timon of Athens*, i, i, 21–5; W. F. J. Knight, *Accentual Symmetry in Vergil*, Oxford, 1939, 105–7, with references.

4. Noel Essex, *Shade Tides and Other Poems*, Oxford, 1939, Introduction, 9–12.

that impressions, sometimes acquired years before, are integrated into poetry when they are consciously forgotten.

But there are times when inspiration does not come; and, in a long poem especially, it may be necessary to make poetry by effort of thought. This process can be called composition. Vergil, as he knew himself, 'composed' the *tibicines*, the 'prop' lines. He may or may not have known that he 'composed' longer passages. But it is fairly safe to say that he did, and we can sometimes decide, tentatively, which they are.

The word 'integration' might reasonably be used to mean the integration of impressions from life. Vergil's true integration, however, preponderantly works on literary reminiscences, large or small. To integrate well, Vergil needed literary reminiscences, and they had to be stored for a long time in his mind. The late E. K. Rand observed that a less successful passage of Vergil may mean that the impressions had not been stored long enough. Sometimes at least Vergil was hampered by having none to store. Macrobius[1] says that Vergil used a weak motive for the start of the war in Latium, the misfortune of Iulus in shooting Silvia's pet stag,[2] because there was no Homeric precedent available. Macrobius was wrong. The motive is not weak, but touching and powerful, characteristically Vergilian in sympathy. And there was a precedent for it, which he missed, not actually in Homer, but in the Cyclic Epic. In the *Cypria* Agamemnon shot a sacred stag at Aulis. Macrobius was right, however, to suggest that Vergil is the better for a precedent. He might have said that Vergil needs literary reminiscences in large numbers, if he is to write his best; the best passages usually prove, on examination, to have the largest number of such reminiscences at their root. In this, Vergil is apparently like Coleridge, Goethe, and no doubt many other poets.

Vergil also integrated from himself, not from others only. It was convenient and natural, and also helpful for the best results, for him to rehandle his former work until he had a newly enriched and softly toned version of it for a new passage. The recognition of this habit, its integrative nature, and its valid utility, is of immense importance for all Vergilian criticism.

The poets reveal each other's ways. Some general remarks of

1. Macrobius, *Saturnalia*, v, 17, 1–5.   2. *A.* VII, 475–510.

Mr T. S. Eliot[1] are as revelatory for Vergil as the psychological comments of Coleridge himself. Writing of Kipling, Mr Eliot says: 'Most of us are interested in the form for its own sake – not apart from the content, but because we aim at making something which shall first of all *be*, something which in consequence will have the capability of exciting, within a limited range, a considerable variety of responses from different readers. For Kipling the poem is something which is intended to *act* – and for the most part his poems are intended to elicit the same response from all readers, and only the response which they can make in common. For other poets – at least, for some other poets – the poem may begin to shape itself in fragments of musical rhythm, and its structure will first appear in terms of something analogous to musical form; and such poets find it expedient to occupy their conscious mind with the craftsman's problems, leaving the deeper meaning to emerge, if there, from a lower level. It is a question then of what one chooses to be conscious of, and of how much of the meaning, in a poem, is conveyed direct to the intelligence and how much is conveyed indirectly by the musical impression upon the sensibility – always remembering that the use of the word "musical" and of musical analogies, in discussing poetry, has its dangers if we do not constantly check its limitations: for the music of verse is inseparable from the meanings and associations of words. If I say then, that this musical concern is secondary and infrequent with Kipling, I am not implying any inferiority of craftsmanship, but rather a different order of values from that which we expect to determine the structure of poetry.' Here, it might be said, Vergil's method, and especially its audially delivered construction, is most precisely defined by reference both to Kipling's method, the opposite to it, and to Mr Eliot's own, which is often, I believe, almost exactly the same as Vergil's. But perhaps this quotation will only seem fully clear and relevant at a later stage of the argument.

When true integration stops, composition may have to begin. It may prove very useful; the attempt to think out a solution may lead to new and good integration, as if by luck, since 'chance', as Agathon said, is 'the friend of art'; a more probable reason is that

1. *A Choice of Kipling's Verse*, made by T. S. Eliot, London, 1941, 18–19.

something in the unconscious has been released for consciousness by thinking. But it is equally possible that the result of composition may be poetry that is weak and strained.

When the inspiration of the unconscious mind failed, Vergil might tell a straight story, derived from some single source such as a handbook of mythology. He might make up a story in an obvious way, and attempt to decorate it. And he might read or say to himself his own poetry from elsewhere, trusting it to start the required process.

We see the results. The boat race in the Fifth *Aeneid*[1] was new. No other boat race in any ancient poem is known. It was conscious invention, to replace Homer's land racing. We find it forced, and even unpleasantly humorous. Vergil may be parodying himself, or, as so often, he may be too deep for us. The passage is quite likely, also, to be very early work. But provisionally we must be dissatisfied, on the standard that Vergil has set. So it is with much of the Ninth *Aeneid*. Vergil has a real emotion, and a picture in his own mind to transmit, not in all the book, but in parts of it; especially the part concerning Nisus and Euryalus, the attached friends who try to find their way through the besiegers of the camp to Aeneas, but are killed. Even here, the only literary foundation was in the Tenth *Iliad*, where Odysseus and Diomedes at night raid the Trojans; and of course the feeling in Homer is very different. Vergil can be watched attempting to integrate his own earlier work, sometimes with rather unnatural and forced developments. Pathos possessed him, and, very interestingly, he reproduces again and again in the Ninth *Aeneid*, in the right and in the wrong places, one of his specially pathetic rhythms, a pause with an elision within the third foot of the hexameter.

True integration works otherwise and is infinitely flexible. It can be classified according to scale. On the smallest scale there are words and phrases; and on the largest scale there is the story, with parts of it often growing out of at least two passages of Homer, with several Greek tragedies helping, and subordinate suggestions from countless other works. Partly by thinking and planning, and partly by letting impressions coalesce of themselves, Vergil would contrive a new form for a story, compounded of

1. *A.* v, 114–285.

all earlier forms, and packed with all the valuable meanings of the past, and reaching, in the blend, quite new meanings too.

It is not impossible to get the impression that Vergil would always use an existing legend faithfully, if he could, inventing only when he must.[1] On the contrary, Vergil, who, like most great poets scarcely ever invented anything, equally rarely, and probably never, followed any legend faithfully. Like Coleridge, he fused the stories and characters, as he fused remembered phrases. Servius[2] partly understood. He observed that Vergil regularly transferred actions and characteristics from one personality to another; as, elsewhere,[3] he observed that Vergil could allude to history, which to Servius included legends, but could not express it directly, because that was against the artistic principles of poetry.

On all the different scales of integration Vergil's poetic process was on the whole homogeneous, and steadily guided by his unconscious mind, in the development of new poetry out of old. It was equally by integration that Vergil built phrases out of words, lines out of phrases, incidents out of other incidents, by isolating and reassembling the attributes and actions of former characters, and, next, large dramatic situations, and finally whole books and poems, all from older elements, redistributed and recombined.

The integration of words, phrases, and lines is a continuous thread, delicately and infinitely complex, running from Homer through Greek and Latin poets to Vergil, then all through Vergil's own work, and onwards to the successors who learnt from him. A phrase may start in some Greek poem, and by combinations and alterations live on until it starts a new history in Vergil's mind, and a sequence of developing appearances in his work, gathering power and depth of meaning on its way. Sometimes, of course, the history of Vergil's expressions might be said to start in Vergil's own mind, for he may be the first to associate together, into a new complex, sounds, thoughts, and words never put to-

1. R. Heinze, *Virgils epische Technik*, Leipzig, 3rd ed., 1928, 239–64; Gino Funaioli, *Sul mito di Laocoonte in Virgilio*, in *Atti del I Congresso Nazionale di Studi Romani*, Rome, 1928, especially 1–7.

2. Servius, *A.* iii, 10.   3. idem, *A.* i, 382.

gether before. But often, and probably most often, the history and ancestry goes back to earlier poetry, sometimes old, and sometimes almost or quite contemporary, as when Vergil exchanges reminiscences with Horace, or adopts and adapts, from Messalla perhaps, or Catullus, or Lucretius, pairs of words, groups of words, and occasionally a whole line. Vergil treats Ennius in the same way; and, in so far as the difference of language allows, Greek poetry also. Sometimes the conscious, and sometimes the unconscious, processes predominate.

It has proved possible to analyse and to classify, according to the different kinds of changes in the adaptation, Vergil's reminiscences of Ennius[1] and Lucretius.[2]

One kind of change which Vergil seems to have sought was in the sound. This is specially noticed by Macrobius[3] and by Servius.[4] Vergil's words are nearly always more musical. For this purpose according to Servius Vergil changed the line of Ennius, *at tuba terribili sonitu taratantara dixit*, 'hark, the trumpet with its alarming note has cried "taratantara"',[5] to *at tuba terribilem sonitum procul aere canoro increpuit*, 'hark, the distant trumpet has crashed its dreadful note with music of the bronze!'[6] Vergil had many other such fastidious motives. He might think a verbal or metrical usage of Ennius unsuitable. Concurrently, he might seek to make words of Ennius more figurative and forcible. Ennius[7] wrote of a fighter's head wrenched from him, and his 'eyes still flickering, half-living yet, longing to find the light again'. Vergil[8] transferred the ideas to a hand cut off, and 'fingers still flickering, half-living yet, trying to clutch the blade again'. He kept many of the words of Ennius; others he characteristically used again in other passages also. Characteristically, too, he had a ready reason for applying the verb 'flicker', *micare*, to fingers. It was a colloquial usage, applied to a game in which players suddenly shewed their fingers, and their opponents had to guess how many would be shewn.

---

1. Sir Maurice Bowra, *The Classical Quarterly*, XXIII, 1929, 65–75.
2. Cyril Bailey, *The Proceedings of the Classical Association*, XXVIII, 1931, 21–39.
3. Macrobius, *Saturnalia*, VI, 1, 6.   4. Servius, *A.* IX, 501.
5. Ennius, *Annals*, 140.   6. *A.* IX, 503–4.
7. Ennius, *Annals*, 472–3.   8. *A.* X, 395–6.

Many derivations are multiple. Ennius, like Vergil, rehandled in 'retractation', or 'reintegrated', his own earlier lines.[1] Vergil might remember each such occurrence of a word-group in Ennius, and apply it himself more than once, with new changes, in his own work.[2] Even then, so sharp is his economy, there might still remain some element, unused, and available for unexpected, and sometimes slight, exploitation in some very different context.[3]

Vergil consciously improved the rhythm and harmony of old lines, by simply applying his fastidious aesthetic conscience. It was, of course, hardly possible for him to be entirely satisfied with any older line, and it was most unlikely, anyway, that it would exactly express his own mood, even if its literal sense needed no alteration. Yet all the time an old line might appeal to him unforgettably, and start his own imagination working. It is usually possible to see some of the reasons why an old line attracted Vergil and why he altered it as he did; even if the possibilities, and the kinds of conscious and unconscious motive, are too many to allow any exhaustive account.

Vergil's most obvious and famous adoption from Ennius is probably the line about Quintus Fabius Maximus Cunctator, who saved Rome from Hannibal in the Second Punic War by *cunctatio*, 'dilatoriness'. Ennius wrote *unus homo nobis cunctando restituit rem*, literally, 'one man, alone, restored to us our whole fortune by dilatory action'.[4] Vergil makes Anchises, in Elysium where beyond death, and before life, the Roman heroes of the future are awaiting their time on earth, address Fabius, and describe him as *unus qui nobis cunctando restituis rem*, 'you who alone restore . . . '.[5] A series of Roman heroes, seen and described, has been working up to an intense moment, a climax after which thought, emotion, and rhythm come for an instant to rest. The steady, inexorable pace of the Sixth *Aeneid* depends on these periodic rests, enforced by a sudden coincidence of word accent and metrical ictus – of which

1. E.g. Ennius, *Annals*, 29, 159, 339.
2. E.g., Ennius, *Annals*, 339; *A.* IV, 482; VI, 797; XI, 201–2; and cf. Lucretius, V, 1205.
3. E.g., *E.* IX, 47, from Ennius, *Annals*, 339, and other passages; cf. *A.* II, 557–8, X, 396, and other passages, from Ennius, *Annals*, 472–3.
4. Ennius, *Annals*, 370.   5. *A.* VI, 846.

there will be more to say later – in the fourth foot.[1] Here the coincidence comes at the middle syllable of *cunctándo*. This coincidence in this place, as will appear later, is characteristic of all
Latin hexameter poetry before Vergil, but Vergil himself miti-
gated its application. It is old-fashioned and suggests the rugged,
hardy past. Words of three long syllables in this part of the line
always have a kind of resolute muscularity, suggesting a determination to force a way through a terrible or difficult task. So
Vergil has *compéllat*, 'addresses', in this place,[2] when in tragic
situations one character forces himself to speak to another while
his heart is breaking. It is tempting to call words of this form in
this place in the line 'will-power words'. And to Vergil, and perhaps to all Romans who had been brought up at school on
Ennius, there was something Ennian about a will-power word.
Accordingly, at this point in the Sixth *Aeneid*, just where a strong
punctuation finished a long, steady period of lines, the impact of
an unexpected line from Ennius himself, reproduced almost unchanged, must have been terrific to Romans. To them the thought
of Fabius, and the tones of Ennius, had great depth of meaning
and strong, evocative association; and the impact can be almost as
terrific for us, if we use our imagination just a little. And Vergil,
according to his way, apparently by doing nothing at all, lets an
overpowering new contrast emerge. The immense weight on
cunctándo, more than any that Ennius laid on the word, starts
thoughts. Fabius saved Rome from Hannibal, by not being afraid
to seem weak and slow, and not putting rumour before safety, as
Ennius also said; and so might Julius and Pompeius, addressed
with deprecation by Anchises near this very place, have saved
Rome from itself, if they had forborne. Vergil allowed much of
his political philosophy to emerge from this Ennian word.

The changes that Vergil made in the line of Ennius are obvious
and simple. The second person, not the third, is needed in the context, and it makes the line more dramatic. So does the present
tense which that change also involves, for Fabius is made to seem
a kind of eternal principle of restraint. Vergil elsewhere[3] writes of

1. W. F. J. Knight, *Accentual Symmetry in Vergil*, Oxford, 1939, 48–59,
77–80.

2. *A.* IV, 304; VI, 499.   3. *A.* IX, 266.

a gift which Dido had given. It is after her death, but he writes a present tense, *dat*; it is a gift which Dido 'gives', or of which Dido 'is the giver'. Perhaps that is because Dido's influence is permanent in the *Aeneid*; in a sense she haunts Aeneas, and haunts Vergil, and us too. There are similar presents in Old Latin, which so uses the same word *dat*, and in other writers. It would be possible to adduce Greek present tenses also for comparison, but the parallels, for once, might not prove sufficiently exact.

Vergil is enabled by his first change to make another change too. To fit the line to the passage, he must have a relative, *qui*, 'who'. That displaces *homo*, 'man', a word normally used in a very general and not very dignified sense. By Vergil's time the word *homo* had declined in status, and Fabius would probably have had to be called not *homo* but *vir*, a word of greater dignity.

That is only a rough account of circumstances, which need fuller statement, and various qualifications; but perhaps it is enough for now.

This particular derivation from Ennius is conscious, on the whole, and not one of Vergil's more unconscious acts of integration. Vergil's unconscious mind might be said to have delivered the line of Ennius to him; but the rest was mainly conscious, obviously enough. The theory of allusion and intended recognition might fit this instance of derivation; as perhaps the theory of retractation might fit the line about Atlas, soon to be mentioned, which Vergil developed from Ennius and Lucretius.

Much simpler is Vergil's alteration, already met, of another line of Ennius, *at tuba terribili sonitu taratantara dixit*, 'but the trumpet, with its dreaded note, said "taratantara" ', or, perhaps, in English, 'tarántaráh'. Vergil could hardly accept *taratantara*, but that was really the only interesting part of the line. Still, he took the line without its last two words, substituting for them *aere canoro*, 'with the music of its bronze'. He thus took from Ennius not much more than the idea of onomatopoeia, and chose onomatopoetic words for himself, without help from him.

The derivations from Lucretius are similar, but this time it is clearer how many small expressions Vergil consciously or unconsciously owed to him. The motives for change are often fastidiously delicate. There are many things in Lucretius which

Vergil does not normally admit to his repertory, for example his long, old-fashioned, compound adjectives, and other old-fashioned forms. Ideas in Lucretius suggest different ideas to Vergil. In three lines[1] Lucretius wrote of kids, and lambs that butt. Vergil[2] uses two of the words, compressed into a reference to kids that butt. Lucretius[3] says that the sun unravels the texture of water with rays, *radiisque retexens*, from *texo*, 'weave'. Vergil[4] twice says that the sun uncovered the world from darkness with his rays, *radiisque retexerit orbem*, the verb being now, however, *retego*, 'uncover'. He kept the sound, but changed the sense, as he did elsewhere, again and again. The influences exerted by Lucretius on Vergil, and Vergil's ways of reacting to them, are too many to assess in full. But however often they are examined, they remain fascinating and revealing too.

There are examples of lines adopted and adapted from Ennius by Lucretius, and by Vergil from both; especially, perhaps, Vergil's *axem umero torquet stellis ardentibus aptum*, 'upon his shoulder twists the pole, ablaze with its fitted stars',[5] of Atlas, one of the lines whose subtle and complex history Sir Maurice Bowra succinctly gives.[6] Even so, this is a very simple case of Vergil's method. Habitually, in large things and in small, he holds contact with the tradition through the centuries, going back often as far as he can, but not sacrificing what has intervened. Elsewhere I have given instances.[7] Hundreds of years of poetic history can leave their signs in a single line.

An unusual example of a simple derivation is a line adopted from Catullus. In his poem *The Lock of Berenice* a hair says to the Queen *invita, o regina, tuo de vertice cessi*, 'Queen, against my will I departed from your head'.[8] Vergil took this comic line for an intensely tragic moment. His Aeneas, in Hades, says to Dido, whom he had loved and left, *invitus, regina, tuo de litore cessi*, 'Queen, against my will I departed from your coast'.[9] Vergil may have forgotten the comic associations; or perhaps, with a characteristic

1. Lucretius, II, 367–9.   2. *G.* IV, 10.   3. Lucretius, V, 267.
4. *A.* IV, 119; V, 65.   5. *A.* IV, 482; VI, 797; Lucretius V, 1204–5.
6. Sir Maurice Bowra, *The Classical Quarterly*, XXIII, 1929, 68–9.
7. W. F. J. Knight, *Vergil's Troy*, Oxford, 1932, chapter IV.
8. Catullus, LXVI, 39.   9. *A.* VI, 460.

and subtle inversion, he has made his tragic line out of the inherently solemn rhythm which helps by contrast to make the line of Catullus a comic success.

From his own earlier poems, and from the *Ciris*, which is conceivably one of them, Vergil took not merely single lines, but groups of lines, to incorporate without change in his later poetry. His practice in this has been established.[1] So he took four charming lines[2] on Nisus and his daughter Scylla, both changed to birds, from the *Ciris*, and set them in the First *Georgics*.[3] So, too, he took from the Fourth *Georgics*[4] his list of the dead to use in the Sixth *Aeneid*,[5] where they wait, like migrating birds, to cross the waters of death to their last home, 'stretching out hands in yearning for the further shore'. And he took from the Fourth *Georgics*[6] a description of Cyclopes at work, and applied it again in the Eighth *Aeneid*[7] with four changes, which might be overlooked. This is the link between Vergil's normal self-integration and self-retractation, and his derivations from others. Except in the last line of the last book, the *Georgics* never copy the *Eclogues* verbally. Occasionally, Vergil uses twice within the *Aeneid* a single line, and still more rarely a group of lines, as of the fleeting ghost of both Creusa[8] and Anchises.[9] Otherwise, these repetitions, from the *Ciris*, from an earlier certainly Vergilian poem, or from within the same poem, are the only known instances of older lines used by Vergil completely without change.

That is a very short account, with the fewest possible examples, but, if we went on, it would be hard to know where to stop, and the enterprise might seem endless.

According to different computations, Vergil reflects Lucretius once in every twelve lines or once in every four or five.[10] Some of the reminiscences consist of pairs of words, coming together in an obvious and perhaps inevitable conjunction, so that they might be called fortuitous. It is not important to decide whether they are fortuitous, or whether Vergil would have used

1. John Sparrow, *Half-Lines and Repetitions in Virgil*, Oxford, 1931, 55–111.

2. *Ciris*, 538–41.   3. *G.* I, 406–9.   4. *G.* IV, 475–7.
5. *A.* VI, 306–8.   6. *G.* IV, 170–5.   7. *A.* VIII, 449–53.
8. *A.* II, 792–4.   9. *A.* VI, 700–2.   10. See p. 100 note 2 above.

some of these phrases if he had never read Lucretius. It is sufficiently certain that the work of Lucretius had sunk so deeply into
his mind that it guided his expression almost as much as the
general quality of the whole Latin language guided it; and yet
Vergil's lines and Vergil's Latin are very different from any other,
all the time.

There is, however, some importance in the question how much
of this particular process was conscious. Here the truth seems to
be, that in general, and all the time, Vergil retained much, or
most, of the poetry of Lucretius in his memory, and could hardly
help integrating it unconsciously every day for much of his life.
But he might sometimes consciously think of a passage of Lucretius, and make of it, not merely a way of saying things, but something to say. He might contemplate a Lucretian complex of words
and sounds and thoughts, and take that complex as his subject, or,
more exactly, as a reality to form one term of an antagonism.
Another reality would then come under contemplation as the
other term. The result is Vergilian poetry, about Lucretius; but
also, perhaps, about the old country gods of Italy. This is a simple
outline of the process by which Vergil created the great passage in
the Second *Georgics*[1] in which he counts happy the scientists and
philosophers who know the origins of the universe and have no
fear of death and the dark; but happy also the country men, who
know their own country gods. There may always be a Vergilian
transference or inversion to help; so that the words of Lucretius
recur, meaning in the context just what Lucretius would not have
had them mean – or perhaps what he had, in spite of himself,
given them the power to mean, in the mind of the Vergil whom he
helped to make.

This more conscious contemplation of former poetry, as the
subject of Vergil's own poetry rather than its inevitable medium,
can be understood from an example which Professor E. K. Rand[2]
has discussed in his sensitive way. Vergil wrote of the moon, *at si
virgineum suffuderit ore ruborem, ventus erit*; *vento semper rubet aurea
Phoebe*, 'but next, if she sheds a colour of red over her maiden face,

1. *G.* II, 475–540.
2. E. K. Rand, *The Magical Art of Virgil*, Cambridge, Massachusetts,
1931, 181.

there will be wind; for with a wind will Phoebe ever go golden red'.[1] That is made from the contemplation of a passage of Aratus, 'You can judge by a moon, all reddened, that the wind is on its ways'.[2] Vergil thought hard about the words of Aratus, and their picture. He meanwhile let his own experience of the moon, and nights before the coming of windy days, strengthen and qualify his contemplation of the Greek words. And there came too a memory of lyric repetition, perhaps from Catullus, or some older Latin poet, with the thought of the maiden, lyric moon; so that lyric repetition of words helped to make the thought and the picture of Aratus what it could be.

There is, I suppose, in the making of the best poetry, at least often, if not always, a triple beginning – the thing, the thought, and the tradition in poetry already existing. Vergil normally needs direct observation and literary antecedent, and when they coalesce, his poetry is made. The late Professor Charles Knapp[3] expressed this very well in an inaccessible article which deserves to be reprinted.

The Vergilian systems of integration can be compared to a set of concentric circles, like ripples made by a stone falling into a pond. Nearest to the centre are systems of words, phrases, and lines. Next nearest are incidents, and other short statements of imagined realities. A character is described in a few words or a few lines as acting in a certain way. How the character and the action came to be evolved is sometimes a surprisingly long and complicated process.

Questions are always being asked about the origins of Vergil's characters, and whether he invented them. In one sense he always invented them, and in another sense he never did.

A fascinating example is Camilla.[4] In Vergil she is a maiden of the Volscians, who lived on the borders of Latium. She was unmarried, and had always lived in the wilds; and now she led a party of her friends to war. Camilla is unknown in literature be-

---

1. *G.* I, 430–1.   2. Aratus, *Phaenomena*, 803.
3. Charles Knapp, *The School Review*, XIII, 1905, 492–508.
4. Catharine Saunders, *Vergil's Primitive Italy*, New York and Oxford, 1930, 92–6.

fore Vergil. Her name existed; a *camillus* was a boy who attended a priest or *flamen*, and the Furii Camilli, a great family in early Rome, used the word as a family name. Vergil[1] derives it from 'Casmilla', which, he says, was the name of Camilla's mother. Perhaps Casmilla was invented to connect the name Camilla with the Greek god Casmilus. Camilla may possibly have been a local nymph. But mainly she is Vergil's creation.

Camilla's lonely upbringing in the wilds has an antecedent in the upbringing of Harpalyce, the Thracian maiden of Greek myth, whose name and quality Vergil uses elsewhere, in a description of Dido. Camilla runs so lightly that she could travel over standing corn without harming the ears. The description is from Homer's lines on the horses of Erichthonius,[2] and still more closely, lines[3] of a lost Hesiodic poem describing Iphiclus.[4] The conception belongs to folk-lore, and something like it is known in Scotland, for example. Perhaps in the Volscian country the corn blown by the wind was thought to betray the presence of some spirit of the corn, and perhaps Vergil took the Greek forms of expression to help him enrich an Italian thought.

But the clearest antecedents of all are in the Amazons of Greek poetry, especially the old Cyclic Epic, about the last days of Troy, which is now lost; and among the Amazons especially their leader Penthesilea, whom Achilles slew, and too late loved, and whom Vergil used in his description of Dido, as he used Harpalyce. But it is hard to think that any Amazon of Greek poetry had Camilla's boyish grace, like the grace of Vergil's Venus, disguised as a huntress; or even perhaps Camilla's feminine, tragic weakness, which caused her death for love of a bright garment that a foeman wore.

But Camilla lived on in poetry,[5] in Dante and in Tasso; and in history too, for a distinguished Dante scholar of the Renaissance, Benvenuto da Imola, tells the story of a fighting Volscian maiden from Privernum of his own times, whom he calls a new Camilla.

---

1. *A.* XI, 542–3. 2. *Iliad*, XX, 226–7.

3. Eustathius, *On the Iliad*, 1206, v. 227.

4. G. Kinkel, *Epicorum Graecorum Fragmenta*, Leipzig, 1877, p. 133, fragment 138.

5. Catharine Saunders, *Vergil's Primitive Italy*, New York and Oxford, 1930, 95–6, citing Henry.

A complicated and instructive system of integration started with old stories of the fall of Troy. I have investigated it else-where.[1]

From various Greek poems Vergil derived some attributes and actions of Cassandra, the Trojan prophetess who was never be-lieved, and used them in his characteristic way. She violently de-nounced the wooden horse in which Greeks were entering Troy. She tried to burn it with a torch; and, torch in hand, danced madly like a bacchanal. Later, during the sack of Troy, she was torn by the lesser Ajax from the temple of Athena. Soon after, Helen was captured in the house of Deiphobus, whom she married after the death of Paris, and who was 'weighted with wine' on the last night of Troy, by Menelaus, who wanted to kill her, but was warned by Aphrodite to consult his own future happiness by letting her live. Earlier in the story, Sinon, the Greek sent in, disguised, to deceive the Trojans into accepting the wooden horse, shone a beacon to guide the other Greeks, returning from Tene-dos, where they had been hiding. In a much later different part of the story, related in the *Odyssey*,[2] Odysseus, having returned to Ithaca, removed the arms from the hall of his own house, so that the suitors could not use them when he started shooting them. He was helped by his son Telemachus, and Athena, who shewed a miraculous light.

Vergil redistributes all those actions. In the Second *Aeneid* Cassandra prophesies very shortly, but her denunciation of the wooden horse and attack on it are transferred to the priest Lao-coon, who throws a spear at it. Cassandra is dragged from the temple of Athena-Minerva, but not much is said of that. The traditions of Cassandra and Helen are entwined; for Aeneas sees Helen hiding in the temple of Vesta, who is a perfect translation of the Trojan Athena, goddess of the city's defence. There Aeneas wants to kill her; but he is restrained by his divine mother, Venus, with a far higher plea than the plea of Aphrodite to Menelaus. For instead of saying, as in the old Greek tradition Aphrodite said, 'Not Helen but Paris is to blame' for the fall of Troy, Venus

1. W. F. J. Knight, *Vergil's Troy*, Oxford, 1932, 71–104, with references; idem, *The Classical Quarterly*, XXVI, 1932, 178–89.

2. *Odyssey*, XIX, 1–40.

says, 'Not Helen, nor Paris is to blame', but the will of gods. Vergil is so close to a Greek original that he strains Latin, and says *non tibi . . . culpatus*, 'not blamed by you',[1] instead of 'not to be blamed by you'; however, he has a slight extenuation, in the old Latin usage, by which the perfect participle was sometimes tinged with a gerundive meaning, so that it connotes the idea of necessity, not fact only.

Venus tells Aeneas to forbear, appearing to him as Aphrodite appeared to Menelaus, and, as her parallel appearance in the First *Aeneid* with its further suggestions shews, as Artemis revealed herself to the dying Hippolytus in Euripides.[2] But the Venus of Vergil is infinitely higher, almost Christian; she rescues her son with her touch, and starts hope again.

That is not all about Vergil's Helen. In the Sixth *Aeneid*[3] she behaves differently. She is in the house of Deiphobus, who is sleeping 'weighted', as in the Greek tradition, not however with drink but with anxiety, *cura*, the same word which Vergil substituted in the account of Aeneas, sleepless, in the Eighth *Aeneid*,[4] to differentiate him from sleepless Dido, of whom in the Fourth similar phrases are used.[5] Of this there will be more to say. In Greek poetry on the fall of Troy, the Trojans were drunk. The drunken sleep of the Trojans, barely hinted in the Second *Aeneid*,[6] is boldly transferred from them to the enemies of Aeneas, the Rutulians killed by Euryalus and Nisus, raiding the enemy at night in the Ninth.[7]

Helen, meanwhile, was also developed. Like Odysseus in the Eighteenth *Odyssey*, removing arms from his hall, she removes the sword of Deiphobus, from under his pillow, as he sleeps. Like Athena in the *Odyssey*, Helen shews a light; but it is a torch, and she shews it in bacchic revelry, having acquired these actions from Cassandra. Helen, however, only pretends to revel. Actually she is signalling to the Greeks, having gained this motive from Sinon, the treacherous Greek who deceived the Trojans, and, helping the other Greeks to enter Troy, sig-

---

1. *A.* II, 601–2; cf. *Iliad*, III, 164–5.
2. Euripides, *Hippolytus*, 1389–1439.   3. *A.* VI, 511–27.
4. *A.* VIII, 19.   5. *A.* IV, 532.   6. *A.* II, 265.
7. *A.* IX, 189, 236; cf. Lucretius, V, 975; Ennius, *Annals*, 292.

nalled to them with beacons. The revelry of Cassandra, partly attributed to Helen in the sixth book, is used much more fully in the seventh for the behaviour of the Latin queen, Amata, maddened by the strain which she undergoes, and by the malignance of gods.

These are a few examples of Vergil's redistribution of actions and attributes to create new characters and new incidents. Everything is both old and new.

The integration of Camilla and Helen is on a small scale, involving comparatively few lines of poetry. There is a sense in which integration can be simpler still, as when Vergil developed an *Eclogue* primarily from the combination of two *Idylls* of Theocritus. That was early in the development of his process. An example on a large scale, with greater complexity, is the tragedy of Dido in the First and Fourth *Aeneid*.

In creating the tragedy of Dido's love, Vergil wrote under strong emotional pressure, which made his integration very pervasive and powerful. From his own feminine intensity, and from who knows what secret and tragic event of his own life, he knew the conflict, and knew the heart of the Dido whom he created. That was within himself. Outside, and in the experience of his own times, he knew the heartlessness with which politicians made and broke marriages.[1] There was Octavia herself, married to Antonius, and set aside. Vergil's scheming goddesses, Juno and Venus, who plotted Dido's love, are like those politicians. Outside, too, there was the lure and danger of eastern luxury, which Vergil had contemplated in the *Georgics*, and contrasted with simple Italian life. The conflicts between love and duty, the moment and the future, are familiar; they have become familiar through Vergil.

But Vergil could not imagine out of nothing, for that would not be imagination. He had to inherit a focal point.

Naevius,[2] in a fragment from some part of his long poem called *The Punic War*, says that someone 'asked how Aeneas had left Troy'. Who asked is not known; quite possibly it was Dido herself, who, with Anna her sister, was mentioned elsewhere by

1. R. S. Conway, *The Classical Review*, XLVI, 1932, 201.
2. Naevius, *Punic War*, I, 19–20.

Naevius.[1] Possibly enough, Vergil owed her name and her association with Aeneas to Naevius. This is the more likely, since it is recorded[2] that the first book of Naevius is the original of the magnificent storm at sea in the First *Aeneid*, when Aeneas is about to reach Africa and Dido. But the storm in Naevius may have come in a different part of the story.

There were other legends of Dido. Servius[3] says that her name meant 'brave maiden' in Phoenician, and was given to her after her death. Her other name, Elissa, is Elath, the feminine of the Semitic El, which means Lord or God. Her brother's name, Pygmalion, and hers are both thought Phoenician. Partly she was a Phoenician fertility goddess, as Mr G. A. Wainwright first explained to me. For that reason, but not only for that, her death on the pyre in Vergil was appropriate; fertility kings were sacrificed by burning, especially in Libya. But long before Vergil Dido had become a real personality. In the third century the Greek historian Timaeus[4] had told the story of her tragic death, before any one associated her with Aeneas. His version is lost, but it was followed by Pompeius Trogus, a writer of the Augustan age, and an abridgement of his account has been preserved by Justinus.[5]

In this legend there was a real motive, lacking in the *Aeneid*, for Dido's conviction that impurity, or marrying again, was for her wrong. Vergil even leaves in his verse a phrase that belonged to the older story; Dido says, 'I was not allowed to live my life, without marriage, without blame, like a beast of the wild' – *more ferae*.[6] But beasts are not 'without marriage', and so the words are not strictly right in their place. However, in Justinus they are also found, and there they fit the context. For there Elissa, as he always calls her, was being compelled to marry Iarbas the African to preserve her people, and saved herself at the last by suicide, that she might not live 'like a beast of the wild'. The phrase remains, with

1. Servius-Daniel, *A.* IV, 9. Cf. Vinzenz Buchheit, *Vergil über die Sendung Roms*, Heidelberg, 1963, 23–58.
2. Macrobius, *Saturnalia*, VI, 2, 31; Servius-Daniel, *A.* I, 198.
3. Servius-Daniel, *A.* IV, 335.
4. *Fragmenta Graecorum Historicorum*, I, p. 197.
5. Justinus, XVIII, 4–6; H. E. Butler, *The Fourth Book of Virgil's Aeneid*, Oxford, 1935, 1–8.
6. *A.* IV, 550–2.

its meaning mysteriously reversed. As Vergil uses it, he is thinking of the unspoilt freedom of the wild country, and perhaps of his
heroine, the soldier maiden Camilla, who, devoted like Hippolytus
to Diana, had there spent in purity her life. After Vergil, the old
tradition revived, and Dido lived on in a pattern of pure fidelity.
Perhaps it is characteristic of Vergil to have made of her a heroine
of passion.

The tragedy of Dido begins with a storm and shipwreck in the
First *Aeneid*.[1] The mood and description come from storms in the
Odyssey, especially in the fifth book. Aeolus, god of the winds, is
involved in both the Tenth *Odyssey* and the First *Aeneid*, but for
Odysseus he puts the winds safely in a bag for him to take, a bag
later untied by the sailors, whereas in the *Aeneid* he releases all the
winds to harm Aeneas, at the request of Juno. It is another characteristic inversion. The storm itself is from the Fifth *Odyssey* mainly,
with echoes of the Twelfth. No doubt it is from Naevius also, and
also from the lost Cyclic epic poem, the *Nosti*, 'Homeward
Journeys'; to the contents of which the First *Aeneid*[2] refers in a
mention of the fate of Ajax, destroyed by lightning on the
Caphyrean rocks.

After the shipwreck in the Fifth *Odyssey*, Odysseus lands in
Scheria. But the landing at Carthage is at a place like Homer's
lovely cave of the nymphs, in the Thirteenth *Odyssey*, when
Odysseus is reaching Ithaca. Aeneas, however, having landed at
Carthage, meets his divine mother, disguised as a young huntress.
This is in part a memory of the meeting between Odysseus and his
protectress Athena, also disguised, on his arrival in Scheria, in the
Sixth *Odyssey*. Next, Odysseus meets Nausicaa, a princess. She be-
friends him, and he goes to the city, enveloped by Athena in a
cloud. So, too, Aeneas goes to Carthage, enveloped by Venus in a
cloud. He has not yet met his Nausicaa. In Homer's source, as
Professor W. J. Woodhouse shewed,[3] Odysseus fell in love with
the princess, and she with him – as she still does, perhaps, in the
Odyssey, at least a little. But Homer has another tale to tell. There
is the wife of Odysseus, Penelope, waiting patiently for him; and,

1. *A.* 1, 65–141.   2. *A.* 1, 39–45.
3. W. J. Woodhouse, *The Composition of Homer's Odyssey*, Oxford, 1930,
63–5.

accordingly, Nausicaa is forgotten. Vergil restored Homer's broken tale. Aeneas meets Dido not on the beach but in the city. They fall in love; and Aeneas stays, more nearly as Odysseus stayed with Calypso, the lonely goddess, than as he stayed in Scheria.

Dido, however, is a queen, and partly recalls Arete, mother of Nausicaa; and to her, as Odysseus to Arete and to Alcinous the king, Aeneas tells his story. The story begins in the second book, about the fall of Troy; it is not from Homer, but from many other sources, mainly Greek plays and, probably, the lost Cyclic Epic. In the third book the story goes on, about the journey from Troy to Sicily by way of Thrace, Delos, Crete, Buthrotum, and a place near Etna, a narrative of which the sources are more obscure, possibly more numerous, and probably more general, including prose works and verbal information. Of the travels there will be more to say.

The love story in the Fourth *Aeneid* is a complex unit. Dido is no longer only Nausicaa, but, at least in slenderest outline, the mythical queen of the Punic story. More really, she is some secret of Vergil's own life; she is also a type of ladies in the Roman world subdued to power, and even, possibly, to a tiny degree, Cleopatra. More than all these, however, her heart, at first, is the heart of Medea in Apollonius Rhodius, of the third century, who is supposed to have been the first to treat delicate feelings 'romantically'. To Medea's first love, Apollonius applies a strange simile of light flickering as it is reflected from a cauldron.[1] The simile is used by Vergil,[2] but not for Dido's love. Most significantly, he detaches it, to be applied, altered, to Aeneas in the eighth book, where he worries, sleepless, as Dido had worried sleepless through him. So Dido for a time is this Medea; but only for a time, even though Servius[3] says that Vergil wholly 'transferred' Dido from Apollonius. For soon there is another change; and Dido, if she is still a Medea, is nearer to the Medea of the play by Euripides than to the Medea of Apollonius, even in her fiercer moods.

From Euripides and Apollonius, though hardly from them only, Vergil learnt that a poet might, and should, look closely into

1. Apollonius Rhodius, *Argonautica*, III, 755–60.   2. *A.* VIII, 22–5.
3. Servius, *Prologue to Aeneid IV*.

the feminine heart, which Vergil himself anyway knew so well. The echoes of Medea continue in the story. Strangely, the god Mercurius, warning Aeneas to go, tells him that there is danger; the fleet may be attacked and burnt. Dido has not thought of doing that. But when Aeneas has sailed she thinks of it; she cries for an attack on the fleet, and afterwards she wishes that she had attacked it. That is how Vergil partly obliterated and then half revived the threat of the Colchians in Apollonius to burn Jason's fleet. The thought of that threat gives to Dido perhaps the supreme expression of her hate, where Vergil allows a peculiar freedom to his power over words and sounds.

Dido talks to her sister Anna, revealing her thoughts, as Phaedra, in the *Hippolytus* of Euripides, talking to her nurse, reveals hers. It is from Phaedra, or some other Euripidean heroine, as prototype, that Dido's love turns to hate, but Vergil makes Dido's hate go beyond the earthly life. Anna, however, is not a nurse, though Dido has with her the nurse of Sychaeus; the only other nurse in Vergil is Caieta, nurse of Aeneas, who gave her name to Caieta, on the Italian coast, and who perhaps recalls the nurse of Augustus, to whom he was much attached. Anna is, however, many other people also. She has a Semitic name, and may well be a mythical figure from Syria originally. Her name is however Latin too. She is Anna Perenna, the functional goddess of the ritual conclusion of the year, *annus*. So a quaint combination was evolved, known to Cato; Anna had fallen in love with Aeneas, and followed him to Latium. It was known to Ovid, and Vergil also; Vergil hints at it, when Dido asks Anna to appeal to Aeneas on the ground of his special friendship with her, almost as if Aeneas thought more of her than of Dido. Meanwhile, Vergil's story is entering the world of Sophocles. Dido and Anna recall his pairs of sisters, Antigone and Ismene in the *Antigone*, and Electra and Chrysothemis in the *Electra*. Like the weaker sisters in Sophocles, Anna does not understand the emotional depth and moral stature of her sister, Dido.

The 'marriage' of Aeneas and Dido stems from the marriage of Jason and Medea in a cave. It seems to be outside the tradition of dramatic poetry. It is in a cave, amid storm and lightning. It is really the old mythic marriage between earth and sky, that makes the fields flower again and the world go on. Lingering yet in our minds are traces of the old awe, and we know in that scene how momentous the union is, and how tremendous the result will be. Mysteriously, nymphs cry aloud. In Apollonius they are not mysterious. It is their cave.

Mercurius, sent from Heaven, tells Aeneas to leave Dido, as in the *Odyssey* Hermes was sent to tell Calypso that Odysseus must go. After that, it is still more exactly the world of Sophocles, whose play, *Ajax*, strongly guided Vergil in the Fourth *Aeneid*. The connexion, long ago observed, is incontestable, and only at first sight hard to believe. Dido, like Ajax who killed the sheep of the Greeks in mad mistake for the Greek leaders, is furious with herself, and hopeless, and resolves to die. In the end, as Ajax falls on the sword of Hector his foe, so Dido falls on the sword of Aeneas, once her dearest, crying to the sun that sees all; they both pray for vengeance, Ajax to the Erinyes, the Furies, and Dido to 'Angels of Dido at her death'; and Dido's long curse is, like the curse of Ajax, half a prophecy. But her curse reaches down Roman history, to Hannibal.

There is still more Sophocles than that. Vergil translated the old Phoenician fertility sacrifice that lingered round Dido into a corresponding Greek fertility sacrifice, which was remembered in the *Trachiniae* of Sophocles, where Heracles dies on a pyre at Oeta's crest.[1] For Dido has her pyre. It belongs to her, but Vergil could have let her die without it. Ostensibly, the motive for it is that Anna should think the pyre a magical plan to destroy, not Dido herself, but her love for Aeneas, and so never suspect the real intention. The plain story does not really need the pyre. But in the version known to Justinus Dido used such a device to save her life from love. Vergil wastes nothing; but it would take a long time to relate the poignancy of the implied contrasts, in a poem where nothing is lost that is still in the stories, and little that has been in them ever before.

Then there is Catullus[2] too, for Dido is his deserted Ariadne, and speaks in some of her tones. Catullus wrote hexameters with a

1. Cf. G. A. Wainwright, *The Sky-Religion in Egypt*, Cambridge, 1938, 6, 49, 64 note 1.
2. Catullus, LXIV, 132–201.

monotonous rhythm, having a nearly regular stress-accent on the fifth syllable from the end of each line. He did not think of restricting it, as Vergil did. However, Vergil restored the rhythm of Catullus for Dido's speeches, turning it into a monotony of extremest poetry, hot hate and misery, and all that desecrated love can be.

The largest of all the schemes of integration, the integration of the whole *Aeneid*, is an immense subject for analysis. There is layer on layer of thought and emotion, coinciding marvellously in the end. The chief layers are the forms and contents of Greek poems, old and new, many books in prose, the current thought and feeling and symbolism of Vergil's own time, much of it not yet written, the Roman tradition of history guided by destiny, and lastly, or firstly, the historical or legendary conditions and events of the Mediterranean world at the end of the age of bronze, and of Italy in the earlier centuries of Rome. These conditions and events offered an outline of story which Vergil adopted as a start, and adapted. Some slight hint of how he adopted and adapted them can be got from comparing the *Aeneid* with two other extant versions of the voyage of Trojans to Latium, and their contribution to the start of Rome.[1]

According to Vergil, Aeneas, in the winter or spring following the fall of Troy, which traditionally happened in the late autumn, set sail with a party of survivors on a fleet which they had themselves built. The numbers are vague; in one place,[2] which belongs to an early conception of the *Aeneid*, Vergil says that there were twenty ships, though elsewhere he seems to imagine a larger expedition.

Aeneas was not the only Trojan to lead an expedition of refugees. Antenor also led such an expedition, and settled in northeast Italy at the mouth of the Timavus, near Vergil's first home.

Aeneas and his Trojans first went to Thrace, but soon sailed south to the island of Delos, sacred to Apollo, where his priest Anius was king. A voice from the temple commanded the Trojans

---

1. Cf. Jacques Perret, *Les origines de la légende troyenne de Rome*, Paris, 1942. A short account of the journey of Aeneas and the authorities for it appears in R. D. Williams, *Aeneid, Book III*, Oxford, 1962, 7–12.

2. *A.* I, 381.

to continue their way, and 'seek their ancient mother'. Anchises thought that this meant Crete, and they sailed there, but there was a plague, and the Penates, gods of his ancestors and his home, appeared to Aeneas in a vision of bright light, to warn him that Crete was not his new home, and he must sail onwards.

On the advice of Anchises they now sailed towards Italy, rounding the south of the Peloponnese and then going north, up the east coast of the Ionian Sea. They landed at Actium, where they celebrated 'Actian Games', and then at Buthrotum in Chaonia. There, to their great surprise, they found Trojans living, ruled by Helenus, a Trojan prince, and Andromache, Hector's widow. They had been captured, but had afterwards been released, and married. Helenus was a prophet, and he gave Aeneas prophetic warnings. Aeneas dedicated in the temple a shield captured from Greeks with an inscription on it. The Trojans at Buthrotum gave to the expedition presents and guides.

Warned by Helenus, Aeneas and his people did not land till they reached south Italy, and then only to sacrifice to Juno. They saw on the coast, in particular, temples of Athena and Juno, and the land of Iapygians and Sallentini. They avoided the Straits of Messina, where Scylla and Charybdis were, and sailed westwards. They landed in Sicily, at a point near Mount Etna. Then they sailed round to the north-west of the island, where some remained, at or near Egesta. In Sicily Anchises, father of Aeneas, died. From there they set sail for Italy, but were driven by a storm to a place on the north African coast near Carthage. There they stayed for the winter. The ships needed repair, the men needed rest, and Aeneas and Dido, queen of Carthage, were in love. In the spring the expedition sailed to Sicily again, and met the Trojans who had already settled there. Aeneas celebrated the death of Anchises which had occurred just a year before, with funeral ritual and games. By a plot of Juno, some women of the party, tired of travel, started to burn the ships. Most of the ships were saved; but the less active members of the expedition settled in Sicily with other Trojans there already, and Aeneas founded the city of Egesta for them. The rest went on to Cumae in Campania, south of Latium, and there Aeneas visited the world of the dead below the earth. He was led by the Sibyl, priestess, there, of

Apollo and Diana, who prophesied the future to him, and brought him to Elysium, a heaven below the earth, where the spirit of Anchises shewed him a vision of great Romans to be. After the return to the upper world, the expedition sailed up the coast and landed in Latium.

They were guided by signs which had been foretold to them. One prophecy was that they would have to eat their tables; and it happened that they put their food on flat cakes, during a meal in the open air; Iulus exclaimed that they were eating their tables, and the fulfilment of the prophecy, probably meaning the end of their journey, was recognized. Having landed the Trojans built a kind of camp, or possibly a city, for Vergil does not make it quite clear which it was. They gained the permission of Latinus, king of the Latins, to occupy a strip of land. Latinus knew of an oracle which required him to marry his daughter Lavinia to a foreign prince. She was engaged to Turnus, chief of the Rutulians; but Latinus, helped by a further oracle, now saw that Aeneas must really be the prince of destiny, and engaged his daughter to him. Inspired by Juno, Turnus, with the sympathy of Amata, the queen of Latium, rebelled, and gathered many tribes in his support. Aeneas was now at war with all Italians near. He went for help to Evander, an Arcadian Greek settled on the site of Rome, and that was his first sight of the place where his descendants were to rule. Before he arrived, the god of the river Tiber appeared to Aeneas in a dream, and promised him success; telling him that he would immediately see a sign which had been foretold to him, a white sow with thirty young. The sign meant that the Trojans had already reached the end of their journey; the number thirty signifying either the number of the old Latin cities, or else the years to elapse before Alba Longa was founded.

When Aeneas arrived, Evander quickly made friends, and shewed him round the place which was later to be Rome. He told him of a visit of Hercules, on the way back from Spain where he had captured the cattle of Geryon, and how he had killed a fiery monster Cacus, who lived on the Aventine hill and had stolen some of the cattle. Evander lent Aeneas an army, under his own son Pallas, and he also suggested that Aeneas should get help from Tarchon, king of the Etruscans, north of the Tiber. He did;

and returning by sea found his camp in Latium heavily attacked. He repelled the attack, and killed Lausus son of Mezentius, the exiled king of the Etruscans, and Mezentius himself; but Turnus had first killed Evander's son, Pallas. There was a truce, to bury the dead, and a chance of reconciliation; but the enemies of Aeneas, under Juno's power, broke the truce. The war started again. Aeneas began to win. Amata, the queen of Latinus, killed herself. Finally Juno gave way, and consented with Jupiter that Aeneas and Latinus should rule together. Aeneas finally defeated Turnus, and killed him in revenge for Pallas. It is implied that afterwards Aeneas, married to Lavinia, was going to share the sovereignty with Latinus, and found the city of Lavinium; that Aeneas would die three years afterwards, and that thirty years afterwards either his son Iulus or, according to another version also recognized, his posthumous son by Lavinia, Aeneas Silvius, having inherited the kingdom, would found Alba Longa. From Alba Longa, Romulus and Remus, descendants of Aeneas, were to found Rome.

In Livy's version,[1] which he wrote probably a few years after Vergil wrote the *Aeneid*, two Trojans, Aeneas and Antenor, were purposely spared by the Greeks. Antenor, with Trojans and Eneti from Paphlagonia, east of Troy, sailed to north-east Italy and settled near the mouths of the Po and the Timavus, where later the Eneti gave their name to the Veneti, whose name appears in Venice. Aeneas with his Trojans went to Macedonia, and then to Sicily; and from Sicily to the Laurentian country in Latium, where they were resisted by Latinus, king of the people of the country, called the Aborigines. Livy then recognizes two variants. In one, Aeneas overcame Latinus, made peace, and married into his family. In the other, the battle was going to begin when Latinus walked out in front, questioned Aeneas, and, pleased with the account of himself which he gave, made peace with him instead of fighting, and gave him his daughter Lavinia in marriage. They founded a city Lavinium, called after Lavinia; and had a son, Ascanius – who was not, in this passage at least, the son of Aeneas and Creusa, as he is in Vergil. Next, Turnus king of the Rutuli, who had been engaged to Lavinia before, attacked Aeneas and Latinus. They defeated Turnus, but Latinus was killed.

1. Livy, I, 1–2.

Turnus appealed successfully to the Etruscans, especially Mezentius, king of the city of Caere in south Etruria. In face of this threat, Aeneas conciliated his allies by combining the Trojans with them under the joint name of Latins. There was a battle. The Latins won, but Aeneas was killed; he was buried near the river Numicius, and called 'Jupiter Indiges', a mysterious name under which he was canonized as a 'hero' or saint. Ascanius was still young, but his mother helped him, and he retained his kingdom. Who he was, Livy is not sure; he was certainly the son of Aeneas, but possibly his mother was not Lavinia, but – as in Vergil – Creusa, the first wife of Aeneas. Anyway, he left Lavinium in his mother's charge, and founded the city of Alba Longa, thirty years after Lavinium had been founded. The Latins prospered; even Mezentius and his Etruscans did not dare to attack them, and there was peace between the two nations, the river Tiber, then called Albula, being the frontier. The monarchy descended in the direct male line from Ascanius to Silvius, from him to Aeneas Silvius, and then to Latinus Silvius, who founded the thirty cities of the 'Ancient Latins', and after whom all later kings of Alba were called Silvius, besides their other names. Of them Livy mentions several, before he comes to the foundation of Rome by Romulus and Remus, sons of Rhea Silvia, a princess in the direct line, and, according to a usual tradition, of the war god Mars. Livy relates that the Palatine Hill, where Romulus founded the earliest Rome, was formerly called Pallantium, after the city of Pallanteum in Arcadia, part of southern Greece; and that long before the foundation of Rome Evander had come from Arcadia and lived on the Palatine, where he had instituted the worship of the Arcadian wolf-god Pan, later to become the Roman wolf-cult of the Lupercalia.[1]

Dionysius of Halicarnassus lived in Rome in the time of Augustus and Livy, and wrote a history of earliest Rome in Greek. He gives a long account of Aeneas, and the legendary background, and details, of his arrival.

The site of Rome, he says, was occupied first by Sicels, and then by Aborigines. They lived in unwalled village settlements on the hills. Then Pelasgian and other Greeks came, and helped them to

1. John Pollard, *Wolves and Werewolves*, London, 1964, 136–7.

secure for themselves, against the Sicels, the country between the two rivers, the Tiber, to the north, and the Liris, to the south, a distance given as a hundred miles. Later, at the time of the Trojan war, Latinus ruled this political unit, and it began to be called Latium. That was sixteen generations before Romulus founded Rome (? 753 B.C.); that is perhaps four hundred and eighty to five hundred years, which gives a fairly early but not improbable date for the Trojan War, in the third quarter of the thirteenth century B.C.

Dionysius cites 'the most learned Roman historians', among whom he mentions Porcius Cato and Gaius Sempronius, for the view that there was a strong Greek element in the population of Italy, and that it had come from Achaea many generations before the Trojan War. Dionysius thinks that they were Arcadians, who crossed the Ionian Gulf led by Oenotrus, son of Lycaon, fifth in descent from Aezeius, son of Phoroneus, dated seventeen generations before the Trojan War. Phoroneus, king of Argos at the beginning of the second millennium B.C., is perhaps the earliest Greek mentioned by any tradition. The brother of Oenotrus, Peucetius, settled with his followers in Iapygia in the extreme south of Italy, and gave their name to the later Peucetii. Oenotrus himself, with the larger half of the immigrants, settled on the west coast of Italy. 'Oenotri' came almost to mean 'Italians' and 'Oenotria' 'Italy'. Dionysius cites Antiochus of Syracuse, of the fifth century, and Pherecydes, of the sixth century, for these movements; so that though they are legendary the authority is good and early. He goes on to say that other Greeks who came to Italy, Pelasgians and Cretans, came afterwards; and to identify places in Italy where there were supposed to be traces of very ancient Greek occupation. The Pelasgians came from Thessaly in north Greece, though they also had an origin farther to the south. They and the Aborigines, more or less combined, occupied cities of central Italy later to become Etruscan. The Siceli were driven out, and went to Sicily, about eighty years before the Trojan War. The name Tyrrhenian or Etruscan now appears. It is sometimes made almost synonymous with the Pelasgian name. But in another legend Tyrrhenus was a leader who came with followers to Italy, after the Pelasgians; Dionysius does not believe in the identification of Etruscans, or Tyrrhenians, with either Pelasgians or Lydians. Soon after, and about sixty years before the Trojan War, according to Roman tradition, Arcadians from Pallantium, led by Evander son of Hermes and an Arcadian nymph, called Themis in Greek but Carmenta in Latin, came to Italy; they were welcomed by Faunus, king of the Aborigines, and allowed to settle on the Palatine Hill, called first Pallantium and then Palatium; but there was also a story that the Palatine was named after a young man called Pallas, son of Heracles, who died and was buried there. The Romans owed to them their cults of Carmenta, and of Lycaean Pan, the Lupercalia.

Soon after, more Greeks came, led by Heracles on his way from Spain, and some settled near the Palatine, with some Trojans among them, whom Heracles captured in the earlier Trojan war, against Laomedon's Troy. Before he left, Heracles killed the giant Cacus who lived on the Aventine and had stolen some of the cows of Geryon which Heracles was driving back to Argos. Dionysius recognizes also different details of the visit of Heracles. He was sometimes said to have left a son Pallas, by Evander's daughter Launa, or Lavinia, and another son Latinus, by a maiden from the far north. Pallas died young; Latinus became king of the Aborigines, and was killed in battle by the Rutulians. As he had no sons, Aeneas, having married his daughter, became king. This, Dionysius adds, happened afterwards.

Aeneas, with Trojans who had escaped from Troy, landed at Laurentum near the mouth of the Tiber. With permission from the Aborigines, they built a city called Lavinium, and, soon after, they and the Aborigines together came to be called Latins. Later again they founded Alba Longa and other cities of the Ancient Latins, and sixteen generations after the Trojan War sent a colony to the Palatine and the neighbouring settlement called Saturnia, where the Arcadians already were.

At the fall of Troy, Aeneas had held out in the citadel, where were the sanctities and the treasure. Then, by agreement with the attackers, he had escaped, with all that he could take, to Ida. His eldest son Ascanius settled for a time in the neighbouring Dascylitis, and then, with sons of Hector, returned to Troy. Aeneas with his other sons sailed to Thrace. Dionysius continues that, according to Hellanicus and Sophocles, Aeneas left Troy for Ida at the order of his father Anchises, who followed the command of Aphrodite (Venus). There were stories also that Aeneas betrayed Troy and so escaped. When Aeneas left Thrace, in one version he settled at Orchomenos in Arcadia. Then he moved on to Italy, where, according to Agathyllus, an Arcadian poet, he had a son Romulus.

In the usual version, according to Dionysius, Aeneas and his men founded a temple to Aphrodite in Thrace, on the promontory of Pallene. Then they came to Delos, and from there to Cythera, where they founded another temple to Aphrodite. The next visits were at Cinacthium, a promontory of southern Greece, and at Zacynthus, an island west of Greece, where the settlement had been founded by a hero called Zacynthus, descended like Aeneas from Dardanus. They sacrificed to Aphrodite, and held games in the place known as 'the race track of Aeneas and Aphrodite'. They moved on to the next island, Leucas, and here again founded a temple to Aphrodite, called Aphrodite Aeneas. They sailed to Actium farther north, and founded another temple to her there. Anchises went on to Buthrotum with the ships, and Aeneas inland to Dodona, where he found Trojans with Helenus, a Trojan prince and prophet who had been captured. Aeneas there dedicated inscribed bronze bowls, of which Dionysius says that some were extant in his day. The party joined together again, and founded another temple of Aphrodite further along the coast.

Taking local guides, they now crossed to Italy, and landed in Iapygia, some at the promontory of the Sallentini, and Aeneas himself at a place called Athenaeum, or the temple of Athena, where the harbour was afterwards called the harbour of Aphrodite. They sailed on, here and there leaving traces of themselves, such as an inscribed bowl, with the name of Aeneas, in a temple of Hera.

They continued west, and landed in Sicily near Drepana, and met Trojans, under Elymus and Aegestus (or Acestes) settled near the river Crimisus; for there had been a former migration from Troy, when Laomedon reigned. Aeneas now helped them by founding the cities of Aegesta or Egesta and Elyma, and leaving there some members of his expedition, either because they were tired of travelling, or because some women burnt some of the ships. Aeneas left traces in an altar to Aphrodite at Elyma and a temple to himself at Aegesta.

Aeneas then went to Italy, anchoring first at Palinurus, called after a helmsman of Aeneas who died there, and putting in at an island called Leucasia, where a female cousin of Aeneas died, and then at Misenum where one of the prominent men, Misenus, died, and then at Prochyta, and Caieta, where another relative of Aeneas died, and also his old nurse. At last they reached Laurentum, where they founded a settlement. This, says Dionysius, is the truth, though there were other versions; that Aeneas never came at all; that it was some other Aeneas; or that Aeneas came, but went back to Troy, and left Ascanius to rule in Italy. He adds that the existence of many graves of Aeneas in many places is no argument against the truth of the legend, since this is a usual phenomenon with important characters.

Two altars erected by Aeneas were shewn near the first settlement. After the first sacrifice, the Trojans ate food off parsley or cakes, used as plates, and one said, 'Why, our own table is already eaten', fulfilling a prophecy, given either at Dodona, or at Erythrae in Asia Minor where there was a Sibyl or prophetess, that the Trojans must sail west till they ate their tables, and must then follow a four-footed guide, and found their city where it rested. They now began to offer sacrifice. A sow was the victim. It broke loose and ran away, for about three miles. Then it rested; and Aeneas decided to found the city there. It was not a good place; but a divine voice from a wood warned him to obey the sign. Another version was that Aeneas saw a vision of his ancestral gods in sleep, giving him the warning. Next day the sow bore a litter of thirty young; the meaning was that in thirty years another city should be founded. Aeneas sacrificed the sow and the litter to the Ancestral Gods.

Latinus, the king of the country, was fighting the Rutulians. He now left them, and came to oppose the Trojans. But before they fought, in the night Latinus was warned by a spirit and Aeneas by the Ancestral Gods to come to terms. They came to terms. The Trojans were to have land, and help the Aborigines against the Rutulians or other enemies. They in turn helped the Trojans to build their city Lavinium, called, according to the Romans, after Lavinia,[1] daughter of Latinus, and, according to some Greeks, after Lavinia, daughter of Anius, king of Delos who had come with the Trojans, and lately died. Aeneas now married Lavinia, daughter of Latinus. Dionysius then traces the lineage of Dardanus founder of Troy to Zeus in Arcadia by way of Samothrace, to prove that the Trojans were akin to the Greeks.

Latinus died three years later. The Rutulians had revolted again under Turnus, a cousin of Amata queen of Latinus, and a deserter from Latinus. In the fighting the enemy were beaten, but Latinus was killed, and Aeneas ruled over his subjects as well as his own. Three years later, however, the Rutulians had their revenge, for, helped by Mezentius king of the Etruscans, they killed Aeneas in battle. His body could not be found. A shrine was built to him, inscribed to him as 'Father God of the Earth Below, who controls the stream of the River Numicius' (apparently an expansion of the title 'Jupiter Indiges', which Aeneas bore after his death).[2]

Opinions may well differ about the general interest of these legends. Criticism has traced their history in part,[3] but it cannot fully extricate their entanglements, or trace the history of their development. Nor can it get very far in the search for some underlying historical facts. Too many unknown quantities are involved for very much certain progress to be made; not that it is impossible to reach some limited results, by long and highly specialized researches.

But there is a particular interest in the legends, especially as they are given by Dionysius. His version is clearly very much like the material on which Vergil worked. Of that, though no one can give

1. The manuscripts of Dionysius of Halicarnassus call this princess 'Launa'. The name seems to be neither Greek nor Latin, and it has been emended to 'Lavinia'.

2. It is now known from an inscription on a *cippus*, LARI AENEAE D(ONUM), 'a gift to Aeneas the Lar', dated in the late fourth century B.C., or the first half of the third, that Aeneas had an early cult in Latium. It was found near Zolforata, perhaps Vergil's Albunea. This is the only example of Lar associated with a proper name. See M. Guarducci, 'Cippo latino arcaico con dedica ad Enea', *Bolletino dei Museo della Civiltà romana*, XIX, 1956–8, 3–13.

3. W. F. J. Knight, *Cumaean Gates*, Oxford, 1936, 149, with references.

a full account of the immense mass of tradition that Vergil had before him, there can be no doubt at all.

It would be possible to make a long and instructive comparison. A very short comparison, though, is enough to shew how Vergil applied his characteristic method here, as elsewhere. He seems to try to neglect tradition as little as he can, but to take every chance to alter it and combine versions together.

Vergil alters the version of the fighting followed by Livy. Latinus, in Vergil, was unwillingly on the side of Turnus, and he survived; in Livy he fought for Aeneas, and he was killed in battle. Vergil combines Livy's variants about the meeting of Aeneas and Latinus. In Livy, either they began by fighting, or made peace at the start and did not quarrel. In Vergil, they made peace at first, and a quarrel came afterwards, followed by peace again.

The comparison with Dionysius is far more complicated, and only a few examples can be given. Vergil seems to have known the versions followed by Dionysius of the fighting in Latium, and to have introduced changes into them as he did into the accounts reproduced by Livy. Latinus, Turnus, Pallas, and Mezentius all appear, but there are changes in the parts which they play, and in the chronology. Hardly anything is exactly the same.

Less obvious but still more interesting are the contrasts in the versions of the travels. In Vergil, the Penates appear to Aeneas in Delos; in Dionysius they appear to him in Italy. In Vergil, Aeneas celebrates Actian games near Actium; in Dionysius he seems to have established a cult, with athletic games, in the island of Zacynthus. In Vergil, Aeneas met Helenus at Buthrotum, and dedicated an inscribed shield at Actium; in Dionysius he met him at Dodona, and there, and afterwards in Italy, dedicated inscribed bowls. The Aeneas of Vergil seems to land for a very short time, on the coast of Italy, but he explicitly sees the very places which the Aeneas of Dionysius visits. In Sicily, according to Dionysius, there have been Trojans for years; according to Vergil, Trojans seem to arrive now for the first time, or else Aeneas has been forestalled by Acestes only recently. The Greek element in Italy is elaborately analysed by Dionysius; Vergil uses Evander, following tradition more closely than usual, but referring to the rest, if

at all, mainly in hints scattered about the second half of the *Aeneid*.
The vision of the Tiber god in Vergil seems to owe something
to various different visions in the tradition. The portents of the
tables that were eaten and the white sow are just slightly different;
in particular, Vergil does not make the sow lead the Trojans, and
he seems not to have finally decided exactly what he meant the
sow to signify. The voice from the wood in Dionysius which
warned Aeneas in Italy seems to have been transferred by Vergil
to Delos, where it is the warning voice from the shrine of Apollo.

These are only a very few of the examples which could be found.
Everything is entirely characteristic. Vergil chooses and uses everything for the imaginative value which it has, or can be made to
have. He clearly began with some version or versions very much
like the story in Dionysius. Most interestingly, the Third *Aeneid*
is closest to such a version, but there are already Vergilian changes.
As the *Aeneid* grew, Vergil's imagination led him farther away
and onwards. The patterns of the *Iliad* and *Odyssey*, and the tale of
Dido, and facts and passions of his own day, and also his own
patient researches into ancient Italian tradition, varied the outlines more and more.

Vergil is not totally unlike all other poets in his process of creation. Perhaps he is supreme in the accuracy and precision with
which his deeper mind delivered poetry in the most authentically
poetic way. Perhaps somewhere in the secret of the Vergilian
process of creation lies the secret of the Vergilian power and
appeal, reaching far on to the future because it reaches far back
into the past, and ranges across the living world into the rhythms
which make mankind akin.

CHAPTER 4

FORM, AND REALITY

I T has been said that the object of all poetry is to bring the mind of man into harmony with the outer world of nature, so that the distinction between the 'I' and the 'it' is broken down. Poets note this distinction, and they are especially sensitive to the frustrations which it imposes. There is mental tension and pressure, till, in poetry's expression and solution, the frustration is overcome and the distinction removed. This is how poets come to be poets at all.

Vergil displays this process with unusual precision. Throughout his work he is conquering areas of experience to be a home for the spirit, instead of being remote and unfriendly to it. There is always his own, friendly world, to which he is trying to annex another world, still strange. Sometimes part of the friendly world is lost, and has to be won again. At the cost of some over-simplification, it could be said that, for Vergil, there are four great tracts in particular; the internal mental world, firstly, of personal experience, and, secondly, of general human experience, which survives in the unconscious mind of every individual, and especially of every poet; and next the outer world, firstly, of the present, of which news is heard in talk or other communication, and secondly, of the past, known mainly from books.

Without theorizing, some of Vergil's mental history can be clearly seen. He began life in a happy home, which he loved all the more because of the threats against it from the outside world. He had to reconcile the home and the threats, and conquer what he could of the threatening world to annex to the world of home. This he did by finding reinforcements in the outer world itself, some in the present and some in the past; in the present he found good as well as evil, powerful friends to help him, and to be worshipped as heroes; and in the past he found feelings like his own, and lines already drawn, which could discipline and classify and organize, and so justify, his own feelings; including both feelings belonging to his own present which his own experience aroused, and also feelings that were more instinctive, and tendencies such as we all inherit from a past, in which the experience has been wider than our own.

Vergil was introverted and shy, and retreated from self-assertion. Possibly like Shakespeare in this, he was strongly influenced by love for his parents, and especially, from certain indications, his mother.[1] He was happy among books and animals, his people at home, and his friends at Rome and Naples. He had a very 'feminine' temperament. Like others with such temperaments, he conceived strong attachments for people, and they for him. His affections spread, less to individual women than to his family and to his comrades and colleagues in work, at home, or at his schools and universities. He is said to have had one liaison only, with a certain Plotia Hieria, and that was held very doubtful even in antiquity. He never married. And he was widely called Parthenias, 'the maiden man', neatly, since he lived half his life near Parthenope in Campania, and also, if this has anything to do with it, since his name, spelt with an *i* as it sometimes was, suggested *virgo*, 'maiden'.

The introverted femininity of Vergil led to tensions, and impulses to violent friendships for equals and juniors, and vigorous reverence for men of importance, both poets and statesmen. He was again in this like Shakespeare, who also made obedience and reverence matters of the affections. Shyness strengthened impulses to protect and to be protected. Both involved at once the satisfaction of self and the effacement of self. For both impulses there were parallels and guarantees in the past, to be got from books; and there was a use to be made of both of them in the present. We may or may not admire Vergil's type. But we can see that Vergil, in the strange words of Robinson Jeffers, 'turned inward' to 'love the people'.

Theocritus and Hellenistic epigrams, besides much other poetry

1. This statement may need apology and perhaps qualification; it is based on a persuasive intuition of the late Professor R. S. Conway and on certain deductions from internal and external evidence; it is probably true that Vergil did not return to his old home after his mother had died and his father had married again.

and the tendencies of the new Roman society, justified strong affections and made them seem normal; and Theocritus further made such affections seem especially at home in beautiful country, so that he thus authorized Vergil to employ these and other affections as a link between the mind and nature.

But meanwhile Vergil himself found in nature proof of the value of restraint. He himself recommends[1] that stallions and bulls should be prevented from mating, if they are to do their work as well as ever they can; and he seems to approve of bees for finding their young in flowers, as he thought, not reproducing themselves by the usual processes.[2]

This belief in restraint is little found in other Latin poets. It may have come to Vergil gradually. There are certainly lines in the *Appendix*, just possibly by Vergil, which are far from fastidious. His certainly authentic poems have a high purity; the only unpleasant innuendo[3] of which he is accused is in a passage of doubtful interpretation. Vergil lived his convictions, and perhaps the repressed, or rather assimilated, impulses strengthened his poetry. The poetry itself is moral, but often erotic, in a healthy, poetic way. The *Eclogues* are full of love interests. They are exquisite lyrics of love and landscape in one, with sometimes a transportation of the loves and landscapes of home into the outer world, when perhaps Cornificius, and perhaps partly Julius Caesar too, become Daphnis, loved by Venus, and when a baby, born to greatness, is to make out of home-love a golden age. The motto of the *Eclogues* is 'Love conquers all', *omnia vincit amor*.[4]

The motto of the *Georgics* is different. Now 'work, remorseless work, has conquered all', *labor omnia vicit improbus*.[5] The adjective *improbus* is sometimes forgotten, when the other words are quoted, but it is important. It is a very Vergilian word, meaning originally 'not *probus*', that is, 'not honest', almost, 'taking an unfair advantage'. It is one of Vergil's colloquialisms. He applies the word to Aeneas, when he ruthlessly exploits success in battle; to a goose that goes on cackling, beyond all reason, all day; and to love itself, which stops at nothing, in driving the human mind and heart to extremes.

1. *G.* III, 209–14.   2. *G.* IV, 197–202.   3. *E.* III, 8–9.
4. *E.* x, 69.   5. *G.* I, 145–6.

Improbus, then, in Vergil suggests a persistence going beyond reason. Work must have such persistence in the *Georgics*; and in the *Aeneid* love has it, all too much. The motto of the *Aeneid* might be satirized as *improbus iste labor victorem vincit amorem* – but it would be a sacrilegiously un-Vergilian parody.

Most of the characters in the *Aeneid* who are made excitingly attractive meet with a sad and violent end. Dido is foremost among them; of the rest, nearly all are attractive young fighters, Nisus and Euryalus, Clytius, Pallas, and Lausus. Such characters clearly appealed most to Vergil. Twice only he promises fame through his poetry, once to Nisus and Euryalus, and once to Pallas. The *Aeneid* confirms the report of Donatus, that Vergil was principally liable to this sort of affection. The same is reported of Sophocles. This characteristic in Vergil indicates the femininity of mind, and the impression made by early association. He was emotionally awake during his education. Like many great poets, he retained what is misleadingly called an adolescent psychology. Some feminine characters are, however, also presented affectionally by Vergil. Camilla, the fighting maiden, is made attractive; but she, like the disguised Venus who met Aeneas near Carthage, is attractive with a certain athletic boyishness. Camilla has a sad end too. Less sad is the destiny of the truly feminine characters, Creusa, first wife of Aeneas, who is given peace in death on the last night of Troy, and Andromache, wife of Hector, found by Aeneas in Chaonia married now to Helenus, and living in a soft quiet sadness not far from peace. Anchises, father of Aeneas, Iulus, his son, and Lavinia, whom Aeneas married dutifully at the end, have comparatively happy destinies. The divine mother of Aeneas is a voice and a presence of heavenly loveliness and blessing. A conclusion is possible. For Vergil, passionate attachments have associations of tragic failure. The calmer, deeply moral affections of the family and the home are creative, and endure. Love demands abnegation, before it comes into its rightful power.

Like, but not quite like, Homer and Shakespeare, Vergil understood the feminine mind best, or at least surprisingly well. If less were known of him, it might be argued that the poet of the *Aeneid*, as it was argued by Samuel Butler of the poet of the *Odyssey*, was a woman. There is something abstract, something as if seen from the outside, in the outward Aeneas and his imperialism. But Vergil's Dido, and the Aeneas whose main self is Dido, Vergil knows. There are his own feelings, brilliant clear; and a secret of his own life, hidden for ever.

Homer inherited the eastern, perhaps Minoan divine pair, the goddess and her male attendant, sometimes lover, sometimes son, Ishtar and Tammuz, Hathor and Horus, Ashtoreth and Adonai, whatever the names in different places may be. Homer did wonders with the formula. He put the interest on the masculine side, and we have Paris protected by Aphrodite, Agamemnon by Hera, and Diomedes, and above all Odysseus, by Athena. The last pair is supremely great. Odysseus, earlier Olysseus, 'Destroyer', of the family of Autolycus, 'the very wolf',[1] the quite wickedly cunning scoundrel of pre-Homeric, Attic, and Vergilian tradition, becomes the wise, loyal, self-dependent hero of Homer, quick to take an advantage on a theory that all's fair in love or war, and that most of life is one or the other; a pattern of gallant, adventurous humanity for all time. And his Athena, little less masculine than Odysseus himself, is to him the very voice of the God who helps those who help themselves; the God in whom those trust, who also keep their powder dry; the God who may be confused with the very courage and clear reason, and the luck, of those who succeed because, in the Greek phrase, their temperament is their destiny.

But Greek myth and poetry had other pairs. The Aeneas of Homer is also protected by Aphrodite; and, in another myth, Heracles has his counterpart, and half his name, in Hera, who was at first his protectress, and then, by one of the strange inversions which are frequent in cult and myth, his persecutor. And to the Latins Aphrodite is Venus, and Hera Juno. Vergil took it all, and added more. He gave to Aeneas the plight and vocation of Heracles, tormented by Juno; Heracles, now Hercules, who had once competed in Roman reverence[2] with the Aeneas of Vergil's Julian day; but his Aeneas is not only a Heracles, but also an

1. J. A. K. Thomson, *Studies in the Odyssey*, Oxford, 1914, 15–19.
2. I owe this fact to the kindness of Dr Harold Mattingly, who in a letter dated 26 October 1942 cites one of the earliest Roman coins, which shews Hercules and the Twins together.

147

Odysseus, listening to a voice of God, and he is the Aeneas of Homer, too, whose protection is a power of love, and who already in the *Iliad* is devout.

But Aeneas is also Vergil's self, facing the devils of a peremptory, wicked, outer world, that commanded him to act, and to face hard things; and he is Vergil's self, guarded and guided by a voice of God. That is how Vergil finds his way, out beyond even Homer. He points back, to the Earth Mother who gave rest to Stone Age man's keenest longing, and forward to, for example, the play by Auden and Isherwood called *The Ascent of F* 6, where the hero, a sophisticated creation of sophisticated modern writers, finds, when all other sanctions fail, at the top of the mountain which he is climbing, not a devil or god, but his mother.[1]

Vergil was brave with the courage that poets need, and he used the excitement of heroic tradition to sustain his courage to face the horrors of the world. He certainly did not like the active exercise of practical courage, which normally comes as an unpleasant surprise to the retiring temperaments that are often, as can be proved by noticing what boys take what books out of school libraries, the most strongly attracted to literary perils and pain. There seems to be a kind of natural compensation; the poets even seem to find a fascination in horrible things, proportionate to their sensitive hatred of them.

His earliest home life left its stamp on Vergil. Obviously he loved the peace and beauty of it. But, at the characteristic age in his childhood, he could hardly help playing soldiers in his mind. He made the literary soldier-game part of his mental home, the patch of friendly territory to which new gains were to be annexed. He was thrilled by the old Roman historical legends, and wanted to write on them. He was thrilled again in contemplation of Octavianus, for all his faults a 'god' and a new Romulus, third in the succession, after the first Romulus, who founded Rome, and Marcus Furius Camillus, who restored her, when she lay prostrate under the invading Gauls; and he planned, as he says at the beginning of the Third *Georgics*, to write on his great deeds. Providentially, he found that poetry must use myth, and

1. W. H. Auden and Christopher Isherwood, *The Ascent of F6*, London, 1936.

wrote on neither, and on both, of his projected subjects in the *Aeneid*.

At first Vergil translated the brave, active, wicked world into an adolescent ardour and pathos of love and landscape, and created symbols. Then he made farming and nature, in a sense, his serious subject; and he took human adventure in politics and war to become the metaphors and similes and comparisons which, as Aristotle perhaps suspected, are at the centre of all poetry. Later still, he reversed the process; he revived his country symbols, and expressed the more realistic, terrible, remote and unconquered heroisms of the *Aeneid* in these pictures of home. But it was at home that the poet was born, and the poet was made; and the story that he had to tell he learnt, or learnt to learn, at that early home; and from that, too, came the manner and shape of its telling, the order and symmetry which his heart demanded, and his brain imposed.

Aristotle says in the *Poetics* that the most important part of a tragedy is the 'myth', or 'plot', μῦθος. What matters most is the story and how it is handled; who kills whom, and why, and how it all ends; not the thrill of poetic words, and music, and impressive spectacle. Aristotle, again, said that the *Prometheus Bound* of Aeschylus was a particularly 'spectacular' play. It was not, however, much noticed by the Greeks. That is because few if any besides Aeschylus himself understood the plot.

It is possible to write a play by almost copying verbally an existing story, and yet by a small twist to make it quite different and quite new. So Shakespeare's work is none the less personal and unique, however closely he follows Plutarch or Holinshed. It is the story that counts; and the story, helped by spontaneous choice of imagery, creates the peculiar world of a play, and its spatial quality. This is proved and explained by the work of Professor G. Wilson Knight; correcting a different, and dangerous, modern view, that the small things matter more, and that the grand structure of a poem is no use at all unless words and phrases are all perfect poetry.

It has often been asked, since Coleridge first raised the question, If you take away from Vergil his sound and rhythm, what is left?

The answer is, everything that matters most. The danger is that the apparently superficial splendour and loveliness will disguise the significance of the structure, and hide its lines. On the other side, the perfection of the poetry, in phrases and single words, in sound, and in rhythm, ought to be just the force that induces in poet and in reader the mood of exaltation in which the great structural lines are best seen to emerge. Perhaps rhythm is everything, if it is taken to include the largest rhythm of all, the rhythm of the whole tale.

The late Professor R. S. Conway rightly judged that the two principles of alternation and reconciliation, and the further description of the principle of reconciliation as 'holistic' in the sense of Field-Marshal Jan Smuts' philosophy, are of cardinal significance in all that Vergil wrote.

The first of these principles, alternation, is seen in the *Eclogues* in word-balances, refrains, and the dramatic dialogue of the odd-numbered poems, alternating with others not in dramatic form. There is balance of character, of present condition and aspiration for the future, and of individual weakness with divine or heroic strength. The *Eclogues* are erotic, and the tension is mainly in unsatisfied love, and the nostalgia of love and lovely country. The reconciliation is a satisfaction of wants. It is explicitly reached, sometimes, simply by the poetry, as in Theocritus Polyphemus says that song is the only cure for love; the mere expression of the want may be enough. At the end of an *Eclogue* it is usually evening; or both sides have done well in the poetic competition, and can leave it at that; or 'the water meadows have drunk enough'; or the country itself gives peace, perhaps because Daphnis will return and make all things grow again, or because Arcadia with its poetry and calm is there for a retreat.

The central success of the *Eclogues* is probably their unification of the human mind and nature in the country into a single harmony. When there is exaggeration, and too forcible treatment of fact, and sometimes, too, when there is not, this unification is often censured as 'the pathetic fallacy'. But it remains at least one of the chief uses of poetry. Vergil continued to achieve this unification in parts of his later work, but in greater subordination to a larger scheme. The *Eclogues* might look like a poetry of escape, based on fanciful wish-fulfilment. The classical tradition of landscape poetry reaches far back in time, through the aspirations of Alexandrian city life, and the relief motives of Greek tragic odes, in which thoughts of far lands and pleasant country give rest from pity and terror, and perhaps more than rest; and it reaches beyond all this, to the psychic wanderings of primitive people, and dreams of the 'detachable soul', which still seem real to invalids in delirium. Vergil, however, tightened up this poetry of relief and made it a poetry of actual and even rational satisfaction through harmony between nature and the mind. There is nowhere else in ancient writing so close a contact between them. Even in Theocritus the contact is less explicit and effective, and, though it is there, and not just incidental, it might still, to some degree, be missed.

So Vergil, by alternation and reconciliation in his first great work, made the mind of man at home in the universe, and reached, just for a time, the destination of poetry – if not yet in the widest poetic world.

The Fourth or 'Messianic' *Eclogue* has a very slight dramatization, in which it differs from the others. Its alternations are of thought, with balances of past and future, and fear and hope, without the help of characters in dialogue. Perhaps there is even a balance between the moods of the different parts of the poem, written at different times. The tensions are released and the contrasts unified in the symbol of the baby, destined to bring a new peace and prosperity. The baby recalls the Eleusinian mysteries, in which there was a declaration that a baby, symbol of new life, had been born to the officiating priest and priestess; and it recalls too the Attic New Comedy, with its foundlings, and their identifications which bring happy endings; which is one result of the psychological impulse which led to many mythic pictures of Holy Families, until the Christian Holy Family came. Perhaps Vergil had already reached his greatest poetic discovery, that the Holy Family, human and divine in one, is enough to unify the explorations of the spirit.

The Fourth *Eclogue* offers a transition to the *Georgics*. The alternation and reconciliation are similar. In the *Georgics* alternations are between the practical needs of the farm, arduous, and, perhaps, to ordinary people, dull, and the splendour within and around practical things, which a poet can see. So Vergil wrote the *Georgics* in balanced masses, alternating practical instruction with passages of imaginative brilliance, which it is a bad mistake to call adornments, or digressions.

The reconciliation in the *Georgics* is not so simple as before. There is too much hard thinking, and consciousness of the wider world and its threats and problems, to allow the unity of mind and nature to be quickly reached. 'The High Father himself ordained that the way of farming should be hard'. Wars and plagues that devastated the farms of Italy could not be met by a mood. The tragic rather than the lyric process must be tried.

So it was; but not fully, until the *Aeneid*. In the *Georgics* a solution is reached partly by a short cut, and partly by retaining the mood of the *Eclogues*, in which the Holy Family is accepted as something like the Word of God. The world in which dreams are to come true, and the golden age, but yet not quite a golden age, is to return, is a world pictured in the unity which the sword of Caesar and the plans of Maecenas made, and framed in the new system of their law. The harmony of composition had for its terms not concepts, but given realities, things that could be touched and known; Italian things and Greek, Pan and Silvanus in one family, almost one person; the animals and the crops and the cottage home, and the quaint old harvest rites. For old ritual, in the *Eclogues* intriguing and attractive, but not very seriously seen, has come to matter more, and to be a thing to cast aside at peril; something to be loved and admired, although, and even perhaps because, it was quaint, and rough, and crude.

Having written the *Eclogues* and *Georgics* Vergil had his destination fixed: the unity of mind and nature, man and men, God and man, in a Holy Family in which law should be a personal thing and justice should live. He had a pattern in the animals, and in the bees, and in the shepherds, too, who reached a balance in their love and in their satisfied longing to be at home in their world. But Vergil was ready, too, to face the tragic vision, and take the tragic way. The farm at Andes, blended now in Campanian landscapes, had become Italy and the Roman world, for in the *Georgics* Vergil was impelled for imagery to outer lands, rich, remote and strange, and their fortunes, ideal and real; imagery which Catullus had used, but not so eloquently. In the *Aeneid* the Roman world had to grow to the universe of human suffering and human hope, where the Holy Family must reign.

The alternations of the *Aeneid*, leading to their reconciliations, are like the dramatic poles of creative antagonism which are associated with the thought of Pythagoras and the poetry of Aeschylus. They are like these, but not quite the same. Both principles are there; it might be well to regard alternations as a matter of the writing and organization; and the antagonistic poles as a matter of the feeling which has entered the poem, and which emerges from it. But the distinction cannot safely be made precise; and no thinking about them can get far, going along this abstract way.

Two hundred years before Vergil was born Callimachus had won his fight with his rival Apollonius Rhodius, and his motto, 'A big book is as bad as it is big', had prevailed. The Alexandrian tradition was still living in Vergil's time, and had become the strongest influence on Latin poets. There were obvious Alexandrian forms to adopt, which were roughly the forms of Vergil's poems, or parts of them. There was the pastoral of Theocritus, Bion, and Moschus, the scientific poems of Aratus and others, and the short epic or epyllion, especially associated with Callimachus and Theocritus. The metre for all these forms was the hexameter, the metre of Homer, but also the metre of Ennius and Lucretius.

Alexandrian poetry in these forms gave a start to Vergil's contemporaries and to Vergil. Pastorals were plentiful, but epyllia and scientific or philosophic poems were rarer.

When Vergil based the *Eclogues* on the *Idylls* of Theocritus and probably also the Greek pastorals of his friend Messalla, he followed an existing form as closely perhaps as any poet ever did. But something revolutionary grew from his work. Others of his time were content to be like their predecessors. Perhaps Vergil was too. But his lyric intensity and natural process of symbolization were immediately released by the attainment of an exactly right traditional form, and his accuracy of association began the long history of his integration by blending two *Idylls* into one. Immediately something far greater emerged. For the *Eclogues* are already universal, poetry of the world and of its conflicting forces, and not of a small corner of it alone.

After the *Eclogues* he took the famous step of returning to the heroic taste of the days of Naevius and Ennius, and of assimilating old Classical Greek material into the Alexandrian schemes which his contemporaries admired. He began with Hesiod, and followed both the Alexandrians and their didactic models. Then, in the *Aeneid*, he allowed the epyllion to grow to Homeric and Aeschylean scale and power, with a Roman depth and range.

The literary form, therefore, which Vergil chose was the short hexameter poem, which could become long, and had already been made at home in Latin. An important adaptation of his own was the special development of the unitary verse group, according to varied principles of internal organization. He also contrived a new scheme of construction, in which dramatic contention and epic narrative are combined in a pattern always real but always fluid and evasive.

But the literary content of Vergil's poems was not to be confined to material which had hitherto found its way into hexameters. The distinction between literary forms in antiquity was fairly sharp, though perhaps it is imprudent to attempt, for example, to say what is and what is not a truly 'epic' line in Vergil. There were quite fixed forms, however, forms which were large and important, and others less considerable, such as the ode of praise, the panegyric, and the wedding ode, the epithalamium, and the birthday ode, the genethlion. There were also, among much else, little pieces called Sibylline oracles, short hexameter poems of strongly unitary rhythm about a dozen lines long, in which wonders to be were foretold.

The Fourth or 'Messianic' *Eclogue* was built by the addition of a wedding or birthday ode, or perhaps a poem in which both were combined, to a different element which is most closely connected with Sibylline prophecy. The result is composite; not all was composed at the same time. It is characteristic of Vergil's method of fusion, and a prophecy of a golden age, guided by a mystic child, later blent with an ode of joy at a wedding and a human baby's birth, is a perfect idea. There are difficulties in the existing poem; and it was only lately that Dr W. W. Tarn,[1] following an

1. W. W. Tarn, *The Journal of Roman Studies*, XXII, 1932, 135–60; cf. Aurelio Peretti, *La Sibilla babilonese nella propaganda ellenistica*, Florence, 1943, *passim*, for the elaborate history of these strange 'oracles'.

intuition of Dr Johnson, worked out the combination of the elements.

The work of Vergil from the *Eclogues* onwards always has a fusion. It is never typical of a single *genre*. The *Eclogues* are pastoral, with something like the allegory of Theocritus, who represented real people under fictitious names. But they are unlike the *Idylls* because they are regularly fusions of more than one of the *Idylls* together, not into a composite construction, but into a new poem of which many of the elements are from former poetry, and some from experience. To what extent Theocritus thus fused earlier work is not clear; he certainly did, a little; but mainly he composed from direct experience and observation.

In the *Eclogues* Vergil used the particular past of the *Idylls* in order to vitalize and generalize in his own poem his own particular experience. He is a good poet partly because he takes that method, the best and perhaps the only good method, to make experience artistic. Poets must, for some mysterious reason, place themselves in a true relation to world poetry, by fixing themselves where they belong in its stream.

Vergil adds to the elements of Theocritus, and especially to his direct observation and his generalization of personal experience, a new lyrical activity, not only lyrical love of the country and of love, but lyrical emotions concerned with many private and indeed public affairs. Vergil, if an exaggeration can be forgiven, wrote the love lyric of Sappho and the political lyric of Alcaeus, both together, in the form of the Theocritean pastoral. The perfect fusion of real in ideal makes any theory that a character in the *Eclogues* exactly represents a character in history as unlikely as it is refractory to proof. This part of the method of the *Aeneid* is already, in the *Eclogues*, nearly complete. There also, realities of history, in the phrase of Professor E. K. Rand, 'shimmer through'; a surprisingly large number of them. In the *Georgics* there is a rest from that kind of representation; but Vergil had already made the method by which, in a fusion of literary sources and personal feelings, real people, and the moods of real people, their moments of moral intensity, and their permanent qualities of character and temperament, impart themselves unmistakably to the ideal realities of the work. No character in Vergil is wholly literary, or wholly derived from an individual in the actual world, but every character partly has both these origins. They are most often rebuilt, out of elements from characters present and past, including Vergil's own self.

In the First *Eclogue* some of Vergil himself is in Tityrus, but he is old, and a slave. Tityrus also occurs in the Third and the Fifth *Eclogues*, and in them he is not Vergil. In the Fifth and conceivably in the Ninth and Tenth there might be some of Vergil in Menalcas, but there is none of him in the Menalcas of the Second and Third. Vergil had reached the stage which poets usually reach after a purely lyrical, personal stage. He had gone outside himself, into the minds of others, and was writing drama. Euripides and Milton are very clear examples of dramatic poets who put themselves, in some moods, into one antagonist, and, in other moods, into another. Vergil did the same at first. Afterwards, he distributed his personality in more Shakespearian complexity. Of course, an autobiographical aspect in the *Eclogues* was inevitable. It is said to be impossible to write a novel which is not autobiographical, and likely, therefore, to look allegorical. But the actualities reproduced may be redistributed so that the apparent allegory is quite illusory. There is an American novel whose characters have been confidently identified as two completely different sets of real people, in two different towns, far apart. This example was given by Professor E. K. Rand to prove the fluidity of 'allegory' in the *Eclogues*. In such a sense all poetry and indeed all fiction might be called allegorical, since they must include elements from actuality.

In the *Georgics*, identifiable elements drawn from actual human individuals are less frequent. But the interaction of personalities has still affected the poem. The tradition to which the *Georgics* belong starts with Hesiod's *Works and Days*, a country poem of the eighth or ninth century B.C. composed in Boeotia to record traditional advice to farmers, how and when to plough, sow, reap, marry, and furnish a farm, with old magical rules of guidance included. Hesiod writes for practical utility, but there is a moral side, the 'gospel of work' as a duty of enlightened self-interest. Further, he addresses his poem to his brother Perses, and has plenty of criticism of his idleness and improvidence to offer;

and he has also private complaints of his own, against the bribe-taking 'kings', apparently the local aristocracy, who ground down the poor; it was now the age of iron, into which the ages of gold, silver, and bronze, and, before bronze, the 'age of heroes', had declined.

Vergil did not discard even these personal interactions. But he made characteristic changes, to introduce, if not dramatized personalities, at least the real needs and emotions of his own world. He could always succeed best by slight but explosively dynamic changes. Here the most frequent changes concern not people but things. Vergil sometimes almost translates Hesiod and other poets verbally; but whereas in the *Eclogues* the plants tend to be Greek from Theocritus, and not even Sicilian Greek, though Vergil is writing of Italy, in the *Georgics* the fauna and flora are more often Italian, and introduced for true practical ends.

But the method of dexterous alteration is applied to personal interactions also. Vergil addressed his poem as Hesiod addressed his, to someone who had need of it; not however to an idle spendthrift, but to Maecenas, Secretary of State for Italy, who persuaded Vergil to write the poem; the difference in the kinds of need, both real, is captivating. Next, Vergil complains, not of a spendthrift, nor of immoral aristocrats who pervert justice, and about whom not much can be done, but of the universal ills of humanity, then powerful and almost triumphant, Mars and pestilence and decay, things that are the rightful enemies of human work and human prayer. Hesiod has interludes of complaint. Vergil has interludes too, digressions they might, wrongly, be called; but they are more like the choric odes of Greek tragedy, partly giving relief and escape, and partly showing the realities of the wider world, in which the action is set, and where the origin and end of that action are to be found. And Vergil made another change, quite simple, but tremendous; he inverted the Hesiodic decline, and wrote of hope, and great, happy ages to come, in an Italy whose past was enough, with work and with prayer, to guarantee her future. Such an optimism is unique in Roman poetry.

Hesiod and Lucretius were in some sense primary for the *Georgics*, and Vergil expresses both of them, to differ from them, and to find his own different way, almost by the very act of expressing them. It is like the process by which a photographic negative is needed to produce a positive photographic print.

By adopting Hesiod and Lucretius Vergil had taken a revolutionary step towards withdrawing from dependence on the Alexandrians. But he did not forget them. For the zones of the sky in his first book he used the *Hermes* of Eratosthenes, who lived in the third century B.C. and for some of his material about bees, and for the actual title of his poem, the *Bee-Keeping* and *Georgics* of Nicander of Colophon, of the second century. These poems of Nicander are lost, but two of his others, on *Treatments for the Bites of Wild Animals* and *Antidotes to Poison*, are extant, and not highly regarded now. However, he was distinguished in his own, and in Vergil's day. Cicero[1] very interestingly says that he was anything but a farmer, and that the excellence of his work on farming was due not to knowledge of farming but to his poetic gift. Characteristically, Vergil chose to rely on a literary scheme, though he knew bees, if he knew anything, very well indeed by direct experience. And characteristically he used the suggestion of Nicander that farming could be treated poetically, not only practically, as Hesiod, on the whole, treated it. Still more characteristically, Vergil combined both methods. A third, and greater Alexandrian poet, who received attention from Vergil and Cicero also, was Aratus, of the third century B.C., a friend of Theocritus. He wrote an astronomical poem called *The Phenomena of the Sky*, based on the similarly named prose work of Eudoxus, and added a treatment of Weather Signs. Cicero translated the poem. It is still extant, for comparison with the *Georgics*, which owe to it the usual suggestions of idea and expression, and perhaps even some of their religious outlook on nature. Aratus begins with a famous and beautiful address to Zeus, from which St Paul quoted the words, 'For it is His very lineage that we are.'

Yet Vergil could have written on farming with no reference to any Greek. Farm books were already established in Italy, and had been since the second century, when the Phoenician work of Mago was translated, and followed by Cato's work on farming, and the work of Vergil's contemporary Varro, which he greatly

1. Cicero, *De Oratore*, I, 16, 69.

used. The tradition went on long after Vergil, to Pliny and Columella and more besides; and in this tradition Vergil might have had an honoured place, even if he had read no Greek, and written no poetry, at all.

The traditional forms which were knitted into the *Aeneid* are so many that they should almost be expressed as a list. Homer is much less primary for the *Aeneid* than Theocritus for the *Eclogues* and Hesiod and other didactic poetry for the *Georgics*; dramatic poetry, the Cyclic Epic, epyllia, the short, Alexandrian epics, from which Vergil reacted to Homeric grandeur and scale, and older Latin poetry from Naevius and Ennius to Lucretius and Catullus, are little less present in the *Aeneid* than the Homeric poems themselves.

Vergil inherited the epyllion with the Alexandrian fashion in which he grew up. He then decided for the classics, old Greek work on a large scale, Homer, Hesiod, and tragedy. This meant an immense task and a risk. He had to write long quantitative poems, which were still not quite happy in Latin, because, among other reasons, stress-accent resisted, as much as in the past or more, the use of quantitative metre. Horace chose the alternative difficulty for his most serious work, the *Odes*; here he wrote, not long poems in hexameters, which he used, roughly, for his satiric work, but short poems in the very hard metres of the early Greek Lyrics, which the Alexandrians generally, if not always, evaded with care. But Vergil did not return to the linear, chronicle form of earliest Latin epic, and the Cyclic Epic of Greece.

Homer made a great part of the *Odyssey* appear as a tale of earlier events told by Odysseus to Antinous, king of the Phaeacians, when he was nearly home. Vergil, perhaps as a second thought, made Aeneas, in the second and third books of the *Aeneid*, tell Dido the tale of the sack of Troy and all the long wanderings, said to have lasted nearly seven years, till at last, like Odysseus among the Phaeacians, having the least travelling and the worst dangers of fighting left to face, he had come to Carthage, as the first book told. It is well known from the strong indications of Vergil's original plan for the *Aeneid* that much or all of the narrative now told by Aeneas to Dido was to be directly related, and that Vergil changed his plan after he had written the third book, but before he wrote the rest. This habit of putting a plot within a plot, and sometimes another plot within that one, is fully developed in Homer; but it became more precise and regular still, but less subtle and elaborate, in the Alexandrian 'little epics' or epyllia, of Callimachus and others, whom the Latin *neoterici* followed. Vergil went forward by that way. The *Culex* and the *Ciris*, which have been attributed to him, are epyllia in scale not unlike several works of Catullus and his contemporaries.

There are other insertions of this kind in the work of Vergil. The end of the fourth book of the *Georgics* is a tale of how Aristacus, a mythical shepherd, lost his bees, and by the help of his mother, the nymph Cyrene, heard from Protcus the tale of Orpheus and Eurydice as an explanation how Eurydice was angry with him for pursuing her, with advice how to create bees anew, from killed heifers. All is lovely and majestic and complete – an exact, if tiny, epyllion, perhaps the best in the world. Then there is in the Eighth *Aeneid* the complete story how Hercules came to the site of Rome and rescued Evander and his Arcadian Greek settlers from Cacus, the volcano-devil. It is an epyllion also. The later part of the same book, the description of the new divinely given shield of Aeneas, is like the central part of an epyllion.

Vergil used his chosen method characteristically. There are always two Vergils, the critic and follower of all predecessors – to apply to him the remark about the two Aristotles, the critic and follower of Plato. Vergil assimilated the epyllion, and discarded it, in the sense that he assimilated it and built epyllia into larger works, which at the same time followed Homeric lines; and he developed them, structurally and in content, with memories of short composition. This fitted well with his own, partly Homeric, process of composition by self-dependent unitary blocks, of a characteristic, spontaneous rhythmic periodicity. Vergil writes a language of which the units are seldom words, as with others, and not so very often lines. The units are letters, syllables, verse-groups and large blocks of groups, even to epyllia and not least whole books.

As usual, the influences converge and blend. The units may look like epyllia or large parts of epyllia. But they are inserted Homerically like the more or less independent passages in the

Iliad, sometimes as long as a whole book; passages carrying the titles, older perhaps than Homer himself, by which, and not of course by serial letters or numerals, the parts of Homer are cited by early authorities. These passages have names like 'The prowess of Agamemnon', or 'of Diomedes', or 'of Menelaus'; 'The recovery of the dead'; 'The fight at the ships'; and 'The embassy to Achilles'. It appears that such pieces were .n at least some poems detachable. There are many stories how early poets appropriated whole poems from each other, to call their own, or insert into their own work, as Creophylus was said to have taken from Homer, or given to him, some of his poetry, and Eugammon to have included in his *Telegonia* a poem called the *Thesprotis*. Accordingly, self-dependent poems inside large epic were traditional from early times. With Vergil, they are, characteristically, old and new, Homeric and Alexandrian also.

The history of symmetrical structure in ancient literature has considerable interest. The most elaborate development is at the very start, in Homer. 'The Pattern of the Iliad', discovered by Sir John Sheppard[1] and Sir John L. Myres,[2] extends throughout the poem, and includes minute details of balancing similarities. The *Iliad* has a pivot, in the middle, and other pivots, in mutual correspondence. On each side incidents and tableaux match. For example, at the beginning an old man, Chryses, appeals to a harsh king, Agamemnon, for the release of his daughter, and at the end another old man, Priam, appeals to another harsh king, Achilles, for the release of his dead son, Hector. The meanings suggested by the implied comparison are a large part of the value and greatness of the poem. Again there are duels one near the beginning between Menelaus and Paris, and another near the end between Achilles and Hector. The first was indecisive, but it was the right way to end the war. The second was the wrong way. That is how Homer makes us think our own thoughts. Vergil does so too, not quite as Homer does, but under his guidance.

The Hesiodic Shield of Achilles has been shewn[3] to have a similar structure, to which is comparable the symmetrical plan in

1. Sir John T. Sheppard, *The Pattern of the Iliad*, London, 1922.
2. Sir John L. Myres, *The Journal of Hellenic Studies*, LII, 1932, 264–96.
3. R. M. Cook, *The Classical Quarterly*, XXXI, 1937, 204–14.

prose works such as the history of Herodotus.[1] Still more startling is the discovery of an elaborate, almost Homeric pattern in the Anglo-Saxon poem Beowulf by Mr E. A. Slade,[2] who was quite unaware that such structures existed elsewhere in literature. In Beowulf subjects and incidents occur in pairs either alternating, as in the form *a b a b*, or in returning symmetry, in the form *a b c d c b a*, with certain variations, and the subordination of pattern to pattern. That is almost exactly the principle of Homeric construction. Why this kind of structure should be found in Beowulf, or indeed anywhere, is still a mystery. How such a mental feat is possible at all is hard to see. Perhaps it is spontaneous, and the artists were partly at least unconscious of what they did; or perhaps originally they invented balanced design to help their memory in oral recitation. However that may be, the appearance of patterned structure in Alexandrian Greek work is more intelligible. There the principle is 'a plot within a plot within a plot'. Catullus has it, especially in *The Marriage of Peleus and Thetis*.[3] There the pattern is a returning symmetry, *a b c d c b a*. In at least one other poem of Catullus the balance is quite as exact. He may have adopted this method partly through a natural development from Alexandrian epyllia, impelled by his own remarkable thirst for many kinds of repetitive rhythm. Whether he owed anything directly to Homeric structure is hard to say.

Such were the tried resources in this technique when Vergil wrote. He did not continue the development further, but characteristically made his structures more varied and fluid. Yet at any moment there may be a sudden balance or repetition. A simile may recall an earlier simile in like, but contrasting, circumstances. A character may compel comparison with a character met earlier

1. Sir John L. Myres, *Who were the Greeks?* Berkeley, California, 1930, 522–5, with references.

2. Mr Slade has not so far as I know published his observations.

3. C. Murley, *Transactions and Proceedings of the American Philological Association*, LXVIII, 1937, 305–17. Professor Ronald M. Smith, 'Temporal Technique in Story-telling Illustrated from India', *Journal of the Bihar Research Society*, XXXIX, Part 3, 1954, 1–24 especially 3–8, finds 'emboxing' also in Indian Epic: he even quotes the late Professor H. J. Rose for the suggestion that 'emboxing does not appear in the West till Hellenistic times, after Greek contact with India'.

in the poem, so that meanings emerge from their similar but different qualities and fortunes.

It has been shewn[1] that the patterned structure in literature agrees with contemporary plastic arts. Homer seems to follow the symmetries of geometric pottery of the eighth or ninth century B.C. Herodotus built his history according to the groups on pediments of temples, which were coming to their greatest perfection in the fifth century when he was writing. An independent but comparable suggestion has been made for Vergil. Dr J. W. Mackail[2] considers that the *Aeneid* followed the structure of a large Roman basilica, the kind of building from which Italian church architecture developed. There is a central nave, with transepts or chapels leading aside from it, represented by books of the *Aeneid* which support the main theme without wholly following its direction.

If so, there is a hint of the change which Vergil made. He introduced time and movement. The other patterns are spatial and static, to be taken in at a glance. The pattern of the *Aeneid* changes as it is observed, like the aspect of a building to an observer walking through it. This difference agrees with a profound quality of the Italian mind, and especially the mind of Vergil, the sense of time and history and ordered development, so rare among Greeks. Vergil harmonized this sense of time in the outside world with the time-conditions of his own mental life, so much of which is present again and again in a memoried phrase.

But there remains some patterned structure in all Vergil's poems. There is the alternation of characters and moods in the *Eclogues*, and of wider experiences and methods of treatment in the *Georgics* and *Aeneid*. In the *Aeneid* there is also a considerable degree of more exact pattern; there the organization of the story in books is reflected in the organization in panels of the pictured shield, which Volcanus made for Aeneas.[3] But Vergil's larger symmetries are principally alternations of mood and action,

1. Sir John L. Myres, *Who were the Greeks?* Berkeley, California, 1930, 505–30, with references; idem, *The Journal of Hellenic Studies*, LII, 1932, 264–96.
2. J. W. Mackail, *The Aeneid*, edited with Introduction and Commentary, Oxford, 1930, xliii.
3. D. L. Drew, *The Allegory of the Aeneid*, Oxford, 1927, 6–41.

punctuated by reconciliations, yet all drawing reality from a mental process and outlook, and moving, and living, in the laws of time.[1]

The *Aeneid* is epic, whatever epic may be; though scarcely three poems exist which fit any available definition of epic equally well. Epic is, of course, long narrative poetry; some epic is 'early', belonging to simple, adventurous societies in a 'heroic' age;[2] but equally some is elaborately artistic, as Homer's on some of its levels, but not all, or as Dante's, or Tasso's, or Milton's. Epic poems are normally dramatic, but they are not meant for stage presentation; they are in verse; and they present a certain kind of human problem. The problem of epic, as distinct from drama, lyric, and satire, and the rest, might be called the problem of hopeless or nearly hopeless courage. There is much more than that in most epics, but that is probably the most constant thing. Epic may arise from an impulse to relieve the tension between individuals and their world, when a new individuality is already emerging from tribal simplicity where individuals think and act alike, and the world is not yet organized to tolerate and control individualism. True individuals make a higher claim on God than any made by men in a less differentiated state. In epic God is challenged, and man resists, till in the end, as the old Scandinavian poets said, 'the wolf eats the world'. The importance, for epic, of this newly found individualism is well attested. But early Roman epic had begun a change. Already in Naevius and Ennius individuals serve a purpose, and epic courage is not hopeless, for it is visibly creating the splendour of Rome. The poets thrilled to the excitement of the heroic days in which they lived. So Vergil too felt, sometimes. Already in the First *Eclogue* the 'god' Octavianus is central. But for Vergil God, man, and epic poetry were less simple than all this.

1. But see now George E. Duckworth, *Structural Patterns and Proportions in Vergil's Aeneid*, Ann Arbor, Michigan, 1962, a very important work presenting not only Professor Duckworth's own striking observations but also a thorough survey, with references of several sorts of pattern-discovery made mainly in the last thirty-five years. I have provisionally left my own text unaltered. See below, p. 425n.

2. H. M. Chadwick, *The Heroic Age*, Cambridge, 1912, *passim*; Sir Maurice Bowra, *Heroic Poetry*, London, 1952, *passim*.

When the *Aeneid* was conceived, Vergil shewed his characteristic habit of acceptance and subtle change. In his Rome, it would be absurd to say that individualism had just emerged, but Vergil somehow scaled up the earlier epic situations, Greek and Roman, to fit his time. It was still a problem of the nearly hopeless courage of the newly helpless individual, incredible though that may at first appear. It is less incredible if it is remembered that Vergil's Rome, after centuries of something that seemed to individuals like free 'democratic' harmony or the hope of it, had relapsed into conditions of master and mass, a new tribal undifferentiation such as Mr H. Stovin has investigated in our modern world, under the name of '*Totem*'.[1] Individuals, more intensely individual than ever, felt the problem of hopeless courage. and the problem. too, of the unknown God who seems not to hear. Rome still had glory. But the collapse of civilization was the predominant obsession in Vergil's day. Mr. H. G. Mullens has shewn that Vergil alone of the poets was hopeful for humanity.[2]

It is completely characteristic that Vergil could only express the present by applying it so that it coincided with a past, which had a very real, but, to anyone else, scarcely recognizable affinity with it. He took Homeric epic, with its grandeur, freedom, and exaltation of man, in relation both to other men, and to God; and with its hopeless courage in the *Iliad*, and nearly hopeless courage in the *Odyssey*. And he took the *Iliad's* slender, mystical hope, and the *Odyssey's* larger, nearer hope, which was yet a hope for a few years only, crushed under the threat of time. From them he made a different hope; a hope that was at the same time both less, for Aeneas is wrenched and racked by the god who must use him; and more, for. in the way of Roman epic, there is a hope for millions, for all time. The *Aeneid*, like the *Iliad*, has a mother and a son, but not only a mother and a son; and like the *Odyssey* an Ithaca of home-coming and a few years of home's happiness; but it is more than an Ithaca, more than a few happy years.

The subtlety of this part of the design is made harder to see by something that looks like Vergil's naïve and diagrammatic treatment of characters and situations. Vergil makes things look simpler

1. Harold Stovin, *Totem*, London, 1935.
2. Hugh G. Mullens, *Vergilius*, December 1940, Number 6, 26–31.

than they are, and disguises his changes. He adopts obvious things unchanged. Names in Vergil, as in Homer, may come from anywhere. A Trojan refugee, or an indigenous Italian, is quite likely to have a name from Agamemnon's army, and this happens not once but frequently. So, too, many scenes and landscapes in the *Aeneid* come straight or nearly straight from Homer or Apollonius, or some other literary source.[1] Sometimes a real place so described was out of reach, a place which Vergil could not have seen, or of which he could not have read any accurate description. If he had lived longer, he might have visited such places and made alterations. But probably the descriptions would have remained typical, like some descriptions in the *Aeneid* of places which Vergil knew well. Even his Latium is partly typical; but here, in his mysterious way, he often combines literary derivation with geographical accuracy.[2]

Occasionally, the typical and the derivative quality is absent. In the Eighth *Aeneid* Vergil describes accurately, but with some anachronism, the site of Rome, and in the Sixth accurately, but with considerable exaggeration, the site of Cumae in Campania. And in the third book he gives a quite real account of the Greek coasts of South Italy. Besides, his imagination plays whimsically with the etymological meanings of place names. In all set descriptions there is much that is not derivative, including sometimes impressionistic touches. Such fusion of the ideal and the real is only one department within Vergil's general integrative method.

The *Iliad* told the story of a man who went too far in the epic individual's pride of courage, and how he was somehow saved;

1. Bernhard Rehm, *Philologus, Supplementband,* XXIV, Heft 11, 1932, especially 62; Anna Gesina [de Tollenaere] Blonk, *Vergilius en het Landschap,* Groningen, 1947, who exactly analyses Vergil's practice in allusions to landscape; Angel Montenegro Duque, *La Onomastica de Virgilio y la Antigüedad Preitálica,* 1, Salamanca, 1949, who argues with great ability that Vergil never invented but always followed genuine historical tradition in the matter of names, an important thesis, of which it is hard to say up to what point it is acceptable.

2. Bertha Tilly, *Vergil's Latium,* Oxford, 1947, carefully compares the localities with the text and proves Vergil's knowledge and accuracy in passages where he writes thus objectively; cf. her notable article, 'The Topography of *Aeneid* IX with reference to the way taken by Nisus and Euryalus', *Archeologia Classica* VIII, 2, 1956, 164–72.

all against a foreground of fighting and stupid hate, honour hourly going too far, and against a background of love and pretty things, kindness, home and nature, faithfulness, gentleness; perhaps this side is really in the *Iliad* the main theme, enhanced and enforced by the horrors and wickedness that pretend to be the real story.

Like Shakespeare, Homer made the metaphors and imagery of his earlier work the plot of his later. The similes of the *Iliad* are part of the background, and they are often of the gentle things that in the end have victory. Homer's obsessions with kind things, right rule, nature, and home, come out as a central part in the *Odyssey*, which is more positively about them, the adventures and dangers and sins all leading that way.

Vergil put his *Odyssey* first and his *Iliad* after, a device intensely Vergilian, which, when it is done, declares its artistic inevitability. Of course Aeneas must travel first and then fight. Chance helps, as when Vergil translates the 'marvellous' or 'splendid' Odysseus, δῖος 'Οδυσσεύς, into the Latin language, and into Trojan sympathies at the same time; for Odysseus, who was to Homer his favourite hero, must be wicked to Vergil, who is on the Trojan side. Vergil has only to write the words in an apparently direct transliteration, *dirus Ulixes*, 'the terrible Ulysses'. *Dirus* has indeed been supposed the same word as δῖος, an original *s* having in the Greek word disappeared, and in the Latin changed to *r*. The identification is wrong, but Vergil's method is none the less illuminated. Meanwhile, by this apparent chance, Vergil has also gone behind Homer to a still earlier tradition, in which the Odysseus whose earlier name was Olysseus, 'Destroyer', and whom Homer transformed, was wickedly cunning and cruel.

In Homer Achilles fights for glory, and his side fights to win back Helen. In Vergil Aeneas fights for a future, and his side fights to win Lavinia, a princess whom he needs, as perhaps Menelaus needed Helen, to strengthen a title to a throne; but he does not really want her, as Menelaus really did want Helen. Those two won their happy home again, and are seen there, in the *Odyssey*. Aeneas is not so shewn; it is hard to be sure that he ever won any very happy home. In the *Iliad* the Greeks are destroying and, if they are making anything, they are only remaking a part of what had been already. Aeneas is making everything; a new city that shall be a world, and a new kind of man. There is consolation in the *Iliad*, in quiet things, and in their triumph when Thetis and Achilles quietly talk, a tragic synthesis, proving beyond appearance and beyond words that somehow all is well. We cannot be sure that the *Aeneid* has even this. Odysseus, sailing west and going into the cave of Calypso, 'her who hides', and even explicitly visiting the world of the dead, is a type of humanity, returning at death to earth, or isles of the dead, by the westward way of the sun.[1] Homer is in some touch with the journeys of Ishtar and Gilgamish, in eastern myth. The symbolism is stronger still, perhaps, in Vergil. Aeneas is held, not by Calypso but by Dido, a livelier love, not a love that he, like Odysseus, is glad to escape. He goes to a home, but a strange, cold, unknown home; and Vergil makes it mysteriously a return, claiming, with some justification, too, that Dardanus, Troy's founder, first came from Italy.

This is peculiarly Vergilian, and especially for the following reason. There is a religion and a poetic truth in all the tales of wanderers coming from the east to Italy before clear history begins. It is not just like other 'heraldic' history, planned to give a respectable origin to people whose antecedents are obscure; like a fifteenth-century genealogy, of which Mr Paul Rainey tells me, where a family is traced to Alexander the Great through Christ and back to Adam and Eve. All have their armorial bearings; after the Fall a figleaf was added to Adam's escutcheon, and an apple to Eve's. The legendary migrations to Italy are not like that. There is some actual history in them. But equally important too is the myth of a westward journey to a land of the setting sun, of rest, and of dreams come true. So some people, who lived there, regarded Italy. And Vergil, taking Homer's broken tales, broken to make Homeric poetry before Italy could take part in any such theme, rebuilt them as perhaps they had been, but added much to them too; and with his sharp economy included, co-incidently with the old picture, a newer picture with new meanings; they can easily be missed, just because they fit the old so well, but they are there all the same. With Vergil, when one motive or reason would be enough, there are always more beside.

1. W. F. J. Knight, *Cumaean Gates*, Oxford, 1936, 1–27, 149–76.

This is, shortly, the Homeric and the pre-Homeric part. Vergil includes it, and evokes from it something a little less human, less ephemeral, perhaps; and something too, rather more statuesque and formal at a first view, and above all more universal and eternal in the sense that great responsibilities are on men, and great results, for all time, depend on the acts of heroes. In man's heroic plight, merely to think of this makes the difficulties seem many times as great; in the heartless confusion of things, with human and divine wills and the energies of nature in conflict, even the way out for a few people is hard to find and follow; but a way out for all mankind is harder still – if there were not Heaven to guide.

Aristotle thought Homer the most dramatic of the poets. He works in narrative, but his situations and characters are as dramatic, in the ordinary meanings of the word, as any could be. The tragic poets of Athens, however, went farther, by being equally dramatic about a more advanced stage of society with more complex impulses and needs, and by compressing their work, to allow many different problems to be stated poetically in a comparatively small number of lines of verse. Vergil, guided by the already more dramatic epic of Ennius, included the conquests of the Greek dramatic poets too.

From Aeschylus he took creative conflict of loyalties, and indeed the Pythagorean formula of antagonisms everywhere, each destined to have a solution of its own, leading to new antagonisms and new salvations.[1] And from Aeschylus, too, he took the long reach of time, and a solution, by living, in the far future, when even God can learn from man. But from this he left something aside. God is for him more Homeric than that, timeless and unchanging. He also added something. He defined and shewed in actual, practical forms the solutions that time could bring. This too might be missed; how intensely the main fabric of Vergil's poetic thought, with its solution by conflict in the mysterious power of time, is Aeschylean. This is, partly, how Vergil is 'holistic', as the late R. S. Conway and Professor T. J. Haarhoff explained, comparing his world-view with the 'holism' of the late General Jan

1. W. F. J. Knight, *Greece and Rome*, v, 1935, 29–40; idem, *The Journal of Hellenic Studies*, LVIII, 1938, 51–4.

Smuts.[1] All is conflict, and the reconciliation which comes before it is too late, for which Thucydides, dominated by the power and the shapes of Aeschylus, austerely pleaded. Jupiter and Juno agree; and the nations fuse and blend. *Tanton placuit concurrere motu, Iuppiter, aeterna gentes in pace futuras?* 'Was it really your will, Jupiter, that nations, destined to live in peace for eternity, should meet in that terrific shock of war?'[2] But the union came.

Without Sophocles, Vergil would not have developed power from innocent suffering, from the distortion of moral states by external forces, and from all the intricacy of the mind. Sophocles taught him, too, to endure to have no consolation, to accept the unredeemed death of greatness, and to hold to ancient piety and law, which became Roman piety and law in the fusion. Again, Sophocles gave him more plot and situation than any other tragic poet. He gave him Dido partly, for she and her sister Anna are partly like pairs of sisters in Sophocles, Antigone and Ismene in the *Antigone*, and Electra and Chrysothemis in the *Electra*; and her death on the sword of Aeneas is the death of Ajax on his own sword, the gift of Hector, given to him before Troy; and, further, she dies on a mysterious funeral pyre, like the pyre of Heracles, on Mount Oeta, where he died. Dido holds on to an immutable law of right, against expediency, and dies for it, like Antigone. In the extant plays of Sophocles there is one answer to all the questions, the translation of Oedipus to a life without death in the *Oedipus at Colonus*. The voice of a god summons him; he recognizes, and accepts, the call; and then his end, we are told, was 'just a wonder'. So too Aeneas in the Eighth *Aeneid* was called in the thunder by Heaven; but called to another life, not beyond death, but here; called to receive his new arms of destiny, from his divine mother. There is much Sophocles, also, in Vergil's Sack of Troy; from the lost *Antenoridae* of Sophocles came the departure of Aeneas from his city, through advice given to Anchises his father by Venus his divine mother. There are countless other influences, and all is, as usual, changed in Vergil; but Sophocles gave much to him, here, too.

1. W. F. J. Knight, *Vergil's Troy*, Oxford, 1932, 21-2, with references.
2. *A.* XII, 503-4.

Euripidean tragedy is nearly always in two moods, the mood of rich sympathy and understanding, with a trust in positive good, beautiful nature, and even the cruel irrational passions of nature and man, and the mood, too, of sharp rationalism, critical and pitiless, sometimes going towards negatives everywhere, as if even the good are bad if you look deeply, and as if there is no true good anywhere, least of all in Heaven, where Gods play with men, and surrender their favourites to each other's spite. The two moods are overlaid, and from the artistic complexity emerging from the poet's complex mind comes the poetry, saying that though nature is lovely there is no comfort, and people, terribly treated, will react in terrible ways. Yet Euripides gives what has been described as the map through the world that tragic poets can give. He shews, whether he means to or not, the things to avoid, the dangers in the mind's mystery. So Vergil could know from Medea and Phaedra how scorned women will attack, and from Odysseus and Menelaus how mean, and worse, those who guide public policy must seem, beside all the suffering of it. Here he combined two Euripidean things, or even three. He made the contrast, between right reason and the dark instinct, as of Turnus devil-possessed, secure, and shewed the pitilessness, and the frightful havoc, of mass impulse, knowing it strangely well. He then turned the binomial subtlety of Euripides upon himself, and made Aeneas in part a Menelaus, a hero with little, sometimes, to say for himself, and with the rational cause left to seem irrational. All the time these two sides are there. It is as if Vergil took as his epic hero some poet of mental structure not unlike the poet Euripides. There are always two opposite things to say. In Euripides the hero of others is not *our* hero, and is shewn wickedly vain; in Vergil the hero of others, shewn in some moods vain and almost wickedly vain, *is* our hero, for we cannot choose but accept. Even the gods of Vergil are a touch Euripidean, especially Juno and Venus, cynically planning to sacrifice Dido. But in Vergil the gods are not simple in duplicity, as in Euripides; Vergil goes back to Homer or beyond, and truly displays our mind and our human predicament, by making the Divine shine through the mythic gods, who, that man may live, die.

Vergil's dramatic construction is nearer to the Attic stage than to Homer. Ennius[1] already used more dramatic speech than Homer, and he influenced Vergil. Vergil has few characters present and speaking at once. In battle, characters succeed each other quickly as in Homer, but normally only Aeneas, Iulus, and perhaps two other characters, such as Dido and Anna or Evander and Pallas, are present at once, and available to speak, and most often only two actually do speak in any given scene. Dialogue, verbally quoted, occurs frequently; there is seldom an unbroken narrative, without dialogue, for very many pages at a time.

Professor R. S. Conway[2] considered that the odd-numbered books of the *Aeneid* are epic narrative, and the even-numbered books are dramatic tragedy. This is not a completely sufficient formula, since both sets of books have both qualities. But in each of the even-numbered books there certainly is an important dénouement, or tragic release, whereas the others end in some suspense. In the second book Troy falls, and tragedy is complete; and then the appearance of Venus and her star, like a theophany at a rite, a divine intervention, almost a *dea ex machina*, brings hope out of final horror. This is a tragedy of a world, and war. The fourth book, Dido's tragedy, is a tragedy of an individual, a tragedy of love; the conflict is between feeling and duty, and much besides; and the solution is a solution less of hope than of despair. The Sixth *Aeneid* has a tragedy less literary than ritual, like the old initiations, known in many parts of the world; they were

1. Ethel Steuart, *The Proceedings of the Classical Association*, XXIV, 1927, 10.

2. R. S. Conway, *Vergil's Creative Art*, London, 1931, 8–13; cf. idem, *Harvard Lectures on the Vergilian Age*, Cambridge, Massachusetts, 1928, 131–40, where Conway takes an important step, revealing a balance between the successive books of each half of the *Aeneid* according to subject: I and VII, arrival in a strange land; friendship offered; II and VIII, each the story of a city – one destroyed by Greeks, the other to be founded with the help of Greeks; III and IX, Aeneas inactive and action centres on Anchises (III); Aeneas absent and action centres on Ascanius (IX); IV and X, Aeneas in action – inner conflict between love and duty (IV); outer conflict with the enemy (X); V and XI, each begins with funeral ceremonies and ends with death – Palinurus (V) and Camilla (XI); VI and XII, Aeneas receives his commission in VI and executes it in XII; see Duckworth, *Structural Patterns and Proportions in Vergil's Aeneid* (p. 164 n. above), 5 and *passim*. This method has now been developed in great elaboration, and many different schemes have been suggested, many of which might be equally true to fact.

designed to give new vitality, by ritual rebirth, to boys or men who were passing an important stage of life, and especially at new manhood, before marriage, and death. Fundamentally, to general human thinking, it is always a new life that is to be won by these rites. In the Sixth *Aeneid*, then, the solution is again different. It is the solution by an after-life, by the eternal value of moral good, and, besides that, by the value of the race, whatever may befall the individual; though the sudden and impressive statement of the theory of reincarnation leaves individual death unreal. But divine justice is still, and remains, a problem not quite solved. Beyond death, all do not suffer fairly. But at the end, by a miracle of poetic ambiguity, Aeneas comes through, or seems to come through, the gate of ivory, the gate of false dreams, or perhaps false 'sleeplessness', *insomnia*,[1] a word which Vergil himself made. Therefore there may still be some delusion, and it may be only pictures that Aeneas has seen. We are not told. But we must think what we must, or may.

The Gates of Sleep are a profound subject; in part they go back through Plato and Homer to Babylonian cult.[2] But it is already clear that they are the fitting end to the 'initiation' in Vergil's sixth book, for initiation ceremonies often finish in sleep for the newly initiated. The Eighth *Aeneid* in one sense continues the initiation. Aeneas has a sacramental meal, as the late R. W. Cruttwell explains, with Evander on the site of later Rome, and joins the feast of Hercules.[3] Evander directly tells him to be like Hercules. He accepts the Herculean role of suffering hero, upholding by his suffering a world: the pattern of Hercules known first from the metope on the temple of Zeus at Olympia, where Hercules takes the place of Atlas, and Athena inspires him to the task. It has all gone to make the *Aeneid*. Aeneas has become by sacrament an Italian and a Hercules. Then he is given his divine arms, like Achilles, when Achilles' own victory over himself, was partly, but only partly, won. We are nearer to the Holy Family again. By the appeal of her love Venus persuaded Vulcanus to

1. *A.* VI, 893–9.

2. E. L. Highbarger, *The Gates of Dreams*, Baltimore, 1940, 1–67.

3. R. W. Cruttwell, *Virgil's Mind at Work*, Oxford, 1946, 69–82, especially 72–6.

make the arms; and with a will and loyalty like the spirit of a poor Italian farmer's wife, he, lord of elemental fire, made them. The shield holds in picture the glory and the deeds of grandsons to be born, beyond the comprehension of Aeneas himself. The symbolism is strong. Aeneas, like Prometheus, and like characters of Greek sculpture at its greatest, must go on, under sanction of the future and the ideal. He is shielded by a glory that is to be, and that he cannot see. He must be content in the dark, knowing whence he has his shield.

Dido the good was broken by external ill; Mezentius, the wicked, in the Tenth *Aeneid*, is built up again into a sympathy and a new strength by adversity. Aeneas kills his son, and then Mezentius himself, and there is all pity for them. Vergil, having written his *Medea*, wrote his *Macbeth*.

The tragedy of Turnus at the end of the whole *Aeneid* is not a new greatness imparted to the wicked, nor a break in the goodness of the good. He sins with *Furor*, insane brutality, to Vergil the greatest sin; but so does Aeneas.[1] Turnus, maddened perhaps by the dark powers, is yet good, a fine bold natural man, not a saint nor a visionary, but wanting only his due, in justice and loyalty and defence of the right. To him, Aeneas must be wrong; to him there are no two ways; the gods favoured the conquering side, but Turnus, like Cato, the conquered. The gods betrayed him, as they betrayed Cato. It is a tragedy of right against right, almost a tragedy of wrong against it. Vergil can teach us much about the nature of right here. Dr Wolf Hartmut Friedrich[2] has worked out the difference in world view between Homer, Vergil, and Lucan; how the idea gradually develops that the side of goodness and right is not always favoured, and how, in Lucan, the great theme is the help that Heaven afforded to the wrong. We are always seeing things happen which might, if we choose, be interpreted so. And Vergil knew it, as well as Lucan; but somehow Vergil learnt to forgive even the gods, and to look to the end.

The odd-numbered books have more steady narrative than the others, and less of the tragic form and release. But some of them

---

1. R. S. Conway, *Vergil's Creative Art*, London, 1931, 15.
2. Wolf Hartmut Friedrich, *Hermes*, LXXIII, 1938, 391–423.

have a tragic movement, in some degree. The seventh is tragic, in a sense; Juno violently infuses hatred and starts war in Latium; but it is the beginning of a tragedy without the end. The ninth book has the tragic end of Nisus and Euryalus; but it is more like something in the narrative part of a tragedy, the 'messenger's speech', than the strictly dramatic catastrophe.

The 'epic' books shew how Aeneas was led on his pilgrimage and the 'dramatic 'stages that he reached, with their tragic issues. Perhaps this is roughly the scheme of the *Aeneid*, its plot, 'myth', or 'organization' – the part of a dramatic poem which Aristotle declared to be the most important of all.

If so, it is quite clear that Vergil made the 'myth'. He was certainly not telling an old story as he inherited it, any more than the Greek tragic poets did; even less, in fact, for they always let the new myth, which they were making, change the old without destroying it, whereas Vergil left scarcely anything in his inherited material as he found it.

Tragedy in epic and in drama gives relief in different ways. Homer brought Achilles and Odysseus to peace after stress in victory, the one over himself, the other over an outer world, for his victory over himself was already won. Aeschylus ranged gigantic forces to face each other and to work themselves out in action, proving where life and strength and hope for the future lay. Sophocles explored the power of moral good to survive human defeat and decay, and the incongruity between the human plight and the human ideal; sometimes he left consolation to the loveliness of the verse alone. Euripides shewed the sadness, which we miss and should not miss, and the goodness of what might have been. The strands were all plaited together by Vergil.

All this dramatic thread is woven in the narrative, which might be said to become less epic and more dramatic when, at violent moments, compression of meaning and swiftness of action increase.

It is hard to know what epic is, because Homer set the pattern of it, and it is very hard to be sure what are our own thoughts of Homer, however reverent and delighted our adoration. But, clearly, in both *Iliad* and *Odyssey* we follow a man on his way; and so we do in the *Aeneid*. Here, however, there are successive, progressive conflicts with real human forces in intellectually clear antagonisms. The epic is dramatized, as Ennius had dramatized his *Annals*. And as, before Ennius, Naevius had written his *Punic War* with a grand purpose in the Roman present,[1] to which mythical beginnings were set to lead, so in the *Aeneid*, after this Roman fashion, there is a clear and brilliant goal, much clearer than in the *Iliad* and much less simple than in the *Odyssey*. The stages make the epic quality of the *Aeneid*. They are not only the tragic conflicts; but also the divine guidance in its several acts of growing revelation, and their gradual effect on Aeneas himself. It is usually said that there is nothing else like that development of a character, in any other ancient book.

The story of the Trojans' wandering leads from prophecy to prophecy and from sign to sign.[2] Providence never ceases to lead.

When Troy was entered by the Greeks, Hector in a dream gave Aeneas the Penates, the home sanctities of Troy, and told him to go on his wanderings and find them a home again. Panthus told him later that all was lost. He fought on. Then, after Priam's death, he found himself alone. He saw Helen, and wanted to kill her. That was at his lowest depth. At that moment his divine mother rescued him and told him to go to protect his family in his home, and how she would guard him. But only when a flame shone on the head of Ascanius, and a shooting star, with thunder on the left, confirmed the omen, would they start. Creusa, lost, met her death; and her ghost told Aeneas that he must go to the Tiber, in a western land. They sailed; and at Delos Apollo told them to seek their ancient mother. This Anchises took to mean Crete; but a settlement there failed, and the Penates appeared in a vision to explain that they must go on to Italy, which Anchises now recognized as the first home of Dardanus, before he came to Troy. They sailed; and a Harpy, a human-headed bird, symbol of pestilent winds, warned them that they were to be compelled by hunger to eat their tables. At Buthrotum on the east coast of the

1. On Naevius see Vinzenz Buchheit, *Vergil über die Sendung Roms*, Heidelberg, 1963, especially 23–53, citing Strzelecki.

2. Dreams are important; Vergil has twice as many in the *Aeneid* as Homer has in his two, longer, poems; cf. H. R. Steiner, *Der Traum in der Aeneis*, Berne, 1952.

Adriatic, Helenus, the Trojan prophet, was found; he gave guidance for the way and for the propitiation of Juno, and mentioned that they would see a white sow with a litter of thirty young pigs when they reached their final home. They sailed past south Italy, landing only once, apparently, and for a short time; but they noted omens which they saw there; and next they came to Sicily, where Anchises died. Then they were driven to Carthage by a storm. There Venus met Aeneas and encouraged him; but some months later Mercurius in a vision told him to remember his destiny and sail away. He landed in Sicily, and held funeral games for Anchises; whose ghost appeared, and told him to visit him at Cumae in the world of the dead. This visit was the next prophetic experience. Then came the arrival in Latium, and an omen of fire on the head of Lavinia, daughter of Latinus, and bees swarming in the citadel, symbolizing the strangers. An oracle given to Latinus at Albunea confirmed the assurance that Aeneas was to be welcomed as the fated prince. Aeneas and his men fulfilled the prophecy about eating their tables. Juno and Allecto started war. The god of the Tiber appeared to Aeneas, and told him of the sow with thirty young. He soon found it, and knew that he had come to his new home. Then he went to fetch aid from the Etruscans, who were prevented from fighting the Rutuli by an oracle saying that they must fight under a foreign leader. Aeneas returned with them, and fought to the end. There were smaller omens, presaging victory and defeat. But, by a regularly progressive revelation, planned by Vergil but not quite expressed in the existing *Aeneid*, their destiny was clear.

Broadly, Vergil found characters and tragic situations in Greek poetry, and the Roman myth in Latin books, poetry and prose, supplying the rest from his mind and experience. The central idea of a spiritual destination to which a man is divinely guided owes something to the *Odyssey* and old poems on Heracles, but not so very much. Into it have coalesced many tales of Greek colonists, guided obscurely by Apollo's oracles and other wonderful signs. Dionysius of Halicarnassus proves that there was already some prophetic guidance in the legend of Aeneas, and an alliance between Aeneas and his Venus-Aphrodite on their way, before Vergil set to it all his strong and delicate hand. But only the poet who had first written the *Eclogues* and the *Georgics* could give the heart and fire to the pilgrimage, and make its progress so divinely matter to the world.

Poets and other writers of fiction are generally noticed either to present realistic characters, or types. Homer and the tragic poets had shewn how to create real people, all different, and how to explore their ways. In Homer characters are universal, not really rare, or very unusual, but both intricate and true; in Aeschylus they are far more typical and simple, the emphasis being on the broad lines and strong forces behind; in Sophocles they are universal partly, but they are also particular and unusual in their moral distortions, and almost specimens of psychological ill-health, permanent or temporary, telling of the germs latent in us, that we do not often clearly know in their activity; and in Euripides characters are sharply defined as ordinary to an extreme and rare degree, what most of us are below the surface, and often, momentarily, even shew ourselves to be; and they are typical not of their class so much as of all humanity, when control is withdrawn and wrong forces applied. The tragic poets can explore further, but Homer makes people most themselves and most real.

Vergil, without adopting characters ready made, allowed traits from characters in other poets to grow up into his scheme. The traditional Odysseus, earlier Olysseus, of the family of Autolycus, 'the very wolf', cunning and pitiless, practical and soulless, almost the opposite to what Odysseus became in Homer's hands, is accepted by the tragic poets sometimes, and by Vergil, with occasional traits from Homer, always. But the plot of the *Aeneid*, in a sense, demands him. It just happened that Vergil's vision forced him back to something like an old, pre-Homeric, form.

The *Eclogues* are often like the *Aeneid* rather than the *Georgics*. In their characters, of course, they must be, for the *Georgics* do not exactly have characters.

The characters of the *Eclogues*, which after all are really lyric poems, do not have to be strongly drawn. But they are distinguished from each other. One shepherd is impatient, another naturally pessimistic, and others sane and ready to recover from all their lyric sorrow. Menalcas is boastful; a reason, it has been suggested, why Vergil can scarcely mean Menalcas to represent himself!

The dramatization is of course simple, and subordinate to the lyrical quality. But there is interest in the characters, because with them Vergil has begun his way of infusing contemporary qualities, emotions, and partial identities into pure literary figures. He is helped by the contiguous representation of real people in the *Eclogues*, especially Gallus in the Tenth. Bits of his friends come to life all the more easily in the imaginary shepherds. Without this experience of the *Eclogues* behind, the *Aeneid* could hardly have been the *Aeneid* at all.

The *Aeneid* was even helped by something like characterizations in the *Georgics*. There the human characters are few and general. So Vergil's impulse to lyrical dramatization went into the animals – the birds whose nests are wrecked by farmers and which weep all night, the ox whose years of faithful service cannot save him from the plague, the bees and the birds, which, in spite of romantic theories, feel a compulsion that they do not understand, and in all their intent activity are more automatic than inspired, and finally the frogs, which, even when they are being eaten by a snake, still insist on having the last word. Vergil's delightful, humorous sympathy with them all has been fully observed by Professor E. K. Rand, and is valuable indeed for its own sake. But it was valuable also as experience for the *Aeneid*, where no brilliance of the imagination is spared from the lavish whole.

There the characters, like the plot or plots, and the words also, grow out of many suggestions. Aeneas already in Homer has high dignity, the divine protection of his love-goddess mother, valour, and righteousness. But the Aeneas of Vergil has the piety and loyalty and tenderness of a true Roman and simultaneously, in the usual way, of Homer's Hector; and he has too the courage and force of Homer's Achilles, and the reflectiveness in some degree, though not the self-dependence, of Homer's Odysseus. There might seem some danger of a character which would be all good, and not human or sympathetic, if the good qualities were thus to be taken from everywhere, and the bad left behind. But Vergil knew how to make Aeneas real and imperfect in a real way, in a way real to men of his, and of later, times; and he made him, unlike most, or even all, ancient characters, grow in moral stature, with time.

The characters in Vergil are always partly dependent on the literary past, but they are very varyingly typical. Aeneas is a symbol to some degree, but not a type of all devoted leaders by any means.

In Troy Aeneas was a man of action, hot in adventure and passionate, but capable of fear; in a storm at sea his will broke and he fell into despair. He gave way to Dido, and left her, not by will-power, but because he must; but by will-power he hid his feelings. He was then more self-reliant, and, at his meeting with Anchises below the earth, he accepted his destiny, and joined his will to the will of heaven. But he could still be anxious and despondent, until his initiation into Italian manhood and leadership at the rites of Hercules. After that he was secure, almost Stoic; but with perhaps more power of emotional pity and sympathy than before, though at the same time his obedience to duty was paradoxically brutalizing him, and he could be cruel, calmly and contentedly. He even planned, in the Tenth *Aeneid*, to kill captives by human sacrifice. In the last lines of the poem he killed Turnus, after relenting, just for revenge, in memory of Pallas, whom Turnus had killed, and because he saw the belt of Pallas, which Turnus was wearing. It was sheer vindictive vengeance. At the end of the *Aeneid*, Rome is sure; but we do not know that Dido would have liked the new Aeneas as much as the old. Aeneas himself is equally, for all we can say, saved and damned by that 'stern salvation of the war', in Gogarty's magnificent phrase. He is not exactly like anyone but himself; but for the subtlety of Vergil, and his Sophoclean or Euripidean indirectness, Aeneas could be discarded, for all his development, as weak, pompous, and cruel. But the world is not so simple, and neither is Vergil, nor Aeneas.

Two things, in particular, can be said. Vergil might have taken Aeneas entirely from life. It simply was not his way. He integrated characters, like all else, largely or mainly from emotions and thoughts as they already existed compressed into literary tradition. Next, he sometimes accepted a type, without further characterization, when that was enough. Achates, who always loyally attended Aeneas, is like Pylades, known from Aeschylus especially, who attended Orestes when he killed his mother, and is almost simply an attendant. Latinus and Amata are a typical old royal pair; but Priam, so brave in his weakness, and Hecuba, so tenderly solicitous for him, are more themselves; and even Latinus, weak and despondent, and Amata, possessed by devils, evince new qualities as the story goes on. Lavinia, their daughter, who, at the age of about fourteen, is soon to marry Aeneas, is little more than a correct child, and so makes her contrast with Dido, so real and so eternally herself, more poignant still. Iulus or Ascanius is not quite like Lavinia. He is a boy of uncertain age; at the departure from Troy he was about nine years old, and, after nearly seven years of travel, in so far as time can be counted, he appears to be about sixteen. The difference ought to be this, but is made to look if anything less. It is Iulus who humanly laughs at noticing that the party ate loaves or cakes used as 'tables', fulfilling the oracle that, when they did this, they would have reached their new homes. He looks handsome, fighting to defend the walls of New Troy in Latium. He leads the 'musical ride' which was the 'Trojan game'. Not much is done to fill in his picture, which is partly a reflection from the much younger Astyanax of Euripides; but his attractiveness, little defined, is yet persuasively indicated. Indeed, most characters are diagrammatic, even Nisus and Euryalus, the affectionate pair who unsuccessfully tried to make their way out from the besieged New Troy in Latium to take a message to Aeneas, then in Etruria, getting help. Their relationship is underlined, perhaps with memories of Harmodius and Aristogeiton, who boldly killed the despot at Athens, and of others, less closely similar. Vergil[1] explicitly promises to them whatever immortality his poetry can give. Yet they are not fully self-dependent characters, but rather outlines, inside which are drawn a few bold, expected strokes. They contain moods and emotions and tendencies, but they do not generate them from themselves. Even Creusa, first wife of Aeneas, whom in old Troyland he left behind and lost, though there the poetry and power and utterly enriched sensitivity and revelation can never in the world be outreached, is still not in her own right herself, but the frame of a harp, with some strings for a few undying notes.

1. *A.* ix, 446–9.

Besides the tradition of epic and tragedy, there was the tradition of comedy. Perhaps comedy created types more than any other form. It is a familiar and obvious remark that the tradition of dramatic types grows from the poets of Attic New Comedy, Menander, Diphilus and the rest, through Plautus and Terence to Molière. But the word 'types' is not likely to mean the same in any two sentences about types. Comedy has to evoke its laugh, or other response, by an unexpected reference to something very familiar. The interest is more than elsewhere concentrated on incongruities, which mean surprise, and have to involve something familiar in life, but not yet elicited to be set in letters. Again types may be outlines, but their content must be convincing and real, since comedy deals in the concrete, seen and directly known, not material already partly abstracted by intellectual activity on it.

With his providentially extraordinary inability to exclude sources of influence and suggestion, Vergil undeniably admits comic precedent even into the centre of tragedy. Hecuba in Troy, just before Priam's death, has the realism of the comic stage; so perhaps has Aeolus, god of the winds, in his obsequious haste to obey Juno; so too have Juno and Venus themselves, when, intriguing comically and heartlessly, they plot, and, with the characteristic comic motive of a substitution, here also owing something to a legend in which the goddess Thetis hid her son Achilles and left a substitute, Venus makes her son Cupid himself impersonate Iulus and charm Dido, to compel Aeneas and Dido to fall into helpless love.

The facts are always worth noticing. And it is always at least possible to think of reasons for them. Hecuba is the more tragic for the comedy; Aeolus is the more obsequious, so that the helplessness of the Trojans, since their foe controls such force, is made impressive; and the heartlessness of the powers, to Aeneas and Dido, as to many condemned in Vergil's own day to dynastic or commercial marriages, is made all the more terrible by such tragically comic irresponsibility. Such *is* the world which poetry must answer.

The success of Vergil is partly due to his willed or spontaneous, perhaps unconscious, patience, in abstaining from cheap effusions, and in waiting till the wealth of his thought and feeling and observation, much of it directly taken from the contemporary world, gathered sufficient literary and traditional material to frame or mould or constrain, and so make artistic and universal, all that his keen artistic and practical vigilance had acquired.

When the form came, it was reinforced by energy that might have made lyric poetry.

By lyric is usually meant spontaneous, personal, effusive poetry, a direct cry of emotion which has found crystallization in a form. Drama is formed by pent emotions issuing in action and conflict. Epic creates a world in great wealth of detail and width of view, in which an individual is watched with concentration on a path through adventures, dangers, and passions. Dramatic conflict may be more spiritualized and mental than epic, where action is normally external.

Such questions are not easy to treat concretely, and there is a danger of playing with words. But there is some sense in saying that the *Aeneid* is unusual in its combination of the three types. There is lyrical observation and direct expression in Homer, but not so very often; he is rather impersonal and objective in dramatization. Vergil thinks through into some characters, and speaks through them lyrically. Perhaps he forgets the characters more than he forgets himself; but that may be unfair. He sees the scene in which they act, and describes it sensitively, out of his own reactions to it. The feelings are not typical, even if the characters sometimes are. Such are the thoughts about all living things, except Dido only, asleep, the beasts, and birds that live on 'miles and miles of transparent mere';[1] and such too are the varying pleas to the austere powers in the stars, 'those fires eternal',[2] and 'the power, if any there is, that takes for its care all whose loving is on terms unfair, some power that is just, and will remember'.[3] Then there are the strange, unexpected sceptical doubts[4] expressed by Nisus to Euryalus, as if he were wondering whether there is really a sanction for self-sacrifice, and if courage and patriotism are worth while, so much recalling the talk[5] of Glaucus and Sarpedon in the Twelfth *Iliad*, and yet, because of a few words, so far away. Often it is in a sort of lyric that the old arguments, Epicurean and

1. *A.* IV, 522–32.   2. *A.* II, 154–5, etc.   3. *A.* IV, 520–1.
4. *A.* IX, 184–91.   5. *Iliad*, XII, 310–28.

Stoic, which once filled Vergil's young thoughts, occur. They have gone to control and give symbols to his feeling.[1]

The lyric feeling makes the tragedy real. It is Roman, deeply compressed, and very complex and aware. Even Euripides is simple compared to Vergil, who of course possesses a deeper past, and a wider present too. It is rather as if the Roman sense of time had quite changed poetry. Vergil could assume the issues without stating them, and release a flood of questions with a tiny hint. He trusts his readers to think what he lets them think. There is a particular example on the other side of the question about Aeneas. We, like others at Vergil's time and since, naturally wonder if Aeneas was really right. Vergil does not say. But he shews the force impelling him. And he shews too the force of right against him, by the insinuations, not perhaps to be accepted, but nevertheless made by characters opposed to Aeneas, Dido, Drances, and Turnus especially. When Aeneas is called a soft oriental, or a pirate, or one who lands in a country not his own, and designs great schemes, in defiance of two rightful kings, so that his plan is 'clearer to himself than to Turnus, who is a king, or even Latinus, king of this very land', ... *manifestius ipsi quam Turno regi aut regi apparere Latino*,[2] there may, indeed, be a defence of Aeneas ready, but we have to remember that such a defence is demanded, and that some could never accept it. This is one of the ways in which a very great poet leads us to see what sort of a place the world is, and 'just how far we can trust anything human' – *humanis quae sit fiducia rebus admonet*.[3] He leads us to wonder, and perhaps to see, how far we can trust the divine. *Tantaene animis caelestibus irae?* 'Have spirits in heaven such violent storms of bitter anger, then?'[4] That is at the beginning of the *Aeneid*. In the middle, Triton, a god, in jealousy kills Misenus, *si credere dignum*, 'if such an act is good enough for our belief'.[5] And at the end Jupiter preserves Italian nationhood, and ordains that the Trojans

1. cf. Viktor Pöschl, *Die Dichtkunst Virgils: Bild und Symbol in der Äneis*, Innsbruck, 1950: in future I cite the English translation by Gerda Seligson, *The Art of Vergil: Image and Symbol in the Aeneid*, Ann Arbor, Michigan, 1962. Pöschl explores certain kinds of symbolism and provides valuable references to modern poetic criticism which elucidate his exposition.

2. *A.* VIII, 16–17.   3. *A.* X, 152–3.   4. *A.* I, 11.

5. *A.* VI, 173.

and Italians shall blend, saying, in monosyllables at first, to Juno, *do quod vis, et me victusque volensque remitto,* 'I grant what you wish; I let you conquer me, and willingly I yield.'[1] With Vergil, we wonder who this Jupiter was, and who this Juno, and then, with him, we look at Rome.

The fusion of everything within a tradition is deceptive. Vergil, in the moods of practical life and of prose, acquired much clear and accurate knowledge. In 26 B.C., after he had started the *Aeneid,* he referred in his letter to Augustus to 'more serious' studies; and if he had lived he meant to give up poetry for science and philosophy. He is recorded to have excelled during his early education in 'mathematics', which probably means astronomy, besides the literary subjects. He stood high among Roman writers on the typically Roman subject, half practical and half scientific, of agriculture. His poems shew real observation of nature, and careful thought about observed realities. Sometimes, in spite of literary integration and typical descriptions of scenery, Vergil displays[2] very precise and accurate knowledge of places known to him by careful exploration. His knowledge of antiquities and especially religious antiquities was equally accurate and still more profound. Vergil even described the sea[3] from his own experience. On the other hand, notoriously, Napoleon decided that he, unlike Homer, knew nothing about war. Even in writing of nature[4] Vergil frequently abandons fact. His plants, though he knew the country so well, are often literary, inaccurately described, or out of place, often in derivation from Theocritus, who writes accurately of eighty kinds that he knew in Cos.

There seems to have been a sharp division between Vergil's practical and his poetical mind or moods. Normally he was very accurate and precise, but in quite different ways, either scientifically and practically, or poetically, one of the two. He was seldom merely muddled. However, at any time poetic necessity and the force of its traditional forms and contents might, in poetic moods, rewrite reality; the boundary is crossed, and poetic necessity has

1. *A.* XII, 833.
2. J. Carcopino, *Virgile et les origines d'Ostie*, Paris, 1919, *passim.*
3. Mary B. Peaks, *The Classical Weekly*, XV, 1922, 201–5.
4. Alice Lindsell, *Greece and Rome*, VI, 1937, 78–93.

exercised supremacy over the apprehended facts, and their natural organization. But equally characteristic are acts of creation in which factual and poetic reality, contemporary and traditional, all coincide. Professor Charles Knapp[1] gave as an example the passage in the Fifth[2] and Sixth[3] *Aeneid* about Palinurus, who fell overboard, and swam to Italy, but was killed by savages at the place which continued to bear his name. Vergil 'has utilized materials got from one passage in the *Iliad* and two passages in the *Odyssey*, combined with matter obtained from local traditions current both in Etruria and Lucania, and yet has put the whole together so skilfully that the ordinary reader does not detect the sutures, besides producing a passage which, though like in details to various other things, is itself in reality a new creation'. Of course it is.

Such reconciliation may be just as clear when it involves direct observation. Many examples are almost too obvious to mention, especially when in the *Georgics*[4] poetry exactly represents, as nothing else could, minute observations of animals, plants and soils. Less obvious is an example[5] in the Second *Aeneid*, where a description of a meteorite or fireball is founded on a passage[6] in the *Odyssey* where a meteorite strikes a ship, on the different ideas about phenomena of the sky among Greeks and Romans, and on the story that the star of Venus guided Aeneas from Troy. Yet his description agrees almost verbally with a description of an actual 'fireball' published in *The Times*[7]; the 'deep yellow glow ... leaving behind a smell of sulphur fumes' is nearly an unintended translation. It is safe to guess that Vergil had seen just such a phenomenon.

This direct observation of contemporary things leads to a further reference to tradition. Politics were urgent, and Vergil had long been interested in them.

When the *Aeneid* was being written, Actium (31 B.C.) had been won; in 27 B.C. the Republic was 'restored'. Vergil could not be slow to wonder about the strange new power so concealed and yet so great, so traditional, and so new. He could not help seeing more

1. Charles Knapp, *The School Review*, XIII, 1905, 492–508.

2. *A.* V, 833–71. 3. *A.* VI, 337–83.

4. Sir A. Geikie, *The Love of Nature among the Romans* ..., London, 1912, 66–7, etc. 5. *A.* II, 692–98.

6. *Odyssey*, XII, 415–17. 7. *The Times*, 12 August 1933, 10.

truth than others. He had generally seen that mankind, whether or not born free, was everywhere in chains; but he got much farther than others in seeing how this came about and what can render it legitimate; and especially also, if anything could, what sort of chains they would have to be.

Direct observation of the facts surrounding his own life led Vergil to the political philosophers, especially Plato, who was a poet also, and could explain the association together of men with men, and under men. There was also, for example, Cicero's work *De re publica* or *Political Theory*. And there were plenty of books of Stoic theory, besides all the books and talks of the Epicureans, Greeks, and Romans too, especially Lucretius, who were helping to give Roman life a friendly, sensitive culture, with a love of nature and a love of peace and calm.

Though Vergil may have thought that he admired philosophy more than poetry, he did not write a prose work to solve the political problem, nor a work in poetical prose, after Plato, nor a philosophical poem, after Lucretius. He is said to have been bad at writing prose. Probably his mind thought most freely when his chosen rhythm of the hexameter defended his thought from interruption by its regularity, and energized and vitalized it by its variety. That is how rhythm works. Unlike Milton, who, though he felt left-handed when he wrote only prose and not verse also, yet wrote prose well, Vergil found verse alone natural. He would be unusual among modern poets.

But there was another strong reason. To Romans, politics were traditionally a matter of emotional pride in their history. This outlook they owed to their own sense of destiny and achievement, perhaps inherited from prehistoric Italian songs,[1] and also to Greeks, who, as Polybius did, explained the Romans admiringly to themselves. But the epic of history in Latin had begun before Polybius, and Naevius and Ennius had made an immense appeal with it. Of course, they owed much to the Greeks. Greek plays had often appealed to patriotic and other emotion evoked by recent history, though seldom, as in the *Persae* of Aeschylus, directly. There were even Greek historical and more or less

1. Augusto Rostagni, *La Letteratura di Roma repubblicana ed augustea*, Bologna, 1939, 45–53, 408–11.

patriotic epics; of them the earliest known is the *Persica*, in which Choerilus of Samos in the fifth century celebrated the almost contemporary victory of Athens over Xerxes. However, the Romans are not known to have owed any large debt to these suggestions. They owed more, perhaps, to Homer; and much to the annalistic habits of Roman civil and religious government, and of Roman family and national pride. Perhaps family pride, and religion, increasingly sensitive and complex, did most to create Roman emotional history, and, through that, with help from the dramatic symbolism of Greek myth and the depth of Latin lyric feeling, to create, in the end, the *Aeneid*.

When Vergil was writing the *Georgics* and the *Aeneid*, much that was discouraging was going on. Octavianus[1] was at first considered as of little importance and not even respectable. He had been as bloodthirsty as, or more bloodthirsty than, Vergil's earlier hope, Julius, and even, perhaps, Antonius. He was cynical, like the rest, in dynastic marriages; and Vergil must have pondered them, as he wrote Dido. Whether or not Vergil, as Servius says, removed from the *Georgics* a passage in praise of his dear friend Cornelius Gallus, because he had been disgraced and had died, there is no doubt that he died, by his own hand indeed, but on account of the anger of Augustus; who afterwards lamented that of all Romans he alone might not be angry with his friends. Vergil might well have conceived bitter feelings for Augustus like the bitterness for Julius Caesar which Catullus, his master in the hexameter, conceived. Instead, he held to the doctrine of Roman and Epicurean friendship, and, as it is hard not to believe, to the Aeschylean doctrine of living evil down; this human Zeus must change, redeemed by human good. But Vergil always saw both sides.

Again the past came to a kind of destined fruition. The world, and Vergil, had been training up to the *Aeneid*. Homer mainly omitted the future, though not, perhaps, eternity, destiny, and the hopeful meaning in time; Pindar's glory was of the day, and the past that made it; Aeschylus left out much tenderness, and the message of simple things; Lucretius offered a life more chill than

1. W. W. Tarn, *The Journal of Roman Studies*, XXI, 1931, 173–99; XXVIII, 1938, 165–8.

he tried to believe, which might well be allowed to stop, all through the world; and Catullus let his heart burn for himself alone. None could lead an army crusading for all mankind. Greek poets could make the real and the ideal coincide in a clear-cut moment; few poets can match with depths of answering and significant moods the depths of a wide world and many ages.

Vergil had not missed the Roman myth and its old poets; he wanted when he was young to write a long poem on the foundation of Rome, and also a poem of contemporary things, about his heroes, directly, as Ennius and Naevius had written annalistic poetry; but he gave up both plans. In the *Georgics* he says that he means to build a marble temple and have Augustus in the middle of it, obviously a poem, under Pindar's architectural figure for a poem, but not so obviously a poem of direct statement and narrative.

In the end Vergil made the decision to which all the experience of all the poets had been leading. All things combined together for good, and he got the secret, as usual, from an overwhelming concurrence of reasons and origins, any one of which would have been a brilliant thought by itself. Like Naevius and Ennius, he took the ancient Roman myth, but made it the main story, not an introduction to an account of historical times. Like them, he put history into the poem, but indirectly, as he had put the world of fact into his Eclogues of fancy. He took Plato's ideal state, organized like bees in a hive; and he took it indirectly from the bees of his own *Georgics*; as in Shakespeare[1] the metaphors of music and tempest, that run through all the plays as metaphors, turn in the end into the very plot of *The Tempest*, so in Vergil Mr R. W. Cruttwell[2] has explained how the bees compared to men in the *Georgics* become in the *Aeneid* men compared to bees. It was therefore not quite Plato's ideal state; it was Italian and of the soil, organic rather than organized, organic beyond any formula Aristotle reached. It was Italy's 'culture pattern', lived in experiment spontaneously and for long, and now made conscious to itself, and to Europe. And it was the ideal, not in remote eternal

1. G. Wilson Knight, *The Shakespearian Tempest*, London, 1932, *passim*.
2. R. W. Cruttwell, *Vergil's Mind at Work*, Oxford, 1946, 51-3, 121, and elsewhere.

calm, but in action, and the taint of action was on it; an ideal made of realities none quite ideal, till the last stone could be put on the temple, and all should be perfectly in place.

There were countless discoveries in which meaning for a city's or a nation's life was to be found; the death of Ajax in Sophocles added on to the deadly moral rigour of Hippolytus in Euripides, and the delicacy of awakening love in the Medea of Apollonius; strange incidents of fighting from many now lost and then little known old epics of Greece; and from Pindar, and not only Pindar, the Heaven of clear air and happiness for the good, a Heaven so strangely rare in Greek books; which yet have their Hades, where, according to the old blended mythical pattern of the ancient east, in the centre Heaven should be, if not in the sky with the Olympian gods. Somehow at Vergil's Cumae it is all there.

Most of all, perhaps, Homer made Vergil; unless nothing could, if all did not. Simple though the idea at least may seem, it was an act of brilliance in Vergil's time to desert fashion and be Homeric at all. Vergil made a bold decision for great poetry, on a great scale. From the tragedy of the *Iliad*, where a man is saved in spite of himself at the cost of his friends, and from the Quest, perhaps the Pilgrim's Progress, of the *Odyssey* where a man comes home, saved because of himself, and saves the best and nearest of his friends, Vergil took something for his Pilgrim's Tragedy of arms and a man who in spite of himself saves his friends, but himself, if we guess right, is lost. Or *do* we guess right?

When, in the earliest *Eclogues* but scarcely before, whatever he may have written before the *Eclogues*, Vergil had once perfected his method of spontaneous artistic fusion of all material, a fusion which invariably implied some alteration of the elements of which the material was constituted, he sustained this method throughout all his work, and scarcely ever admitted to finished poetry any inherited fact or thought or mental picture without his characteristic fusion and alteration.[1]

This method produced the fairy tales 'which are the only true

1. But cf. Anna Gesina [de Tollenaere] Blonk, *Vergilius en het Landschap*, Groningen, 1947.

stories', that is, true myth, in which the unconscious mind of past and present illuminates, and energizes with emotion, the facts of the selective and partly delusive experience presented by ordinary life. The difficulty, always experienced in any attempt to find even small complete systems of everyday fact in Vergil's poetry, is a sign that his poetry is purely and thoroughly artistic. Vergil had got further than his predecessors towards being thoroughly and purely artistic almost or quite all the time.

Accordingly, the Italy of the *Eclogues* might be called the Greek Sicily of Theocritus, which was partly pictured from the island of Cos, where he also lived, translated into the half-Greek landscape of the Campanian Italy where Vergil lived and wrote. That is not all. Vergil's early life, passed some years before far to the north, had left emotions which were for long stored and compressed. They were energized again by new experiences, such as the mental adventures in the 'Garden Academy', including the news of the confiscations of land. But they found symbols for their expression in the landscape not of north Italy but of Campania, and Campania, too, coloured by the idiom and rhythm of Alexandrian poetry. This poetry for us seems to be mainly the poetry of Theocritus. But there was very much more. Euphorion must have exercised a strong influence, sometimes mediated by Latin contemporaries of Vergil, certainly Gallus, and almost certainly Messalla, who wrote Greek poems with the mind of an Italian.

The totality therefore is not a picture of Vergil's Italy, but a picture of the contents of Vergil's mind, a mind expressed in many idioms, both Italian and Greek, and fully active only under the influence of rhythms which streamed, branching, from many poets' moods. Yet the ill goat that cannot keep up with the rest,[1] and the first love of a boy in his twelfth year for a tiny girl, in a garden,[2] are quite straight from the facts of the common day. For in such moments ordinary things break into fairyland and come to be really alive because of this other world where they truly belong.

The *Georgics* are some return to a kind of realism. The pictures of the crops and ditches and animals and cottages compose a total picture of a real Italy. But everything is coloured by contrasts, for it is all framed by a world of imagination; and accordingly nothing

1. *E.* I, 13.   2. *E.* VIII, 37–41.

is entirely actual. The sheep of the farm are themselves changed, when Vergil, appealing to Pales, goddess of pasture, says that now for such a majestic subject he 'must speak in deep-toned harmonies' – *magno nunc ore sonandum*.[1] But in the *Georgics* Vergil is nearest to a straight depiction of actual things. It is a matter of proportion. Here the elements, combined and fused, are larger. They are altered for the fusion at their edges; but the unaltered core of them is greater, and has space for the actual within its content. It remains true that in Vergil's mature work everything is fused and changed.

The *Aeneid* returns towards the degree of fusion and alteration found in the *Eclogues*, and goes beyond it, though it normally does not go beyond the *Eclogues* in a certain surrealistic tendency that they have. That is, the elements of actuality fused in the *Aeneid* are smaller than the elements so fused in the *Georgics*. They have normally a smaller unaltered core. The sheep belonged to one time and place and were actual. But a group of sailors or soldiers in the *Aeneid* is normally different, with characteristics of several places and times, perhaps, and nearer to shepherds in the *Eclogues*, who are not exactly either real or even literary shepherds, and who, though they are partly both, may yet be also, to some degree, leading figures of contemporary Italy.

So too the places, and also the customs and elements of culture, in the *Aeneid* are normally altered for and by their fusion. The heroes of the *Aeneid* are not as Homer's heroes were when they lived on earth, if they ever did, nor even quite as Homer pictures them. It is impossible to say that the characters of prehistoric Italy which Vergil introduced have any particular claim to be like the chiefs who lived in Italy in Trojan times. Nor is there the least reason to believe that any Phoenicians like Dido and her friends lived at those times in north Africa. The dates are wrong for one thing; and, among much else, these characters owe too much to the mind of Sophocles and other Greeks, and to Vergil's own.

The whole scheme, however, of a voyage of Trojans from Asia to the western Mediterranean is not out of all touch with prehistory as far as it is known.

The *Aeneid* does not closely follow any existing system of facts,

1. *G.* III, 294.

or any existing literary tradition. In it all inherited material is changed, much or little. But a great number of facts, and many traditions, literary, and oral, were blended and changed to make the poem. Vergil's mind generated a world of its own according to its peculiar schemes of rhythm, colour, and moral contrast. The facts and traditions all contributed a part of themselves to the activity of Vergil's mental world. But his mind retained control, and did not suffer coercion from the material.

The framework of the *Aeneid* is a complex of movements in the Greek heroic age. Cultures clashed and impinged, and there were migrations and wars, from which ancient tradition was not wholly wrong to trace the political and cultural conditions of classical times.

Early in the twelfth century B.C. according to Eratosthenes, or about a generation earlier according to Dr Carl Blegen's excavations, destruction came on the city of Troy. Archaeologically, Homer's Troy is Hissarlik VIIa. Schliemann, the first excavator, thought it Hissarlik II, and his expert manager, Dr Wilhelm Doerpfeld, thought it Hissarlik VI – the second and sixth city, from the bottom, on the site. There is no certain reason why Troy should not have fallen, as Homer and the other poets say, to an attack of raiding Greeks, perhaps 'Achaeans', bearing a very late Mycenaean culture.

It was a time of violent movements. Peoples from Asia Minor, Syria, perhaps Crete, with others from Greece, among whom were Achaeans, are known from Egyptian records to have attacked Egypt in Trojan times. There were three big attacks, in the thirteenth and early twelfth century. Hittite records prove that an Achaean power was in touch with Asia Minor well before and during the thirteenth century. Tribes that attacked Egypt had names which almost certainly appear later towards the west of the Mediterranean. There were the Shakalsha, the Tursha, the Shardina, and the Mashwasha, whose names are convincingly seen surviving among the Sicels of Sicily, the Tyrseni or Etruscans in Etruria, the Sardinians, and the Maxyes, a tribe living on the north African coast.

Perhaps then a true record of a migration by sea from Troy or near Troy to the western Mediterranean in the twelfth century B.C.

may have survived. It certainly might have occurred. That, however, until recently was always denied. It was assumed that a long voyage at such an early date was impossible; and that the story of Aeneas was purely fanciful. It is now known, from contemporary drawings on pots, that the Egyptians had very practical ships about two thousand years earlier; and also that in Trojan times wars were fought with the help of large navies. Even earlier, there was a culture known as the 'basket ware' culture, which, according to the finds, must have spread from the west to the east of the Mediterranean before 4000 B.C., and well before Egyptian civilization was fully established; and it must have been carried on ships. There is other evidence. About a thousand years before the Trojan War, Early Helladic pottery came from Greece to the south-east and east coasts of Italy, where it has been found; and about two centuries before the Trojan War Minoan and Mycenaean pottery begins to appear in south-east Italy and Sicily. A large volume of varyingly credible legends recorded by several writers represents in various forms the movements which the pottery might imply.

Whether any such movement actually came to Latium is a different question. But there are strong signs that one came to Sicily. The work of Dr Ludolf Malten has thrown much new light on the subject.[1]

Sicilian names, for example, of the river Crimisus, and the city Elyma, recall an eastern tribe called the Solymi, which belongs to Asia Minor; and there was a cult of Venus at Eryx, with her two doves, which certainly came from the east Mediterranean. It is now believed that Dardani, cousins of the Trojans, who mainly lived not actually in Troy, but, as Homer says, farther inland, sailed to Sicily in Trojan times, about 1200 B.C. or soon after. If so, they may well have had with them the name of Aeneas, either as the name of a leader, or of someone, or something, else.

The name occurs as an epithet of Venus-Aphrodite in several places, in Aenea, Aineia, a Greek city in Thrace, and Aenus, Ainos in north-east Greece. Other Dardan names occur in Arcadia, and there are traces of them, too, on the eastern coast of the Adriatic.

---

1. Ludolf Malten, *Archiv für Religionswissenschaft*, XXIX, 1931–2, 35–59; cf. W. F. J. Knight, *Greece and Rome*, VI, 1937, 70–7, with references.

Dardani came down from the north, and split. Some went to the Troad, and some of their descendants sailed to Sicily afterwards. Other Dardani went by land further to the west, and left signs of themselves in Thrace, north-east Greece, south Greece, and Illyria.

All these places except Aenus, which might be represented, as well as Aenea itself, by the landing of Aeneas at Aenea, are exactly or approximately indicated by Vergil, whose Aeneas travels on the sea by the places at which there were traces of his people, though some of these traces are really due to movements by land, not by sea. Aeneas, in Vergil's plan, could not easily reach Arcadia by sea; but he has with him an Arcadian called Salius, who in other stories joined him in Arcadia, but whose presence with Aeneas in Sicily Vergil, characteristically, leaves unexplained.

Classical literature has little to say of all this at first. Homer gave Vergil the name and figure of Aeneas, son of Anchises and Aphrodite, and perhaps something towards his character too; for Homer's Aeneas is religious, loyal, and a good fighter, though he is not strongly characterized. There is no precise knowledge of the west as yet; and, though the *Odyssey* has plenty of memories of it, it is still fairyland unless, after all, according to some modern views, it is actually centred in Sicily. The first mention of Italy is in the Hesiodic *Theogony*,[1] where Telegonus, Agrius, and Latinus are sons of Odysseus and Circe. The passage has been suspected, but needlessly; it implies that a legend of Latium existed by the seventh century B.C. The next notice is more interesting still, but also doubted. There is a 'Trojan picture',[2] a *tabula Iliaca*; an earthenware tablet, dated at about the end of Vergil's life or a little later, and found at Bovillae near Rome. It is modelled to represent the Trojan War, and it is inscribed with the names of the poets and poems whence the information used had been derived. It contains a picture of Aeneas starting from Troy with his family, and led by

1. Hesiod, *Theogony*, 1011–16.
2. U. Mancuso, *Atti della reale Accademia dei Lincei*, Fifth Series, XIV, viii, 1909–11 (1911), 662–731; R. W. Cruttwell, *Virgil's Mind at Work*, Oxford, 1946, 2, 113–20; for the coins of Segesta in Sicily, B. V. Head, *Historia Numorum*, Oxford, 1911, which shews that as early as about 240 B.C. Segesta was glad to assert kinship with Rome.

Hermes, with the words 'Aeneas starting for Hesperia', the Western Land; and it attributes the incident to a poem called the *Sack of Troy*, by Stesichorus. Stesichorus lived in Sparta, and later at Himera in Sicily, in the seventh and sixth centuries B.C. If there is no mistake, a legend of Aeneas sailing for Italy or Sicily was already known in Sicily among the Greeks at that date. This conclusion has been resisted, with the argument that the Stesichorus mentioned must be a later poet of the same name. But that is neither proved nor probable.

That Aeneas was known as a traveller and founder at least early in the fifth century B.C. is shewn by a coin of Aenea, Aineia, in Thrace, of that time. On it Aeneas is shewn with his family, starting from Troy. There is also a very important terra-cotta group,[1] existing in several copies, found at Veii; it is of Aeneas in hoplite's uniform with Anchises on his shoulder but no Penates. The date is the first half of the fifth century B.C., when clearly the story was already known.

The first historical Greek settlement in Italy was Cumae, founded perhaps at the end of the ninth century B.C., and the first in Sicily was Naxos, founded late in the eighth century B.C. A legend that Aeneas led a migration to Sicily or Italy is not known to have existed then; but it had already arisen not very many generations afterwards. There is no sign of further interest in it, however, for some time; then it became noticed, in relation to the rising power of Rome.

Timaeus, of Tauromenium in Sicily, a learned but romantically minded historian of the third century B.C., took the legend very seriously, and offered proofs, from what he had seen at Rome, especially 'Trojan pottery', that the Romans really were descended from Trojans. The strict Polybius derided him, and denied that he even went to Rome; Mommsen called him one of the people 'who are on no matter so well informed as on the unknowable'. In the same century a Greek tragic poet Lycophron wrote a poem called *Alexandra*, a violent and heavy work, still mainly extant; it is like a caricature of Aeschylean majesty and mystery. The poem contains a long prophecy by Cassandra on the future greatness of Rome, and it fully recognizes that Aeneas came from Troy to be

1. Charles Picard, *Revue Archéologique*, XXI, 1944, 154–6.

the first founder of the Roman race. It may have been written soon after the first trade treaty between Egypt and Rome made in 273 B.C.

Aristotle was interested in Rome, and called it a Greek city. He was aware of a legend that its foundation was due to Greeks, returning from the Trojan War with Odysseus, who were compelled to remain because Trojan captive women burnt their ships. This incident, with variations, is surprisingly frequent. It is localized at Aenea and in Sicily as well as in Latium, and Vergil uses it, perhaps twice; once in Sicily, where the Trojan women, tired of travel, burn some of the ships, and stay in the island; and perhaps again in Latium, where the ships of Aeneas, to save them from being burnt by Turnus, are transformed by Cybele into nymphs of the sea.

In the third and second centuries B.C. the legend of Aeneas was already current in Rome. Naevius and Ennius began their epic histories with it. It developed quickly in various forms, and was freely used to justify Roman claims. On account of it the worship of Cybele was brought to Rome (205 B.C.), and soon afterwards (197 B.C.) the Aetolians recommended themselves to Roman friendship on the ground that they alone of the Greeks had not fought against Troy.

The legend now changed less quickly, until in the first century B.C. it was adopted by the Julii, who are thought to have developed it further. They made it support their claim to divine ancestry, and a leading share in the foundation of Rome.

The forms of the legend which Vergil is likely to have found are shewn clearly by the short version of Livy and by the longer account of Dionysius of Halicarnassus. Both wrote soon after Vergil. He treated this material as he treated the poetry of Homer and Sophocles, on the principle of the integrative redistribution of attributes and incidents.

No other version, of course, contains all the elements found in Vergil's. His plan of combination went farther than any previous plan, and his version is accordingly in some respects farther from factual coherence.

There are two main anachronisms in the *Aeneid*. The Trojans on their way to found the Roman future could not have met

Phoenicians building Carthage, or Etruscans long established in Italy.[1] There is a tradition that Utica, neighbour and mother city of Carthage, was founded about the eleventh century B.C. But there is no reliable evidence for that. Carthage itself was certainly founded first in the ninth or eighth century B.C., possibly in about the same generation as Rome; it was even sometimes said that Rome and Carthage were founded on the same day. The date of the foundation of Carthage is clear enough both from known history of Phoenician enterprise, and the archaeology of the site. If Aeneas came straight from Troy after the sack, he came about three hundred years too soon to meet Carthaginians on his way.

There are similar anachronisms in Vergil's assumptions of the presence of Greeks in Italy, but their implications are less precise. There may well have been Greeks, though not quite in all the places implied by Vergil.

On the whole, Aeneas, travelling perhaps at the beginning of the twelfth century B.C. or even earlier, found according to Vergil culture and political geography not of that time, the 'heroic age', but of 'the age of colonization', some four or five centuries later. There are already Greeks settled on the east, south, and west coasts of Italy, in the places colonized by Greeks in the eighth and seventh centuries B.C. The southern cities were passed by Aeneas on his voyage. The eastern city, Arpi, founded by Diomedes in the legends, comes into the story afterwards, when Diomedes refuses to send help against his old enemy Aeneas. Most important of all is Cumae near Naples, where Aeneas visited a temple of Apollo and Diana, and was taken to the world of the dead by the Sibyl, a priestess and prophetess with a Greek name, Deiphobe. The name itself is apparently Vergil's invention. It is based on different but similarly formed names of sibyls elsewhere. But Cumae is anyway Greek for Vergil; he refers in fact to the foundation of the city from the Greek island of Euboea; though he does not assert that the Greek city existed when Aeneas reached the site. Greek Cumae can be precisely dated. It is the earliest of the Greek colonies in the west, and pottery found there proves

1. See p. 53 above and p. 200 n. below.

that its foundation or at least occupation by Greeks occurred at the end of the ninth century B.C. There is every reason to doubt the very early date, in the twelfth century, which Vergil implies, and which other ancient notices endorse; the proof rests on negative evidence, but this time it is strong.

Vergil also suggests the existence already in Sicily of the later Greek colonies. He mentions their names in the Third *Aeneid* in the narrative of the voyage of Aeneas; and even refers to the ancient fame in horse racing of Acragas, as if it belonged to a time before Aeneas; it really belongs to the fifth century B.C., when Pindar was celebrating the victories of its sovereign Hiero.

There remains the settlement of Evander and his Arcadians on the Palatine Hill where Rome was afterwards to be. There is no proof that Greeks were there in the twelfth century B.C., and in the literal sense it is unlikely. On the other hand, there is no doubt that some Greeks were at Rome at or soon after its foundation; and there happens to be a remarkable correspondence between the legends of Rome and the legends of Arcadia. For example, the adventures of Romulus and Remus are like the adventures of Telephus. Sir Arthur Evans has shewn many similarities subsisting between the religions of Rome and of the Aegean Bronze Age. There may be some fact behind the story of Evander, perhaps a common racial element in Greece and Latium. It is to be remembered that some legends brought Aeneas himself from Arcadia, and that Dardanus was supposed by Vergil and other writers to have come from Italy to found the Dardan race of Troy. The persistence of various stories of similar tendency is some argument for supposing that they represent an underlying fact; but it is little help in deciding just what this fact may have been.

Still more mysterious are allusions in Vergil to Greek origins of Etruscan cities. It is possible that in later times, perhaps in the eighth or seventh century, Greek families came to live in them, as the Corinthian family of Tarquinius Priscus was said to have settled in Etruscan Tarquinii. Or there may really have been very early Greek settlements. On the whole the Etruscans were most probably a race which sailed from Lydia in Asia Minor to Italy in the eighth to seventh centuries B.C.[1] They may have already mingled with Greeks and acquired some Greek culture in their Asiatic home.

Simple explanations are seldom sufficient for anything which Vergil says. It is not enough to assume that he merely committed anachronisms for artistic purposes. It is more likely that he did so, but at the same time had other reasons also.

Actually, he seems to have acted as he did in the *Eclogues*, and made his poem, which is apparently simple, represent two or more different systems of conditions, as if they were really one simple system. He described, in the colours of the historic cities of the 'age of colonization', not only those settlements, but others, almost forgotten, which had occurred long before, and he added features and allusions from quite recent and even contemporary times.

The pre-history of Italy is complicated. Vergil deserves praise for his surprising success in finding an artistic expression of it.

There are palaeolithic remains in north Italy, and there was a neolithic population which lasted with little change, as elsewhere, for thousands of years. The early inhabitants are on the whole likely to have been akin to the historical population of Liguria, in north-east Italy, and the Iberians of Spain.

Early in the second millennium B.C. northern tribes began to penetrate south, and after about nine hundred years they had spread into most parts of Italy. They, or many of them, were the ancestors of the modern Italians, and are usually called *Italici*. The first invaders (*c.* 2000 B.C.) cremated their dead; the later (*c.* 1000 B.C.) inhumed theirs.

These tribes were apparently related to the tribes from the north who invaded Greece and Asia during the same centuries. All seem to have spoken Indo-European dialects, some of which came to be known as Latin, Greek, and Sanskrit.

The invaders of Italy soon began to bring a bronze-age culture with them. The earlier elements came from Switzerland, where they had lived in pile dwellings on lakes. They did the same in north Italy, and, when they settled in places where there were no lakes, they built similar dwellings on dry land. These settlements

1. There seems to have been an earlier wave, in the thirteenth century B.C.: G. A. Wainwright, *Anatolian Studies*, IX, 1959, 197–213.

are known in Italian and other languages as *terremare*, the plural of *terramara*, a word meaning 'marly earth', from a quality produced in the soil from the remains of long occupation. The most southerly *terramara* is near Tarentum, Taranto, in the instep of Italy, near the heel.

The Italici eventually constituted large tribal groups, which have left their names to districts of modern Italy. Of them the most important was the Umbro-Sabellian group, a strong and prolific population which occupied the mountains of Umbria in north-eastern central Italy, and spread down the east coast towards the south, occupying the Sabine country east of Rome, and further south Samnium. The Latins, occupants of Latium, on the west coast of central Italy, were a parallel group also descended from the Proto-Italici; the Latins lived in thirty cities, of which one was Alba Longa; and colonists from Alba Longa founded Rome. Interspersed with the Italici were remnants of the old neolithic population.

This ethnic situation was presently altered by the arrival of Etruscans from Asia Minor, though we cannot be very certain of the dating. They occupied the country north of Latium, mainly near the west coast, and expanded north to the valley of the Po, and south, through or round Latium, to Campania. Eventually (*c.* 700 B.C.), they occupied Rome itself, perhaps combining a number of villages to form the first city.

Not so very long after the Etruscans were installed in Italy, successors of the Italici began to come from the north. They were the Celts, or Gauls. They exerted pressure on the Etruscans, and occupied the valley of the Po, and land to the south towards the east coast of Italy. It is possible that some of these Etruscans and Gauls were among Vergil's ancestors. The Gallic pressure continued and increased, and one of their raids temporarily occupied Rome early in the fourth century (390 B.C.). But they were really an advantage to the Romans, for they weakened the Etruscans, and helped the Romans to overcome their power.

More obscure are other racial influences, coming by sea from the east.

Before the Italici came, 'Early Helladic' (? 2200 B.C.) and other pottery found on the east and south-east coast of Italy shews that there was contact with Greece and Illyria to the north of Greece.

When the bronze-age world of the Minoans and Myceneans collapsed or decayed during the period after 1500 B.C., Minoan and Mycenaean influence spread westward. It is proved by pottery found in south-east Italy and Sicily. But whether this influence spread north up the eastern or western coasts of Italy is more doubtful. Probably it did, especially on the east.

There was also without doubt the mysterious movement by sea to Sicily of people from the neighbourhood of Troy, who may well have included Dardani, and brought with them the name Aeneas and the worship of Aphrodite.

At the end of the bronze age, intercourse with the east revived after a lapse, and it has been said that the whole Italian iron age developed under strong influence from the Aegean. The main evidence for the localities of this influence is the discovery of Greek geometric pottery of the tenth, ninth and eighth centuries B.C. in south Italy. It is earliest (c. 950 B.C.) at and near Tarentum, and Croton to the west of it, and a little later (c. 825 B.C.) at Cumae, near Naples, far up the western coast.

The Etruscans continued to be in increasingly close touch with Greek lands. And by the eighth century or earlier some contact with Phoenician traders had started.

When the Italici had begun to be firmly settled in Italy, there were many small towns and villages, supported by agriculture and pasture, some designed on the principles of the pile-dwelling, and each closely united, and planned geometrically, for defence. The dead were either buried or cremated, a distinction which has led to the suggestion that the Italici were of two different racial groups. Their religion was an early form of the later religion of Latins and Romans, but without Greek influence. Their culture was simple, but of some refinement. Weapons and utensils were often well made of bronze. Dress was very simple, fastened by *fibulae* or safety pins, which the Italici were perhaps the first to use – they are a rare example of an invention found earlier in Italy than in Greece. They have left no sign of advanced political or military organization, and none of literature; though in the north of Italy the culture of the Villanovans, the most advanced Italici, reached great refinement at the end of the bronze age.

Presumably Minoan and Mycenaean culture, which pottery proves to have travelled as far as Italy and Sicily late in the bronze age, retained there at least in some degree its usual attributes of artistic and practical power, with a high degree of political and religious organization, and of skill at sea, and, at need, though they were peaceful people, at war. But there is no proof that this influence had more than a superficial effect on the fringe of Italian and Sicilian civilization; though there is some indication, in similarity of religious and social practices, that an element of population, living at and near the later Rome, was in some way ultimately akin to the Minoans and Mycenaeans.

The real active life of an advanced, vigorous and organized Italy begins for us, and perhaps for ancient scholars and poets too in so far as they understood the past, at a time when the Etruscans were firmly established in north and central Italy, and the Greeks, a few generations later, on the coasts of south and west Italy and Sicily. These processes occurred from the ninth to the sixth century B.C.; traditionally it was about the middle of the eighth century B.C. that Rome was founded. These are the centuries whose culture, on the whole, Vergil recreates by imagination. But blended with his picture are many later things, and also many whispers of a more distant past, which are heard in legends preserved by several ancient writers besides Vergil, and give hints of movements, situations, and active life at the time of the Trojan War, when Aeneas took on him the Trojan destiny, or even earlier times still. The world of the *Aeneid* is in this not very different from the world of other epics, especially of Homer's poetry. There, too, the ages meet: the heroic age of Troy's fall, and the age of Homer himself. In the *Aeneid* almost the same two ages meet; and with them, also, the age of Vergil himself, centuries after, and all the intervening centuries, and the future too.

Vergil, like Pindar and Euripides, for example, was a keen, acute, and devoted investigator of antiquity. He had the advantage of learned scholars to whom he could refer, especially Marcus Terentius Varro, who commanded in Spain against Julius, was forgiven by him, and later was made by Augustus chief librarian of his new public library. Vergil had earlier documents to use, such as Cato's *Origins* and Varro's *Trojan Families*, and he exploited local information.

He got by these means no unitary, historic picture of a single age in Italy's past, but instead a great many single elements, some perfectly historical.[1]

For example, Vergil, alone of ancient writers, emphatically asserts[2] the very ancient Italian custom, exemplified by the earliest graves, at the beginning of the first millennium B.C., in and near the Roman forum, of combining, or associating without great interval of time, the rites of cremation and inhumation at a place where the 'cremating' and 'inhuming' peoples met.[3]

He clearly reproduces facts of earlier warfare. Certain strange and obscure weapons are correctly attributed in the Seventh *Aeneid* to those tribes who used them; but there is no likelihood that they were anything like as early as the graves of the forum. The armies employ mounted infantry, meant to do their actual fighting on foot, not chariots only, as in Homer's heroic age, nor true cavalry fighting on horseback, as in the later historical wars of Rome, from the fourth century onwards. Mounted infantry, with some survival of chariots, is probably right for the eighth, seventh and sixth centuries B.C. Vergil reproduces the conditions of the same period in the material of weapons. They are mainly of iron, not of bronze, as usually in Homer. Other characteristics are later. Vergil's fighters bear heraldic emblems, especially on their shields. The custom points not to any heroic age but to Greek Campania of about the fourth century B.C. But again Greek influence cannot be excluded. Greeks of the Classical Age had emblems on their shields; such emblems are as powerful and symbolic in the *Seven against Thebes* of Aeschylus as they are in the *Aeneid*.

Almost everywhere in the Italy of the *Aeneid* there are signs of settled civic life, some organization, and wealth. Rich clothing and gold colour the battle pictures. Silver is more rare. This too represents the conditions of the Etruscan age, especially as disclosed on

1. Catharine Saunders, *Vergil's Primitive Italy*, New York, 1930, *passim*.
2. *A.* XI, 203–9.
3. Franz Altheim, *A History of Roman Religion*, translated by Harold Mattingly, London, 1938, 94–100, etc.

such sites as Tusculum and Praeneste, to the south and south-east of Rome.

To balance this picture there is another, going with it, a picture of the hardihood of Italian country folk and mountaineers, and their poverty and energy. That picture is equally true of many parts of Italy at most times, but truest of societies which were not assimilated to the civic life and wealthy ways of Etruscans and Greeks.

In the Seventh *Aeneid*, Vergil presents a 'gathering of the clans', and in the Tenth some account of the Etruscan contingents who followed their king Tarchon to help Aeneas. These passages recall Homer's 'catalogues' of the Greek ships and contingents, and the allies of the Trojans, but they are not nearly so historical. Homer seems here to have adopted tradition as he found it, but Vergil reconstructed what was recorded, a thing very difficult to do for shortage of material. Accordingly, Vergil used almost every breath of tradition that he could find. Some was local tradition; Vergil disliked missing any chance to introduce a reference to genuine local antiquities. But he was always willing to introduce these references in secondary forms, not only as Greek influence had in very early days modified them, but also as they had developed after literary treatment by Greeks and others in later times. There is therefore much conflation of Greek myth and legend, and many Greek names occur among Italian allusions. There is regularly a great advance in personalization. Messapus and Juturna were, by their Italian rites, water spirits: but in the *Aeneid* they take part in the war, the one as a human chieftain and the other as the divine sister of Turnus. They drew from their old characters their new. To Messapus belonged the horse-form appropriate to an earth and a water divinity, and so he becomes very much a 'horse-taming hero', son of Neptunus. Juturna's very name suggests in Latin 'a help to Turnus'; and so she becomes his sister, and helps him in his last fight.

Much of the mythical creation had been done before Vergil, some by Greek influence on Italy before ever Rome began. But even so it might be said that Vergil had a unique power of creating myth, with its full emotional and moral value and the symbolism of truth, by his own single mind, a power normally exercised

collectively, by the work of many minds through many generations.

However important the 'myth' or story of a poem may be,
scarcely less important, unless it chances to be after all the same
thing, is what the poet chooses to talk about on the way. Poems
put readers and hearers into moods in which they see and feel new
truth about the world; and they normally do so largely by presenting things to them with strongly real and noticeable qualities and
identities. The very mention of something suggestive, however
loosely the mention may be attached to the story, contributes to
the story's success.

Poets can be distinguished by their personal obsessions – the
things of which they cannot help writing, pictures in their mind
which they must express, and which tend to evoke in the percipient the same mood again and again. In ancient poetry the
individual gods helped in this way. Each was a complex of poetic
suggestion. Places could be used like this also. Whether anything
like the variety of significant percurrent imagery lately disclosed[1]
in English poetry is to be found in the poetry of Antiquity is not
yet known; but the same method, applied to it also, would
certainly have successful results.

Gold is the most important substance for Vergil, and he introduces it freely for all kinds of purposes, usually with the obvious
implication of wealth, light, and life, in contrast to some tragic
disaster. Equally schematic are his typical numbers. Again and
again he uses the numbers three, seven, twenty, and a hundred,
and they are nearer to imagery than to numerical statements. It
would be easy and interesting to work out the different kinds of
interest and awe, which the different numbers evoke.

Place names caught Vergil's imagination. He is readily driven
by emotional thoughts concerning power to think of Mount
Rhodope in Thrace, and the Acroceraunian Mountains in Epirus,
that 'Thunderbolt Headland' which he associates with storms.[2]

1. G. Wilson Knight, *The Wheel of Fire*, London, 1930, etc.; cf. Viktor
Pöschl, *The Art of Vergil: Image and Symbol in the Aeneid*, Ann Arbor,
Michigan, 1962.
2. See below, pp. 243–5.

The storms in Vergil are not easy to interpret. Bad weather seems in general to be for him as for Shakespeare a kind of cosmic accompaniment and signal of a failure in human love and friendliness. In the *Eclogues* when Daphnis dies the green things wither, an old classical motive going back to the supposed dependence of nature on the strength of divine priest-kings, which left strong traces in Greek tragedy. The enmity between storms and happy homes is obvious and literal in the *Georgics*; interestingly, the farmer is told that there is much useful work to do indoors; and the force with which the imagery of storm is delivered leaves no doubt of its poetic reality.

In the *Aeneid*, a storm is the instrument by which Juno seeks to destroy Aeneas but by which he is in fact driven to Carthage and Dido; he is compared to an oak, which storms cannot uproot, when he obeys heaven and will not stay with her; and there is a storm when he is sailing away, a storm in which, according to one of two conflicting versions in the *Aeneid*, Palinurus the helmsman fell into the sea. Whether there is some deep symbolism here, of the steering will deranged by passion, it is not yet possible to say, till Vergil's imagery is better understood.

Then there are trees, and especially the laurel. It grows both in Priam's palace, the start of the voyage of the Trojans, and in the palace of Latinus, its end. The meaning is suggested by the late R. W. Cruttwell,[1] and is shortly this. The laurel is deeply fixed and most ancient in Mediterranean culture; it has magic power, and roots humanity to the soil of its home. It suggests the oldest homes of men in huts and cattle in pens, it gave health – Epidaurus, the city of healing, was called after it (*l* often becomes *d*) – and it is near the start of the earth religion, of rescue and prophecy, which Apollo at Delphi inherited. There must be a laurel in a home secure and blessed by Heaven. Augustus knew, and he had a laurel, of which a miraculous tale was told.

Vergil found much of his imagery ready in current religious tradition. A thrill of doubt and fear comes when he mentions lawless magic; and a thrilled sense of duty and responsibility when he mentions sacrifice. Perhaps the frequent omens have a value as

1. R. W. Cruttwell, *Vergil's Mind at Work*, Oxford, 1946, 52–4, 133–4.

imagery too; there is a sudden renewal of faith and the reality of the divine guidance each time an omen is met.

A similar force of emotion is evoked when gods appear. The first hint of Juno releases a flood of fear. Her implacable persecution of Hercules and Aeneas his successor, and her favour to Greeks and Carthaginians, spring to life. Opposite are the emotions when Venus appears, softly touching her son, and all the new world to be, with rescue from heaven. With her in the rhythms and tones and words a soft golden light is shed, in contrast to the metallic sounds with which Juno is always introduced. Apollo is not like either. He is a god of light and hope, and beautiful; but he is terrible too in his power. He was worshipped almost above Jupiter by Augustus; and he was more important in the earlier than in the later draft of the *Aeneid*.

Long ago it was noticed[1] that when Aeneas descended to the world below, the labyrinth on the gate of the temple at Cumae symbolized the winding ways below the earth, and that, deep down, beyond hell, when Elysium is reached, the flowers and the bees in the sunlight there are symbols of life. The observation has been very productive.

Vergil's flowers are often literary and symbolical, as when, after Homer and Sappho, Vergil compares a young fighter at his death to a broken flower. In the *Eclogues*[2] there is once a great colourful mass of flowers and fruit, united for allegiance to some one loved; flowers are grown for their own sake in the *Georgics*[3] by the old pirate settled near Tarentum, no less than fruit.

Of the bees and the labyrinth there is more to say.

Vergil in the *Georgics* compared bees to men and in the *Aeneid* men to bees.[4] He takes the form and organization of a bee community, where each lives for all, as the start of human association. For him the beehive town of the bees is a miniature of the beehive

1. Margaret G. Verrall, *The Classical Review*, XXIV, 1910, 43–6. Cf. T. J. Haarhoff, 'The Bees of Vergil', *Greece and Rome*, VII, 1960, 155–70; Robert Coleman, *The American Journal of Philology*, LXXXIII, 1962, 55–71; and H. Malcolm Fraser, *Beekeeping in Antiquity*, London, 1931, 2nd ed. 1951.

2. *E.* II, 45–55: cf. T. J. Haarhoff, 'Vergil's Flower Garden', *Greece and Rome*, V, 1958, 67–82, a delightful and revealing article.

3. *G.* IV, 130–8.

4. Cruttwell, ibid., 51–2, Ch. IX, 115–26, Ch. X, 127–42.

hut town of men, the typical form of very early human settlement
in the Mediterranean lands, and perhaps the form of earliest Rome,
where the 'cottage of Romulus' and the round temple of Vesta,
symbol of the earth, the city, and the fire on the king's hearth,
survived to recall the old beehive life of men. The bees live in a
service which is perfect freedom, and men should too. They rightly
symbolize[1] the freedom of saints in Vergil's Elysium, when death,
symbolized, in contrast, by all kinds of binding restraint, is passed
and overcome. The arrival of the Trojans in Latium is presaged by
a swarm of bees in the citadel of Latinus, on a laurel tree.

Almost correlative with the bees is the labyrinth, the very picture of restraint, obstruction, and bewilderment. It has through
most of history symbolized the entry to the cave tomb, or the
entry to the earth mother, and to life again after. It has symbolized
too the defences, human and superhuman, of the civilized city,
within which a beehive life goes on. But Vergil uses this symbolic
complex in greater detail than that.

Among Vergil's recurrent images are the circular and labyrinthine movement.[2] Circles, or encirclements, are intimated in the
wall of Troy,[3] Vesta's temple,[4] the round grave, encircled by a
snake,[5] the rivers and Cyclopean walls of Hades,[6] the circumam-
bulation of a victim round the fields, and round an altar,[7] the rings
on the shield of Aeneas,[8] a spinning top,[9] encirclements which
are a love charm,[10] and the circular movements of the fighting
heroes, especially in the last fight of Mezentius.[11] The more
tortuous movements are in the Trojan Game, with the labyrinth
and the course of the dolphins to which it is compared,[12] the labyrinth on the temple gate at Cumae,[13] and the wanderings of Aeneas
from Troy, expressed in words[14] which could equally mean the
wanderings of a maze, the very meaning, in some contexts, of Troy's
name.

1. *A.* VI, 707–9.
2. Cruttwell, ibid., Ch. VIII, 83–97 and elsewhere: some of the ensuing
examples are more explicit than others – for example all cyclopean walls are
not circular but all contain the element *cyclo-* in their name, which is enough.
3. *A.* I, 483, etc.   4. *A.* II, 567–8, etc.   5. *A.* V, 84–93.
6. *A.* VI, 132, etc.; 630–1.   7. *G.* I, 345.   8. *A.* VIII, 448–9.
9. *A.* VII, 378–83.   10. *E.* VIII, 73–8.   11. *A.* X, 882–7.
12. *A.* V, 580–95.   13. *A.* VI, 14–33.   14. *A.* X, 110.

The images go back to an earlier layer of thought[1] at which the circle was magical, and sharply distinguished the outside of a hut or settlement from the inside. It is symbolic of defence and sanctity. So is the labyrinth, but it is more complicated. Partly it represents the circle, and partly the cave, or the tomb, which was at first a cave, or the earth, which is the universal mother. This is a wide department of old folk-lore, which has had an immense effect on the creation of myth and on the subsequent psychology of mankind; and it is intensely remembered and realized by Vergil.

Associated with the artificial labyrinth for Vergil is the picture of underground passages and cavities. They had been associated by Lucretius with volcanoes and with rivers, and with volcanoes by another poet also, the poet, reputed to be Vergil, of the strange poem called *Aetna*. The poem as it stands is probably later than Vergil, but some of it at least is earlier, and it may contain a poem on Etna by Vergil himself, from which it has been expanded. At any rate, Vergil's imagination was captured by underground passages and cavities. He mentions them in describing the home of Cyrene to which Aristaeus went,[2] the river basin of the Tiber,[3] Mount Etna and the Liparae Islands,[4] Hades,[5] and the home of the volcano giant, Cacus, at Rome.[6]

Vergil's imagination, deeply rooted in the past, readily inherited and retained volcanic symbols, for both in Italy and in Crete, in which Vergil takes a mysterious interest, volcanic and seismic phenomena were in strong control before history begins. They are attached for him to the ideal complex of labyrinths, circles, and rivers; but they have a further importance, also.

This was first suggested, and proved, by the late R. W. Cruttwell.[7] Throughout the *Aeneid* there are two forces, which he calls the Volcanic and the Vestal. There is war and peace, the outer world and the home. Aeneas has responsibilities in both; he is Volcanically armed for Volcanic war, and initiated 'Volcanically' at Cumae and on the site of Rome; and all the time he preserves the 'Vestal' life of his family and his people, and builds the home life of

1. W. F. J. Knight, *Cumaean Gates*, Oxford, 1936, *passim*.
2. *G.* IV, 333–56.   3. *A.* VIII, 65–7.   4. *A.* VIII, 416–23.
5. *A.* VI, 236–67, etc.   6. *A.* VIII, 241–6.
7. R. W. Cruttwell, ibid, 98–112.

his city to be. The dwellers in the city and in the home are past, present, and to come. As the late Professor H. J. Rose[1] has shewn, the Italians of the early iron age buried their cremated dead in urn-fields where they could take part with the living and defend them. The primitive custom had been to bury the dead actually in the house. Vergil, in his picture of the Rome which was to be for all the world a home, and was so regarded, nearly four centuries later, by Claudian and others,[2] brilliantly shews in Elysium all the Roman family, past, present, and to come, together in a single vision. What Aeneas carried from Troy has been acutely if precariously conjectured by Mr Cruttwell. He carried a hut-urn, an urn to contain cremated ashes in the shape of a miniature hut. The round hut was primitive in the Mediterranean, and is known before the thirtieth century B.C. in Crete. There are also hut-urns, dated before the twentieth century B.C., found in the island of Melos. The round hut was similar in Sardinia and elsewhere. In Italy, it was the pattern of the long-preserved sacred 'beehive' hut of Romulus, and of Vesta's round temple. So the round hut-urn that Aeneas carried with the images of the gods of Troy, the ashes of her heroes, and her sacred, undying fire, might well represent the continuity of past, present, and future, and within the Vestal circle keep safe from Volcanic dangers the life of Rome to be. There are still villages of 'beehive huts' in Italy.

In the *Georgics*, Vergil conquered for poetry Italian agriculture, already almost a traditional subject for prose since the translation into Latin from Phoenician of Mago's works. Agriculture meant discipline, and the hardness of old Rome. Cato, the typically hard, wrote on agriculture. Vergil took, therefore, encouragement and exaltation from heroic life in books and elsewhere. He drills his fields like troops. The vines march up the hills.[3] Diamond formation, right in battle, must be strictly kept in the fields too. A poor farmer's life, with few possessions, and much to be done, suggests to him the fine picture[4] of the steely Roman soldier, carrying everything with him and hung round with equipment 'like a Christmas tree' as our soldiers say, marching, marching, and then quickly in

1. H. J. Rose, *The Classical Quarterly*, XXIV, 1930, 129–35.
2. T. J. Haarhoff, *The Stranger at the Gate*, London, 1938, 291–2.
3. *G.* II, 276–87.   4. *G.* III, 339–48.

position, dug in, before the enemy could ever have guessed. Italy is the home of hard, resolute men;[1] Marsians, always troops of first quality; prolific Sabellians, who spread through half Italy with their habit of the 'sacred spring', sending a whole age-class of manhood out when the order was given; all of which Vergil characteristically expresses in two words, *pubem Sabellam*, 'prolific manhood of Sabellians';[2] Ligurians, too, inured to hardships; Volscians with their short spears; and the home of all great Romans too, the Scipios who made themselves hard – how, Vergil had to write the *Aeneid* to guess; and, last of all, Augustus Caesar, still going the old Roman way, and winning at that moment the distant east for Rome. The subjects of Vergil's poem on war and politics often correspond with the imagery of his country poems; whose subjects in turn provide the imagery for the great poem of politics and war.

Vergil's cows and bees, and other creatures, are regularly humanized. A bull fights for dominion and for love, is defeated, and trains hard for revenge. Vergil looks into the heart of birds, that foretell weather changes by their behaviour, playing, *nescioqua praeter solitum dulcedine laeti* 'revelling in some rare, mysterious joy';[3] but he decides that they are not, as some thought, inspired, but, in Professor Rand's phrase, just 'self-important but automatic prophets'. Nor will Vergil allow divine inspiration to bees. They work and work, like a perfectly organized human community; with utter loyalty to their 'kings', but in risk of sedition if there are two 'kings'; fighting valiantly, and terrifically, but peaceful at once if a little dust is thrown on them; intent, at cost of life, that 'the fortune of their house' should 'endure'; *stat fortuna domus*,[4] said Vergil, and made the thought a key to Heaven's gates in the *Aeneid*.

To make country things his own and understand them, with contentment, Vergil applied to them literary heroism, and literary wisdom. So he talked of them in human metaphors. Afterwards, in the *Aeneid*, he had to make heroisms, more real and horrible, his

1. *G.* II, 167–72.   2. *G.* II, 167.

3. *G.* I, 412; cf. John G. Landels, 'The Two Cultures in Vergil', *The Proceedings of the Virgil Society*, II, 1962–3, Lecture Summary No. 61.

4. *G.* IV, 209.

own, and to find a place for them in the home country of his mind. So he applied to them metaphors from the country, reversing his process. A fight is like conflicting winds, or like a battle between bulls; sailors preparing to sail are like ants at work; an army is like cranes; and a pursuit is like the pursuit of a pigeon by a hawk.

Characteristic of early thinking and early poetry is a direct comparison of the unknown to the known. Apparently, humanity in a simple stage of development no less than in a scientific age regards the explanation of a thing as the first step to control of it, perhaps magical. That is seen especially in the old Finnish epic, the *Kalevala*. And the explanation of a thing is obviously helped by a knowledge of what it is like. Accordingly, epic poetry regularly has many similes, that is, short passages comparing, to some well-known state of things, a new state of things, which has just occurred in the narrative. At the stage which Homer has reached, there is nothing primitive about similes. They are artistic devices, controlling delicately and powerfully the mind of the percipient, as the poet wills. They create effects by reinforcement, contrast, and general enrichment of the moment's mental world. Sometimes they afford relief in hot action. On the whole, they are part of imagery, and work like other imagery.[1] All imagery is ultimately, at the same time, both comparison and also just what the poet chooses to mention; and what the poet chooses to

1. Cf. W. Elmslie Philip, 'Virgil's Similes, an Example of his Artistic Perfection', *The Great Tradition* (Lectures to the Exmouth Virgil Society, Spring 1945), 1945, II: Vergil 'used simile to regulate the thematic material of his poem, to bring out contrasts of character and of situation, and to bring out the human and emotional element in his story. By choice of language, and by masterly use of it, Virgil's similes are knit with their context. By connexion of subject and of ideas, simile is linked with simile, and a contrast visualized with telling effect. By the massing of similes the full power of pictorial imagination is called in to create a dramatic climax. There is little anywhere in narrative or epic poetry to compare with the closing scenes in the Twelfth Book of the *Aeneid*, where simile plays a vital role.' It is to be hoped that Mr Elmslie Philip's extensive work on the similes will soon be published. Cf. Viktor Pöschl, *The Art of Vergil; Image and Symbol in the Aeneid*, Ann Arbor, Michigan, 1962, whose valuable treatment of all this subject and especially similes is in sympathy with certain British habits of thought.

mention, in a certain order and rhythm, almost *is* the poem. That sounds obvious, but it has been almost as much unnoticed as it is important.

Alternation and reconciliation normally occur together in similes. A new world of comparison alternates with the world of action; and the comparison reconciles the action to perception, by the relief, and also by the picture given of something known.

The similes are sometimes far from ornamental, but are intrinsically authentic art. Like early, simple people who found it easier to see a river as a bull that was also a man than simply as a river, poets see things most satisfactorily, or indeed only, in partial identity with something else; and that is the root of metaphor and simile. Vergil understood a battle best if he saw it as some kind of storm, or forest fire. These great images run right through his work, as a poetic obsession; we have lately learnt that these great recurrent images are, more than any other part of their art, the very language of poets.

Some similes have great expressional density. It has been noticed that Homer's similes start with a single point of similarity, and develop themselves in more or less complete detachment from the thing that suggested the comparison, but that Vergil's similes continue in similarity, making contact at several points. Homer's similes, like much else in Homer, are nearer to an early condition of thought, in which ideas suggest ideas and those ideas more ideas, so that in the excitement of the moment the start is forgotten, sometimes even at the cost of syntax. Shakespeare makes fun out of this habit of thought, in speeches of the Nurse in *Romeo and Juliet* and Mistress Quickly in *Henry IV*, *Part* 2. Vergil's tendency is to make realities acceptable and tolerable by a coincidence as exact as possible with known, friendly realities. He diverges pictorially like Homer; but he also arrays a multiple correspondence, and sometimes achieves an exact and elaborate symbolism.

When Aeneas, having reached Latium, tries to sleep, but is prevented by anxiety, his thoughts, says Vergil,[1] flit like light reflected from a cauldron, in rays that shine straight up to the ceiling. This simile is much the same in Apollonius,[2] where it indicates the flicker of a first love dawning in Medea's mind.

1. *A.* viii, 18–25.   2. Apollonius Rhodius, *Argonautica*, iii, 755–60.

The contrast is powerful at the start. Aeneas has a mind sensitive to hopes and fears, not quite unlike the young Medea's, in spite of the greatness thrust upon him. In a way he is passive, too; the light is reflected light; he does not really want to plan and worry, but he has to follow the divine guidance, and do his part. The contrast comes from the tremendous importance of Aeneas for the future. He must decide right, for the hope of Rome, and human civilization. Medea stakes only the happiness of herself, and her home.

There is another comparison; in fact two. Once elsewhere a cauldron of water is a symbol; when the thoughts of Turnus are compared in a simile[1] to a cauldron that boils, and sends upwards dark clouds of smoke and steam, while the room must, of course, be lighted red by the fire. Turnus has been inspired with hate and fury by Allecto. His thoughts boil violently, and emit darkness from themselves, against a red glare, not light reflected from the divine sun.

Now at that other landing, in Africa, Aeneas disobeyed, and then, overwhelmingly convinced by the god Mercurius himself, obeyed at last. There were no two ways for him. But, there in Africa, it was Dido who had to plan; and she was planning for her death, not, as Aeneas in Latium, for life. She then, and Aeneas after, when all other living things had rest and forgetfulness, explored in thought every way, and, like his, her mind was tempestuous.[2] Again and again the same words and rhythms are used, with a very Vergilian change; for Dido's mind was tempestuous with a tide of fury, but the mind of Aeneas was a tide of 'cares'.

Dido is threaded through the later part of the *Aeneid* like a memory of the country, gained in Vergil's early life, and retained from the *Eclogues* or the *Georgics*. Here it is hard to miss the force in the comparison. Aeneas is suffering at his landing in Italy the same tribulation that he himself inflicted on Dido when he landed in Africa. His suffering is more creative than hers, but he is less blameless; though Turnus, who has most right on his side, is yet somehow, with his *furor* and his *violentia*, less blameless and less creative than either. All have their due sympathy.

Dido is evoked, when Iulus rides a horse she gave,[3] or Aeneas

1. *A.* VII, 461–6.　　2. *A.* IV, 522–32.　　3. *A.* V, 570–2.

presents a bowl given by her;[1] when Cleopatra, victim, like her, of a 'marriage', is 'pale with the death to come',[2] described in almost exactly the words in which Dido has been described; Dido is there in other echoes, thought, sound and rhythm, too; but, above all there is her meeting with Aeneas in Hades,[3] when, in the agony of his last talk to her, and in his fright at her resolute fury with him, he saw his last hope of her, if any had lingered, depart.

There is another side to the question. Dido was a danger to New Troy, as the Greek attack had been destructive to the old. The two thoughts are exquisitely linked by a pair of similes, each a memory of country things.

Aeneas, the veil withdrawn by his divine mother, sees all Troy settling into the fires; and falling, like an old mountain ash, attacked all round by farming men, with axes of steel; its trunk yields to the shock, and its crest nods; then down it comes, trailing havoc behind.[4]

When Dido entreats Aeneas to stay, he is like an ancient oak, blown every way by winds; the leaves wave violently, but the roots – the very words are from the *Georgics* – stretch as deeply down as the crest towers high, and hold firm. So did the *mens*, the instinctive, visionary will, of Aeneas hold.[5]

Troy is attacked by men with steel, and Aeneas by the winds of passion, which are like Shakespeare's metaphorical tempests. Troy is on the crests, too high, too proud; the Troy of Laomedon forsook her gods; Troy, lacking root, had to fall. Aeneas, by grace, we could say, by the loyalty that *pietas* forced on him – he was *pius Aeneas*, 'Aeneas the true' – could stand. For his father was Anchises, not Laomedon, and he stood firmly on a truer, Dardan, past, and listened to deeper voices in his heart. So he stood firm; and the tears, and not Dido's only, rolled helplessly.

Country memories continue to contribute the blend of thought with thing, and the assimilation of the new and strange to the familiar and the already won.

In the Fourteenth *Iliad*, to save the Greeks whom Zeus was leaving to defeat, Hera beguiled Zeus back to his old love for her and distracted him. In the Eighth *Aeneid*,[6] Volcanus – the Latin of

1. *A.* IX, 265–6. 2. *A.* VIII, 709. 3. *A.* VI, 450–76.
4. *A.* II, 624–31. 5. *A.* IV, 437–49. 6. *A.* VIII, 370–406.

Hephaestus – is so beguiled by Venus – the Latin of Aphrodite –, but to make arms, not to neglect the war. In the Eighteenth *Iliad* the shield of Achilles is made by Hephaestus, because Patroclus, killed fighting and bearing the arms of Achilles, has lost them; Achilles needs new arms, whereas Aeneas only needs better ones; both times the arms are made through the entreaty of the hero's mother, in the *Iliad* Thetis, and in the *Aeneid* Venus; but Venus appeals with love, and not, as Thetis, with the recollection of a debt owed to her.

Having got so far, it was just the time, says Vergil,[1] when a cottage woman in Italy, trying to keep her home together for her family in loyal purity, will wake the sleeping fire, and work, and keep the maids working, weaving on, and adding all the night time to their working.

Then – like her, just as active, and at the same late hour, up rose the god whose might is fire, to make those arms for the Prince of Destiny, whose mother was Love, and whose hand must be strong. He called to his Cyclopes, volcano powers, Thunder, Lightning, Fire-anvil were their names – *Brontes*, *Steropes*, and *Pyracmon*, stripped 'to the limbs'. They were making thunderbolts for Jupiter, an 'aegis' for Minerva, and a chariot for Mars. 'Put all that away', he said. 'There are arms to make, arms for a man, to make him bold. Now you need all your master skill.'

So they made the arms in the volcano's heart, those elemental powers of metal, and might, and fire. It was just like a mother, a small farmer's wife in Italy, who works and works, and will not give way. The work was done, with a will like hers.[2]

Not many parts of the *Aeneid* have so good a claim to be, not just nearly, but quite, Vergil's greatest. That is, for the idea alone, the story, the 'myth'; without counting the majesty of the verse, and the little things, like 'arms for a man', reminding us that the destiny of 'arms and a man', the opening words of the poem, is not failing. Perhaps Vergil remembered his earlier passages, where he had talked of comparing small things to great; once, a small

1. *A.* VIII, 407–42.

2. R. S. Conway, *The Proceedings of the Classical Association*, XXV, 1928, 34–5, quoting A. W. Verrall.

town to Rome herself,[1] and later bees, at work, to Cyclopes in their cave.[2]

Vergil was guided more by audial and intellectual than by visual images, but his visual images are also strong, and sometimes they initiate and control his creation. It would often be possible to discover when it is that they do.

Perhaps the visual dominates most in the *Eclogues* before the audial images have gathered momentum. There, there are lovely clear images of sight. 'See how the bullocks are bringing home the plough hung from the yoke, and the sun declining doubles the shadows' length';[3] 'and now the roofs of the farms in the distance are smoking, and the shadows that fall from the mountains are larger now';[4] 'an apple Galatea shies at me, the naughty, dashing off to the willows, and wanting to be seen first all the time'.[5]

Vergil, in the *Georgics*, really saw a horse's 'clear cut head, short barrel, and fat quarters',[6] and, with a miracle of expression, how a high-bred horse, at a trumpet call, 'cannot stand still; his ears a-quiver, his legs trembling, as he holds, compressed and rolling, clouds of fire, up in his nostrils', *stare loco nescit*; *micat auribus et tremit artus, collectumque premens volvit sub naribus ignem.*[7]

In the *Aeneid* the visually sharp sometimes comes as a change. 'Dido herself, so lovely, pouring a wine-offering from the bowl in her hand, right between the horns of a white-gleaming cow', is clearly seen, doing what rites she can in hope of keeping her joy, or 'pacing before gods' faces there, near their fat altars', and as she 'gazed, mouth open, questioning the breathing flesh' of the sacrifices.[8] Clearly seen, too, is the priestess whom she consulted, 'that priestess, hair astream, telling in voice of thunder her thrice hundred gods',[9] the priestess who fed the dragon that guards the tree, 'sprinkling wet honey drops, and poppy charged with sleep'.[10]

The Third *Aeneid*, otherwise so close to earlier work, is remarkable for clear pictures; especially 'the harbour went bending back

1. *E.* i, 23.　　2. *G.* iv, 176.　　3. *E.* ii, 66–7.
4. *E.* i, 82–3.　　5. *E.* iii, 64–5.
6. *G.* iii, 80; cf. the delightful treatment of this slightly unexpected thoroughbred by Mlle A.-M. Guillemin, *Virgile, poète, artiste et penseur*, Paris, 1951, 158–9.
7. *G.* iii, 84–5.　　8. *A.* iv, 60–4.　　9. *A.* iv, 509–11.
10. *A.* iv, 483–6.

from the south-eastern waves, to form a bow; with barriers of rocks, afoam with the salt spray, hiding it behind, where towered crags let down their pair of arms, their wall; the temple shrinking back away from the shore';[1] and 'Petelia, little town, resting firmly on its own ring wall',[2] for the town seen from the sea, with its wall at the foot of its little hill, looked as if the wall were supporting the town, perched on it.

But throughout Vergil's work at any moment a clear visual image may come. In the Eighth *Aeneid* the Tiber is 'grazing his banks, as he cuts rich farming land;[3] and in the Tenth a hero, Halaesus, crouches to attack, 'gathering himself into the arms about him', *seque in sua colligit arma*,[4] another miracle of expression.

There is a special kind of visual perception in Vergil, concerned with works of art. He sees them when he describes them. Examples are the carved cups in the *Eclogues*,[5] and in the *Aeneid* the pictures on the walls at Carthage,[6] which made Aeneas weep as in similar circumstances the lay of a minstrel made Odysseus weep; and then the sculptured temple-gate at Cumae,[7] many emblems, especially on shields, in the later books of the *Aeneid*, and figureheads of ships in the fifth book and the tenth. Above all, there is the shield of Aeneas,[8] divinely made, like the shields of Achilles in Homer and of Heracles in Hesiod. It is perhaps not quite safe to say that only the shield of Achilles could actually be constructed. Vergil's shield would be complicated, but its panels are well designed, in balanced, artistic composition. And all the time it gives something like an allegorical microcosm of the whole *Aeneid*.[9]

Another kind of visual apprehension in Vergil is his description of dreams. Above all, there is the nightmare of Dido,[10] dreaming that, pursued by Aeneas, she is going down a long road alone, looking for the Tyrians in a waste land. That is a real dream, seen by Vergil himself and perfectly told. Much of the Sixth *Aeneid* may be dreamland, but some certainly is, especially the inspiration of

1. *A.* iii, 533–6. 2. *A.* iii, 401–2. 3. *A.* viii, 62–3.
4. *A.* x, 412. 5. *E.* iii, 35–43. 6. *A.* i, 450–93.
7. *A.* vi, 20–33. 8. *A.* viii 625–731.
9. D. L. Drew, *The Allegory of the Aeneid*, Oxford, 1927, 6–41.
10. *A.* iv, 465–8.

the Sibyl by Apollo,[1] who rides her, like a horse. That is a well-known dream experience, from which it has been actually supposed that the word 'nightmare' is derived. Finally, there is the frightful experience of Turnus, fighting his last fight in a terrible, unhappy dream, a world gone mad, with no gods left to trust.[2] All is mystical, as Professor W. A. Laidlaw suggested to me. The whole *Aeneid* ends in a nightmare world. Vergil found new meanings in Homer's death of Hector, when by a trick of Athena Deiphobus his brother was there, and then vanished, and he had no spear, though the spear of Achilles was miraculously given back to him after a throw. Homer may have been tapping a dream experience; Vergil certainly was, and infusing into the Homeric mould a direct dream vision of frustration and hopelessness.

Vergil's poetry of the ear is harder to miss than his poetry of the eye; but often, when the waves of sound fill the world, and it is hard to be ready for the sharper visual images, even when they are there, yet recurrent imagery still appeals to sight and communicates a light and a colour, spread over all the scene.

In the *Eclogues* the landscape pictures bring their own colour, hot sunshine and deep shadow, with often a splash of more, perhaps when the names of flowers, their contrasts asserted, are introduced. The visual scene is mainly sunshine, and how things seem in sunshine in different moods; and the hot Campanian midday may melt into the sunshine of evening, the softening of the light helping the structure of the poem to soften a sadness or bring a conflict to rest.

Light-imagery in the *Georgics* is not so strong, but more varied. It does not often help to create a world of some predominant colour tone; more usually the moments and even single objects bring their own colour, adjectival to themselves only. There is so much of the country in the *Georgics*, and so much, and so rapidly, of the country's changing moods. You see the lightning flash out of the clouds, and a world all brown with rain; or some grey, misty, watery tract of land; or sunshine in an orchard.

The dominance of unifying colour imagery belongs rather to dramatic poetry; it cannot help the *Georgics* as much as it can help the *Eclogues* and *Aeneid*, which, here as in other matters, agree

1. *A.* VI, 77–80.   2. *A.* XII, 614–96, 728–90, 843–952.

together in some contrast with the intervening poem. But at the end, the *Georgics* provide something like an instructive exception to their own rule. The fourth book ends with the story of Aristaeus, who lost his bees, and heard from Proteus, through the advice of his mother Cyrene, a nymph below the sea, the cause, and the way to a remedy. Here dominant colours can be found, and especially a cool green pervading shimmer in Cyrene's world on the sea's floor.

Throughout the *Aeneid*, there is nearly always some dominant light or colour, sometimes recalled from Vergil's earlier work, and sometimes new. In the first and third books there are landscapes and seascapes coloured like sights in the *Georgics*; and the over-civilized red and gold of Dido's imperial home had also been practised in the *Georgics* before, so that we may be reminded that they are in contrast with the destiny of Aeneas, as they had been in contrast with Italian country homes. The colours in the second book during the last night of Troy are sharper and stronger, and they are a great part of that book's majesty. Mainly, there is an alternation of black darkness in the lost city with sudden scenes of bright or blazing light. Sometimes there is clear moonlight, which Vergil is artist enough to forget when black dark is needed; sometimes the hot red glare of the burning, the colour of the flames speaking of the blood that is being shed; and once there is the lovely, kindly sunlight of home, the home of the *Eclogues*, and of heaven, the heaven that the sixth book is to proclaim; and it shines out on Aeneas when his own divine mother comes to save him in all the murk, and the blood, and the glare. There are more changes too; a different light in the home of Aeneas when he tries to persuade his family to come with him; a new light in the sky when a shooting star foretells hope for them; then dark again, in their flight; a gleam of arms; and a ghostly light, matching high, thin vowel tones, when the wraith of the lost Creusa, his wife, appears to Aeneas; and last the new fresh cleansing light of dawn, when the morning star arises, and life begins anew out of death. In the fourth book, there are old colours from the first book, and from the *Georgics*; they are more elaborate and less bold than the colours of the fall of Troy. Of colours in the fifth book there is less to say, though they are there. The sixth is richer in them, with great variation at first; then a steady dark gleam, like sea depths or woods in a weak moon, ghostly, grim; and later the bright, pure sunshine of heaven, with white-robed figures of saints and heroes, yet to live, or whose life is done.

In the second half of the *Aeneid* the tonality is enriched. There are stately homes, rich fighting dress and armour, colourful ships, colourful birds, and the blood of battle. The battle scenes are full of red-purple and gold. How rich and vital, we say, was the Italy which Aeneas found. Then comes the end; and perhaps nowhere else do tones of colour and light take such great part in the message that Vergil tells. The brightness of the battle melts into a weird grey. Only by a cloud is Turnus at first saved. Smoke rises from the burning city. A light of death and dream pervades the world of Turnus; deluded by a spirit of evil, in the form of a deathly bird of night, he has nothing secure to his sight or his touch. Weapons betray him; his divine sister leaves him; his mind is beset by sight and memory of friends swept helplessly from him in his helplessness. But Aeneas is real, towering over him, brutal and vindictive now; and Turnus is real to himself, and to us, when he takes the point, and his spirit flies.

A thorough examination of the imagery of Vergil has long been wanted, and is still to be done. But work has begun. The late R. W. Cruttwell discovered some dominant intellectual conceptions of Vergil's mind, as they spring from ancient and half-forgotten cult and superstition, especially the labyrinthine circles and spirals, and the antagonism between things 'Volcanic' and things 'Vestal', which condition Vergil's thinking with geometric and dynamic forms. Miss Janet Bacon[1] has started a different line of research.

1. J. R. Bacon, *The Classical Review*, LIII, 1939, 97–104. Interest in many kinds of Vergilian symbolism is increasing fast; cf. for example Vinzenz Buchheit, *Vergil über die Sendung Roms*, Heidelberg, 1963; Francesco Arnaldi, *Studi Virgiliani*, Naples, undated but about 1944, with its fine sense of Vergilian symbolism; Viktor Poschl, *The Art of Vergil: Image and Symbol in the Aeneid*, Ann Arbor, Michigan, 1962 (see p. 184 n. above), perhaps the first book devoted to this subject; Benjamin Farrington, 'Vergil and Lucretius', *Acta Classica, The Proceedings of the Classical Association of South Africa*, 1, 1958, 45–50; and of course the pioneer work of the late R. W. Cruttwell, *Vergil's Mind at Work*, Oxford, 1946. F. W. H. Myers, 'Virgil', *Essays: classical*, London, 1883, and many reprints, already, exactly though shortly, estimates Vergil's symbolic method.

She has examined the eighth book of the *Aeneid*, and found in it a pervasive quality mainly imparted by insistence on colour and a mental mood.

Aeneas sails to the mouth of the Tiber, and up the Tiber, to the site of later Rome. There he makes friends with Evander and his Arcadian Greeks, and is shewn the marvels of the site, already old, and already historic. Jove is there; and Hercules had come there, and saved the Arcadians from the volcanic fire devil, Cacus. Aeneas, as Miss Bacon discovers, is 'in Wonderland'. All is bright and new. It is a fresh, and freshening, turn of his destiny. He accepts the burden of Hercules and Herculean service. There is a thrill, and a glory now; not, except in the first part of the book, anxiety and dreariness, and memories of lost Dido.

In this first part of the book are frequent touches, linking this moment to others, in earlier and later parts of the poem. Phrases recall firstly the vision of dead Hector in the second book, when he warned Aeneas to escape from Troy, and gave him the Trojan sanctities to take with him, and secondly another vision in the third book, when the Penates themselves, the gods of the Trojan home and Trojan state, appeared to Aeneas, directing him to Italy. This time it is the god of the river Tiber that appears to him again in a vision in the night.

When the main story begins, all is light and colour and tranquillity, a tranquillity new to Aeneas. He had no idea that he could find such peace, or indeed such a friend as he, according to Dr T. R. Glover[1] 'the most solitary figure in literature', now found in Pallas, Evander's son. It is better than at that other landing, at Carthage, now. All is colour, and all is wonder; the chief word for wonder occurs four times as often in the eighth book as it occurs, on an average, in the rest of the poem. And after this book Aeneas scarcely wonders at all. The light-imagery proves that it is a new world. 'The Julian house has come out of darkness and wavering light, through storm, into the brilliant state of semi-divinity. This light-sequence is an epitome of the whole book and in some measure of the whole *Aeneid*. The light, like the wonder, is most noticeable in the eighth book. Up to this, except for some beautiful dawns and a fine day for the funeral games in Book V, light has

1. T. R. Glover, *Virgil*, London, 3rd ed., 1920, 221.

been fitful: flashes of lightning, occasional glitters, the smoky light of torches, lamps in Dido's banqueting-hall, the lambent fires that burned Troy, the "lux maligna" of an uncertain moon, the tail of a comet, the portentous flame round the head of the child Iulus, the supernatural fires that lit the dangerous liaison with Dido.' There have been a few moments of clear, steady light: as when Aeneas came out of the cloud that concealed him at Carthage, when the Penates appeared to him, and when he came to the Elysian fields of heavenly sunshine. 'But there has been nothing like this growing brightness; Aeneas has led his life in the shadow.' Now he and his world glitter; and it is Turnus who, at the very end of the *Aeneid*, 'passes into the shadow . . . It is Virgil's last word.'[1]

1. J. R. Bacon, *The Classical Review*, LIII, 1939, 103.

CHAPTER 5

LANGUAGE, VERSE, AND STYLE

VERGIL is great partly because the aspects of his art converge and cohere so well that it is extremely difficult to discuss them separately.[1] Thus his language, metre, rhythm, and style of expression are all so fused together that they are not individually obtrusive. His metre, the hexameter, helps to make his language, and is part of the style; and the style, whatever may reasonably be meant by the word, is not really separable from the hexameter. There remain however some signs in Vergil's work that the conflict between metre and language, so obvious in most of his predecessors, had not been quite surpassed. The fusion is not so faultless that it has reached the enervating facility of Vergil's successors. But metre is only part. In and near Vergil's life-time much happened to Latin prose style. Its development was partly but not wholly connected with the controversy between the Asianists and the Atticists. In Vergil's early years Atticism began to prevail, after long years of eclipse.

Cicero himself had a great share in developing the periodic structure characteristic of classical Latin, and then in starting the devolution of it, back, or on, to the word-order normal in Late Latin and the Romantic Languages, and in modern English, too. The periodic structure was partly artificial in Latin, and due to Greek oratory; but as usual there are two sides, and Latin really had a tendency to accept and augment such influence, through its psychological habit of making statement not precede, but follow description. English and other modern languages say, 'we saw that immediately'; but classical and in fact early Latin, 'we that immediately saw', describing the action first, and stating the fact of it at the end.

1. Cf. T. S. Eliot, *What is a Classic?*, First Presidential Address (1944) to the Virgil Society, London, 1945, who correlates the genius of Vergil with the condition of human culture attained when he was writing.

This was the tendency, and when it was developed by organizing not only words but also phrases and clauses in this order, and by an active preference for emphasizing what was important by reducing the number of main statements, and therefore for subordination rather than co-ordination, it produced the characteristic period of classical Latin prose. It is noticed, however, that even Cicero does not, most often, fully subordinate clauses. He subordinates a number of parallel clauses, which follow each other, to a main clause, of which the most important part, often the main verb, is at the end of the sentence, and often, but not always, he uses characteristic Latin word-order within the clauses. He is less inclined to subordinate clauses to each other by enclosing each clause within another clause logically prior to it. This further step is said to be characteristic of Livy, who wrote when Cicero's latest speeches had already begun the devolution towards our modern word-order. A thoroughly periodic structure may have been less easy for an audience to understand; although a little practice and experiment in Latin conversation shews, even now, that Latin word-order is quite wrongly supposed to be much harder to understand in speech than English order. After all, German, in its order, comes in between English and Latin: it often has what in English would count as an inversion.

Almost equally important for Vergil's verse were the new periodic prose and the old repetitive poetry. Any examination of all Vergil's certainly authentic work suggests that there is something which can be called the mould which principally limited and conditioned his poetic process. If it is possible to distinguish form and content, this is the form. The form was not merely a negative limitation; it imposed habits of thinking and feeling, and created and intensified proclivities. Vergil seems increasingly to have owed to this form his peculiar readiness of response, and the characteristic movement of his poetic activity. It became engrammatic.

The form is the Vergilian period or movement, a group of hexameter lines, built together so that the group, not the single line, is the unit. It is hard enough to imagine the real Vergil without the hexameter, which he used as no one else ever used it in the three works that are certainly his; but, after some observation and reflection, it is probably harder still to imagine him in his maturity without his still more characteristic verse-period.

It has been noticed that in Homer the single line is much more unitary than in Vergil, and that Vergil by contrast builds long structures, which belong naturally to a far later stage of development; and of course much is usually said about Vergil's art of varying the pauses, so that they come at various places in the line, and less often, than in most other poets, at the end. Such observations are most valuable. However, the Homeric hexameter is already beginning to form into groups, small, as for example the five lines[1] in which the first advance of Achilles on Hector is described, or longer, and built of smaller units, as the account[2] of the storm which wrecked the raft of Odysseus.

I should suggest that verse-groups are characteristic of passages with which Homer himself had most to do, not passages such as the *Catalogue of Ships*, which he inherited, for there the single lines are more independent, and composed, rather than integrated, into their sequence. That some lines of Homer are more smooth and fluent, more integrated, as I should say, from traditional words and sounds, is the important observation of Professor W. J. Woodhouse,[3] who well compares these traditional elements to pebbles, worn smooth in centuries, by water's flow. And it is in such spontaneity and fluency that Homer's verse-groups are made. A finished, unitary verse-group is the result of true poetic processes, and particularly of integration.

Again, in a few of the more emotional and fluent passages of Lucretius, especially his great beginning,[4] there are self-subsistent unitary verse-groups, but at other times, as in Homer, single lines are less coherent with each other, and, concurrently with this, '*enjambement*', the run-over of one line into the next without a pause, is less frequent. An examination of *enjambement* in Lucretius by Professor Karl Büchner[5] has enlightened his method of com-

---

1. *Iliad*, XXII, 131–5.   2. *Odyssey*, V, 291–8.
3. W. J. Woodhouse, *The Composition of Homer's Odyssey*, Oxford, 1930, 232–44; cf. W. F. J. Knight, *American Journal of Philology*, LXII, 1941, 302–13.
4. Lucretius, I, 1–43.
5. K. Büchner, *Beobachtungen über Vers und Gedankengang bei Lucrez*, Berlin, 1936, especially Chapter 1.

position; for him, as for Vergil, the flow of poetry sometimes stopped, and waited to be started again when the time came. Already pauses in the middle of the line had started to become natural and spontaneous, and, as Professor F. W. Shipley[1] shews, that is why hiatus is easier at the usual pauses.

But on the whole, Vergil was the first Latin poet to build lines into longer structures which became the finished units of expression. His predecessors in Latin hexameter verse had mainly for their unit the single line. Dr J. W. Mackail[2] well compares three periods, of Lucretius, Catullus, and Vergil.

'The moulding of Latin into foreign metres was a laborious task, and the Latin hexameter had hitherto tended to heaviness and monotony. Melodiousness of single lines, within a restricted range of pattern, had been mastered by Catullus, continuous movement in successive waves by Lucretius. But complex harmony and the periodic structure remains unachieved.' 'Both in the Lucretius and in the Catullus, it will be observed, the single line is the rhythmical unit; the only approach to periodic structure is that the last two lines have no pause between them; they alter the rhythm only by what might be called a super-Alexandrine, a single line of double length. In the Catullus, the single-line rhythm repeats itself placidly, like the successive ripple of a slack tide on a smooth beach. The melodiousness is complete; but nothing comes of it. Each line might quite well be a line of Virgil's; but the effect of the whole is as un-Virgilian as possible.

'In the Lucretius, on the other hand, the rhythms are so managed that their effect is cumulative. He can get more volume both of weight and of sound into a given compass than any other Latin poet, perhaps than any other poet at all: and he can pile line on line with certainty to get massed effects. In the surge of the

1. F. W. Shipley, *Transactions and Proceedings of the American Philological Association*, LXIX, 1938, 134–60; Dr Ernst Badian further emphasizes to me the merit of Cicero's poetry. Cicero experimented with 'echo-words'; his *enjambement* is quite free at times, and deliberately used for a swift rush of action; and his sound-values are carefully planned for effect. In this he is only comparable with Vergil himself.

2. J. W. Mackail, *The Aeneid*, edited with introduction and commentary, Oxford, 1930, lxxv–lxxviii, citing especially Catullus, LXIV, 62–7, Lucretius, V, 1188–93, and Vergil, *A*. XII, 542–7.

successive phrases here there is no monotony, but continuous and rising magnificence.

'But in Virgil's more intricate and more consummate art, the line, even when it consists of a single phrase, is always felt as part of a larger periodic structure. ... By constant variation of stress and pause, by a fugal mastery equalled in our own language by Milton alone, he established the golden mean between the monotony of the earlier Latin hexameter and the tripping movement – itself becoming monotonous in its turn – into which it was metamorphosed, before it settled down into a sterilized convention, by the facile adroitness of Ovid.'

Perhaps Vergil learnt the verse-group or paragraph most directly from Theocritus, because Theocritus was dramatic. He lived in Sicily; and Italy and Sicily had strong popular dramatic tendencies. In the fifth century B.C. Epicharmus, the comic poet, and Sophron, the writer of realistic mimes, had lived in Sicily. It is likely that Greeks in Sicily and elsewhere developed a pastoral folk-poetry in which performers answered each other in verse, as characters in English ballads answer each other. This 'answering', 'amoebaean' poetry may well have begun very early; Homer says[1] that at a feast of the gods Muses sang, answering each other; and a modern monument at Catania in Sicily, to the poet Stesichorus of Himera, who lived in the seventh century B.C., attributes to him, on the authority of Aelian, the invention of pastoral poetry.[2]

Theocritus often but not always makes his characters speak in small verse-groups. Sometimes each speaks one, and sometimes a character with a long speech divides it into three- or four-line units, especially noticeable when they are marked by a refrain. Vergil accepted from Theocritus the refrain, and the tune of it all, including the verse-group of perhaps three to five verses. Such units are obvious in the *Eclogues*. But the fourth *Eclogue*, the 'Messianic' *Eclogue*, probably the last to be written, in which Vergil prophesies a golden age to be, has verse-groups which shew in rhythm and organization an influence similar but not quite the

1. *Iliad*, I, 604.
2. E. K. Rand, *The Magical Art of Vergil*, Cambridge, Massachusetts, 1931, 168; Aelian, *Varia Historia*, X, 18.

same, the influence, as Professor R. G. Austin[1] has proved, of Sibylline oracles, which have a parallel development in style to the *Idylls* of Theocritus. These oracles affected Vergil; but, as usual, he accepted more than one influence when one alone would seem quite enough; and he visibly and audibly echoed in the same *Eclogue* a poem of Catullus,[2] *The Marriage of Peleus and Thetis*, in which Catullus, too, had begun to use short verse-groups, marked by a refrain which Vergil explicitly remembers. The same influences acted on both poets, except that Vergil derived them through Catullus as well.

Having accepted the unitary verse-group, Vergil developed it in great elaboration, far beyond any other poet of hexameters. He gave his verse-groups rhythmical symmetry which makes them comparable to the strophic systems of Pindar, or the later stanzas of 'ottava rima' or 'royal rhyme', or of heroic couplets, as Pope perfected them. Vergil began making epic verse periodic, and introducing into its symmetries, such as had been used in other forms, but were absent from the looser epic verse of his predecessors.

Vergil was early in his life dominated by Catullus[3] and others of the neoteric school. Catullus had an exceptional thirst for symmetry, which he satisfied on different scales. In the single verse[4] Catullus adopted the balance of the golden line; a pair of nouns, each with an adjective, and a verb, the verb in the middle, and each pair divided by it, and partly in each half of the verse. Vergil in his early period wrote such verses; as *mollia luteola pingit vaccinia calta*, 'paints the soft irises with yellow marigold',[5] two adjectives, a verb, and then the two nouns.

This arrangement of words in the line is not Lucretian. But it has become frequent already in Catullus and the early work of Vergil.[6]

1. R. G. Austin, *The Classical Quarterly*, XXI, 1927, 100–5.

2. Catullus, LXIV.

3. For the influence of Catullus on Vergil, see R. E. H. Westendorp Boerma, 'Vergil's Debt to Catullus', *Acta Classica, The Proceedings of the Classical Association of South Africa*, I, 1958, 51–63, an important article.

4. Arthur M. Young, *The Classical Journal*, XXVII, 1931–2, 515–22.

5. *E.* II, 50.

6. Arthur M. Young, *The Classical Journal*, XXVII, 1931–2, 515, note 1, citing E. K. Rand, *Harvard Studies in Classical Philology*, XXX, 1919, 126: on the Neoterics, see Luigi Alfonsi, *Poetae Novi*, Como, 1945.

It is possible that Cicero started it in his poems; they were much more important for the development of the Latin hexameter than is usually supposed; and some fragments shew his advanced skill in word-order of this kind.

The golden line can be brought into relation with much of Vergil's technical history. It is a useful line for Catullus, whose verse-groups allow a very sharp unity to the lines in them; but Vergil gave to his verse-groups so sharp a unity of their own that so unitary a line must oppose the unity of the group. Accordingly Vergil gradually repressed the golden line, making its structure looser and looser according to a detectable devolution,[1] until word-order became preponderantly a function of the verse-group, not of the single verse. In Vergil's later style, if a golden line, or a line like one, occurs, it is usually at the end of a verse-group, asserting unity by rhythmic punctuation.

In the golden line, and similar structures, Vergil secured something which he could abandon gradually; and in the technique of verbal responsion he found an influence to help other influences, from earlier Latin poetry and elsewhere, for guiding him to his practice of internal rhymes, by which he binds verses, but still more verse-groups, together. His adaptations are most characteristic. The rhymes, however, must wait.

From a practice in which unitary lines, including occasionally golden lines, were not abnormal, Vergil went on towards a word-order less constricted by the structure of the verse. In this he reflected a part of the history of Latin prose, when it was inclined to abandon the periodic structure. Like Caesar, Vergil came to substitute co-ordination for subordination in the structure of his sentences. Both writers say 'and', and add a new main verb, far more often than many people think; Caesar, perhaps, developed co-ordination concurrently with Cicero, and Vergil after both, but before Livy had developed subordination in his particular way.

Vergil's co-ordination, especially in his later style, and at dramatic moments, sometimes helped his formation of verse-groups into their unity. As he developed co-ordination of syntax, he reduced what is, perhaps, a form of subordination, the fixed

1. Arthur M. Young, *The Classical Journal*, XXVII, 1931-2, 515-22.

structure of words within the verse. He remained free to return partially and momentarily to such regularities. It is noticeable that in passages of intense creative spontaneity, even more characteristic of later than of earlier work, he applies musical responsions in the form of rhyme which seem like the revival of old memories in which were retained the echo of the golden line.

The period or group of hexameters, then, is the form, and the strange, curt, rich, whimsical Latin language is the material. How Vergil managed them is, I suppose, the 'style'.

Vergil, from the start of his certainly authentic poems, was strict. Everything must be tight, firm, and compressed, but also musical. There must never be too many vowels or too many consonants, or the wrong ones, or the wrong number of short or long syllables, or pauses in the wrong place, either at the end of the line or elsewhere. Former poets, whose work is known, with the possible exception of Cicero and the poet of the *Ciris*, had never aspired to anything like that. The contrast is immense; yet even Vergil did not really quite master his material, one reason why he is so great. But this carefulness is a small part of the matter.

The poems in the Vergilian *Appendix* are in iambics, hendeca-syllables, elegiacs, and hexameters. However many, or however few, may be by Vergil himself, and though some anecdotes about other elegiacs attributed to him are apocryphal, Vergil could hardly help writing in the more informal metres at first. But perhaps he was unusual, for his time, in abandoning all other metres in favour of hexameters so soon. Vergil's language is a hexameter language. The style is the man, but with Vergil it might be said that the metre is the man, and the style is the metre. Having found the hexameter, Vergil thought and felt in it, and saw the world through it. It was not his slavery, but his freedom, and his power.

From the *Eclogues* onward Vergil settled down to hexameters and hexameters only. The chief reason was that the Alexandrians and Italians before Vergil had made the hexameter the metre for almost any sort of work, as it had been at first, but as it definitely was not in Classical Greek times. Then, it was the heroic metre of epic, and the didactic metre of instruction, genealogical, proverbial and practical, and philosophical. It was kept from propaganda, satire, and lyric, and from drama, except very rarely. It belonged to what was ancient, or severe; its use for philosophy by Empedocles and others is an interesting development from its use by Homer and Hesiod, who were regarded as instructors.

The hexameter was used for an immense number of Greek poems, early, classical, Hellenistic, and late, from before Homer who lived in the ninth century B.C. till Johannes Tzetzes, at about A.D. 1150, and after. Perhaps not much less than a hundred thousand lines survive still; at one time at least a million and probably much more were in circulation. Hexameters were natural for subjects which could be treated in prose, but had been traditionally treated in verse since the time when there was no prose. They had an important use in hymns, addressed to Apollo and Leto at Delos and to other gods, too, elsewhere, which were used to introduce recitations of epic; as in sacrifices, the gods were to taste first, and the worshippers have something to enjoy afterwards. And oracles given by independent poet-prophets, and by official priests as at Delphi, were in hexameters; many oracles were believed the work of poets such as Orpheus and Musaeus, before Homer.

After the Greek classical age, the use of hexameters was expanded again, and became more various. Satires were written in hexameters, and poetry that could be called lyric. Homer's hexameters had been perfectly successful in expressing lyrical moods, and so had the hexameters of later poets, as in the fragment of Alcman, in which he longs to be a bird of the sea. Professor E. A. Havelock[1] emphasizes the difficulty of the early Greek lyric metres for later Greek poets, to whom quantity had become an unnatural and artificial principle of metre, since stress-accent had prevailed over it in about the third century B.C.; that is at least one reason why the Hellenistic writers abandoned more complicated metres in favour of the simpler and more homogeneous hexameter form.

Latin hexameter poetry began with Ennius, who sought to copy the Homeric hexameter. Later it continued with Lucilius, the

1. E. A. Havelock, *The Lyric Genius of Catullus*, Oxford, 1939, 88–9, 132–44; Kenneth Quinn, *The Catullan Revolution*, Melbourne, 1959, *passim*.

founder of Latin satire, who before the end of the second century
B.C. had begun to write freer hexameters, already more remote
from the Ennian and Homeric, but by a direct development from
them; contemporary or nearly contemporary Greek hexameters
were not needed to help, but may have contributed something.
By Vergil's time the influence of this later Greek poetry had
become important. The Roman literary world knew Alexandrian
work in hexameters well, especially 'little epics', 'epyllia', long
and learned hymns more literary than religious, and pastoral idylls,
that is, 'little pictures' of a part of life. Here there was lyricism,
dramatic treatment of real, contemporary people, quaint and
remote learning, poetic escape, introspection, and refinement of
sentiment. They were all assets, to Roman taste. The not very long
hexameter poem, in the Alexandrian manner, but with remote
reference, if needed, to earlier Roman tradition and to Homer
indirectly, was a natural thing in the first century B.C. This was
often the poetry written by the very men whose lectures the
Roman poets heard, and, as Havelock says, even if it was artificial
for the Greeks to write such poetry it was not artificial for Romans
to emulate it. An influence that helped was the lively interest in
foreign religions and their evocative symbolisms, and especially,
for some poets, the interest of the Sibylline oracles.

These Sibylline oracles were short pieces, obscure and curt or
longer and more explicit, but usually limited to about a dozen
lines, which circulated in great numbers in the last two centuries
B.C. and after. They were not very ancient or authentic, and rather
a fashion than a very serious literary or religious phenomenon. A
source of diffusion was Syria, among other places. Here the spirit
of Hebrew prophecy found its way into the little Greek hexameter pieces; a not very Greek religious fervour, otherworldli-
ness, and even adventism, can be seen in them. They found
friends in Egypt, where they expressed the aspirations of people
who expected from Cleopatra and her descendants the start of a
golden age. Nor was it hard for the Sibyllines to find friends in
Italy, where the 'Sibylline Books' were the final appeal for Roman
state religion. The Roman Sibylline Books, in the legend, had
been offered by a Sibyl, nine, then six, then three for the same
price, to Tarquinius Priscus, first Etruscan king of Rome; who

bought them at last, before the Sibyl burnt them all, as she burnt the first six.

Sibyls, prophetesses who in the myths were half human and half divine, were known on the fringe of the Greek world in its early days. Some were said to have lived before the Trojan war in Asia Minor; there had been Sibyls in Asia, and one at Delphi; and tradition located another at Cumae, in Campania. There was interest, therefore, in Sibyls among Italians. Now when the Temple of Jupiter on the Roman Capitol was burnt down in 83 B.C., the official Sibylline Books were burnt with it, and a new edition had to be compiled. There was no difficulty in finding Sibylline oracles; what were collected seem mainly to have been the short Greek hexameter pieces, which were already current, and undoubtedly multiplied now in response to the demand. It is doubtful whether much distinction was made between old and new and between Italian and foreign Sibylline oracles. And the style of the Greek oracles affected Roman poets, especially Catullus and Vergil.

Long before Vergil Latin poetry had become self-conscious and critical. Plautus and Lucilius mocked grand writing.[1] But perhaps it was Lucretius who first devised a characteristic Latin hexameter, not merely an adaptation of the Greek, and made it a form in which almost anything could be said, sometimes in boldly colloquial language and sometimes with exquisite delicacy and great depth of feeling; it must anyhow seem so to us, because he alone of Vergil's predecessors wrote a long serious poem which has survived. Latin poetry had now achieved lyrical delicacy, fervour, and high intent together, and had for the first time become itself. Vergil had to react against what he found; he was so different from others, and so much had happened. He reacted against Catullus by opposing and surpassing his limited individual aspiration, and against Lucretius by exalting the spirit and active life; and also against both of them, in modifying the quite amazing repetitive qualities of their styles. But he took for his own work what each of them had won for Rome.

There seems no end to the blending in Vergil's method, and the superimposition of form on form; anything but vacant spaces, or

1. W. B. Sedgwick, *The Classical Quarterly*, XXI, 1927, 88–9.

a thin stream of simple meaning. Vergil was going to write hexameter poetry on a serious, or a grand scale, and under practically all the literary classifications under which Greek and Latin poets had written it. In a way he worked backwards, from contemporary Latin, and Greek Sibylline and Theocritean, to Hesiodic, and lastly to Homeric use and style, gathering up the experience of the world as he went. There were other literary influences which Vergil used, not all poetic. Vergil presupposes among all else the history of oratory, which had been in controversy during the fifty years before his birth. The oratory of Appius Claudius Caecus, in the early part of the third century, remained, and was praised, for all its deficiencies. Later, after practice in politics law, and drama, oratory at Rome fell under two distinct Greek influences, the severe Attic and the richer Asianic styles; they were discussed with interest, and at first on the whole the Asianic won. The interest was so keen because a characteristic polarity of Latin is between severe direct statement or understatement and passionate exaggeration, inclined to become admittedly formal and conventional. If Caesar is on the whole much more restrained than Cicero, yet the two forces can easily polarize in the same writer, even in contiguous passages, or the same passage. The Greeks as usual taught the Romans what they were doing and how to do what they were bound to do. It was said in antiquity that Vergil wrote at different times according to all the four styles of prose oratory, and that he had the merits of all the great Attic orators.

Vergil, like the rest, had opportunities to acquire the current habits of thought and expression in spoken and written prose, Latin and Greek. Mlle A.-M. Guillemin[1] shews how Vergil adopts the forms of businesslike, ordinary expression, for example to narrate military operations, and even to describe the respectful obedience of lesser to greater divinities, like Roman soldiers taking orders from officers. Speeches are like speeches of the forum and senate, fervid, or reasoned point by point, and technically correct; even including the speeches of Aeneas and Dido to each other. And Dido's last words,[2] recalling her life and work, are like a Roman epitaph. That it should all fit into

1. A.-M. Guillemin, *L'originalité de Virgile*, Paris, 1931, 117–22.
2. *A.* IV, 651–62, especially 653–8.

the poem so well is a sign of the authentic reality of the poetry.

There is a sense in which the ancient literary manners were extraordinarily conventionalized and a sense in which they were not. From Aristophanes and Aristotle to Longinus and beyond, critics expected books to have abstract qualities such as dignity, intensity, exaltation, accuracy and moderation in figurative expression and in proportion, and propriety in choice and disposition of words and phrases. There was less interest in the problem how these qualities cohere, how for instance an unexpected word can by contrast increase 'sublimity', and how sense, sound, and rhythm work together for good. 'Inspiration' and 'genius' covered much. Vergil's own most appreciative readers, in the early centuries after him, supposed that they were admiring him, not for what we should call true poetry, but for his use of language, his oratorical power, and even his grammatical accuracy. We are now much more inclined to ask how Vergil devised a language of sense and sound to express in perfect fusion the great, growing, system of his vision.

The languages and metres of ancient poetry exercised much control over the thought. Homer's was a style 'which does the thinking, and creates the poetry, for you', in Goethe's phrase. New forms, lyric, dramatic, and the rest, soon found a natural manner and a set of expectations and requirements. But the usual polarity of 'convention and revolt in poetry', the description under which Professor John Livingston Lowes[1] has investigated these conditions, was in antiquity just sufficiently intense – not excessively, as in England recently, nor insufficiently, as in the less popular medieval poetry. Revolt is generally some way of being 'unpoetical' in poetry, especially with every-day ideas and words and rhythmical forms. Archilochus in the eighth or seventh and Hipponax in the sixth century B.C., founders – after Homer, perhaps – of poetic attack, put streams of everyday anger into verse; and Archilochus was classed near Homer for merit. Pindar, using the most rigidly elaborate verse-structure ever made, more than once inserted the most ordinary, ephemeral personal references.

1. John Livingston Lowes, *Convention and Revolt in Poetry*, London, 1930, *passim*.

There had been a long tradition of oral Latin poetry of several kinds; but in appearance, for us, Latin poetic style almost starts with drama, freely translated from Greek, but Italian in direct natural statement of lively but common thoughts in obvious, unabashed words. The Latin of Plautus and Terence was praised for centuries. The Italian depth, and aspiration, and Italian caustic vitality, always tried to extend language and make it more useful; and it was a rigid language, not, like Greek, ready and willing to be extended. Lucretius, very much as Italians of Dante's time did also, blamed the poverty of the inherited speech, and Plautus calls Latin barbarous, a word not wholly technical or conventional or indifferent, but having at least a hint of disparagement. Yet as Théophile Gautier says best, 'Yes, from a form rebellious to the toil, verse, marble, onyx, enamel, emerge the more beautiful.' And it was by accepting with ardour the popular language, and obeying its laws, that Dante learnt, above all from Vergil, his *bello stile*; not a manner adopted from others, but a manner of his very own, made under guidance from the great principles and qualities of the past.

In adapting their recalcitrant language, Latin poets often shewed a certain whimsical devilry – as Ennius, with his *cere – comminuit – brum*[1] and the spondaic 'hexameter minimus', *olli respondit rex Albai longai*,[2] Lucretius with his grotesque words, as *homoeomereia* at the end of a verse, and Catullus with his all-embracing admission of Greek metrical forms and extreme experimentation. The poets were tempted indirectly to satirize themselves and their work. It was a kind of double but simultaneous awareness, of subject and object, which were more distinguishable to Latin writers, and not, as among Greeks, coincident. Ovid has it in the *Fasti*, but not usually in the *Tristia*, and the lack makes that work boring. In Lucan the habit is there, but he is also boring in spite of it, because the duplicity goes too far, and weakens the force of the primary meanings.

The question here really expands into three – how poets evaded, and how they used, the difficulties of their language, and how they followed their propensity towards a double meaning. The questions

1. Ennius, *Annals*, 609.   2. ibid., 33; cf. 623.

are particularly applicable to Vergil, who seems to have had an interest in language for its own sake unusual in a poet.

He uses his language with a peculiar sensitivity to its qualities. Latin had for centuries aspired mainly to plain inescapable prose statement, confined rigidly to fact, without suggestions. Vergil writes like that at intense poetic moments. It is pure prose when Dido is introduced – *talis erat Dido . . . instans operi [regnisque futuris]*, 'such was Dido . . . busy at work planning [her kingdom to be.]'[1] There is a hush; after swift rhythms that have gone before, the reader needs no more impulse to his imagination, which spontaneously defies the damping effect of the language of prose. So too, when Jupiter finally yields, so that harmony may begin for Latium, he says, in monosyllables that are famous, *do quod vis*, just 'I give what you want',[2] as bare as bare can be.

Vergil admits an occasional paradox or oxymoron, suggesting Lucan, such as *una salus victis nullam sperare salutem*, 'for conquered men the sole salvation is to know salvation cannot be for them'[3] at the fall of Troy, or a less paradoxical, rhetorical contrast like Juno's resolution, *flectere si nequeo superos, Acheronta movebo*, 'if I cannot bend the powers above, I shall start Hell's river of pain',[4] or a crisp proverb, this one from Terence, *audentis fortuna iuvat*, 'fortune helps those who dare'.[5] But Vergil uses this group of duplicities rarely, and it is not important, except when it is no longer itself, but has turned into statements, which are simply of high rational density, not strictly paradoxical at all.

Compression into density of meaning is the main principle of Vergil's expression. To achieve it he exploits as far as ever he can the nature of Latin speech and thought.

Latin has comparatively few words. The art of writing Latin was, and still is, principally the art of making two or three words, chosen to go together, have quite definitely a meaning far more than the total of the meanings of each word, added together. Latin words are ready for this, since many have had to be words of inclusive content, by themselves meaning not very much, but seeming to have empty spaces in them, in which, when the right word comes near them, they can suddenly generate a new and often

1. *A.* I, 503–4.   2. *A.* XII, 833.   3. *A.* II, 354.
4. *A.* VII, 312.   5. *A.* X, 284.

unexpected meaning. It is best to consider now some specially Vergilian passages, but without implying that Vergil is not often much more ordinary.

All languages have favourite words. In Latin among the favourite words, characteristic and much used, are *facere*, 'to do', *habere*, 'to have', and *res*, 'a thing', often in the sense of 'a thought'; it is connected with *reri*, 'to think', as 'thing' and 'think' are connected in English and German. *Facere* is briefly expressive when Vergil can say that Volcanus, on the shield of Aeneas, *fecerat . . . procubuisse lupam*, 'he had worked the story how a she-wolf sank down and was there . . .',[1] with the Roman twins. A hero gives arms to a younger hero, *donat habere viro*, 'gave him the arms, to be arms that a man might wear'.[2] Here the meanings are at least latent, not newly generated, but elicited by the proximity of other words. *Habere* means 'have' and 'hold', and so own and wear, proudly; *donat* implies a sense of 'owning' and *viro*, which is dative of recipient and simultaneously dative of advantage, has the connotation, or denotation, of active courage in the world itself, which helps to generate also the meaning of 'wear'.

Res, and other words subordinately, make the famous *sunt lacrimae rerum*.[3] Aeneas arriving at Carthage sees pictures of Trojan fighting painted on the walls; emotion overcomes him, and he says, *sunt hic etiam sua praemia laudi, sunt lacrimae rerum et mentem mortalia tangunt*, which seems to mean, in prose, not much less than, 'There is no denying that even in this far land honour gets its due, and they can weep at human tragedy; the world has tears as a constituent part of it, and so have our own lives, hopeless and weary; and the thought how things have always their own death in them breaks our hearts and will and clouds our vision.' That seems to be it, in the sense that it is hardly possible to deny that any of those meanings are there; and anyhow no one has translated the line more shortly with any great prospect or even

---

1. *A*. VIII, 630–1.   2. *A*. V, 262; cf. IX, 362.

3. *A*. I, 462; cf. Robert Speaight, 'The Virgilian Res', Presidential Address to the Virgil Society, 1958; my over-translation here should perhaps have been reconsidered, but the sense in which it is intended may be to some extent endorsed by Luigi Alfonsi, 'Sunt lacrimae rerum et mentem mortalia tangunt', *The Classical Journal*, Malta, IV, 1950, 19–22.

expectation of success. The first of the two lines might seem to limit the statement to the particular plight of the Trojans. But almost the whole point is that in the second the meaning expands to all the world.

The explanation, shortly, seems to be this. *Rerum* controls; it means 'things' in the sense of *any* things undefined and therefore *all* things and so the world, and the world as you both see it and think about it, as in *rerum cui prima potestas* of Jupiter, 'who has the sovereign authority over the world',[1] which implies the connotation of 'think', and *rebus nox abstulit atra colorem*, 'the black of night stole all colour from the seen world',[2] which implies the connotation of 'see'. Yet still strong is the particular suggestion not of all the world, but of our own wordly fortunes, as in *fessi rerum*, 'heart sick at the thought of the failure and weariness always theirs'.[3]

In *sunt hic etiam* ... and *sunt lacrimae rerum* ..., *sunt* at the beginnings underlines real, enduring existence, as in *sunt geminae somni portae*, or *sunt geminae belli portae*, that is, 'there is no denial that there are gates . . .' – 'of sleep', [4] and 'of war'[5]; or *sunt apud infernos tot milia formosarum* in Propertius,[6] 'it must be true, in their thousands, with the folk below – "all the lovely dead are there"', as Gogarty represents it. *Mens* is an inclusive word also. It is not, however, vague. It means thinking of an active quick kind, mainly by imagination, sometimes prophetic, as in *heu, vatum ignarae mentes*, 'sad, how prophets' vision could not know'.[7] So it is in *magnam cui mentem animumque Delius inspirat vates*, 'the prophet god in Delos breathes into her the spirit's visionary might',[8] of the inspiration of the Cumaean Sibyl before she prophesied to Aeneas. There is an implication of motive power in *mens*. Catullus says *nec potis est dulcis musarum expromere fetus mens animi*, meaning something like 'my spirit's energy of imagination cannot deliver the lovely ripe fruit of poetry'[9] in the time of sadness. The meaning 'will', apparently the practical decision which follows intuitive, imaginative apprehension, appears in *mens inmota manet*, of Aeneas, resolved to leave Carthage, 'his will remained unshak-

1. *A.* x, 100.   2. *A.* vi, 272.   3. *A.* i, 178.
4. *A.* vi, 893.   5. *A.* vii, 607.   6. Propertius, ii, 28c, 3.
7. *A.* iv, 65.   8. *A.* vi, 11–12.   9. Catullus, lxv, 3–4.

able'.[1] Another important meaning of *mens* is memory, and that contributes too.

Mortalia is 'mortal things', obviously enough, but it is different from 'things that are going to die', *moritura*; the whole word is death, with an adjectival suffix closely associating the meaning with the understood noun; things, that is, not which death would as if by accident visit, but which have seeds of death in them, always. The adjective is like *fatalis* in its intimacy of characterization.

This, then, is the way I should analyse one of Vergil's elaborate systems of meaning. The more nearly you have in your mind what Vergil had in his – it is hopeless enough, of course, to get very near – the more closely you approach the full significance. And the first thing for us to do is to remember other occurrences of the same words in the *Aeneid*, and let them communicate to our minds as much as they will take of what was in the mind of Vergil. Experience has shewn that it is infinitely more risky to exclude possible meanings, if they are appropriate and Vergilian, than it is to admit all the meanings that can be discovered.

The scope of *res* can be assumed by another word. In *si ... fortuna sequatur*, 'if fortune should really go our way',[2] another meaning of *res*, 'reality, fulfilment, fact', as in Livy's *clamoremque res est secuta*, 'the fulfilment, success, of the plan followed',[3] contributes to the meaning of *fortuna*, by adding the thought of reality and fulfilment to the thought of fortune.

In these usages external meanings are added to words through the relations of other words to their internal meanings, actual and potential. Another way of using words in combination is this. The Latin perfect participle is not fully described as a verbal adjective, normally passive and past-perfect in meaning. It can be more strongly predicative, and carry in its predication the sense of what in English would be a noun. *Mortuus Romulus* is more likely to mean 'Romulus is dead', or even more characteristically 'the death of Romulus' than 'dead Romulus'; so it is with Horace's *ademptus Hector*, 'the removal of Hector',[4] and with Milton's Latinism, 'ever since created man ...'. The same action occurs when the gerundive is used as a present or future participle passive,

1. *A.* IV, 449.   2. *A.* IV, 109.   3. Livy, II, 65, 3.
4. Horace, *Odes*, II, 4, 10.

a regular extension of the primary meaning 'needing to be ...' into a secondary meaning, 'being ...', or 'about to be being ...'.

There is a shadow of such predication, with its change of the logical subject of the sentence, in the present participle active. Livy[1] has a sentence illustrating all three; his *ab urbe oppugnanda Poenum absterruere conspecta moenia, haudquaquam prompta oppugnanti*, 'but from any attack on the city itself the Carthaginian commander was deterred by the mere sight of the defences, so uninviting to an attacker', or even, by a kind of fusion of two fusions, '... by the uninvitingness to an attacker, or attack, of the sight of the walls' – the 'death of Romulus' raised to the third power –, perhaps, '... by the most uninviting aspect presented by the walls themselves to any threat of attack'. All this is far from easy to get right; but I hope these remarks can at least indicate some of the strange grammatical, semantic, and logical opportunities which the Latin language offered for Vergil's exploitation.

Now, if the most is to be made of this power in words, it has to be apprehended, consciously or unconsciously; and much of Vergil's hard, conscious thinking went to the apprehension of the power in words by a clear comprehension of facts about them. The facts concern what they mean, how they came to mean it, and what they might mean. To say that Vergil uses words etymologically does not express the whole truth but it is a convenient and legitimate way of referring to his practice in this matter.

The simplest kind of etymological use is this. When Vergil uses a proper name, he is inclined to add an adjective which denotes the meaning of the word from which the proper name is developed.[2] Among many places in Sicily whose names he treats etymologically is Selinus, which he calls, *palmosa*, 'palm-leafed',[3] because the name means parsley or celery, suggesting to some extent palm-leaves. He talks of *Hernica saxa*, 'Hernican stones',[4] because the Hernici,

1. Livy, XXIII, 1, 10.

2. Bernhard Rehm, *Philologus, Supplementband*, XXIV, Heft 11, 1932, 26–8, 37–9, 103–6: cf. Anna Gesina Blonk, *Vergilius en het Landschap*, Groningen, 1947, *passim*.

3. *A*. III, 705: no doubt the similarity between the two sorts of leaves might have been closer.

4. *A*. VII, 684.

a tribe south of Rome, not only lived in stony country, but were called 'stone men', for that is what, in the Oscan language, their name means. There are many examples, most of them quite certain. Vergil piquantly calls old Carthage 'ancient'[1] in one place and 'new'[2] in another. There was a 'New Carthage' in Spain. But the Semitic name Carthage originally meant simply 'New Town'. There is no doubt that Vergil knew, and was remembering, that. He calls an Italian town, Graviscae, *intempestae*, 'inclement', 'with bad weather'.[3] No reason has been suggested. Probably he elicited the idea of the adjective from the apparent element *gravis*, 'burdensome', 'unpleasant', or 'unfavourable', in the name, and used it subject to other ideas about the place which have been forgotten.

A very pleasant etymological use, depending on Greek and on a cross-reference within Vergil's work, is *campi . . . Geloi*, 'plains of the laughter town', almost 'those plains of laughter'.[4] Gela, the Greek city in Sicily, has a name which is the root of the Greek verb for 'to laugh'. In Vergil's Hades there is a rather remarkably named area, the 'plains that mourn', *lugentes campi*.[5] Without entering into the long discussion which these two expressions really demand, it is easy to see that they help to account for each other, and together reveal what was at some time in Vergil's mind.

Another example, which is not quite certain, is also interesting enough to mention. Vergil writes of 'the isle of Aeaean Circe', *Aeaeae . . . insula Circae*.[6] From analogy, the adjective Aeaea, usually of course meaning 'of Aea', the name of Circe's island, might be expected to carry a meaning contained in the name Circe. And in fact there is such a meaning for it to carry; and again in a Semitic language, for in a Semitic language a word so spelt would mean hawk, the very meaning of κίρκος, *kirkos*, in Greek, which is ultimately Circe's name. This is part of M. Victor Bérard's theory of Phoenician place names in the Mediterranean; it was related to this passage of Vergil by Father Espinosa.[7]

1. *A*. I, 12.   2. *A*. I, 366.   3. *A*. x, 184.

4. *A*. III, 701.   5. *A*. VI, 441

6. *A*. III, 386; Victor Bérard, *Calypso et la Mer de l' Atlantide*, Paris, 1929, 293; idem, *Nausicaa et le Retour d'Ulysse*, Paris, 1929, 287–8, 486–8.

7. Aurelio Espinosa Pólit, *Virgilio, el poeta y su misión providencial*, Quito, 1932, 69, note 2 continued 70.

Nearer to certainty is the etymological application of the adjective *durus*, 'hard', applied to Atlas,[1] the personified mountain, who, as Vergil in the same line says, holds up the sky. The name Atlas is the same as a Greek word meaning 'holding', 'enduring', an intensifying prefix α-, *a*-, and the verbal adjective or participle τλάς, *tlas*, from τλῆναι, *tlenai*, 'endure', cognate with the Greek word for 'talent', which was originally the weight which a man could endure to lift or hold up. Vergil's line expresses the meaning in the name Atlas, in a relative clause. It expresses it however again in the word *durus* which means sometimes 'hardened', hardened either to do, or to endure. It is scarcely deniable that *durus* here means 'enduring', 'hardened to endure' the weight of the sky, a close translation of the name Atlas.

As before with *lacrimae rerum*, cross-references within Vergil's work give help. Vergil calls the Scipios *Scipiadas duros bello*, 'men of Scipio's line, who harden themselves to war',[2] not simply 'hard', which the Scipios were not. They hardened themselves to endure both doing and suffering, though they were naturally gentle. That does not give an etymology, but another passage does. Anchises, in the vision of the future in the world beyond, shews to Aeneas *geminos*, *duo fulmina belli*, *Scipiadas*, 'that pair of Scipio's line, twin thunderbolts of war'.[3] That is etymological, since the name Scipio is cognate with the Greek word for sceptre, σκῆπτρον, *skeptron*, which is a meaning of the Latin name, and also for a thunderbolt in one of its variations. That the etymology was known is shewn by representations of thunderbolts on a coin of the Scipios.[4]

These three passages co-ordinate themselves and suggest how Vergil thought and wrote, and how he should be read. There is a serious risk of misunderstanding and indeed mistranslation if such undoubted tendencies in Vergil are missed or forgotten.

The etymological habit intensifies and enriches the meanings of passages, and modifies their moods. When Vergil is talking about the weather and its signs, he enlivens and makes delicately

---

1. *A.* IV, 247; R. W. Cruttwell, *The Classical Review*, LIX, 1945, 11; id. *Vergil's Mind at Work*, 133.

2. *G.* II, 170.   3. *A.* VI, 842–3; Cicero, *Pro Balbo*, 15, 34.

4. H. E. Butler, *The Sixth Book of the Aeneid*, Oxford, 1920, note on *A.* VI, 842.

humorous this serious subject by calling the clouds 'fine weather' clouds, *serenas*, and the south-east wind 'wet', *umidus*, because its name was Auster, which he with others derived from a root meaning 'dry', a root appearing in the English, and indeed the Greek, word 'austere'; and finally by calling the north wind, whose name Aquilo meant 'black', *clarus*, which is something like 'brightly clear', and almost 'white'.[1] The winds had colours in Celtic folk-lore, and there are signs of colours for them in Latin, as in Horace's *albus Notus*, 'the white south wind'.[2]

This passage proves Vergil's etymological interest, all the more because though he might have easily found the theory of Auster, it was not argued till lately[3] that Aquilo was associated with *aquilus*, 'black', before the time of later writers, who lived well after Vergil. This raises two further questions. Vergil may have supposed the words cognate, thinking rationally about them, or he may have been content to associate them irrationally, from their similarity of sound. This is a large question, which must wait. The other question is large also. So far, I have had to over-simplify Vergil's poetic process. When he called the black wind white, it was not merely through a wish or an instinct to make a usefully paradoxical pun, but also through a Homeric suggestion, also to some extent etymologized.

Professor H. J. Rose[4] has explained, in amplification of my own view, that Vergil, besides all the rest, derives the idea of a white wind from Homer's 'North wind, father of a clear, high air', Βορέης αἰθρηγενέτης.[5] Vergil's north wind cleared the sky and was therefore whitening, or white, partly because it really did so, according to his own observation, partly because Homer said something like it, and Vergil analysed Homer's word better than others have analysed it, and partly, too, because the Latin word for north wind invited the contrary adjective. This is entirely characteristic. Vergil normally has a great complexity of reasons,

1. *G.* i, 460–3; W. F. J. Knight, *The Classical Review*, XLVIII, 1934, 124–5.
2. Horace, *Odes*, i, 7, 15–17.
3. W. M. Lindsay, *The Classical Review*, XLII, 1928, 20.
4. H. J. Rose, *The Classical Review*, XLVIII, 1934, 170.
5. *Odyssey*, v, 296.

when to anyone else any one of them might seem enough. 'Art is the friend of chance, and chance of art.'

Vergil sometimes seems more intent on a Greek original than on the Latin which he writes. Aeneas, cheering his men after a wreck, says *neque enim ignari sumus ante malorum*, 'since, as you know, we are not hitherto ignorant of afflictions',[1] *ante*, 'hitherto', being really 'before', and so hardly right with 'we are', in the present. The Greek of it is in the *Odyssey*, οὐ γάρ πώ τι κακῶν ἀδαήμονές εἰμεν, 'we are not people who are yet without the knowledge of afflictions that comes of learning', or, still more literally, 'we are not unlearned yet of afflictions'.[2] The adjective, meaning 'not having learnt', contains a past tense in it. Therefore 'yet' is rational. The translation into Latin just loses that shade of meaning, and leaves an irrationality, of no importance of course, and indeed rather piquant and pleasing.

There is another similar compression of two senses into one, this time purely Latin, apparently, in *iam dudum sumite poenas*, literally 'exact punishment long since',[3] an imperative. In the indicative, Latin, like related languages, uses a present tense for something which has been going on a long time, and still is going on. This time what is and has been going on is a necessity; but the necessity is expressed by an imperative, implying 'you ought to have exacted punishment a long time ago and the need or desirability of doing so has been going on all the time till now, and still is going on.' It is one of Vergil's more remarkable ingenuities of compression.

The analysis of Greek words, as a step to the etymological use of Latin words, is shewn in the invention of a word for a dream. In Latin a dream is *somnium*, but there is also a word *insomnia* for sleeplessness. Vergil uses a word *insomnium* in the plural, *insomnia*, to mean dreams. Through the ivory gate of sleep the spirits send false dreams, *insomnia*.[4] Dido says, *quae me suspensam insomnia terrent?* 'What are these dreams that affright me, so anxious?'[5] That ought to mean, if anything, 'What sleeplessness ...?' But primarily at least, the word means dreams. The reason[6] is that

1. *A.* I, 198.   2. *Odyssey*, XII, 208.   3. *A.* II, 103.
4. *A.* VI, 896.   5. *A.* IV, 9.
6. A. Meillet, *Esquisse d'une Histoire de la Langue Latine*, Paris, 1928, 219–20.

Vergil has made an equation between the Latin word, in which *in-* should mean a negative, and the Greek word for a dream ἐνύπνιον, *enhypnion*, also neuter with a plural in -α, -*a*, also ending with the word ὕπνος, *hypnos*, sleep, and beginning too, with a corresponding prefix, ἐν-, *en-*, *in*; but it corresponds to *in-* in the sense of 'in', not in the negative sense, and the Greek word legitimately means something that happens in sleep, and so a dream. Vergil has analysed and Latinized a Greek word by its parts, and adopted a Latin word which corresponds etymologically, but is actually new, and might be called wrong, even.

Of this there is much to say. The process of Vergil here has been rational in analysis and associative in synthesis. The impulse may have been instinctive, as if Vergil forgot his own language. In a sense he often did; or rather forgot certain claims that it made on ordinary people. But there is also a possible reasoned motive. Dido may be meant to have been frightened both by dreams, and, intermittently, by sleeplessness. *Suspensam* suggests it. Then *insomnia* means both, and Vergil has again made a word mean two things at once, partly because another word induces and elicits one of the meanings.

The word *insomnia* for dreams now got into the language. This is important, for parallels for Vergilian usages which come from later writers are always liable to be misleading because they may be dependent on Vergil alone. That is how, when Aeneas and his friends were looking at the pictured legend of the Cretan labyrinth on the temple gate at Cumae, the word used, *perlegerent*, 'they would have read all to the end',[1] has been misunderstood as 'they would have looked at . . .', simply because Ovid, himself misunderstanding Vergil, used the word *perlegere* to mean 'look at'. Of course, till Ovid misunderstood it, it meant 'read to the end'. Vergil meant what he said, as usual. The Trojans *read* a very important message from those pictures in bronze and gold.[2]

There have already appeared certain signs of irrational association of ideas taking part with rational processes. It is probable that really there is no irrationality in any but bad poetry, and that association, as Berkeley held but Locke denied, is a source of

1. *A.* VI, 34.
2. W. F. J. Knight, *Cumaean Gates*, Oxford, 1936, *passim*.

knowledge. The reasoning is there, but concealed; that is, in the finished poem. It is possible, but perhaps not quite certain, that truly irrational processes occur, and are useful as steps, apparently fortuitous, to the compressed rationality of the final result. Certainly, to everyday apprehension, a large part of Vergil's normal process looks irrational in a superficial sense.

Association works well, or even perhaps best, in a dreamlike consciousness, in which there is access to surrealistic material in the unconscious mind. In his early enthusiasm Vergil was perhaps more inclined than later to accept association, and leave it, without making it appear superficially rational. There are the well-known instances in which he is supposed to have 'translated' Theocritus wrongly; πάντα δ' ἔναλλα γένοιντο, 'may everything be put upside down!'[1] produces *omnia vel medium fiat mare*, 'may all things become a mid waste of sea',[2] because ἔναλλα, 'inside out' or 'upside down', suggests ἐν ἁλί, 'in the sea'. There is, of course, no fair complaint. A chance association suggested a good but quite different idea. Even if Vergil honestly deceived himself about Greek, as he may have deceived himself about the Latin word, *insomnia*, there is still no fair objection; except, perhaps, to the singular verb.

Association involves usually or often former poetry, imaginatively remembered, but prose writings or even ordinary talk will often serve. There is an early passage in which poetry need not originate the association. A despairing wanderer says 'some of us . . . shall come to Oaxes' either, 'in Crete', or, '. . . sweeping chalk down', *pars . . . rapidum Cretae veniemus Oaxen*.[3] Oaxes may be a town in Crete, or a river, sweeping chalk down, since *rapidus*, from *rapere*, 'seize', elsewhere in Vergil means 'seizing' in the sense of 'scorching', of the sun, which catches at you, and *creta* is a word for chalk, here possibly objective genitive after an adjective derived from a verb. There was however no town in Crete called Oaxes and no river anywhere of that name. But there was a town in Crete called Oaxus or Axus, and Crete is called by Apollonius Rhodius Oeacian, Οἰαξίς. There were rivers in Asia called the Oxus, the Araxes, the Jaxartes, and the Orontes, and one at least is

1. Theocritus, *Idylls*, I, 134.   2. *E.* VIII, 58.   3. *E.* I, 65.

known to have swept down, not chalk, but loam. It is quite clear that Vergil's Oaxes is a compound of the town and one or more of the rivers, probably all;[1] there is an exact parallel in Coleridge, who, as Professor Livingston Lowes proved,[2] created Mount Abora in *Kubla Khan* from many originals, some not mountains at all, by associating them together.

The meaning of Oaxes, whatever Vergil thought it to be, could of course elicit from *Cretae* or *cretae* either the meaning 'Crete' or the meaning 'chalk'; and so also it could elicit from *rapidum* either the developed, usual meaning 'swift', or the etymological meaning 'snatching', 'carrying off', 'sweeping down'. Probably Vergil created this complex at different times, not all together, and assumed, however little he may have expressed them to himself, at the different times, different meanings for the words. It is hard to say which meaning is the right meaning now. *Cretae*, 'in Crete', a genitive for an ablative – Crete is a *large* island, and would need a preposition in prose – might seem strange; but Greek regularly uses a genitive for the country in which a town is, and Vergil himself says *Libyae* for 'in Libya'.[3] The truest meaning is probably 'Oaxes, swift river in Crete', but it is scarcely a sensible question to ask, except for one reason, which concerns the next problem to be faced. Vergil often leaves a doubt of his meaning. Here the doubt matters little; either translation is imaginatively satisfying, and nothing much depends on which is chosen. Elsewhere the doubt matters more; and sometimes the doubt itself is very important to the poetry. That is, Vergil's words may be authentically ambiguous. If there is an apparent ambiguity, either one meaning is right and the other wrong; or both are equally right; or both meanings are there, and should be accepted, but one meaning is the main meaning, and the other belongs to the penumbra of suggestion which so often surrounds Vergil's words. 'Penumbra' in this connexion is one of the late Professor R. S. Conway's felicities; and to him is due the very valuable advice, that we should always decide which is the main meaning, when-

1. W. F. J. Knight, *The Classical Review*, LI, 1937, 212–13.

2. John Livingston Lowes, *The Road to Xanadu*, London, 2nd ed., 1933, 373–6.

3. *A.* IV, 36.

ever Vergil leaves more than one open. It is nearly always true that all possible meanings are there, and should be noticed, but that one is the main meaning, and should be distinguished from the others. For all his suggestions and associations, Vergil is still precise, and few tasks need more precision than the attempt to understand him.

Vergil's ambiguities are partly a result of the qualities of the Latin language which enable it to express more than might be expected. But neither the poet nor the language are different in kind from all other poets and languages. The ambiguities of English poets have been detected and classified into no less than seven types by Professor Empson;[1] who observes that the eighteenth-century editors of Shakespeare normally emended his text by restoring not what he wrote, but what he read, or what first occurred to him, before he had fused prosaic ideas into suggestive poetry. That meant that if they found 'sermons in stones, books in the running brooks' they would be inclined to emend it to 'sermons in books, stones in the running brooks', which a continental scholar is actually said to have done. So *Cretae veniemus Oaxem* has been emended to *certe veniemus ad Oxum*, which is exceedingly comic, if the true meaning of *certe*, 'at any rate', is remembered. Poetry is often, or even normally, made by altering simple and plainly reasonable prose statement, and sometimes the process by which it is made in a poet's mind looks just like the process by which texts are corrupted. Dr Wolf Hartmut Friedrich[2] has acutely shewn how supposed corruptions in the plays of Seneca are frequently uncertainties in the poet's mind, which have remained, as he left them, not fully or not sufficiently resolved, in his text. Interest in the subject is increasing, and there is a book on classical ambiguites by Professor W. Bedell Stanford[3].

Vergil probably learnt how to use what may roughly be described as ambiguity and the etymological use of words from Sophocles, when he learnt from him much about subtle loveliness of sound. Sophocles, besides his tragic irony, which is his main

1. William Empson, *Seven Types of Ambiguity*, London, 1930, 102–9.
2. Wolf Hartmut Friedrich, *Untersuchungen zu Senecas dramatischer Technik*, Borna-Leipzig, 1933, *passim*.
3. W. Bedell Stanford, *Ambiguity in Greek Literature*, Oxford, 1939.

kind of ambiguity, uses words etymologically.[1] There is in Vergil an almost 'Sophoclean irony', in passages where his imagination was in contact with the imagination of Sophocles, especially in the parts of the *Aeneid* about the last day of Troy, and about Dido and her death. Sinon, trying to make the Trojans pull the wooden horse into Troy, tells them that he will pay a 'great' reward;[2] in one of the lost plays of Sophocles which Vergil was certainly using 'great', μέγας, *megas*, in Greek, would equally mean 'terrible'. So, too, Priam, telling Sinon, 'you shall be one of us', *noster eris*,[3] implies a double meaning in Greek like 'you shall be our friend' and 'you shall be in our midst'. Other instances are clearer still.

Dido pleads with Aeneas not to leave her, and sends Anna to plead for her. He stands firm like an oak tree, its leaves and boughs blown by strong winds; *mens immota manet, lacrimae volvuntur inanes*, 'his deeper will stayed, unshakable, and the rolling tears were useless'.[4] *Mens*, the instinctive will, controlled and guarded by the vision, is the will of Aeneas. It is not said whose tears rolled. The structure of the sentence would suggest that they are the tears of Aeneas. But we only know for certain that Dido was weeping. So it is often assumed that they are her tears. But if so, it is strange Latin, without a possessive pronoun to explain that they are not the tears of Aeneas. Mainly, of course, they are his tears; but there are moments in the poem when it is well not to be too sure; and there are readers, also, who had better not be too sure at any time; and anyhow they are not his tears only, but hers too, if we need to think so, and, again if we need to think so, the very fountain of tears of all the world.

Aeneas did mind leaving Dido, and part of his tragedy is that he must seem, even to readers, not to mind, or not certainly to mind. One of Vergil's difficulties was to make a strong silent man, or one who visibly becomes a strong silent man, a tragic hero, for a tragic hero can scarcely be too strong and silent to be able to explain himself, and still remain dramatically interesting. Yet

1. Lewis Campbell *Sophocles* edited with English notes and introductions, Oxford, 1879, 1, 87–107, especially 99–101.

2. *A.* 11, 161.   3. *A.* 11, 149.

4. *A.* iv, 449; cf. Viktor Pöschl, *The Art of Vergil; Image and Symbol in the Aeneid*, Ann Arbor, Michigan, 1962 46–7. 185–6.

Vergil succeeded, partly through the sheer power of his intellect, shewn here in the omission of one demonstrative pronoun in the genitive case.

Vergil follows the device of ambiguity again, when Aeneas meets Dido in Hades, and for the last time, and takes away no kind word, no word at all, even, just an averted glare. His last words to her are *quem fugis? extremum fato quod te adloquor hoc est*, meaning something like 'From whom are you turning away? This is the last thing which I speak to you by fate',[1] not a very communicative translation, but capable of containing further meanings. The first two words are noticeable. They remind us that the last time that he saw her, Aeneas turned away, indeed fled away, from Dido; and now it is she who turns from him. The two words can also mean 'What had the man become from whom you turn away?', that is, 'Don't you see', or 'do you think', 'that I am a different man now?' That, if it is right, starts us thinking. The next words are cryptic. They may be 'It is fate's fault I am talking to you, but it is the last time', or 'It is only by fate that this is the last time I talk to you'; but it is a little strange as Latin, even Vergilian Latin, if so; *extremum fato* come together so impressively; and *quod te adloquor* looks more like 'my speaking to you' than 'what I say . . .' or 'that I speak . . .'. I doubt if the words can be prevented from having any of these meanings; but I doubt still more whether they can help meaning 'This talk to you is the last happiness that fate can ever let me have'. It was not like that when Achilles lost Briseis, or Odysseus left Calypso. When Dido goes, seen for the last time, Vergil does say that Aeneas wept.

Another characteristic of Vergil's language is this. Phrases, and even single words, sometimes, which are otherwise hard to understand, have an ancestry and a history, in Vergil's mind and on his pages, which it is often possible, and, if so, always worth while, to trace, for in that way much that is obscure can be clarified.

The Greeks, in the Second *Aeneid*, attacked Troy 'buried in sleep and wine', *somno vinoque sepultam*,[2] a use of *sepelire* found in prose, and Rutulians in the Ninth are similarly described, *somno vinoque soluti*, 'relaxed by sleep and wine'.[3] Ennius[4] and Lucretius[5]

1. *A.* VI, 466.   2. *A.* II, 265.   3 *A.*. IX, 189, 236.
4. Ennius, *Annals*, 292.   5. Lucretius, V, 975.

used similar phrases. In the sixth book, Aeneas and the Sibyl had to pass Cerberus, the watch dog of Hades. The Sibyl threw him a piece of drugged food, and he quickly went to sleep. Aeneas dashed to the door, *custode sepulto*, 'as soon as the guardian was safely buried';[1] not, of course, in the earth, but in the equivalent of 'sleep and wine', as we know from Vergil's use of the complete phrase in the Second *Aeneid*, but as, without the other passage, we could not have been sure of guessing.

The wooden horse climbed into Troy, *feta armis*, 'pregnant with arms',[2] these words at the beginning of a line. Later in the poem two heroes guard the gate of the Trojan camp in Latium *freti armis*, 'relying on their arms',[3] the words again at the beginning of the line. The text has been emended to *animis* 'courage' for *armis*, quite wrongly, since *armis* so obviously fits Vergil's style and method. He was thinking of an attempted entry through defence walls. And that reminded him of the wooden horse. So *feta armis* came back to him, and controlled his choice of words. He made, as usual, the smallest change.

In the *Georgics* Vergil writes, *ut silicis venis abstrusum excuderet ignem*, 'to hammer out the fire thrust deep in veins of flint',[4] a fine description, starting from Homer's σπέρμα πυρός, 'seed of fire'.[5] He also has *saeva leonum semina*, 'lion cubs, fiery atoms of ferocity',[6] if that is anywhere near the translation of words meaning literally 'fierce seeds of lions'. We can however at least see clearly some of the poetic value which *semina* may have, of minute but explosively powerful things. These two passages coalesce in the Sixth *Aeneid*, *quaerit pars semina flammae abstrusa in venis silicis*, 'some of them went in quest of the atoms that breed the flame, thrust deep in veins of flint'.[7]

Explaining how to recreate bees by spontaneous generation from killed bullocks, Vergil says that a time comes when 'creatures, quite marvellously, can be seen', *visenda modis animalia miris*.[8] This became associated in his mind with a group of words identical in metrical form. In grafting, he tells how farmers 'teach' a cutting from another tree 'to grow into the moist bark',

1. *A.* vi, 424.	2. *A.* ii, 238.	3. *A.* ix, 676.
4. *G.* i, 135.	5. *Odyssey*, v, 490.	6. *G.* ii, 151–2.
7. *A.* vi, 6–7.	8. *G.* iv, 309.	

udoque docent inolescere libro.[1] Anchises in the Sixth *Aeneid* says that souls in Purgatory have to be purified of many taints that during life on the earth inevitably 'grow into their souls, quite marvellously', *modis inolescere miris*,[2] two rather noticeable expressions coming together. Vergil found it easiest to write by listening to more than one original at once, and the originals were often from his own work.

There comes a time, says Vergil, when, but for human energy in picking fruit, degeneration of the fruit trees naturally sets in.[3] Everything 'falls away, grows worse again, ebbing, with the undertow back', *in peius ruere ac retro sublapsa referri*;[4] like a man rowing upstream, who, the moment he stops rowing, is swept quickly back downstream.[5] For 'the moment . . .' Vergil uses *atque*, normally 'and', but capable of the other meaning. The *at* in it was originally an interjection; Vergil, as usual, understood the word from the inside. For 'row' he uses *subigit*, 'drive from under', almost an 'etymological' meaning; he uses the word again for Charon, punting his boat, 'driving it from below' and perhaps also 'controlling' it,[6] another meaning, with his punt pole or boat hook. More important is a fuller reminiscence in the Second *Aeneid*. 'From the very moment', says Sinon, when the Palladium, the luck of Troy, was impiously stolen by Odysseus and Diomedes, 'the hopes of the Greeks trickled away, ebbing, with the undertow back', *ex illo fluere ac retro sublapsa referri*.[7] The first two words and the first two letters of the next are different; otherwise it is the line in the *Georgics*, applied now to human things from a first use about the land and nature. Clearly, the original metaphor is from an ebbing tide; futility is expressed by the falling rhythm of *ruere* and *fluere*, with elision; and the spirit and feeling of a Platonic thought concerning nature is proved to be exactly right, through its charge of old meanings and with a tiny change, for an ebb in the affairs of men. The still earlier history of the thought and its form may be long, going back to the literal backwash of the sea, possibly the sea that drew Odysseus, as he tried to land, back from the rocks at Scheria.[8]

1. *G.* II, 77. 2. *A.* VI, 738. 3. *G.* I, 197–203.
4. *G.* I, 199–200. 5. *G.* I, 201–3. 6. *A.* VI, 302.
7. *A.* II, 169. 8. *Odyssey*, V. 420–1.

This way of thinking and creating runs right through Vergil, shewing how dangerous it is to say, as has been said, of such similarities, 'the words are alike, but the thought is different'. The thought is always partly different, but it is also in some part of it the same, or words so nearly the same would not be used. If that is accepted, it becomes possible to find why similar words are used, and that reveals the fuller meaning. Sound dominated Vergil, and to understand him we must know how he heard the sound, and how it contained and conveyed to him his thought.

Apollo in the Sixth *Aeneid* magnificently masters the Sibyl's prophetic brain, 'crushing her to shape', *fingitque premendo*.[1] There is nothing wrong with that; it is admittedly terrific; but it is tempting to ask how Vergil thought of it. The answer is that he had been practising such sounds for such a meaning.[2] In the *Georgics* he has to talk of a countryman looking after trees; and for 'and he prunes them to shape', he brilliantly, but more obviously, says, *fingitque putando*.[3] Years of evolution, in which both conscious and unconscious thought played their part, went into the making of Vergil's great expressions.

Sometimes the final achievement is far richer than the earlier stages. In the *Georgics* there is *truncos sensere valentis*, 'found that the trunks had grown strong',[4] and *Grai vertere vocantes*, 'the Greeks translated and called . . .',[5] both happy, but neither exploiting the loveliness of the soft vowels as Vergil must all the time have felt that they could be exploited. But at last they were quite perfectly exploited, when in the *Aeneid* two doves of Venus guided Aeneas to the Golden Bough; *ipsa sub ora viri caelo venere volantes, et viridi sedere solo*, 'right up to his eyes, they came, came flying from the sky, and settled where the ground was green'.[6] Down and straight,

---

1. *A.* vi, 80.

2. For all this topic see F.-X. M. J. Roiron, *Étude sur l'imagination auditive de Virgile*, Paris, 1908; there is of course always the possible effect of phrases from other writers, known or unknown; here it is hard to know at what point in the process Vergil may have been influenced by words reported from Varius, *Fingitque morando*.

3. *G.* ii, 407.   4. *G.* ii, 426.   5. *G.* iii, 148.

6. *A.* vi, 191–2; Lucretius vi, 833: since *venere volantes* occurs here in Lucretius, Vergil may simply have taken the words from him; or, not less characteristically, he may have worked his way back to these through other

down and straight again they flew, and up, and alighted, all softly, as birds of Venus should. You can see and hear them. Vergil has found the full use for the music of his brain.

Charon's eyes 'glare starkly', *stant lumina flamma*.[1] This is strange; eyes do not usually stand, though *stare* is a very favourite Vergilian word, with many meanings, especially 'be still', for example of the sea, a Greek idea originally. If eyes 'stand', it is surprising that they should do it 'with flame'. There is an alternative reading, *stant lumina flammae*, 'eyes of flame stand', which is inferior in authority, but sometimes chosen. That it is unnecessary is proved by a phrase later in the poem. 'They see that the sky towers with a dust cloud', 'they see in the sky a towering cloud of dust', *iam pulvere caelum stare vident*.[2] That is more than half-way from prose to the poetry of Charon's eyes. The dust stands straight, a great streak of it, into the sky. That is, the sky itself looks a towering streak, and it is by means of the dust that it so appears. This characteristic transference is like *totumque adlabi classibus aequor*, 'all the sea's expanse aglide with shipping',[3] where the sea of course is still, and the 'fleets' are gliding. So the sky, 'stark towering with dust', is, perhaps, credible. Charon's eyes are like the sky in being suddenly impressive to the sight, intensely real in their steady, stark, stiff, 'standing' glare. They glare, of course, with flame; for Vergil's Charon is not only the Greek ferryman of Aristophanes, but more than half his Etruscan self, Charun, the Etruscan torturing death-devil, no ferryman at all. But Vergil has meanwhile got something else quite right. For the name Charon or Charun in Greek means something like 'bright eyed'.

Evander 'passed all the shape of Aeneas in review', 'gazed at him all over', *totum lustravit lumine corpus*.[4] *Lumine* ought to be *luminibus* to mean 'eyes', as Dido 'strayed with voiceless eyes all

similar-sounding word-groups; if he took his two words directly from Lucretius, the passages remain interesting: in Lucretius *volantes*, used as a noun, designates the birds which are killed by the atmosphere above Lake Avernus, whereas Vergil applies *volantes* as an adjectival participle to the life-giving doves of Venus, a typical inversion.

1. *A.* VI, 300: cf. Sir Frank Fletcher, *Vergil, Aeneid VI*, Oxford, 1941, pp. 56–7, who chooses *flammae* and takes it as nominative plural.

2. *A.* XII, 407–8.   3. *A.* X, 269.   4. *A.* VIII, 153.

over' Aeneas, *totumque pererrat luminibus tacitis*.[1] How *lumine* comes, is seen from *postera Phoebea lustrabat lampade terras . . . Aurora*, 'the morrow's dawn with the torch of Apollo's sun was washing all the earth'.[2] *Lustrare* and *lumen* could now easily attract each other. But *lustrare* does not mean 'look at', if it is the dawn, with the sun's torch. There is an intermediate reference. 'Sun, who review with purifying flames all works of the world', said Dido, *Sol, qui terrarum flammis opera omnia lustras*.[3] Vergil was remembering Sophocles, whose Ajax, about to die like Dido by the sword, appealed to the sun, the all-seeing. So here *lustrare* means both 'purify' and 'see'. It is a very Vergilian word; it is connected with *luere*, 'atone', and its first meaning is to 'wash'; its next meaning is to 'purify', as by walking up and down to purify an army ritually; and so just to 'walk up and down', or 'wander'. In Vergil's mind *lustrabat lumine* went together; perhaps he connected the words etymologically. He assumed, poetically, that with *lustrare* – whatever it might mean, for he did not analyse it every time – *lumine* was sure to be all right, especially when he could remember a similar phrase used with *luminibus* in the plural.

The association from which Vergil developed an expression was often predominantly an association of sound. What happened was this. With, or possibly more or less without, a rhythm, a sound attracted Vergil. He used it in some place where the feeling belonging to it was appropriate; as perhaps he had in mind *canibus lacerasse marinis*, 'to have torn with hounds of the sea',[4] from the *Ciris*, of Scylla, when he wrote *manibus supplex orasse supinis*, 'to have prayed with upturned hands,[5] in the *Aeneid*, of Iarbas, the Numidian who wanted to marry Dido, and prayed to Jupiter in his hate of Aeneas. From the *Ciris*[6] Vergil also apparently took four complete verses, which he used in the *Georgics*,[7] about the fate of Scylla, turned into a bird, to be pursued by Nisus, whom she had wronged, also turned into a bird; and much more besides.

Now the *Ciris* might just possibly be by Vergil, or it may be by

1. *A.* IV, 363–4.
2. *A.* IV, 6–7; cf. II, 564, 754 (with Servius); III, 658.
3. *A.* IV, 607. 4. *Ciris*, 61; *E.* VI, 77.
5. *A.* IV, 205; cf. IX, 485. 6. *Ciris*, 538–41. 7. *G.* I, 406–9.

someone else, perhaps his friend Gallus. That makes no difference
at present. Sounds came into Vergil's mind equally from the
work of himself and of others; and he used them. In this instance
he had to say that Iarbas prayed, and he might have used any one
of dozens of sound complexes to say it. The one he chose is
enjoyable for itself, and for the reminiscence in it. Readers can
easily find out for themselves reasons why they like it, if they do.
But it is really part of the earlier discussion, already passed, on
Vergil's process of evolving expressions from his own former
thoughts and phrases.

In the *Georgics*, it is told how a ploughman will knock against
empty helmets on an old battlefield. The helmets fell off, or the
human remains decayed, and left them. The words are *galeas . . .
inanis.*[1] The word *inanis* suggests frustration, because it is very
often 'empty' in the sense of 'vain'. You might possibly remember the empty helmet which Menelaus, in the *Iliad*,[2] found
in his hand, when in the duel the chin-strap of Paris, whom he was
dragging by his plume, broke. If so, the sense of frustration in the
Vergilian passage may be emphasized by the reminiscence, and
prepare you for the shock of a passage in the *Aeneid*, where Iulus,
son of Aeneas, rides up and pleads with the women of the expedition who are burning the ships; and he throws his empty
helmet on the ground, *galeam proiecit inanem.*[3] The literal sense is
almost absurd. He could hardly have thrown on the ground a
helmet with his head in it. This is one of the times when sound
takes charge of sense, and the sense of the sound is almost all the
sense there is. The process here is extremely associative, like a
surrealist picture rather than a surrealist poem. But it is not unlike
the process which led to *Oaxes* in the First *Eclogue*. There sounds
and associations produced an imaginary idea; here the sound of
inanem, with associations in Homer and Vergil himself, produced
a new meaning momentarily emerging from an ordinary word to
the exclusion of its literal significance. Vergil must want the word
to mean, if anything, 'helpless' or 'pathetic', to imply 'with a
gesture of helpless appeal'. There is not much doubt that this is

1. *G.* i, 496.
2. *Iliad*, iii, 369–76.
3. *A.* v, 673; A.-M. Guillemin, *L'originalité de Virgile*, Paris, 1931, 141–2.

how the word came to be used in this extraordinary way.[1] There might well be doubt whether it is a pardonable thing to have done. But, the more used to Vergil we are, the more we are likely to accept his meaning from this surprising communication. Such complete sacrifice of literal rationality is rare, though not quite unparalleled. Vergil never meant to write like James Joyce, but to some degree he prepared a way for him.

Sound association has created and left in the text of Vergil a phrase which mystified all commentators, till Mr J. R. T. Pollard saw that it was an example of this surrealism. Vergil says that Allecto travelled through the air, *caeli convexa per auras*, 'convex of heaven on the winds'.[2] The manuscript authority for this extraordinary expression is very strong indeed. *Convexa*, of course, means 'convex', and as an adjective in the neuter plural is used commonly enough elsewhere with *caeli* for the vault of heaven. Vergil meant to say something like 'conveyed' on the air, 'riding the air', but, instead of 'conveyed', he said 'convexed'. In his mind were the ordinary uses of *convexa* for 'vault of heaven' and some correct phrase for 'riding' such as *auras invecta tenebat*,[3] '(Juno) was holding [her course] riding the winds', literally, 'held the winds, riding,' a phrase that occurs a few pages before in the same book. Needless to say, emendations have been attempted; as usual, as if to restore something like the words of which Vergil had been thinking when he wrote his surprising phrase.

More often sound works on the creative imagination of Vergil with the cooperation of other impulses. I choose an example which seems specially interesting; but it is controversial. When Aeneas first landed on the soil of Carthage, shipwrecked, he fortunately found a herd of stags. He started shooting and did not stop till he 'laid out seven gigantic, fine stags victoriously on the ground', . . . [*cervorum*] *septem ingentia victor corpora fundat humo*.[4] *Fundat* is subjunctive, from *fundere*. But it might also mean 'founded', 'laid foundations for', 'attached firmly to', from *fundare*. *Humo* means, strangely, *from* the ground, which seems

---

1. *A.* v, 673: the possibility that *inanem* means a helmet used for a sham unreal fight, the Trojan Game just concluded and mentioned as *belli simulacra* in the next line, *A.* v, 674, seems to me less likely.

2. *A.* VII, 543.   3. *A.* VII, 287.   4. *A.* I, 192–3.

wrong, and as *humi*, not *humo*, normally means 'on the ground' in Latin, though there are examples of *humo* in poetry, *humo*, which is the reading of the manuscripts, is usually emended to *humi*. But it is not difficult to see how Vergil reached his strange expression. Ultimately it is due to a reminiscence of sound. To Vergil, associating by sound *fundat*, subjunctive, and *fundat*, indicative, the word meant at this moment 'plant', 'root to the spot'. The anchor, with its gripping teeth, 'founded' the fleet when it first came to Italy, *fundabat*.[1] Aeneas put the stags immovably on the ground, rooted to it, not by anchors or anything like that, but by their own weight. The difference between the stags alive and galloping and the same stags dead and motionless could well be expressed by the thought that they suddenly became rooted or anchored to the ground, almost as if they had foundations in it, like a building. Next comes something else. Vergil had already written, or at least had thought of writing, that after the sack, 'all Troy smokes from the ground', *omnis humo fumat Neptunia Troia*.[2] To say 'from the ground' is natural and right for the contrast between Troy standing and alive, and Troy dead and burning. At this point Vergil, with visual imagination this time, saw the pictures together, Troy smoking, and the stags, dead on the ground, smoking too, with the steam of the warmth of life and action just done. He was used to looking closely at animals, and had noticed the steam coming from them, as he shews elsewhere.[3] And now, or earlier in the process, sound helped. To one of Vergil's kind of imagination, who was remembering *fumat humo*, 'smoking from the ground,' it was almost inevitable to say, if he said *fundat* – whether from *fundere* or *fundare*, so alike in sound – *fundat humo*, meaning almost 'anchored, smoking from the ground'. Vergil, for unusual reasons, chose a word and a form which were together also unusual, but not impossible.

This is a good passage for indicating the complicated system of different impulses through which Vergil must sometimes be understood. It is not unique and anyone who disagrees about it can find others. Perhaps it may remind us that he had a visual, as well as an audial, imagination, both working together. Sometimes

1. *A.* VI, 4. 2. *A.* III, 3. 3. *G.* II, 542.

he visualized very sharply indeed, but perhaps not always; it is a question that has been met already. The passage may remind us, too, that Vergil's peculiar poetic process must always be remembered, when a question of a reading arises. He may at any time surprise us by saying 'Sermons in stones' instead of 'in books', or even something stranger still.

Vergil's language is guided by audial imagination, and directed towards compression, which gives emotional and intellectual density. Like the otherwise very different Thucydides, he can achieve 'more ideas than words'; like him, he lets silence speak to heart and mind; but the proportion of thought to emotion is necessarily different in the 'ideas' of a poet.

As compression enabled Vergil to elicit more and more meaning from words in themselves and in their proximity to other words, so also it is compression which guided Vergil in his choice and his changes of grammar and syntax. He used the history of words and constructions in both Latin and Greek to help him to achieve compression.

Metrical value and compression of meaning, old Latin, and also but much less, Greek practice, recommended to Vergil syncopated forms of verbs, and he has many, such as *placida compostus pace*,[1] 'laid calm in gracious peace', *compostus* for *compositus*, *accestis*, 'you have approached',[2] for *accessistis*, and *qui Paridis direxti tela* 'who guided the bow of Paris',[3] *direxti* for *direxisti*; there is another reading, *derexti*. The hard, consonantal words are worth more than mere convenience. Two lines after *direxti* is another example, *gentis repostas*, 'nations secluded from the world'.[4]

The compression, which affects Vergil's grammar and syntax, is partly controlled by metre. In classical Latin, present participles on the whole have their ablative in -*i*, except when they are in the ablative absolute construction. Vergil readily uses -*e* in *ocior* ... *ventos aequante sagitta*, 'swifter than an arrow that keeps pace with winds'.[5] To provide the two short syllables which metre demands in this part of the verse, Vergil would have had to introduce an unwanted word but for the form in -*e*. He also uses the form for an

1. *A*. I, 249.　　2. *A*. I, 201.　　3. *A*. VI, 57.　　4. *A*. VI, 59.
5. *A*. X, 248.

adjective of this character when it is not a participle, as *Laurente*, 'Laurentian',[1] for *Laurenti*. Perhaps this is scarcely irregular. The rules for -*i* and -*e* were not rigidly fixed in Vergil's time, so far as they concerned adjectival forms.

Vergil uses a fourth declension dative, in -*u* for -*ui*, as in *curru subiungere tigris*, 'yoke tigers to a chariot'.[2] Compression is gained; for without this dative the metre might have imposed a long periphrasis.

Vergil does not usually employ forms that belong purely to earlier Latin, but he does at times. Some of his metrical variations suggest the past rather than the present. Occasionally he uses the old first declension genitive in -*āī*, common in Lucretius; as *aurai simplicis ignem*, 'fire of air's purity'.[3] He also several times uses *ollus*, old equivalent of *ille*, 'that' or 'he', as known for instance in the old funeral formula, *ollus quiris leto datus*, perhaps, 'that Roman has been sent on his way to death', 'has died', that is. Vergil, however, though he uses the word several times, only uses it in the nominative plural and dative singular, *olli*, and in the dative plural *ollis*, as *olli . . . procumbunt*, 'they fall to their task',[4] *olli . . . respondit . . . Latinus*, 'to him Latinus replied',[5] and *igneus est ollis vigor*, 'they have a fiery energy'.[6] Once there is a form of the old verb *fuo*, the Greek φύω, from which the perfect tenses of *esse*, 'to be', were formed, in *Tros Italusve fuat, nullo discrimine habebo*, 'whether he be Trojan or Italian, I shall hold it in no distinction',[7] that is, 'it will make no difference'. Another old verbal form is *faxo*, 'I shall make', 'see to it', 'guarantee', common in comedy. It retains the -*s* of old futures, like Greek, as in πράξω, *praxo*, 'I shall do'. Vergil has the old future in *ego foedera faxo firma manu*, 'I shall make our treaty sure by my own might'.[8]

Several times, too, Vergil uses the old present passive, or deponent, infinitive in -*ier*, as in *summa dominarier arce*, 'hold sway at the citadel's crest'.[9] It found its place naturally in hexameter rhythms, and, like most Vergilian usages, it may have been at least helped towards adoption by its readiness to fit the metre. Once,

1. *A.* XII, 547.   2. *E.* V, 29.   3. *A.* VI, 747.
4. *A.* V, 197–8.   5. *A.* XII, 18.   6. *A.* VI, 730.
7. *A.* X, 108.   8. *A.* XII, 316–7; cf. IX, 154.
9. *A.* VII, 70.

if an ancient opinion is correct, he uses *dii* for *diei*, an old genitive of *dies*, 'day';[1] and once, apparently, a genitive *die*.[2]

Vergil has two examples of tmesis, the separation of a prefix from a word. Here again no single origin can be asserted. Ennius has the notorious *cere- comminuit -brum*, 'split his brains', the word *cerebrum* being shamelessly split too. Alike in Homer and Lucretius some prefixes are not closely bound to their words; in Homer's language they have not reached that stage, and are naturally free. In Greek tragedy they have already become attached, but sometimes become detached again. It is mainly but not purely through Lucretius that Vergil has *inque salutatam linquo*, 'and whom, with no goodbyes said to her, I leave',[3] for *insalutatamque*, and *inque ligatus*, 'tied from moving',[4] for *inligatusque*.

Ablatives often provide a useful short syllable, and Vergil uses them for a great variety of meanings. Since the appropriate preposition would often lose more space than the use of the ablative gains, he freely omits prepositions, and especially prepositions meaning 'in', 'at', or 'from'. This practice of Vergil is so general and obvious that the long treatment which it would need is hardly worth while. Perhaps one particularly pleasing example will serve here. Neptunus found that Aeolus had started a storm without his permission, 'and he lifted from the crest of a wave his head, serene, looking forth over the deep', *et alto prospiciens summa placidum caput extulit unda*.[5] The ablative *unda* is very natural, but the other ablative, *alto*, has always been hard to understand. It might have meant 'lifted from the deep', but there is already *unda* to provide that meaning. It might mean 'looking forth from the deep', but that is forced and strange, especially with no noun for *alto* to qualify. It cannot naturally mean 'looking forth over the deep', unless Vergil has extended his use of the ablative without a preposition farther even than is usual for him.

Now one Vergilian use of the ablative has been called 'ablative of motion within a place', like *toto properari litore*, 'there is hurrying all over the shore',[6] though here the ablative without a preposition could be simply a poetic ablative of place where, or

1. *A.* 1, 636; Aulus Gellius, IX, 14, 8.   2. *G.* 1, 208.
3. *A.* IX, 288.   4. *A.* X, 794.   5. *A.* 1, 126–7.
6. *A.* IV, 416.

even a normal ablative, excused its preposition by *totus*, a regular prose usage. The ablative *alto* probably means 'over the deep', as if the gaze of Neptunus passed, that is, moved over it, when he looked. Vergil allowed himself this strange ablative because it afforded an economy of words. He already had the verse *prospiciens summa flavum caput extulit unda*, 'looking forth she raised her gold-haired head from the crest of the wave',[1] which he had used of Arethusa in the *Georgics*. He could fit it into its new place, substituting *placidum* for *flavum*, with such neat economy, only because he allowed himself the rather daring ablative *alto* to fill a place at the end of the preceding line. He had elsewhere often used *alto* at the end of a line, but in more normal circumstances.

Vergil also omits prepositions with the accusative, meaning 'to', especially after verbs of motion, as ... *remeabo inglorius urbes*, 'without my glory to the cities ... I shall return'.[2] As so often, when Vergil goes forward, he also goes back, for there is usually something old in his innovations. Here he is using the accusative in a way appropriate to Latin, as regular accusatives for 'motion to', without a preposition, shew; they survive, notoriously, in names of towns and small islands, and in the words *domus*, 'home', and *rus*, 'country'. But, as so often, there is Greek influence too, for Greek poetry frequently leaves out prepositions, which are needed in prose, with all cases. It is well known that originally cases had to sustain their meanings without the help of prepositions, which were developed comparatively late.

A very famous class of Vergilian usages concerns the accusative case, carrying a more or less adverbial meaning. In classical prose there are slight survivals of such a use in *quid?* 'why?', literally something like 'in relation to which?', *quod*, 'because', literally something like the same thing, without the question mark, and *nihil*, 'not at all', literally 'in respect of nothing'. There is some antecedent in old Latin; but as usual the influence is Greek too, for Greek prose and poetry freely use accusatives which are to some extent adverbial accusatives, or accusatives of respect. Vergil adopted such accusatives inevitably, since they are a great

1. *G.* IV, 352.
2. *A.* XI, 793. For uses of the accusative, see the fine treatment in E. C. Woodcock, *A New Latin Syntax*, London, 1959, 1–14.

help to compression. And with them he sometimes used middle verbs, that is, verbs passive in form but in meaning neither active nor passive, but partly both. Again the origin is double. The middle voice existed in old Latin; and of course in Classical Greek of all kinds it is most frequent.

Accusatives which can be widely classed as adverbial are not very easy to classify and understand exactly, especially as Vergil uses them.

There is firstly the cognate accusative, an accusative object which contains the same idea as the verb and is thus akin to it, as in *itque reditque viam totiens*, 'so often goes and returns his way'.[1]

Perhaps it is by an extension of this accusative that such an accusative is possible as in *aeternum vale*, 'farewell for all time', as if it meant 'farewell an eternal farewell'.[2] But here *aeternum* may be purely accusative of length of time, since *vale* in Latin means 'be well'; the strict meaning may be 'be well for an endless time'. It is hard to be sure how much the exact original meaning of *vale*, 'be well' 'fare well', was always remembered. Catullus wrote *in perpetuum, frater, ave atque vale*, as if he meant literally 'fare, my brother, for ever well', rather than 'good-bye . . .'[3] Vergil looked inside words according to his etymological habit; but it remains possible that here he simply compressed the usual phrase *in aeternum* into an adverbial accusative.

More certainly comparable to cognate accusatives are the true internal accusatives, adjectives in the neuter, qualifying no expressed substantives, and acting as objects to verbs, as in *horrendum stridens*, 'with her frightful shrieking',[4] and *nec mortale sonans*, 'speaking in no mortal tones'.[5] The natural explanation is that these quotations literally mean 'shrieking a horrible shriek' and 'sounding a not mortal sound'.

There is an interesting extension of this accusative in *nec vox hominem sonat*, 'and there is no human creature in your voice's sound',[6] a noun this time, not an adjective. The literal meaning is 'and your voice does not sound a man', and so 'your voice has not got a man in its sound'. It is to be supposed that there is an ellipse. 'To sound a man' is 'to indicate a human creature with

1. *A.* VI, 122.   2. *A.* XI, 98; cf. 97.   3. Catullus, CI, 10.
4. *A.* VI, 288.   5. *A.* VI, 50.   6. *A.* I, 328.

sounds', or 'to convey by sounds the idea of a human creature', a quite Vergilian compression of a phrase into a word. There are Greek usages which might have helped, perhaps two in particular, one of which is remembered in this very context. Aeneas is addressing his divine mother Venus, who has appeared to him on the Carthaginian coast disguised as a human huntress, and he says that she is surely a goddess. Later she declares herself, *vera incessu patuit dea*, 'a goddess indeed she proved herself by her very walk to be'.[1] *Patuit dea*, literally 'she was open as a goddess', is from the Greek φανερὰ ἦν θεὰ οὖσα, 'she was obvious being a goddess', that is, 'she was obviously a goddess'. That is in the first book of the *Aeneid*. In the last, Turnus recognizes his divine sister Juturna, and says *nequiquam fallis dea*, 'uselessly do you try to disguise that you are a goddess',[2] literally, 'you deceive or escape notice being a goddess', a normal Greek construction, λανθάνεις θεὰ οὖσα, which Latin reproduces with an enforced compression, since in Latin there is no participle meaning 'being'.

The Greek nominative appears again in *sensit medios delapsus in hostis*, 'he realized that he had slipped into the midst of enemies'.[3] Greek uses a nominative of the participle after verbs of perception if the subjects of main and subordinate clauses are the same; 'he realized that he had slipped' would be ἤσθετο ἐμπεσών, like Vergil's Latin.

Such constructions, suggested by the required meaning, may have combined with thoughts of adjectives in the internal accusative to produce *hominem sonat*.

There is another construction like *hominem sonat* in *parte alia Marti currumque rotasque volucris instabant*, 'elsewhere in their cave the Cyclopes were pressing on a chariot for Mars, and winged wheels for it'.[4] *Instare* takes a dative. The accusatives are due to the thought that they were pressing on with their task, and their task was the chariot and wheels. This time the accusatives might be called in apposition to a cognate accusative understood.

Comparable, perhaps, is a passage already considered, *fecerat et ... fetam ... procubuisse lupam*, 'he (Vulcanus) had made too [a part of the shield of Aeneas] picturing how a she-wolf, preg-

1. *A.* I, 405.   2. *A.* XII, 634.   3. *A.* II, 377.
4. *A.* VIII, 433-4.

267

nant, had sunk down,'[1] literally 'he had made . . . that the she-wolf had . . .' *Facere* must here mean 'to make a picture telling a story', and the accusative and infinitive can be called in apposition to an object understood. The picture and the story are nearly equivalent anyhow; they are not even irregular Latin; indeed Vergil writes of 'reading a picture'[2] (on the gates of the temple at Cumae). As usual, there is here, too, a Greek side, for the Greek for 'make', ποιεῖν, the origin of the word 'poet', readily means 'make poetry' or 'tell in poetry a story', followed by an accusative and infinitive; and it is used, too, of creating pictorial art.

Another accusative hard to explain with complete certainty is in *intonuit laevum*, 'it thundered on the left'.[3] Probably that is internal or cognate; 'it thundered a left-hand thunder'. But Vergil sometimes makes intransitive verbs transitive, and transitive intransitive. He has, thus, *clipeum . . . intonat*, 'makes his shield thunder',[4] and *verbera insonuit*, 'cracked her whip'.[5] So possibly *intonuit laevum* was to him 'it made to thunder the left "thing",' that is, ' "part of the sky".'

When Vergil writes *cetera parce, puer, bello*, 'in all else, my boy, refrain from the war',[6] he makes *cetera* an adverbial accusative, 'as to the rest'. *Parcere*, 'spare', of course, takes the dative. It can be argued that *cetera* is cognate, 'spare all your other sparings', but it is safer to trace it to the natural tendency of earlier Latin to use the accusative adverbially, as in the prose use of the singular *ceterum*, 'for the rest', sometimes in the sense of 'however'; and perhaps still more to the Greek τὰ ἄλλα, 'in other respects', clearly the original of *cetera Graius* of Achaemenides, who was 'in all else', obviously, 'a Greek'.[7]

Vergil's more complicated accusatives owe something to a natural tendency of Latin, something to Greek, and much to himself.

The Greek middle voice has often to be considered also, and the old Latin middle voice remembered. Vergil writes *ferro accingor*, 'I am girt',[8] that is, 'I gird myself with my blade'. He also writes *ferrum cingitur*, 'he girds to himself his blade'.[9] In the first

1. *A.* VIII, 630–1.   2. *A.* VI, 34.   3. *A.* II, 693; IX, 631.
4. *A.* IX, 709.   5. *A.* VII, 451.   6. *A.* IX, 656.
7. *A.* III, 594.   8. *A.* II, 671.   9. *A.* II, 510–1.

the person is the direct object; in the second the sword is the direct object, and the person the indirect. Both are legitimate significations of the middle voice in Greek, and from them come many usages of Latin poets, and especially Vergil.

When the person who does the action is the indirect object of the middle, the direct object may be a part of the person, as in *nigro circumdata turbine corpus*, 'herself shrouded in blackest cyclone storm',[1] literally 'having surrounded for herself her body . . .' The middle has another meaning, as in *pictus acu tunicas*, either 'having embroidered his tunic',[2] or, perhaps more rightly here, 'having had his tunic embroidered', and so 'wearing an embroidered tunic'.

The common use of perfect participles explicable as middles with direct objects is close to a use of adjectives. In *lacerum . . . ora*, 'torn in the face',[3] *lacer* is almost a verb; but it would be forced and wrong to suggest that it is in any sense middle. Still less would it be right to suggest this for *nigrantis terga*, '[bullocks] with black backs',[4] and little more for *nudus membra*, 'his limbs bare'.[5] These 'accusatives of the part affected' may be traced partly, but only partly, to old Latin; middle usages, Latin and Greek, may have helped; but, still more, common Greek prose usages, one of which Vergil not only translates but even transliterates in *Cressa genus*, '(a slave girl) a Cretan by race',[6] Κρῆσσα τὸ γένος. To an extent hard to fix, this explanation may often partly apply to accusatives equally explicable as direct objects to middle verbs. In *manus iuvenem . . . post terga revinctum*, 'a young man with his hands tied behind his back',[7] the explanation by the middle is unlikely. The verb is clearly passive, and the phrase something like a close translation of a Greek passive participle, with a Greek accusative of the part affected or accusative of respect.

Characteristically Vergilian is transference, the application of an idea to one word which naturally belongs to another; and transference affects middle constructions, as in *lacrimis . . . perfusa genas*, 'with tears streaming over her cheeks'.[8] Here it would be more natural to say *lacrimas*, for the tears are poured, and *genis*, for they are poured on the cheeks; however, the *per-* of *perfundere* can im-

1. *A.* XI, 596.   2. *A.* XI, 777.   3. *A.* VI, 495.
4. *A.* VI, 243.   5. *A.* VIII, 425.   6. *A.* V, 285.
7. *A.* II, 57.   8. *A.* XII, 64–5.

ply an accusative *genas*. The transference is clearer in *lacrimis oculos suffusa nitentis*, 'her shining eyes brimmed with tears'.[1]

In *perque pedes traiectus lora tumentis*, '[dead Hector . . .] and his feet, all swollen, pierced through with thongs',[2] there may be a transference, the natural expression being 'having been pierced through his feet with thongs', not 'thongs through his feet', according to Latin usage. *Lora* is not a natural accusative unless *traiectus* is middle, and it is object to it. But Hector did not pierce his own feet; Achilles did. *Traiectus pedes* would be simple, *pedes* being an accusative, perhaps Greek, of the part affected. On the other hand *traiectus*, 'pierced' or 'put through', makes *per*, 'through', natural. This, and the illogical feeling that *traiectus* is a middle like many other middles in the *Aeneid*, combined to make the transference easy. Or possibly *lora* is object to *-iectus*, meaning 'allow to throw or pass', so 'having allowed [someone] to pass thongs . . .'.

There is perhaps a similar transference in *puppis . . . Phrygios subiuncta leones*, '[the ship] with Phrygian lions linked [at her prow, as figurehead]'.[3] This, literally, is the 'ship linked as to Phrygian lions'. More logical would be 'linked as to her prow with lions'. Here the lions may be regarded as part of the ship; it was actually the lions that were linked, heraldically together, each side of the stem. But grammatically the ship was linked, and the part affected, the prow, might have expected to be added, in the accusative, with the lions in the ablative. Conceivably, *subiuncta* might be middle, as if the ship linked its own lions.

Vergil extends the normal Latin objective genitive after some adjectives, such as in *peritus belli* 'skilled in war', and as in *Phoebi nondum patiens*, 'not yet consenting to endure Phoebus' power',[4] to other adjectives, especially participles. Greek poetry has genitives with many shades of meaning which might have helped. In *veri . . . effeta senectus*, 'old age that has no more fertility of truth', 'can bear no more truth',[5] *veri* is also an objective genitive after an adjective containing a verbal idea. In *fortunatus . . . laborum*, 'enviable for', or 'happy in,' 'your duties faced',[6] the genitive is a genitive of origin or cause, principally Greek, for Greek uses a genitive freely after verbs meaning 'admire', 'envy', 'count happy'. It can be

1. *A.* I, 228.   2. *A.* II, 273.   3. *A.* X, 156–7.
4. *A.* VI, 77.   5. *A.* VII, 440, 452.   6. *A.* XI, 416.

called a genitive of the source of emotion. Or it may be near the principal original meaning of the genitive, the meaning of an expanse of existence, within which something has a place – the whole book, of which something noticed is one chapter. Here the duty faced constitutes a kind of mental world, and the good fortune exists because it has a place in the world of duty faced. The phrase is continued with *egregiusque animi*, 'and rare in spirit', 'of rare spirit'.[1] This genitive is also a genitive of the whole world to which a part belongs, the world being high spirit, and the part being the distinction in that quality. Meanwhile, the construction is helped by the normal prose use of the 'characteristic genitive', as in *vir magnae virtutis*, 'a man of great courage'. Vergil may be said to have simply transferred the adjective from the noun in the genitive, guided by his habit of using genitives in their original partitive sense, and helped by Greek usages which were nearer than Latin usages to the broad original meaning. This original meaning probably appears in *fessi rerum*, 'weary at their plight'.[2]

A genitive takes part in a difficult line, *iustitiaene prius mirer belline laborem*, 'Is it for his justice, more, that I should admire him, or admire his exertion in the war?'[3] So Drances thinks of Aeneas. *Iustitiae* is a Greek genitive of cause, or the source of emotion, as with other verbs such as 'pity . . . for'. The object, 'him', is understood. Then the construction changes. Vergil often writes -*ne*, the interrogative particle, at the beginning of the second part of a question where *an*, 'or', might be expected, as in *pelagus Troiamne petemus*, 'shall we make for the ocean, or Troy?';[4] he also uses *anne*, as in *filius, anne aliquis magna de stirpe nepotum?* 'is he a son of mine, or some one from the lordly lineage of my descendants?'[5] – asked in Elysium by Aeneas about the spirit of Marcellus. In this way Vergil saves an introductory particle, and has one of them, not two. After *belline*, then, by a change of construction, *laborem* is direct object to *mirer*. However, other readings, *iustitiane* and *laborum*, are well attested. If they are right, *iustitia* is ablative of cause, and *laborum* the Greek genitive of the source of emotion. It is at least unlikely that the right reading, whatever it may be, has the two nouns in the same case.

1. *A.* XI, 417.   2. *A.* I, 178.   3. *A.* XI, 126.   4. *A.* X, 378.
5. *A.* VI, 864.

The dative case originally indicated something like a third party in a transaction, without clear definition of the relation to the action in which the third part stands. Later the relation came to be more clearly defined, and most Latin datives can be described as datives of advantage or of disadvantage.

Vergil is characteristically true to the nature of Latin in his extensions of the dative.

There is a remarkable dative of disadvantage, or perhaps an ethic dative, denoting a mental effect, in *et hosti ante exspectatum positis stat in agmine castris*, 'and, for the enemy before all expectation, [the Roman soldier] stands in marching ranks, his camp already made'.[1] The troops are there, for the enemy's surprise and alarm. Another explanation may be right, or partly right. The dative may be a dative of the agent after the perfect passive participle, a usage regular in Greek and common in classical Latin, which Vergil employs elsewhere as in *nunc oblita mihi tot carmina*, 'all those poems have now been forgotten by me'.[2]

When Vergil writes *longe illi dea mater erit*, 'his goddess mother will be far from him',[3] literally 'for him', an ablative with *ab* 'from' would have been expected. To quote every relevant parallel would be too long, but something can be said shortly. The dative seems to imply separation. It could be called an old-fashioned dative of undefined relationship; but it was used by Vergil under various suggestions. He was partly thinking of the dative of disadvantage after *deesse*, 'to be wanting to', 'to fail', a meaning which is implicit here. There may have been a thought, too, of a possessive dative, 'he will have his goddess mother far away'. The use of the adverb *longe* is perhaps colloquial.

In Vergil's phrase *curru subiungere tigris*, 'to yoke tigers to a chariot',[4] *curru* being an old form of *currui*, the dative is a dative of advantage, as if the tigers were yoked for the good of the chariot. This dative in Vergil tends to return to the old dative of motion to. He writes *subiere feretro*, 'they placed themselves beneath the bier',[5] very nearly 'went under' it. In these instances the use of datives with other verbs compounded with *sub-*, and also with

1. *G.* III, 347-8. 2. *E.* IX, 53. 3. *A.* XII, 52.
4. *E.* V, 29. 5. *A.* VI, 222.

verbs compounded with *in-* and other prepositions, may have made the dative seem natural.

Extensions of the normal dative after verbs of giving helped the tendency to a 'dative of motion to'. *Pelago . . . praecipitare*, 'to throw headlong into the sea',[1] and *fer cineres . . . rivo . . . fluenti*, 'bring ashes . . . to the flowing streamlet'[2] are like 'give to the sea' and 'give to the flowing streamlet'. Less like any kind of giving is *praedam . . . ales proiecit fluvio*, 'the bird flung its prey away into the river'.[3]

Finally, a 'dative of motion to' must be frankly recognized in *it caelo clamor*, 'a shout rose to the sky',[4] and *facilis descensus Averno*, 'easy is the descent to Avernus'.[5]

It is often said that the reflexives, *se* and *suus*, 'himself', 'his own', 'herself', 'her own' and so on, must refer to the grammatical subject of the clause and normally of the main clause. This is not strictly true, for the rule often has to be broken for the sake of sense, and reference to the logical, not the grammatical, subject was certainly permissible, from the early poet Naevius onwards. At any rate, this freedom is conspicuous in Vergil, especially for the nominative of *suus*, as in *stat sua cuique dies*, 'each has his own appointed day',[6] and *responsa reposcit ordine cuncta suo*, 'required full answers, each in its own right place'.[7] Sometimes there is some strain, as in the famous and sublime *quisque suos patimur manis*, 'each of us bears the destiny which is his own spirit in death',[8] where the subject of the verb is in the first person, and *suos* is of the third person. Here, too, there is much gain in compression.

An example of double influence, from older Latin and from Greek at the same time, is in the characteristically Vergilian use of two or three *-que*s for 'both . . . and . . .'. The first *-que* is the Greek τε; they are ultimately the same word, as *quis?*, 'who?', is the same as τίς; and *quis*, 'anyone', the same as τις. The original meaning of *-que* and τε was something like 'just' or 'precisely', not 'and'; such meanings, other than 'and', remain in many words, as *quicumque*, 'whoever'. Vergil understood this *-que* unusually well, for he actually uses *atque* to mean 'immediately',[9] not 'and',

1. *A.* II, 36–7.   2. *E.* VIII, 101.   3. *A.* XII, 255–6.
4. *A.* XI, 192.   5. *A.* VI, 126.   6. *A.* X, 467.
7. *A.* XI, 240–1.   8. *A.* VI, 743.   9. *G.* I, 203.

building up the meaning out of *at*, originally an interjection like 'oh!', and -*que*, 'just', 'oh! just' apparently meaning to him 'There! At the moment . . .' However, unlike Greek τε, -*que* in Latin should not strictly mean 'both', but only 'and'. It is not certain that in Latin it ever exactly means 'both'. But it is commonly used in a position in which 'both' would be appropriate, not only by Vergil, but by others, from Naevius onwards. Ennius already has *divumque hominumque*, 'both of gods and of men also'.[1] In the corresponding Greek phrases, such as ἀνδρῶν τε θεῶν τε, again 'both of gods and of men also', the meaning is nearly or quite 'both . . . and . . .', and the Latin version must have come to nearly the same thing from Greek influence. But the earliest Latin writers had already started that, or a similar process, and not certainly through Greek influence alone, for there too a -*que* appears, more or less redundantly used.

An obvious and simple example of Vergil's principle of compression in syntax is his use of *quippe*. Here he might be said to compress his syntax to the extent of removing it altogether, and of using *quippe* without its appropriate syntax, so that it means not less but more.

By no means always, but most often in ordinary classical Latin *quippe*, meaning something like 'inasmuch as', is used with a relative, *qui, quae, quod*, or with a participle. Vergil has the word several times, but always absolutely, like a co-ordinating conjunction, or an adverb. The expression is therefore shorter, and, further, meanings vary subtly. Often it is not the usual Latin *quippe* at all. Juno's *quippe vetor fatis* is 'oh, but, I suppose, it is by fates I am forbidden'.[2] Iarbas, the Numidian who wants to marry Dido, says in his reproach to Jupiter, *nos munera templis quippe tuis ferimus*, 'of course, we go on bringing gifts to those temples, just because they are yours'[3] – though we get no good from them. *Quippe* is not satisfied by 'just because'. It wants 'of course' too.

Vergil chose *quippe* to represent the Greek δή, *de*, a particle mainly emphatic and ironical. *Templis quippe tuis* almost means 'temples wrongly supposed to belong to you'. Why Vergil chose *quippe* for this use is a subtle question. He needed his delicate dexterity to make Latin come so near to the sensitivity of Greek.

1. Ennius *Annals*, 249.   2. *A.* I, 39.   3. *A.* IV, 217–18.

Obeying the motive of compression, and again depending on both Greek and partly on Old Latin authority, Vergil characteristically used the infinitive where *ut* or *ne* with the subjunctive are classical, especially after verbs of commanding, persuading, preventing, and so on, as in *admittier orant*, 'they entreat to be admitted',[1] *monet succedere Lauso Turnum*, 'she warned Turnus to go to the help of Lausus',[2] and *parce pias scelerare manus*, 'refrain from staining with sin true hands'.[3] Not far from this use is the infinitive of purpose, perhaps mainly Greek in origin, very often used with *dare*, as *dedit gestare*, 'gave him to carry'.[4] Comparable to this infinitive is the infinitive after a noun containing a verbal idea, as in *amor casus cognoscere nostros*, 'passion to learn our adventures'.[5] The infinitive is treated as a noun in the accusative, object to a verb, actual or virtual.

Similarly, the simple present infinitive, regarded as an accusative object, occurs regularly after verbs which in prose require for their object a phrase composed of an accusative and a future infinitive, as *promitto occurrere turmae*, 'I volunteer to go and face the squadron'.[6]

Historic infinitives are frequent, as in *nos pavidi trepidare metu*, 'we, alarmed, made haste in trembling dread'.[7] But Vergil's use of them is not significantly different from their use in ordinary classical prose.

The subjunctive is regularly in Vergil replaced by the imperative after *ne* and *neve*, *neu*, in prohibitions, as in *ne me terrete*, 'affright me not'.[8] This clearly facilitates compression, and is all the more natural in Augustan Latin because it is the regular construction in Greek.

Apart from the imperative for subjunctive after *ne* in prohibitions, Vergil's use of moods and tenses is nearly always classical.

The chief exception is in indirect question; here, following both Greek and old Latin usage, Vergil occasionally replaces the subjunctive with the indicative, as in *viden ut geminae stant vertice cristae*, 'see you how on his crest the twin plumes stand?',[9] and *ne quaere doceri . . . quae . . . fortuna . . . mersit*, 'search not to be told . . . what

1. *A.* IX, 231.	2. *A.* X, 439–40.	3. *A.* III, 42.
4. *A.* XII, 211.	5. *A.* II, 10.	6. *A.* XI, 503.
7. *A.* II, 685.	8. *A.* XII, 875.	9. *A.* VI, 779.

fortune plunged [them into such misery]'.[1] The text at such places is often emended, but to do so is nearly always, and perhaps quite always, wrong.

Frequently a subjunctive form of *esse*, 'to be', in a compound tense is omitted, against the rule for classical prose which normally omits only indicatives; as in *quaerit . . . quae passus terraque marique*, 'he asked what he had endured on land and sea',[2] *sit* or *esset* being understood. Compression is similarly gained when two perfect participles, one the predicate, are used without *et* and a copulative verb, as *superis immissa . . . Allecto . . . bacchata*, 'Allecto released upon the world above has made her revelry . . .'[3]

In 'if' -clauses, where a future or future-perfect indicative would be expected, Vergil sometimes uses a present indicative, as in *si pereo, hominum manibus periisse iuvabit*, 'if I die', or, perhaps, 'if my death is upon me, it will be pleasure that I have died at human hands'.[4] Of course, the present has variations of meaning, sometimes near to a deliberative subjunctive; and anyway the present tense, expressing future time in such clauses, is far more legitimate in classical prose than it is often supposed to be.

Another similar habit of Vergil's is also not strictly irregular. He puts past unfulfilled conditions into a kind of historic present, making them appear like future remote conditions, as in *ni docta comes . . . admoneat . . . irruat*, 'if his learned guide were not to warn him . . . , he would dash in upon them'.[5] The natural meaning would be, 'if his learned guide had not warned him, he would have dashed in upon them', with imperfect or pluperfect subjunctives. It is hard to say exactly whether the form of the sentence is changed, or whether it is simply put into historic presents.

Vergil has many examples of the so-called irregular conditions, as *si fata deum, si mens non laeva fuisset, impulerat ferro Argolicas foedare latebras, Troiaque nunc staret, Priamique arx alta, maneres*, 'if decrees of destiny, that gods have made, and their will and vision had not been sinister then, he (Laocoon) even now had forced home his

---

1. *A.* VI, 614–15.   2. *A.* X, 161–2.   3. *A.* X, 40–1.

4. *A.* III, 606; cf. Javier de Echave-Sustaeta, *Estilística Virgiliana*, Barcelona, 1950, an attractive monograph, mainly on Vergil's conditional clauses.

5. *A.* VI, 292–4.

blow with the point of steel, his spear, to smash the hiding of the Greeks (in the wooden horse); and Troy would now have been standing yet, and you, tall citadel of Priam, would have still remained'.[1] The indicative, *impulerat*, as is usually and rightly said, brings it home to us that the deed was as good as done. A further explanation is that two thoughts are expressed together, and something is left unsaid. Laocoon had already driven the spear into the wooden horse; and, if destiny had been kind, it would have let the spear break the horse open. It is as if a conjunction such as *ut*, 'when', had preceded *impulerat*, and after it *foedare* had been *foedavisset* – 'having driven home the blow, he would have smashed the place of hiding'.

All 'irregular conditions' have similar explanations. There is always the omission of a thought, or the combination of two thoughts together, in compression; and often both. The writer begins as if he were going to say one thing, and goes on to say something not quite the same. Vergil of course, uses the 'irregularities' to multiply meanings in a small space. They are due to the guiding rule of compression, and Vergil's instinct to follow it.

In Latin, perfect tenses can be used instead of presents to give further qualification to a verb. Such uses are economies of expression, and natural to Vergil, apart from the occasional consideration that a perfect form might be delivered to him with the imagined rhythm that came, even if it did not most easily fit the sense. These perfects mainly suggest that an action is rapidly over, over as soon as noticed, but there are other effects also. Some are brilliant poetically.

The 'gnomic' perfect, or perfect of proverbial or general statement, expresses what has been found by experience to occur regularly. This is the function of the Greek 'gnomic' aorist, which has influenced Latin. Vergil uses the perfect in exactly this way in *illius immensae ruperunt horrea messes*, 'the harvests of such a farmer are boundless, and always burst his barns'.[2]

More often, when Vergil uses a perfect rather unexpectedly, he is exploiting some possible meaning in his own way. Sometimes his perfects represent a present state resulting from a past action. That is the regular meaning of the perfect in Greek, and it is found,

1. *A.* 11, 54–6.　　2. *G.* 1, 49.

with some verbs and in some phrases, in most kinds of Latin. There is *noscere*, 'to get to know', and its perfect *novi*, 'I have got to know' and therefore 'I know now'. Vergil develops this perfect in *sub terra fovere larem*, '[bees] prove to have made their warm home under the ground',[1] literally they have 'nursed', 'caressed', or 'made warm' their home. This is brilliant. It expresses the interested surprise of one who uncovers a bees' nest, and suddenly thinks how all this home life has been going on unnoticed all the time, started perhaps long ago. Then there is *cum messis inhorruit et cum frumenta . . . turgent*, 'when [spring comes and] the harvest stands, suddenly bristling, and the corn . . . is swelling . . .'[2] literally 'when . . . the harvest has bristled, and the corn . . . is swelling . . .' The function of the perfect is again poetically expressional. The spring comes; and, almost before you realize that, you see the effect of it. You suddenly find a bristling harvest has sprouted already, and you will notice that the grains in the corn ears have begun to swell. There is such a feeling in *aeriae fugere grues*, 'the cranes of the sky are fled',[3] suggesting that the sky is suddenly empty of them, and they have gone before you had time to notice; though here the tense is really a normal perfect.

A characteristically Latin idiom is the use of the perfect to denote a present state which is the negative result of a past action. Cicero said of the conspirators whom he arrested *vixere*, 'they have lived', that is, 'their life is done', that is, 'they are dead'. Such a laconic, half-cynical understatement is natural in Latin, and not least in the Latin of Vergil, who writes *fuimus Troes, fuit Ilium . . .*, 'we the Trojans are no more, and Ilium is no more',[4] literally 'we have been (and so are no longer) and Ilium has been (and is no longer)'.

The gerund, or gerundive, in Latin is a form capable of much adaptation to new use. Thus *faciendus* means 'having to be done', and then 'able to be done', 'likely to be done', 'about to be done', and even 'being done'. A substitute is thus provided for verbal forms which are otherwise wanting in Latin. Now the secondary meanings of the gerund form may creep up to the surface in most Latin, early, classical, and late. Vergil was characteristically ready to make use of them.

1. *G.* IV, 43.　　2. *G.* I, 314-5.　　3. *G.* I, 375.　　4. *A.* II, 325.

For example, he says *volvenda dies, en, attulit ultro*, 'the days as they roll past have brought it to us of their own will'.[1] That is, 'days that have to be rolled', or 'are about to be rolled', or 'are being rolled' (in the future). There is, strictly, since the last meaning is required here, a combination together of two secondary meanings of the gerundive form; for in classical Latin the meaning of obligation is, I suppose, primary. It is another example of Vergil's habit of understanding words from the inside; or perhaps of his sense of old Latin, if such is the earliest meaning of the form. Vergil uses the gerundive again in this way in *volvendis mensibus*, 'as the months roll', literally 'the months being rolled'.[2]

More frequent are more normal uses, which equally help compression of meaning. Gerunds are used with unexpected prepositions, not only with *in* or *ad*, as in classical prose. An example is *ante domandum*, 'before taming them'.[3] An almost exact parallel to *ante domandum*, in which a perfect participle is used, is *ante exspectatum*, 'before expectation',[4] literally 'before the having been expected thing'. Here again Vergil exploits Latin grammar for meaning; quaintly, since 'before' is applied to a past form, which implies a contradiction between 'before' and 'after'. *Exspectatum* has almost lost its tense in its quite possible and in fact natural meaning, 'the expectation of the thing', which is implicit here. As usual, there is something to add; for in old Latin the perfect participle passive could carry a gerundive tinge of meaning, with a suggestion of obligation, and this also may have influenced Vergil.

More frequent are normal uses of the impersonal gerund in the ablative, such as *virisque adquirit eundo*, 'and acquires new strength just by its moving'.[5] Such expressions happily compress meaning, but are not irregular usually. There is, however, *cantando rumpitur anguis*, 'a snake is overcome by singing',[6] that is, not by its own singing, which ought to be the meaning, but by some one else's. Servius explains that this is a 'passive gerund'.

Vergil uses a gerundive in the dative of purpose in *qui cultus habendo sit pecori*, 'what care is needed to maintain and tend our flock'.[7] This dative so used is old, and mainly legal and constitutional, as

1. *A.* IX, 7.   2. *A.* I, 269.   3. *G.* III, 206.   4. *G.* III, 348.
5. *A.* IV, 175.   6. *E.* VIII, 71.   7. *G.* I, 3-4.

in the phrase *dictator legibus scribundis*, 'dictator for the purpose of codifying laws'. It is rich in curt compression.

Language is a quaint mystery, a bridge over what Hegel called the 'ugly black ditch' between matter and mind. Vergil bridged the ditch well. That is partly because he wrote as if he knew that 'words are fossil history'.

At the beginning of the third century B.C. the history of Latin literature starts for us with the lost speeches of Appius Claudius Caecus, the first named Latin writer. This was the time when Italy was approaching unification under Rome, and Greek influence, which strongly impregnated the fabric of Latin culture perhaps as early as the foundation of the city, was about to become very strong again, and self-declared, and explicit. The Greek effect on Latin literature was not, however, as sudden and sovereign as it is usually supposed. It had worked its way in for centuries, and had already made a large contribution when Latin literature was – to us, now – prehistoric and anonymous.

This early 'literature', of the eighth to the fourth century, was so far as is known oral, not written down. It included something like heroic lays, sung at banquets, which Cato and Cicero mention, and rough dramatic performances. Very possibly prose and verse were mixed. The verse was 'Saturnian', properly a name for any old Italian verse. One usual form is sometimes compared to 'The king was in his counting house, counting out his money'. Like Anglo-Saxon poetry, it was scanned according to a certain arrangement of stress-accents, without apparently a strictly limited number of unstressed syllables. Gradually quantity forced its way in, partly, but perhaps not wholly, through Greek influence, and slightly altered some Saturnian verse. But stress-accent never lost its life altogether in Latin poetry; scansion by quantity alone only started, so far as we know, when Ennius invented the Latin hexameter, and quantity was at no time completely dominant in all Latin poems.

Latin developed qualities of style in the prehistoric period when, probably, prose and accentual verse were mixed. The style was founded on forms of repetition, not only the metrical recurrence of a scheme of stresses, but also alliterations, rhymes, and assonances; as in many other languages, such as Welsh and Erse, at a characteristic stage. When in the third century B.C. Latin literary history begins for us, this stage has been reached and its qualities permanently consolidated; they never quite disappeared, even from highly polished poetry in Greek metres. The history of Latin poetic style, and to some extent prose style too, is partly a history of the principles of repetition. Their use was sometimes restricted, but it revived again, so imbedded in the language was it.

There is a sense in which all Latin literary creation was formal and schematic, with jealously guarded purities and precisions; and in this respect prose and verse should not be too sharply distinguished. Verse was more repetitive; but prose style influenced it. Active development had continued for centuries before the names of the first known poets meet us; they were Livius Andronicus whose first play is dated 240 B.C., and Gnaeus Naevius, said to have produced his about five years later. Besides plays, Livius translated the *Odyssey*, and Naevius wrote an epic on the First Punic War. Latin epic and drama were old, when the movements of the first century B.C. were at their height.

Livius Andronicus, the captive from Tarentum, besides translating Greek plays, decided that the *Odyssey* was more amusing for the sons of his patron, Livius Salinator, to learn than the Twelve Tables of Roman law, and proceeded to translate it for them. But he never thought of such a thing as a Latin hexameter. The ordinary Latin metre, which may itself owe something to the Greek, was the Saturnian. The most famous Saturnians are the line of Naevius on the Metelli, how 'quite automatically Metelli become consuls at Rome', *fato Metelli Romae fiunt consules*, and their reply, 'The Metelli will give Naevius the poet a spanking', *dabunt malum Metelli Naevio poetae*.[1] The scansion is not fully understood, but clearly it is mainly by stress-accent, though at some time quantity partly affected it. So it is in Latin comedy, but here Greek iambic and trochaic metres and others too, are used; the first is like the metre of *Paradise Lost*, but with six, not five, feet of two syllables each, and the second is the metre of

1. E. H. Warmington, *Remains of Old Latin*, London and Cambridge, Massachusetts, II, 1936, pp. 154-5; the first of the two lines may be an iambic senarius.

Tennyson's poem *Locksley Hall*. It is however likely, but incapable of proof, that Latin already had similar metres long before, perhaps themselves due to very early Greek influence. They certainly fit the Latin language admirably, and give it a chance to use its numerous long syllables and its tendencies to rhyme and assonance, and to that parallelism of sound and idea which is already obvious in the primeval Hymn of the Arval Brothers to Mars, a composition in such old Latin that it might almost be supposed written in another language.

Ennius boldly introduced the Greek six-foot line, the hexameter, into Latin from Homer, and he fitted Latin words into it, according to quantity of syllables, not stress-accent. Each of the six feet of a hexameter is either a dactyl or a spondee, the syllables being respectively long, short, short, and long, long, $- \smile \smile$ and $- -$. The difficulty was to get enough short syllables. So Ennius, though he sometimes contrived plenty of dactyls, as in *at tuba terribili sonitu taratantara dixit*, 'hark! the trumpet with alarming tones said tarántaráh'[1] – here with a characteristic alliteration and onomatopoeia –, sometimes admitted also the not very desirable *hexameter minimus*, without a single short syllable, as *olli respondit rex Albai Longai*, 'to him replied the king of Alba Longa'.[2] Homer, who is freer than classical Latin poets, has at the most one such verse.

Ennius was busy enough making Latin fit hexameters at all, and, still more, in making his whimsical but deep and majestic sense of poetry come to expression in this extraordinary medium. He was naturally very free with the rules. Over a hundred years later Lucretius still had a hard problem, with his subject of atomistic materialism, but he succeeded in making his verse flow more freely, finding ways of increasing the short syllables. For this, he sometimes used long words, as in one of his overpoweringly great lines, *insatiabiliter deflevimus, aeternumque* ..., 'we have wept and wept, never satisfied in the weeping, and for eternity [no day shall take the grief from our heart]',[3] and, by perhaps the most elaborate known system of verbal repetitions, he would exploit time after time in a single passage the short syllables of a single word.

Vergil settled down to a hexameter of his own, according to strict rules, and established for himself a normal line, which he

1. Ennius, *Annals*, 140.   2. ibid., 33.   3. Lucretius, III, 907.

could vary within limits to express a wide range of feeling. The hexameter has six feet, each either a dactyl, long, short, short, – ˇ ˇ, or a spondee, long, long – –, except that the fifth foot is usually a dactyl, and the sixth a spondee or trochee, long, short – ˇ. The metre is determined by quantity, that is, length of syllables, alone. There must be a break between words, or 'caesura', inside the third or fourth foot, but not after the first syllable of the fifth or sixth. There must be no hiatus; a syllable ending in a vowel or -*m* at the end of the word elides before a vowel at the beginning of the next. Earlier writers had elided syllables ending in -*s*; Vergil did not. The last rule Vergil kept invariably; but he reserved the right to break the others.

Elision, by the way, is Vergil's special province. It has even been held that he alone of ancient classical poets was glad to use it, and planned to use it, as an instrument of art, and that all the others thought it an unpleasant necessity sometimes, but tried to avoid it. Even Vergil has very little elision in the *Eclogues*. Then, in the *Georgics* the art of elision appears already perfect, though examples are still less frequent than in parts of the *Aeneid*. There, there may be perhaps half a page without any. Perhaps they cluster thickest in passages of violent movement and activity: it is a valuable exercise, to look for elisions, and find where they come in greatest number, and what is their artistic effect, as for example *sed picis in morem ad digitos lentescit habendo*, 'but [rich soil] clings like pitch to the fingers of anyone holding it',[1] the slurred elision suggesting stickiness.

The normal Vergilian hexameter may well be represented by
– ˇ ˇ | – – ˇ ˇ – || – – | – – ˇ ˇ | – –
arma virumque cano, Troiae qui primus ab oris.[2] Not only are the ordinary rules obeyed, but the distribution of short syllables, where a choice is open, follows Vergil's most frequent practice. For example, the first foot is a dactyl, and the fourth a spondee. A spondee in the first foot and a dactyl in the fourth foot are both slightly less usual, but neither is irregular. The arrangement of words in the metre governs the incidence of stress-accent, which

1. *G.* ii, 250.
2. *A.* i, 1; for Latin verse in general see now H. A. B. White, *Latin Scansion for Schools*, London, 1960.

is regular if the metre, including the breaks between words, is regular; here the incidence of stress-accent is regular, and normal, or nearly normal, also. There is a stress-accent on the first syllables of the first, second, fifth and sixth feet, and on the second syllable of the third; but in the fourth foot there is none at all. According to the researches of Miss Avery Woodward,[1] this is one of the most usual schemes; it would be equally, or slightly more, usual, if there were one less accent on a first syllable of a foot early in the verse. On this question of accent there will be more to say. The line is normal also in 'caesurae', the breaks between words in the middle of feet. A caesura should occur either in the third or fourth foot. Here there is, as often, one in each.

It is well known that Vergil made lines blend into periods and paragraphs by carefully varying the breaks between words and pauses in the sense, so that they occur in different places in the lines, and so that the sense could be freely continued from one line to the next. It must have been a hard effort, since the lines spontaneously given to him by his memory must have been mainly lines with pauses at the end, and with breaks between words predominantly in regular places, especially after the first syllable of the third foot and after the first syllable of the fourth foot.

The caesura in either of these feet after the first syllable is called 'strong'. There may be a 'weak' caesura, after the first short syllable of a dactyl, in either of these feet. Such lines were less easy, natural, and frequent. There is a weak third-foot caesura and a strong fourth-foot caesura in *quidve dolens regina deum tot volvere casus.* . . .[2] There is a strong third-foot caesura and a weak fourth-foot caesura in . . . *venturam et nostros ea fata manere nepotes.*[3]

Vergil took more care than his predecessors to avoid a pause at the end of the line, but only when such a pause was undesirable; more than half the lines in the *Aeneid* have a pause at the end. In very perfect and finished passages there is sometimes a pause at the end of nearly every line, as in Sinon's sacrilegious vow in the Second *Aeneid*,[4] where he calls the stars to witness that his lies are

1. A. Woodward, *The Philological Quarterly*, xv, 1936, 126–35.
2. *A.* i, 9.   3. *A.* ii, 194.   4. *A.* ii, 154–9.

true. Here the rhythm partly depends on a balance of line with line; two begin with the same word. In the succeeding passage,[1] the plan happens to be different. The verse moves faster; and of eleven lines only three or four can be said to have a pause at the end.

Breaks between words coinciding with the partition between metrical feet are avoided in all Greek and Latin hexameter verse to some extent. Vergil avoided them more carefully than his predecessors. There is one place where such a break between words, if there is also a strong pause, almost destroys a line; that is, right in the middle, at the end of the third foot. Vergil avoids a break here altogether, except in a very few lines, such as *pulverulentus equis furit*; *omnes arma requirunt*, 'mad from battle, dust-covered from the horses; all longed for their arms',[2] and *Dardanides contra furit. Anxuris ense sinistram* ..., 'The Dardanid faced them in fury. [He struck off] Anxur's left hand with his sword'.[3] The line depends for its unity on having an emphatic caesura within the third or the fourth foot. A break between the third and fourth foot turns a hexameter into two equal short lines. Vergil, of course, usually mitigates his obedience to his own rules. As he admits a pause of sense at the end of a line when it is required, so, too, he admits a break at the middle point of a line; and especially when the pause in sense is not too strong, as *effigiemque toro locat haud ignara futuri*, 'stationed on the bed ... his portrait, knowing well what was to be'.[4]

There are some rules which are not certain, because they are broken often. A monosyllable may combine with another word to make the fifth foot, so that in a sense there is a break after the first syllable and in a sense there is not, as in *et pede terram*, 'with his foot ... the earth'.[5] If the last two words only are taken together the rule is badly broken; but it is usually safe to take the first two together, and consider the rule saved. Vergil rarely allows more than one weak caesura, or break between words

1. *A.* ii, 160–70.   2. *A.* vii, 625.   3. *A.* x, 545.
4. *A.* iv, 508.   5. *G.* iii, 499.

after the first short syllable of a dactyl, in a single line. Ennius

did not mind this, as in *visus Homerus adesse poeta*, 'I dreamt that
the poet Homer was before me'.[1] Vergil did, except in about a

dozen verses, as *conlapsos artus atque arma cruenta cerebro*, 'all falling,
limbs and weapons bloody with brain'.[2] But it is hardly a rule.

There are some regular licences with words. *Deinde*, 'then', may

be either *deinde* or *dein*, two syllables or one. *Proinde*, 'accordingly',

two syllables, occurs. So *deerit*, 'will be lacking', can be *deerit*, and

aureus, 'golden', in the cases which end with long syllables, is

always two syllables, as *aurei*, for it would not otherwise get into
the verse without elision. Some words would not get in at all
on their real quantities. So Vergil always scans *semianimis* as

semianimis, *ariete* as *ariete*, *religio* as *religio*, and *Italia* as *Italia*,

though he usually makes the *I-* short in the adjective, *Italus*,

'Italian', writing *per gentis Italum*, but *Itala regna*. There are variations, not so necessary, in Greek proper names; Vergil has

Athos once and *Athon* once, the long *o* being right; *Orion* and

Oriona rightly, once each, but *Orion* more often; and *Sychaeus* once

but otherwise with a short *y* in the name.

Most metrical irregularities are to some extent deliberate and
part of Vergil's art, though many of them are due to his instinctive memory of rhythmic units. We get so used to regular metre
that an irregularity gives an awakening shock, and we are ready
to notice what sort of irregularity it is.

Perhaps the least intellectually significant irregularities are in a
Greek scansion of Greek words, especially proper names. Vergil
often uses *hymenaeus*, 'wedding song' or 'wedding', once early in

the line, *hic hymenaeus erit*, 'this shall be their wedding',[3] but all the
other times at the end of the line, where a four-syllable word is

not normally allowed, as in *Lacedaemoniosque hymenaeos*, 'a wedding

1. Ennius, *Annals*, 6. 2. *A.* IX, 753. 3. *A.* IV, 127.

with a Spartan queen',[1] here plural with little change of meaning.

So also he puts long Greek proper names at the end, as in *saltantis Satyros imitabitur Alphesiboeus*, 'Alphesiboeus will copy prancing satyrs'.[2]

Greek practice allowed this, and other variations too, which Vergil sometimes adopted. Hiatus is common in Greek hexameters after the first syllable of a foot. Vergil accordingly writes *pati hymenaeos*[3] at the end of a line; the *-i*, of course, would be expected to elide before the *hy-*. Greek hexameters often have spondaic fifth feet. Vergil adopts this practice, too, for Greek words, especially, as in *atque Getae atque Hebrus et Actias Orithyia*.[4] *Orithyia* begins with two long syllables. In this line, which is very Greek in shape, there is also a hiatus; the *-ae* of *Getae* does not elide, before the *a-* of *atque*. In Latin, it would be expected to elide. In Greek it would not; but if it occurred later in the foot, without the ictus, it would be shortened. Vergil adopts both these practices in *Glauco et Panopeae et Inoo Melicerti*, 'to Glaucus and Panopea and Melicertes, son of Ino' (a sea deity).[5] But this is truly irregular, because the *-o* of *Glauco* is not even in a first syllable, with the ictus. Vergil was adapting a line of Parthenius, Γλαύκῳ καὶ Νηρῆι καὶ εἰναλίῳ Μελικέρτῃ, 'to Glaucus and Nereus and Melicertes in the sea'. The trouble was in the 'and'. Καὶ begins with a consonant. But *et* does not. However, Vergil's choice of the word *Inoo* is quite typical of his simpler ingenuity.

There is a distinction between Latin and Greek in short final syllables also. In Greek they are lengthened before double consonants, and λ, *l*, μ, *m*, and ρ, *r*. In Latin they are not; but, before a spirant and a guttural or dental as *sc-*, *st-*, *z-*, they may not remain short either. Therefore different words have to be used if desired words involve this dilemma. An exception is *nemorosa Zacynthos*.[6]

---

1. *A.* iii, 328.   2. *E.* v, 73.   3. *G.* iii, 60.   4. *G.* iv, 463.
5. *G.* i, 437.
6. *A.* iii, 270; cf. xi, 309: z was soft in Latin almost like English *s*; see W. R. Hardie, *Res Metrica*, Oxford, 1934, to supplement the too brief statements here.

Vergil lengthens final vowels occasionally, and especially in the Homeric arrangement of two or more words joined by -que, representing τε, occurring after each of them. He writes terrasque tractusque maris caelumque profundum, 'lands and expanses of sea, and the depth of sky'.[1] The first -que is lengthened before tr-. Sometimes the vowel is lengthened before a single consonant, which in Greek is possible, and often not irregular, as in liminaque laurusque dei, 'the god's own threshold, and his laurels there'.[2]

Many of Vergil's metrical irregularities are transferences of Greek usages to Latin words. Occasionally he ends with a four-syllabled Latin word, as in femineo ululatu, 'with the wailing that women make'.[3] Here there is a hiatus too. Or, again with a Latin word involved, he puts a spondee in the fifth foot as in cornua velatarum obvertimus antemnarum, 'we turned that way the arms of our sail-clad yards'.[4] There was an Italian town Antemnae; the name is apparently the same as the word for 'yards'. Vergil uses it as a Greek word might be used, at the end, with a hiatus, in turrigerae Antemnae, 'Antemnae with the towers it wears'.[5]

Vergil here has a hiatus in which a long syllable remains long, as often in Greek, when the long syllable is the first in the foot, and so carries the ictus. He writes, too, spem ferre tui, audentior ibo, 'to bring hope of you, the more bold shall I go'.[6] He sometimes shortens a long syllable in hiatus, the normal practice in Greek hexameters and old Latin, already met in Panopeae, a Greek name. It occurs again with Greek names, as in flerunt Rhodopeiae arces, 'the high fastnesses of Rhodope wept',[7] and Pelio Ossam, 'on Pelion Ossa',[8] and with Latin words, te amice nequivi conspicere, 'yourself though, friend of mine, I could not see'.[9] The last quotation is

1. E. iv, 51.   2. A. iii, 91.   3. A. iv, 667.
4. A. iii, 549.   5. A. vii, 631.   6. A. ix, 291.
7. G. iv, 461.   8. G. i, 281.   9. A. vi, 507–8.

from the meeting with Deiphobus in the Sixth *Aeneid*, which is in some ways Vergil's most perfected passage. There is thus little doubt that the irregularity here is intentional; and other signs suggest that most of the irregularities are.

He also allows a short syllable at the end of a word which ends with a consonant and would naturally require a consonant at the beginning of the next word if it is to become long, to count as long even when the next word begins with a vowel; as in *pampineo gravidus autumno*, 'teeming with autumn's wealth of vine'.[1] This, at the beginning of the second book of the *Georgics*, which was certainly revised carefully, is another of the proofs that metrical irregularities are often or usually intentional. There is an irregularity in the opening of the first book of the *Georgics*, also, just as certainly intentional, [*qui cultus habendo*] *sit pecori, apibus quanta experientia parcis*, '[what care is needed to maintain and tend] our flock, how much experience we need to guard our thrifty bees,[2] where the *-i* would be expected to elide before *a-*.

Some of the short syllables thus lengthened have a further reason for being long. Several times *-or* is lengthened, as in *et furiis agitatus amor et conscia virtus*, 'and love tormented by forces that make mad, and goodness that knew itself good',[3] and *-is* is lengthened in *sanguis animusque sequuntur*, 'blood and the spirit came out with it (a spear) too'.[4] Here the vowels are normally short in classical Latin. But in earlier Latin they had been long, and Vergil might be said to return to the earlier quantity. Sometimes, however, the lengthened syllable had never been long, as in *fer sacra, pater, et concipe foedus*, 'bring, father, instruments of sacrifice, and make the treaty ours'.[5]

Once only Vergil leaves a short open vowel unelided and

---

1. *G.* II, 5: the strange slow rhythm is surely expressive; we are made aware of great loads of fruit, almost too heavy to handle; cf. the notes on elisions in Virgil, *Aeneid* IV, Oxford, 1955, and *Aeneid* II, Oxford, 1964, edited by R. G. Austin.

2. *G.* I, 4.   3. *A.* XII, 668.   4. *A.* X, 487.   5. *A.* XII, 13.

lengthens it too; it is in the last line but one that Turnus, ultimate foe to Aeneas, speaks, before his last encounter, *sancta ad vos anima atque istius inscia culpae descendam*, 'no, holy the life that I shall be, with never a thought of guilt like this, when I go down to you [ghosts below]'.[1] There is no need of emendations, such as *sancta ad vos anima atque istius nescia culpae*, or the insertion of *a!* before *atque*, to remove the unique lengthening of the last syllable of *anima* in hiatus. It is a tremendous moment; Vergil's metrical practice has been working up to be ready for it, with something new.

It is uncertain how much these metrical variations have an expressional effect; though the shock of the last of them, like a gasp, drawn into a suppressed wail, can hardly be missed. The rest have an aesthetic effect, clearly enough; they give a new, gracious, unexpected pleasure, perhaps especially in the musical and mysterious Greek names.[2] A vowel unexpectedly long may suggest an expressive pause. A spondaic ending may give solemnity. But just how much of the effect of most direct irregularities is expressional is not easy to say. There is one kind, however, which is very clearly expressional, the addition at the end of a syllable outside the metre, to be elided, against the ordinary rule, before a vowel starting the next line. The extra syllable joins the lines closely, and can make them suggest continuity or suspense or a threat, as in *quo super atra silex iam iam lapsura cadentique imminet adsimilis*, 'while above him a black, hard stone, at any moment like to slip and looking as if it already fell, impended'.[3] The -*e* of *cadentique* elides before the *i* of *imminet*, as if at the moment of the last rest and first movement. There is only one instance in which

1. *A.* XII, 648–9.

2. L. P. Wilkinson, *Golden Latin Artistry*, Cambridge, 1963, 11–13; the Romans explicitly enjoyed Greek names; see also, for all these aesthetic questions in Latin verse, another fascinating book, N. I. Herescu, *La poésie latine. Étude des structures phoniques*, Paris, 1960; cf. also W. F. J. Knight, 'De nominum Ovidianorum Graecitate', *Orpheus*, VI, 1959, 1–4.

3. *A.* VI, 602–3.

a final extra syllable cannot elide, *quin protinus omnia perlegerent oculis . . .* , 'Why, straightway they [Trojans looking at the gate of the temple at Cumae] would have read on, every pictured word . . .',[1] but here it is more likely that the *ia* of *omnia* form one syllable, as in *aurei*, which also occurs at the ends of lines. The Trojans would still be reading, but for Achates' and the Sibyl's interruption, and the line would refuse to end but for the synizesis.

The effect of some of the less violent abnormalities is easier to detect. There is the line with a full stop right in the middle, which makes it feel as if it had no caesura, though it has, *Dardanides contra furit. Anxuris ense sinistram . . .* 'The Dardanid faced them in fury. [He struck off] Anxur's left hand with his sword'.[2] Apparently the division and the hurry of dactyls at and after it, mean expressively a sudden dash after a pause. A more impressive line has its only caesura after an *et* beginning a new phrase, *armaque corporaque et permixti caede virorum,* 'arms, bodies, and, with the human carnage blent . . .'[3] This delivers its shock. It seems to have no caesura, and all at the start is tumbled and chaotic, full of weight and mass and detail.

There is a brilliant line that owes much to a pause in the fifth foot where no pause is usual, and the equivalent of a four-syllable word at the end, *immittit; sonuere undae, rapidum super amnem . . .* , 'He threw; the waves' roar sounded; over that tearing river [went Camilla]'.[4] Camilla, the soldier maiden, was in her babyhood tied to a javelin and thus thrown across a river by her father into safety from enemies. Vergil has succeeded in the impossible task of representing by sound the impressions of a baby in this unusual position. It is a new world, and the sound, especially of *rapidum super amnem,* with the unusual pause after *rapidum,* declares it. You can hear the muffled roar of unseen waters, to the descant of your beating heart.

Monosyllables end lines sometimes. Their effect is variously estimated. They normally mean that the first syllable of the sixth

1. *A.* VI, 33-4.   2. *A.* X, 545.   3. *A.* XI, 634.   4. *A.* XI, 562.

foot has no word-accent, except when the monosyllable is *est*, with 'prodelision' of the *e* after a vowel ending the preceding word, the *e* disappearing, not the vowel before, as in elision. So *est*, with its prodelision, hardly counts, since it does not alter the stress-rhythm. More interesting is such an ending as *opum vi* 'with might of resources',[1] which concentrates weight on two narrow points in two consecutive syllables, contrasted in vowel tone, *vi* making -*um* sound darker. The effect is again clear. Then three monosyllables meaning animals come at the end, *mus*, 'mouse', in *exiguus mus*,[2] 'the tiny mouse', and *bos*, 'ox', in *procumbit humi bos*, 'the ox fell full on the ground',[3] and *dentesque Sabellicus exacuit sus*, 'in Sabine land wild boars whet keen their tusks'.[4] It is not fanciful to think that the same kind of ending helps to express the apparent insignificance of the mouse, the weight of the ox, and the violent, swinging action of the boar. Expectations, and the very subtle effect of relations between vowels and consonants in adjacent words, control the meaning within limits; the short *a*'s and *i*'s of *Sabellicus exacuit*, with their incisive consonants, are very different, as preparation for the final word, from the ponderous *u*'s and *m*'s of *procumbit humi*. The regular description of Jupiter, *divum pater atque hominum rex*, 'father of gods and of mankind sole king',[5] may perhaps assert supremacy and dignity by the lonely monosyllable. But on the whole the effect of monosyllables ending lines is not very easy to describe precisely.

One of Vergil's ways of binding verse-groups together is to manipulate the stress-accent which Latin words normally carry.[6] He arranges that the first syllable of the fourth foot of a line shall be a syllable which has a stress-accent when that will help the rhythm. One specially important way is to let a sequence of lines, forming a unitary paragraph, have no stress-accent in this place until the last line. This gives a strong beat at the end, releasing

1. *A.* XII, 552; L. P. Wilkinson, *Golden Latin Artistry*, 224.
2. *G.* I, 181; cf. Quintilian, VIII, 3, 20.
3. *A.* v, 481.   4. *G.* III, 255.   5. *A.* x, 2.
6. W. F. J. Knight, *Accentual Symmetry in Vergil*, Oxford, 1939, *passim*; on stress-accent, see now L. P. Wilkinson, *Golden Latin Artistry*, 89–96.

power pent up in the earlier lines. Such a paragraph has been called a 'released movement'. Released movements are common all through Vergil, especially in long and solemn narrative passages. They give a sense of steady, rhythmic marching, and break the strain of maintained solemnity. The other most usual pattern has been called an 'alternation'. In it, lines with an accent on the first syllable of the fourth foot alternate with other lines which have no accent there. There are expanded alternations, with two lines or more balancing two or more, up to six or seven in some of the schemes, which extend to twenty lines, and have a subtle and elaborate complexity which is a marvel. The patterns are found combined and varied in many ways, but the alternation and released movement are primary. They chance to correspond with two principles of Vergil's mind which have been already noticed, the tendency to alternate arrangement in general matters, and the tendency to reconciliation, which is exactly the effect of the released movement. The presence of stress-accent at the beginning of a foot has been called homodyne, and the absence heterodyne. There are therefore homodyned and heterodyned lines and feet, and the quality in which they vary has been called texture. In general, besides the fourth-foot patterns, texture has an expressional value. Homodyned lines are free, and likely, especially if they are dactylic, to run very quickly; heterodyned lines are constricted and lack freedom, and are likely, especially if they are spondaic, to move slowly.

Once more, Catullus had been preparing the ground for Vergil. In some of his informal poems he arranged for emphasis of stress and of metre to coincide all or nearly all the time, to give a colloquial effect. He even played with the accent, especially in the famous couplet in which the words of the first line occur in the second, but with the accent in the opposite relation to the metre.[1]

The patterns of texture seem often unconscious, rhythms 'given' with the rest of the poetry, often unconsciously. As M. Paul Valéry says,[2] the rhythm may often come first and the rest afterwards, including words and thoughts.

1. Catullus, LXII, 21–2: *qui natam possis complexu avellere matris, complexu matris retinentem avellere natam.*
2. Paul Valéry, *Poésie et pensée abstraite*, Oxford, 1939, 13–21.

Nearly all Latin words have a stress-accent, which is normally on the same syllable on which it would be if the word were English; the accent is on the last syllable but one, if the last but one is long, and otherwise, if the word is long enough, on the last but two. This is called the Law of the Penultima.[1]

The hexameter imposed emphasis on the first syllable of each foot, an emphasis called metrical ictus. There might or might not be a stress-accent on that syllable. There may, then, be harmony between stress-rhythm and metre, when stress and ictus coincide; and that is called homodyne. Or there may be conflict, when stress and ictus fall on separate syllables; and that is called heterodyne. Homodyne makes the line free, ready, and smooth. Heterodyne makes it constricted, reluctant, and rugged. Meanwhile dactyls and spondees also have an effect, dactyls increasing speed and spondees reducing it.

Latin poetry began with stress and went on to quantity, for the purpose of using Greek metres. When Vergil was born there seems to have been a contention between the two principles, developing or about to develop. There was a tendency away from quantity, seen in the readiness with which Catullus wrote in iambic and hendecasyllabic metres in which stress and ictus often coincided, and indeed he apparently sought the coincidence there, as he did also in the hexameter. Vergil restored quantity by giving stress its due, and using it, neither denying it, nor letting it dominate. He made stress in relation to ictus, due to quantity and metre, a new instrument, both aesthetic and expressional; though Catullus had already played with one of the possibilities.

Expressionally, homodyne gives the line freedom and denotes freedom, physical or psychological, as in *ímpius haéc tam cúlta novália míles habébit*, 'shall a wicked man of blood own these ploughed lands, so neat with all our care?'[2] Here there is a freedom of indignation.

---

1. W. Beare, *Latin Verse and European Song*, London, 1957, doubts that Latin had precisely a stress-accent: P. J. Enk, *Mnemosyne*, VI, 1953, 93–109, shews effectively that if Latin did not exactly have a stress-accent it had what amounted to the same thing.

2. *E.* I, 70.

Expressionally, heterodyne gives the line constriction and reluctance, and denotes obstruction and effort, physical or psychological, as in *appárent rári nántes in gúrgite vásto*, 'there could be seen
scattered figures swimming on that expanse of water',[1] where hard,
slow effort is rendered, and ... *expédiunt féssi rérum, frugésque
recéptas* ..., 'they fetched out [food and utensils] weary at their
hopeless plight, and [prepared ...] the meal saved from the
waves',[2] where there is slight effort that hopelessness makes to
seem great.

This variation of lines according to their texture is hard to
separate from their variation according to their metre. Lines, the
same metrically, can have quite different effects on account of
texture. There are two famous lines describing Cyclopes, spondaic but for the fifth foot; I call such lines 'Cyclopean Lines'. One
of the two is mainly homodyne, *mónstrum horréndum, infórme,
íngens, cui lúmen adémptum*, 'monstrous creature, appalling, shape-
lessly vast, with its eye's light stolen away'.[3] The effect is free,
irresistible movement. The other line is mainly heterodyne, *illi
ínter sése múlta vi brácchia tóllunt*, 'they, in unison, mightily raised
their arms [with hammers, working at the forge]'.[4] It expresses,
obviously, great effort overcoming great resistance.

Texture combines with metre. It helps the powerful expressive-
ness of metrical irregularities as in *túne ílle Aenéas quem Dardánio
Anchísae* ... ? 'are you, you, the great Aeneas, born to Dardan
Anchises [by gentle Venus ...] ... ?'[5] That is what Dido said,
realizing with a wonder almost in spite of herself, that here, in the
life, was the Aeneas of whom she had heard so much. All combines, the heterodyne of mental conflict extended even to the
fifth foot, the spondaic ending, and the hiatus of *-o* before *A-*. It
is an extreme instance of what all these instruments in Vergil's
hands can do.

1. *A.* I, 118. 2. *A.* I, 178. 3. *A.* III, 658.
4. *A.* VIII, 452. 5. *A.* I, 617.

Stress-accent was always trying to control the hexameter, and by at least the fourth century A.D. it completely did, in the work of some poets, for example Commodianus, who was quite ignorant of metre, but composed hexameters that closely followed Vergil's distribution of stress-accent.[1] In the earlier history of the metre, it was accent that made the rules for breaks between words at the ends of lines. The poets felt that stress and ictus must coincide in the fifth and sixth feet, to give definition to the ends of lines and prevent one merging with the next.

Vergil saw or felt that if the fourth foot was homodyned regularly, as Lucretius and Catullus homodyned it, there would be too emphatic a definition. So he reduced homodyne in the fourth foot, using it a little more than half as often as the other two, and using it, when he did, frequently for a special purpose.

Of Vergil's use of pure sound much has always been said. Metrical irregularities contribute to it comparatively rarely; but they should be counted as part of the enormously intricate system of expressional variations which the Vergilian hexameter provides.

One of the most famous onomatopoeic lines, that is, lines representing sense by sound, is *quádripedánte pútrem sónitu quátit úngula campum*, 'with a four-foot clatter the hooves [of horses] crumbled and quaked the plain'.[2] The dactyls render speed, the heterodyne with accents on short syllables a kind of tumbled confusion, and the *u* sounds a dark, dull, thudding noise, expressing the sound of hooves on soil. The verse is used again,[3] changed a little.

Elsewhere the telling word *quadripedans* is used with a metrical irregularity, as a five-syllable ending, and with much sharper sounds from vowels and consonants. The words are *perfractaque*

---

1. Cf. L. P. Wilkinson, *Golden Latin Artistry*, 108–10, for Theodulph's two poems, one according to quantity, and one according to stress, that is stress as it normally occurred in quantitative verse; and Otto Skutsch, 'Sound and Sense in Virgil', *Virgil Society Lecture Summaries*, No. 33, a very revealing and also objective statement concerning vowel sounds.

2. *A.* VIII, 596.   3. *A.* XI, 875.

quadripedantum pectora pectoribus rumpunt, 'crash went breasts of four-foot horses bursting horses' breasts'.[1] There are four *p*'s and four *t*'s, three of them in a combination *ct*. The long words, the word-breaks after dactyls, and the homodyne, give the effect of a steady situation, which no one tried to stop, of violent, continuous destruction.

Different kinds of sound and different kinds of energy are regularly applied together to render meaning; vowels, consonants, metre and texture all helping. There is *exoritur clamorque virum clangorque tubarum*, 'arose, then, shouting from men, and blare from trumpets'.[2] The *a* sounds in *clamor* and *tubarum* help most; they have however quite different effects, due to the vowels and consonants near to them. Another startling use of a bitter, frightening *a* is in *sulpurea Nar albus aqua*, 'the river Nar, white with sulphurous water',[3] that heard the trumpet of war.

Characteristically Latin in repetition of words, and characteristically Vergilian in their exactly and delicately modulated sadness, are two passages where *e* sounds are used. One is on a hero's death in battle, *te nemus Angitiae, vitrea te Fucinus unda, te liquidi flevere lacus*, 'sad for you, Angitia's forest, the Fucine lake, so glassy, with just a wave, and those translucent meres, they wept for you'.[4] The five long *e* sounds are made distant and soft in sadness by the seven sounds of *i*. In *te veniente die, te decedente canebat*, 'of you [Eurydice] he [Orpheus] still was singing, as the day came, as day departed, too',[5] the *e*'s are more self-dependent. Of fifteen syllables, eleven have *e*'s. The sadness, accordingly, is richer, warmer, nearer. This effect is quite certain, and habitual in Vergil; but here it is applied more strongly than anywhere else. In both these quotations the metre is entirely regular, and not even in any way unusual.

Vergil read everything, and listened to everything, for the song in it. Fashionable Alexandrian verse might well be worth saying

---

1. *A.* XI, 614–15.   2. *A.* II, 313.   3. *A.* VII, 517.
4. *A.* VII, 759–60.
5. *G.* IV, 466; on such sound-values see L. P. Wilkinson, *Golden Latin Artistry*, Cambridge, 1963, Ch. 11, 7–45, with which my account should be compared, and N. I. Herescu, *La poésie latine. Étude des structures phoniques*, Paris, 1960.

over and over again, and copying in Latin, for the song in it only. All his life Vergil copied sequences of metrical Greek proper names, partly for their other associations and suggestions, but mainly for the song in them, as Milton did, though Milton liked a different kind of song. The other associations were however important. Surprise, and remote mystery were there. So was a lyric delicacy, as in *Clioque et Beroe soror, Oceanitides ambae*, 'Clio and her sister Beroe, children of Oceanus, both';[1] or a metallic, ancient grandeur, as in *at Danaum proceres Agamemnoniaeque phalanges* . . . , 'but the chiefest of the Danai, and rank on rank that Agamemnon led . . . ';[2] or a statuary of cold, past pathos, through a mist of drying tears, as in the vowels of *Parthenopaeus et Adrasti pallentis imago*, 'Parthenopaeus, and, a pale ghost there, Adrastus'.[3] The great wealth of names in *Amphion Dircaeus in Actaeo Aracyntho*,[4] of Amphion, whose song a shepherd in the *Eclogues* emulates, impresses us with the exaltation of a poetic power in distant lands and times. Often enough, poetry must have mystery for its own sake, imparting a consciousness to its readers that they are delighting in a wonder, and in not knowing all. But gradually sound slips into sense more and more, rather as the old Latin way of translating from Greek slipped into being the characteristic way of creating European poetry.

The music of Greek verse gave Vergil names, vowel memories, and sometimes rhythms; but here we do not know enough about how Greek poetry sounded to Italians of Vergil's time. Probably Latin poetry carried for Vergil sounds more capable of evoking meaning in general and especially intellectual density. That is partly due to easier familiarity, partly to the 'penumbral' nature of Latin expressions, and partly to the ready intercourse between spoken Latin and the tune of existing Latin verse.

Vergil built his sound alphabet chiefly from earlier Latin hexameter poetry. In it were sounds and rhythms, many fortuitous, but most of them at least potentially significant. Vergil heard significances which were there, or might have been there, and used the sounds as if the significances really were there.

With, or nearly with, the rhythm, there usually came to Vergil sound associations of vowels and consonants, an important part of

1. *G.* iv, 341.   2. *A.* vi, 489.   3. *A.* vi, 480.   4. *E.* ii, 24.

Vergil's 'self-repetition'. Vergil had a peculiarly keen audial imagination, which worked creatively. Sounds which he had heard, or evolved himself, stayed in his memory, and recurred, either as they already were, or with the suggestion of other sounds. That is, Vergil often said what he said not because he thought out ideas and then expressed them, but because a sound came into his imagination, and he felt an urgent need to express that sound, and with it the suggestions of feeling and thought which it carried with it, or evoked. As rhythm often came first, so often did sounds of vowels and consonants. The two, of course, are varyingly different or nearly the same. The paradox is that the sense often comes after, determined by the sound or rhythm.

The sound complexes of Vergil have been classified very thoroughly by the late Father F.-X. M. J. Roiron, S.J.,[1] who invented the name *imagination auditive*. To some extent the question still remained how such a process could be legitimate and poetic. Actually, it is quite a normal source of poetry. We can guess that meanings are attached in the minds of poets, and of readers familiar with them, to sounds and rhythms, and that, when the right circumstances are there, the meanings latently carried emerge. The sounds carry meanings as coins carry values, representing many very different things; but the right article can still be bought, and so, too, the right value emerges from the sound, when the right associations co-operate.

Part of the truth may also be that the music of sound and rhythm enlivens the consciousness, and makes it ready for ideas and comprehension.[2] Thus some of the content may come not from sound and rhythm, which merely prepare the mind, but from something else. The sound is not exactly a necessary nuisance, but it is partly independent of the meaning, and a step by which it is reached. It is however usually enjoyable for its own sake; and indeed in Vergil the whole complex, rhythm, sound, thought, and feeling, is nearly always perfectly harmonious, each part co-operating so that there is one whole and it is hard to believe that there are any parts at all.

1. F.-X. M. J. Roiron, S.J., *Étude sur l'imagination auditive de Virgile*, Paris, 1908, *passim*.
2. W. F. J. Knight, *Poetic Inspiration; an approach to Vergil*, Exmouth, 1946.

Vergil's effects of sound are, however, partly due to Homer and the other Greeks. Homer sometimes has rhyme and assonance;[1] he especially allows parts of hexameters, or whole hexameters, to end alike. The effect is lovely, and could not be missed; but it does not happen very frequently. In most Greek poetry, with the possible exception of very late epic, there is some evasion of it; it is said that rhyming verses are a sign of humour, irony, or parody, as the four rhyming verses of the drunken speech of Heracles in the *Alcestis* of Euripides.[2] The Alexandrians had remarkable word balances, for example Callimachus in his *Hymn to Zeus*.[3] But, as usual, there is a distinct Latin side to the question, and this time it is the stronger. As Mr W. B. Sedgwick[4] explains, Latin poetry had an instinct for rhyme, partly due to the nature of the language. Long trochaic tetrameters, the metre of Tennyson's *Locksley Hall*, started in Latin Comedy or before, and went on till they broke into two to form some of the usual metres of medieval Latin hymns. The rhymes were already there, it might be said; for at all times these trochaics had strongly tended to rhyme their middle with their end, or the ends of two successive lines together, or even two ends of lines, and two middles also. There may have been here a result of popular habit or popular taste; but it is at least certain that the practice of irregular rhyme is thoroughly characteristic of the people and still more of the language, which is rich in similar endings. The question was whether such tendencies should be used. Lucretius, as Dr Rosamund E. Deutsch[5] has shewn, exploited them to an astonishing degree. Vergil, with his habit of exploiting all chances, and yet of mitigating extreme tendencies of predecessors, was certain to exploit these tendencies of Latin, but to keep them under control.

It has been recently said that Vergil's rhymes and assonances are too strong for modern taste. That was said not far from the time when Mr T. S. Eliot was developing his technically very

1. A. Shewan, *Classical Philology*, xx, 1925, 193–209.

2. Euripides, *Alcestis*, 782–5.   3. Callimachus, *Hymn to Zeus*, 91–6.

4. W. B. Sedgwick, *Greece and Rome*, i, 1931–2, 96–106.

5. Rosamund E. Deutsch, *The Pattern of Sound in Lucretius*, Denton, Texas, 1939, *passim*; cf. now Thomas Halter, *Form und Gehalt in Vergils Aeneis*, Munich, 1963, whose observations of schematisms in Vergil are in line with Dr Deutsch's observations.

Vergilian poetry in exactly this direction, even going farther than Vergil in a whimsical acceptance of sound for what looks like its own sake, with rhymes, final and internal, and massed assonances. Other modern poetry, English, and Spanish also in South America, as Father Espinosa has explained, has gone far in the Vergilian way of rhymes which are not quite rhymes. Like everything else, rhyme and assonance can be overdone, as in the comic French poem, said to have been written by a pedantic schoolmaster in love, who thought the use of the past subjunctive a mark of refinement, and who made several lines end in *-assiez*, and the last with '. . . *vous m'assassinassiez*'. At a certain stage Welsh had an elaborate structure of sound-balances. Mr N. Horton Smith tells me that Hungarian religious chants are offensive in their excessive rhymes. There may be even something primitive about such poetry. But that does not mean that we should be surprised that Vergil did not reject the flaming enrichment of the audial reality which he perceived, or that the technique should be revived today by the more Vergilian poets.

The suggestion of remembered sound can direct the composition of a new passage, even if the rational relation between the old and new passages may not be obvious. Sometimes, however, the rational relation is obvious enough. In the *Aeneid*, Aeneas thinks thoughts of hate about Helen who has brought destruction on Troy, his home,[1] and later Dido, in love with Aeneas and now deserted by him, speaks about him words of hate.[2] Both times, in what Aeneas thinks about one woman, and in what another woman says about Aeneas, and nowhere else in all Vergil, hate is expressed by a great intensity and profusion of the sounds *s*, *ss*, and *x*. It is worth while to notice what Vergil does twice only. Each passage unmistakably increases the impression of the other, by an intellectually definable meaning carried accurately by sound. The emphasis is this time not on the process by which the verses were created, but on the effect of the finished verses, partly dependent on a similarity of sound, which is recognized by at least a large number of readers. But creative process and finished effect are both normally, and perhaps always, involved together, if in varying degrees.

1. *A.* II, 585–7.   2. *A.* IV, 604–6.

301

A single sound does not always have the same emotional value. It depends on many sorts of context. But the usual estimates of the individual values of sounds associated with Mallarmé, Rimbaud, and Dame Edith Sitwell can be approximately true for particular poets within limitation. For Vergil, certain sounds regularly rouse similar emotions provided that we have learnt to interpret them not from theory or caprice, but from Vergil himself, and provided also that there is nothing in the metre of the verse, or other sounds in it, to conflict with the impression, or distort it.

The sound of *a* is often tragic and sad at close range, actively, as in *moriamur et in media arma ruamus*, 'let us plunge right into the swords and die'.[1] The *a* may be directed by other sounds in proximity to a more remote sadness, as in *Parthenopaeus et Adrasti pallentis imago*,[2] already met. There the *ae*, *e* and *i* sounds have an effect. All are sad, *ae* bitterly, *e* richly, glowingly sad, with tears warm as afternoon light; the *i* is the most remote of all, the salt of tears fainting in mist.

These sounds normally occur together, as in the words of Aeneas to Dido *nec me meminisse pigebit Elissae*, 'and I shall like remembering Elissa'.[3] Here there is an important point for Vergil's audial imagery. He calls Dido Elissa in the later part of the Fourth *Aeneid*, not Dido. Why he does so was asked in Antiquity, but little came of it; there was a suggestion that Elissa was Dido's name in her youth, and that it thus helps the pathos. It does, but scarcely for that reason. Clearly, the sounds are right; *e*, *i* and *ae*, readily available in one word, and giving exactly the kind of sadness needed.

Vowels sometimes are less mixed; as in the already met and amous *te veniente die, te decedente canebat*, 'of you as day came [Eurydice], of you, as day declined, he [Orpheus] still was singing';[4] but such mass distribution is rather surprisingly rare.

Sounds of *o* and *u* render strength, darkness, stern sadness, and solemn, reverberating fear; as in many occurrences of *tuorum*, *suorum*, and *umbrarum*. *Cape dona extrema tuorum*, says Andromache at Buthrotum to Aeneas, 'accept the last presents we of your kin can give';[5] Aeneas, in burning Troy, cries, *Iliaci cineres et flamma*

---

1. *A.* II, 353.   2. *A.* VI, 480.   3. *A.* IV, 335.   4. *G.* IV, 466.
5. *A.* III, 488.

extrema meorum, 'ashes of Ilios, flame that was last sight to me of all I ever held dear';[1] and Turnus, very near to his death, in tones heard nowhere else in all Vergil, says ... *descendam magnorum haud umquam indignus avorum,* '. . . down I shall go; but one, still, who never once has shamed his great ancestors'.[2]

In these instances consonants help, especially *m*, which the Romans explicitly considered solemn. Adjacent letters always make a difference to vowels, and, strictly, should always be considered. A change of consonants affects *o*. In *tendebantque manus ripae ulterioris amore,* 'stretching hands in a longing for the further shore[3] [beyond the waters of death]', everyone agrees about the two sounds of *-or-*. They are quite different from *-or-* associated with *-um*. Here the very short light vowels are important. They let the *o* sounds fall heavily and seem very long in contrast; so that they force themselves into a normal world, instead of creating a world of their own dark solemnity.

Vergil's audial imagery has four predominant moods, firstly, sad sounds of *u, ae, e,* and *i,* secondly, solemn sounds of *o* associated sometimes with *u* and *m,* thirdly fiery, resonant and metallic sounds of *a* and *e* associated with *m* and *n* and frequently rhyming, and fourthly consonantal effects of *c, p,* and *t,* with short vowels, rendering forces and impacts rather than qualities in mass.

Other sounds are less predominant, but not less important, as the violent concentrations of *s* expressing hatred in the thoughts of Aeneas about Helen, and in the words of Dido to Aeneas.

The consonantal mood of forces and impacts is seen in the dream of Hector, *perque pedes traiectus lora tumentis,* 'his feet all swollen, and pierced, where the thongs went through'.[4] The violence of movement, when Hector was dragged behind the chariot, is suggested; as violent impacts are expressed in *perfractaque quadripedantum pectora pectoribus rumpunt,*[5] a striking passage, inevitably mentioned here more than once.

Few audial moods are so active as the associations of *m, n, a,* and *e,* often in rhymes. Aeneas saw Helen *limina Vestae servantem et tacitam secreta in sede latentem,* 'clutching Vesta's threshold, silent, biding there in her seat apart'.[6] It is definite, fiery in the

1. *A.* II, 431.   2. *A.* XII, 649.   3. *A.* VI, 314.   4. *A.* II, 273.
5. *A.* XI, 614–15.   6. *A.* II, 567–8.

glare of the burning city, and colourful, with a richness of blood.

These are not the only rhymes. In rhyming, *ae* often takes a firm or cruel sound, in association with solemn vowels and consonants, as if it meant not sadness but acceptance of sadness, for yourself or another; as Juno's *funestaeque iterum recidiva in Pergama taedae*, 'death's firebrands again to burn the citadel of a Troy founded anew';[1] and as in the description of the Gates of War, *sunt geminae belli portae (sic nomine dicunt) religione sacrae et saevi formidine Martis*, 'There are twin Gates of War, for so are they called by name; hallowed by holy dread, and the fright of war's heartless god'.[2] There are four sounds of *ae* in two lines.

In alliteration, one letter has always proved uniquely impressive, *v*, the Latin consonantal *u*. Vergil, like Lucretius before him, has even been thought to have used it excessively. It is better to see how he uses it expressively. To him it is soft, a letter concealing more than it says, with recessions of sadness, fear, and pathos; or just softness, airy and feathery. So he says of the doves of Venus, *ipsa sub ora viri caelo venere volantes et viridi sedere solo*, 'right to his face they came, flying down from the sky, and settled where the earth was green'.[3] But he also says, of Dido's nightmares, how from the shrine of her first husband, *voces et verba vocantis visa viri*, 'she dreamt he was calling to her, calling, speaking';[4] and of the nightmare of Turnus near his end, in his own words, *vidi oculos ante ipse meos me voce vocantem Murranum*, 'I have seen before my very own eyes Murranus, calling, calling aloud to me ...'[5] Those whom, perhaps, Aeneas hurt most of all, came to similar dream-experiences on their way. Perhaps many of us can recognize from our own delirious dreams this very sense and mood.

There is a certain regularity in the use of audial moods. Juno is fierce, decisive, dark, everything that does not fit the vowel tones of *Elissa* and *Sychaeus*. Her appearances have their special audial quality. In the First *Aeneid*, 'even in those times that goddess yearned and strained that Carthage, could the Fates allow, should have dominion over every race', *hoc regnum dea gentibus esse, si qua fata sinant, iam tum tenditque fovetque.*[6] The consonants gather;

1. *A.* VII, 322. 2. *A.* VII, 607-8. 3. *A.* VI, 191-2.
4. *A.* IV, 460-1. 5. *A.* XII, 638-9. 6. *A.* I, 17-18.

there are eleven contiguous pairs of them within words; and they are the stronger and more wiry for the very short vowels which give them their way.

In the seventh book, when Juno stirs the fury of Allecto to start war in Latium, such decisiveness of sound recurs, as in *aurasque invecta tenebat*, 'rode the air upon her course',[1] *stetit acri fixa dolore*, 'pierced with a sharp pain, still she stood',[2] *effundit pectore dicta*, 'spoke from her heart a stream of words',[3] *odiis aut exsaturata quievi?* 'or, my hate glutted, have I sunk to peace?',[4] *haec ubi dicta dedit, terras horrenda petivit*, 'so saying, sight of dread, down to the earth came she',[5] *virgo sata Nocte*, 'maid, daughter of the dark',[6] and *at saeva e speculis tempus dea nacta nocendi . . .*, 'but now from her place of watch the heartless goddess, finding the moment to do the harm . . .'.[7]

Alliteration, rhyme, assonance, and metre itself are all forms of repetition; of which another form is the recurrence of an idea. Repetition of both sound and thought occurs when a word is repeated, or a whole verse, as in a refrain.

Vergil soon learnt the refrain from Theocritus, balanced expression from old Latin and Hellenistic epigrams, and the most elaborate 'self-repetition', in most of the senses, from Lucretius and Catullus. There were many other poets, whose work is lost, who were developing and varying these and other discoveries during Vergil's youth.

In the *Eclogues* he used all that he had learnt, with some restriction. In the *Georgics* he restricted the repetitions more. In the *Aeneid*, they came back; not quite the same, but fused, and melted, and more finally and eternally Vergilian.

It is clear that sounds may be brought into relation with each other both in different passages alike in emotional tone, and in the same passage, close together. This is our return to the topic of rhyme and assonance, that is, reminiscence of sound at short instead of long range. Rhyme occurs most easily between the ends of the first and second halves of a verse when in one place there is a noun and in the other an adjective agreeing with it. In penta-

1. *A.* VII, 287. 2. *A.* VII, 291. 3. *A.* VII, 292.
4. *A.* VII, 298. 5. *A.* VII, 323. 6. *A.* VII, 331.
7. *A.* VII, 511.

meters, and in hexameter 'golden lines', this is perhaps most likely of all. Vergil rejected pentameters, and also abandoned the golden line for most of his work, but he often kept the rhyme characteristic of it, in spite of his changes in structure and word order.

First are true rhymes, before a caesura and at the end of a verse, as *descendo magnorum haud umquam indignus avorum*.[1]

It is rare for both the two last syllables in each of a pair of words to rhyme. More often one syllable rhymes, with a slight similarity in another; there is then a single-syllable rhyme and a double-syllable pseudo-rhyme, as in the words of dead Palinurus, when Aeneas met his ghost, *paulatim adnabam terrae*; *iam tuta tenebam*, 'by slow stages I was swimming towards the land, and now I was coming to win its safety',[2] *-bam . . . -bam* being rhymes and *-abam . . . -ebam* pseudo-rhymes, if we like to look at it that way – *consonancia* and *assonancia* as they are well called in Spanish.

Rhymes, pseudo-rhymes, and other kinds of repetition, very interestingly preponderate in highly emotional passages which have also elaborate patterns of texture.[3] They are both kinds of rhythm, which intense emotion seems to generate automatically and to add to the usual rhythms of metre. The meeting with Palinurus is an example of such highly emotional passages.

When Aeneas encounters Deiphobus in the world beyond death,[4] the texture-pattern is the most elaborate in all Vergil; and there are rhymes and assonances, as *vix adeo agnovit pavitantem ac dira tegentem supplicia*, 'scarce quite he recognized him, trembling, and seeking to hide the ghastly mutilations on him . . . ',[5] and *tunc egomet tumulum Rhoeteo litore inanem constitui et magna manis ter voce vocavi*; *nomen et arma locum servant*; *te, amice, nequivi conspicere et patria decedens ponere terra*, 'then, myself, on the Rhoetean shore, a cenotaph barrow I erected for you, thrice calling with loud voice on your shade; your station there your name and arms are keeping; but you yourself, friend of mine, I could not see, to lay you, at departure, in soil of home'.[6] It is not easy, after examining that whole passage intently, to think that Vergil's rhymes and

1. *A.* XII, 649; cf. XII, 373.   2. *A.* VI, 358.
3. W. F. J. Knight, *Accentual Symmetry in Vergil*, Oxford, 1939, *passim*.
4. *A.* VI, 494–534.   5. *A.* VI, 498–9.   6. *A.* VI, 505–8.

assonances are too much for modern taste – certainly not when they are so clear an instrument of the supreme master's power.

Dido's spoken epitaph on herself[1] has a rhyme-system of six -*i* sounds, effectively and variedly placed within four lines; and it finishes, in the next but one, with -*ae* sounds at the middle and end. When Aeneas meets Dido in Hades,[2] he speaks with rhymes of -*o* in the first line, and -*am* in the second, each time at the middle and end, with a slight rhyme of -*i*, and a memory of the -*o*, recurrent in the nine lines following.

Another comparable passage is the scene in which Aeneas suddenly sees Helen at the sack of Troy. There is the pattern of texture, and many rhymes and assonances, not confined to single verses. Many have sounds of -*am*, -*antem* and -*entem*, as the first three lines, of which the second is [*limina Vestae*] *servantem et tacitam secreta in sede latentem* [*Tyndarida aspicio*], 'clutching [Vesta's threshold], silent, hiding there, in her seat apart, Tyndareos' daughter I saw'.[3] There follows [*dant clara incendia lucem*] *erranti passimque oculos per cuncta ferenti*, '[the bright blaze gave light to me,] straying as I cast eyes about, on all things everywhere'.[4] The rhymes here join the first and last words in each of two lines.

In these emotional, repetitive passages, all the kinds of repetition often come together. A steady, even story is followed by a moment of intense and important activity. The verse changes. Rhymes, assonances, and alliterations begin. Words are repeated. And probably there is a pattern of texture as well. The intensity of emotion delivers poetry in a corresponding intensity of many kinds of rhythm.

After Aeneas and Latinus had come to terms, and all was peace and welcome, Juno in the sky, observing, talked to herself in anger, hate, and determination to reverse the success.[5] The verse is rapidly strengthened. There are rhymes, especially of *o*. Then she swooped to earth, and called Allecto the Fury from Hell.[6] It is a compact verse-group of eight lines. Of the first four, two have one pair, and two two pairs each, of rhyming words. The next line has two parts, one starting with *odit*, and the other with *odere*. The next two lines have three phrases introduced by *tot*, *tam*,

1. *A*. IV, 653–8. 2. *A*. VI, 456–66. 3. *A*. II, 568.
4. *A*. II, 570. 5. *A*. VII, 286–322. 6. *A*. VII, 323–9.

and *tot* again, another repetition. The first seven lines are an alternating pattern of fourth-foot homodyne, punctuated by an additional line of homodyne at the end.

After the long story, told by Evander to Aeneas on the site of Rome, about the visit of Hercules, when he destroyed Cacus, the scene and mood change sharply. Venus persuades Vulcanus to make arms for Aeneas, in a paragraph[1] of lines which has force and loveliness and delicate balances, working up to strong, rich rhymes in *ergo eadem supplex venio et sanctum mihi numen arma rogo, genetrix nato,* 'but now, you see, I come to you, myself I come entreating you, a power holy to me; and I ask arms, a mother asking, for a son'.[2] There follows a repetition of *te,* starting successive groups of words. The reply of Vulcanus[3] begins with parallel clauses, whole lines, and parts of lines. Soon come three lines, made parallel by their first words, *quicquid, quod,* and *quantum,* the second[4] with a triple rhyme of *-o, quod fieri ferro liquidove potest electro,* 'whatever can be made with steel or molten white gold', and the third ending with an *-o* as well.

But, in looking for irregularities and surprises, and the infinity of devices characteristic of Vergilian verse, there is a danger. Once seen and understood, they should not be too sharply isolated. They are part of Vergil's splendour, with all that is deeper and wider than they. There is a real risk that the glory of things seen and heard may make us forget to look and feel and think beyond.

Vergil's language and verse and all that can be included in those conceptions, infinitely varied and complex though they may be, yet constitute a unity which is hard to denote except by calling it Vergil's 'style'.

To talk about the style of a writer may perhaps be out of date and even unscientific, at least in the sense that the old idea of style does not fit well with our present habits of thought. The general acceptance of the notion that the style is the man is in itself a confession that there is something tautological in any talk about style.

1. *A.* VIII, 370–86.   2. *A.* VIII, 382–3.   3. *A.* VIII, 395–404.
4. *A.* VIII, 402.

Yet writers can write differently. They may write sometimes to express one mood and at other times to express another. They may faithfully represent the mood that is theirs at the moment. Or they may be less direct and ingenuous, and express a mood which they have themselves induced, or which they have simply fancied to be their mood. They may, that is, pretend, and in dramatic poetry they almost must pretend. They adopt a personality which is not strictly their own. If we knew more about imagination, we might say that one of its tasks is to enable an artist to adopt a mood or personality that really belongs to some one else, real or fictitious.

Writers, then, are expected to use 'the right words in the right order' in respect to their own real or assumed personality and mood. If the ability and mental state of a writer are given, the manner of writing, or the style, should follow. It might be reasonable to understand by style a manner of matching mood and personality by words and word-order.

There are then three determinants. Style, if the word is admitted, is controlled by the language used, by the permanent personal limitations and abilities of each writer, and by the present mood of each writer, either real and spontaneous, or induced, or even assumed.

The qualities and limitations of the Latin language are familiar enough. Among them are the force and weight in the words, long or short, with plenty of strong consonants and long vowels, and an irrepressible stress-accent. There is also a terse economy, for which many reasons can be suggested. For one, the Italians, living in a world of intercourse by mutual agreement, needed precise legal expressions of fact and circumstance, without ambiguity and secure against evasion. Such expressions were needed also in the ritual of a religion where everything might depend on exact detail. The life of disciplined and practical restraint and will required firm simplicity of statement and discouraged figurative expansions of language. But such needs were to come. The Italians and especially the Romans were presently committed to the task of keeping pace with the thought of more advanced neighbours, Greeks and Etruscans, in a language not nearly versatile and opulent enough for the purpose. A solution was found in the typical Latin method of using the latent internal significances of words, and the significances generated by words in their special relations to each other, so that word-groups could mean far more than the total of the meanings of the constituent words. That depended on a use of suggestion, and produced in turn something like the opposite of the situation with which it all started, for Latin precision and singleness of meaning led eventually to Latin suggestion, innuendo, and ambiguity.

Vergil's personal and permanent qualities and limitations were closely involved with the emotions of his life-history, and also with his experience of sound and rhythm in Latin and Greek verse. His normal style is controlled by rhythmic forms of sound, and enlivened by certain kinds of love and hate and intellectual interest. The result is mystifying, because it is at once narrow and comprehensive. Vergil is recorded to have been a poor writer of prose; naturally, since his mind needed verse rhythms to enliven its activity. Hexameter writing and hexameter thinking limited his style.

For all his love of trees, Vergil could not, in his poetry, say 'trees', *arbores*, in the nominative, vocative, or accusative plural, since the word would not fit into the hexameter; nor could he use the name *Hercules*, unless he used it in the genitive or ablative singular, *Herculis*, *Hercule*, or in the accusative or dative with a varyingly unpleasant elision. Such situations made Vergil use synonyms or periphrases, with different secondary effects.

The inability to say 'trees' must have reinforced Vergil's inevitable tendency to prefer the particular to the general. This tendency, like others, is common to people near the 'primitive' state of culture, and to poets. There are, for example, tribes of the Pacific who have no name for 'tree', but only names for those particular trees which they use for any purpose, and which are therefore detached from the manifold of undifferentiated experience. It is a mark of good poetry to be concrete and individual, in itself and in its references. It is a mark of Vergil's poetry. And here the restraint of metre has helped the tendency.

Vergil had to find synonyms for Hercules, especially Alcides, 'son', really grandson, 'of Alceus', literally 'Mighty in Battle', and

Amphitryoniades, 'son of Amphitryon'. The first helped Vergil's suggestive method; the meaning of the name could enforce the point of a story or reference and the majesty of a thought or picture. The second is a long, heavy, impressive word, filling nearly half a line; it increases the force of a narrative, and significantly suggests the parallel name for Aeneas, Laomedontiades, 'son', really grandson, 'of Laomedon'. There is much in the comparison of Aeneas and Hercules, and the chance which is the friend of art, especially Vergil's art, contributed to the comparison. Again and again fixed laws of metre, rhythm, or rhyme, instead of enslaving poets, increase their freedom.

It was the sound, metre, and rhythm, of course, which mainly carried to, and carried in, Vergil's mind the originals of earlier poetry, poetry of others or his own, out of which he integrated his new work. Without the containing and energizing metre and rhythm the integration could not go on. Much of Vergil's poetry is cross-referenced by his audial imagination in this way. He often says, just a little differently, what has been said in Latin hexameters before. His style, as Dr van Gelder explained, is governed by self-repetition. But enough has been said already about self-repetition of this kind.

Vergil's permanent qualities and limitations, as they affected his style, are too many to enumerate, and some are insufficiently known. It is clear that by nature or education he had the habits both of close observation and reasoning and also of associative self-suggestion. Much of his style depends on the latent possibilities of words. His brilliant, compressed expressions are due to clear, sharp, thinking, possibly years before the expression was formed, and possibly never conscious. There is a profound and acute rational knowledge of words behind *se . . . induet in florem*, 'clothes itself into flower', perhaps 'draws on, and over it, its flowering time'.[1] Such intrinsic, reasoned, and observed metaphors are not very frequent in the work of Vergil, but they are characteristic of him. Some examples of this class, different, but alike in principle, are these: *hi . . . vix ossibus haerent*, 'these [lambs] scarcely cling to their own bones', that is, 'have scarcely any flesh clinging to their bones',[2] a geometrically correct expression

1. *G.* I, 187–8.   2. *E.* III, 102.

311

which yet seems violently metaphorical; *sollicitanda tamen tellus,* 'yet you must never leave the soil in peace';[1] *alitur vitium vivitque tegendo,* 'the blemish [an ulcer] is fed and draws life from the concealment';[2] *huc ... resoluta referri omnia,* 'that to this [soul of all the world] all life, dissolved again [in death] is carried home';[3] *summa sequar fastigia rerum,* 'I shall follow just the high points of the story [in telling it]';[4] *versa pulvis inscribitur hasta,* 'the dust took the writing of the spear reversed',[5] of Troilus, dragged behind his stampeding chariot; *hinc spargere voces in vulgum ambiguas,* '... hence onward [Ulixes] sprinkled upon the multitude his two-wayed hints ...',[6] that is, set remarks circulating, to discredit Sinon; *et sidera verberat unda,* 'lashing the stars with whips of the wave';[7] *pendent ... minae ... murorum,* 'those threats of battlements stayed in their suspense',[8] when Dido, attending to Aeneas, neglected the work of building; *in nubem cogitur aer,* 'into a cloud the heavy air was compressed';[9] *dente tenaci ancora fundabat navis,* 'with its teeth, that hold, the anchor already was making foundations for the ships';[10] *primam ... [vocem] loquentis ab ore eripuit pater,* 'at the first moment, as he spoke, his father caught from his lips those words';[11] *exstinctos faucibus ignes,* '[gazing] where the flames from the jaws [of the dead Cacus] were damped out now,'[12] literally 'at the extinguished fires in his jaws' – almost a limiting case of the Vergilian extension of inherent metaphor, and comparable to Ezra Pound's beautiful thought, 'She was like one who had been there and was gone' – ; *collecta fatigat edendi ex longo rabies,* 'mad urgency to eat, gathered from far back, torments him [a wolf]',[13] as if the hunger had been being 'collected' or 'amassed' from far back on the path of his life, and increased continually; *mole sua stat,* '[Mezentius] stood in the stability of his own massive weight';[14] *experto credite quantus in clipeum adsurgat,* 'believe it, from one who has experience, how giant his might, as he leaps up behind his shield',[15] as if the shield were dashing ahead and he, Aeneas, leapt to overtake it – a powerful picture – ; and *irasci in*

1. *G.* II, 418. 2. *G.* III, 454. 3. *G.* IV, 225–6.

4. *A.* I, 342. 5. *A.* I, 478. 6. *A.* II, 98–9.

7. *A.* III, 423. 8. *A.* IV, 88–9. 9. *A.* V, 20.

10. *A.* VI, 3–4. 11. *A.* VII, 118–9. 12. *A.* VIII, 267.

13. *A.* IX, 63–4. 14. *A.* X, 771. 15. *A.* XI, 283–4.

cornua temptat, '[a bull] seeks to charge his horns with fury',[1] literally 'to be angry', or 'pour his anger', into them. Here and elsewhere Greek originals may well have helped towards the result.

This exploitation of these more closely knit metaphorical possibilities in words is one of Vergil's permanent characteristics. Interestingly, he used it most in the *Georgics*, and especially in passages of direct observation without much literary suggestion.

Many of these permanent characteristics are very obvious and well known. Vergil likes to intensify and clarify meaning by putting contrasted words together, a frequent practice in Latin made easy because Latin word-order is very variable. He says of a bull, *pingui macer . . . in ervo*, 'thin and wasted in a richly supplied stall';[2] of the wooden horse, *monstrum infelix sacrata sistimus arce*, 'grim, on our hallowed citadel, we halted the uncanny thing';[3] and *parvumque patri tendebat Iulum*, '[Creusa] held out to me, his father, little Iulus' (when she was persuading him to leave Troy).[4]

There is another very Vergilian extension of a natural Latin figure of speech, hypallage or transference. Vergil sees the whole ideal complex in a single blended view. Accordingly an adjective may be attached to an unexpected noun. It does not matter much, since the point is the presence of some quality in the whole complex. The balance of the sentence may suggest the transference; sometimes a noun ought to have two adjectives with it, and, to avoid that, for it is not liked in Latin except in certain special usages, one adjective is detached to qualify some other noun, without loss of effect, or even with increased effect. Often metre dictates the construction of an adjective. This indifference sometimes leads to amusing problems in textual criticism.

Dido asks Anna to gain her just a little more time to be with Aeneas.[5] 'This is the last indulgence I entreat', she says, and then, *quam mihi cum dederit cumulatam morte remittam*,[6] 'and when he has given it to me, I shall release it for him, crowned with the interest of death'. And Anna went backwards and forwards taking the pitiful messages between Aeneas and Dido.

1. *A.* XII, 104. 2. *E.* III, 100. 3. *A.* II, 245. 4. *A.* II, 674.
5. *A.* IV, 433–5. 6. *A.* IV, 436.

Here there is at least one doubt and at least one ambiguity. The best available manuscript, the Medicean, *M*, reads *cumulata*, and opens the question of Vergilian transference. *Cumulare* means 'heap up' or 'put the top or crown on a heap', or on anything else. According to *M*, Dido would repay the indulgence or favour with 'heaped death'; according to the other manuscripts, she would repay it 'heaped with death'.

There need not be any serious difference. Even in prose, there is not much difference between *cumulo te laudibus*, 'I heap you with praises', and *cumulo laudes in te*, 'I heap praises on to you'. Accordingly, Dido may be going to repay the indulgence of a little time 'with death heaped' or 'heaped with death', that is, 'with death added as interest', or 'increased by way of interest with the addition of death'. It is only when ambiguity is considered as well as doubt that the difference is at all serious.

Dido is telling Anna that if Aeneas gives her more time she will repay the debt, either when death has been 'heaped', or when the debt has been 'heaped' with death. Dido does not want to tell Anna her plans for killing herself. We may understand that Dido will repay Aeneas by giving him all the rest of her life, that is, by giving him her own death by way of interest on the loan of a little time. But neither Anna nor Aeneas must understand that. They must think something which the words might also mean, and which gives no secret away. What the reader may think is communicated by both the readings. Anna and Aeneas are to think that Dido will repay the debt with interest at death, whenever death should come. That is more like *cumulatam*, because that reading can be separated from *morte* more easily. There are many complications, such as the ancient and popular conjecture *dederis*, 'when you [Anna] have given ... '. But on the whole Vergil seems to have written *cumulatam morte*, and positively meant it to be mistaken for *cumulata morte*, which makes the more tragic secondary meaning more clear, by readers, or rather listeners, who according to the ancient practice were to hear the *Aeneid* read to them.

It is easy to understand how Vergil's own nature, and the Latin language itself, tended to transferences. Sometimes, however, they become to some extent irrational and even metaphoric.

The stomach or barrel of the wooden horse is called *curvam compagibus alvum*, 'a barrel curved with fitted timbers',[1] whereas it was really a curved thing made of fitted timbers, or an unqualified thing made of curved timbers; *curvis compagibus* would be prose sense. There is of course a poetic rationality. The figure is visual. The horse bulges widely, and with the bulge are noticed concurrently the separate planks. Prosaically, the bent planks make the horse's barrel. Poetically, the planks make the barrel bulge and bend. It is a direct grammatical rendering of the well-known poetic kind of causation.

Poetic causality accounts for much in Vergil, including transferences. The transferences need not always contain so close a visual, audial, or tactile rationality, for sometimes they are simply a neat way of adding further constituents to a total picture. But, as usual with Vergil, it is always worth while to see if the fullest possible meaning is there.

Transference is one among many 'figures of speech', which from contemporary times onwards have furnished classical categories for the discussion of the manipulation of words by ancient writers. Our present interest has a different orientation, since we are inclined, rightly or wrongly, to ask questions with 'why?' rather than 'how?'. Repetition of words is a 'figure of speech', anaphora. We, less content with classifications and comparisons than the ancients, try, wisely or foolishly, to ask and answer why poets repeat words. Perhaps we are only asking 'how?' in another way, and end by merely devising more detailed classifications.

Zeugma is a figure of speech which continues to need its ancient name. By zeugma a word is linked to two others, appropriately to one, but less appropriately to the other. It is a method of economy used by Vergil several times, and might be called characteristic of him. He writes *fugam Dido sociosque parabat*, 'Dido made ready flight, made ready her comrades too'.[2] It is a different kind of preparation each time. The verb is more metaphorical with the first of the two objects. So, too, the verb is not equally metaphorical with its two objects in *amissam classem, socios a morte reduxi*, 'I reclaimed his lost fleet, and reclaimed his comrades from death',[3] that is, 'danger of death'.

1. *A.* II, 51.　　2. *A.* I, 360.　　3. *A.* IV, 375.

Of the other figures of speech, two may be mentioned. One is asyndeton, by which words, phrases, and clauses are joined without the co-ordinate conjunctions or connective particles which are frequently almost obligatory in classical Latin prose even when they would seem out of place in English. Poetry however is freer, and any Latin poet can begin a sentence without 'and' or 'but' or 'for' or 'therefore'. Vergil freely joins small clauses with 'and' and possibly an implied comma. On the whole he is in contrast with the more argumentative Lucretius in his tendency to avoid some of the usual connectives at the beginning of sentences. 'Therefore' and 'because' and even 'for' are seldom in place. On the other hand, Vergil very often begins a sentence with *at*, a strong, sharp, exclamatory 'but', which had originally been an interjection, and very often he introduces a new phase of his story with *interea*, 'meanwhile'.

Chiasmus is a pleasing figure by which the second of two pairs of words occurs in a reversed order. There may be a noun and then a verb followed by a verb and then a noun. In prose and in elegiac verse the figure is often used very obviously and directly. Vergil tends to use it with subtlety, partly obscuring the order and the correspondence of the words; as in *Phyllida mitte mihi*; *meus est natalis, Iolla*, 'send Phyllis to me; for my birthday it is, Iollas',[1] where *mihi* and *meus* and the two verbs *mitte* and *est* are sufficiently different to soften the figure of speech. Here, and normally in Latin, chiasmus and asyndeton go well together. Sometimes Vergil uses the two figures with full emphasis and precision, above all in *laudato ingentia rura, exiguum colito*, 'you shall be content to admire great estates, but you shall yourself cultivate one that is small'.[2]

Horace,[3] in attributing to Vergil's poetry *molle atque facetum*, which seems to denote or connote qualities of sympathy and quick-witted humour, clearly indicated qualities which should be apparent to us in Vergil's manner of writing, or 'style'.

Vergil's humour is another difficult question. He has little in common with the loudly humorous Latin writers, and there are no signs that he could achieve a strong laugh as well as Catullus could. If some of the incidents in the Fifth *Aeneid* were as funny to

1. *E.* iii, 76.   2. *G.* ii, 412-13.   3. Horace, *Satires*, i, 10, 44-5.

him as they are sometimes supposed to have been, he was capable of a heavy, derisive, cruel humour. Strangely, that is possible. But it is by no means proved, and unlikely. Whatever precisely Horace meant by attributing to him – before the *Aeneid* was written – *molle atque facetum*, heavy, cruel humour is denied by the phrase. The true and typical Vergilian humour is the humour of the *Georgics*, the wayward, whimsical readiness to find a smile in comparisons of animals and men. True to a favourite modern explanation of humour, Vergil finds the ridiculous in a conjunction of the human and the mechanical. His animals are partly mechanical and partly human like the sea birds which Professor Rand calls 'the self-important but automatic prophets of changing atmospheres'. There appears the slightly sardonic Latin tendency to think two thoughts at once.

Intimate, in the heart of Vergil's words, is his delicate, sadly reflective kindliness. His depth of sympathy with human suffering is renowned for ever. He feels with the hurts of animals and powerless things, and thinks with the brains of the plants and trees. Yet he seems strangely insensitive sometimes. He does not appear to wince at the pain of some animals, even the poor bullocks beaten to death for the spontaneous generation of bees in the Fourth *Georgics*. He does not even seem to wince at the horrors of battle, horrors which he himself makes emphatic again and again. Napoleon said that Homer knew warfare well, but that Vergil knew nothing about it at all.[1] However that may be, Vergil knew farms and the suffering of animals. Perhaps he was not so spontaneously and irrepressibly sorry for them as Lucretius was. Perhaps he had disciplined and moralized his sympathies, in obedience to Stoics, or Epicureans, or even the practical needs of the farm. Farming people are notably kind-hearted and cruel too. But yet Vergil, seeking a direct cause for the war in Latium, found it in the accident by which Iulus shot a pet stag. Macrobius thought the motive weak. It is easier to think it an example of Vergilian greatness. That, says Vergil, with the reticence of the style that is the man, is what even a sport, if it is cruel, may bring.

1. The late Field-Marshal Earl Wavell, 'Arms and the Man', Presidential Address to the Virgil Society, 1948, disagrees; he finds indications that Vergil's military knowledge was good.

To the inevitable question whether Vergil wrote a natural or a conventional and artificial style, there is scarcely an answer at all. His 'style' is an elaborate system, gradually developed by himself and others from natural and artistic adaptations of word-order, sound-effects, favourite words, and favourite combinations of words, always controlled by metre and rhythm, but grown to be a natural language for Vergil himself, as it is for readers familiar with him. It was partially at least a mixed style, combined out of countless spoken and written idioms of different places and ages. The Romans of the time liked it immediately. Agrippa, who thought it rather a grotesque and dishonest style, was very much in the minority. Readers seem to have been so well imbued with the existing poetic tradition that poetic and spoken styles appeared equally natural to them. In that sense the situation was like our nineteenth-century situation. A certain quaint formalism was spontaneously accepted from poets.

But in another way Vergil was a bold and violent modernist. He coerced words and their meanings, and used unexpected licences. This and his dependence on rhythm and sound for their significance and almost for their own sakes must have made him seem as Hopkins and Eliot seem to us. Above all his style has reality. He has something to say and he says it. Economy and compression remain his first characteristics, and they are the means to reality and significance.

Vergil's Latin is mainly, at the start, the Latin of his poetic contemporaries. Comparison with Catullus shews that either these contemporaries, perhaps including Cicero, or Vergil himself, refined the language by limiting it to certain forms by the exclusion of many that were current. Catullus writes the imperatives *inger* for *ingere* from *ingerere* and possibly *dice* for *dic* from *dicere*. He certainly has *face* for *fac*. Vergil would have insisted on the classical forms *ingere*, *dic*, and *fac*. But it is hard to understand the immense reputation which he gained as a purist and grammarian, for he allowed himself irregularities, including old-fashioned and colloquial expressions, and even positive inaccuracies.[1]

The reminiscences of old and popular Latin in Vergil are not very many. Some have been met, such as *ollus* for *ille*, and infini-

1. See Appendix 1.

tives in *-ier*. One old form is, however, of special interest now, since it was criticized, and helps to shew how Vergil was regarded.

In the Third *Eclogue* Vergil wrote *dic mihi, Damoeta, cuium pecus? an Meliboei? non, verum Aegonis,* 'come, tell me, Damoetas, whose flock is it – not the flock of Meliboeus?' 'No, it is Aegon's'.[1] *Cuium* is the nominative singular neuter of an old interrogative adjective, *cuius?* meaning 'belonging to whom?', 'whose?' It was so old-fashioned and unusual that, according to Donatus, a parody was written, *dic mihi, Damoeta, cuium pecus? anne Latinum? non, sed sic homines nostri nunc rure loquuntur,* 'Come, tell me, Damoetas, whose flock is it? Is that really Latin?' 'No, but that is how people like me now speak in country places.' The joke is not exactly brilliant, but it is significant that it was made. Oddly the adjective *cuius* is actually used by Cicero.

Less than Catullus, but more than Horace in his fully artistic poetry, Vergil accepts colloquial expressions. His style is rooted partly in old Latin but more still in contemporary Latin, written and spoken, and Greek too, old and new. It is rather the exception than the rule when any strong or unusual expression of Vergil comes from one of these sources only.

Colloquialisms are not normally easy to detect, because other influences blend, and because Latin has not the kind of distinction between written and spoken language which makes detection easy. Some colloquial Latin could never get into a great poem, but some could be so at home there that it might be called as literary as colloquial. In Vergil, *hoc habet,* 'he's taken the knock!',[2] is colloquial enough. It is what the crowd said of gladiators who met a decisive blow. When Juno has made Allecto the Fury inspire the Latins to resist Aeneas, and the Fury asks if she would like more still to be done, Juno, at that terrific moment, says, *terrorum et fraudis abunde est,* perhaps, 'the panics and the crimes will do nicely now',[3] though here obviously, the true translation, if it could be found, would have to be a more diluted expression.

The chief effect of colloquialisms on Vergil is more general. Latin, like all languages, has favourite words, among them *dare,* 'to give' or 'put', the two meanings of two distinct verbs in Indo-European represented in Latin by the single verb *dare.* Vergil

1. *E.* III, 1–2.   2. *A.* XII, 296.   3. *A.* VII, 552.

might have avoided *dare* as trivial. Instead, he made a favourite of it; it may occur twenty or thirty times in a book of the *Aeneid*, in a great variety of meanings, one in particular being something like 'to put a thing in a position to be available for something'; as *immotam . . . coli dedit*, of the once floating island of Delos, 'put in a position to remain fixed and be inhabited';[1] or, alternatively, 'gave to Delos the privilege that it should be fixed and inhabited', as if *ei*, 'to it', and *eam*, 'it', as accusative subject to *coli*, had to be supplied. This is a habitual form of phrase in Vergil. He gets compression by taking the short, colloquial Latin word *dare* and constructing it with an explanatory infinitive, a usage derived mainly from exalted Greek poetry. *Dare* is useful in such phrases as *qua data porta*, literally 'where a way out had been put available',[2] and *daret leto*, 'commit, send on the way, put, to death',[3] the old Latin funeral formula, as in *ollus quiris leto datus*.

There is a common colloquial use of *morari*, 'delay', 'waste time', 'worry about', as in *de pecunia nil moror*, 'it isn't the money I'm worrying about'. *Moror* and its noun *mora*, like *dare*, are short and have short syllables, and are valuable for compression of thought. Accordingly Vergil uses them freely, as in *et esse nil moror*, 'and I don't worry that I should be',[4] that is 'if I really am [hostile to you as you think]'. Vergil reaches great power with *mora*, as in *pugnae nodumque moramque*, a hero, Abas, 'who knots and fixes the fight',[5] never letting it break up into movement through his defeat.

Vergil's ability to express his moods according to his own momentarily and transitorily active characteristics depended to a great extent on the accumulation, through his life, of many poetic resources, available to be evoked again. To old resources Vergil continually added more.

Latin is a language of few words; and, except for agricultural terms and names of trees and plants, Vergil himself used very few words, even for a Latin writer. He did not use a quarter the number that Shakespeare used. His art lay in combining his few words so as to elicit a great variety of meanings. His less permanent and more momentary qualities of style are functions of this method of art. Vergil found as he developed his powers many different

1. *A.* iii, 77.   2. *A.* i, 83.   3. *A.* v, 806.
4. *A.* xi, 364–5.   5. *A.* x, 428.

methods. He came in the end to have countless resources in store. He went back to his own past for them, and used them to create and enrich new moments in his final poem.

The ancients, as I remarked before, distinguished styles mainly by the qualities of simplicity and elaborate decoration, and of everyday levity and solemn severity. Vergil was said to be master of all these styles in their four accepted classifications. He was also said to command the styles of all the nine great Attic orators. Their special qualities included rhythm and degrees of co-ordination and subordination of clauses.

To us these distinctions are not the most interesting. We are inclined to ask instead how an effect that we feel is produced. The more such questions are asked about Vergil, the harder to answer they seem. It is perhaps hardest of all to say just how the delight of the *Eclogues* is communicated.

Gradually, on reflection, the history of Vergil's 'style' becomes clearer. It can be traced according to different criteria.

One criterion is the kind of relevance.

In the *Eclogues* almost any thought may occur in almost any line. They are perpetually going off at a tangent. The relevance is a relevance of pure poetry. The connexion of thought is emotional, lyrical, associative, as in the choral odes of much Greek tragedy; or even more, since in the tragic odes one thing leads to another perceptibly, while in the *Eclogues* even the association of ideas often seems sudden and arbitrary. That is how much of the delight comes. We are pleased to see what unexpected beauty there is in a way-ward, impulsive allusion, at a passionate moment, to an un-suspected part of this new world of imagination. That is, there is a poetic discovery of new and real relations. They are what poetry, and science too, exist to discover.

There is more than might be supposed in this question of poetic relevance which is apparent irrelevance. Like other poetic things it begins at a 'primitive' stage, perhaps from the kind of impulse which produced metaphor and simile. Later come poetic competitions, in which poets ask each other, and answer, poetic riddles, quite disconnected. The Greek *Competition between Homer and Hesiod* is of this sort. It is preserved by a late writer, but the main part of it was probably composed well before the fifth century B.C. It is very much like part of the Third *Eclogue*;[1] there, when Damoetas asks where the sky extends three cubits only, and Menalcas replies by asking where flowers grow inscribed with the names of kings, there is a keen and complex delight at the thought of the intriguing, apparently irrelevant mysteries, on which the prizes or bets in the poetic competition depend. There is a sense of possessing a new and unexpected world, or at least of peeping over a fence at a fresh new heaven in the garden next door. It is a childish delight; children enjoy apparent irrelevances; in that they are both 'primitive' and poetic. It is possible that the joy of surprise and mystery is helped by the old folk-lore revived in the *Eclogues*. The sky three cubits broad is really the ancient Italian symbol of the world or sky, equally called *mundus*. It was a kind of ceremonial grave for offerings to earth powers, opened once a year. There is old folk-lore, too, in the flowers inscribed with names of kings; perhaps they were first marked with the blood of Hyacinthus, or even Adonis.

A more mature kind of surprise, more explicable by what are supposed normal poetic mechanisms, and less dependent on anything 'primitive', is the not less beautiful passage in the Second *Eclogue*. 'Oh, dear, whatever did I want for my poor self?' says Corydon; 'Mad fool, I have let north-east winds in on my flowers, and the wild boars into my clear water springs'.[2] Whatever rational structure of metaphorical or allegorical meaning may be attributed to such acts of poetry, the lovely surprise of them retains its rights.

All the time sound and rhythm reinforce the surprise values. They alone are a delightful surprise, even if the meanings of the words are not understood.

Strangely, in the *Georgics* the units of poetic detonation are both larger, and smaller too. The intrinsic, reasoned metaphors, which declare their relevance to careful thought – the expressions like *se . . . induet in florem*[3] – are minute. The main other sort of imagery is in great panels or expanses, passages a page long perhaps, or more, in which the wider worlds of fact or imagination are disclosed in their relation, partly obscure, to the work of the farm. The inescapable poetic love of obscure metaphoric relevance finds its outlet in two main channels, but not these only. The need for

1. *E.* III, 104–7.   2. *E.* II, 58–9.   3. *G.* I, 187–8.

outlet is urgent, since for much of the time the *Georgics* follow a path dictated by fact; in contrast to the *Eclogues*, which are like Alice's wonderland.

This question of scale needs recognition. It is really the question answered by Mr T. S. Eliot for Dante, when he said that the Divine Comedy does not have, or need, minor imagery in its verse since the whole poem is a single grand metaphor. So, perhaps, is Shakespeare's *Tempest*, the play in which the dominant imagery of Shakespeare's earlier work has now become the actual plot.

Meanwhile in the *Georgics* another technique of comparison is developing, for the work of the farm is compared by simile and by percurrent metaphor to the life of politics and war.

Thus the *Eclogues* have a dreamlike, unitary quasi-irrelevance, which goes well with the occasional surrealism of their use of words. The quasi-irrelevance of the *Georgics* is nearer to the rationality of prose and is built on several different scales. The *Aeneid* is like the *Georgics* in the multiplicity of scale, and in the substructure of prose-like reasoning to which it adheres. It is like them also in its simile and metaphor, the more obviously relevant kinds of quasi-irrelevance. But it retains in readiness the more unconscious, spontaneous method of the *Eclogues*, with their power of surprise. In the *Aeneid* Vergil relived some of their life, most of all in the third book, but not there only.

The poetic style of the *Aeneid* depends, as all poetic style must, on emotions and comparisons. Intrinsic, reasoned, verbal metaphor is used as in the *Georgics*, and so are the broad panels of the wider world within which the narrative has its fuller meaning. Such a panel may be on the scale of the passage in the First *Aeneid*[1] where Jupiter proclaims the Julian future of Rome, perhaps about a page long or more; or on the scale of Evander's narrative of Hercules in the Eighth *Aeneid*,[2] almost a complete epyllion. But 'style' on this scale is almost structure. More strictly 'stylistic' is the development of the minor metaphor which runs through verbal expression.

The style of the *Aeneid* in this sense varies widely. Partly, it is a question of what the ancients called ἦθος, *ethos*, 'temperament', 'moral tone', or 'moral and temperamental mood'. The *Aeneid* is

1. *A.* I, 254–96.   2. *A.* VIII, 184–305.

fully dramatized and its 'style' reflects the character and situations. That may mean that the comparative faculty is used to refer a character to its type. Vergil works by signals. A soldier in a battle speaks as soldiers in battles are supposed to speak, the poetical quality of the language being used to make it at least seem terse and direct. That is seen in *pars belli haud temnenda, viri, iacet altus Orodes*, 'Men, there lies Orodes, so proud and tall, no contemptible part of the enemy's power, which we have to beat to win the war';[1] the translation looks expanded, but probably it scarcely goes beyond the full meaning which Vergil, by poetic means, has compressed into what appear to be terse, direct, and masculine words.

Sometimes it is hard to imagine a passage occurring anywhere but in the *Aeneid*. The line about Orodes is like that. At other times the *Aeneid* draws on the resources already won in earlier poetry. Dido says that her dead husband, Sychaeus, keeps her fidelity and love, and there is none for any but him; *ille meos, primus qui me sibi iunxit, amores abstulit: ille habeat secum servetque sepulchro*, 'that one who first joined me to him took away for ever any love there might have been in my life. So let him have it all in his own keeping, guarding it – just for the burial'[2] – that is, either to share his grave, or to await Dido, when she should come to hers. There are exquisite delights in this. The first line has the tone of the *Eclogues*. Words suggest the *Eclogues*, *ille*, *primus*, *iunxit*, *amores*, and especially *amores*. In the plural it is just a little like *amours*, slightly frivolous. Dido uses it anything but frivolously, but, in Vergil's mystifying way, even then it means something like a serious, tragic equivalent of the American 'love life', that is, the whole erotic side of life, all the chances of love that life has to give. Vergil has enabled himself to mean something new by adopting something quite different from his own *Eclogues*. Equally important is the metrical rhythm. The line has the dancing movement characteristic of pastoral poetry. The reminiscence of the *Eclogues* is poignant indeed. Dido and Vergil too both seem to be looking back to lighter days of sunshine and flowers, when there was hope for them.

If there is any doubt of the reminiscence, it is removed by the contrast of the succeeding words. One, *secum*, recalls the Fourth

1. *A.* x, 737.   2. *A.* iv, 28–9.

Georgics,[1] where Orpheus had his lost Eurydice 'all to himself, alone' as he sang about her on the shore. There is, however, a loneliness of the *Aeneid* in it too. Aeneas told the Sibyl, before he went to the world of death, *omnia praecepi atque animo mecum ante peregi*, 'I have forestalled all of it, by working through all of it in my own thoughts alone'.[2] The concluding words fully belong to the *Aeneid*, in their stern finality, and the triple alliteration of *s*; and they make the earlier reminiscence of the *Eclogues* unmistakable by the contrast. To some extent the conception of 'style' is indispensable in questions like this.

Here a variation of 'style' grew out of different emotions. In the *Aeneid* emotions find an orchestration of notes ready for their expression. By a few touches Vergil can refer a passage to one of many generalized moods, as he can classify a character by some slight reference of the character to a general type. There is nothing whatever mechanical in this; at the most there is a touch of 'classical' abstract schematization, without which the arts usually soon come to decadence. The gain in compression and expressive reticence is immense.

Vergil's 'silences' are famous, especially since Dryden explained them. Vergil can generate with his words a meaning which outlasts them, and seems to be in the air after the words have ceased. Strangely, this is a quality of much French work, in prose and in poetry too, 'classical' work not less than 'romantic'.

Of this it is hard to find a better instance than one of the unfinished lines, to be mentioned later. In the Second *Aeneid*, Venus withdraws the veil from the eyes of Aeneas, and he sees the divine forces at work on Troy's destruction – *apparent dirae facies inimicaque Troiae numina magna deum*, 'there loomed most terrible aspects then, the great powers divine that were not friends to Troy'.[3] The final syllable, in the depths of its dark sound, seems to send reverberations to eternity. Other unfinished lines have similar effects, especially the confident words of Turnus to the disguised Fury Allecto, *nec regia Iuno immemor est nostri*, 'and regal Juno still remembers me'.[4] It is at least likely that Vergil, having at first intended to complete these lines, finally ceased to want to complete

1. *G.* IV, 465.   2. *A.* VI, 105.   3. *A.* II, 622–3.
4. *A.* VII, 438–9.

at least some of them, which supply so greatly their own silent completion.

After Dido's declaration that Sychaeus has taken all her love with him to the grave, there is a Vergilian silence; and then, *sic effata sinum lacrimis implevit obortis*, 'so she spoke; and then the tears welled and broke, streaming on to her dress on her breast'.[1] In the silence before this line, as we find after, Dido's emotions have been revealed; Vergil has said nothing, but everything is suddenly clear, how stirred Dido had been, hardly able to talk at all of the old love, and already weakening before the new. Homer could do it; and perhaps Dante and a few more. Webster's famous line, 'Cover her face; mine eyes dazzle; she died young', has the same kind of reticence. Again and again Vergil leaves silence to speak of Dido.

With some risk of irrelevance, a peculiarly interesting kind of Vergilian restraint can be set beside the silences. Vergil carefully avoids some words, or uses them very rarely indeed. The word *servus*, 'slave', he never uses at all, though he uses the feminine *serva* twice.[2] Servants are usually called by the far kinder and more generous words *verna*, 'home bred slave', *famulus*, 'household slave,' and *minister*, which means something like 'junior assistant'. A word which Vergil hardly ever uses is *barbarus*, which is supposed originally to have meant 'unintelligible' and so 'foreign and uncivilized', and which came to mean 'brutal'. Vergil applies it, in the words of a speaker in the First *Eclogue*, to some veteran who is to be given a confiscated farm. He uses it again in the First[3] and in the Second *Aeneid*,[4] for the land of Carthage, which at first repelled the shipwrecked Trojans, and, in the form *barbaricus*, for 'barbaric' gold decorating door posts at Troy. It is usually and sensibly supposed that Vergil thought that there should be no slaves and allowed none in his poetic world. How far a similar explanation for his restraint in using *barbarus* is right is not quite clear.

An obvious revival in the *Aeneid* of the 'style' of the *Georgics* occurs when similes of country things or other references to them are introduced, and when there is peaceful contemplation of opu-

1. *A.* IV, 30.   2. *A.* V, 284, IX, 546.   3. *A.* I, 539–40.
4. *A.* II, 504.

lent prosperity, normally in visions of the future under the Julian House. The *Georgics* have a quiet, periodic, majestic, balanced movement, with less varied and violent emphasis than is characteristic in the *Aeneid*.

To enumerate, however, the qualities of style which are characteristic of the *Aeneid* is not easy. One or two can be detected with some security, and some are developed rather from the *Eclogues* than from the *Georgics*.

In the *Georgics* Vergil had invented his characteristic period, verse-group, or movement, and he continued to use it in the *Aeneid*. Perhaps he was more inclined there, and especially in his latest style, to avoid single lines and couplets by adding lines to make a movement of at least three.

But the *Aeneid* remembers the *Eclogues* in the intense personal feeling with which lyrics help tragedy. Perhaps too the *Eclogues* communicated to the *Aeneid* a wider range of musical surprise; perhaps these musical tones are in the *Eclogues* more decorative and self-subsistent, and in the *Aeneid* more significant.

Implicit in this development is the development of the repetitive principle. Self-repetition might almost be called as important as emotion and comparisons as a constituent of poetry. Perhaps it is a necessary accompaniment or correlative of emotion, and perhaps it is also just one of the many methods of comparison. It is an immense subject partly met already; and here the thinnest further outline must be enough.

The *Eclogues* balance words and sentence-form. In the passage of the riddles about the *mundus*, 'world', 'sky', or 'ritual, public grave', each speaker begins his couplet with *dic quibus in terris* . . ., 'say in what lands . . .'.[1] Earlier, three consecutive couplets have begun with *qui* . . ., 'he who . . .'.[2] The First *Eclogue*[3] begins with *Tityre, tu* . . ., 'Tityrus, you . . .', goes on to two lines each beginning with *nos* . . ., 'yet we . . .', and returns to *tu, Tityre*, 'while you, Tityrus . . .'. In the Fourth, two consecutive lines begin with *iam* . . ., 'now . . .';[4] the first and third of a movement of four lines begins with *te* . . ., 'you . . .';[5] two consecutive lines begin with *occidet*, 'there shall perish . . .';[6] the first and third of a

1. *E.* III, 104, 106. 2. *E.* III, 88, 90, 92. 3. *E.* I, 1–5.
4. *E.* IV, 6, 7. 5. *E.* IV, 11, 13. 6. *E.* IV, 24, 25.

three-line group begin with *aspice* . . .!, 'look and see . . .!;[1] and of the last six lines[2] the first two begin *Pan etiam Arcadia . . . iudice . . .*, 'Even Pan, with Arcadia to decide [the poetic competition] . . .', the next and next-but-two start with *incipe, parve puer . . .*, 'Begin, little boy . . .', and the last line is built of two parts, balanced by *nec . . . nec . . .*, 'neither . . . nor . . .'.

The schematization of the *Eclogues* by word-balances and repetitions reaches back through Sibylline verse to Hebrew and through Catullus and Lucretius to old Latin, and forward to the *Georgics*, where it is restricted, and to the *Aeneid*, where it is applied occasionally in changed forms with great effect. Once in particular at an unexpected moment in the solemn Sixth *Aeneid*[3] it occurs with another characteristic of the *Eclogues*, aposiopesis, a sudden end to a sentence before it has reached its correct finish, and a change in the construction. Several sentences in the *Eclogues* are so stopped and changed, but none in the *Georgics*, and proportionately only a few in the *Aeneid*. But in the passage of the Sixth *Aeneid* both the balance and repetition, and the aposiopesis, occur. Aeneas, pleading to go to the world below, says in short, 'If Orpheus could win his bride back from Hades by help of his lyre, if Pollux redeemed his brother by taking turns in dying, and went the way back and forth so often – why need I talk of Theseus and great Hercules? My lineage also comes from supreme Jupiter'. The first and third of the five lines begin with *si*, 'if', and the fourth and fifth have a repetition of *quid . . .?* 'why . . .?'. The conditional clauses are broken, and never have their main clause, which is replaced by a sudden, formally irrelevant question. On all this I should like to quote the late Dr J. W. Mackail.[4]

'In the minute tessellation of the *Eclogues* there are traces of the influence of the old Latin rhymed accentual verse; and two lines in the *Lydia*, a piece by an unknown contemporary poet, *luna, tuus tecum est: cur non est et mea mecum? luna, dolor nosti quid sit: miserere dolentis*, suggest, though this may be only a fancy, a stanza from some old Latin ballad . . . So much of this influence still lies beneath the surface in Vergil's own mature poetry as to give to

1. *E.* IV, 50–2.   2. *E.* IV, 58–63.   3. *A.* VI, 119–23;
4. J. W. Mackail, *The Aeneid*, Oxford, 1930, lxxix.

its music a faint but perceptible colour, which in the mechanized hexameter of the Silver Age has disappeared.'

The word-balances of old Latin have some detectable origins. One is ritual repetition, as in the ancient Arval hymn to Mars, where for example *satur fu, fere Mars*, which may mean 'be satisfied, fierce Mars', is repeated, and as in the charm quoted by Varro which was intended to cure bad feet, *terra pestem teneto, salus hic maneto*, 'let the earth keep the disease, and let health remain in my feet.' The charm suggests too another origin, a natural delight in jingles and assonances much helped by the Latin language, so rich in similar terminations. There is no doubt that this natural delight was exploited in popular verse, especially the long tetrameters which are represented in surviving Latin comedy. These tetrameters naturally fall into two parts, which tend to rhyme. From them eventually developed medieval Latin hymns, at least in part. Meanwhile something like a popular tradition had affected Lucretius, whose poetry is an elaborate structure of alliterations, rhymes, and other repetitions. Catullus has an almost unparalleled thirst for balance and repetition, and he satisfied it differently in the two different sorts of poetry which he wrote. In his Alexandrian, mythological, learned narrative poetry he adopted a structural symmetry from Callimachus, which, as Catullus elaborated it, recalls the immensely complex but less rigid pattern of the *Aeneid*. In his direct, short, passionate, colloquial lyrics Catullus used a symmetry of much smaller scale.[1] There he took verbal suggestion from one or two of his lines to energize his imagination for the creation of others; and the pieces grow out of blended self-repetition, and give his poetry 'internal regularity' by this means. He writes *sed obstinata mente perfer, obdura*,[2] and, several verses later, *at tu, Catulle, destinatus obdura*.[3] Two whole poems,[4] in particular, are cross-referenced so. This technique also asserts the unity of the single verse. The repetitions of Lucretius[5]

1. J. van Gelder, *De Woordherhaling bij Catullus*, The Hague, 1933, *passim*.
2. Catullus, VIII, 11.   3. Catullus, VIII, 19.
4. Catullus, VIII and XXIX.
5. Rosamund E. Deutsch, *The Pattern of Sound in Lucretius*, Denton, Texas, 1939, *passim*; with both books, Dr van Gelder's and Dr Deutsch's, cf. now Thomas Halter, *Form und Gehalt in Virgils Aeneis*, Munich, 1963, and N. I. Herescu, *La Poésie latine*, Paris, 1960.

are just as remarkable; but they rather act between verses, sometimes across a long interval.

Vergil was affected by all the methods of repetition, balance, and
symmetry, but he restricted most of them at most times as he
restricted the Catullan golden line and the Catullan habit of
regularly writing hexameters with a stress-accent on the first
syllable of each fourth foot. In structure the *Ciris*, whether or not
Vergil wrote it, is like the longer poems of Catullus. The Fourth
Eclogue, perhaps the most Catullan of Vergil's certain poems, recalls the hexameters of Catullus in phrases, in the unity of single
lines, in schematization of balanced word-order, and in the quality
of the verse-groups; but not, interestingly, in fourth-foot accent.
It also recalls the lyrics of Catullus in the partial construction of
new lines out of the verbal elements of earlier lines in the poem.
With Lucretius Vergil shares the rhyme-systems, but he does not
use his verbal repetition across a wide interval.

The *Georgics* are built rather of periods than stanzas, and this
kind of repetition is less evident. On the whole it is a lyrical
method and less fitted to the *Georgics*, where repetition is more
remotely implicit, or diffused, or missed because of its structural
scale. The earlier kind occurs, however, as in a couplet of which
the first line is in two parts each beginning with *primus* and ending
with an imperative, and the second line contains another *primus*
and an imperative of similar form, 'you be the first to dig the
soil . . .'.[1] Soon after, two parts of a line, and the next line itself,
begin with *iam* . . ., 'now. . . ;'[2] and presently the same repetition
occurs with *hinc* . . ., 'hence . . .'.[3]

The last two instances help to shew how Vergil developed
varied pauses and rhythmic punctuation. Lines are divided more
variously in the *Georgics*, and a new group of words after a pause
may start at many different points of the line. Vergil became insistent about this for a time; he was less insistent in the *Aeneid*.
The real process, of course, was the transference of unity from the
single line to the period or paragraph. Part of this process was the
variation of pauses within the line and some avoidance of them
at the end of the line; but a further part was a certain intensifi-
cation of the unity of the last line in a period, so that unity there

1. *G.* II, 408–9.   2. *G.* II, 416–7.   3. *G.* II, 514–5.

contributed to the unity of the whole passage. The last line, then, is given a rhythmic punctuation.

There are various ways of doing this. In the *Eclogues* a period may end with a golden line, or a quasi-golden line, which at least gives some definition at the end of a succession of lines, each of which tends to have a rather emphatic unity of its own. This use of the 'golden' schematism continued even in the *Aeneid*. Another method is to break up the last line but one, and emphasize the partition, as in the line in which *primus* and the imperative are repeated; and then to end with a line which is less strongly divided, such as the line which contains a single *primus* and continues to an imperative at the end. The first line is schematically almost two lines, and the second very positively one, all the more for the contrast. Vergil often distinguishes a last line from a last but one in this kind of way. A variety is the use of a last line which gains unity from division into three parts, not two, like *emicuit parmamque ferens hastamque trementem*, '[the statue of Athena] darted forth, holding her shield, and her spear all quivering'.[1] The triple division contradicts the usual division of a line into two, which is normally due to a strong third-foot caesura, here absent. A further method of rhythmic punctuation is to use at the end of a period, after a line or lines with no stress-accent on the first syllable of the fourth foot, a line, or a pair of lines, having a stress-accent in that place. A development of this is the use, at the end, of a line with many stress-accents on the first syllables of feet, as *Ascraeumque cano Romana per oppida carmen* in the *Georgics*, 'I sing my song like Hesiod's from town to town of the Roman lands',[2] and, in the *Aeneid*, *Albanique patres atque altae moenia Romae*, 'our fathers at Alba, and proud, battlemented Rome'.[3] The effect is not confined to passages which are strictly released movements.

In the mature style of the *Aeneid* Vergil had partly freed himself from his willed insistence on the unity of the period, and from his early subjection to the balances of the *Eclogues*. He was used to the wayward surprises of his imagination, to the reasoned intrinsic metaphors which he could make out of simple words, and to the straight narration of thought, fact, and fiction according to the

1. *A*. 11, 175.   2. *G*. 11, 176.   3. *A*. 1, 7.

331

sequence and rationality of prose. These, and many more, practices, artifices, methods or predilections had become spontaneous. They might blend together, or come separately into play, when the *Aeneid* had grown to the supreme power of its culminating orchestration.

The chief advance in the *Aeneid* is force. There has been force earlier, as in the description of the storm in the First *Georgics*. Power there has been too, as in the delicate and solemn pathos so vital at the end of the Fourth *Georgics* in the tale of Orpheus and Eurydice. The *Eclogues* are sad and pathetic and touching and thrilling, but they do not carry a world's sorrow, as the *Georgics* can, though even there the pain is softened by restraint and harmony. Vergil in the *Aeneid* goes beyond what is supposed to be the 'classical' restraint, and accepts harmonies that are tumultuous. It is possible that he is the greatest of poets, and possible, too, that a reason for that is his ability to apply supreme power by force and by soft means also. Force and power themselves do not go readily together.

There is generally an impression that Vergil has more power than he is willing to use, as if he could never come to the end of his resource. There are long passages of subdued emotional vigour. But sometimes he withdraws the control, and releases with irresistible impact his full power by means of all his force.

At such times sound takes command, and sound almost is Vergil's style then. There are rhymes, assonances and pseudo-rhymes, elaborate patterns of stress-rhythm, and a sense of freedom and impetuosity in which mere metre is almost forgotten. The metre seems to exercise only light restraint. The words fall into a natural, almost a conversational order, and find whatever pauses they choose. There are seldom metrical irregularities. The tiny, intrinsic, reasoned metaphors are little wanted. All this seems to have become old and dull and almost childish to the mature Vergil at his moments of supreme and ultimate sovereignty. He is doing harder things; or they are being done through his lips by the breath whose might kindles the universe.

What these passages of both force and power achieve can be roughly guessed. They emit a kind of glow, each of different light, often bold and fiery in colours of red and gold. They raise humanity to a mystical world, where all is stronger and intenser and there is no check to dynamic realities. In this world it is not the little metaphors, but symbol in giant forms that speaks. And it speaks in, or with, or by, rhythmic symmetries that are almost too subtle, too remote from ordinary things, to detect, but are yet somewhere near the heart of life, where the mind comes in touch with truth.

Of this kind is the death of Laocoon,[1] the death of Priam,[2] the Helen scene and the ensuing appearance of Venus and the vision which she shewed,[3] the death of Dido[4] – a passage of more than a hundred lines –, the meeting with Deiphobus in the world of the dead,[5] much of the vision which Anchises shews to Aeneas,[6] much, too, of the mission of Allecto the Fury, sent by Juno to start war in Latium, up to the moment when Juno herself opens the gates of war,[7] and then the making of the arms of Aeneas,[8] and the death of Turnus.[9] These are passages of force and power, comparable, for all their variety of tone, in style. Within the passages, the style may change, and many lines may deliver power otherwise.

In the appearance of Venus to Aeneas at Troy, just after the fierce force of the Helen scene,[10] the power is softly applied. So it is at the other appearances of Venus as the divine mother of Aeneas, when she appeals to Jupiter for him,[11] when she meets Aeneas, shipwrecked in Africa,[12] and when she persuades Volcanus to make the arms for him.[13] There is much variety of tone, but it is all a rescue, soft and faithful, the rescue of home and young love. But it is not the style of the *Eclogues*. Some of the tones recall them. But Vergil has gone on far from that time. The style is blended out of emotions remembered in tranquillity. When Venus met Aeneas after his shipwreck, she was disguised as a hunting girl, quite boyish. When she talks to Jupiter and Volcanus she is almost a young, half naughty, fortunate Dido. But when she fully declares herself to Aeneas, at the end of the meetings in Africa and

1. *A.* II, 199–233.   2. *A.* II, 526–58.   3. *A.* II, 567–623.
4. *A.* IV, 584–705.   5. *A.* VI, 494–534.   6. *A.* VI, 752–892.
7. *A.* VII, 286–640.   8. *A.* VIII, 370–453.
9. *A.* XII, 614–49, 843–952.   10. *A.* II, 588–93.
11. *A.* I, 227–9.   12. *A.* I, 314–34, 402–9.   13. *A.* VIII, 370–406.

at Troy, she is a true mother, with all a mother's sovereign power
to rescue and shed a spell of sweetness; but regal, too. Vergil's
own loves, of perhaps three kinds, were blended into Venus, and
taught him to write of her. What was left went to make the young
soldiers who die, and Ascanius; and went to make Dido. But
much is safe for ever in Vergil's Venus.

This direct creation of style by emotion is like the creative
process of the *Eclogues* in the importance given to vowel values,
but different in a rich depth of tone, as in *divinum adspirat amorem*,
'adding a breath of divine love',[1] and *comae divinum vertice odorem
spiravere*, 'her . . . hair breathed from her head a scent of heaven';[2]
and also in the almost prosaic simplicity which Vergil uses sometimes in his greatest poetry, as in *cui mater media sese tulit obvia silva*,
'and there, right in the wood, his mother came to meet him',[3] and
in *cum mihi se non ante alias tam clara videndam obtulit . . . alma
parens . . .*, 'when, there before me, at no other time before so
visible, my own kind mother came to meet my sight'.[4] Here the
intervening words are too serious for the *Eclogues*, *et pura per
noctem in luce refulsit*, 'just shining on me, in a pure stream of light,
through the dark';[5] like *rosea cervice refulsit*, 'shone with the delicate
hue of her neck',[6] at the earlier meeting. Somehow the pace is
slowed, and the lines are charged with meaning even when they
are simple and light, without specially rich vowel colour, and,
notably in this style, without repetitions.

The expression of pathos for which Vergil is famous also seems
to come straight from deeply felt and richly remembered emotion,
without very much detectable dynamic method. Of this there is,
however, some. The habit of reading Vergil develops attention to
full meanings of words, with implications. Accordingly, simple
words, in close proximity to other words, significantly related by
contrast or otherwise, are spontaneously given great strength by
readers so trained by Vergil himself, who, like other great artists,
is brilliant at getting the work done for him. Daedalus had twice
tried to picture on the gates of the temple at Cumae the death of
his son Icarus, but *bis patriae cecidere manus*, 'twice those hands sank
from the trying, for they were a father's hands',[7] trying to depict

1. *A.* VIII, 373.   2. *A.* I, 403–4.   3. *A.* I, 314.   4. *A.* II, 589–91.
5. *A.* II, 590.   6. *A.* I, 402.   7. *A.* VI, 33.

his own son's death. When the trumpet-call to war was heard afar in Latium, suddenly, without transition, Vergil says *et trepidae matres pressere ad pectora natos*, 'and mothers trembled, clasping to their breast their sons'.[1] Here it is not so much that Vergil says this, as that he thought of saying it, and picked that idea out of all the ideas possible; and perhaps above all that he said it suddenly, inconsequently, with a surprise, as often he said more trivial things in the *Eclogues*. Here, as not always in the *Eclogues*, the relevance is terrifyingly, bitterly clear; but the brilliance is won by a partial recourse to the old, apparently inconsequent, way. Vergil often revives it in the *Aeneid*, for example, when he suddenly evokes some myth, and it is only afterwards that we realize the point of it. He evokes the Centaurs in writing of Hercules;[2] and we remember that in Greek sculpture they represented barbarism, and he the courageous fight for true civilization. Pathos in one sense at least may depend on Vergilian silence, as in *tendebantque manus ripae ulterioris amore*, 'stretching out hands in longing for the further shore',[3] of the dead who could not yet cross the river of death; for here something is left unsaid which holds the heart of the pathos: that though they wish indeed that they were alive, yet they would rather reach the land of death than wait, halfway; and that, helpless and hopeless, they can do no more than the gesture of longing. Of the effect of the vowels in this line, much has been said here and elsewhere, but little decided. Perhaps it is at least helped by contrast of very long and very short syllables, and a kind of monotony in the repetition of a sound.

The strong passages of power exerted by force may include the best that Vergil ever did, but need not. Nor need such passages as the appearance of Venus, or the lines of supreme pathos, be the greatest. But if another class is added, then there is little doubt that in these four roughly divided kinds of passage at least the larger part of Vergil's supreme triumphs can be found.

The passages of the fourth class are like the first in fluidity, freedom, regularity, and rhythmic pattern, but unlike it because such passages lack the most forcible elements, rhyme and assonance, with their rich colour tones, and perhaps balanced repetition of other kinds, and also the sharp, fierce, impacts of vowels and

1. *A.* VII, 518.   2. *A.* VIII, 293–4.   3. *A.* VI, 314.

consonants. These passages are often exquisite units of thought and expression and rhythm, from perhaps four to thirty lines long, with a soft, blended, delicately-coloured perfection, reproducing a mood of acute and lovely consciousness. Most of them have a pattern of stress-rhythm. Among them are the passage in praise of Italy in the Second *Georgics*,[1] the first paragraph of the whole *Aeneid*,[2] the end of the Fifth *Aeneid*[3] where Palinurus falls from the ship into the sea, and lines at the end of the Seventh[4] on the fighting maiden Camilla. Each presents a harmonized picture, which nothing can change.

Saint Augustine[5] was surprised to see Saint Ambrose reading quietly to himself, and making no sound. That was in the fourth century A.D. This is one of the indications of the immense importance of sound and pronunciation in ancient literary work. Poetry was not itself, unless it was heard aloud. So also today faults in the pronunciation of Vergil's poetry can spoil the appreciation of it. We must somehow hear it whenever we read it. And at the same time we must have a satisfactory, though inevitably an individual, theory about the kind of language Vergil writes, and the kind of thought and feeling in it. That involves an attempt to discover what is the kind of English into which, according to our careful individual judgement, it is least offensive, and least unreal, to translate Vergil.

There are many contradictory ways of pronouncing the ancient languages, and it is hard to assert confidently what, precisely, the ancient pronunciations were. But it is quite wrong to say that, since complete certainty is out of reach, it is useless to try to pronounce Greek and Latin as they were pronounced in classical times. There is plenty of evidence to shew, without much risk of serious error, how Latin in particular was spoken. This is now understood, even in England, where, until not so long ago, Latin was always pronounced as if it had been English.

Pronunciation is well known. Roughly, the vowels and consonants are as they are in Italian; but *c* and *g* are hard, the Italian pronunciation of *gl* and *gn* is absent, and diphthongs have

1. *G.* II, 136–76.   2. *A.* I, 1–7.   3. *A.* V, 835–71.
4. *A.* VII, 803–17.   5. St Augustine, *Confessions*, VI, iii, 3.

their own sounds, especially *ae*, like 'aye', or possibly between 'aye' and French è, *oe*, like 'oy' in 'destroy', and *au* like 'ow' in 'how'.

Less well known, but becoming better known continually, is the care needed to give full value in pronunciation to every letter, every quantity, and every stress-accent. Pronunciation of literary works was an art among the Romans, presupposed by the creation of the works. If Latin poetry is not pronounced accurately and well, it becomes something quite different from its true self, and cannot be successfully understood.

In reading Vergil aloud it is important to give emphasis evenly and regularly not only to the first syllable of each foot, but to all the long syllables, and to all stressed syllables also. The metre must not take entire control; prose rhythm must be maintained at the same time. The short syllables must be pronounced clearly, not almost eliminated, as in English they often are.

Vergil, like most other poets but not all, read well. He read his own poems with great beauty of effect and great power, *lenociniis miris*, 'with amazingly attractive appeal', as Donatus says. He meant it to be read aloud; and of course that was the usual Roman method of first publication. Clearly, he wrote for reading aloud, and unless Vergil's poetry is read aloud by us, the poetic act of communication is not complete. If it is to succeed, the poetry must be read with clearest pronunciation of every letter, equal or almost equal emphasis for both stress and ictus, and with careful variation of pace and power.

Vergil's style is musical, intellectual, conventional, colloquial, archaic and modernistic. It is hardly to be expected that an English style, corresponding in all its qualities, could be found or invented for the translation of Vergil. It is possible to secure some of the required correspondences, but certainly not all at once.

The translation of Vergil into English requires careful consideration of the available principles, and careful choice between them. You can translate the approximate meaning of the Latin into an old-fashioned English, as the custom was a few years ago; or into English natural at our own time, producing the poetic effects which you think Vergil would have produced if he had been a contemporary Englishman, as Dryden translated Vergil, or Pope Homer. Or you can attempt to reproduce the sound and rhythm of Vergil, at the cost of the sense. As for the sense itself, you can construe the words literally, taking the clearest, common-sense meaning; or you can attempt to suggest the poetic surprises in the words by poetical language; or you can sometimes even attempt to represent Vergil's double meanings, or even his silences, for which Dryden so highly praised him. It is very difficult indeed to follow two principles at once. It is best to choose whichever one seems to represent Vergil most truly and completely.

Then there is the question of verse or prose. Blank verse is obvious, but hard to write well. Rhymed couplets have good qualities, but they are quite different in rhythmic span from the Vergilian paragraph or period, and have strong associations remote from Vergil. Long lines and ballad metres become monotonous in a way most unlike Vergil. All metres sacrifice Vergilian rhythm and freedom. But good translations have been made in all of them, or, if not good translations, good poems, founded on Vergil. That is one of the great decisions; whether the rendering is to be verbally accurate, or poetically like the original.

There seem two good plans, a verse translation giving the poetic mood and force of the original, with some corresponding values of sound and rhythm, and a prose translation, which attempts to elicit as much as ever it can of the meaning of all the words and cases and tenses and moods. The last I prefer; though it has to be long, and to sacrifice almost all the Vergilian brevity and compression, it seems to get the utmost possible amount of Vergilian effect, though the kind of effect that it gets best may not be the most important.[1]

The style is another question. Vergil is not pompous or pedantic. He writes directly and metaphorically, transferring words and extracting meanings, sometimes content with his own characteristic exploitation of ordinary words and idioms, but inclined to go back to old words and old meanings deliberately or instinctively. It is a muscular and modern style. A translation should use words common in modern prose and avoid archaism, and any sort of poeticalness for its own sake. The translator, like Vergil,

1. This I have attempted to do in a Penguin translation of the *Aeneid*, Harmondsworth, 1956, with reprints.

should think above all of expressing the full meaning in minute precision. Dignity can still be saved. Unobtrusively, ugly words, and sentences ending with a preposition, can be avoided; and by unremitted listening sensitive and varied rhythm can be won.

There are problems to solve. Often a verb must be translated by a noun or a noun by an adjective, or an 'and' by an 'of', or a finite verb by a participle. It is important to reduce the number of 'ands'. An example of these difficulties is *magnam cui mentem animumque Delius inspirat vates aperitque futura*,[1] literally 'into whom the Delian prophet inspires a large mind and spirit and discloses things about to be'.[1]

It is very unlikely that any word but the simplest can be trusted to have its obvious vocabulary meaning. *Magnus*, partly through Latin and partly through Greek associations, will in a poetic context mean 'impressive' or 'powerful' as well as, or instead of, 'great'. Both *mens* and *animus* are often said to mean 'mind'. It is possible that both do mean 'mind' sometimes; but it is much more important to remember that *mens* is 'energetic imagination' and *animus* 'the wind of the spirit', than to agree that 'mind' is a word which might sometimes stand for those concepts, as they are hurriedly handled in ordinary prose usage. But to say 'powerful vision and spirit', if sufficient, is unnatural. The 'and' is wrong. The Delian inspired one thing, not two; it is a hendiadys. The 'and' must go, and an accusative noun must become a genitive or an adjective. But in English adjectives are normally more intrinsically expressed than in Latin. It is reasonable for an important part of the meaning to be expressed by an adjective. So I would make *mentem* an adjective, and *magnam* a noun, and say 'the spirit's visionary might'.

In Latin, and above all in Vergil, a single word is much nearer to serving as a whole sentence than in any of the other more familiar languages. *Delius* and *vates* are somehow more than the 'Delian prophet'; they might be 'the prophetic god born in Delos', but that is heavy, and 'god', strangely, is a word to avoid in translation, because 'a god' is remote from most of our talk, and has associations of artificiality. 'He of Delos, the prophetic' might be better. *Inspirat* hardly can be quite 'inspire'; it is two thousand

1. *A.* VI, 11–12.

years nearer to its origin in *in-* and *spirare*, 'breathe into'. Vergil is inclined to work etymologically; and, though it is a risk, it seems to me much the smaller risk of two to say here 'breathes into her'.

Aperitque futura is easier. It is fairly obvious that the *-que* must go, and that the verb must become a participle. *Futura* is dark and threatening with uncertainty, and possibly the quality of the word, here at the end of an important sentence, needs reinforcement. One way, and a Vergilian way, is to use an old emotional charge allusively, and say, remembering H. G. Wells' terrifying film, 'revealing things to come.'

Poets of the old proud lineage, says Flecker, sing to find our hearts, they know not why. But they find them; and perhaps it is because their lineage is old and proud.

They do it with a song, for there must be rhythm. It seems that they reach back to old times when humanity shared the same rhythms, so that they can still awake some old rhythm in whose pervasive echo humanity can still be one, and, awakened, see. Vergil, says Professor Corso Buscaroli,[1] does not mean to 'recall anything to our *memory*'; he means '*to make us see*'. He, and the other great poets, too, create a rhythm which possesses us, because it touches us where we are all alike, and have been all alike for thousands of years. When the rhythm possesses us, we see.

What happens is a mystery. We do not observe the parts of our minds where rhythms make us one. We do not even observe the rhythms. The mind which we know in ourselves, and the rhythms which we detect and analyse in the work of Vergil, are much more obviously unique than universal, personal to ourselves and to the poet. But there must be something else, obscure, and deeper; or these new, unique minds of ours would never recognize, and accept, as their own long loved and comprehended riches, the strange new tones and cadences which every great poet finds.

Clearly, the event is double. Like the icebergs, our minds have the greatest part of themselves below the surface. The poet's rhythm puts us into a mood in which our conscious mind has access to our unconscious. There is something that we do not

1. Corso Buscaroli, *Virgilio, il libro di Didone*, Milan, etc., 1932, p. 324 on *A.* IV, 473.

know happening. The ancient rhythms, lost to sight amid the orchestral complexities of the great masters, are there, awaking a response in us. Then the poet of the old lineage makes all things new. He has found new rhythms, new tones. The spirit's eyes and ears are open, and there is access to the unconscious soul of truth in us. There the new rhythm enters and is built on to the old. We, too, are made new. We are made to hear, and so to see.

CHAPTER 6

POETRY AND MANUSCRIPTS

VERGIL's way of writing, and the qualities of his poetry, are reflected, and are also enlightened, by the transmitted text of his poems, and its condition and problems.

The texts of ancient writers have survived in very various conditions, some hopelessly corrupt, and some, among them the texts of the New Testament and Vergil, in excellent condition, with comparatively few possibilities of serious doubt.

Ancient writing is preserved on inscriptions, of which the earliest in Greek lettering, inscriptions at Thera and at Abu Simbel in Egypt, are dated not long after 650 B.C.; the inscriptions at Thera may be older.

In Italy there are traces of a scarcely legible inscription, in which the word *rex*, 'king', is identified, on a stone found under the 'Black Stone' in the Roman Forum, and dated to the sixth century B.C.

The earliest copies of classical literary documents are on papyri found in Egypt, and the first is a lyric 'nome', the *Persians* of Timotheus, written not long before the date of the surviving fragment, in the fourth century B.C. Other papyri are little later, and there are some for all the following centuries till the sixth century A.D.

Some papyri are the only authority for a text, for example papyri of Bacchylides and of the *Constitution of Athens*, by Aristotle. But most classical texts depend mainly on vellum *codices* or books, not scrolls, *volumina*, the earlier form. Codices began about the first century A.D., and in the next two centuries became general. Scrolls, *volumina*, were usual before. They continued in some places, especially towards the east; in the monastery of Vathopedi on Mount Athos scrolls of the early centuries can still be seen, resting fearlessly on open shelves in a small room.

The best manuscripts of the New Testament, even before the

Codex Sinaiticus, of the fourth century, was discovered, and the best manuscripts of Vergil, have few serious competitors. Editors of texts are sometimes quite well off when they have one or two good manuscripts of the twelfth, eleventh, or perhaps the tenth century A.D. At such dates writing is beautifully clear, sometimes like the upright copybook hand of the most modern typewriters.

Editors of Vergil, however, have fared much better. They have no less than seven manuscripts of the sixth century and earlier. None are quite complete, and some are fragmentary; but the three most complete, the Medicean, *M*, the Palatine, *P*, and the Roman, *R*, form a positively majestic triad. They were actually written before the development of minuscule and majuscule book hands, and are in bold and most attractive Roman capitals.

Even they are not the earliest. The most ancient of all is apparently *Augusteus*, *A*, of the third or even the second century. It has only eight surviving leaves, containing fragments of the *Georgics*, and four lines of the *Aeneid*.[1] The leaf containing the lines from the *Aeneid* is possibly now lost. There is some mystery about it. The lines were copied from the leaf before it disappeared. *A* scarcely affects the text of Vergil, as constituted from other manuscripts. The next oldest, probably, is the fragmentary manuscript of the early fourth century, called *Schedae Vaticanae*, *F*, *schedae* being 'pages'. It contains 1,906 lines only, but there are fragments of all the books of the *Aeneid*, except the tenth and twelfth, in length from 14 to 167 lines. *F* is very valuable. Probably a little later, but still of the fourth century, are two palimpsest fragments, *Schedae rescriptae Veronenses*, *V*, fifty-one leaves, with 1,320 lines, some indecipherable, and the *Schedae rescriptae Sangallenses*, *G*, eleven leaves, with 266 lines, including fragments from the first, third, fourth, and sixth books of the *Aeneid*, in bad condition however, and hard to read.

Next are the three chief manuscripts. *Palatinus*, *P*, of the fourth century, about contemporary with the palimpsests, is nearly complete, but has some leaves missing. On the whole, it is the best manuscript of them all. However, the vulgate, or ordinary text which has been most generally adopted was based by Nicolas Heinsius in 1676 on *Mediceus*, *M*, of the early fifth century. It has

1. *A*. IV, 302–5.

many corrections, made by several hands starting soon after it was copied, and continuing for two centuries after. It is the most complete, and almost, if not quite, as good as P. Then comes *Romanus*, R, of the fifth or early sixth century, which is less complete than P and M, since most of the second, third and sixth books of the *Aeneid* are missing, and which was copied by a less competent scribe than they.

Most often, these manuscripts are enough to constitute the text. The late J. W. Mackail[1] estimates that in the *Aeneid* there are less than a dozen instances 'in which the necessity for altering the text materially against the unanimous evidence of the primary manuscripts is so clear that alteration has been generally accepted and has become the modern vulgate'. Most often there are three or four of these primary manuscripts available for every passage.

The later manuscripts are very numerous. Some can be traced to the archetypes of P, R, and V – the originals from which they were copied. One, *Gudianus*, γ, preserves otherwise unknown readings of the archetype of P, but they are mainly matters of detail.

The six earliest manuscripts are not far in time from their original. There was probably one authentic text of the *Eclogues*, the *Georgics*, and the *Aeneid*, which was rapidly multiplied in copies from the moment of publication. The texts of the *Eclogues* and *Georgics* received Vergil's final corrections; the text of the *Aeneid* did not, but a single version only seems to have been published by Varius and Tucca, and to have been the only one in circulation for some years.

Some ancient texts may go back to original variants, both equally authentic, as Saint Augustine seems to have allowed different versions of the same text to circulate. The text of Vergil, however, was originally one. Aulus Gellius[2] records that Valerius Probus, in the first century A.D., saw a manuscript corrected by Vergil himself, and learnt from it how Vergil spelt certain words. Elsewhere[3] Gellius says that he can readily believe people who claim to have seen a text written out by Vergil himself. Vergil's family is supposed to have possessed copies written or corrected by Vergil for two or three generations at least. Even then, there was

1. J. W. Mackail, *The Aeneid*, Oxford, 1930, lx.
2. Aulus Gellius, XIII, 21, 1–12.   3. ibid., IX, 14, 7.

clearly much interest in details, and there still is. The latest full edition of Vergil, by Professor Remigio Sabbadini,[1] makes new progress with Vergil's spelling and grammar, and in due course it should lead to more progress still.

From Vergil's lifetime onwards manuscripts of his work multiplied rapidly and continually and hundreds still survive; and ever since the first printed edition, the *editio princeps*, issued by Sweynheim and Pannartz at Rome, undated, but probably about A.D. 1467, printed editions have followed each other rapidly, sometimes at the rate of at least one a year.

But though manuscripts of Vergil are good, early, and in close relation to the authentic original editions of the poems, that does not mean that there are no difficulties in constituting Vergil's text. On the contrary, it has special difficulties of its own.

It is beginning to be realized that mistakes in the transmission of copied documents are not so absolute and detectable as they used to seem, partly because you cannot be sure that a writer wrote what you think he ought to have written. That is a simple way of indicating a complicated matter.

Almost everything depends on what sort of text and what sort of writer it is. The Alexandrians, in starting textual criticism on Homer, were guided, Aristarchus especially, by a personal judgement about what was, and what was not, good enough for Homer to have said. Since ancient critics, as Mr H. D. Lucas once well explained in a lecture, had very little sense of time and history, the Alexandrians failed to make enough allowance for changing ideas, and also, perhaps, for the Homeric method of composition, in so far as it can be estimated. Homer undoubtedly went over his poetry, some of it his own in a much stricter sense than other parts, again and again, and various versions might be equally Homeric. But others, too, had been doing something like the same thing to some of the material before, and others again, the rhapsodes who recited Homer, were to do it after. When Homer died, there existed texts of his poems, possibly written, more or less as he wished them to be. But additions and excisions and

1. *P. Vergili Maronis opera*, R. Sabbadini recensuit, Rome, 1930: cf. the revised edition, with the collaboration of L. Castiglioni, Turin and elsewhere, 1945.

alterations might be made, not easily distinguishable from the variations which Homer had himself at different times approved. The main task of the Alexandrians was to mark for rejection lines which had been added, as many were, by rhapsodes, and their main difficulty was in deciding who had made the additions, if they were additions, Homer himself, or another. They could not realize, as we can, how like a rhapsode's or a copyist's mistake a change of mind by an author himself may be.

The complications here have been revealed by Dr Wolf Hartmut Friedrich in his work on Seneca's plays and Professor William Empson in his book on the ambiguities in English poets;[1] their statements have been mentioned here already. A writer may never decide what his text should be, or he may decide this in his own mind, but yet leave on his page variants, without shewing which is to be chosen. Further, he may actually compose his work by a method which is in aspect very like textual corruption, but is really a most authentic poetic method. That is, he may accept into his mind rational ideas, and alter them until they become poetry, but cease to be rational or coherent. Copyists appear to do much the same thing, with this great difference, that the poets make poetry this way, and the copyists usually something which has not this compensation. The difference is easier to miss than it should be.

The texts of the *Eclogues* and *Georgics* were carefully published during Vergil's life-time and immediately became school books. There is not much doubt usually, except in small matters, what Vergil's final decisions were. The uncertainties which exist are due not to Vergil but to copyists. The *Aeneid* on the other hand was not published by Vergil, though he read probably the second and fourth book, and certainly the sixth book, to the family of Augustus. At his death, he left it unfinished. He wanted it burnt, but he was persuaded, or overruled, by Augustus, and it was decided that his friends, Varius and Tucca, should edit it, on the strict understanding that they should excise passages not required, but add nothing. That is the account of Servius.

1. Wolf Hartmut Friedrich, *Untersuchungen zu Senecas dramatischer Technik*, Borna-Leipzig, 1933, *passim*; William Empson, *Seven Types of Ambiguity*, London, 1930.

The literary executors did their task well. They had manuscripts written by Vergil himself or by his secretary, Eros. They were not, however, definitive texts in every part of them. There were alternative lines in the margin, or suggestions for additions and excisions; and some passages had a ring round them, meaning that they must be removed. The executors, loyal to Vergil's ardent wish that lines which he regretted should be suppressed, certainly tried to publish nothing of which they were not sure that he would approve. There was, however, the possibility of doubt; in the text of the *Aeneid* Vergil's final decision could not always be known.

Servius records four instances of passages which were rejected, implying that they were not the only ones. The first,[1] also mentioned by Donatus, is a set of four additional lines before the beginning of the *Aeneid*, fitting on to it, in which Vergil explains that he who wrote on shepherds and farmers, now writes on arms and a man, and which Varius is said to have removed. The second[2] is the Helen scene, where, at the sack of Troy in the Second *Aeneid*, Aeneas sees Helen and wants to kill her – till his divine mother appears and restrains him, and directs him to his next, real duty. Servius in his *Life* says that Varius and Tucca removed it. The additional introduction at the beginning of the *Aeneid* may well be rejected. It is charming, but Vergil is likely to have preferred, on second thoughts and reasonably, the impersonality of epic. The Helen scene was, according to Servius, rejected possibly because it contradicted an account of Helen given in the sixth book, and possibly because the desire to kill a woman was too unchivalrous for Aeneas. Without any doubt it must stand. If Vergil himself meant to reject it, he was wrong, as poets often are about their own work. Though the passage has actually been thought the work of an imitator, not Vergil, it is overpoweringly Vergilian and one of the most indispensable things in the *Aeneid*. There is only one course, boldly to print it in its place, and feel sure that Vergil would have changed his mind. Of other such rejected passages, two are certainly known.

1. Servius, *Prologue to Aeneid I*.
2. Servius, ibid.; cf. R. G. Austin, *The Classical Quarterly*, xi, 1961, 185–98.

One is a group of three verses in the Third *Aeneid*,[1] good, but spoiling the story, for the Trojans are lost in a storm at sea, and the unwanted lines explain that they were near specific places on land. The other is a group of four lines describing the Gorgon Medusa in the Sixth *Aeneid*.[2] Both passages are preserved by Servius, who says that the first of the two was found 'ringed in the margin', and that the second was 'left by the poet and removed by those who corrected the text', presumably the first editors. Why the passage about the Gorgon was removed is uncertain. Perhaps it seemed too much like the later description of Tisiphone.[3]

In the *Aeneid*, therefore, there are two sources of uncertainty, due to copyists, and also to Vergil himself. In the other poems there is in general only one, due to the copyists. The copyists of Vergil do not cause much trouble, but they cause it in a special way.

The text of Aeschylus has suffered because the Attic Greek of his period and especially the Attic of Aeschylus himself has been little understood by anyone, ever since his time. Aristophanes, less than two generations after his death, finds plenty of humour in his language. To this day, though progress is being made more quickly now, knowledge is simply insufficient; and the copyists did not know Aeschylus nearly well enough to copy him rightly.

The copyists had quite sufficient reasons to copy Aeschylus wrongly in their ignorance of his language, but they were helped sometimes by knowledge of his metres. The copyists of Pindar were in the same kind of plight. The language of Pindar is, however, except in details, easier than the language of Aeschylus. But his metres are harder, and indeed from classical till modern times were so entirely misunderstood that it was not suspected that Pindar wrote metrically at all.

Thus the copyists of Pindar and Aeschylus failed because they did not know and understand the texts well enough. Those who handled the text of Homer, however, though there was much that they did not understand, knew it rather too well than not well enough. Rhapsodes had to know much epic, Homeric and other,

1. Servius-Daniel, *A.* III, 204.   2. Servius-Daniel, *A.* VI, 289.
3. *A.* VI, 555–8.

very well indeed. They count as the earliest transmitters of the text; and they expanded the text and perhaps corrupted it too by adding lines from other passages, and making other changes, just because, in a sense, they knew epic poetry too well.

The same thing is true of Vergil, perhaps in unique degree. There have always, from the beginning, been people with their minds full of Vergil, hardly able to refrain from reciting him at length. The result from the start was this. Copyists and others wrote in the margin of copies parallels from elsewhere in Vergil which a current passage suggested. These parallels might sometimes displace the right text, so that copyists wrote at a given place not what Vergil had written there, but something which he had written elsewhere, and which the present passage had recalled to some reader. This happened also when no parallels were written in the margins, simply because the minds of copyists were so full of Vergil that they were almost as likely to copy their thoughts as the words of the manuscript before them.

This was all the more easy because of the audial imagination which Vergil himself used, and habitually develops in others. That is, Vergil himself normally wrote down something which was suggested to him by the sound of earlier Latin verses, either by other poets, or, increasingly as time went on, by himself. Vergil wrote what the many Vergilian and other passages in his mind suggested to him; and so did the copyists. The result is that it is sometimes really difficult to distinguish the uncertainties caused by copyists from the uncertainties caused by Vergil himself. Both often write what is unexpected because they have in their minds other Vergilian passages. On every page this must be remembered.

So far this is not unlike the conditions of Homeric criticism. Sir Maurice Bowra[1] has explained the complications of Homeric repetitions. About every third line of the *Iliad* repeats either another line of it, or a part of another line. Homer's expressional alphabet consists of 'epic formulae'. Probably Vergil repeats himself still more often. But the exact repetitions are smaller. Homer would repeat a whole passage of several complete lines exactly as they were elsewhere. Vergil, as Heinsius observed, hated the

1. Sir Maurice Bowra, *Tradition and Design in the Iliad*, Oxford, 1930, 123.

exact repetition of epic formulae, but relied on audial suggestion. Mr John Sparrow has shewn that Vergil very rarely repeats himself exactly; only about thirty lines occur twice in the *Aeneid*. The rule does not apply to Vergil's own earlier work; occasionally he even incorporates in the *Aeneid* three or four lines from the *Georgics*, without any change. Vergil, in all his certainly authentic poems, used lines from the *Ciris* very freely.[1] That is some argument for the view that he wrote the *Ciris* himself, but did not publish it for a long time.

There is therefore some guidance when the text of Vergil is in doubt through a possible reminiscence by a copyist. If Homer has the same line or lines in two places, other things being equal it is exceedingly likely that in both places they should stand. If Vergil has the same line or lines in two places within the *Aeneid*, it may almost be assumed either that he really did alter either one or the other, or that he would have made an alteration, if he had finished his revision. It is thus often easy to say that a variant is right because it is not exactly the same as a passage elsewhere. But it is dangerous to cut out repeated lines, for Vergil may have meant to change them very little.

This habit of Vergil is in close relation to the discovery of Mlle A.-M. Guillemin.[2] She notices, as I mentioned before, that a strong influence in Latin poetry is 'competition', ἀγών, *agon*, in Greek, by means of 'retractation', *retractatio*, the practice of rehandling the same motive again and again, in not quite the same words.

As usual, the Latin language has something to do with all this; and so have the early translations from Greek into Latin, though, as Professor F. Leo and Professor T. J. Haarhoff explain,[3] the Latin word for translating, *vertere*, *vortere*, 'turn', never meant mere translation but always something more. But this free translation did set the Latin writers to the task of finding the best way to say something rather than the task of finding something to say; Lucilius, already, attacked a hundred kinds of 'solecism'. Perfect

1. John Sparrow, *Half-Lines and Repetitions in Virgil*, Oxford, 1931.

2. A.-M. Guillemin, *L'originalité de Virgile*, Paris, 1931, 125–47.

3. T. J. Haarhoff, *The Stranger at the Gate*. London, 1938, 170–88, especially 179, with references.

expression became the object, and then the habit and then the rule, all the more because the difficulty of rendering Greek ideas in the naturally narrower range of the Latin language compressed the spring of ingenuity and feeling. The habit and rule went on, till in the later Roman Empire the attempt to say something had been practically abandoned in favour of the duty of saying anything or nothing well or fairly well; and in the Europe of the sixteenth century it was positively immoral, except for a revolutionary, to attempt to say in Ciceronian Latin anything that Cicero had not said.

The results of the method of retractation might of course be bad; but they might also be immensely good, because of the discipline, compression, and finish which the method imparted. Vergil as usual had an advantage, because earlier poets, perhaps Lucilius and Catullus especially, had been infusing popular and colloquial language into poetry, and Catullus and others had shewn anew how to succeed in the Italian practice of rendering Greek ideas without losing either Italian intensity or Greek lyric grace.

Retractation meant competition on the part of the poets, sometimes with other poets, and sometimes with themselves. Vergil especially competed with himself. It was almost a part of his lyrical 'tendency to repetition', besides being the result of what might be called the convention of retractation. Vergil sought difference in sameness; of this the clearest examples are in the immense number of ways in which he described the beginnings and ends of speeches, and sunset, and sunrise. Homer has only a few ways, and repeats himself regularly. The changes which Vergil made in what he had himself said before are like, but not quite like, his alterations of Lucretius and Ennius.

The Vergilian process is sometimes conscious retractation, the intellectual solution of a problem of taste; but obviously sometimes there is a drift towards unconscious integration. Either way, the facts must be remembered in textual criticism. Sometimes a variant is preferable just because it is not quite the same as a similar passage elsewhere. Occasionally the question arises whether of two identical lines in different contexts one should be excised. Excision is seldom right, if manuscript authority for both lines is good. There is an organic authenticity in Vergil's self-suggestion, so that, if a line occurs in two passages which are mutually supporting by a poetic coherence, an identical line, repeated from elsewhere, can safely be regarded as part of Vergil's mood, and something which he was likely to alter slightly, not to reject. In Vergil, the reasons why a thing *is* so tend to coincide with the reasons why it *ought to be* so. Accidents are not quite accidental.

There is a further interest here, also textual, at least more or less. Some of the retractations are not single lines about sunsets, but considerable incidents, which appear in pairs. There is similarity of general form and story, and varying similarity of words. The questions arise, whether one passage, of each pair of passages, should be removed; which passage is derived from the other; and which, if either, is the one to be excised.

A tendency to such duplication is one form of Vergil's tendency to repetition, and his self-suggestion. Dido has a sister Anna, who was partly a divine creature of Roman religion, Anna Perenna. So Camilla, the fighting maiden, finds it easy to have a sister also, similarly named, for she is Acca, and similarly, at least in part, a Roman divinity, Acca Larentia. Accordingly, it is both possible and probable that Vergil sometimes, if not always, wanted pairs of incidents to remain. At first he got a suggestion from somewhere, and when the time came worked it up into an incident. Meanwhile its applicability in another place occurred to him, and at some time he worked it up differently for that place. He might even put both passages into their contexts before realizing that both were valuable, possibly expecting to remove one of them later, until one day he read the whole poem, and only then found that the double use of a single suggestion would have to stand, either because the story had come to depend on both, or for another reason.

It is probably in this way that the incidents of Palinurus and Misenus came both to be needed in the *Aeneid*. At the end of the fifth book Palinurus, the flagship's helmsman, falls overboard, touched by the wand of the god of sleep, and seems to be drowned. In the sixth book Aeneas meets him on the borderland of the dead world, for he is unburied; and he tells his tale, and asks for burial. Perhaps he had the burial afterwards. But, before that place in the sixth book, the Sibyl had told Aeneas that he must bury 'a friend'. Aeneas found Misenus, who was lying dead on the shore, killed by the god Triton. Aeneas buried him, before entering the depths. But no mention of Misenus has occurred in any such context as this. There are thus two incidents of unburied friends, each having the name of a place in Italy, Misenum, the naval station, and Cape Palinurus, famed for shipwreck. Both were suggested by Elpenor in the *Odyssey*,[1] who was unburied at the entrance to Hades because he was killed by falling off Circe's roof.

It is possible to see why both the incidents came to be necessary. Neptunus, Vergil explains, required the sacrifice of one life for all, and Palinurus is the sacrifice. He is, too, a commentary on Apollo's prophecy; Apollo promised that he should reach land, and he did, but was killed by a wild tribe there. He fell with the tiller, broken off. That is a motive from the most ancient Epic of Gilgamish, a myth of initiation like the Sixth *Aeneid*, retained in Vergil's imaginative memory;[2] for there Gilgamish, in quest of his ancestor in the world below, lacked an important part of his boat, to cross the waters of death. The symbol survives. Again, the name of Palinurus marks a point of history, the terrible shipwreck in the first Punic War, 255 B.C. We do not have to understand everything to see that there was enough here to prevent Vergil from abandoning Palinurus. In fact, we have only to read the lines of soft, utter loveliness about his death,[3] and the others, of no less amazing majesty, on the meeting with him below,[4] to be immediately convinced that they could never be sacrificed. Palinurus belongs to an early plan of the poem. The voyage is from Libya,[5] not Sicily; and Apollo has the importance[6] that he has in the Third *Aeneid*.

Misenus is just as important, for he is part of the symbolism shewing that Aeneas must satisfy ritual needs before he finds the golden bough and goes forward to the world of the spirit.[7]

1. *Odyssey*, XI, 51–83; XII, 8–15.
2. W. F. J. Knight, *Cumaean Gates*, Oxford, 1936, 1–27, especially 28.
3. *A.* V, 833–71.   4. *A.* VI, 337–83.   5. *A.* VI, 338–9.
6. *A.* VI, 341–8.   7. *A.* VI, 149–235.

Misenum was the later naval station; Vergil needed these references. Misenus was son of Aeolus, and challenged gods to competition with his shell trumpet. This is part of the myth of earthquakes in ancient volcanic days, when the shell trumpet was the warning of an earthquake; but that is something which must wait till more of the late R. W. Cruttwell's work on these matters appears. Part of the passage about Misenus comes into Donatus' story, already met, how Vergil composed poetry. He had left, as we have seen, the first part of a line, *Misenum Aeoliden . . . ,*[1] incomplete. Then, long afterwards, inspiration suddenly came, and the completions, *quo non praestantior alter aere ciere viros* and finally *Martemque accendere cantu,*[2] were written down, apparently on two different occasions. Clearly, Vergil wanted to keep Misenus, if he so waited for the perfect completion of lines about him.

There are two other pairs of passages which have been specially mistrusted, because it is not immediately clear that both passages of each pair are essential.

One pair is this. An association of ideas which occurs at the death of Dido,[3] when she sank down to die and a cry was raised as if all the city had been falling down, recurs for the death of Amata,[4] queen of Latinus, who killed herself in despair, when it was clear that Aeneas, not Turnus, would marry her daughter Lavinia. Latinus is shocked at her death and at the fall of the city.[5] It is sometimes possible to trace the way by which thoughts and words go from an original, more prosaic condition, in some earlier work of prose or poetry, or some heard remark, or some plain rational experience of Vergil himself, onwards through some less obvious and prosaic condition, to their final application in pure poetry to a situation in which they are surprising to prosaic thought. That happens partly here. Dido's death is also associated with a city's fall; but the sequence of events is not nearly so clear; and now the thought of the fall of the city is much less appropriate, since unlike the city of Amata Carthage was not at war. The poetry, however, is far more intense. Poetically, the confused events are expressive; and there is poignancy in the suggestion

1. *A.* VI, 164. 2. *A.* VI, 164–5. 3. *A.* IV, 663–71.
4. *A.* XII, 593–611; cf. *A.* XII, 54–80, 659–60. 5. *A.* XII, 609–10.

of the fall of Carthage destined to happen centuries later. Vergil contrived the death of Amata, and then, chance as usual being the friend of art, saw that the motive could be applied to Dido, far less obviously, but far more powerfully. It is very possible that he then wanted both passages to remain, because Amata would now, by the echoes, remind readers of Dido, with the poignant thought that here was another woman who had died pitifully before the advance of Aeneas and of the Rome that was to be. This is not the only place, late in the poem, where Dido's ghost lingers haunting in the dark.

That seems the right account of the history of this motive in its two latest stages. The earliest stage is less certain, but it is likely to be an incident in one of two mysterious Greek poems, now lost, but used by Vergil for his Sack of Troy.[1] From Quintus Smyrnaeus it is clear that one of these poems gave an account, which Vergil used for Amata and Dido, of the hopeless prophetess Cassandra at Troy, believed by none; and how she tried to warn the Trojans, became mad with failure, and collapsed. The similarities are very close; and the ideas are here exactly appropriate, especially as then it was the famous fall of Troy that impended.

The case here, for Vergil's method, is not perhaps very strong. The second pair of passages has a stronger one. Sinon,[2] appearing in Troyland to outwit the Trojans by his talk and persuade them to take in the wooden horse, and Achaemenides,[3] a companion of Odysseus who was left behind in Sicily, and encountered Aeneas and his men there, are presented with similar thoughts and words. Both appeal for pity and give an account of themselves. Characteristically, the words are sometimes alike when the thought is different; Vergil normally accepts a verbal complex, and lets it suggest quite new meanings to him.

As before, the process has gone further in one of the two passages. Achaemenides is more literal, and Sinon more imaginative, with poetry far more intense and grand. Clearly what happened is this. Again the primary original source seems to have been in one of the two lost poems about Troy; and it concerned Sinon.

1. W. F. J. Knight, *The Classical Quarterly*, xxvi, 1932, 178–89.
2. *A.* ii, 57–198. 3. *A.* iii, 588–654.

Vergil accepted the ideas and images, and, according to the principle which Servius knew better than many of ourselves, applied them to a quite different character in a new situation, Achaemenides, who may also owe something to the Philoctetes of Sophocles. That was in the third book of the *Aeneid*, composed before Vergil conceived the idea of his second book, on Troy, as it now is. Later, when he had settled down to the second book, by a characteristic stroke of genius, he did something, which seems obvious now, but which was, for its strange, inverting brilliance, extraordinary; he applied material concerning Sinon to none other than Sinon himself; not however the Sinon of whom he had read, but a far richer, and fully Vergilian, Sinon, profiting by his transformation through Achaemenides.

Most people think that the third book is far from finished, and that Vergil might have changed it greatly. But, since he liked pairs of incidents, it is probable enough that Achaemenides would have remained. There is again a poignancy in the suggested comparison. Sinon is master, and wicked; Achaemenides is helpless, sincerely needing rescue; both are Greeks, bitter foes; but the Trojans shew mercy both times, and the second time they are proved right not to have learnt their lesson. It is all Vergilian.

These passages raise questions that are textual, more or less, but, characteristically, not only textual. So it is with apparent gaps, where lines seem missing; and also with lines that may be called rhythmical additions.[1] Vergil, at one stage of his career, probably late, is thought to have extended his natural movements of two or three verses by an additional verse, not really necessary to syntax, sense, or rhythm. Milton is said to have done the same. That is, when sense and rhythm have come to a natural stop, they are continued, as if to make both more rich and full, by another line. Whether Vergil would have left these additional lines, or whether he might have added more, is unknown; and the question is precarious, since it depends on a subjective sense of the right length for a movement. On the whole, it seems likely that at some late stage Vergil accepted, as satisfying and now natural to him, the rhythmic span of the verse-group of three or four

1. J. W. Mackail, *The Aeneid*, Oxford, 1930, liii–liv.

verses, and that he sometimes made additions, to prevent an appearance of too many self-dependent single lines and couplets.

Most of the textual problems in Vergil are not quite so strange as these.

A very large number of variant readings in the text of Vergil concern single letters. Decision has to be made between such forms as *voluntur* and *volvantur*, *partem* and *partim*, and *trementis* and *frementis*. Often both will stand equally well, without spoiling sense, grammar, or metre.

There are many passages in the *Aeneid* where a few lines have been thought out of place, and transposed by editors. The transpositions are generally convincing on the whole. When Vergil died, the text of the *Aeneid* was still partly fluid, and passages in the margin could easily be copied in the wrong place. A good example of a convincing transposition is in the Tenth *Aeneid*, where Juno substitutes for Aeneas a wraith. Turnus pursues the wraith on to a ship, which Juno now sets adrift. In the best manuscripts, two lines[1] about the wraith occur after two lines[2] about Aeneas. They fit better, with a smoother change of subject, the other way round, and on comparatively weak manuscript authority they have been convincingly transposed. Other transpositions are purely conjectural, but still convincing, or at least attractive, for example more than one attempt to improve the order of lines about a hero Aventinus, in the Seventh *Aeneid*;[3] as they stand in the manuscripts, they occur misleadingly after the subject has been to some extent changed. But there is never any proof that these transpositions are right. It is always possible that, if Vergil had found lines out of place, he would have made other changes besides, or instead of, altering their position.

The most interesting textual problems concern passages which have been supposed intolerable as they stand, but to which no satisfactory alternative is authenticated. The Fourth *Eclogue* ends with the words *cui non risere parentes, nec deus hunc mensa dea nec dignata cubili est*, 'one on whom his parents never smiled no god has counted fit to share his table, nor any goddess fit to share her bed'.[4] The sense seems to require that the baby who is to be a

1. *A.* x, 663–4.   2. *A.* x, 661–2.   3. *A.* VII, 666–9.
4. *E.* IV, 62–3.

brilliant success must begin life with a smile of recognition for his parents. Therefore a different reading, recorded by Quintilian[1] but in none of our manuscripts, arose in antiquity, *qui non risere parentes* ... 'those who never smiled at their father and mother ...' This transfers the smile to the baby. But then a plural relative, *qui*, has a singular antecedent, *hunc*. There is nothing strange in that, especially in the *Eclogues*. But, if this is the right reading, it could easily have suggested as an emendation the reading found in all the manuscripts. If so, it was probably an emendation by the original editors. All this, however, is conjecture. The manuscripts may well be right; their reading is quite intelligible to all who realize what divine power, to guide and to exalt, there was in a parent's smile for Vergil.

There is a fascinating problem in the Third *Aeneid*. The Trojans had landed in Sicily, and had just embarked again in fear of the Cyclopes. They felt like setting sail in any direction, so frightening was their experience. Then Vergil says, *contra iussa monent Heleni, Scyllam atque Charybdim (inter utramque viam leti discrimine parvo) ni teneant cursus*, 'but against that the instructions of Helenus warned them not to hold their course between Scylla and Charybdis, since between those two the way was a way to death, with a narrow margin'.[2] The punctuation and interpretation is due to Kvičala, and adopted by the Oxford Text. It depends on the assertion of Priscian, Tiberius Donatus and Servius that here *ni*, usually 'unless', is an old Latin form for *ne*, 'lest', 'not to'. Ancient variants include *monet, movent, Scylla, Charybdis, ne*, and *nec*. The best attested reading has been cleverly kept by the discovery that *ni* can mean *ne*. The sense is right, since the lines clearly explain that the Trojans would not have minded where they went, except that Helenus had warned them not to go by way of Scylla and Charybdis, that is, the Straits of Messina. So they sailed westwards along the south coast of Sicily.

There is, however, another possibility, which does not need the assumption that there are brackets and that *ni* is for *ne*. It is possible to translate the lines, 'Against this, the instructions of

1. Quintilian, IX, 3, 8.
2. *A.* III, 684–6; cf. for a different but very attractive interpretation, Vergil, *Aeneid* III, edited by R. D. Williams, Oxford, 1962.

Helenus warned them that, if they did not keep their course (that is, continue westwards), then, between Scylla and Charybdis, the way had on both sides only a narrow margin of safety from death'. That is probably more Vergilian. It assumes quick subtle changes of Vergil's unconscious thought, but little besides. The variants arose because such rather surrealistic writing is not easy to paraphrase or translate rationally.

In the Seventh *Aeneid* there is a problem, already mentioned. Allecto is ungrammatically described; *deserit Hesperiam et caeli convexa per auras Iunonem victrix adfatur*, 'she left Italy, and, convex of heaven on the winds, triumphant, addressed Juno'.[1] Vergil, as Mr J. R. T. Pollard explained, has let himself say *convexa*, 'convex' instead of *convecta*, 'carried' or 'riding', or something like that. He was led to do so by his habit of writing *caeli convexa* as the 'vault of heaven', which goes well with the idea in *victrix*, 'triumphant'. No wonder there have been many ancient and modern conjectures. But Vergil is entitled to his bad grammar, when he pleases to use it.

A famous question concerns the unfinished lines,[2] which stop before the end, and leave a gap. There are fifty-seven of them in Vergil, or perhaps fifty-eight, if a doubtful one[3] is counted. They are unknown elsewhere. There is little doubt that Vergil did not originally intend to leave any lines incomplete. The unfinished lines are not always most frequent in the least finished books. There are ten in the second book, seven in the third; two each in the sixth and the eleventh; and one in the twelfth.

It seems that Vergil, when after long thinking a flow of finished poetry came, reached the end of the spontaneous flow sometimes in the middle of a line. So the line remained unfinished, until a new flow could start at this particular place. Years of waiting might be necessary. The unfinished lines are like the *tibicines* or 'props', temporary lines which Vergil, according to Donatus, inserted at places where he could not at once solve his problem, 'in order that nothing might delay the impulse of creation', *ut ne quid impetum moraretur*. In antiquity some

1. *A.* VII, 543–4.
2. John Sparrow, *Half-Lines and Repetitions in Virgil*, Oxford, 1931, 21–52.
3. *A.* V, 595.

ill-advised attempts were made to complete the unfinished lines.

All the unfinished lines but one, *quem tibi iam Troia*, 'whom to you now from Troy',[1] as Donatus noticed, give a complete sense. Five are detachable and trivial, as if they were signs that a line must be later inserted. Five others are also detachable, though they continue the sense. Seventeen are part of a unit, a line and a half long, which is itself detachable; the units may have been inserted by editors from the margin. Twenty-nine are undetachable, organically part of longer and necessary, but sometimes apparently unfinished, passages.

That Vergil did not originally plan to leave lines incomplete is no proof that he never changed his mind. Some are so beautiful, and complete themselves so perfectly by the eloquent Vergilian silence which they leave behind them, that it is quite possible that Vergil, here as elsewhere, intentionally accepted an artistic success which he had accidentally, as it seemed to him, achieved.

In very small matters there is some uncertainty about Vergil's text. Among them is spelling. Gellius records the existence of a manuscript of which Vergil himself had corrected the spelling, and he gives instances of the spellings preferred. But Quintilian has left a warning to any who would make Vergil's practice rigidly regular by emendation, 'confessing their own ignorance by their attempt to disparage ignorance in the copyists' – *et dum librariorum insectari volunt inscientiam, suam confitentur*,[2] a criticism adaptable for wider meanings.

Classical Latin, to be correct, insists on some original, uncompounded, spellings for prefixes, such as *admoneo, adpono*, not *app-*, and *inmundus, inmitto*, not *imm-*; on an accusative plural in *i*-stems *-is, urbis*, not *-es*; and on *-i*, not *-ii* in the genitive singular of nouns in *-ius*, such as *fluvi*, not *fluvii*. These are probably the spellings preferred by Virgil and indeed the occurrence of the uncontracted genitive in *-ii* has been taken as evidence that the three lines[3] of Vergil in which it is found are spurious. Only one,[4] however, is at all likely, and that is not very likely, to be spurious; and the reason is not the *-ii* but weak manuscript authority, and the

1. *A.* III, 340.   2. Quintilian, IX, 4, 39.
3. *A.* III, 702; *A.* IV, 640; *A.* IX, 151.   4. *A.* IX, 151.

occurrence of almost the same line elsewhere.[1] Care was, indeed, taken about spelling in antiquity; but inscriptions, even of the classical age, shew a wide variety, and Gellius, in the passage where he traces the accusative plural form *orbis* to Vergil's own authority,[2] says that Vergil and others chose spelling, and even grammar, sometimes, to satisfy their ear. For a time, it seems, the rules became stricter. Saint Augustine used classical spelling; but the tradition of accuracy had then already decayed again, and manuscripts of the eleventh century have much the same false Latin spelling as our own books of a few generations ago.

Accordingly, the question of Vergil's spelling is not quite simple. The primary manuscripts are a guide, but they are not regular; Professor Remigio Sabbadini in his latest edition has now shewn that, as Gellius thought, Vergil himself was not quite regular either, and varied his spelling, perhaps sometimes for the aesthetic value of different sounds.

The textual criticism of Vergil is a pleasant puzzle. But it is more than that, for it is a contact with the mind that made the poems, living on in the lovely script of the great primary manuscripts, and living on in us, when by right judgement we are guided to choose a reading well. Very intimately must we know Vergil, if we are to feel, and therefore choose, aright.

But it is not only so that Vergil has left his soul on earth.

1. *A.* ii, 166.   2. Aulus Gellius, xiii, 21.

CHAPTER 7

VERGIL AND AFTER

VERGIL immediately made a great reputation with the *Eclogues*, and increased it with the *Georgics*. He had the full support of Maecenas and Augustus all the time; among important men, only Agrippa disliked his work, which was too modern for one so conservative and practical, blaming Vergil, as we saw, for inventing a new kind of affectation, *cacozelia*. The *Aeneid* was not published in Vergil's lifetime, though he read some of it, the usual way of first publication. He read probably the second and fourth books, and certainly the sixth, to the family of Augustus; Octavia fainted when he came to the passage in the sixth about Marcellus, who had been destined to succeed Augustus, but who died not long before Vergil.

While Vergil was still alive, the *Eclogues* and *Georgics* became school books. Q. Caecilius, a freedman of Cicero's friend Atticus, is said to have introduced Vergil in a school for boys over fifteen which he founded in Rome in 26 B.C. From then onwards Vergil's poetry, including the *Aeneid* as soon as it was published, has never ceased to be taught in schools. Martial mentions the kind of copies used for this purpose, or given as presents. Some had Vergil's portrait as a frontispiece.

The *Aeneid* was ardently awaited. Propertius wrote, *cedite, Romani scriptores, cedite Graii, nescio quid maius nascitur Iliade*, 'Give place, all writers of Rome and writers of Greece, besides, for now there is something coming to birth greater than the *Iliad* itself'. Too much must not be made of this praise, since Propertius is almost equally complimentary to quite unimportant work.

When the *Aeneid* was published, it was accepted without hesitation, and read universally, in a large number of copies, which were quickly made. It became a principal school-book, as it has been ever since. Quotations from it are found written on the walls of public baths at Rome and streets at Pompeii, some of which date from a very few years after the publication. The speakers of the time immediately began to quote it freely.

We can still see ourselves in the best poetry, and in Vergil's especially. Vergil's contemporaries could see themselves in it too, and not entirely through chance, or the nature of things.

Vergil at first wanted to write an epic on the kings of Alba, before Rome was, and he also planned an epic on the deeds of Augustus. That was when his enthusiasm for the Julian party was not yet fully criticized by himself. About the time when he finished the *Georgics* his view changed, or at least admitted some conflict of impulses.

Servius says that the last part of the Fourth *Georgics* was originally the praise of Cornelius Gallus, but that when Gallus, who now held a high administrative appointment in Egypt, having been suspected of inefficiency or excessive ambition and reproved by Augustus, committed suicide in fear and despair, Vergil removed the passage about him, and substituted the little epic about Aristaeus, Orpheus, and Eurydice. The story has usually been accepted. As we have seen, doubts have been cast on it, and it can hardly be true. But there is no doubt that Gallus, to whom the Tenth *Eclogue* was written, was one of Vergil's greatest friends, perhaps quite his greatest, and that Vergil was devoted to him. And there is no doubt that his death was in a sense due to Augustus, who was bitterly sorry, and lamented that he alone of all Romans could not be angry with his friends.

It cannot be asserted that Vergil sided with either Gallus or Augustus. It is scarcely conceivable that he fully turned against either. But he must have felt bitterness, and strong sympathy with Gallus. That can be taken as certain. And there are plentiful signs that while he was writing the *Aeneid* he perpetually pondered questions of right and wrong, and applied them to the régime. This régime he had once wholeheartedly accepted, and in most moods could still accept; but in other moods Vergil, perhaps more than anyone else, could not help remembering the blood and tears and old glories overcast.

Signor Francesco Sforza[1] has shewn that it is possible, even if incorrect,[2] to regard the whole *Aeneid* as a disguised attack on Augustus. He believes that the reason why Vergil tried to prevent its publication was repentance, due to the great kindness shewn by Augustus to him in his last illness.

And, in fact, there is support for such a view in the countless passages of the *Aeneid* in which the imperial leadership looks cruel or mean. But there is as much support for the opposite view also, or more, since the glories of Rome's future elicit again and again from Vergil sublime and spontaneous poetry. Whatever Vergil's conscious judgement may at different times have been, his poetic insight, not fully under the control of his will, gave an automatic assent. It was for him to find, if he could, how this assent could be right.

The conflict started in the years after Actium, when propaganda was shameless. How shameless it was has lately appeared through the work of Dr W. W. Tarn, who has proved in particular how the truth about the Battle of Actium itself was lost to history through tendentious falsification. Horace seems to have forced his poetry into conformity against his real sympathies. Vergil and Horace are usually classed together as propagandists; but there is a distinction. Both, it might be said, honestly and rightly, and not only through the personal kindnesses of the rulers, decided to support the régime, which was for both the best, or the only, thing to be done. But the plan could not easily be carried through with perfect sincerity. Both poets tried to be sincere; Horace made a commendable, and Vergil a brilliant, attempt; and Vergil, on account of his exceptionally powerful and subtle intellect, succeeded.

Almost anything that can be said of Vergil is a part of one side of the truth. 'The allegory of the *Aeneid*', perpetually sought in Antiquity and the Middle Ages, and partly discovered and first, in a new sense, fully stated by Professor D. L. Drew,[3] is like that.

1. Francesco Sforza, *The Classical Review*, XLIX, 1935, 97–108; idem, *Il più prezioso tesoro spirituale d'Italia: l'Eneide*, Milan, 1952, which restates and amplifies his views.

2. W. S. Maguinness, *The Wind and the Rain*, VII, 2/3, 1951, 124–35.

3. D. L. Drew, *The Allegory of the Aeneid*, Oxford, 1927, *passim*.

There is in the *Aeneid* plenty of evidence to recommend his theory, as there is to recommend Signor Sforza's. Aeneas is what in Vergil's mind Augustus himself came to be, the representative, in a more poetic plan, of the central figure of the never written contemporary epic. Of this central figure Vergil had thought, and his mind was full of the results. Perhaps they had proved unsatisfactory, so that, by telling the superficial truth directly, the deeper truth must be disguised; and only the substitution of poetic myth for history could restore the poetic reality, which was still securely held. So, in Aeneas, Augustus 'shimmered through'. He has the devotion to duty of Augustus, and many other qualities which Augustus tried or pretended to shew, or perhaps really had; courage and friendliness and self-restraint and faith in religion and in the family. He has his faults too; a hot, irrational cruelty at first in Troy; a hardness of heart, perhaps too easily imposed on him by heaven, at Carthage; and a colder cruelty in the fighting in Italy, when he is capable of sheer revenge on Turnus, and even plans,[1] but only plans, to sacrifice human captives at the funeral of Pallas, as Achilles sacrificed Trojans to dead Patroclus, and as in 40 B.C. Augustus himself, if a report is true, at Perusia sacrificed with horrors Etruscan aristocrats.

Other characters are partly representative also. Dido is a lovely eastern queen, for whose sake it seemed easy to abandon empire, but a marriage with whom might have great significance for future power. So far she is in a position like Cleopatra's; but most of Dido is very different from most of Cleopatra. Aeneas is attended and helped by the loyal Achates. Augustus had a loyal friend in Maecenas. But that hardly amounts to allegory. Augustus thought much of his daughter Julia, and was bitterly disappointed at her evil life; he thought much of his adopted son and heir Marcellus, and was bitterly disappointed at his death. Aeneas has a son Iulus, who never once disappoints him; his disappointment is in Dido, and she is mainly part of the life, not of Augustus, but of Vergil. Augustus regarded Julius Caesar as his father, and professed devotion to him. The real father of Aeneas, Anchises, could hardly be more different than he is from the great Julius,

1. *A.* x, 517–20; xi, 81–4; Suetonius, *Augustus*, xv; W. F. J. Knight, *The Classical Review*, xlvi, 1932, 55–7; xlvii, 1933, 169–71.

with his contempt for tradition, his free thought and vicious living, his vanity, his brilliance, and above all his inimitable sense of humour. The memory of Julius is already in the *Aeneid* not quite sacred. He is no longer even partly the Daphnis of the *Eclogues*, if he ever was; nor the Caesar of the *Georgics*, whose death is a disaster for the world, marked by terrible signs in the sky. Anchises in Elysium implores him, and Pompeius, to forbear, and not to start civil war.[1] The process has begun by which Augustan and later poets increasingly disparage him. To Pompeius Vergil is more sympathetic, for there is no doubt that he saw Pompeius, dead on the shore of Egypt, in the dead Priam, unexpectedly described as dead and headless on the Trojan shore. Cato, too, has already begun his literary future fame in the *Aeneid*. On the shield of Aeneas he is seen as the law-giver of the good; and in the First *Aeneid*[2] there is a striking and unique simile in which the waves, calmed by Neptunus, are compared to a riot, calmed by a grave, respected orator, who need not be Cato, but who poetically reflects the mood in which Cato is traditionally admired. There is even a slight hint, lately very well appraised by Mr Hugh G. Mullens,[3] of Livia, the empress, in Lavinia, the almost suppressed bride whom Aeneas wins. It is, however, the young Livia; the great and free influence for good, exercised by Livia afterwards, was yet to come.

The *Aeneid* is not, therefore, exactly an attack on Augustus, nor is it exactly an allegory. It is, however, in close and effective relationship to the contemporary world and its policies and morality. The late Professor R. S. Conway[4] explained what was really happening. Poets, said Shelley, are the unacknowledged legislators; in O'Shaughnessy's poem, 'the movers and shakers of the world for ever, it seems'.

Horace, and Vergil far more, shewed to the Government and especially Augustus a picture of the world, in which the broad moral facts appeared as great structural lines, which may be missed in the confusion of phenomena but which it is the task

1. *A.* vi, 826–35.   2. *A.* i, 148–53.
3. H. G. Mullens, *Vergilius*, iii, 1939, 12–15.
4. R. S. Conway, *The Proceedings of the Classical Association*, xxv, 1928, 19–38.

of great poetry not to display, but to allow to emerge, from the presentation of a story. 'You may make the laws of the people', thought Vergil, 'if I may make their songs.' And he made them for more than one people.

Augustus changed greatly. The elder Seneca[1] records how in his later life he bitterly repented of the excesses of his youth. He could still be hard, especially to his own family, Julia, Tiberius, and others. He was perhaps still a little vindictive, like the matured Aeneas. While he was writing the *Aeneid*, Vergil saw this and other dangers. It is hard for us to read the *Aeneid* without seeing such dangers as Vergil himself saw; and there is no doubt that he influenced Augustus, and led the leader of Rome.

To do this, it was useless to dictate. *Natura non vincitur nisi parendo*, 'nature can only be overcome by obedience to nature'. So it is with most powerful men. Vergil accordingly allowed his poem to express frankly the great qualities of the leader and the régime, but he included also subtle hints, which might be missed, yet might be accepted, consciously or unconsciously. Augustus might without knowing it be led to live up to his picture in the *Aeneid*, and to avoid faults which Aeneas avoided, or did not avoid. At least, the plan had considerable success.

Vergil kept his balance and did not let momentary emotion sway him beyond reason in either direction. He rather let it compress thought into poetry. To express his great array of meanings he partly depended on his unique power over words, grammar, and syntax. There is an example in the reference to the Tarquins and Brutus in the Sixth *Aeneid*, *vis et Tarquinios reges animamque superbam ultoris Bruti fascesque videre receptos?* – 'do you wish to see also the kings called Tarquin, and the arrogance of the soul in Brutus, who took the vengeance, and how he recovered the rods of sovereignty?'[2] There has always been a controversy over the meaning of this, because it has been felt either that the *animam superbam*, 'arrogance in the soul', belongs immovably to Tarquinius Superbus or the Tarquins generally, or else, if, as the Latin incontestably requires, it must be taken with *Bruti*, the

---

1. Seneca, *Suasoriae*, 43.
2. *A.* vi, 817–8; W. F. J. Knight, *The Classical Review*, xlvi, 1932, 55–7; xlvii, 1933, 169–71.

adjective must have a good meaning like 'proud', which, especially in Vergil, it has not. The answer is that Vergil daringly says what he means with the subtlest suggestion of allusion. Characteristically, he had made a slight and most unexpected change, with immense consequences; and he has said softly, but definitely, that the extreme republicans, in his day and at the foundation of the Republic, were arrogant and tyrannical. Before the murder of Caesar there was much thought of the old Brutus. Messages, addressed to him, and begging him to awake, were written on his statue in Rome; and were of course intended to stimulate the Marcus Brutus then alive to rescue the Republic from Caesar. Vergil knew that it was the men who mattered, more than the form. Merely restoring the Republic would do no good, if the Republicans, like the old Brutus who executed his own children for conspiracy, had tyranny in the soul. For that is what he means; as the late R. S. Conway explained,[1] *anima* is a deep, unconscious, instinctive part of the soul, where the real quality of a man resides.

Vergil preferred a religious faith and a family loyalty to constitutional form.[2] He returned to universal human principles after a time of rationalism, when attempts were made to make it impossible for bad men to do harm rather than to prevent men from being bad at all; the result had been chaos, with six civil wars in about sixty years. That the Roman Empire began with good order, on human principles, and, whatever the violence and scandals in the capital, maintained that order and those principles in many lands for centuries, is partly the work of Vergil.

The effect of Vergil in literature began on his own friends and on their friends, his immediate successors.

In poetry, Vergil and Horace, in co-operation to some extent, created a new idea and a new pattern of poetry that is classical, in the sense that it must use to the utmost every possibility of perfection. After them the ideal was misunderstood by many, who

1. R. S. Conway, *The Classical Review*, XLVI, 1932, 199–202.

2. There is a certain strength and sanity in Vergil's, and Aeneas's, religious faith and moral code; cf. E. C. Woodcock, 'Virgil's Philosophy of Religion', *Virgil Society Lecture Summaries*, Number 44, 1957; P. Boyancé, *La Religion de Virgile*, Paris, 1963.

thought too much of their superficial neatness and too little of their depth and truth. There even exists today an ingenious opinion that Vergil and Horace ruined Latin poetry by substituting their new kind for the more spontaneous and fiery tradition which the lyrics of Catullus might otherwise have started. If there is some truth in this, it is the fault of the followers who found neatness and glitter easier to see and to make their own than the greatness beneath.

Ovid, Publius Ovidius Naso (43 B.C.–?17 A.D.), is the first important successor to Vergil. Ovid did not know Vergil personally; he says that he had just seen him, no more. But he accepted, with some comprehension too, very much from Vergil, including Vergil's conception of the mission of Rome and the interest of Rome's past, and some of Vergil's precision in expression and command over the possibilities of Latin. He developed, too, quite marvellously and in many directions, the Vergilian repetition; but it led him into tautology. Yet Ovid's poetry is really the opposite to Vergil's. It is full of Vergilian phrases; but Ovid writes on one level, not many, and without the penumbra of secondary suggestions on which the Vergilian depth relies.[1] Ovid is 'classical' in the usual popular sense; whereas in the usual popular sense Vergil is 'romantic'. It would, however, be easy to find ways of saying that Vergil is the more 'classical' of the two, and Ovid the more 'romantic'.

Ovid was caught by momentary enthusiasms which he derived from Vergil, but he had not Vergil's selfless poetic, moral, and heroic ardour. Perhaps his sense of humour, whimsical and doubly aware in the mature Latin way, was too pervasive to let him be a great poet. Certainly he was too selfish, too much inclined in the last resort to take nothing seriously but himself. He had not established a harmony between the mind and the outer world, except by certain easy methods, applicable only to easy terms. He was not epic or tragic.

1. Ovid has probably been underestimated: see Hermann Fränkel, *Ovid; A Poet Between Two Worlds*, Berkeley, California, 1945; L. P. Wilkinson, *Ovid Recalled*, Cambridge, 1955; and Douglas F. Bauer, 'The Function of Pygmalion in the *Metamorphoses* of Ovid', *Transactions and Proceedings of the American Philological Association*, XCIII, 1962, 1–21.

But he had immense merits. It is almost true to say that he shewed the future one way of using a part of Vergil's instruction. He isolated the play of sharp wit, and developed to the utmost its power to say simply, gracefully, and humorously, that sort of simple thing which had to be said, and said in that way, to have a value. Perhaps Ovid passed on a little of Vergil in his very great influence on the future.

For that influence he had. Even in the Middle Ages he was widely read and taught. The Church actually permitted his immoral love poems to be counted a part of moral philosophy! Perhaps more than any other poet he provided the Renaissance with its vitalizing, if erroneous, conception of the nature and merits of classical literature, especially its imagery and dexterity.

On the other side was Livy, Titus Livius (59 B.C.–17 A.D.), whose home was at Patavium, Padua, not far from Vergil's. His prose epic of the march of Rome is Vergilian in conception and language beyond any other work of literary or other art. It is Vergilian in the depth, significance, rhythm, and dignity of its Latin, and in the sense of the continuity and the vital development of organic Roman society, under men guided by gods. It has the Vergilian faith in normal human values, and some of the Vergilian sympathy. But there is much that it lacks, especially the hope which Vergil kept, for all his knowledge of despair.

Later poets returned to Vergil's epic structure from Ovid's casual unities on smaller scales.[1] But they all seemed to make mistakes which Vergil avoided. Lucan's *Pharsalia* is a historical poem of the Civil War which Julius won. It has its moral, that the old things which gods should guard are in fact defeated by the wicked and the new. Like Vergil, and unlike Ovid, Lucan has this interest. He even makes prophecies and omens count in the development of his tale. His language is epigrammatic and mono-tonously brilliant. Quintilian said that he was a better model for orators than poets. Above all, Lucan did not create a myth.

Statius wrote shorter poems in praise of the emperor and others, and a long *Thebaid* on the legends of Thebes. With less ability than Lucan, he was more of a poet, and perhaps he had

1. For the differences between these poets see the admirable short account of Luigi Alfonsi, *Letteratura Latina*, Florence, 1958.

more varied and authentic emotions to impel him.[1] But they were not deep enough, or closely enough in touch with his intellectual mind, to make great poetry. Silius Italicus, in his long *Punic Wars*, sought to be more Vergilian than Lucan, but with only slight success.

Calpurnius Siculus and Nemesianus wrote apparently Vergilian pastorals, charming often, but just not what the *Eclogues* are, quite unique, and the incontestable product of a single, unmistakable, mind.

Valerius Flaccus, alone of Vergil's successors, prevailed over the grave difficulty which beset them all, the difficulty of producing great art when the medium is fully under technical control.[2] He has some of Vergil's depth, weight, and reflective power.

Vergil made the younger Seneca the fine tragic poet that he is beginning to be recognized to have been. Like Valerius, he had to write in Vergil's words. But he could not, as Vergil could, give infinite complexity of meaning and sensitivity, on many planes, to his tragic themes.

Vergil's power of suggestion, and of extensive and incisive meaning expressed by the fewest words generating their effect by internal and external relations, was inherited above all by Tacitus. His prose histories, deeply bitter and cynical against the sins and follies of the great, are built by Vergilian words and usages, for an almost exactly opposite end. Perhaps it is only the negative side of the same thing. But Vergil could never have written out of bitterness alone. Besides, he was not overcome with evil, but overcame evil with good.

In the fourth and fifth centuries A.D. there are still some tones of the Vergilian ardour, when, with Vergilian words, Claudian and Rutilius admire the greatness of a Rome that had made of a world a home.

Vergil's domination of literary style led to the cento, a poem composed entirely of old lines rearranged to give quite a different

1. Statius has also probably been underestimated: see the able and sympathetic expositions of Dr A. J. Gossage, especially 'Statius and Vergil', *Virgil Society Lecture Summaries*, No. 47, 1959.

2. Cf. Dr H. MacL. Currie's effective estimate of Valerius as a true poet, 'Virgil and Valerius Flaccus', *Virgil Society Lecture Summaries*, No. 48, 1959.

meaning. Very many writers wasted much ingenuity on this absurd enterprise for over a thousand years. Even in the nineteenth century the cento was not dead, for a cento of Latin verses was then composed, celebrating Nelson's victories, in which a line applied by Juvenal to Hannibal on his elephant was reapplied to Nelson on his flagship the *Lion* – *cum Gaetula ducem portaret belua luscum*, 'when the African beast was carrying the one-eyed leader'! Earlier centones often redistributed Vergil's lines to tell Biblical stories.

Meanwhile Vergil and his work became subjects of intellectual interest. The story of their strange adventures in the medieval mind has been told in the permanently indispensable work of Domenico Comparetti; to which the researches of Dr R. Palgen among others are now adding something new.[1]

The main interest in Vergil was at first educational. Vergil was, strangely, a model for the teaching of grammar and rhetoric. Grammar was for the young, and it was linguistic. Rhetoric was more philosophical and advanced. It was the art of good speaking, but it was partly based on the interpretation of classical works, not the mere ability to read and understand them; its teachers assumed in the learners the knowledge that teachers of grammar could impart.

At least as early as Quintilian, Vergil was accepted as the supreme authority on such questions as the genders of nouns, questions which were becoming more and more important, and were destined to become important beyond all reason. Throughout the Dark Ages and the Middle Ages this importance was maintained, and Vergil was the guide to grammar. But the grammarians were not very successful. Ignorance and mental chaos increased with a rapidity which is hard to believe. Books on grammar were written, and copied with expansions; and the more they were read and copied, the greater the ignorance and confusion became.

So it was, too, with rhetoric and interpretation. At first Vergil's

1. Domenico Comparetti, *Virgilio nel medio evo*, Rome, 1872 (and translations); R. Palgen, *Das mittelalterliche Gesicht der Göttlichen Komödie*, Heidelberg, 1935, with references on page 3.

poetry was used as a source for examples of the figures of rhetoric, the set forms in which language was traditionally used for persuasion. But the interest of persuasion grew less as the importance of public speaking declined, and interest shifted more and more to interpretation.

Vergilian interpretation began in his own times and never stopped. In the third and fourth centuries the long commentaries of Tiberius Donatus and Servius, and the one wrongly ascribed to Probus, were written. They too were copied and expanded.

The commentary of Servius, the greatest help which commentators to this day possess, is full of interpolations added in transcription, and it is not always certain which are the comments of Servius himself. The work is of varying, but immense, value. It is long, filling three quarto volumes of print. On the whole, Servius himself was sensible and even clever; he was very learned, and freely cites by name earlier commentators. But he is fanciful too, and is already inclined to the allegorical kind of interpretation which was later to reach almost the greatest depths of absurdity that the human mind has attained.

The general interest in Vergil had always involved some controversy about his merits. He had scarcely died when there was a name, 'Vergiliomaniac', for a devoted admirer of Vergil, and another, 'Vergiliomastix', literally 'scourge of Vergil', for anyone who disparaged him. The first disparagements were for his supposed plagiarism. Later complaints were sometimes directed against his polished refinement, and in the age of Hadrian, when old things were in fashion, Cato's prose was preferred to Cicero's, and the poetry of Ennius to Vergil's. The attempt of the emperor Caligula to abolish for ever the honour paid not only to Vergil, but to Homer, Plato, and other great authors, was an isolated act of madness.

The defenders of Vergil found victory on the whole easy, though opposition has always eventually revived again. The controversy was productive, because it led to thought. The *Attic Nights* of Gellius include many results of this thought in the interesting material concerning Vergilian topics which they contain. Macrobius, in the first half of the fifth century, wrote a still more useful work, the *Saturnalia*, in which he defends Vergil against detractors. He transcribes without acknowledgement much material from earlier writers. Of the many works principally devoted to Vergilian criticism which existed, the *Saturnalia* of Macrobius is the only one which survives.

The work of Macrobius may be said to belong partly to the old tradition of comparison between authors, represented by Quintilian and Longinus, but partly to the rhetorical tradition of interpretation. There were some people who claimed to explain any passage in Vergil, and meanwhile it was becoming famous that there were twelve passages in Vergil which could not be explained. It was even said that Vergil made these passages inexplicable on purpose, to puzzle posterity. Vergil was now fairly safe from blame. He was established as second only to Homer, and little, if at all, inferior to him.

The general impression given by all this is that the real depth of Vergil was never understood in antiquity, because there was too much interest in form and classification, and not enough in the 'imaginative solidities'. But already an instinct for a deeper comprehension was appearing, and appearing, paradoxically, in some of the greatest absurdities with which the name of Vergil has been connected.

Allegory already existed in a very simple form in Theocritus. The name of a fictitious shepherd may disguise the name of a real poet. There is a touch of this allegory in Vergil's *Eclogues* and *Aeneid*, but it is very slight, and fused and blended in lyrical and tragic emotions.

Allegorical interpretation of the poets was of course already old. It had been spontaneously applied to Homer in the sixth century B.C., and not, as the late Professor Jonathan Tate[1] has shewn, simply in defence of him. It was soon applied to Vergil. Servius has some excesses of allegorical interpretation; but the greatest of all were achieved by Fulgentius, in the sixth century, a Christian who wrote a book in which a sneering and overbearing Vergil was supposed to appear to him and communicate the most grotesque interpretation of the *Aeneid* as a kind of philosophical allegory of human life and progress. Yet all the time the attraction

---

1. J. Tate, *The Classical Quarterly*, XXVIII, 1934, 105–14.

to allegory proved that Vergil was felt to be more than a master of grammar and rhetoric.

Vergil had at once been accepted by the early Christians as a Christian before the time, and a prophet of Christ. Constantine the Great made strong use of the Fourth *Eclogue* in the speech with which he established Christianity as the religion of Rome. Saint Augustine was deeply imbued with Vergil, accepted him as a prophet, and 'wept for Dido when he should have been weeping for his own sins'. He did not see that there was no incompatibility, and that acceptance of the Vergil of the Fourth *Aeneid* was like the acceptance of Christianity itself. His great work *The City of God* is not far from the tradition of the *Aeneid*.

The Vergil of Christian legend has two origins.

One is in local tradition at Naples, which remained attached to the region of Vergil's second home, and grew and grew, and was found and recorded by later medieval travellers.

The other origin was scholastic, and emerged from the adoration of Vergil as a master of grammar and rhetoric, and from allegorical interpretation.

In the medieval stories, Vergil became a magician, who performed great miracles. He was especially an astrologer. Augustus and other Romans appear as medieval monarchs and knights, their historical relationships and chronology hopelessly confused. Mainly, Vergil is a Christian saint or sage, who takes un-Christian revenge on sinners. But sometimes he is surprised in a most undignified and immoral love intrigue, and duly takes his revenge on those who discovered him.

The medieval distortions of the story of Vergil constitute, even more than the allegory, one of the most extraordinary and bewildering vagaries of the human mind ever recorded. For the further facts of it it is necessary to refer again to Comparetti's great work; but there is a short version of these, and of earlier, and still more interesting, developments by Dr J. W. Mackail,[1] which I am generously allowed to quote here in full.

'The whole of post-Virgilian Latin literature, in prose as well as in poetry, is saturated with Virgilian quotations, adaptations

1. J. W. Mackail, *The Aeneid*, Oxford, 1930, lxx–lxxii.

and allusions, as much as English literature for the last three hundred years has been with Shakespeare, and even more.

'Not only so; but the *Aeneid* became a sort of Bible. The famous *Sortes Vergilianae*, a method of seeking in it for supernatural guidance, came early into vogue. The phrase as well as the thing was already established a century after his death, perhaps sooner. Not only the practice, but a large measure of belief in its efficacy, lingered on into the seventeenth century. Oracles were sought by formal and ritual consultation of the *Aeneid* in temples. It took, for this purpose, the place of the discredited Sibylline Books. Hadrian, according to his biographer, consulted both, and received from both the prophecy of his future elevation to the principate. Clodius Albinus received his *sors* from two lines of Virgil in the temple of Apollo at Cumae; Alexander Severus his in the temple of Fortune at Praeneste: the great Illyrian Emperor Claudius his, towards the end of the third century, "in the Apennines", not only for himself but for his descendants, the Imperial house of Constantine.

'Virgil, indeed, was thought of and treated as in some sense deified, and able from the other world to exercise control or intervention in human affairs. His birthday, like that of Augustus, was registered in the calendar as a saint's day. Poets, like Statius and Silius Italicus, worshipped at his tomb as at a shrine. Alexander Severus placed his bust in the *lararium* or family chapel of the Imperial palace, where divine honours were paid to it. This worship would have ceased with the decay of paganism; but it was taken over by the Christian Church. The Fourth *Eclogue* was accepted and proclaimed as a direct prophecy of the birth of Christ. It was so expounded, in an address to the whole Christian population of the Empire, by Constantine after he had decreed the recognition of Christianity as the State religion. Thenceforth it was taken for granted, and almost became an article of faith. St Augustine not only accepts this doctrine, but actually cites Virgil's own mention of the Sibylline prophecies – the *Cumaeum carmen* of the Fourth *Eclogue* – as authentic proof of the genuineness and validity of those earlier predictions. In the second childhood of Latin letters, the construction of centos from Virgil was a favourite and elaborate occupation. Masses of these have been preserved. Many were ingeniously forced into a Christian sense, and actually made use of in churches. Pope Gelasius at the end of the fifth century, when making an authoritative revision of the Canon of Holy Scripture, is said – though on the evidence of doubtful documents – to have found it necessary to exclude these from the Canon by name.

'Legend after legend was invented on the strength of this belief. St Paul was said to have visited Virgil's tomb on his way from Puteoli to Rome, and to have wept at the thought that he had died before the Light had come into the world. The story was incorporated in the special office for St Paul's day at Mantua. In the Christmas services at Rheims, "Maro, prophet of the Gentiles", was called on with the prophets of the Old Testament to bear witness to Christ. Popular fancies ran into still greater extravagances. Virgil the prophet became Virgil the magician. Round his name grew a mass of fantastic tales, which, originating perhaps at Naples, spread all over Europe. They bulk largely in the *Gesta Romanorum*, the most widely popular of all medieval books. They were the foundation of many romances in prose and verse from the twelfth century onwards. One of these, *Les Faictz merveilleux de Virgille*, passed through edition after edition in the early days of printing in France, and was translated into nearly all the languages of Europe.'

The adoration of Dante for Vergil is majestic. His is a very different world, governed in our modern imagination by the portraits of Dante, especially Giotto's portrait of him in his youth, by the records of the hot ferocity of Florentine politics, and perhaps by memories of visits to Florence, and to Sienna too, where, on a Roman pinnacle of a hill, the Middle Ages live yet, and the Roman she-wolf guards the northern limit of medieval Rome.

Dante, wandering in rocky woodland, thoughtful, met in the imagination the tall grave figure of his 'sweet master', the 'sublime teacher', 'supreme excellence of man' – *il dolce maestro mio, alto dottore, virtù somma*. Always there is a startling exultation of reverence in his succession of names for Vergil. The Irish poet of our times, Gogarty, says, 'I turned to human grandeur's most exalted voice for reasons, and not the least, that Vergil led a soul estranged from Hell'. Dante was not the first or last poet to let

Vergil lead him; and he led him, as far as human grandeur's most exalted voice can lead, to the brink of Paradise, but not beyond. So the Sibyl, who suggests human ritual, led Aeneas to a brink of Paradise. There she handed him to a father's love, to lead him onwards; but Vergil took Dante to the love of Beatrice. The greatest spirits go upwards and forwards, and each moves daringly to another stage, though somehow all keep pace together. Dante had not Vergil's utter sweetness of sympathy, and was not so Christian there; but he went past Vergil in accepting, according to the Christian romanticism of the Middle Ages, and making central to his poem, a land where dreams come true. There was no smile from Dido for Aeneas in the world beyond death.

Dante replaced the Vergilian form and structure, and its fluidity within half-seen guiding rules, with a sharp regularity, all circles, and circles within circles, hierarchic, mounting upward, from the deeps of Hell where weeping processions of the condemned move in gloom,[1] to the focal supremacy, where Beatrice shone, and there was God, the love that moves the sun and stars. Somehow Vergil helped Dante to see love the brighter for hate, and helped him in spite of his difference of spirit and poetic organization.[2]

Dante, like Vergil, assimilated the past and made it different. His process is integrative, as the investigations of Dr R. Palgen have shewn. Dr Palgen is independent of Professor J. Livingston Lowes, who yet himself suggested the application of his method to Dante; but the agreement is close. And the relation of Dante to his past enlightens the relation of Vergil to his. In a sense both were themselves just because they *were* the past that they inherited and contained.

As Vergil turned the Theocritean Greek word for 'inside out' into a Latin word for 'the sea' because sound suggested the new idea, a change which has been considered a bad linguistic mistake, so Dante was equally helped by ignorance, temporary or permanent, of Vergil's language. It has been said that Dante found

1. G. Wilson Knight, *The Christian Renaissance*, 1962, 258–9.
2. See J. Sheehan, 'Catholic Ideas of Death as found in *Aeneid* VI', *Classical Folia*, XVI 1962, 87–109, who compares Vergil's Limbo, Hell, Elysian Fields, and Purgatory with the teaching of the Roman Catholic Church and especially of the early Fathers.

Vergil about as easy as a modern Englishman without special knowledge finds Chaucer. So Dante, finding in Vergil *quid non mortalia pectora cogis, auri sacra fames?* 'to what do you not drive brains of mortal men, accursed hunger for gold?'[1] wrote, *per che non reggi tu, o sacra fame dell' oro, l'appetito de' mortali?*, 'why do you not take control of the hearts of mortal men, holy hunger for gold?'[2] It is an extreme instance. *Sacer*, 'sacred', may mean 'holy' or 'accursed', as *sacré* in French. It is clear that Dante mistranslated Vergil. This is natural in a poet, though some poets happen to be interested and competent in linguistic accuracy. More interesting is the inversion, and yet at the same time the extension, of the Vergilian spirit. Vergil hated corruption and sinning for money; such sinners are deep in damnation in his Hell. Yet he achieved some acceptance of the world's evil. He trusted less to denunciation and suppression of evil, than to the defeat of it by living, and living down. Like Aeschylus, he is near to Walt Whitman's vision[3] of the minute good that drives the great mass of evil from the world – 'Roaming in thought over the Universe, I saw the little that is Good steadily hastening towards immortality; and the vast all that is call'd Evil I saw hastening to merge itself and become lost and dead.'

Dante made his peace somehow with evil, but not as Vergil made his, if he ever did. Dante accepted acceptance, as the Church did; it might almost be true to add, following Vergil. Vergil sometimes denounced the sinner, but sin was everywhere, even in the ideal of Aeneas, if it was an ideal, and in his action. So he made a world in Chekhov's phrase, 'where it would be strange not to forgive'. Dante went farther, and less far. For him acceptance meant repression, and he revelled in the unforgivingness of Hell; but it meant indulgence too, and he came to let even greed control, if it was for good.

Like Vergil, Dante is not easy to understand. It is hard to see how, if he liked Vergil, he could have liked Hell, 'the supreme proof of the mercy of God'. Perhaps Professor G. Wilson Knight

1. *A.* III, 56–7.   2. Dante, *Purgatorio*, XXII, 40–1.
3. Walt Whitman, *Roaming in Thought (After reading Hegel)*. Meanwhile the *Aeneid* is tragic also; see W. S. Maguinness, 'The Tragic Spirit of the *Aeneid*,' Presidential Address to The Virgil Society, 1955.

is right to say that after all in Dante's Hell, by the strange allegorical indirection of the medieval mind, there are not really living, suffering men, but their sins, the venomous by-products of souls and minds repressed and frustrated in the world.[1] Vergil too, of course, has his Hell. How real it is, and just how he meant it, is hard indeed to say. Certainly, Aeneas comes, from seeing the visions below earth, out from the gate not of horn, for true dreams, but of ivory, that seems in his words to be the gate for dreams that are false. Perhaps there is some truth in Dr J. W. Mackail's theory, that in Vergil's world below earth they are all pictures that are seen, like frescoes on walls of an old Minoan palace, to which he compares the house of Dis.

The romantic movement that spread from Provence in the twelfth century affected the conception of Vergil in the later Middle Ages, and the *Aeneid* was regarded as an allegory of love. That helped the rather different romanticism of the Renaissance to assimilate Vergil naturally. Vergil now represented not Christianity, but the best that had been in Paganism. He was not, however, chosen for such supreme adoration as in the Middle Ages. There was plenty of competition from other writers. But that the humanist Marco Girolamo Vida, in his Latin poem *De Arte Poetica*, devoted especial praise to Vergil is proof enough that the Renaissance knew that priceless lessons were to be learnt from him still.

His effect on Spenser, however, is immediately plain, and immensely important to the English tradition of two kinds of poetry; poems of love and the country, and the long epic of moral action. The old medieval allegory was still alive in Spenser, reinforced by new contact with Vergil in a clearer mental atmosphere. And Spenser must surely owe to Vergil some of the music of his verse.

The Elizabethan dramatists, including Marlowe and Shakespeare, wrote out of Vergil as well as Seneca.

There followed Milton with his *Lycidas* and his attempted epic of acceptance and docile worship of a God whom his own poetic

---

1. G. Wilson Knight, *The Christian Renaissance*, London, 1962, 194.

spirit had outlived. Milton learnt some of Vergil's harmony of music and grandeur, and tried to learn his full success.[1] Then Dryden came, and translated Vergil into rhymed couplets. The result is a poem of Dryden's age, which is not to us very Vergilian. But there was another result, for the work of translation gave Dryden a comprehension of Vergil's poetry which has helped to develop and maintain Vergilian scholarship since.

Since the seventeenth century, Vergil has been almost part of the English poetic tradition. He contributed especially perhaps to Gray, Pope, and Tennyson, and most recently to Eliot, Gogarty, and Noel Essex.

When printing was invented, the text of Vergil was one of the first to be printed. The *editio princeps* was the work of Sweynheim and Pannartz, and appeared at Rome undated but long before the end of the fifteenth century, probably in or about the year A.D. 1467. Soon editions were coming out every year, and continued to do so for centuries. In the seventeenth century a Spaniard, de la Cerda, published a very stately edition with a profound and enormously learned commentary, in three thick folio volumes.[2] It is sad that de la Cerda should be so rare and to most people inaccessible. The editions of Heyne, Leipzig, 1767–75 in four volumes, and of Ribbeck, Leipzig, 1859–68, in five, are still indispensable. The first is the foundation of subsequent commentary and the second of subsequent textual criticism. There is still no full English edition later than Conington's, London, 1858–98, in three volumes; Volume I appeared in 1858, Volume II in 1863, and Volume III with the collaboration of Nettleship in 1871; Nettleship published his revisions of Volume I in 1881, Volume II in 1884, and Volume III in 1883; and Haverfield finally revised Volume I and published in 1898. There are more recent texts,

1. See, on this epic tradition, Sir Maurice Bowra, *From Virgil to Milton*, London, 1945, and now Franz Josef Worstbrock, *Elemente einer Poetik der Äneis*, Münster, 1963; cf. perhaps *Virgilio Eneida Libro 11*, Introducción y Comentario de Javier de Echave-Sustaeta, Madrid, 1962, 18–38.

2. Juan Luis de la Cerda, s.j., of Toledo, published his three volumes at Madrid in 1608, 1612 and 1617 (Library of Congress catalogue). A second edition came from Lyons, first volume in 1619, second in 1612, and third in 1617; and a third from Cologne, complete, in 1628 (reissued 1647 and 1680). In the Lyons edition the dedicatory epistle of the second volume is dated 1610.

especially the Teubner and the Budé texts, and of course the Oxford text; the most recent, and probably the best, is by Remigio Sabbadini, and a new edition of it revised with the collaboration of L. Castiglioni.

So long do commentaries tend to become that books of the *Aeneid* are now usually edited singly. The chief single editions are E. Norden's, of the Sixth *Aeneid*, Leipzig and Berlin, 1924, Corso Buscaroli's of the Fourth, Rome, etc. 1932, Arthur Stanley Pease's, also of the Fourth, Cambridge, Massachusetts, 1934, and R. S. Conway's of the First, Cambridge, 1936. Professor Conway had begun to edit the whole of Vergil, but the work was stopped by his death. J. Henry's *Aeneidea*, 1873–92, will always be valuable. Meanwhile, more complete editions of individual books of the *Aeneid* have lately appeared in Great Britain, Book VI by Sir Frank Fletcher, Book XII by Professor W. S. Maguinness, Books III and V by Mr R. D. Williams, and Books II and IV by Professor R. G. Austin. All, though they are on a small scale, are of high quality and of high general utility, alike for the young and for mature scholars.

Vergil has been deeply admired almost universally since the Renaissance by poets, scholars, and critics in almost all civilized countries, and not least in France during the seventeenth and eighteenth centuries. The German scholars have been on the whole an exception, and, though they have worked hard and most usefully on Vergil, they have often misunderstood him and failed to apprehend the power of his poetry. But this has now been changed.[1]

To read Vergil, two kinds of attention are especially needed, attention to the force of the poetry and its richness, which assert and communicate positive values, and attention to the details, however tiny and apparently irrelevant, of the expression, for they may impart the secret of his thought, and whenever Vergil uses an

---

1. There has been almost a German revolution in favour of Vergil lately, German scholars emphasize the contribution of Professor Friedrich Klingner, especially in his book *Römische Geisteswelt*, Munich, 1961; first edition Munich, 1943. Cf. Viktor Pöschl, *The Art of Vergil; Image and Symbol in the Aeneid* (see p. 184 n. above), 91–138, where he treats Turnus poetically, not politically, accepting the fact that Vergil is a poet, and opposes Heinze's view.

unexpected word or form or phrase, it must be noted with the most extreme care.

It is not possible for one individual to explain to others what is to be derived from a great poet, except very broadly, because great poetry has many layers of meaning and different minds get different things from it. But it is possible to find some of the special appeal that a poet of the past has for a particular age, and it is especially easy to see the interest of Vergil's poetry for our own times.[1]

'The only thing', said Hegel, 'that we learn from history is that no one ever learns anything from history.' Perhaps we are beginning to learn the lesson, and give it effect and upset the epigram. There have, anyway, been many attempts in the last hundred years to learn from history by comparing periods of antiquity with modern times. Long ago the Germans saw in republican Rome the ideals of the First Reich. Later, a parallel to modern liberal democracy was found in classical Greece, and a parallel to the complexity, social and economic, of modern states in the Hellenistic empires. Early in the twentieth century the Rome of Cicero was thought like Edwardian and later England, in its imperial range and political and financial scope and elaboration. In the last few years this kind of interest has increased, and the unsuccessful communism of early Greece, and Greece of the third century B.C., and unconstitutional autocracy in both Greece and Italy, have been keenly investigated with at least some expectation of practical lessons for today. Plenty of warnings have been given that parallels are seldom as close as they seem, and that arguments from analogies are dangerous; and, with the experience gained and caution learnt, comparisons should be increasingly valuable, especially as our own times really reflect more and more the tendencies of antiquity.

Greeks suffered notoriously because they could not achieve restraint, and could not enforce it on powerful individuals. Yet they invented the mottoes of 'nothing must be overdone' and 'know yourself', which contain the secret; they fixed the nature of

1. G. B. Townend, 'Changing Views of Vergil's Greatness', *The Classical Journal*, Iowa, LVI, 1960–1, 67–77, eloquently shews how Vergil has been admired by different ages for quite different reasons.

the sin that hurts, ὕβρις, *hybris*, that can scarcely be translated except as 'un-Christian behaviour'; and they produced great writers of whom almost all explained with perfect clarity the dangers with which man threatens man. Homer and Euripides shewed the pathos and horror of cruel things, and Aristophanes their folly. Aeschylus and Thucydides taught how time must help, and can help those especially, who know how to pause in time. The universe is a process and so is society. Opposites can be reconciled; that is how the process anyhow goes on, and if man works in obedience to that law, it is best for him. It is madness to throw away slowly won gain; reversion to savagery is all too quick.

But the Greeks did not sufficiently understand time, and concrete, simple things, or the need, in Pope's words, of 'wild nature's vigour working at the root', not for evil, but for good.

Vergil epitomized former experience and discovery in a time like ours, when it had become clear to many that two things must be held fast, unresting activity of the moral sense and moral consciousness, and deep trust in organic, inherited culture. Vergil had rare powers of combining apparent opposites, and he used them in this. It was his main problem. In his world and in his poetry men must be good and hold hard, not digressing from established ways in pursuit of a concept of the mind, but relying on concrete things, in which scarcely any at that time except a Roman and a poet could see the real strength and the truth. Much of the confusion at the end of the Republic seems, at least in the histories which at present we are able to write, to be due to Tiberius Gracchus, who, like Polybius, tried to fit Greek theory on to Roman society, not, however, cautiously and for purposes of theory like Polybius, but for quick and active reform. He underestimated, like most old reformers, the unseen, unintelligible forces in organic society, and could not see that sometimes, and for the present, it is best to leave ill alone. Not that he entirely failed; but he gave more semblance of right and reason to Marius and Sulla than was their due.

Vergil knew the philosophers and owed very much to them. They had sunk into his poetic thought, and came out in poetry sometimes. But they were not all. He made of them a commentary on the realities that can be known with the heart, which to him were central, and guides in a world where clearest appearance is often most delusive. He was not an irrationalist, surrendering to unreason; but he could be rational about the irrational things.

We, also, have been over-confident in the expanding powers of civilization, and we have assumed that if a plan seems at one moment sure to work then it will work. We have often sought to change society according to what we imagine are its rational needs, without remembering that there may be countless other needs, satisfied by nature in gradual, experimental development, which are not accessible to our reason and interest, but which, forgotten in too rational and exclusive plans, and unsatisfied, will soon take revenge; usually in a violent reaction which takes too much account of irrational forces, and, by working too quickly as rationalism worked too quickly, precludes alike the advance of reason and the preservation of emotional truth.

Vergil's hero, *pius Aeneas*, is not Aeneas the Good but Aeneas the True. *Pietas* is loyalty, and more; it is being true to all that can claim, not only, as in official Roman religion, material dues, but obedience in devotion and affection. Principally a Roman must be true to the gods, true to Rome, and true to his family and clients. Vergil examined the idea of *pietas* and found in it, as he learnt to understand it, the central salvation. Like his contemporaries, we have wondered which of many conflicting duties should be done, and have been inclined to Carlyle's advice, to do, in times of doubt, the duty that is nearest. That is Vergilian; but in the sense that doing the nearest duty will, under Providence, mean that the more distant duty will be done too. In Carthage Aeneas is not called *pius* till he has decided to leave Dido; then he is called *pius* again. He has been true to his gods, his country, and his father and son, but not to Dido. He wins Italy, and the will of Jupiter is done.

Plenty of Romans believed in this delicately pervasive *pietas*; Cicero said that it could be infringed by a mere expression of countenance. And there were countless philosophical expressions before Vergil's time of most or even all of the doctrines which he might be thought to have held. So also it is said that everything in the Sermon on the Mount has an antecedent in earlier teaching.

That is not the point. Prophets and poets select and organize; and then they infuse emotion and will into doctrine. Hearers and readers then accept convictions and practical tendencies which are not imposed, but which grow up in their own hearts and minds.

There must be leadership for human society, and it must be under Heaven. Some individual good must be sacrificed, sometimes individual conscience too, apparently, for the individual does not know all, and must rely on loyalty. But the Heaven that guides the leader wills that he should, as Homer knew, be a father to his people, and translate the harmony of the family into political strength. That is the opposite of the main direction of the Greeks, but it is a natural consequence of Italian history. Cicero claims that the Italians were not supreme in any other merits except two, religious faith, fear, and observance, and something which he expresses in the words *hoc domestico nativoque sensu*, perhaps 'the ties which hold us to our home and all to which we owe our birth'.

The Christian quality in Vergil, so famous in the world ever since, has itself antecedents. It is hard to find in Christianity itself anything, except the whole of it and its quality and power, which was not in part anticipated. Even the Trinity was known in Hellenistic religion, but with Sophia, Divine Wisdom, as the Third Person. The Cynics were devout and sweet-natured in their self-abnegations. The asceticism of the pagan world, though not much is normally heard of it, was as violent sometimes as any in the Middle Ages.

But the God who was a merciful father, whose son saved the world from sin, was never quite reached. Yet a god was sacrificed for the sake of man according to Babylonian myth, already old two thousand years before Christ. God, or a son of God, Dionysus, Adonis, Polydeuces, was always dying; there was the tomb of Zeus himself in Crete. Sin, not merely ritual impurity, progressively became the taint from which the initiate in mysteries must be free; at Eleusis in the fifth century B.C. the process had gone far. In the third and second centuries B.C., at the sanctuary of Asclepius at Epidaurus, purity of heart came to be explicitly required of those who came for health to the god. Prometheus and Hercules both suffer more and more, as the mythical tradition develops, for the salvation of man.

By mysterious degrees the conception of a heaven in the sky, already in Homer beginning to be detached from Olympus, and already the eternal home of a hero, Heracles, whose ghost was in Hades, came to be quite strongly developed before Vergil's time. The Orphics called themselves sons of earth and starry heaven, and some of them believed in an ascent of the purified soul to the sky. They widely spread the theory of reward and punishment after death, especially in South Italy. In Cicero's *Dream of Scipio*, sanctioning the laws and customs of Rome, there is a Platonic heaven, of spheres and orbits, to which great Romans are to go after death, to live in bliss; but they must wait patiently, and serve loyally on earth.

The world beyond the grave was more real to republican Romans, as Professor B. Farrington has shewn,[1] than used to be supposed. It is strong in the poetic feeling of Propertius; and it was a real and current belief, used by the Government as an instrument of rule, which, again as Professor Farrington has shewn, Lucretius attacked. But the other world was a confusion to thought. Antiquity retained the primeval instinct to imagine it deep in the earth, originally deep within the earth mother herself, to whom the dead seemed to return. But a Garden of the Gods, first known in the *Epic of Gilgamish*, forced its way into the myth, and a place was found for it in the earth, beyond the rivers of Hades, in a place with its own sun. Pindar in the Second *Olympian* already has the picture, which seems to be Orphic, but of course has origins far earlier than the Orphic name. The Garden of the Gods was not always underground; it was in the west, beyond the ritually imagined Pillars of Heracles, perhaps an island, like Porphyry's Island of Cronos.[2] So the world of the dead was entered from an island already in the *Odyssey*. The dead set with the sun.

1. B. Farrington, *Science and Politics in the Ancient World*, London, 1939, 160–216.

2. Cf. Maria Helena Monteiro da Rocha-Pereira, *Concepções Helénicas de Felicidade no Além de Homero a Platão*, Coimbra, 1955; W. F. J. Knight, 'The After-Life in Greek and Roman Antiquity', *Folk-Lore*, LXIX, 1958, 217–36; cf. Vittorio D. Macchioro, *From Orpheus to Paul*, London, 1930.

In Homer the dead are in their world for ever, weak ghosts. Pythagoras and Plato spread the conception, world-wide outside Greece, of a continuance of life in other bodies, at intervals, to go on for ever, or eventually to cease. In Plato there is already a picture of the whole universe in the scene of life beyond the grave; but it is doubtful whether the sky is clearly the place of rest for any human spirit. There is, however, a divine judgement, deciding the fate of souls, not, as in Homer, mere jurisdiction among the dead. Minos and Rhadamanthys are judges of the dead and decide their future; or else an unnamed divinity, acting under Necessity and Fate.

Fate was a difficulty for ancient religion, even greater than the confusion about the after-world. Vergil merged the confusions into a poetic picture coherent emotionally, but scarcely otherwise; and he similarly merged, by a newer insight, fate, and God.

A god limited by fate cannot be like the Christian God. And fate, especially after the Stoics had developed their theory of it, was hard to consider moral. Vergil joined two things. He attached the sense of destined national greatness, which was inherent in the Roman myth, to the Greek conception of fate. So fate might not be moral, but it yet guarded and guided Rome.

Vergil expressed the conviction which others already felt that the advance of Rome was good for the world, and a moral enterprise. Therefore, fate, or fortune, or destiny, all conceptions which had developed in Greece and Italy mainly after classical Greek times towards a point at which they might take the place of divinity, became moral, because it guided a moral process apparently for moral purposes. So fate approached God again, and there was a partial return to the Homeric world-view, in which Zeus and fate are both in a sense supreme, and the obvious possibility of conflict between them is most often not considered. Vergil had only to go a step further and make fate the instrument of the Supreme God. Sometimes he does so. 'The fates', says Jupiter, 'will find a way'; and it is 'the fates of Jupiter' that ordain.[1]

1. See Rosemary M. Arundel, *Philosophies in the Aeneid*, a thesis submitted to the University of London for the degree of M.A. in Classics, 1956, which gives useful lists of *fatum* and other such words as they occur in Vergil, and discusses them.

Vergil has used, once more, the internal nature of a word; for *latum* is a participle of *fari*, 'say', and ought, as Vergil saw, to mean oracle, ordinance, or command. But Vergil is not normally quite precise with concepts; and he retains also the other meaning of fate, for the eternal laws that are not transgressed, as the laws that forbid return across death's waters.

Vergil's Jupiter is father of gods and men, and speaks 'with the countenance with which he makes the skies go blue'; telling Venus not to fear, for she has the fate of her people assured, never to be moved. Jupiter himself is true to the vision of the holy family; Rome starts secure on her way, when Jupiter and Juno are reconciled about her. Jupiter's will is law, but he asks co-operation. And he suffers; his own son, Sarpedon, had to die. He too, in some way, is bound, self-bound, perhaps. And that is something which we still do not quite understand.

Vergil's Juno is the Greek persecutress of Heracles, Hera; and also the special divinity of women at Rome. She defends women, Dido, Amata, and Lavinia, but it is little for their good. She seems like a mysterious inertia in things, resisting progress and making it more painful than it might have been. She is like instinct that is too strong in the defence of the outworn and old. There is much that is hard to understand in Vergil's Juno; but it is easy to detect some of the mental reality which she, in the manner of true mythic personalities, represents.

The Venus of Vergil is like the two kinds of love in Byron; or perhaps the two elements in it, the incestuous and sadistic, and the divine and lovely. The mother of Aeneas prevails. She is invincible; and she, rather than Juno or blind fate, guides, with Jupiter, the world. Perhaps it is not inconceivable that Vergil learnt to think so, not only from the professed lineage of the Julii, from his own experience, from Greek religion, especially Orphism, and even from Ionian physicists before, but also from the great opening passage of Lucretius, the 'atheist', where he entreats Venus, ruler of the world, to help him.

Yet the other Venus is in Vergil too, the heartless Venus who entraps Dido. If we like, we may infer that love rules the gods; but man, if he can see, must rule his love.

Apollo is specially interesting in Vergil. At one stage he was intended to be more important than he is now in the *Aeneid*; for in the early third book he is the guide, and there are references elsewhere to consultations of his oracle in Lycia which are not narrated in the text. He is consulted at Delos, however, in the Third *Aeneid*, and at Cumae in the Sixth, where his prophetess the Sibyl leads Aeneas below the earth to Anchises.[1] Yet it is rather as a forerunner of Apollo at Cumae, as at Delphi, that the ancient Sibyl speaks and guides; Apollo is later. And Apollo here is in part a strange old Italian god of the world below, Vediovis, favoured by the Julii, besides his bright Greek self. Still Aeneas prays and makes his vows to Apollo, assuring him of high worship in the city to be. And it was so. Apollo was the favourite deity of Augustus, and in his regard almost superseded Jupiter. For he was a god of brightness and youth and song, an armed god of peace, fit to guide and defend an age when the world was to be young again. He guided the hand and arrow of Paris to take the life of Achilles; and in Italy he once takes a small part in the war. Vergil might have said more of Apollo if he had finished the *Aeneid*. Or he might not; since Apollo had a large place in the original plan, represented by the Third *Aeneid*, but a smaller place in the rest of the poem. Perhaps Vergil had begun to think, as Aeschylus thought, that Apollo alone is not enough.

Vergil's gods are grand or lovely or both, and it is possible to accept them in the imagination often poetically, and sometimes religiously. They are true to humanity, and, as the best pagan theologies will, they constitute a symbolic psychology. Jupiter, Venus, and the Fate of Rome are together supreme, and worshipful, almost as a trinity.

But they are not the cause why Vergil was so soon thought a natural Christian at heart, evincing more than others that the soul is naturally Christian: *anima naturaliter Christiana*. Partly, it was an inevitable conclusion from the Fourth *Eclogue* and its almost Biblical imagery that Vergil foretold the birth of Christ. The truth

1. For Vergil and the Sibyls cf. J. B. Garstang, 'Aeneas and the Sibyls', *The Classical Journal*, LIX, 1963, 97–101; for the Sibyl of Cumae cf. John Pollard, 'Delphica', *The Annual of the British School at Athens*, LV, 1960, 195–9; and for Sibyls in general, idem, *Seers, Shrines and Sirens*, London, 1965, 106–7.

of the matter seems to be that the Hebrew Bible and its thought were little known in Italy; but that the Sibylline oracles of the Greek east could have transmitted almost the same thought and imagery; and that Vergil, sensitive as few have been to the past and the present, chose the image of a baby to mark the golden age, as the early Christian generations themselves chose to contemplate not only the Christ of manhood, but also the Babe at Bethlehem. There was a necessity in it for both.

Saint Paul was reputed in the legend to have wept over Vergil's grave, wishing that he could have met him in life. But they would not have been in complete agreement. Vergil's outlook, as Sir Robert Falconer[1] has shewn, would have proved to be in some conflict with the teaching of Saint Paul. The *pietas* of Vergil and his trust in civilizing Rome, are in contrast to the πίστις, *pistis*, 'faith' or 'belief' – the translation once more is hard – so much stressed by Saint Paul, and to some degree also with Saint Paul's not quite invariable mistrust of the temporal order, and his reliance on redemption through Christ.

Yet when in A.D. 325 Constantine imposed Christianity on the Roman world, he enlisted Vergil to help. Vergil had bridged the gap between the sublime moral and religious attainment of classical antiquity, and the uncompromising presentation by Christians of the sanction which they drew from a world beyond earth, a sanction, however, which could guard, enliven, and expand the attainment of the past. It was not of slight importance that Constantine read at his great conference a Greek translation of the Fourth *Eclogue*. The early Christians needed Vergil's help, Saint Augustine perhaps chiefly, but not he alone. Their quarrelling, as one of them quaintly admitted, made life like Hell. They needed the Vergilian humanity and dignity. More important still, without Vergil the worlds seen and unseen could never have approached so near in thought and act together, and the long tradition of the ideal City of God, that descends through Saint Augustine and Pope Gregory the Great to Milton and our own times and our own future, could not be so intimate a part of our assumptions and the hopes in our plans. It would have been harder to say, with

1. Sir Robert Falconer, *The University of Toronto Quarterly*, VI, 1936–7, 18–32.

Mr Lionel Curtis, that all true politics are the attempt to base our lives on the Sermon on the Mount.

It is clear why Vergil had to see the good of the present, and elicit it, if not make it, by looking at the past. And it is clear too that he had to look at a composite, blended past, in order to draw from it, and draw straight, the strong lines of hope in the present. He had to give back something like the superstition which the late Dr W. R. Inge said that we now suffer for losing; he had to make it true, however, and so make a myth of it, a fairy-tale and more besides; one of the fairy-tales that are the only true stories. And he had to make the Roman world a family again, a family of families as it had been round the most ancient cottage of Rome's primeval kings. So, like but unlike modern nations and their speakers, he found the need of a personal head, a leader and father who might look half-divine: one sort of the old, dim truth; which because it is so old can help to bring in the new.

The past, awake in Vergil, directed him to a focus for strong loyalty; and in the end he found Octavianus, the Augustus to be, and fitted his mind to the acceptance. Adopted by the great Julius Caesar, Octavianus inherited the Julian devotion to Venus the goddess of love, and added to that a peculiar devotion to Apollo, god of light and loveliness. So the Rome of Vergil had a little of what the England of Elizabeth might have, a kind of erotic force to sustain in imaginative loyalty. Voltaire has the irreducible statement that 'only love is good, only misery is true'. Something more than misery may be true; but love, if all goes well, cannot be less than good. This love, the spring of duty and loyalty, has always tried and tried to enter the heart of politics and all the religions. In the old east and among savages civilized love tried to be represented by unrestraint at rites; and Pindar proves that this solution was applied even in Greece, at Corinth. Greek cities, as the late C. G. Jung says, were held together by their special kind of affection, and, as love names on pottery shew, the return to normal impulses synchronized with the decay of the city state in the fourth century; though even then Thebes, while her power was greatest, had her Sacred Company, bound together in loyalty by strong affections between its members. Already farther from mere biological sex, and nearer to the more selfless affections and devotions of the Christian ethic, was Epicurus, whose most famous saying is, 'all the world dances with friendship'. Zeno the Stoic, like Plato before him, made 'love' the principle of unity in ideal civil organization. Lucretius, rejecting the gods and goddesses, prayed first and only to the power of love that no poet can reject. He is said to have died in 55 B.C., the year that Vergil is supposed to have assumed the dress of manhood; and already, well developed in the Rome of bloodshed and wickedness, with its cynical power-marriages, and the new high finance, was something that might return and return, and outlast them all: the new Roman kind of friendship, explicit in the writings of Cicero, Catullus, Horace, and Vergil. This kind of friendship, a real care for others, spontaneous, but highly valued and guarded by will-power and restraint and attentively fostered, was something new and progressive. Partly, it was soundly based on what might be called the genuine and inspired sociological research of Epicurus and his followers, especially in the 'Garden Academy'. We are keenly working towards the ideal of it now, and without knowing it we are trying to follow the rules which Philodemus left to Siro, and to Vergil, and through them, and the rolls of his works lately found at Herculaneum,[1] to us.

But Vergil had to be in part a Stoic too. Ages are marked by their polarity, and Vergil's age, like ours, had its cruel and terrible side, which was far more obvious, and must have seemed to be winning, but was really far less permanent and real. Octavianus was himself at first hardly respectable; any wholehearted respect that his party deserved was more easily rendered to its other members. The future divine leader was only raw material. Vergil had the intuition to see beyond; he supplied the gentler influences and contributed the workmanship. Others helped, but Vergil above all had the courage to hope and the brilliance to see.

In some moods there is a temptation to believe that somehow, though the blood and tears might, and should, have been saved, it was worth while; there is an easy way to take, if we agree with the English Philosophical Radicals, who, reacting from the ideas of the French Revolution, maintained that the suffering of many must be endured if necessary, and that there is value and im-

1. Norman W. De Witt, *Classical Philology*, XXXI, 1936, 205–11.

portance in a good life lived by a few; life must go on, and its quality cannot be judged by counting. But that is too near to the worst things in Aristotle to content us for long; and Christianity, and Vergil, tell us better.

Vergil has been called 'holistic' by the late R. S. Conway and Professor T. J. Haarhoff. He looked for a whole, and found or made one; both found and made, in some sense. He did so in the Pythagorean and Aeschylean way by facing and reconciling opposites. Of them, there were many pairs – the Greek and the Italian, the old and the new, the kind and the cruel. That is not all. There were the two philosophies, Stoic and Epicurean, of which almost too much had been made by Roman enthusiasm for Greek thought. There was involved here another pair, in a sense more important, the new reason and the old faith, 'the origin of the world' and 'country gods', as Vergil said – a pair which almost corresponds to the mind and the heart, each with its own authority. And there was this pair – the little world of Vergil's home, and the big world, wicked perhaps but wonderful, that broke in upon it with a shock; and there was, subordinately, yet another pair, the world of books, and the world of things.

There were all these influences, antagonisms, and compulsions. But Vergil himself was more than any causes that can be found for him, and ultimately beyond definition and explanation except as himself.

There is much interest in the task, which has been well done by a succession of scholars, of finding in Vergil Epicurean and Stoic thoughts and phrases. It has been supposed that he went through an Epicurean phase, and later settled down to an outlook nearer to Stoicism. With part of his mind he probably did follow some such path. But it is important to see that a poet, as a poet, cannot exactly follow any systems, because any poetically felt and expressed beliefs are more or less sure to be beliefs that cannot be expressed as a system, or in any way but poetry. The quality of the feeling is intrinsic to the thought, but additional to it. Poets think what can be expressed poetically; they do not think and express poetically what might be expressed otherwise. The poetic exaltation with which a belief is held makes it different from any belief held unpoetically. That is why orthodoxies are so different from the spirit of their poetic and prophetic originators.

But when Vergil comes to a dramatic moment at which a character must speak in a particular sense, he normally makes the character say remembered thoughts and words, characteristically changed. That is how fragments of Stoicism and Epicureanism recur, just like the fragments of Homer or Ennius. Some characters at some moments drift towards those two outlooks. Iarbas, Dido, Nisus, and Euryalus have occasion to fall into a mood in which Epicurean opinions are natural. Aeneas, after the first part of the *Aeneid*, is normally in a position in which he has to try to think and speak rather as a Stoic might. Vergil characteristically does not work everything out from the start, but uses the inherited alphabet of words and beliefs. Many Stoic phrases are associated with Aeneas; but Sir Maurice Bowra[1] has well shewn that in nature and sentiment Aeneas is very unlike any Stoic. There is more truth in saying that he was an Epicurean, for though with Stoics he believed in a spiritual world under divine control, his emotional life was always in some harmony with the broad, cultured, sensitive, and sympathetic Epicureanism of Siro's Garden.[2]

From the Stoics Vergil may well have taken some of his respect for character, his belief in a divine ordinance and in duty, his interest in prophecy and omens, and some of his thoughts concerning the world beyond the grave, and his ideal of the brotherhood of mankind.

From the Epicureans he may have derived some of his love of the delicate things in life, his belief in the possibility of human harmony and tranquillity, and his interest in nature and science, and his conception of human progress from simple beginnings.

Thus the ideal of human friendliness and co-operation was a point of real if not apparent agreement between Stoics and Epicureans; and it belonged not less to Vergil himself and much of his own world.

The Epicureans were almost Christian in their characteristic temper. But they believed in a mechanistic universe, neither

1. Sir Maurice Bowra, *Greece and Rome*, III, 1933, 8–21.
2. Charles N. Smiley, *The Classical Journal*, XXVI, 1930–1, 660–75.

originated nor controlled by divine power. And they denied the immortality of the soul.

Vergil believed in a universe divinely created and divinely controlled according to laws, both physical and moral. And he believed in the immortality of the soul. Like most of ourselves, he was prepared to accept the contradictions involved. He realized that however strong the evidence for determinism, physical and moral, limited free will is still a fact; and he did not define the degree to which free will and divine guidance can be coincident. His picture of the world certainly included a life after death, partly determined by moral character shewn on earth. He also accepted the validity of prayer, quite obviously, again and again; it was a 'chance prayer' which won for Aeneas the divine guidance under which he found the golden bough. Yet Vergil also writes as if prayer cannot deflect the decrees of fate.

Poetry might almost be defined as the method by which truth can be reached and expressed even when it involves contradictions. By poetry Vergil reaches the prayer 'Thy will be done'. And the poetry alone, with no direct statement of the command, produces in us a state of mind in which we know that we must love our enemies, and want to love them.

Vergil's reputation as a natural Christian had many origins, but to us his chief claim to it is in his humanity and sympathy. No tremendous demand of patriotism and Roman destiny makes him forget the blood and tears or accept them with reconciliation. It has often been said, but Father Espinosa[1] has made the thought far more real and impressive than it has been before, that Vergil's sympathies are incomparably deeper and wider than any other pagan's, almost different in kind; and his sympathies gave him a law for living, requiring that the heart, as Keats too demanded, should be a perpetual guide to the mind. Vergil went farther than Keats, and saw and faced the difficulties; but he followed his heart nevertheless.

There is truth in the view, best maintained by Father Espinosa, that Vergil had a providential mission to prepare the world for Christianity. He gave Christianity a chance to accept, and to

1. Aurelio Espinosa Pólit, *Virgilio, el poeta y su misión providencial*, Quito, 1932, *passim*.

change, as he accepted and changed inherited thoughts and phrases. Vergil formed the long past into a scheme of life in which Christianity 'would not be a surprise', and still more, in which a certain orthodoxy could be Christian. He made a picture of right living in which old human values and principles were preserved, and in which that which is Caesar's could be rendered unto Caesar, and unto God that which was God's; what he left unsaid was Christianity's say. This 'orthodoxy', in the subtle and profound sense in which Dr Theodor Haecker[1] attributes it to Vergil, and by which he distinguishes the Vergilian tradition from various disastrous humanisms and materialisms of later times, may almost be taken as Vergil's supreme discovery.

There is no reason to imagine that Vergil, however truly he may have been 'a Christian at heart', was therefore always saintly. There is evidence that he could take offence, in the story that because the people of Nola were as he thought unfair to him in the matter of a water-supply, he removed from the *Aeneid* a reference to their city.[2] And, both as farmer and poet, it is clear that he could be hard when hardness was needed. But nothing was more deeply characteristic of him than his deep and tender sympathy, sensitive to all beauty and all sorrow. In many moods Vergil saw tragic pity and beauty broken so poignantly that he scarcely saw beyond. But equally characteristic were his poetic discipline and courage. He revealed a world with room for pride in heroic greatness, and a faith in it, happier, perhaps even stronger, than Milton's, because clearer-eyed for the little things which to understand is to forgive. Aeneas was not a lonely Samson; but Aeneas and Anchises together, while Anchises lived, were more.[3] Vergil won the pride, and paid its price; and with full right he could send down all ages imperial tones. Italy is 'the ancient land, having might by her arms, and by richness of her soil', *terra antiqua potens armis atque ubere glaebae*.[4] Already in the *Eclogues* there is to come one

1. Theodor Haecker, *Virgil, Father of the West*, London, 1934, 60–70.

2. A. Maiuri, 'Virgilio e Nola', *Quaderni di Studi Romani*, Rome, Istituto di Studi Romani, 1939.

3. L. J. D. Richardson, *The Proceedings of the Royal Irish Academy*, XLVI, Section C, No. 2, 1940, 85–101, especially 88–90.

4. *A.* III, 164.

who 'will guide by inherited greatness in him a world which that greatness brought to peace,' *pacatumque reget patriis virtutibus orbem*.[1] With his heart Vergil said Jupiter's words, 'Let there be a Roman stock and its might from Italy's manhood growing', *sit Romana potens Itala virtute propago*.[2] He had obeyed the command of the Sibyl, 'You, give not way to tribulation, but face it, the more daring for it, and go on,' *tu ne cede malis sed contra audentior ito*.[3] So Vergil learnt to give his mighty aid. Gogarty 'turned to human grandeur's most exalted voice for reasons'; and so may our world, the world which, as the late Dr Otto Neurath happily said, is Stoic and Epicurean too, polarizing into its true self on those two poles; 'knowing how to love beauty, and how to resign it.'[4]

The great poets have all faced the delights and the dangers which we must choose and refuse and which govern our living and thinking. They can direct our minds to take, in action, the next step forward. If we think not, there is nothing for it but to read them again.

1. *E.* IV, 17.   2. *A.* XII, 827.   3. *A.* VI, 95.
4. Cf. Pierre Boyancé, *La Religion de Virgile*, 1963, especially 175–7.

VERGIL'S LATIN

(This Appendix is reprinted from *Acta Classica, Proceedings of the Classical Association of South Africa*, 1958, Vol. 1, an issue dedicated to Professor T. J. Haarhoff.)

PARADOXICALLY, if one word had to be found to indicate the method by which Vergil became a great, or even the greatest, lord of language, that word would be 'compromise'. Compromise seems a dull, or even a mean, method. Right-minded people, and people of spirit, can be expected to say that they hate compromise. Yet compromise was Vergil's way to the unique Vergilian Latin, the tones of human grandeur's most exalted voice.

Vergilian compromise is easier to accept as a principle when two other principles or tendencies of Vergil's mind are remembered, the tendencies to alternation and reconciliation. Vergil liked to give close attention to one thing or one character or one interest, and then equally close attention to its opposite. When such attentions are repeated in turn, they alternate. When, eventually, claims are balanced, and some constructive equilibrium is found for them, there is progressive reconciliation. This mechanism is to be expected in any artist; but it is peculiarly characteristic in Vergil. He shows its operation on many scales, from the arrangement of letters, words and verses to the manipulation of great tragic forces. What happens is much more than mere compromise; but compromise is the start, and the method for part of the way. At the far end of the way is Vergil's 'universality'.

Vergil remained himself, and characteristically himself, in every phase and aspect of his immense artistic activity. This sounds obvious; but it can be forgotten, and if it is, mistakes follow. Nor is it a fact which is easy to remember in full, and understandingly. The number of considerations which Vergil held in view and harmonized is so vast that our intellect and imagination are strained.[1]

This characteristic operation of Vergil's mind seems to be the result of his moral nature. He was shy, doubtful and meditative, and afraid of being over-confident. With humility, however, he combined the highest integrity. Therefore he wished to be thorough, and not to act unfairly or allow anything that he did to be below standard or shabby. These propensities might well have paralysed his self-expression; but fortunately he had other advantages, including a will-power strong even by Roman standards, and a force of intellect scarcely to be imagined.

None of this is irrelevant to the complex and elusive question of Vergil's language. The finished mastery of his poetry is deceptive, and obscures the intricacies of its origins.

The basis of Vergil's Latin is Ciceronian practice. Indeed, his Latin is perhaps fundamentally nearer to the Latin of Cicero's prose and verse than to any other kind of Latin known to us.[2] Being rational and logical, Vergil preferred to start with a Latin of such resource and lucidity that no outline of thought need be

1. I have made very free use of J. Marouzeau, *Traité de stylistique latine*, Paris, 1946, to which I refer in the notes as *M*, and also A. Cordier, *Études sur le vocabulaire épique dans l'Énéide*, Paris, 1939. To them I owe many references and some conclusions. They should be consulted for the bibliography of the subject. Since independence was impossible, and I needed to argue from material presented by them, I have gratefully followed their presentation. Closely relevant to the present subject is Andrew J. Bell, *The Latin Dual and Poetic Diction*, London and Toronto, 1923, a provocative but instructive work with much concerning 'the figures'. The observations of L. A. S. Jermyn, *Greece and Rome* xx, 1951, 26-37, 49-59, seem to me indispensable.

2. Eduard Fraenkel, *Atti e Memorie della reale Accademia Virgiliana di Scienze, Lettere ed Arti di Mantova*, N.S. Vols. 19-20, 1926-7, 217-27, stresses the parallel and comparable importance of Vergil and Cicero to Petrarch, 'gli occhi de la lingua nostra', and considers them to have been mutually sympathetic. He does not say very much about their similiarity of language, but his observations are constructive, not least on *Catalepton* X as a highly skilful and characteristic exercise by Vergil in developing and parodying Catullus I V. Some small agreements of conscience, if that is the word, between Cicero and Vergil are worth noticing; for both *equidem* must mean 'I indeed', not simply 'indeed', and 'igitur' must not stand first in a sentence, where Cicero has it, I believe, only about twice; cf. also Karl Büchner, *P. Vergilius Maro, Der Dichter der Römer*, Stuttgart, 1955.

obscured, and no rational relationships need be misrepresented. Latin has not quite the precision of Greek; but Cicero's best prose comes near to the ideal. Accordingly, Vergil on the whole accepted as a substratum Cicero's judgement on the accidence of nouns and verbs, the syntax of moods and tenses, and to some extent the choice of vocabulary; and Cicero could sometimes even furnish him with a metaphor capable of poetic use. Lucretius, though his Latin has even been thought not altogether unlike the Latin spoken in Rome in his own day, and Catullus, with his inclination to rather reckless experiments, could never have accepted so much of Cicero's Latinity.

Vergil compromised from the start. For one thing, he perpetually compromised between Greek and Latin. At any time a phrase derived from or affected by a passage in Cicero or any other Latin writer might be changed by the influence of a Greek writer or Greek writers. That was continually happening, and it has to be assumed. For example, when Vergil writes *rumpit uocem* he recalls Greek phrases such as φωνὴν ῥηγνύναι. Servius is therefore wrong, or incomplete, in saying that what Vergil did was merely to invert a correct expression such as *rumpit silentium*.[1] Again, *sensit medios delapsus in hostis*[2] is not less a Greek construction because, besides its occurrence in Catullus and Horace, it is also old Latin; Plautus wrote *daturus dixit*.[3] The Greek background can never be safely forgotten, and all ancient and modern scholars who compare Vergilian expressions exclusively with Latin antecedents run a serious risk, a risk which must always be recognized even if it cannot always be avoided.

Apart from Greek, Vergil had plenty of other Latin to balance with Cicero's, even if Cicero's was his substratum; and it is a serious probability that he tried to read it all, and did read a great part. When he was writing the *Eclogues*, the Greek of Theocritus and other Hellenistic poetry gave him most of the necessary material, but he was already making use of early and classical Greek poetry including lyric and tragedies, and Latin poetry also, especially the poetry of Catullus and Gallus, and perhaps several other 'neoterics'. The *Eclogues* already show Vergil hard at work according to his characteristic method. He was already

1. Servius, *A.* II, 129.   2. *A.* II, 377.   3. Plautus, *Asinaria*, 634.

'compromising' between opposites, and especially combining and compressing together derivations from different passages of earlier literature. One result is the comparative frequency even in the *Eclogues* of phrases and sentences hard to translate according to one exclusive sense or to any received Latin usage. Vergil could perfectly easily have given us plain sense and a thin stream of meaning. But he had a different conception of his art.

The *Georgics* required the use of Hesiod, perhaps Aristotle, certainly Theophrastus, Hellenistic didactic poets, Cato, Lucretius and countless others, including Cicero's Latin translations of Greek poetry and both poetry and prose by Varro. All or nearly all affected Vergil's Latin. Among the compromises which now strained his language was the very arduous adjustment of it to both literary material of many ages and direct, familiar knowledge of the country and the farm.

Material for the *Aeneid* came from literary works in Greek and Latin, in poetry and prose, and numerous beyond all computation. Among them, in particular, were Latin poems in the Roman epic tradition, in which the *Aeneid* was to take a place. Vergil duly accepted their influence, but without neglecting other influences. There are here good examples of his compromises, and of his careful and sensitive judgement. He had to decide how much to accept, and how to use the material provided by the tradition, such as rare and archaic words, epic formulae and long compound adjectives. These questions have been elaborately investigated, and lists and statistics published.[1] Vergil learned from Hellenistic innovations, but diverged. He accepted the Hellenistic practice of hard thinking in the choice and vital use of words, but not to the extent of abandoning epic tradition or even some epic formulae. He purified the epic style which Ennius, Lucretius, Cicero in his poetry, and others offered for his use. He even admitted expressions more appropriate to Latin drama, not only tragedy but also comedy. But he remained traditional, and an epic poet. He did not carry classicism to the degree of purification reached in Horace's Odes, and perhaps later emulated by Lucan; he did not normally allow, as even Ovid was inclined to allow, old, obscure or unexpected forms and expressions to creep into the verse with-

1. Cordier, *passim*, especially 142–51, 285–301.

out strong reasons for their admission, and, as Quintilian would have advised, he was carefully moderate in his archaisms. To reach his destination in an extreme of power, Vergil travelled by countless middle ways.

Archaic and formal usages, familiar from old Latin epic, sometimes set Vergil's Latin in obvious contrast with the Latin of Cicero's prose. Macrobius, agreeing with Quintilian and perhaps going farther, was right to insist that old Latin can very often explain Vergil's apparent innovations. Vergil no doubt liked the traditional flavour, and agreed with Quintilian's belief that the sense of antiquity adds a certain majesty.[1] But, as always, Vergil's motives are subtle and even elusive. His habit of compromise was a means, not an end. To achieve it to his own satisfaction, he needed three other principles of art. His poetry must be musical, and musically expressive. It must also be visual and tactile. Vergil normally wrote concretely of solidly imagined people, things and actions, avoiding the loose play of abstract ideas. Finally, but no less important, the meanings must be compressed and condensed into a short space and few words.

Vergil's tendency to compromise, which might also be described as a willingness to consider everything and despise nothing, gave him great freedom to be expressive. It led him to diverge from his predecessors in small matters and in great. For the sake of musical sound he allowed many old genitive forms in *-um* instead of *-orum*, such as *deum*, *virum* and *magnanimum*. When, at the death of Turnus, *-orum* stands at the end of both the first and second halves of a single verse, it is unique.[2] Vergil nowhere else allows the syllable to occur in exactly these places.[3] Ovid was

1. Quintilian, I, 6, 39.
2. *A.* XII, 648–9:
      sancta ad vos anima atque istius inscia culpae
      descendam magnorum haud umquam indignus avorum.
Similarly unique is *A.* XII, 903–4:
      sed neque currentem se nec cognoscit euntem
      tollentemve manus saxumve immane moventem.
3. Close, but different, are *A.* III, 549, *A.* VII, 18, *A.* XI, 361; by contrast, Ovid uses these sound-complexes very freely and devalues them; see W. F. J. Knight, 'Ovid's Metre and Rhythm', *Ovidiana, Recherches sur Ovide*, edited by N. I. Herescu, Paris, 1958, 106–20, especially 114.

characteristically more tolerant, and used such impressive sound-effects more freely and less thoughtfully, so making them less impressive. Vergil wanted his poetry to present and emphasize the concrete; accordingly, he used far fewer verbally formed nouns ending in *-men -minis*, *-tura* and *-tus* than Lucretius. The nouns ending in *-tus* were favoured little by Vergil but much by Livy, who seems to have learnt much from Vergil, and afterwards affected Vergil in his turn.[1] The nouns in *-men -minis* were of course a great help to versification, as Ovid found; he used them in immense numbers and variety. Interestingly enough, Vergil was more ready to use them if they had, or could have, a concrete meaning, as *gestamen* and *tegimen* or *tegmen*. Like other Latin poets he developed the use of nouns, especially, but not only, eloquent short nouns which may almost personify qualities and actions, to express what prose might express by verbs.[2] Another revealing practice is Vergil's care to substitute other verbs, with richer and more vital visual content, for *est* and *sunt*, as *iacet*, *ibat*, *incedo*, and most of all *stat*, *stant*.[3] Vergil did not invent the practice, but he extended it. As for compression of meaning into a short space, examples are everywhere.

Most often, when Vergil writes unusual Latin, this desire for compression is the reason, or one of the reasons. He was always trying to compress; '*et est sermo in compendium coactus*', as Servius well described it.[4] Vergil used the word *pone*, 'behind'. It was not contemporary literary Latin, but old, and possibly in Vergil's time a rustic survival.[5] But it was very much shorter than *a tergo*. Still shorter, for its wealth of meaning, is *ilicet*. Vergil uses it with enormous tragic effect to mean something like 'all was lost', or 'no hope remained'.[6] But it was not fashionable. It belongs to old

1. Augusto Rostagni, *Da Livio a Virgilio e da Virgilio a Livio*, Opuscoli Accademici, Serie Liviana IV, Padua, 1942.

2. Bell, 155–8; Vergil should be carefully compared with other writers in his exploitation of *cor*, *fatum*, *fides*, *horror*, *lis*, *mens*, *mos*, *numen*, *spes*, and other such nouns; a new use of nouns was one of the many lessons learnt by Tacitus from Vergil ('in some sense Vergil touched off the Silver Age' – J. R. T. Pollard); cf. many notes in Vergil, *Aeneid* II, edited by R. G. Austin, Oxford, 1964.

3. *M*, 146.   4. Servius, *A*. I, 639.

5. *M*, 195, citing Stolz-Schmalz-Hofmann, *Lateinische Grammatik*, Munich, 1928, 500.

6. *A*. II, 424.

Latin, especially the Latin of the law courts and comedy.[1] In Terence it means something like 'the court rises'; all can go home. What is astonishing is that Vergil should have drawn from such a word such overpowering tragic and poetic force. He also used *magis atque magis*, a despised expression, with high poetic success. He even went so far as to adapt the very informal *ecce tibi*, writing *en perfecta tibi*, at a moment of high intensity;[2] but, as usual, the artistic gain is great.

Vergil's humility and readiness to compromise led him to such daring and such achievement. Indeed, it sometimes looks as if his unwillingness to call anything common or unclean caused him to become not only capricious and unconventional, but positively provocative, if not impertinent. However, even so his poetry does not fail, and the price paid is nothing compared to the profit in compression and explosive poetic power.

There are some examples of Vergil's receptive catholicity which, though they show no great distortion of normal Latin, are sufficiently instructive to be specially mentioned. Writing of a thoroughbred horse, Vergil says that he 'replaces soft legs', or 'feet,' 'on the ground', or 'replaces his legs', or 'feet', 'softly', the proleptic adjective being beautifully expressive, *mollia crura reponit*.[3] The meaning of *mollis* in this context has of course been discussed. It is more important to look at the adjective in another context. For Ennius uses the same words, *mollia crura reponunt*, but of *grues*, 'cranes': *perque fabam repunt et mollia crura reponunt*.[4] The birds, walking about and picking up beans, are comic; the thoroughbred is not, but exquisitely beautiful in form and action. What exactly Vergil has done, why his daring choice of a derivation has enabled him to express the very nearly inexpressible, and how he has altered Latin to do so, would need a long inquiry. But Vergil's daring gave him, as usual, success. No one can really fail to see the picture presented.

In such examples Vergil sometimes makes use of meanings and suggestions, appropriate in an older context but less obviously

1. Servius-Daniel, *A.* II, 424: ILICET confestim. mox. sane apud veteres 'ilicet' significabat 'sine dubio actum est'. . . . Terentius (*Adelphi*, 791) . . . *rescivit omnem rem, id nunc clamat, ilicet.* idem (*Eunuchus*, 54–5) *actum est, ilicet, peristi.*
2. *A.* VII, 545.   3. *G.* III, 76.   4. Ennius, *Annals*, 556 Vahlen, 3rd ed.

appropriate in his own, new, context, to make his own intended meaning more exactly clear. Again there is paradox. Vergil writes of Juno, 'an incessant affliction for the Trojans', as *Teucris addita Juno*.[1] The verb is unexpected. Perhaps it suggests Socrates, 'applied', like a gadfly, to the Athenian democracy. But it is known where Vergil found it. It was in Lucilius, who wrote *si mihi non praetor siet additus atque agitet me, non male sit*,[2] 'If, with all the rest to put up with, I had not the Praetor, too, on my hands, tormenting me, it would not be so bad.' This is not the only rather surprising Lucilian echo in Vergil. The very inappropriateness of the old associations is made to add force and precision to Vergil's poetry. Again, conventional Latin is very lightly altered.

By being reconditely allusive Vergil made his poetry defiantly direct. He was praised in antiquity for excelling in all the styles of rhetoric, even though he wrote poetry, not rhetorical prose. It does not follow that he always obeyed the expressed and authoritative rules for good writing.

Quintilian has a rule against *mixtura verborum*, which roughly means 'too many words out of the natural place in a sentence', and he accuses Vergil of disregarding it when he wrote *saxa vocant Itali mediis quae in fluctibus aras*.[3] This is not very terrible, especially if it is the only bad case which Quintilian could find. There is here, however, a notable case of Vergil's care in choosing the middle way. Quintilian's *mixtura* is a fault which often beset many good Roman poets, though usually in tolerable measure; but it is not unlike that 'interlacement of word order' which is praised as a practice valuable to Vergil for the enrichment of meaning, as of course it is.[4] He could, however, dispense bril-

---

1. *A.* VI, 90.
2. Lucilius, XIV, 469–70 Marx; Macrobius, *Saturnalia*, VI, 4, 2.
3. Quintilian, VIII, 2, 14; *A.* I, 109; *M*, 322.
4. J. W. Mackail, *The Aeneid of Virgil*, Oxford, 1930, Intro., lxxxiv: 'It is in the manipulation of language that Virgil stands apart from other poets. His sensitiveness to language is unique, more especially the way in which he perpetually – it might almost be said, in every line of the *Aeneid* – gives words and phrases a new colour by variation, sometimes obvious, sometimes so delicate as to escape notice, of the normal or classical diction. Language always remains with him a fluid medium, and he handles words so as to make them different. The interlacement of order, to which a highly in-

liantly with the practice of interlacement as he could, apparently, with every other device; and so achieve the sweet, heavenly power of his verses beginning *devenere locos laetos* ... , where Aeneas at last reaches the homes of bliss.[1]

There was an amusing difference of opinion concerning the repetition of words.[2] Quintilian noted that the best writers did not greatly worry to avoid repetitions, though some people were quite childish in their efforts to find synonyms.[3] The Auctor *ad Herennium* had already observed that synonyms were regularly used by writers to avoid repetitions, but he himself liked repetitions and classified their uses.[4] Cicero to some extent concurred.[5] As usual, Vergil himself partially agreed with both sides. His repetitions are sometimes exquisitely artistic according to many classifiable schemes, as *videmus Italiam. Italiam primus conclamat Achates, Italiam*, ... [6] in three verses, *ab Iove ... Iove ... Iovis*[7] in two verses and *nocte ... nocte ... nocte ... noctes*[8] in four. There can be great

flected language like Latin lends itself, is carried by him to the utmost limit, and the phrase within which no division by punctuation is possible may extend over several lines. Words which are logically or syntactically inseparable may be at long distances from one another, and his cross-patterns of language, while they seldom fail to convey the effective meaning desired, almost defy analysis. It was this which led his detractors to say that he did not write Latin; and there is this much of truth in the criticism, that his Latin is a language of his own, and one in which he was, up to the last, perpetually experimenting.'

Cf. however Fraenkel (see p. 400 note 2 above), 226 with notes 1 and 2 for Vergil's freedom from such awkward arrangements as Catullus, LXVI, 18; *non, ita me divi, vera gemunt, iuverint*; Vergil shows a slight tendency to such writing in the *Eclogues*, but scarcely any after them. A thorough inspection of hyperbaton throughout Vergil might reveal secrets concerning his mind and thought.

1. *A.* VI, 638–9:
    devenere locos laetos et amoena virecta
    fortunatorum nemorum sedesque beatas.
cf. *M.* 335. 'C'est là un des exemples les mieux faits pour montrer le rôle que peuvent jouer les bons écrivains dans la défense de la langue, en réagissant contre ceux qui par l'abus des procédés de style aboutissent à la négation même du style.'

2. *M*, 267–76.   3. Quintilian, VIII, 3, 51; X, 1, 7.
4. *Auctor ad Herennium*, IV, 42, 54.
5. Cicero, *De Oratore*, III, 54, 206; *Orator*, 39, 135.
6. *A.* III, 522–4.   7. *A.* VII, 219–20.   8. *G.* I, 287–90.

poetic might in a repetition, as *inde domum, si forte pedem, si forte tulisset*.[1] And yet again Vergil often admits casual repetitions in great frequency and, to us, rather offensively as *solemus . . . solebam . . . solent*[2] in five verses. Meanwhile, his care to find synonyms is often thorough and successful, as when in fourteen verses eleven words mean water in some form, and nine of them are different.[3]

Vergil freely used parataxis when constructing clauses, though a simple sequence of statements was accounted *sermo inliberalis*. Vergil could write elaborate paragraphs. But on the whole he inclined to a narrative structure nearer to Caesar's habit than to Cicero's or Livy's, with many connectives meaning 'and'. Poets, of course, are not expected to write in prose periods, though Lucretius and Catullus both exhibit long and elaborate paragraphs. But there is a special interest here. Vergil tended to return to old Latin structure, even to the use of present participles in the nominative to end sentences, and in word-order which approached modern English. It is indeed probable that, by organizing sentences in this way, Vergil altered the course of the literary future, and even helped to decide the shape of medieval Latin and the languages of modern Europe. There is here another example of Vergil's attention to both of two extremes. This time he was inclined to favour both, in different passages.

There was apparently a rule discouraging the excessive use of pronominal words, and words lacking a solid content of meaning.[4] Latin is rich in such words, and perhaps especially forms and derivatives of the relative pronoun. They are useful for emphasizing, with brevity, the rational organization of a sentence with an almost mathematical logic, and that is something which Latin likes to do. The free use of such words belongs apparently to old Latin, and especially old legal Latin. It was not considered good in literary Latin or artistic oratory in the classical period. Vergil has not much of this fault, but he did not always try to avoid it. There is the famous *quae cuique est fortuna hodie, quam quisque secat spem . . .*[5] As usual, that which, occurring elsewhere or used by another, might have been a fault, is turned to high poetic effect.

1. *A.* 11, 756.   2. *E.* 1, 20–25.   3. *G.* IV, 360–73.
4. *M*, 109–15, citing E. H. Sturtevant on 'grammatical machinery'.
5. *A.* x, 107.

There may be no great merit in *nos tamen haec quocumque modo tibi nostra vicissim ...*[1] But Vergil's practice represents a restriction of the practice of Ennius, as in *quicquam quisquam [quemquam], quemque quisque conveniat, neget*,[2] a verse admittedly from a drama, not epic; and even when he meant to echo Ennius he never went as far as Ennius would freely go.

When Vergil wrote strangely, he apparently obeyed his own judgement, for all his diffidence, without much caring for pedantic critics. He used the adjective *cuius -a -um*; *dic mihi, Damoeta, cuium pecus? an Meliboei?*[3] A reply came in the form of a parody: *cuium pecus? anne Latinum? non, verum Aegonis: nostri sic rure loquuntur*.[4] It is a foolish complaint. The adjective *cuius* was good old Latin, had probably survived outside Rome, and was indeed used by Cicero. Vergil used *hordea* in the plural, otherwise not known.[5] The answer offered, 'by Bavius and Maevius' as Servius pleasantly says, was *hordea qui dixit, superest ut tritica dicat*.[6] It seems rather childish to us. Vergil may well have had Latin authority for *hordea*. But he was probably more or less thinking in Greek, as he often did, and using the plural as Greek used it for more than one type of grain, as τὰ ἄλφιτα.

Poetry, in Vergil's day, had advanced farther than poetic criticism. There certainly seems to have been much rather pedestrian appreciation going on in antiquity, and in later antiquity. Macrobius, however, has passages which, from our point of view, are appreciatively in the right direction, even if some secrets of classical poetry had been lost before the later writers lived.[7]

A list, partly taken from Servius, which Macrobius gives shows the kind of Vergilian phrase which seemed to other Romans unusual, but also well, *bene, pulchre*, contrived. Examples are: *recentem caede locum*,[8] '*nove dictum*'; *caeso sparsurus sanguine flammas*,[9] that is, '*qui ex caesis videlicet profunditur*'; *corpore tela modo atque oculis vigilantibus exit*,[10] that is, '*tela vitat*'; *exesaeque arboris antro*,[11]

1. *E.* v, 50.   2. Ennius, *Scenic Fragments*, 422 Vahlen, 3rd ed.
3. *E.* III, 1.   4. Donatus, *Life of Vergil*.   5. *G.* I, 210.
6. Servius, *G.* I, 210: *hordea – usurpative*. Bavius et Maevius: *hordea qui dixit, superest ut tritica dicat*.
7. Macrobius, *Saturnalia*, VI, 6, 1–9.   8. *A.* IX, 455–6.
9. *A.* XI, 82.   10. *A.* v, 438.   11. *G.* IV, 44.

'*antro*' for '*caverna*'; *frontem obscenam rugis arat*,[1] '*arat non nimie sed pulchre dictum*'; and *vir gregis*[2] for '*caper*'. Macrobius exclaims: '*et illa quam pulchra sunt: "aquae mons"*,[3] *"telorum seges"*,[4] *"ferreus imber"*[5] *ut apud Homerum* λάϊνον ἕσσο χιτῶνα'. He likes *dona laboratae Cereris*,[6] *oculisve aut pectore noctem accipit*,[7] *vocisque offensa resultat imago*,[8] *pacemque per aras*,[9] and *paulatim abolere Sychaeum incipit*.[10] On the verse *discolor unde auri per ramos aura refulsit*[11] he writes: '*quid est enim aura auri, aut quem ad modum aura refulget? sed tamen pulchre usurpavit*'. Of *simili frondescit virga metallo*[12] he says '*quam bene usus est "frondescit metallo"*.' On *haud aliter, iustae quibus est Mezentius irae*,[13] he writes: '*odio esse aliquem usitatum, irae esse inventum Maronis est*'. He notes that *Iuturnam suasi*[14] is unusual for *Iuturnae suasi*.

Macrobius' list and comments may seem simple and obvious. But they show how Vergil's language appeared to intelligent readers in antiquity, and help to indicate what seemed, or indeed were, at least some of the differences between the Latin of Vergil and the Latin of others. The list shows Vergil never letting anything alone without hard thought and at least some act of originating will. Occasionally there is perhaps an appearance, deceptive or not, of change for the sake of change and no more. More often in these and other such instances there is compression of meaning, a clear enrichment of content, and an access of emotion, drama, music, or colour, due to an unexpected word or usage.

The practice is something like a great extension of the normal figure of *abusio*, κατάχρησις, that is, the sudden use of an unexpected word.[15] Caesar advised writers to avoid an abnormal or unusual word, *inauditum et insolens verbum*, like a dangerous rock at sea.[16] Fronto was not content with usual and ordinary words, *solitis et usitatis verbis*.[17] He advised out-of-the-way words, *verba non obvia*,[18] and disagreed with Cicero, who thought that in the best orators very few unexpected and improbable words, *insperata*

1. *A.* VII, 417. 2. *E.* VII, 7. 3. *A.* I, 105. 4. *A.* III, 46.
5. *A.* XII, 284. 6. *A.* VIII, 181. 7. *A.* IV, 530–1.
8. *G.* IV, 50. 9. *A.* IV, 56. 10. *A.* I, 720–1.
11. *A.* VI, 204. 12. *A.* VI, 144. 13. *A.* X, 714.
14. *A.* XII, 813–14. 15. *M,* 177–8. 16. Gellius, I, 10, 4.
17. Fronto p. 50, ed. Naber. 18. Fronto p. 98, ed. Naber.

atque inopinata verba, could be found.[1] These writers were thinking mainly of vocabulary and words in themselves unfamiliar, the true *abusio*, rather than words unexpected in their context. But the interest is not the less for that. There was clearly, and had long been, a useful difference of opinion. One of the points at issue was whether we should write smoothly, or surprisingly, administering shocks. Characteristically, Vergil took everything into consideration, and might almost be said to have devised a way to secure the advantages offered by both the opposing doctrines. It is as if he had set before himself the ideal of compression, and then, subject to that ideal, had worked out his compromise of usual words, unusually manipulated.

This policy led to a great number of small divergences from Ciceronian Latin, many of them indicated by Servius, and many, too, revivals of old Latin practice. When Vergil uses a mood or tense which would not be expected in Ciceronian prose, for example an indicative in indirect question, as *ne quaere doceri . . . quae forma viros fortunave mersit*,[2] or *viden ut geminae stant vertice cristae?*[3] or a very sharply significant perfect tense, as *tum res rapuisse licebit*,[4] there are usually antecedents in old Latin. Other variations, as *quem dat Sidonia Dido*[5] (for *dedisset*), and 'mixed conditional clauses', are no doubt Vergilian, but most of them are near to the general tradition of Latin expression, and some are Vergilian in the sense that Vergil exploited constructions which, like other parts of the Latin language, had already achieved a compression of complex meaning.[6] This, as a general tendency of Latin, can be seen in other matters, including a number of single words; the adjective *lentus* is almost a poem in itself.

A few of Vergil's genders were noticed in antiquity as irregular. He was apparently alone in making *damma*, usually meaning 'doe', masculine; this was apparently because he wanted the sounds of *timidi dammae*, without a rhyme. The genitives of Greek names, as *Achillei* or *Achilli*, were said to be inventions of Vergil, created

---

1. Fronto p. 63, ed. Naber.
2. *A.* VI, 614–15; for such questions see *Virgilio Eneida Libro II*, edited by Javier de Echave-Sustaeta, Madrid, 1962, 38–64.
3. *A.* VI, 779.   4. *A.* X, 14.
5. *A.* IX, 266.   6. Bell, 140 and *passim*.

to give the right sound. But his third-declension datives in -*e*, fourth-declension datives in -*u*, and perhaps a fifth-declension genitive in -*ē* are from old Latin; so, directly or indirectly, are the syncopations *direxti, repostas*. None are very startling, except perhaps *aspris* for *asperis*. So probably are some usages of the gerund which might seem strange. Servius, explaining *ardescitque tuendo*,[1] calls the gerund 'passive', as also in *frigidus in pratis cantando rumpitur anguis*;[2] this is in contrast to *cantando tu illum* [sc. *superabis*]?,[3] which he calls 'active'. Of course, *cantando rumpitur* might be a retention from some expression *cantando rumpas* or *rumpere potes* after a Vergilian adaptation. The best parallel from another writer is *erumpendo naves incendunt*, from the *Bellum Hispaniense*;[4] some such source may have influenced Vergil. No principle seems to be infringed by *volvenda dies*,[5] and *inter agendum*[6] is correct; both may perhaps be called old-fashioned. Vergil's extended use of cases, especially the dative and ablative, and his omission of prepositions, are particularly characteristic and important, but no more can be said about them here.

Miscellaneous details are plentiful. Old-fashioned are Vergil's active verbs which might normally have been deponent, such as *populat* for *populatur*, and perhaps some intransitives which might have been transitive, as *siliqua quassante, volventia plaustra*, and *volventibus annis;* other unusual forms are *recens* as an adverb; *multa*, plural, adverbial, for *multum; ambo* and *duo* as accusatives; *adeo* meaning something like 'indeed', and *atque* involving some such sense as 'suddenly'; *proprius* meaning 'appropriate' or 'correct' rather than 'his own'; *puto* in an old Latin sense, 'ponder'; and such old forms as *stridunt* for *strident* and *stetērunt* for *stetērunt*.

Vergil preferred to treat Latin as timeless, and as still fluid, that is, still more fluid than it actually was in his own time. He was not only using language, but also creating language, as a poet should. He was perhaps capricious and self-willed; but to a poet *quidlibet audendi semper fuit aequa potestas*. The main thing was to have the greatest possible volume of material to use, and the most extensive resource. Vergil used old Latin as he used contemporary

1. *A.* I, 713.   2. *E.* VIII, 71.   3. *E.* III, 25.
4. *Bellum Hispaniense*, XXXVI, 3.   5. *A.* IX, 7.   6. *E.* IX, 24.

Latin. There were two words for 'son', *natus*, poetical, and *filius*, prosaic. He used both; but each only in contexts which were appropriate.[1] He similarly used the more dignified *proelium* and the less dignified *pugna*, both appropriately, and not far apart.[2] But he used the prosaic *fluvius* very freely, and did not clearly distinguish it from the more poetic synonyms; a word may be useful for itself, apart from any associations. At, or near, the opposite extreme, are such phrases as *Anchisa generate*, which seem to be principally valued for their Ennian quality. They are occasionally used in considerable numbers, and contribute importantly to some elaborate Vergilian passages.[3]

1. *M*, 167.   2. *M*, 193.

3. L. R. Palmer, *The Latin Language*, London, 1954, 112–14, on *A*. x, 100–10:

> tum pater omnipotens, rerum cu prima potestas,
> infit (eo dicente deum domus alta silescit
> et tremefacta solo tellus, silet arduus aether,
> tum Zephyri posuere, premit placida aequora pontus):
> 'accipite ergo animis atque haec mea figite dicta.
> quandoquidem Ausonios coniungi foedere Teucris
> haud licitum, nec vestra capit discordia finem,
> quae cuique est fortuna hodie, quam quisque secat spem,
> Tros Rutulusne fuat, nullo discrimine habebo,
> seu fatis Italum castra obsidione tenentur
> siue errore malo Troiae monitisque sinistris …'

Professor Palmer writes: 'Virgil's archaisms are used with delicate and deliberate artistry. As with Lucretius, they are dictated by the theme. It is noteworthy, for instance, that the form *fuat* occurs in Virgil only in a speech of Jupiter (l.c.), a passage worth examining in the present context. The words of the *Pater Omnipotens* are introduced by the archaism *infit*. The scene is sketched with alliteration of Ennian intensity:

> eo dicente deum domus alta silescit.

The speech itself opens with an impressive 'dicolon abundans':

> accipite ergo animis atque haec mea figite dicta.

His judgement, which begins with the majestic polysyllable *quandoquidem*, 'in as much as' (never used by Cicero in his speeches, nor by Caesar), has the balanced binary structure rooted in the language of religion and law. In the last line we sense the *dolo malo* of the *leges sacrae* and the *sinister* of the language of augury. Thus the archaism *fuat* finds its setting in a majestic context where the father of gods and men sits in the judgement seat. Marouzeau has pointed out a number of instances where such archaisms colour the language spoken by the gods: *quianam* is used by Jupiter (*A*. x, 6), *moerorum* by Venus (*A*. x, 24), *ast* by Juno (*A*. 1, 46). No better illustration could be found of Quin-

Ellipse is part of the reason for many Vergilian irregularities. Sometimes it may count as the whole reason. On *occumbere morti* Servius says *novae locutionis figura et penitus remota*, rather strong language, and quotes Ennius, *morti occumbant obviam*.[1] It is hard for us to realize that the Romans felt that the loss of *obviam*, though there is still an *ob-* in the verb, made so much difference. Even in this phrase, apparently, Vergil was quite audacious in his continuous and insistent search for brevity and compression.

There are three adjectives which, differentiated in classical Latin, had all according to Servius meant 'large' or something like it in old Latin. They are *dirus, indignus,* and *saevus*.[2] Servius may well be inexact. But if the words did once have wider meanings, it may be that Vergil took advantage of a certain ambiguity when he wrote *indigno cum Gallus amore peribat*,[3] or when he

tilian's dictum 'verba a vetustate repetita . . . adferunt orationi maiestatem aliquam' (1, 6, 39).

'The Sibyl, too, speaks a language not of this world:
> olli sic breviter fata est longaeva sacerdos;
> "Anchisa generate, deum certissima proles ..."

The whole passage (*A.* VI, 317–36) describing Aeneas' arrival at the Styx is particularly rich in archaic colouring: *enim* 'indeed', the assonance *inops inhumataque*, the anastrophe *haec litora circum*, the archaic significance of *putans*, the locative *animi*, and finally the phrase *ductorem classis*, where an antique gem in a modern setting of *glossae* forms the splendid line
> Leucaspim et Lyciae ductorem classis Oronten (334).

In this passage we may note, further, the Ennian reminiscence *vada verrunt* and *vestigia pressit*; the patronymic expressions *Anchisa generate, Anchisa satus,* which were a feature of Latin epic style from Livius Andronicus on; the syntactical Graecism (this a "gloss") *iurare numen*; and finally the un-Latin *-que ... -que*, which is a 'calque' coined by Ennius as a convenient hexameter ending on the lines of Homeric expressions such as ὀλίγον τε φίλον τε, πόλεμοί τε μάχαι τε, etc.'

I hope so long a quotation will be forgiven. Professor Palmer's comprehensive and rounded commentary is particularly valuable here since my treatment in the text is selective and fragmentary.

1. Servius-Daniel, *A.* II, 62; Ennius, *Scenic Fragments*, 135–6 Vahlen, 3rd ed.; but cf. also Ennius, *Annals* 398 Vahlen, *occumbunt multi letum ferroque lapique*; perhaps even in this small matter Vergil struck a balance between two Ennian phrases. In general ancient criticism tends to overlook the double parenthood accountable for many, or most, Vergilian inventions.

2. Servius *ad G.* I, 37, *E.* VIII, 18, *A.* I, 4 and *A.* II, 226.

3. *E.* X, 10.

applied *saevus* to Juno.[1] The adjective *dirus* is more interesting. It is thought to have come to Rome from Umbrian and Sabine neighbours of the Romans, so that it may not have been fully understood.[2] Vergil noticeably used it to mean neither 'terrible' nor 'large', but something nearer to 'excessive' or 'exaggerated', tending to 'uncanny', 'grotesque', 'unnatural', as in *dira cupido*,[3] an 'excessive', perhaps even 'impertinent', desire[4]. It is possible that in these three instances Vergil used antiquity and obscurity to increase his freedom, just as he used simple verbs in preference to compounds, for instance the older form *tendere*, which has necessarily more possible meanings than *contendere*, so that his art of ambiguity, light allusion, and penumbral meanings could be helped. But Vergil was equally capable of finding *contendere* in an old passage and adapting it as *tendere*. It is hard to keep pace with the constructive agility of his mind.

Servius does not apparently quote Sallust when he comments on Vergil's gerundives such as *ardescitque tuendo*; but elsewhere he cites more parallels from Sallust than from any other writer. It is unnecessary to suggest that he does so because Sallust was in particular use as a school text. More probably Vergil admired Sallust's artistic treatment of the Latin language, and joined him in enterprise and experiment. Cicero complained of historians whose only merit was their brevity; Vergil thought that there was much to be said for that quality, and certainly sympathized with Sallust in his liking even for Cato's Latin. Servius, or Daniel's Servius, quotes Sallust for *requierunt*, intransitive,[5] *aevoque sequenti*,[6] the meaning of *cultus* in *qui cultus habendo . . .* [7] (two quotations from Sallust), the fifth-declension genitive in -$\bar{e}$ (*diē*),[8] the use of *forent* for *essent*,[9] *falsus* meaning 'deceptive',[10] a possible form *vinus* (οἶνος) instead of *vinum*,[11] the meaning 'un-

---

1. *A.* I, 4, *et al.*   2. Servius-Daniel, *A.* III, 235.

3. *A.* VI, 373; cf. *G.* I, 37 and *A.* IX, 185.

4. This interpretation arose, indirectly, from a comment on the word by Mr John D. Christie.

5. Servius, *E.* VIII, 4.   6. *E.* VIII, 27.   7. *G.* I, 3.

8. *G.* I, 208.   9. *G.* I, 260.   10. *G.* I, 463.

11. *G.* II, 98; Servius has apparently misunderstood Vergil, but that is irrelevant here.

truthful' for *vanus*,[1] *certos* meaning 'reliable men'[2] (two quotations from Sallust), *fidens animi*,[3] *foedavit voltus*,[4] and *vos agitate fugam*.[5]

This is a selection from notes in the earlier part of Servius' commentary; a full list would be long. There cannot be serious doubt that Vergil, from the *Eclogues* onwards, worked in sympathy with Sallust's experiments, and learnt from him procedures which were important in determining his own treatment of language throughout his lifetime, especially his choice of words, and of contexts for them. Sallust helped to teach Vergil the extension of the figure of *abusio* which was to become characteristic of all his work.

Agrippa's famous criticism of Vergil's Latin[6] is of course hard on Vergil, but it seems to have been an honest reaction to carefully observed facts; too carefully observed, perhaps, for passivity might have allowed receptive sympathy to grow. Others too have been misled. However, Agrippa helps to show that Vergil's Latin seemed very peculiar to at least some contemporaries, and to confirm our own conception of what Vergil's peculiarities were.

By far the greater number of Vergil's first hearers and readers accepted him with whole-hearted acclaim. Latin was still, even then, experimental. There was scarcely yet a standard Latin, as there has been a standard English for two hundred and fifty years. But Vergil's contemporaries, if well read, must have noticed echoes of many periods and many writers, almost continuously. The less well-read probably found his Latin about as remote and strange as we find the Authorised Version of the Bible, or a little less so; and perhaps sometimes it seemed to them about as artificial and elaborate as Gerard Manley Hopkins' poetry seems to us.

But all alike, and at all times, could and should have been

1. *A.* 1, 392. 2. *A.* 1, 576. 3. *A.* 11, 61.
4. *A.* 11, 286. 5. *A.* 11. 640.

6. Donatus, *Life of Vergil*: '*M. Vipsanius a Maecenate eum suppositum appellabat novae cacozeliae repertorem, non tumidae neque exilis sed ex communibus verbis atque ideo latentis.*' There is very little at all offensive in this famous notice except the words *suppositum* and *cacozeliae*. There is even a pleasing suggestion of the middle way in *non tumidae neque exilis*, and the remaining words might almost be taken as an acknowledgement of Vergil's success.

captivated by the Vergilian music; and most have been. The music depends on the Latin, and the Latin would not have all its music if Vergil's artistic mind had not been so capacious.

After all, to judge of Vergil's Latin it is not so necessary to read Servius and other commentators as to read Vergil himself, and other Latin poets for comparison. If we do so, and look out not for oddities but for the ordinary, regular, personal quality of the text before us, we notice something in Vergil which sets him apart from the rest, and which can be called part of his universality. The other poets are always themselves, and perhaps even a little self-conscious sometimes. Each has a style, and sometimes it seems an exaggeratedly individual style. Vergil, of course, leaves fingerprints everywhere. But they are less important. What is important is the catholicity, the intellectual capacity, the patience which enabled him to amass all the resources which his vision required, and the economy and variety with which he used them.

Being so greatly gifted, he could, with a small vocabulary and under fairly rigid rules, do something different every moment. Variety of expression is one of his great secrets of success. He had the full power of rare genius to break the rules and 'snatch a grace beyond the reach of art'.[1] Sheer resource, and abundance of material at his immediate command, gave him immense flexibility, even though he often seems formal. He needed all of it, because in his art not only syllables but even single letters counted; not only vowels but also consonants; not only quantities but also accents; and so on, beyond the limits of our knowledge. Pauses must not be too regular. They can, however, be regular in the right place for a short passage which is poetically, dramatically and emotionally such as to require just such pauses. Dactyls, spondees and elisions must match the iridescent flash of the many-sided systems of thought, which they must follow, and in their turn engender. Comedy and tragedy must co-operate to create truth within a two-word phrase. Elemental forces must conflict and crash about us in the story, and the life of whole worlds must seem to us tangibly at stake. Yet the artist himself must keep something in reserve and never lose control, but coldly check himself against excess in strengthening or pro-

1. Alexander Pope, *An Essay on Criticism*, 153.

tracting or repeating any single note. It is, oddly enough, the end of the way of which compromise was the beginning. But it was always a compromise composed of fairness and honesty, a sympathy for finding a value in all things, a courageous will to pay any price however high, and unresting effort never withheld until everything needed, everything that could conceivably be needed, and needed for a task never imagined before, had been acquired. *Tantae molis erat.*

APPENDIX 2

VERGIL'S SECRET ART

(This Appendix is reprinted from the *Proceedings of the Virgil Society*, I, 1962, and from *Rivista di Cultura classica e medioevale*, VI, 2, 1964, 121–39.)

A WARNING, as wise as authoritative, has lately been issued. It is our duty, and our delight, to read Vergil. But, if so, then some of the closer examinations of his text, especially some recent arithmetical explorations in which his poetry is shewn to be organized according to exactly corresponding numbers of lines, are not merely tedious but worse: they remove Vergil farther from our poetic enjoyment, and reduce him to a field for statistics.

In face of this, it is clear what would be the worst thing to do. That would be to abandon Vergil the inspired, and inspiring, poet, and to hand his text over to computers. It would be better to ignore the more damaging results of research, and continue as before, reading, enjoying, profiting. But there exist other people, who will not all be content to ignore the less attractive discoveries, all the more because these discoveries are mainly true facts, and can hardly now be disproved. A third way is best, to try to fit the new facts into their place in the whole scheme of Vergil's art. They might thus be cut down to size. It might then be possible to live with them, without excessive distraction from the deeper appreciation of his poetry.

After all, Vergil's achievements and abilities are already recognized to be so vast and so multifarious that no single further discovery concerning his methods should make more than a moderate difference to the general estimate. After a little adjustment, tentative and perhaps not very successful, each new wonder can recede into the whole immense mystery of Vergil, leaving it as, or nearly as, it has always been. 'It is a strange peculiarity of Vergil', wrote Macrobius, 'that he is invulnerable to criticism and unaffected by praise.'

Vergil planned deliberately. It is now well known that the

supposed intentions of a poet are by no means the most important question to be asked about him, if not indeed the question which is, of all questions, the least worth asking. Certainly the wind of inspiration bloweth where it listeth. It blew for Vergil. Yet Vergil had his intentions, and his plans, and a method in his inspiration; and much of all this was Vergil's secret, unknown to other people.

His literary biography is known in outline, and is very fairly reliable, since Vergil's own friends collected at least some material about him which was handed on to his ancient commentators and biographers, and has so reached us.[1] There are gaps and uncertainties, especially about dates, but they are not fatal. The information is, I think, ample to show that Vergil, whatever else he may have been, was a real poet, not a mere propagandist.

Modern methods can elicit enough internal evidence, even including style and feeling, to prove that Vergil's supposed early poems in the so-called Vergilian *Appendix* were not, except for perhaps three or four, written by Vergil.[2] Of these exceptions, one is the famous parody of Catullus IV, *Catalepton* x. Catullus had written a poem in praise of his yacht:

> *phaselus ille quem videtis, hospites,*
> *ait fuisse navium celerrimus.*

Vergil wrote a parody about the successful career of a mule-driver,' Sabinus', who actually became a consul:

> *Sabinus ille quem videtis, hospites,*
> *ait fuisse mulio celerrimus.*

Vergil retained as many of the actual words of Catullus as he could, but changed the others to fit Sabinus the muleteer. He was already interested in fitting words together and solving verbal problems.[3] He began with humour, ingenuity, and a love of

1. K. Büchner, *P. Vergilius Maro, Der Dichter der Römer*, Stuttgart, 1955, 6–17.

2. ibid., 41–160.

3. E. Fraenkel (*Atti e Memorie della reale Accademia Virgiliana di Scienze, Lettere ed Arti di Mantova*, N.S., vols 19–20, 1926–7, 217–27) well emphasizes the importance of the parody as an exercise for Vergil.

words. Another early poem, *Catalepton* v, almost certainly by Vergil, in which he says goodbye to the teachers of rhetoric because he is going to Naples to learn Epicurean science, shews the same propensities. The parody shews something else too. No one can certainly identify the muleteer who became a consul. Vergil already knew how to make his poetry ambiguous. He had begun to acquire what Keats called 'negative capability'.[1] 'That is', wrote Keats, 'when a man is capable of being in uncertainties, mysteries, doubts, without any irritable reaching after fact and reason'. W. B. Yeats went further: 'The more a poet rids his verses of heterogeneous knowledge and irrelevant analysis, and purifies his mind with elaborate art, the more does the little ritual of his verse resemble the great ritual of Nature, and become mysterious and inscrutable. He' (that is, the poet) 'becomes, as all the great mystics have believed, a vessel of the creative power of God.'[2] These ideas fit Vergil, at least to some extent. Clearly this 'negative capability', especially when on a smaller scale, often depends on a dexterous use of single words. Vergil used fact and reason to protect himself and his reader from excessive fact and reason.

Taken together, these two interests, verbal manipulation and 'negative capability', already constitute an important part of Vergil's characteristic style, already discernible, even before he wrote the *Eclogues*.

In his early years Vergil is said, no doubt truly, to have been interested in many subjects, as poets usually are, including mathematics. He certainly had the good poet's ability to amass knowledge. His passionate love for his family, his home, the countryside of Italy near and far, and the old history of Roman glory, is not in doubt. He was soon planning his future poetry;

1. Keats, Letter to George and Thomas Keats, Sunday, 21 December 1817: 'I had not a dispute but a disquisition with Dilke on various subjects; several things dove-tailed in my mind, and at once it struck me what quality went to form a Man of Achievement, especially in Literature, and which Shakespeare possessed so enormously. I mean Negative Capability, that is, when a man is capable of being in uncertainties, mysteries, doubts, without any irritable reaching after fact and reason – Coleridge, for instance, would let go by a fine isolated verisimilitude caught from the Penetralium of mystery, from being incapable of remaining content with half-knowledge.'

2. Rosamund E. Harding, *An Anatomy of Inspiration*, Cambridge, 1948, 71.

and already he knew that he had to work his words hard, and make the reader do his part. At some time, but perhaps not quite yet, Vergil understood his own genius, and made his secret plans.

Presently he read the Greek pastoral poems of Theocritus and others. He was swept away by their music, as we are credibly told. From now on the music of words is so central to his art that it may even be paramount, and from now on Vergil's poetic method is determined. The purpose here is to try to see how Vergil can possibly have contrived so intricate an art as he did contrive. The *Idylls* and the *Eclogues* begin to shew Vergil's plan.

He was joining, of course, the world of the Greek Hellenistic poets, and their adherents the Latin 'moderns', *neoterici*, who were producing free translations of Greek originals. Catullus freely translated Callimachus. Romans had been freely translating Greek poets for two hundred years. Free translation from the Greek can be found in Vergil. But so far as I know it is confined to small units of poetry, a line or two or less than a line, and is always part of a longer but not necessarily very long passage which is not merely a translation but much more than that.

The *Idylls* and the *Eclogues* provided Vergil with nearly all the main principles of his procedure, and started him on his characteristic co-ordination of hard thinking and inspiration. He now learnt, first, word-music, and then that balance of form in thought and expression which is central to pastoral poetry, in which it is normal for one goatherd to speak or sing and another to answer him. This addiction to balance pervades Vergil. He balances ideas, and, helped by Sallust, who was one of Vergil's more important teachers in the condensed use of Latin, carries the process so far that he regularly contrives to let two different and even contrasting meanings reside together in a single phrase or even a single word – as when he lets a word which he coined himself, *insomnia* (*Aeneid* IV, 9), neuter plural, mean both sleeplessness, *insomnia* feminine singular, and dreams, *somnia*, neuter plural. On the way to this extreme is the very important step taken when he did not translate Theocritus but blended two or more Idylls together. All the time he was helped by what he knew already, how to fit words together ingeniously, and also how to leave obscurities and ambiguities in his finished poetry. Surely all this, especially the care to avoid direct translation and to blend elements into something new, is based on conscious intention. It is deliberate policy. It seems also to be Vergil's own secret. Even Horace hardly understood it, though he believed in putting words together ingeniously, *callida iunctura*. The typical case is this: Tibullus and all the other poets who mention her present a Sibyl who is a single, known, Sibyl, whereas Vergil makes his Sibyl a blend of several known Sibyls.[1] Vergil consciously realized that, as André Gide wrote, 'The whole problem lies just in that – how to express the general by the particular – how to make the particular express the general'.[2]

Vergil would have agreed with Coleridge's requirement in *Biographia Literaria*, XIII, that the 'secondary', or poetic, imagination 'dissolves in order to recreate'. But Vergil seems generally to begin with an exact combination of not less than two existing elements. The death of Priam is a simple example. One old Greek epic said that Neoptolemus, or Pyrrhus, dragged Priam from the altar to kill him. Another said that he killed Priam actually on the altar. Vergil as usual made these sources modify each other. He kept 'altar' and kept 'drag'. But he made Pyrrhus drag Priam to, not from, the altar, and kill him there. This is more horrible still, and Vergil was also enabled to gain other poetic effects by the change. Goethe is said to have maintained that a poet ought to accept as much as possible from his sources, and alter everything so accepted, but always with the slightest possible alterations. It is strange how modern poetic theory fits Vergil so much better than most of the ancient beliefs about poetry. Vergil was an inventor.

But there were still more suggestions in Greek pastoral poems which Vergil could use. There was allegory, not very much of it but enough to shew that in a pastoral poem a countryman, a goatherd or another, could be made to represent some real person, perhaps a living poet. Obviously this suited Vergil. But he did not abandon his 'negative capability' and his ambiguity. That

1. J. H. Waszink, 'Vergil and the Sibyl of Cumae', *Mnemosyne*, Series IV, I, i, 1948, 43–58; characteristically, Vergil alone blended several Sibyls together.
2. I owe this quotation to Professor John J. H. Savage, *Transactions of the American Philological Association*, xci, 1960, 364, note 14.

is why there is so little agreement among those who try to identify the characters in the *Eclogues* with real people, poets or politicians especially; it has even been argued with exact learning and much intellectual power that Galatea is Sextus Pompeius and Amaryllis Marcus Antonius.[1] There is always at least some ancient evidence on which these identifications can be based. It still seems most probable that, as Servius thought, Vergil does not use allegory, but only suggestions emerging from partial similarities, with no exact equivalences. Vergil may even have hoped that several different schemes of suggestion would 'shimmer through' – E. K. Rand's brilliant phrase – leaving the choice to the reader. Certainly Tityrus and his mission in the First *Eclogue* appear as a blend of two distinct characters in two different situations. This example is simple. Less simple is the Fourth *Eclogue*, itself a combination of two poems of different kinds, where two or more schemes for the ages of man (of which at least one, Hesiod's, is inverted) are combined, and where a great number of identifications for the baby are possible. Here 'negative capability' is so powerfully used that it is actually legitimate to identify the baby as the Messiah: such, by nature and design, is Vergil's art. Had Vergil – in Yeats's words – 'become a vessel of the creative power of God'?

Vergil's set plan of combination, especially condensed combination, and of ambiguity with 'negative capability', runs all through his work on all scales. It appears in single words, in the *Eclogues* and after, as when *depellere*, of lambs, is 'wean' or 'drive down' – whereas 'drive up' would have been expected in the context – and *insere* might be either 'plant' or 'graft'. Vergil regularly chose words on this very principle.

If characters in the *Eclogues*, though not strictly allegorical, can suggest real, living poets and politicians, and, quite legitimately, different people to different readers, there may still be much more to find in the Eclogues. They may be poems about poets and poetry. They can also be about human life and the wide world. It is gratifying to think, and likely enough, that the Sixth *Eclogue*

1. J. J. H. Savage, ibid., lxxxix, 1958, 151ff.; cf. ibid., xci, 1960, 355ff. This article is of great interest for its treatment of Agrippa's judgement on Vergil's style, his *cacozelia*.

is actually about the history of civilization and its phases.[1] There may be many simultaneous meanings in Vergil. And he certainly may well have constructed his poems in far more elaborate and intricate symmetries than any suspected in his text before about a generation ago.

Patterns of structure in hexameter poetry, when a unitary passage of a certain number of lines is followed, immediately or after an interval, by another passage of exactly equal length, or of a proportionate length according to a fixed formula of proportion, were not invented by Vergil. They are not unknown in Homer, Apollonius Rhodius, and Catullus. They are often associated, of course, with 'emboxing', when two passages of equal length about the same subject are separated by another passage about another subject, which may, itself too, be so divided. The practice is also recognized in *Beowulf*[2] and ancient Indian epic.[3] According to the most thorough examinations Vergil operated this method in the *Eclogues* very elaborately indeed.[4]

In deciding how may lines should be comprised in his paragraphs or line-blocks, short or long and up to lengths of hundreds of lines, he certainly followed, often exactly but sometimes approximately, the 'Golden Ratio', the ratio of $1/0.618$. Not only Vergil but apparently many other Latin poets wrote according to

1. C. G. Hardie, '*Eclogue* VI'; *Virgil Society Lecture Summaries*, No. 50, 1960.
2. See p. 162 above.   3. See p. 162 note 3 above.
4. George E. Duckworth, *Structural Patterns and Proportions in Vergil's Aeneid*, Ann Arbor, Michigan, 1962, who, besides his own notable discoveries, surveys this whole question of patterning and gives references. The symmetry of equivalent numbers, as when the Fourth *Eclogue* is found to consist of seven-line paragraphs with a twenty-eight-line block in the middle, is hardly deniable. Balances of book with book or poem with poem according to subject-matter (above pp. 161-4, 172n., below p. 426) certainly exist, and exist in several different schemes, as different scholars identify them; some schemes are no doubt more authentic and significant than others; some may be accidental. So, according to certain critics, are the hundreds of symmetries according to the golden ratio which have been exposed. This can hardly be entirely so: too many of the symmetries positively exist; attractive examples, all based on the golden proportion of 21 : 13, are Vergil, *Aeneid* IV, 672-92 and 693-705, *Aeneid* XII, 919-39 and 940-52, and Horace, *Ars Poetica*, 1-294 and 295-476. At the time of writing (August 1964) the debate concerning these golden symmetries is sharp, but it seems that they can hardly be quite disproved, though some restatement may be needed.

this same golden ratio, which was also applied in ancient architecture and music and in medieval and Renaissance painting.

These balances by numbers of line occur throughout Vergil. They were first noticed in the First *Georgics*, where Father Guy Le Grelle observed that the lines given to 'Works' (*Georgics* 1, 43–203) are in 'golden ratio' to the lines given to the 'Days' (*Georgics* 1, 204–463).

There are also balances according to subject. Eight of the *Eclogues* stand in a returning symmetry about *Eclogue* v, which is itself outside the scheme, and is paired with *Eclogue* x; v is about a shepherd who has become a god and x about a friend who has become a shepherd: meanwhile, I and IX are about country life and the confiscation of a farm, II and VIII about love, III and VII about music and a singing match, IV and VI about important religious and philosophical subjects, IV being about the future and VI about the past. There are other schemes: for example, I, II, and III correspond in subject to VII, VIII, and IX respectively; all these are realistic, contrasting with IV, V, and VI which are about gods and contain fantasy; and x, sharing the characteristics of all, reconciles the central group with the other two.

The *Georgics* have similar balances: I and III end gloomily, II and IV hopefully; the messages they give are: I War, II Peace, III Death and IV Resurrection. *Georgics* I and II are about the less animated growths of vegetation, and III and IV about the more animated creatures, the animals, birds and insects. *Georgics* I and II have long prefaces, III and IV short; I, 231–58 gives the topography of the sky (including, at 240 f., references to Scythia and Libya) and III, 339–83 gives the topography of Libya and Scythia; I, 125–46 describes the labour of a farmer and IV, 125–46 the labour of an old gardener; and I, 2 and IV, 2 mention Maecenas and so do II, 41 and III, 41.

Balance and symmetry belong to the arts. In some works, and most obviously in large musical works, there is a vast and various mathematical structure.[1] In large poetic works a comparable

---

1. Dr Hazel van Rest (now Mrs David Harvey) has kindly told me that medieval German poems are carefully disposed in numerical symmetries, some copied from ancient works; she refers to Ernst Robert Curtius, *Europäische Literatur und Lateinisches Mittelalter*, Berne, 1948, Excursus xv,

structure should not cause surprise. It is present in T. S. Eliot's *Four Quartets*. But in poetry the underlying mathematics are harder to detect. They can yet contribute to aesthetic effect, even on readers unaware of them. Vergil especially, as Yeats advised, 'purified his mind with elaborate art'.

Such elaborate art must certainly involve conscious planning and calculation.[1] Vergil positively decided to blend his sources, on a large scale and on a small, down to the scale of single words and even parts of words. He decided to condense his language down to an explosive compression. He both naturally and deliberately adjusted his poetry to permit obscurities and ambiguities, leaving his readers to furnish themselves with precise meanings;

Zahlenkomposition, 493–500, and several other authorities. Meanwhile, Spenser's elaborate composition according to balanced numbers of lines has been well established in detail by Dr Alastair Fowler, *Spenser and the Numbers of Time*, London, 1964. Certainly, poets of many ages have applied numerology in their poems.

1. Thinking that plastic evidence was also needed, I questioned Mr Michael Ayrton, the artist, who has both practised and explored the art of the golden ratio, or 'golden section.' He generously wrote a reply of great interest. Here I can only offer some excerpts. 'If Vergil made use of the Golden Section in any way similar to the use made of it by painters and architects, one factor seems to me cogent. He must have used it in a fashion more complex in detail and more integral to the whole structure of his verse than the numbering of lines or episodes, however related, would imply.' In painting, the proportion, if used, must run right through the picture, on large and small scales. 'To make the postulate valid Vergil must presumably have used the division not only in large but in little. At some point *in each line* . . . a golden division should occur. Does it? Ideally the number of letters should be so related to the line. . . . Unfortunately the schemata which have gradually evolved in European art are so ingrained in our visual tradition that at various times since the Greeks all sorts of pictures may be analysed by "golden" rectangulation in a manner which would seem to prove that the system had been employed, when in fact it was not in the artist's conscious mind. . . . If he (Vergil) put words, phrases and lines in the right place and in the right order, as a result of being a great genius with a superb ear, it might be quite possible to impose a system on him posthumously which would fit pretty closely but would only prove him a natural harmonist.' This, from an artist who had never read of patterns in Vergil, seems to me of very great importance. The question of the golden symmetries is even less simple than it seems. I agree that the patterns, or most of them, are there. But much more has to be said about them.

and some of them were so expressive, and seemed so concrete, that they have been explained as allegorical. Further, Vergil planned his poems to allow an exactly balancing number of lines for unitary passages, arranging the answering line-groups in complex variety. He also had regard to the position of the word-accent in his lines, especially in the fourth foot of each hexameter, a technique apparently harmonizing with the general scheme for lines in numerical equivalence or other fixed proportion. He arranged poems and books to stand in a sequence patterned according to subjects, or themes, balancing and contrasting.

In all this patterning there seems little room, so far, for anything besides the method of conscious head-work, despised by Goethe and not admitted as even a possible method for true poetry by Plato in the *Ion*, total inspiration being essential. Ennius was perhaps more Platonic: he notoriously owed his poetry to sleep, and drink, obviously his way to inspiration. Poets certainly differ in their methods. But meanwhile Vergil, strange though it may be to recall in this context, is especially famous for the inspired kind of poetic creation. He 'stepped into the stream of rhythm and harmony' as Plato would have wished. The dominance of his 'auditory imagination' has been elaborately established. Even the highly-patterned *Eclogues* grew from a passionate love for the word-music of Greek pastoral, enjoyed, no doubt, in what Schiller called 'a musical mood', the first stage of oncoming inspiration for him. There are signs of this kind of mood in the many oddities of language in the *Eclogues*, where Vergil seems to have been too dreamy even for grammar or at least correct Latin. Schiller's second phase of inspiration is a vision of 'picture-sparks'. Perhaps they too intervened before Vergil returned to the highly rational adjustments which his poetry, especially, needed.

It is recorded that when he was writing the *Georgics* he used to deliver every morning 'a great number of lines', and spend the rest of the day 'licking them into shape', till he was left with a few, highly polished. In this he was perhaps like Milton, who also dictated poetry in the morning, having on the previous evening read some 'choice poets', either for recreation or 'to store his fancy against the morning', as his nephew, John Phillips, records.

That Vergil, like Coleridge and many more, composed poetry

in 'the deep well of unconscious cerebration' by the recombination of 'hooked atoms of thought' has been argued persuasively. Some of his poetry came out, like Coleridge's *Kubla Khan*, without 'going through' his 'head at all', to use Noel Essex's description of her own poetic process. The problem was not how to create the poetry, but how to draw out into consciousness poetry already made but still in the unconscious mind. This is exactly the theme of the famous anecdote about the half-line 'Misenum Aeoliden' (*Aeneid* VI, 164) and how Vergil completed it with two successive flashes of insight while his secretary was reading the book to him. Vergil, surely, was like Coleridge, Milton, and also Ennius but without the drink. He had no lack of sheer inspiration, if that is a fair term for poetry made by 'the secondary imagination' dissolving and recreating material existing in the unconscious mind.

Vergil himself understood his own imagination, and applied conscious thought to his unconscious mental processes. That was an important part of his secret. His composition was, therefore, in stages. He first observed, and read. Secondly, he allowed his unconscious mind to work on its store of material. Thirdly, he dictated and corrected the poetry which came into his consciousness. The problem is to discover which parts of the work were done at each of the stages.

When Vergil was writing the *Aeneid*, he first prepared a prose version. Racine wrote a prose version for at least one of his plays. Alfieri regularly wrote a prose version: his stages were 'ideare, stendere, verseggiare'.[1] For his other works Vergil may or may not have first written prose: perhaps he wrote a little prose, sometimes, as W. B. Yeats did; and perhaps he kept long notes, from the books he read. Some operations clearly belong to a prose version or notes. Among them is the deliberate plan which Vergil made for the *Aeneid*. It was to be 'a structure of great and heterogeneous complexity, including both Greek and Roman names and subjects, and designed to express both the legendary facts of early history and also the history of Augustus and his family'.[2] Vergil was now to operate, on a very large scale, exactly

1. I wish to thank Professor P. J. Yarrow for this information.
2. Donatus, *Life of Vergil*.

the same principles of combination, compression and multiple significance on which he had decided when writing the *Eclogues*. The whole scheme of the *Aeneid* works on the same principle as Vergil's invented word *'insomnia'*. And it must have been consciously devised, often with the help of prose.

However, there are signs of versified preliminary work in the *Georgics*, where some passages (II, 346–50, 350–3) appear to be short indications of longer passages in Theophrastus.[1] Each is a kind of heading. Vergil intended to expand these headings, so covering in his own way the material in Theophrastus. This material had probably been consigned to the unconscious mind for dissolution and recreation. If these observations are correct, they suggest that Vergil sometimes wrote preliminary notes in verse.

On the whole Vergil seems to have planned all his outlines and at least his larger structures in a mood of conscious thinking. There was so much of this to do that he may have found the task of fixing exactly corresponding numbers of lines for balanced passages only one more task, and a task to him not unbearably arduous. He is already known to have matched lines with lines and passages with passages by his distribution of word-accent, in coincidence with metrical ictus in the fourth foot of his verse, 'fourth-foot homodyne'.[2] And now this patterning by accent apparently harmonizes with the patterning by numbers of lines, which was discovered much later. The accentual symmetries had seemed spontaneous and unconscious. They now appear to be more conscious work, though no doubt liable, as is all conscious work, to sudden assistance from the unconscious. Here there are examples of one technique which must have been deliberate, and of another too which, were it not for this separate evidence, might have been spontaneous and not consciously willed.[3]

1. I wish to thank Mr L. A. S. Jermyn for this suggestion: perhaps I may here express profound gratitude for his other kindnesses, especially his selfless service to the Virgil Society.

2. W. F. Jackson Knight, *Accentual Symmetry in Vergil*, Oxford, 1939.

3. As I said above, there is a sharp controversy concerning some of the patterns and proportions. I provisionally assume, and indeed believe, that they will on the whole survive criticism. To what extent they were consciously devised and applied may be more doubtful than I imply. See above p. 427n.

How Vergil planned the *Aeneid*, and composed it by the careful direction of his own exceptional powers, is a problem both complex and subtle. He may have made elaborate notes with long extracts from books read, and the prose draft may have been long and full. Many lines may have been contrived by ingenious jigsaw-manipulation. Many delicate meanings may have been calculated thoughtfully. But the greatest passages do not look like this. They are surely discharged in a stream of inspiration. Quite evidently the sources are forgotten, and it is a re-creation based on elements from them, which is present. They are sensuous, not intellectual; they are determined not by thought but by sound, and dominated by Vergil's 'auditory imagination'. Vergil knew that they would be, and prepared.

The more his preparation is understood, the more astounding it is. For his Dido, he probably copied out earlier poetry concerning Ajax, Ariadne, Heracles, Medea, Nausicaa and even Dido herself, next learnt it by heart, and then slept on it, allowing his unconscious mind to dissolve the material and recreate it in a new combination, now becoming great poetry, and indeed depth poetry.[1] This he may have dictated, after sleep, each morning, and then corrected. He must have known that Ennius drew his poetry from sleep, as Keats in *Sleep and Poetry* (348) stated explicitly that he did. However, usually more time is needed for gestation. Between the collection of the material and the dictation of the poetry five, ten, or more years may normally have elapsed. But reading, on the evening before composition, could still be valuable for 'working up' – Blake's phrase – 'the vision'.

The sources for Dido converge on Dido. This is normal. So is divergence. Sources are dislocated and dissolved; and their elements are redistributed. Convergence and divergence are complementary. Thus Vergil, most consciously aware of the law which he had created and accepted, broke up the Cassandra of the old Greek epic. He transferred elements from her to Laocoon, to Dido, to the Sibyl, to Helen in his Sixth *Aeneid*, and to Amata. This is so tidy and economical that it looks deliberate. But dream-

1. The contemporary novelist, Mrs Elizabeth Jenkins, writes down her problems at night in the form 'I want to know ...'. In the morning she has the answer. She considers it a year later.

poetry, direct from the unconscious, can be tidy and economical too. Coleridge's *Kubla Khan*, certainly produced in sleep, is very tidy and economical, and very much compressed also.

Here and elsewhere a certain dream-association, or some sense of allurement linking memories together, some mysterious poetic attraction, perhaps, may have exercised an appeal at a very early stage in the process.[1] There is an astonishing example in some place-names intricately used by Vergil in his account of the beginning of the war in Latium. Two Latin heroes are killed, Almo and Galaesus (*Aeneid* VII, 531–9). Both were at first rivers, the Almo near Rome and connected with Cybele, and the Galaesus flowing into the gulf of Tarentum, a place which interested Vergil when writing the *Georgics*. Soon after Vergil mentions another hero, also on the side of the Latins, Oebalus, son of Sebethis, nymph of the small river Sebethus which flows into the sea near Naples (*Aeneid* VII, 733–6). Oebalus was also the name of a Spartan king, said to have been the founder of Tarentum, called by Vergil Oebalian in the *Georgics*, just before the mention of the river Galaesus there (*Georgics* IV, 125–9).

The proposal is that Vergil associated these names together, perhaps quite early in his career. He had certainly seen all the three rivers before he wrote the *Aeneid*. At some unknown time a reason for the artistic association of the names occurred to Vergil. All the three localities were important in the Second Punic War, and associated with Hannibal. So Vergil, in recounting the war between Aeneas and the Latins, contrived to suggest also allusions to the Second Punic War, the war with Hannibal.

Now the Spartan king Oebalus was the father of Tyndareus by a water-nymph Bateia. Tyndareus was father of Helen. Bateia was also the name of Teucer's daughter. Teucer was a king of Troy, and by his daughter Bateia, whom Dardanus married, became the ancestor both of Paris and Aeneas, so helping Vergil to make the war in Italy fought by Aeneas parallel not only to the Second Punic War but also to the Trojan War itself. It is a kind of literary counterpoint.

Such is a small, uncertain, glimpse of an astonishing part of

1. The following paragraphs are based on Robert W. Cruttwell, *Virgil's Mind at Work*, Oxford, 1946, 41–54.

Vergil's secret art. He let his very complex structure arise not mechanically but organically. At certain stages there are unconscious associations, offering possibilities. These possibilities Vergil pursued with a keen sense of the relevant and an economy which forgot nothing. The result is like the veins on a leaf, but to say this is superficial, for the comparison needs many leaves, interpenetrating.

Meanwhile the movement is also a chain-reaction. Teucer's Bateia is the Myrine whose tomb was outside Troy; in Homer Aeneas leads Trojan forces past it on one side and Ascanius leads Phrygian forces past it on the other side (Homer, *Iliad* II, 811-15, 819-21, 862-3). Vergil calls the place an ancient mound of Ceres, and it is used not for dividing a marching army but as a meeting-point for the refugees escaping from Troy (*Aeneid* II, 713-16). The smaller technique of variation continues. The genealogies are of course continually exploited. Aeneas arrived at the mound with his Penates, and Vergil calls them here 'Teucrian Penates'. Now Dardanus had a brother Iasus, Iasius, or Iasion. Both were born at Cortona in Italy. Dardanus married Bateia at Troy. Iasius lay with Demeter-Ceres 'in a furrow', according to some authorities in Crete. Their son was Plutus, "Wealth". Now Dionysius of Halicarnassus has a story that certain gods appeared to Aeneas in Italy, encouraging him. Vergil transferred the incident to Crete, where the Trojans landed by mistake. And he linked it with the tradition of Iasius. He combined the obscure gods who appeared to Aeneas in Italy with the Plutus who was the son of Iasius and Demeter-Ceres, and neatly turned them into the Penates, Teucrian and Roman. They speak to Aeneas, telling him to go to Italy, birthplace of Dardanus and their own father, Iasius (*Aeneid* III, 147-71). The *Aeneid* grows like an oak from an acorn, according to the intricate and peremptory laws of its growth.

It is recorded that when Vergil could not solve a problem and create a good line he would write a temporary line, a 'pitprop', 'so that nothing might delay the onrush' of the poetry. Clearly, then, Vergil produced poetry in a spontaneous, rapid stream. The Romans used to ask whether poets were born or made, whether poets wrote 'by nature' or 'by skill', '*poeta nascitur an fit?*', '*natura scribit* [*poeta*] *an arte?*' Vergil characteristically reconciled the two functions, and directed his own inspiration. He was not content with the precepts of either Plato or Horace alone, or the practice of either Ennius or Catullus. He used both.

Longinus called Theocritus 'the most felicitous of poets'. Vergil could equal him in felicity but not all the time. His method of intense compression of meaning involved risk. Some years ago a distinguished scholar argued that Ovid's clear and precise poetry is the right sort, but Vergil's is the wrong sort, being less precise in outline and sometimes obscure. It is more likely that Vergil was simply doing something harder, and succeeding nearly always, but not quite always. He was not, as Longinus called Apollonius Rhodius, 'dead safe'. Longinus adds 'But who would not rather be Homer?' We could add, 'Or Vergil?'

Vergil's ardour for compression – *et est sermo in compendium coactus* as Servius would say – evoked the strictures of Gellius, or his character, the redoubtable Favorinus. To describe Etna, Vergil (*Aeneid* III, 570–7) used Pindar's description (*Pythian* I, 40–50), and, according to the accusation, made nonsense of it. Vergil, though famed for his incomparable elegance, has left many unpolished lines which are quite unworthy of him. The lines on Etna, says Favorinus, are the worst of all. Indeed, Vergil has hardly even begun to compose them. Pindar is luxuriant enough; Vergil is unbearably inflated. Pindar at least keeps to fact, and says that Etna emits smoke in the day-time and flames at night. But Vergil, being too busy looking for words noisy enough to satisfy him – a blow for 'auditory imagination' – positively confused day and night together. Pindar's snake-like streams of lava are correct. Vergil's 'black cloud smoking with a cyclone of pitch and white-hot ash' is just not in the scheme of things. What is white-hot cannot smoke, neither can it be black. Favorinus thinks that the best defence would be to accuse Vergil of a vulgar error in supposing 'white-hot' to mean no more than 'hot'. When we come to Vergil's 'stones and rocks hoisted aloft', and then 'melting, groaning, and crowding together in the sky', our experience as readers is infinitely more fantastic than any that the Trojans could have undergone on the spot. Gellius – or Favorinus – is very stern.

From a modern standpoint Vergil is easily defended. He was inventing a new kind of poetry, with richer meanings, closer reasoning, the effects of atmosphere, and a certain surrealistic impact. Ways are opened to metaphor, ambiguity, and atmosphere. Vergil behaved like Picasso, when Picasso shews together two things which in nature cannot be seen together, or develops Velasquez' portrait of Philip II to make his own version. Vergil of course did not copy Pindar. He used him to detonate his own imagination. As a painter, having seen an actual landscape, does not copy it but creates a poem in paint about the landscape which he has seen, so Vergil created his poetry partly as poetry about the poetry of the past. According to Goethe the best things in any work of art are what are taken from tradition. Vergil found the right way to take them.

There is a view, held by Sir Joshua Reynolds, that artists must examine the great works of the past if they are to create good works themselves. Vergil made much use of earlier passages which are by no means great. He found many in Apollonius.

When the Jason and Medea of Apollonius get married in a Cave of the Nymphs there is nothing mysterious.[1] Everything is clear and rational, a plain attractive narrative. The comparison with Vergil is important:

> *speluncam Dido dux et Troianus eandem*
> *deveniunt. prima et Tellus et pronuba Iuno*
> *dant signum. fulsere ignes et conscius aether*
> *conubiis, summoque ulularunt vertice Nymphae.*

> (*Aeneid* IV, 165–8).

The Nymphs are obscurely remote: yet originally it was in their cave that the wedding took place. There is plenty more to notice, especially in what Vergil carefully does not say, and in his order of ideas. Several of Vergil's great and numinous passages make use of some very plain narratives in Apollonius.

Comparisons with Apollonius often illustrate Vergil's secret

1. For this comparison with Apollonius Rhodius I acknowledge the help of Mr Preshous and his thesis on the subject, which I hope will be published soon; cf. J. D. M. Preshous, *The Sources of Vergil's Aeneid with special reference to Apollonius Rhodius*, Bristol University Thesis, 1961; and see Markus Hügi, *Vergils Aeneis und die hellenistische Dichtung*, Berne, 1952.

methods of thought and of choice. There are good examples in, and behind, the famous *insomnia*,

Anna soror, quae me suspensam insomnia terrent?

(*Aeneid* IV, 9).

The complicated subtlety here was developed from some long, expansive expressions in Apollonius. After a description of all the rest of the world asleep (*Argonautica* III, 744–50), Apollonius writes,[1] 'In her yearning for Jason, fretful cares kept her (Medea) awake' (III, 752). There is also: 'Meanwhile the maiden lay on her bed, fast asleep, with all her cares forgotten. But not for long. Dreams assailed her, deceitful dreams, the nightmares of a soul in pain' (III, 616–18). There is, too, Medea's speech on awakening: 'Chalciope, I am terrified for your sons. I am afraid that father will destroy them out of hand, strangers and all. I had a little sleep just now, and in a nightmare that is what I saw' (III, 688–91). If Vergil's line is rightly translated and understood, he is seen to have expressed in five words many lines of Apollonius, and added, by his peculiar art, a suggestive mystery which allows the reader to imagine far more, even, than can be found in the prolix Apollonius. A characteristic stroke of genius, in substituting a question for a statement, greatly helped. Besides the compression, that is, the convergence, there is as usual divergence. The thought 'fast asleep with all her cares forgotten' (III, 616 with 744–50) is transferred by Vergil to his picture of all the world, men and animals, asleep, but not Dido, and joined to a much altered version of the description in Apollonius of the sleeping world (*Argonautica* III, 744–50: *Aeneid* IV, 522–32). '*Brevis esse laboro, obscurus fio*', said Horace. Vergil, with his queer taste for paradox, discovered that he liked, and could use, obscurity. Medea in Apollonius could not keep her mind off Jason: 'The whole scene was still before her eyes – how Jason looked, the clothes he wore, the things he said, the way he sat on his chair, and how he walked to the door. It seemed to her, as she reviewed these images, that there was nobody like Jason. His voice, and the honey-sweet words that he

1. I gratefully use Dr E. V. Rieu's Penguin translation.

had used, still rang in her ears' (*Argonautica* III, 453–8). Vergil has

> *multa viri virtus animo multusque recursat*
> *gentis honos: haerent infixi pectore voltus*
> *verbaque nec placidam membris dat cura quietem*
>
> (*Aeneid* IV, 3–5)

and

> *quis novus hic nostris successit sedibus hospes,*
> *quem sese ore ferens, quam forti pectore et armis!*
>
> (*Aeneid* IV, 10–11).

Again a question saves space and adds mystery. This time a great deal of Apollonius is suppressed: Vergil surely liked Apollonius, who deserved it, but he was writing a different kind of poetry. He excluded detail, as when in the second *Aeneid* he reduced a long, dreary list of multifarious killing, which he found, apparently, in some old Greek poem on the sack of Troy, to

> *crudelis ubique*
> *luctus, ubique pavor, et plurima mortis imago*
>
> (*Aeneid* II, 368–9).

These examples should be added to countless verbal usages, mainly metaphorical and resulting from combination and compression, such as *caeso sanguine*, 'blood from slain victims' (*Aeneid* XI, 82), *tela exit*, 'avoids the weapons' (*Aeneid* V, 438), and *occumbere morti*, 'meet death' (*Aeneid* II, 62), a mixture of Ennius *morti occumbant obviam* (Ennius, *Scenic fragments*, 135–6 Vahlen, 3rd ed.) and *occumbunt multi letum ferroque lapique* (Ennius, *Annals*, 398 Vahlen, 3rd ed.).[1]

Taken together, this material may be allowed to suggest how Vergil thought. He knew his own mind and his own laws for working. He read generally, and he read specifically. Particularly he read, for the poetry concerning Dido, the *Argonautica* of Apollonius. He or a secretary may have copied out many lines of this poem as notes. Now the effect of the material from Apollonius is not only decorative; it is also structural. Therefore it must have been used already for Vergil's prose draft. It has been truly

1. See above, p. 414n.

said that without Apollonius the *Aeneid* would have been entirely different.

It was mainly when Vergil turned his prose into verse that he effected his smaller combinations and compressions. Excision and abbreviation are characteristic of 'head-work'. Long gestation gave him a stream of verse each morning. Unconscious cerebration and memory had already adapted the source-material to fit – approximately – the new story, or the new form of the story. But compression, explosive power, and 'elegance', as Gellius would say, were not perfect. It was principally while 'licking his rough lines into shape' that the omissions, the abbreviations, and the compressions were achieved, as Vergil said the lines over, aloud, to see what would come.

He always liked compression. But it has now been suggested that he was subject to a further influence, which could have enforced it – the need to organize the parts of his work by 'the golden ratio' in the number of their lines.[1] Perhaps even this heavy additional burden would have been, to Vergil's enormous intellectual power, tolerable enough. To us, if it helped him to perfect his incomparably thoughtful style, it is a blessing.

There exists a very good short edition of the Fourth *Aeneid* with a commentary which almost or quite ignores the relation of Vergil to Apollonius. Certainly, Vergil had to depend on sources. But a reader may well ignore his dependence on them and treat other matters as so important that the interest of smaller-scale technique fades. The Dido whom Vergil created with such immense toil is eloquent, however little that toil is remembered. Like Allecto,[2] Dido carries profound meaning for the nature and history of mankind.

Dido is a Graeco-Roman heroine, but still more she is, and had been, a Phoenician goddess, Anat-Elishat, her two names providing both Dido's other name Elissa and the name of Dido's

1. See above, pp. 425–6.

2. Allecto is exquisitely integrated from Greek plays, extant or lost, concerning Dionysus, from Homer's Eris, 'Strife', Euripides' Lyssa, 'Madness', and Ennius' Discord, besides, no doubt, much more; and she carries these powerful significances with her; see W. F. J. Knight, 'The Integration of Allecto', *The Classical Journal* (Malta), III, 1948, 3–4.

sister, Anna.[1] Now in early times goddesses, not gods, had been dominant in Mediterranean lands. But, through the arrival of migrating peoples of Indo-European speech, gods everywhere prevailed over goddesses – everywhere except at Carthage. Carthage, therefore, represents an older order. It is supported by Juno the Roman goddess who is especially a goddess of women. Against Carthage and against Juno, Rome and the Roman Jupiter must prevail.

There is surely some truth in the view advanced by Erich Neumann that rituals of initiation have as part of their intention the purpose of enlivening the progressive, masculine element in societies and preventing this from relapsing into a more static condition, the matrix of the feminine.[2] If such was the purpose, that is sufficient here. The purpose need not have been well conceived. Perhaps the feminine element is unjustly maligned as an influence for mere stability. Socrates thought it the source of prophecy. But the symbol existed, and is mightily used by Vergil. Rome has to go forward, and 'pass the whole earth under laws', *totum sub leges mitteret orbem* (*Aeneid* IV, 231). Instinct and passion are not enough; clear judgement and will and cerebral control must lead. Vergil could have told the story without Dido. Others did. Or he might, with others again, have made Dido a heroine not of passion but of self-sacrifice. But he preferred to serve the deepest truth. Even then, the end is in, not victory, but reconciliation.

Perhaps we cannot see very clearly into the secrets of Vergil, his lonely art, which made him unique, the one and only Vergil whose power reaches always farther, and always, however his readers and their times may differ, prevails.

1. E. Paratore, 'Nuove interpretazioni del Mito di Didone', *Studi e Materiali di Storia delle Religioni*, xxvi, 1955, 71–82; cf. C. Picard, *Les religions de l'Afrique antique*, Paris, 1954, 26–55.

2. E. Neumann, *The Origins and History of Consciousness*, Pantheon Books, New York, 1954.

INDEX OF NAMES

Accius, Lucius, 67

Actium, 63, 79, 91–2, 94, 132, 138, 141, 186, 364

Aelian, 229

Aeschylus, 33, 43, 47–8, 149, 153, 169–70, 175, 178, 180, 187–8, 348, 379, 384, 390
  Prometheus Unbound, 67
  Prometheus Bound, 149
  Persae, 187
  Seven against Thebes, 204

Agathon (poet), 111

Agathyllus (poet), 138

Agrippa, M. Vipsanius, 63, 79–80, 89, 91, 101, 318, 362, 416, 424n

Albinus, Clodius, 376

Alcaeus, 42, 155

Alcman, 233

Alexander 'Polyhistor', 81

Alexander the Great, 14–15, 22, 29, 31, 50, 168

Alfieri, Vittorio, 429

Alfonsi, Luigi, 9, 33n, 51n, 68n, 78n, 230n, 240n, 370n

Altheim, Franz, 74n, 204n

Anacreon, 42

Anat-Elishat, 438

Anchises, 97, 115–16, 119, 132–3, 138, 146, 170, 172n, 176–7, 180, 195–6, 216, 255, 333, 365–6, 390, 397

Anderson, W. B., 90n

Andes (Pietole), 54, 58, 152

Andronicus, 81

Anna, 129–30, 170, 313–14, 352, 439

Antiochus of Syracuse, 136

Antonius, Lucius, 60, 75

Antonius, Marcus, 24, 59–63, 69, 74–5, 77, 83, 86, 91, 125, 188, 424

Apollo, 32, 36, 47, 55, 92, 97, 131, 133, 142, 176, 198, 207–8, 220, 233, 256, 339, 353, 389–90, 392

Apollodorus, 71

Apollonius Rhodius, 49, 105, 128–30, 153, 166, 190, 214, 249, 425, 434–8

Aratus, 67, 82, 121, 153, 158

Archias, A. Licinius, 81

Archilochus, 237

Aristarchus, 345

Aristogeiton, 181

Aristophanes, 32, 43, 237, 257, 348, 384

Aristotle, 15, 18, 29–30, 33, 48, 102, 149, 160, 169, 175, 189, 197, 237, 342, 394, 402
  Poetics, 149
  Constitution of Athens, 342

Arnaldi, Francesco, 222n

Arundel, Rosemary M., 388n

Arval Brothers, Hymn of the, 282, 329

Ascanius, *see* Iulus

Atkins, J. W. H., 80n

Atticus, 81, 362

Attila, 39

Auden, W. H., 104, 148

Augustus Caesar (Octavianus), 16, 52–3, 59–61, 63–4, 73–80, 88–91, 93–4, 97, 129, 148, 152, 164, 185, 188–9, 207, 212, 346, 362–7, 375–6, 392–3, 429

Austin, R. G., 9, 230, 289n, 347n, 382, 404n

Avitus, Q. Octavius, 102

Ayrton, Michael, 427n

Bacchylides, 342

Bacon, Janet, 222, 223, 224n

Badian, Ernst, 9, 228n

Bailey, Cyril, 114n

Baudouin, Charles, 106n

Bauer, Douglas F., 369n

Beare, W., 46, 294n

Bell, Andrew J., 400n, 404n, 411n

Bellum Hispaniense, 412

Benecke, E. F. M., 100n

Benvenuto da Imola, 122

Beowulf, 162, 425
Bérard, Victor, 244
Bergson, Henri, 31
Berkeley, George, 248
Bibaculus, M. Furius, 64, 67
Bignone, Ettore, 9
Bion, 153
Blake, William, 431
Blegen, Carl, 193
Blonk, Anna G. de T., 166n, 190n, 243n
Bowra, Sir Maurice, 9, 114n, 118, 164n, 349, 381n, 395
Boyancé, Pierre, 368n, 398n
Bridges, Robert, 65
Brown, B. Goulding, 9
Browning, Robert, 105
Brutus, M. Junius, 23, 61, 71–2, 75–6, 86, 368
Buchheit, Vinzenz, 126n, 176n, 222n
Büchner, Karl, 9, 52n, 68n, 85n, 227, 400n, 420n
Bury, J. B., 34, 35n
Buscaroli, Corso, 340, 382
Butler, H. E., 126n, 245n
Butler, Samuel, 146
Byron, Lord, 109, 389

Caecilius (of Novum Comum), 64
Caecilius, Quintus, 362
Calidius, Marcus, 69–70
Caligula (Gaius Caesar), 373
Callimachus, 49, 51, 85, 153, 160, 300, 329, 422
  Hymn to Zeus, 300
Callinus of Ephesus, 51
Calpurnius Siculus, 371
Calvus, C. Licinius, 67, 69–71, 76
  Zmyrna, 67
Camillus, M. Furius, 148
Campbell, Lewis, 252n
Carcopino, Jérôme, 185n
Carlyle, Thomas, 385
Carthage, 15, 96, 127, 132, 146, 159, 177, 198, 207, 219, 224, 240–1, 244, 260, 354–5, 365, 385, 439
Cassius, Gaius, 61, 75, 81, 86
Castiglioni, L., 11, 345n, 382
Cataudella, Quintino, 9
Cato, M. Porcius, the elder, 129, 136, 158, 211, 280, 373, 402, 415
  Origins, 204

Cato, M. Porcius, the younger, 20, 23, 174, 366
Cato, P. Valerius, 64, 67
Catullus, C. Valerius, 45, 51, 58, 64–74, 76–8, 80, 85, 104–5, 114, 118–19, 121, 130–1, 153, 159–60, 162, 188–9, 228, 230–1, 235, 238, 241, 266, 293–4, 296, 305, 316, 318–19, 328–30, 351, 369, 393, 401, 408, 420, 422, 425, 434
  The Lock of Berenice, 118
  The Marriage of Peleus and Thetis, 70, 162, 230
Catulus, Q. Lutatius, 66
Cerda, J. L. de la, 381
Chadwick, H. M., 164n
Chaucer, Geoffrey, 101, 105, 379
Chekhov, Anton, 379
Chesterton, G. K., 15
Choerilus of Samos, *Persica*, 188
Christie, John D., 9, 11, 415n
Cicero, M. Tullius, 13, 21–3, 45, 50, 56, 59–61, 67, 69–70, 72, 74–5, 80, 158, 187, 225–6, 228n, 231–2, 236, 278, 280, 318–19, 351, 362, 373, 383, 385–7, 393, 400–3, 407–10, 413n, 415
  Auctor ad Herennium, 407
  De Consulatu Suo, 67
  De Finibus, 80
  De Re Publica, 187
  In Pisonem, 80
  Somnium Scipionis, 387
Cinna, C. Helvius, 64, 67, 74
Claudianus, Claudius, 211, 371
Claudius Caecus, Appius, 20, 236, 280
Claudius Gothicus, Emperor, 376
Clayton, F. W., 23n
Cleopatra, 63, 91, 128, 216, 234, 365
Clodius Pulcher, P., 59
Coleman, Robert, 90n, 208n
Coleridge, S. T., 44, 101–6, 109–11, 113, 149, 250, 421n, 423, 428–9, 432
  Ancient Mariner, 104
  Biographia Literaria, 103, 423
  Dejection, 103
  Kubla Khan, 103, 109, 250, 429, 432
Columella, L. Junius Moderatus, 159
Commodianus, 296

Comparetti, Domenico, 100, 372, 375
Conington, John, 381
Connolly, Cyril, 9
Constantine the Great, 375-6, 391
Conway, R. S., 125n, 144n, 150, 169,
   172, 174n, 217n, 250, 366, 368,
   382, 394
Cook, R. M., 161n
Cordier, A., 400n, 402n
Cornificius, Quintus, 70, 72, 145
Crassus, M. Licinius, 23, 58, 91
Crawford, O. G. S., 17
Creophylus, 161
Crome, J. F., 56n
Crump, M. M., 96n
Cruttwell, R. W., 173, 189, 195n, 207,
   208n, 209n, 210-11, 222, 245n,
   354, 432n
Currie, H. MacL., 371n
Curtis, Lionel, 392
Curtius, E. R., 426n
Cynics, the, 18, 386

Dante Alighieri, 105, 122, 164, 238,
   323, 326, 377-80
Delphi, 35-6, 207, 233, 235, 390
Democritus, 18, 65
Deutsch, Rosamund E., 300, 329n
De Witt, Norman W., 393n
Dido (Elissa), 96, 117-18, 122, 124-
   32, 142, 146-7, 159, 168, 170-2,
   174, 180-4, 188, 192, 207, 215-
   16, 218-19, 221, 223, 236, 239,
   247-8, 252-3, 257-8, 274, 295,
   301-4, 307, 312-14, 324, 326,
   333-4, 352, 354-5, 365, 375, 378,
   385, 389, 395, 431, 437-9
Diogenes the Cynic, 18
Dionysius of Halicarnassus, 44, 135-
   42, 177, 197, 433
Diphilus, 49, 182
Doerpfeld, Wilhelm, 193
Dolabella, P. Cornelius, 81
Donatus, Aelius, 52, 56, 61, 64, 79,
   82, 84-5, 87-8, 90, 92, 95, 97,
   102, 107-8, 146, 319, 337, 347,
   354, 359-60
Donatus, Tiberius Claudius, 358, 373
Donne, John, 104-5
Drew, D. L., 163n, 219n, 364
Dryden, John, 325, 337-8, 381

Duckworth, George E., 10, 164n, 172n,
   425n
Duque, Angel M., 166n
Dwyer, J. J., 9

Echave-Sustaeta, Javier de, 276n,
   381n, 411n
Edwards, W. A., 102n
Eleatics, the, 18
Eleusis, 32-3, 151, 386
Eliot, T. S., 9, 100-1, 104, 111, 225n,
   300, 318, 323, 381, 427
   Four Quartets, 427
Elissa, see Dido
Ellis, R., 10
Elysium, 115, 133, 208-9, 211, 271,
   366
Empedocles, 65, 233
Empson, William, 251, 346
Enk, P. J., 9, 294n
Ennius, Quintus, 19, 49, 66-7, 94,
   106, 114-18, 153-4, 159, 164,
   169, 172, 176, 187, 189, 197, 233,
   238, 253, 264, 274, 280, 282, 286,
   351, 373, 395, 402, 405, 409,
   413-14, 428-9, 431, 434, 437
Epicharmus, 229
Epictetus, 18
Epicurus, 18, 21, 60, 65-6, 393
Epidius (teacher of Vergil), 59, 69
Eratosthenes, 158, 193
Eros (secretary of Vergil), 108, 347
Essex, Noel, 109, 381, 429
Etruscans, the, 15, 30, 37, 53-4, 78,
   133-7, 140, 177, 193, 198-205,
   257, 309, 365
Eudoxus, 158
Eugammon, 161
Euphorion, 51, 67, 73, 106, 191
Euripides, 19, 48-9, 51, 124, 128-9,
   156, 171, 175, 178, 180-1, 184, 190,
   203, 300, 384
   Alcestis, 300
   Hippolytus, 129
Evans, Sir Arthur, 199

Fabius Maximus Cunctator, Q., 115-17
Faictz merveilleux de Virgille, Les, 377
Falconer, Sir Robert, 391
Farrington, B., 21n, 222n, 387
Faustus, Perellius, 102

Favorinus, 434
Flecker, James Elroy, 340
Fletcher, Sir Frank, 257n, 382
Fordyce, C. J., 70n
Fowler, Alistair, 427n
Fraenkel, Eduard, 77n, 400n, 407n, 420n
Frank, Tenney, 53, 56n, 70n, 72n, 73n, 86
Fränkel, Hermann, 369n
Frazer, H. Malcolm, 208n
Friedrich, Wolf Hartmut, 174, 251, 346
Fronto, M. Cornelius, 410
Fulgentius, Fabius Planciades, 374
Funaioli, Gino, 113n
Fundanius, 70–1

Gallus, Cornelius, 52, 62, 70–4, 77, 81, 85–6, 90, 179, 188, 191, 259, 363, 401
Garden Academy, The, 60, 76, 80–1, 86, 191, 393, 395
Garstang, J. B., 390n
Gaster, Theodor, 40
Gautier, Théophile, 238
Geikie, Sir A., 186n
Gelasius, Pope, 377
Gelder, J. van, 45, 311, 329n
Gellius, Aulus, 344, 360–1, 373, 434, 438
Gercke, A., 95n
Gesta Romanorum, 377
Gide, André, 423
Gilgamish, The Epic of, 40, 168, 353, 387
Gilkes, Martin, 106
Giotto, 377
Gjerstad, E., 15n
Gladstone, W. E., 100
Glover, T. R., 223
Glucker, John, 10
Goethe, Johann Wolfgang von, 95, 100, 110, 237, 423, 428, 435
Gogarty, O. St. J., 180, 241, 377, 381, 398
Gonçalves, Francisco R., 9
Gordon, Mary L., 55n
Gossage, A. J., 371n
Gracchus, Gaius, 69
Gracchus, Tiberius, 384
Granarolo, J., 68n

Gray, Thomas, 101, 381
Greece, 14–15, 22, 27, 31, 33, 40, 91, 135, 193–5, 199–200, 202, 383, 388, 392
Gregory the Great, Pope, 391
Guarducci, M., 140n
Guillemin, A.–M., 101, 107, 218n, 236, 259n, 350

Haarhoff, T. J., 9, 11, 31, 90n, 169, 208n, 211n, 350, 394, 399
Hades, 190, 209–10, 216, 244, 253, 307, 353, 387
Hadrian, Emperor, 373, 376
Haecker, Theodor, 397
Halter, Thomas, 45n, 300n, 329n
Hammurabi, Code of, 27
Hannibal, 115–16, 130, 372, 432
Hardie, Colin G., 10, 85n, 425n
Hardie, W. R., 287n
Harding, Rosamund E., 421n
Harmodius, 181
Harrison, Jane, 47
Harvey, Mrs David, see Rest, Hazel van
Hatt, Mrs E. M., 9
Haupt, M., 70n
Haury, Auguste, 85n
Havelock, E. A., 233–4
Haverfield, F., 381
Head, B. V., 195n
Hegel, G. W. F., 280, 383
Heinsius, Nicolas, 343, 349
Heinze, R., 46n, 113n, 382n
Hellanicus, 138
Henry, J., 122n, 382
Heraclitus, 18, 35
Herculaneum, 60, 393
Herescu, N. I., 290n, 297n, 329n, 403n
Herod the Great, 90
Herodotus, 26, 31, 35, 162–3
Hesiod, 27, 34–5, 106, 122, 154, 156–9, 195, 219, 233, 402, 424
Works and Days, 156
Heyne, C. G., 381
Hiero of Syracuse, 199
Highbarger, E. L., 173n
Hipponax, 237
Hirtius, Aulus, 81
Hirtzel, F. A., 10
Hofmann, J. B., 68n, 404n

Holinshed, Raphael, 149
Homer, 26, 30, 32–5, 40–2, 46–8, 50,
    99–100, 104, 110, 112–13, 122,
    127–8, 146–8, 153, 159–69, 171–5,
    178–9, 183, 185, 188, 190,
    192, 194–5, 197, 203–5, 208,
    213–14, 220, 227, 229, 233–4,
    237, 246, 254, 259, 264, 282,
    300, 317, 326, 337, 345–6, 348–51,
    373–4, 384, 386–8, 395, 425, 433–4
    Iliad, 40, 78, 100, 112, 142, 148,
        161, 165–6, 168, 175–6, 183, 186,
        190, 216–17, 259, 349, 362
    Odyssey, 40, 46, 49, 55, 67, 100, 123–4,
        127, 130, 142, 146, 159, 165,
        167, 175–7, 186, 190, 195, 247,
        281, 353, 387
Hopkins, G. Manley, 318, 416
Horace (Q. Horatius Flaccus), 13–14,
    19, 57–8, 70–1, 76–80, 101, 114,
    159, 242, 246, 316–17, 319, 364,
    366, 368–9, 393, 401–2, 423, 434
Horrox, Lewis, 9
Hortensius, Quintus, 69–70
Hose, H. F., 9
Hügi, Markus, 435n
Hunt, Terence J., 10

Imhotep, 27
Inge, W. R., 392
Isaiah, 81
Isherwood, Christopher, 148
Ishtar, The Descent of, 40, 168
Italicus, see Silius Italicus
Italy, 24, 27, 37, 49, 59, 61, 63–4, 75,
    77, 84, 89–91, 93, 97, 107, 120,
    131–2, 136, 138–9, 141–2, 152,
    157–8, 168, 176, 189, 191–2, 194–6,
    198–205, 210–11, 217, 223, 229,
    234, 261, 280, 336, 342, 365,
    383, 385, 388, 390–1, 433
Iulus (Ascanius), 110, 134–5, 137, 139,
    146, 172, 176, 181–2, 215, 224,
    259, 317, 334, 365, 433

James, B. Scott, 9
James, L. G., 9
James, William 44, 103
Jeffers, Robinson, 144
Jenkins, Mrs Elizabeth, 431n
Jermyn, L. A. S., 400n, 430n

Johnson, Samuel, 100, 155
Joyce, James, 260
Julia (d. of Augustus), 365, 367
Julius Caesar, 23–4, 53, 58–60, 69–72,
    74–5, 81, 83–4, 89, 93, 116, 145,
    188, 203, 231, 236, 365–6, 368,
    370, 392, 408, 410, 413n
Jung, C. G., 392
Juno, 97, 125, 127, 132–4, 147, 171,
    175–6, 182, 185, 207–8, 239, 274,
    304–5, 307, 319, 325, 333, 357,
    389, 406, 415, 439
Justinus, 126, 130
Juvenal, 372

Kalevala, 213
Keats, John, 35, 56, 396, 421, 431
Kellett, E. E., 101
Kinkel, G., 122n
Kipling, Rudyard, 111
Klingner, Friedrich, 382n
Knapp, C., 121, 186
Knight, G. Wilson, 11, 88n, 103, 109n,
    149, 189n, 206n, 378n, 379, 380n
Knight, W. F. Jackson, 26n, 40n, 48n
    63n, 100n, 109n, 116n, 118n,
    123n, 140n, 168n–70n, 194n,
    210n, 227n, 246n, 248n, 250n,
    290n, 292n, 299n, 306n, 353n,
    355n, 365n, 367n, 387n, 403n,
    430n, 438n
Kvičala, J., 358

Laevius (poet), 66
Laidlaw, W. A., 220
Landels, John G., 212n
Landor, W. S., 101
Latium, 15, 97, 110, 121, 129, 131–4,
    136, 141, 166, 175, 177, 181, 194–
    5, 197, 199, 201, 209, 214–15, 239,
    254, 305, 317, 333, 335, 432
Lavinium, 97, 134–5, 137, 140
Leech, D. J. G., 46n
Le Grelle, Guy, 426
Leo, F., 350
Lepidus, M. Aemilius, 60
Lewis, C. Day, 104
Lindsay, W. M., 246n
Lindsell, Alice, 185n
Livia, 366
Livius Andronicus, 46, 106, 281, 414n

Livy (Titus Livius), 13–14, 20, 78, 134–5, 141, 197, 226, 231, 242–3, 370, 404, 408
Lloyd, L. J., 105n
Locke, John, 248
Longinus, 237, 374, 434
Lowes, J. Livingston, 44, 102–3, 237, 250, 378
Lucan (M. Annaeus Lucanus), 21, 95, 174, 238–9, 370–1, 402
Lucas, H. D., 345
Lucilius, Gaius, 233, 235, 350–1, 406
Lucretius Carus, T., 21–2, 51, 58, 65–6, 72, 87, 100, 114, 117–20, 153, 157–9, 187–8, 210, 227–8, 235, 238, 253, 263–4, 282, 296, 300, 304–5, 316–17, 328–30, 351, 387, 389, 393, 401–2, 404, 408, 413n
Lycophron, 196
Lysias, 69

Macchioro, Vittorio D., 387n
Macedon, 15, 22, 134
Mackail, J. W., 163, 228, 328, 344, 356n, 375, 380, 406n
Macrobius, 52–3, 79, 94, 110, 114, 317, 373–4, 403, 409–10, 419
Maecenas, Gaius, 52, 62–3, 71, 75–80, 89, 152, 157, 362, 365, 426
Magia Polla, 55
Mago, 158, 211
Maguinness, W. S., 364n, 379n, 382
Mahabharata, The, 95
Maiuri, A., 397n
Mallarmé, Stéphane, 302
Malten, Ludolf, 194
Mancuso, U., 195n
Manilius, 65, 87
Mantua, 54, 61, 64, 73–4, 83, 89, 377
Marcellus, M. Claudius, 91, 94, 271, 362, 365
Marius, Gaius, 384
Marlowe, Christopher, 380
Marouzeau, J., 400n, 404n, 406n–8n, 410n, 413n
Martial (M. Valerius Martialis), 362
Martins, F., 9
Mattingly, Harold, 74n, 147n, 204n
Meillet, A., 247n

Menander, 49, 182
Messalla Corvinus, M. Valerius, 62, 71, 75, 83, 86, 114, 153, 191
Metelli, the, 281
Milo, Titus Annius, 59
Milton, John, 52, 94, 101, 156, 164, 187, 229, 242, 298, 356, 380–1, 391, 397, 428–9
Lycidas, 380
Paradise Lost, 94, 281
Mimnermus, 34, 51
Misenum, Cape, 90, 139, 353–4
Mohenjo–Daro culture, the, 26
Molière, Jean-Baptiste, 182
Momigliano, Arnaldo, 15n
Mommsen, Theodor, 196
Moore, R. W., 9
Moschus, 153
Mullens, H. G., 165, 366
Murley, C., 162n
Murray, John, 50
Myers, F. W. H., 46n, 222n
Myres, Sir John L., 161, 162n–3n

Naevius, Gnaeus, 46, 49, 94, 107, 125–7, 154, 159, 164, 176, 187, 189, 197, 273–4, 281
Naples, 55, 62, 64, 72, 82, 84, 86, 88, 144, 198, 202, 375, 377, 421
Napoleon Bonaparte, 185, 317
Nelson, Lord, 372
Nemesianus, 371
Nettleship, H., 381
Neumann, Erich, 439
Neurath, Otto, 398
Nicander of Colophon, 158
Nietzsche, F. W., 45
Nisbet, R. G. M., 80n
Norden, E., 382

Oaxes, River, 249–50
Octavia, 61–2, 90–1, 94, 125, 362
Octavianus, *see* Augustus Caesar
Olympia, 32–3, 35, 173
Olympus, Mount, 387
Orphics, the, 32, 36, 387, 389
O'Shaughnessy, A. W. E., 366
Otis, Brooks, 46n, 49n
Ovid (P. Ovidius Naso), 25, 43, 59, 67, 78, 80, 85, 129, 229, 238, 248, 369–70, 402–4, 434

Pacuvius, Marcus, 67, 70
Paetus, *see* Thrasea Paetus
Paetus, L. Papirius, 81
Palgen, R., 372, 378
Palmer, L. R., 413n–14n
Pannartz, Arnold, 345, 381
Pansa, C. Vibius, 81
Paratore, Ettore, 9, 22n, 33n, 52n, 439n
Parthenius (teacher of Vergil), 55, 81, 287
Parthenope, 64, 144
Paul, E. & C., 106n
Pausanias, 33
Peaks, Mary B., 185n
Pease, A. S., 382
Penates, the, 132, 141, 176, 196, 223–4, 433
Pereira, M. H. M. da Rocha, 387n
Peretti, Aurelio, 154n
Perret, Jacques, 131n
Perses (brother of Hesiod), 156
Petrarch, 400n
Phaedrus, 60, 80
Pherecydes, 136
Philip II, King of Spain, 435
Philip, Elmslie, 213n
Phillimore, J. S., 51n, 57n
Phillips, John, 428
Philo of Alexandria, 19
Philodemus, 60, 76, 80–1, 393
Picard, C., 196n, 439n
Picasso, Pablo Ruiz, 435
Pindar, 32–3, 46, 104, 188–90, 199, 203, 230, 237, 348, 387, 392, 434–5
Piso, L. Calpurnius, 81
Pizzani, H., 22n
Plato, 17–18, 26, 28–30, 33, 37, 43, 109, 160, 173, 187, 189, 373, 388, 393, 428, 434
  Cratylus, 43
  Ion, 428
  Republic, 37
Plautus, T. Maccius, 20, 46, 67, 106–7, 182, 235, 238, 401
Pliny the Elder, 101, 159
Plotia Hieria, 144
Plotius Tucca, 64, 71, 75–6, 91, 344, 346–7
Plutarch, 149
Poincaré, Henri, 44, 103

Pólit, S. J., Fr. Aurelio Espinosa, 42, 99–100, 244, 301, 396
Pollard, J. R. T., 9, 135n, 260, 359, 390n, 404n
Pollio, C. Asinius, 52, 62, 70–1, 73–5
Polybius, 20, 187, 196, 384
Pompeius, Sextus, 61, 63, 79, 89–91, 424
Pompeius Magnus, Cn., 23, 58–9, 83, 116, 366
Ponticus, *Thebaid*, 78
Pope, Alexander, 230, 337, 381, 384, 417n
Porphyry, 387
Pöschl, Viktor, 51n, 184n, 206n, 213n, 222n, 252n, 382n
Pound, Ezra, 104, 106, 312
  Homage to Sextus Propertius, 106
Preshous, J. D. M., 435n
Priscian, 358
Probus, M. Valerius, 73, 76, 344, 373
Propertius, Sextus, 51, 71, 77–8, 94, 106, 241, 362, 387
Prowse, Keith, 10
Punic Wars, the, 20, 49, 53, 281, 353, 432
Purgatory, 255
Pyrrhus, King of Epirus, 15
Pythagoras, 153, 388

Quinn, Kenneth, 49n, 68n, 233n
Quintilian (M. Fabius Quintilianus), 57, 358, 360, 370, 372, 374, 403, 406–7, 413n
Quintus Smyrnaeus, 355

Racine, Jean, 43n, 429
Radhakrishnan, Sir S., 16
Rainey, Paul, 168
Rand, E. K., 44, 102, 107, 110, 120, 155–6, 179, 212, 229n–30n, 317, 424
Rapisarda, E., 9
Rehm, Bernhard, 166n, 243n
Renan, Ernest, 54
Rest, Hazel van, 426n
Reynolds, Sir Joshua, 435
Ribbeck, Otto, 381
Richards, I. A., 103
Richardson, L. J. D., 9, 397n
Rieu, E. V., 436n

Rimbaud, Arthur, 302
Robinson, E. A., 10
Roiron, S.J., F.-X. M. J., 256n, 299
Rome, 13–15, 19–24, 30–1, 49–51,
    53–4, 58–63, 72, 76–9, 82–4,
    87, 89–91, 115–16, 131, 133–6,
    144, 148, 160, 164–6, 173, 180,
    185, 189, 195–9, 201, 203–5, 209–
    11, 215, 218, 223, 234–6, 244,
    280, 308, 323, 355, 362–4, 367–70,
    375, 377, 381, 383, 385, 387–93,
    401, 409, 415, 432, 439
  early history, 13–15, 30–1, 53–4
    (as legend 131–4)
  foundation, as told by Dionysius of
    Halicarnassus, 135–40; Livy,
    134–5; Vergil, 131–4
  philosophy at, 19–24
Ronsard, Pierre de, 43
Rose, H. J., 9, 53n, 162n, 211, 246
Rostagni, Augusto, 187n, 404n
Rousseau, Jean-Jacques, 26
Rutilius Namatianus, 371
Rykwert, Joseph, 26n

Sabbadini, Remigio, 10–11, 96n, 345,
    361, 382
St Ambrose, 336
St Augustine, 336, 344, 361, 375–6,
    391
  City of God, 375
St John, 19
St Paul, 158, 377, 391
Sainte-Beuve, C. A., 46n
Salinator, M. Livius, 281
Sallust (C. Sallustius Crispus), 65,
    415–16, 422
Sallustius, Gnaeus, 65
Sappho, 42, 44, 104, 155, 208
Saunders, Catharine, 121n, 122n,
    204n
Savage, John J. H., 80n, 423n, 424n
Saxo, 39
Schiller, Friedrich von, 428
Schliemann, H., 193
Schmalz, J. H., 404n
Scipio Aemilianus Africanus, P.
    Cornelius, 19
Scipios, the, 212, 245
Sedgwick, W. B., 235n, 300
Seligson, Gerda, 184n

Sempronius, Gaius, 136
Seneca the elder, 367
Seneca, L. Annaeus, 21, 87, 101, 251,
    346, 371, 380
  Ad Lucilium, 87
Servius Honoratus, 52–3, 61, 73, 75–6,
    82, 85, 87, 89–90, 92–5, 97, 109,
    113–14, 126, 128, 188, 279, 346–8,
    356, 358, 363, 373–4, 401, 404,
    409, 411–12, 414–17, 424, 434
  Life of Vergil, 97, 109, 347
Severus Alexander, M. Aurelius, 376
Sforza, Francesco, 364–5
Shakespeare, William, 16, 52, 88, 101,
    109, 144, 146, 149, 167, 189, 207,
    214, 216, 251, 320, 323, 376,
    380, 421n
  Henry IV, ii, 214
  Henry VIII, 16
  Macbeth, 16
  Richard II, 88
  Romeo and Juliet, 214
  The Tempest, 189, 323
  Timon of Athens, 109n
Sheehan, J., 378n
Shefton, Brian, 9
Shelley, Percy Bysshe, 54, 100, 109, 366
Sheppard, Sir John T., 161
Shewan, A., 300n
Shipley, F. W., 228
Siculus, see Calpurnius Siculus
Sikes, E. E., 67n, 69n
Silius Italicus, 371, 376
Siro, 60, 80, 82, 86–7, 393, 395
Sitwell, Dame Edith, 302
Skelton, John, 105
Skutsch, F., 85n
Skutsch, Otto, 51n, 296n
Slade, E. A., 162
Smiley, Charles N., 395n
Smith, N. Horton, 301
Smith, Ronald M., 162n
Smuts, Jan, 150, 169
Snell, Bruno, 76, 77n
Socrates, 16–19, 34, 406, 439
Solon, 30
Solovyef, V. S., 28
Sophists, the, 34, 43
Sophocles, 43, 48, 74, 129–30, 138,
    146, 170, 175, 178, 190, 192,
    197, 251–2, 258, 356

Sophocles (*contd*)
  Ajax, 130
  Antenoridae, 170
  Antigone, 129, 170
  Electra, 129, 170
  Oedipus Coloneus, 170
  Trachiniae, 130
Sophron, 229
Sortes Vergilianae, 376
Southan, Joyce E., 9
Sparrow, John, 119n, 350, 359n
Speaight, Robert, 240n
Spenser, Edmund, 380, 427n
Stanford, W. B., 251
Statius, P. Papinius, 370, 376
Steele, R. B., 101
Steiner, H. R., 176n
Stesichorus, 196, 229
Steuart, Ethel, 172n
Stolz, F., 404n
Stovin, Harold, 165
Strzelecki, L., 176n
Stubbs, H. W., 9
Sturtevant, E. H., 408n
Suetonius Tranquillus, 52, 107
Sulla Felix, L. Cornelius, 24, 384
Sulpicius, Servius, 75
Sumeria, 25–7, 40
Swannick, Mrs G., 9
Sweynheim, Conrad, 345, 381
Syme, Sir Ronald, 63n, 65n

Tacitus, P. Cornelius, 39, 371
Tarn, W. W., 154, 188n, 364
Tarquinius Priscus, L., 199, 234
Tarquinius Superbus, L., 367
Tasso, 122, 164
Tate, Jonathan, 374
Tennyson, Alfred Lord, 101, 282, 300, 381
  Locksley Hall, 282, 300
Terence (P. Terentius Afer), 46, 67, 107, 182, 238–9, 405
Theocritus, 49, 51, 106–7, 125, 144–5, 150–1, 153, 155, 157–9, 185, 191, 229–30, 249, 305, 374, 401, 422, 434
  Idylls, 49, 107, 125, 153, 155, 230, 422
Theognis, 27, 34
Theophrastus, 402, 430

Thomson, J. A. K., 147n
Thrasea Paetus, P. Clodius, 21
Thucydides, 31, 36, 170, 262, 384
Tiberius Caesar, 367
Tibullus, Albius, 51, 70–1, 77–8, 423
Tilly, Bertha, 166n
Timaeus, 126, 196
Timagenes, 81
Timomachus, 87
Timotheus, *Persians*, 342
Torquatus, Manlius, 81
Townend, G. B., 383n
Trebatius Testa, C., 81
Treves, Piero, 9
Trogus, Pompeius, 126
Trojan War, the, 136–7, 194, 197, 203, 235, 432
Troy, 20, 27, 89, 93, 95–6, 109, 122–5, 128, 131, 134, 137–40, 146, 159, 168, 170, 172, 176, 180–2, 186, 193–9, 202–3, 209, 211, 216, 221, 223–4, 239, 252–5, 261, 277, 301–2, 307, 325–6, 333–4, 347, 355–6, 365, 432–3
Tucca, *see* Plotius Tucca
Twelve Tables of Roman Law, the, 30, 46, 49, 281
Tzetzes, Johannes, 233

Vahlen, J., 10
Valerius Flaccus, C., 371
Valéry, Paul, 293
Valgius Rufus, 71–2
Varius Rufus, L., 64, 70–1, 75–6, 91, 97, 256n, 344, 346–7
Varro, M. Terentius, 69, 158, 203–204, 329, 402
  Trojan Families, 204
Varus, Alfenus, 61, 64, 71, 73
Varus, P. Quintilius, 64, 73, 76
Velasquez, 435
Ventidius, Publius, 90
Venus, 84, 93, 97, 122–5, 127, 138, 145, 147, 170–3, 177, 182, 186, 194, 208, 217, 256–7, 333–5, 389–90, 392
Vergil, *see* Subject Index, Vergil
Verrall, A. W., 217n
Verrall, Margaret G., 208n
Vida, Marco Girolamo, 380
Villon, François, 43

Virgil Society, The, 11, 40n, 85n,
  212n, 225n, 240n, 296n, 317n,
  368n, 371n, 379n, 419, 425n, 430n
  (of Exmouth, 213n)
Voltaire, 99, 392
Volterrenus, Elbius, 78

Wainwright, G. A., 25n, 53n, 126,
  130n, 200n
Warmington, E. H., 10, 281n
Waszink, J. H., 423n
Wavell, Earl, 317n
Webster, John, 326
Webster, T. B. L., 40n
Wells, H. G., 340
Westendorp Boerma, R. E. H., 230n
White, H. A. B., 283n
Whitman, Walt, 379
Wilamowitz-Möllendorff, U. von,
  69n

Wilkinson, L. P., 290n, 292n, 296n,
  297n, 369n
Williams, R. D., 131n, 358n, 382
Woodcock, E. C., 265n, 368n
Woodhouse, W. J., 127, 227
Woodward, Avery, 284
Wordsworth, William, 105, 109
  Intimations of Immortality, 109
Worstbrock, Franz Josef, 381n

Xenophanes, 34
Xenophon, 34
Xerxes, 188

Yarrow, P. J., 429n
Yeats, W. B., 109, 421, 424, 427, 429
Young, Arthur M., 230n, 231n

Zeno, 393
Zoroastrianism, 19

SUBJECT INDEX

Ablative case, 264–5

Accent, word, *see* Stress-accent

Accusative case, 265–70

Adjectives, compound, 118

Aeneid, The, alternation and balance in, 153
  colour imagery in, 220–2
  composition of, 63–4, 92–8, 429–31
  intention of Vergil to burn, 64, 91
  poetic style of, 323–4
  popularity of, 362
  publication of, 64, 91–2, 346–7, 362
  'rejected' passages in, 347–8
  relation to the *Iliad* and *Odyssey*, 165–9
  story of, 131–4
  transpositions in text of, 357

αἰδώς ('shame'), 30

Allegory, 156, 322, 364, 374–5, 380, 423–4, 428

Alliteration, 282, 304–5, 307, 329

Anachronisms, 197–200

Analogy, 43

Anaphora, 315

Anomaly, 43

Aposiopesis, 328

Appendix Vergiliana, The, 61–2, 81–8, 105, 145, 232, 420–1

Archaisms, 118, 263, 318–19, 403, 412

Asceticism, 18, 386

Association, of words (including 'ambiguities'), 247–51, 258
  of sound, 258–61, 298–302, 332
  of names, 432–3

Assonance, 282, 300–1, 305–7, 332, 335

Asyndeton, 316

Bees, 9on, 189, 208–9, 212, 317

Bisexuality, 122, 144, 146, 333

Catachresis ('abusio'), 410–1

Chiasmus, 316

Christian affinities in Vergil, 16, 375–7, 390–1, 396–7

City-states, 13, 22, 25–7, 29, 36, 42, 50, 392

Colloquialisms, 319–20

Comedy, 35, 151, 182, 300, 329

Compression, 247, 262–3, 267, 274–6, 311, 404, 434, 438

Conditional sentences, 276–7

'Contaminatio', 46

Copyist errors, 348–9

Cyclic Epic, the, 46, 110, 122, 127–8, 159

Dative case, 272–3

Eclogues, The, alternation and balance in, 150–2
  as a school book, 346, 362
  autobiography in, 156
  date of composition of, 61–2, 428
  'relevance' in, 321–3, 335
  symmetry in, 425–6

Editions of Vergil, 345, 381–2

Ellipse, 414

Epicureanism, 18–19, 21–4, 60, 65, 72, 80–1, 86, 183, 187, 317, 393–5, 398, 421

Epithalamium, 154

Etymology, 166, 240–50, 258–60, 266, 340

Fate, 33, 388–9

Femininity, 125, 144, 146–7

Genethlion, 154

Genitive case, 270–1

Georgics, The, alternation and balance in, 151–2
  as a school-book, 346, 362
  date of, 63, 428
  style of, 88–90
  symmetry in, 426

'Golden Ratio', 425–6, 427n, 438

Grammar and syntax, 262–80

Hebrew literature, 43, 81, 234, 391

Hendiadys, 339

451

Hybris, 36–7, 384
Hypallage, 313 (and
    'transference'), 314–15

Imaginative power, 332–3
Imitation in poetry, 99–104, see also
    'Integration'
Inspiration, 108–10, 428–9
'Integration', 46, 104–6, 110–15,
    119–20, 131, 438n

Manuscripts, 314, 342–5
Metaphors, 167, 213–14, 311–15,
    321–3, 331–3, 437
Metre and prosody:
    caesura, 283–6, 291, 331
    'Cyclopean Lines', 295
    elision, 283, 287, 290
    enjambement, 227–8, 284
    Greek usages, 286–8, 290
    heterodyne, 293–5
    hexameter, 225–8, 230–6, 282–96,
        298, 310, 329, 425;
        uses of, 153–4, 226–7, 232–3
    hiatus, 228, 283, 287–8, 295
    homodyne, 293–4, 296–7, 308, 430
    ictus, 115–16, 294–6, 430
    lengthening of short syllable, 287–9
    prodelision, 292
    quantity, metrical, 233, 280, 283,
        286–90, 294
    'Saturnian' verse, 280–1
    synizesis, 286, 291
    synonyms enforced by metre, 287,
        310–11
    trochaic tetrameters, 300
    verse-endings;
        hypermetre, 290–1
        monosyllables, 291–2
        polysyllables, 286–8, 296
        trochaic fifth foot, 287–8, 290
    see also Stress-accent,
        Poetry: 'verse-groups'
Middle voice in Latin, 268–70

νέμεσις ('retribution'), 31
Nominative, Greek, 267

Onomatopoeia, 117, 282, 296
Oracles, see Prophecy and oracles

Oratory, 69, 236
Oxymoron, 239

Parataxis, 408
Pathos, 112, 302, 332, 334–5
Penultima, Law of the, 294
Philosophy, Greek, 17–18, 33
    Vergil and philosophy, 18, 33n, 187
'Pietas', 385, 391
πίστις ('faith'), 391
Plagiarism, 99, 373
Plot ('myth'), 149, 175, 205–6, 217
Poetry:
    Alexandrian, 49, 51, 64, 66–71, 77–8,
        80, 84–6, 105, 153–4, 158–60, 162,
        191, 232, 234, 297–8, 300, 329, 422
    'allusive' theories of, 102
    'amoebaean', 229
    Anglo-Saxon, 280
    characters and types in, 178–9, 423
    classical and romantic, 43, 325, 368–9
    English tradition of, 380–1
    epic, 41–2, 44–5, 49–50, 105, 164–5,
        172, 175–6, 183, 187–8, 213, 425
        (Indian, 95, 162n, 425)
        see also Cyclic Epic
    epyllia, 70, 73, 85, 153–4, 159–60,
        234, 323
    'golden lines', 230–2, 306, 330–1
    lyric, 44–5, 68, 183–4
    Medieval, 105
    'neoteric', 51, 66–8, 230
    pastoral (bucolic), 51, 75, 324, 423
    philosophical, 21, 65, 232–3
    'relevance' in, 321–2, 335
    'silences', 325–6
    'tibicines' ('props'), 107, 110, 359
    unfinished lines, 325–6, 359–60
    'verse-groups', 226–7, 229–32, 292
    see also Alliteration, Assonance,
        Compression, 'Golden Ratio',
        Hypallage, Imitation, Inspiration,
        'Integration', Metaphors, Metre,
        Onomatopoeia, Repetition,
        'Retractatio', Rhyme, Rhythm,
        Similes, Sound, Stress-accent,
        Symmetry
Prepositions, avoidance of, 264–5
Pronunciation of Latin, 336–7
Prophecy and oracles, 21, 32, 133,
    139, 176–7, 207, 233–5

Prophecy and oracles (*contd*)
  ('Sibylline oracles', 154, 230,
  234–5, 328, 376, 391)

Reincarnation, 17, 173
Religion, ancient, 22, 24–5, 30–8,
  202, 385–8 ('Deities' in Vergil
  388–90; 'Initiation' 172–3;
  'Mysteries', 26, 32–3)
Repetition, 305. 307–8, 327–30, 349–50,
  407–8
'Retractatio', 101, 107, 115, 119–20,
  350–2
Rhyme, 231–2, 300–8, 329, 332, 335
Rhythm, 150, 293, 298–9

Similes, 167, 213–15, 321, 323, 326
Sound values (and association),
  258–61, 298–302, 310–11, 332,
  361, 434
Stoicism, 14, 18–23, 33, 35. 48, 50,
  184, 317, 388, 393–5, 398
Stress-accent in poetry, 115, 233,
  280, 283–4, 292–4, 296, 309,
  331
Surrealism, 260, 434–5
Symbolism, 89, 168, 174, 177, 188,
  207–10

Symmetry, 161–4, 230, 329–30, 333,
  425–8, 430

Textual criticism, 345, 351–2, 354–61
Tmesis, 238, 264
Tragedy, Greek, 36, 47, 171, 175
  of Dido, 125–30
  of Turnus, 174
Translation, problems of, 337–40
Trees in Vergil, 83, 310
'Trojan game', the, 93, 181, 209

Vergil, characteristics of, 187, 310
  Christian affinities in, 16, 375–7,
    390–1, 396–7
  friendships of, 72–80
  literary influences on, 43, 48, 100,
    114–22, 125–31, 153–62, 169–71,
    422, 435–7
  philosophy of, 18–19, 21, 60, 174, 187,
    394–6
  and prose, 187, 310
  psychological characteristics of,
    144, 146, 334
    see also Bisexuality

'Will-power' words, 116

Zeugma, 315